META-ANALYSIS FOR PUBLIC
MANAGEMENT AND POLICY

The Instructor's Guide for *Meta-Analysis for Public Management and Policy* includes the following:

· Microsoft Excel .csv files containing the data necessary to replicate all of the example analyses in the book, including the school voucher meta-analysis in chapter 8
· Stata command files that allow readers to replicate all of the example analyses in the book, including the school voucher meta-analyses in chapter 8
· Sample syllabus for a graduate seminar in meta-analysis, tailored for public management, public policy, and the social sciences
· PowerPoint files that can be used as is or customized to deliver classroom lectures that cover the following:
  · Introduction to meta-analysis and meta-analysis in public management and policy (effectively, the book introduction plus additional items from chapter 1)
  · Literature searches for meta-analysis (effectively, chapter 2 from the book)
  · The calculation and combining of effect sizes in meta-analysis (effectively, chapter 3 from the book)
  · The basics of meta-regression analysis (effectively, chapter 4 from the book)
  · Advanced meta-regression for public management and policy (effectively, chapter 5 from the book)

The Instructor's Guide is available free online. If you would like to download and print a copy of the Guide, please visit: www.wiley.com/college/ringquist

META-ANALYSIS FOR PUBLIC MANAGEMENT AND POLICY

Evan J. Ringquist

Edited by
Mary R. Anderson

JOSSEY-BASS
A Wiley Imprint
www.josseybass.com

Cover design by Jeff Puda.

Published by Jossey-Bass
A Wiley Imprint
One Montgomery Street, Suite 1200, San Francisco, CA 94104-4594—www.josseybass.com

Limit of Liability/Disclaimer of Warranty: While the publisher and author have used their best efforts in preparing this book, they make no representations or warranties with respect to the accuracy or completeness of the contents of this book and specifically disclaim any implied warranties of merchantability or fitness for a particular purpose. No warranty may be created or extended by sales representatives or written sales materials. The advice and strategies contained herein may not be suitable for your situation. You should consult with a professional where appropriate. Neither the publisher nor author shall be liable for any loss of profit or any other commercial damages, including but not limited to special, incidental, consequential, or other damages. Readers should be aware that Internet Web sites offered as citations and/or sources for further information may have changed or disappeared between the time this was written and when it is read.

Jossey-Bass books and products are available through most bookstores. To contact Jossey-Bass directly call our Customer Care Department within the U.S. at 800-956-7739, outside the U.S. at 317-572-3986, or fax 317-572-4002.

Wiley also publishes its books in a variety of electronic formats and by print-on-demand. Some material included with standard print versions of this book may not be included in e-books or in print-on-demand. If the version of this book that you purchased references media such as CD or DVD that was not included in your purchase, you may download this material at http://booksupport.wiley.com. For more information about Wiley products, visit www.wiley.com.

Library of Congress Cataloging-in-Publication Data
Library of Congress Cataloging-in-Publication Data has been applied for and is on file with the Library of Congress.
ISBN 9781118190135 (pbk.); ISBN 9781118227657 (ebk.); ISBN 9781118240496 (ebk.); ISBN 9781118265253 (ebk.)

Printed in the United States of America
FIRST EDITION
PB Printing   10 9 8 7 6 5 4 3 2 1

CONTENTS

FIGURES, TABLES, AND EXHIBIT

Figures

Tables

Exhibit

PREFACE

It took twenty-five years to write this book. I was introduced to meta-analysis in 1987 at the Inter-University Consortium for Political and Social Research Summer Program at the University of Michigan. At the time, I was intrigued by the power of the idea of meta-analysis—a suite of statistical techniques for drawing generalizable conclusions from a set of sometimes inconsistent original studies. At the same time, I was struck by the fundamental limitations of the techniques, especially when applied to the types of original studies that are the stock in trade of the social sciences. I left Ann Arbor with the impression that meta-analysis was attractive but ultimately not very useful for social scientists, although I vowed to monitor progress in the field.

I returned to meta-analysis in 2000, and have taught graduate-level courses in the field since. The past decade or so has been an exciting time for meta-analysts, as the statistical techniques of meta-analysis have developed rapidly, particularly in the area of meta-regression. These developments, coupled with recent advances in econometrics and the ever-increasing quality of quantitative research in the social sciences, have produced an environment in which the techniques of meta-analysis now can be used effectively to not only synthesize the results from original quantitative research in public management, public policy, and the social sciences but also account for systematic variation in the conclusions from this original research.

Meta-Analysis for Public Management and Policy was written with the hope that it might encourage public management and policy scholars to rethink how their research can contribute to evidence-based management and policy, and ultimately inform more effective governance. It was also written with the hope that it might encourage scholars in the social sciences generally to think more carefully about (1) the production of cumulative knowledge in their respective disciplines and (2) the production of knowledge that is useable by practitioners. Meta-analysis offers a set of tools to help scholars meet all of these goals.

The Audience for the Book

The primary audience for the book is the next generation of researchers in public management and policy—that is, graduate students in public policy, public affairs, public management, and public administration programs. While some of the material is moderately technical—especially in chapters 5, 6, and 7—advanced or highly skilled master's students should find the material accessible, as should all Ph.D. students. To make full use of the techniques offered here, students should have had a basic statistics course and a two-semester (or a very good one-semester) course in applied regression analysis and extensions of the general linear model. A second audience for the book is current researchers in public management and policy. This audience includes academics, researchers in government, and analysts working at policy research organizations. Any researcher interested in generating cumulative knowledge to inform decision making will benefit from using the techniques described in the text. A third audience for the book is researchers in the social sciences more generally, particularly in disciplines closely related to public management and policy: political science, economics, and sociology. Scholars in these fields devote somewhat less attention to problem-focused research and the production of knowledge useable by practitioners in government. The research methods and products produced by political scientists, economists, and sociologists, however, are often nearly identical to those of public management and policy scholars. Moreover, the ability to build cumulative knowledge from original studies is no less important for the type of theory-driven basic research that is more common in these fields. That is, meta-analysis is as useful for fostering scientific progress as it is for fostering evidence-based decision making.

The Plan of the Book

The Aim of the Book

This book is written with three aims in mind. First, I wanted to write a textbook that would introduce readers to the design and execution of meta-analysis within the framework of public management, public policy, and the social sciences. Chapters 1, 2, 3, 4, and 6 serve this aim. Apart from some differences in emphasis and presentation consistent with the substantive focus on policy and management, these chapters could appear in any standard meta-analysis textbook.

Second, I wanted to write a book that would integrate the statistics of meta-analysis with advanced techniques in econometrics that are more familiar to social scientists. The goals of this integration are twofold: to offer researchers in public management and policy a set of sophisticated techniques for conducting meta-regression analysis using effect sizes from the types of original studies common in these fields, and to systematically assess the most common approach to meta-regression in the social sciences—the FAT-MST-PET-MRA techniques from economics (Stanley 2001, 2005). Chapter 5 offers readers a set of advanced meta-regression techniques customized for public management and policy, while chapter 7 reports on extensive Monte Carlo analyses of the elements of the FAT-MST-PET-MRA approach. The conclusion from chapter 7 is that researchers should avoid the economics approach to meta-analysis in favor of the more traditional approach developed in the fields of statistics and medical statistics.

Third, I wanted to offer readers a set of original meta-analyses that employ the techniques developed in chapters 1 through 7 to answer important questions in the fields of public management and policy. In chapter 8, Tatyana Guzman, Mary Anderson, and I offer a meta-analysis summarizing the effects of educational vouchers on student academic achievement. In chapter 9, Ed Gerrish and Po-Ju Wu present a meta-analysis of the effects of performance measurement systems on the performance of public organizations. Chapter 10, coauthored by Joe Bolinger and Lanlan Xu, offers a meta-analysis summarizing evidence of the effects from the deconcentration of federal public housing on the life outcomes of recipients of federal housing assistance. In chapter 11, David Warren and Li-Ting Chen provide a meta-analysis of the relationship between public service motivation and the performance of government agencies. We believe that these are the first meta-analyses to address any of these questions.

Empirical Examples

I use two recurring examples in chapters 1 through 7 to illustrate the techniques of meta-analysis. The first is a meta-analysis of the empirical literature on environmental justice. The original article (Ringquist 2005) is one of the twenty-seven meta-analyses published in the fields of public administration and policy since 1980 (see table I.1). The central question in environmental justice research is whether actual or potential environmental risks are distributed disproportionately with respect to race and class. Typical operationalizations of these general questions examine whether polluting facilities are more likely to be located in communities with large percentages of poor or minority residents, and whether levels of pollution are higher in these communities. A spirited debate took place in the academic literature during the 1990s over whether environmental inequities existed. The sample data set used here contains 680 effect sizes from forty-eight original studies measuring race-based environmental inequities. The original article concludes that there is strong evidence of race-based environmental inequities, but that the magnitude of these inequities (that is, the conditional average effect size) is substantively small.

The second empirical example considers a contentious issue in education research and policy—the effects of educational vouchers on student academic achievement. Advocates argue that vouchers will increase student academic achievement either by allowing students to attend higher-performing private schools (the private school effect) or by forcing existing public schools to improve to avoid losing students and revenue (the competition effect). As was the case with the topic of environmental justice, a spirited debate took place in the academic literature during the 1990s and 2000s regarding the effectiveness of vouchers. Working with Mary Anderson and Her Sung Kum, I presented a conference paper in 2002 synthesizing the evidence regarding the effect of vouchers to that point (Ringquist, Anderson, and Kum 2002). At that time, however, I felt that the relevant empirical literature was neither large enough nor mature enough to support a published meta-analysis. I returned to this question in 2010, and the results are presented in chapter 8. In addition, I use the example of educational vouchers in chapters 1 through 7 to illustrate the practical application of the techniques of meta-analysis.

Computational Approach

There are a handful of very good statistical software programs specialized for meta-analysis, including Comprehensive Meta-Analysis, Review Manager (RevMan), and MetaWin. In my experience, these packages have difficulty managing the type of effect sizes and conducting the types of analysis that characterize meta-analysis in public management and policy. Therefore, all of the data management and statistical analysis in the book are conducted using the Stata statistical software package. I chose Stata for three reasons. First, Stata is one of the most common, if not *the* most common, of the statistical packages used by researchers in public management and policy. Readers are more likely to adopt the techniques in this book if they can be executed within a familiar computing environment. Second, while Stata does not currently include commands for meta-analysis, members of the Stata Users Group (SUG) have developed a handful of very useful meta-analysis ado files that can be downloaded from the Stata website and integrated in Stata versions 10.0 and above. Moreover, Sterne (2009) has collected excellent documentation for these user-written commands. While useful, the SUG meta-analysis ado commands cannot estimate the meta-regression models introduced in chapter 5 and used in chapters 8 through 11. This is not surprising, since these commands were written by researchers in medical statistics. Management and policy scholars work in a different statistical environment from that of most meta-analysts. Thankfully, it is a relatively simple matter to adapt the statistics of meta-analysis to make use of data coded from original studies in public management and policy. The third reason for using Stata is that it is easy to write command files for the statistical routines necessary for estimating the meta-regression models introduced in chapter 5 and the Monte Carlo simulations in chapter 7. The Stata command files and data sets necessary to replicate all of the analyses in chapters 3 through 8 are available on the companion website maintained by Jossey-Bass.

Acknowledgments

My first debt in crafting this book is to my colleague Mary Anderson. Mary believed in this project for ten years, never (publicly) giving up hope that our early work together on meta-analysis would see the light of day. In addition to contributing original material to the introduction, conclusion, and chapter 8, Mary served as counsel to the other members of the research team and edited (and re-edited) all of the chapters in the volume. Just as important, Mary served as a trusted adviser and proved an inexhaustible well of good humor as I struggled to make this book a reality.

My second debt is to the members of the research team that collaborated on the book. Joe Bollinger is a student in the joint Ph.D. program in public policy at Indiana University; Ed Gerrish, Tatyana Guzman, Dave

Warren, and Lanlan Xu are students in the Public Affairs Ph.D. Program at Indiana University; and Li-Ting Chen and Po-Ju Wu are Ph.D. students in the School of Education at Indiana University. Each and every one of these students is an intellectual marathoner. Conducting an original meta-analysis is not for the faint of heart. Though I warned each member of the team that the project would require three times the effort they expected up front, in reality the project demanded even more from them. They met deadlines and produced outstanding content while never uttering (publicly) complaints about the unreasonable expectations placed upon them by the senior author. Weaker colleagues would have cracked. My team barely flinched.

My third debt is to the professionals who helped develop the ideas in the book and prepare the manuscript for publication. Alison Hankey and her team at Jossey-Bass have been absolutely first-rate. Alison believed in the project early on, allowing me to write the book I wanted to write. Her support and firm guidance were invaluable in moving the manuscript to the finish line. Fran Berry, Carolyn Heinrich, and Michael McGuire were far too patient as I droned on about the possibilities of meta-analysis in public management and policy research, serving as sounding boards and providing ideas for original meta-analyses that might be included in the book. The School of Public and Environmental Affairs at Indiana University allowed me to teach the two-semester course in meta-analysis that provided both a proving ground for the ideas in the book and a training ground for the research team. Many schools wouldn't have allowed a faculty member this type of flexibility. But SPEA is a special place. Colleagues at SPEA and elsewhere who reviewed sections of the manuscript also deserve a special note of thanks: J. S. Butler, Joshua Cowen, Brad Heim, Haeil Jung, Jim Perry, Jonathan Plucker, David Reingold, and Justin Ross.

My deepest debt, for this book as for most things in life, is to my wife, Laurie, and daughters, Rachel and Hannah. They showed levels of patience, forbearance, understanding, and support that I didn't deserve as I abandoned my roles as husband and father in favor of my roles as researcher and author. Writing a book adapting the techniques of meta-analysis for public management and policy has been a first-order professional goal, but it came at the opportunity cost of nine months of missed soccer games, dance recitals, movie nights, and bedtime stories. As a reader, I hope you conclude it was worth it.

November 2012   Evan J. Ringquist
                                                                          Bloomington, Indiana

THE AUTHORS

Evan J. Ringquist is professor and director of the Ph.D. program in public affairs and joint Ph.D. in public policy in the School of Public and Environmental Affairs at Indiana University, where he also holds affiliate appointments in the Department of Political Science and West European Studies. Ringquist received undergraduate degrees in political science, economics, and biology from Moorhead State University, and received M.A. and Ph.D. degrees in political science and an M.S. degree in land resources from the University of Wisconsin-Madison. Ringquist served as the co-editor of the *Journal of Policy Analysis and Management* and on the editorial boards of *Policy Studies Journal, Social Science Quarterly*, and *State Politics and Policy Quarterly*. Ringquist has published three books and more than forty articles and book chapters examining the implementation and effectiveness of environmental policies, the distribution of environmental risks and the contributions of policy decisions to these distributions, democratic influences in policy making, and bureaucratic politics and behavior. Some of this research has been funded by the National Science Foundation, the U.S. Department of Energy, and the German Marshall Fund of the United States. Ringquist has served under contract or as a consultant to the U.S. Environmental Protection Agency, the U.S.

National Park Service, and numerous state governments and nonprofit organizations.

Mary R. Anderson is an assistant professor of government and world affairs at the University of Tampa. She holds a B.A. degree in history and political science from the University of Central Florida and M.S. and Ph.D. degrees in political science from Florida State University. Her research interests focus on political decision making. More specifically, she studies political behavior, such as voting and public opinion, with an interest in how psychological factors influence such decisions. Her work has been published in the *American Political Science Review, Journal of Politics, Political Behavior*, and *Political Psychology*. She lives in Tampa, Florida, with her husband and three children.

META-ANALYSIS FOR PUBLIC MANAGEMENT AND POLICY

INTRODUCTION

Meta-Analysis for Public Management and Policy

Evan J. Ringquist and Mary R. Anderson

"Meta-Analysis is not a fad. It is rooted in the fundamental values of the scientific enterprise: replicability, quantification, causal and correlational analysis. Valuable information is needlessly scattered in individual studies. The ability of social scientists to deliver generalizable answers to basic questions of policy is too serious a concern to allow us to treat research integration lightly. The potential benefits of meta-analysis methods seem enormous"

(BANGERT-DROWNS 1986, 398).

"We get the impression that meta-analysis is on the brink of becoming a major part of the evidence base underlying important questions about which programs or policies work (or not)"

(CORDRAY AND MORPHY 2009, 478).

There are two perspectives on how scientific research generates knowledge. The first views science as a largely solitary enterprise. Individual researchers or research teams, inspired by a brilliant insight, toil tirelessly to nurture that insight until it becomes a singularly influential article, book, or report that improves our understanding of the world. Especially valuable studies might even be seen as "critical tests" in the Poppernian sense that they distinguish between competing theories of physical or social phenomena. In the public mind, at least, our highest scientific honors go to researchers embodying this perspective (for example, the

Nobel Prize). The second perspective views science as a cooperative, collective endeavor. Knowledge advances through the accumulation of countless small pieces of evidence offered by countless investigators. As eloquently articulated by Cooper, Hedges, and Valentine (2009, 4), "the moment we are introduced to science we are told it is a cooperative, cumulative enterprise. Like the artisans who construct a building from blueprints, bricks, and mortar, scientists contribute to a common edifice, called knowledge. Theorists provide our blueprints and researchers collect data that are our bricks." These two perspectives are not mutually exclusive, or even in conflict, and we would guess that most scholars view the research enterprise through both perspectives. We would also assert, however, that most researchers view their own work through the first perspective, implicitly expecting that once new knowledge is generated, the accumulation process will take care of itself.

Vast increases in the number of researchers, the proliferation of research outlets, and the power of information-processing technology have led to exponential growth in the production and dissemination of scientific research. An inevitable consequence of this growth is that the conclusions from scientific research sometimes conflict. We find ourselves in a situation described by Morton Hunt in which "virtually every field of science is now pervaded by a relentless cross fire in which the findings of new studies not only differ from previously established truths but disagree with one another, often vehemently. Our faith that scientists are cooperatively and steadily enlarging their understanding of the world is giving way to doubt as, time and time again, new research assaults existing knowledge" (Hunt 1997, 1).

A similar story can be told about research in public management, public policy, and the social science disciplines that contribute most to research in these fields: economics, political science, and sociology. The growth of research output has been no less impressive in public management, public policy, and the social sciences than in the natural sciences. The number of scholarly articles published in these fields has grown by an order of magnitude over the past generation. New academic journals providing outlets for higher-quality or "more relevant" research have been started (for example, *Journal of Policy Analysis and Management, Journal of Public Administration Research and Theory*, *Perspectives on Politics*, *The Journal of Economic Perspectives*, and so on). In addition, reports by public policy research firms and think tanks have proliferated during this same period.

This impressive increase in research output, however, has not been accompanied by a commensurate increase in confidence regarding the validity of the most common theories in public management and policy, or in the ability of scholarship in these fields to move forward in a cumulative fashion. That is, an increase in research output has not been accompanied by a comparable increase in scientific progress. Moreover, this increase in research output has not transformed researchers in public management and policy into go-to resources for policy makers. Stated differently, the increase in research output has not made this research more relevant or useful to management and policy practitioners. To the contrary, "over the years . . . many policy makers have been disappointed with the assistance they have obtained from behavioral and social science research. The major problem has been that different research studies on the same question have reported conflicting and contradictory findings and conclusions, leaving policy makers puzzled as to which findings were correct and which should be chosen as the foundation for policy recommendations" (Hunter and Schmidt 1996, 324). Borrowing again from Morton Hunt: "The resulting intellectual melee does serious injury to science and society. For one thing, it impedes scientific progress. As the volume of research grows, so does the diversity of results, making it all but impossible for scientists to make sense of the divergent reports even within their own narrow specialties. . . . For another, when legislators and public administrators seek, through hearings and staff research, to study a pressing issue, they can rarely make sense of the hodge-podge of findings offered them" (Hunt 1997, 5).

While science as a collective enterprise may be self-correcting, the products of scientific research are not self-organizing. Cumulative knowledge does not arise organically. Aggregating scientific results, like generating these results in the first place, requires agency and effort. *Meta-analysis* provides a set of tools for this task. Meta-analysis is a systematic, quantitative, replicable process of synthesizing numerous and sometimes conflicting results from a body of original studies. Using meta-analysis, researchers can (1) calculate an average effect size that summarizes the weight of the evidence present in the original research on a particular question and (2) account for why empirical results vary across original studies. Meta-analysis is used routinely in evidence-based medicine to better inform health care and health policy choices, and is used with increasing frequency to guide the choice of education interventions. Despite its promise, meta-analysis is used very infrequently in public management and policy research.

We believe the time is right for policy and management scholars to embrace meta-analysis as a set of tools for advancing theory and inform-ing practice. First, the statistics of meta-analysis have developed to a point where they can integrate the results from original studies in these fields. Second, public management and policy research is making greater use of field experiments and high-quality quasi-experimental methods, the results from which are more amenable to being combined using meta-analysis. Finally, we are witnessing a movement in support of "evidence-based policy making," while at the same time public managers face increasing pressure to "manage from data." Meta-analysis provides a set of methods for synthesizing large amounts of evidence in a way that is useful for managers and policy makers.

Introducing Meta-Analysis

The origin story of meta-analysis traces the technique back to Sir Karl Pearson's 1904 study in which he combined the correlation coefficients from several original studies examining the effectiveness of vaccines for typhoid fever in order to obtain a more precise estimate of the relationship between vaccination and reduction in mortality.[1] Although there was sporadic progress in the statistics for combining research results over the next seventy years, the modern era of research synthesis was inaugurated by Gene Glass's landmark study of the effectiveness of psychotherapy treatments. Glass standardized and averaged treatment effects across 375 original studies using a process he dubbed "meta-analysis" (Glass 1976, 1978; Smith and Glass 1977).

As is true of many technical innovations, Glass's procedure for combining results from original studies was devised to address a particular problem. It was not until a decade later that Hedges and Olkin (1985) established the statistical theory that underlaid Glass's procedure and several other techniques of meta-analysis. The next decade saw the development of relatively distinct branches of meta-analysis in different fields of study. Meta-analysis in education followed on the innovations of Glass. Meta-analysis in psychometrics, by contrast, developed a set of techniques for adjusting the results in original studies to correct for differences in scale reliability, measurement error, and measurement range restrictions (Hunter and Schmidt 1990, 1996). The foundations of meta-regression were also laid during this period by Larry Hedges and others (Hedges 1982; Hedges and Olkin 1985; Cooper and Hedges 1994b). Since the late 1990s, advances in the techniques of meta-analysis have occurred largely in the field of medical statistics, led by researchers such as Colin Begg, John Copas, Julian Higgins, and Jonathan Sterne (for a review, see van Houwelingen, Arends, and Stijnen 2002). The emphasis on meta-analysis in medical statistics has been driven by the movement toward evidence-based medicine.

These developments in the techniques and application of meta-analysis have largely bypassed the fields of public management and policy and the associated social science disciplines of economics, political science, and sociology. There have been few meta-analyses completed in these fields and little attention paid to developing methods of meta-analysis for the types of original studies produced by researchers in these fields.

The Institutionalization of Meta-Analysis

In just the past generation meta-analysis has become institutionalized within the research community. Evidence of this institutionalization can be found in the tremendous growth in the use of meta-analysis in the scholarly literature. Figure I.1 presents a graph of the number of articles

FIGURE I.1. NUMBER OF ARTICLES PUBLISHED EACH YEAR IN THE "META-ANALYSIS" TOPIC CATEGORY AS REFERENCED BY THE SOCIAL SCIENCES CITATION INDEX

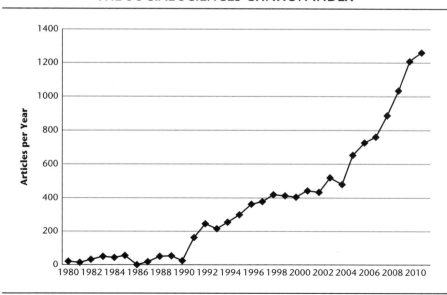

FIGURE I.2. NUMBER OF ARTICLES PUBLISHED EACH YEAR WITH *META-ANALYSIS* IN THE TITLE AS REFERENCED BY GOOGLE SCHOLAR

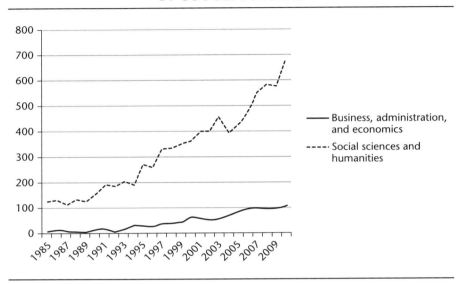

referenced under the topic heading "meta-analysis" in the Social Sciences Citation Index (SSCI) between 1980 and 2011. Using the search phrase *meta-analysis* should identify virtually all entries that use meta-analysis, since the Cochrane Collaboration (see below) recommends that all publications that use meta-analytic techniques use the phrase *meta-analysis* in the title. The number of meta-analysis articles referenced by SSCI stayed in the double-digits throughout the 1980s, but between 1991 and 2000 the number of articles increased 150 percent, from 162 to 400. In the next decade the number of meta-analysis articles nearly tripled, from 440 in 2001 to 1,257 in 2011. During the same period, SSCI recorded an equally dramatic rise in the number of publications in the "policy" topic category, from 2,454 in 1990 to 18,748 in 2011, an eightfold increase. Figure I.2 shows a similar pattern resulting from a search of Google Scholar. From 1985 through 2010, the number of scholarly publications with the term *meta-analysis* in the title rose from 12 to 102 in the Business, Administration, and Economics category (a ninefold increase) and from 128 to 676 in the Social Sciences and Humanities category (more than a fivefold increase).

TABLE I.1. CUMULATIVE NUMBER OF ARTICLES IN JSTOR DATABASE PUBLISHED SINCE 1980 THAT INCLUDE ANY OF THE SEARCH TERMS IN THE TITLE OR ABSTRACT

Academic Discipline	Meta-Analysis	Meta-Analytic	Research Synthesis
Public Administration and Policy	27	2	1
Economics	35	7	0
Political Science	25	8	3
Sociology	62	33	6
Education	360	81	112

While the publication of research in public policy and of research using meta-analysis has boomed since 1990, the growth trajectories of these two have been largely independent. That is, there has been comparatively little growth in public policy research that uses the techniques of meta-analysis. A search of the SSCI database for 1990 finds no articles that are listed jointly in the "meta-analysis" title field and the "policy" topic field. By 2011, only twenty-four articles were jointly listed in these areas. Moreover, meta-analysis has been slow to penetrate the disciplines that contribute to research in public management and policy. Table I.1 reports the cumulative number of articles archived by *Journal Storage* (JSTOR) since 1980 in the fields of public administration and policy, economics, political science, sociology, and education that include the terms *meta-analysis, meta-analytic*, or *research synthesis* in the title or abstract. Across the hundreds of scholarly journals included in the JSTOR database, economics, political science, and public administration and policy each published roughly one meta-analysis article per year over this period. Sociology journals published roughly three meta-analysis articles per year. By contrast, journals in the field of education published an average of over eighteen meta-analysis articles per year between 1980 and 2010. If meta-analysis is a growth industry in scholarly research, public management and policy scholars have done little to capture market share.

Additional evidence of the institutionalization of meta-analysis is found in the development and growth of international research organizations with the goal of improving the quality and quantity of meta-analytic research. Four of the most noteworthy of these organizations are the Cochrane Collaboration, the Campbell Collaboration, What Works Clearinghouse, and Meta-Analysis of Economics Research Network.

The Cochrane Collaboration

Established in 1993, the Cochrane Collaboration is an international network of more than twenty-eight thousand individuals, many of them researchers, with the goal of improving the quality and efficiency of health care worldwide through the generation and dissemination of high-quality research syntheses in medicine and other health care services (www.cochrane.org). Three products of the Cochrane Collaboration are especially worthy of note. First, the organization publishes *Cochrane Handbook of Systematic Reviews of Interventions*. The *Handbook* is essentially a how-to guide and best-practices manual for conducting high-quality meta-analyses in medicine. The *Handbook* is also used extensively by nonmedical researchers as a reference for the statistics of meta-analysis and as a guide for the effective presentation of the results from meta-analyses. Second, the Cochrane Collaboration publishes *Cochrane Reviews*, an extensive set of high-quality meta-analyses of health care interventions and health policy topics. Currently numbering more than four thousand, most Cochrane reviews meet the best-practice guidelines laid out in the *Handbook*, and they provide a rich base of information for evidence-based health care decisions. Third, the Cochrane Collaboration partners with Wiley-Blackwell to publish two peer-reviewed journals, *The Journal of Evidence-Based Medicine* and *Evidence-Based Child Health*, both of which feature prominent research articles emphasizing the techniques of meta-analysis.

The Campbell Collaboration

Established in 2000, the Campbell Collaboration (www.Campbell collaboration.org) is a sister organization to the Cochrane Collaboration. The Campbell Collaboration (C^2) is named in honor of Donald Campbell, the highly regarded social scientist who famously encouraged researchers to think of public policies as social experiments and to evaluate them as such. In contrast to the Cochrane Collaboration, C^2 has an explicit focus on public policy and encourages the production and dissemination of high-quality systematic reviews of policy research in the areas of criminal justice, education, social welfare, and international development. The Campbell Collaboration is a much smaller organization with far fewer collaborators and little or no paid staff. Moreover, C^2 has (thus far) produced nothing like the *Cochrane Handbook* or the set of *Cochrane Reviews* for researchers and practitioners in public policy. Nevertheless, C^2 collaborators and members of C^2 committees include many of the leading figures in meta-analysis, such as Betsy Becker, Harris Cooper, Julian Hedges, Mark Lipsey, Terri Pigott, Hannah Rothstein, and David Wilson.

What Works Clearinghouse

Established in 2002, What Works Clearinghouse (WWC) is an initiative of the U.S. Department of Education's Institute of Educational Sciences (ies.ed.gov/ncee/wwc). Administered by Mathematica Policy Research, one of the world's leading public policy research organizations, WWC both commissions and conducts systematic reviews of empirical research on educational interventions and education policy for educators and policy makers. While not all WWC reviews are formal meta-analyses, many are.

Meta-Analysis of Economics Research Network

Meta-Analysis of Economics Research Network (MAER, www.hendrix.edu/maer-network) is a relatively new collaboration of researchers from the field of economics. MAER has the aim of increasing the quality and quantity of meta-analysis in economics, largely through the FAT-MST-PET-MRA approach to meta-analysis, evaluated at length in chapter 7. While MAER does not publish Cochrane-like reviews, the organization does publish a bulletin summarizing recent meta-analysis research in economics and holds an annual workshop and colloquium.

A Role for Meta-Analysis in Public Management and Policy

A Role for Meta-Analysis in Improving Scholarship

When applied to questions in public management and policy, the tools of meta-analysis can help build bodies of cumulative knowledge and provide more precise and robust guides for action. Meta-analysis can advance scholarship in these fields in at least four ways.

Problem Identification. One way of distinguishing public policy research from more disciplinary-centered research is that the former is often problem-focused while the latter is more frequently motivated by theoretical concerns (Lasswell 1951). Given its emphasis on practice, the same might be said for research in public management. While good management and policy research is also grounded in theory, this distinction is important if for no other reason than that research in these fields often focuses on measuring the magnitude and scope of public problems. Individual original studies can contribute to problem identification and to measuring the magnitude of the problem in certain contexts. By synthesizing these original studies, meta-analysis can derive an estimate of the overall magnitude of the problem, map the scope of the problem, and determine whether the problem is more serious in some contexts than in others, as in the following scenarios:

- An original study can determine whether hazardous waste incinerators are inequitably distributed with respect to the race and class of community residents, but meta-analysis is better suited to measuring environmental inequities from all sources of potential environmental risk, and to determining whether these inequities are larger for certain risks or for particular groups.
- Individual studies can measure whether the range of a particular animal species or its breeding patterns have changed in response to increases in temperature, but meta-analysis can aggregate the results from multiple studies to determine whether there are large-scale patterns in species' range and breeding patterns consistent with the predicted effects from global climate change.

Measurement. Many important policy and management decisions hinge on accurate measurement of specific quantities of interest. For example, the wisdom of implementing a proposed regulation depends in part on the social benefits from the regulation. Estimating social benefits, in turn, requires accurately measuring nonmarket values. Individual studies can provide estimates of these values in particular contexts, but meta-analysis can aggregate estimates from individual studies into more robust and precise measures, as in the following scenarios:

- A study of wage differentials in a single industry or labor market can produce a measure of the statistical value of a life, but a meta-analysis of many such studies can provide a more accurate measure of this concept across the entire economy, and can determine whether this value differs across regions.
- A hedonic pricing model for a single community can provide an estimate of the social benefits from pollution control, but a meta-analysis of many such studies can produce a more accurate measure of these

benefits across the entire society, and can determine whether these benefits vary geographically.

· Individual studies can measure the cost savings from privatization of service provision in certain locales, but a meta-analysis of many such studies can provide a more comprehensive picture of the estimated fiscal benefits from privatization.

Program Evaluation. Vast amounts of scholarship have attempted to assess the consequences of policy interventions and management reforms, and the practical value of these efforts has increased as a consequence of, among other things, the 1993 Government Performance and Results Act (GPRA). Single original studies can evaluate a handful of outcome measures for individual policy and management actions, often in limited geographic areas. By synthesizing the results from these studies, however, meta-analysis can provide a bigger-picture view, evaluating the effects of management and policy reforms across multiple outcomes and geographic areas. Meta-analyses may also be able to help identify which program variants or elements are most and least effective, as in the following scenarios:

· An individual study of the New York City educational voucher program can determine whether vouchers improved math scores for students in this school system, but a meta-analysis of many voucher studies can measure the overall effect of educational vouchers and determine whether vouchers are more or less effective at building math skills compared with building reading skills.

· An individual study may be able to assess the effectiveness of a single federal job training program, but a meta-analysis of many studies may be able to provide evidence regarding which job training programs are most and least effective.

· An individual study may be able to examine the effect of contract design on contract performance in a particular government agency or municipality, but a meta-analysis of many studies may be able to produce general lessons about the most effective method of matching contract design to program context.

Hypothesis Testing and Theory Building. Practical sensibilities notwithstanding, scholarship in public management and policy is often keenly interested in building and testing theory. Meta-analysis can contribute in a meaningful way to theory development by aggregating the results from original studies that provide singular tests of hypotheses from these theories, as in the following scenarios:

- The Advocacy Coalition Framework (ACF) was offered as an empirically testable theory of policy making and policy change (Sabatier and Jenkins-Smith 1993). While the predictions from the ACF have been tested in a handful of contexts, a meta-analysis of original ACF studies could provide powerful evidence regarding the validity and generalizability of this theory.
- Bureaucracies that are representative of the clients they serve (racially, socioeconomically, ideologically, and so on) are theorized to be more effective and responsive than less representative bureaucracies (see, for example, Meier, Wrinkle, and Polinard 1999). Dozens of empirical studies have attempted to measure the effects of representative bureaucracy across levels of government and program areas. A meta-analysis synthesizing results from these studies could help establish whether the hypothesized benefits from representative bureaucracy are present, and whether these benefits differ across contexts.
- There is an ongoing debate in the public management and policy literature about the relative effectiveness of top-down versus bottom-up policy implementation designs (see, for example, Elmore 1979; Mazmanian and Sabatier 1989; Maynard-Moody, Musheno, and Palumbo 1990; Hill and Hupe 2009). Most tests of these perspectives examine implementation success in a single policy area or within a small number of agencies. A meta-analysis of the body of research in this area could help establish empirically the conditions under which top-down or bottom-up implementation styles are more effective.
- The use of meta-analysis for hypothesis testing and theory building is also especially helpful in the core social-science disciplines of political science (such as synthesizing the evidence regarding the effects of negative campaign ads on voter turnout), economics (for instance, synthesizing the evidence regarding the theory of Ricardian equivalence), and sociology (such as synthesizing the evidence regarding the characteristics and conditions associated with effective social movements).

A Role for Meta-Analysis in Improving Professional Self-Image

In one of the few explicit treatments of the role of meta-analysis in public policy decisions, John Hunter and Frank Schmidt paint a bleak picture of the contributions of social scientists to the policy-making process.

Hunter and Schmidt describe a cycle in which social scientists identify new and important questions having policy relevance. Initial studies examining these questions provide clear answers regarding, for example, the effectiveness of social policy interventions. Subsequent studies cast doubt on these initial conclusions, however, and with the proliferation of studies comes a proliferation of conclusions. The best efforts of ever-larger groups of social and behavioral researchers generates confusion and uncertainty rather than clarity. In the end, researchers conclude that the phenomena being studied are "hopelessly complex" and move on to other questions. After several repetitions of this cycle, social and behavioral scientists themselves become cynical about their own work and express doubts about whether behavioral and social science in general is capable of generating cumulative knowledge or answers to socially important questions (Hunter and Schmidt 1996, 325–326).

Although Hunter and Schmidt were writing within the field of psychology, public management scholars will surely recognize the angst about the perceived inability of the field to progress through the building of cumulative knowledge. While the perspective that public management (or public administration) should aspire to the production of scientific knowledge is not universal within the field, it is the dominant perspective. In their definitive summary of theoretical perspectives within public administration, Frederickson and Smith assert that research in public administration "aspire(s) to be *scientific*, using the word 'scientific' here to mean a kind of formal rationality by which the insights and decisions of one generation form the foundation for the inquiries of the next generation. Knowledge, then, becomes collective and cumulative" (Frederickson and Smith 2003: 3–4). For half a century, scholars in public administration have lamented the field's inability to live up to these aspirations, and have characterized much of the research in the fields as faddish and non-cumulative (Mosher 1956; Perry and Kraemer 1986; Houston and Delevan 1990; Overman and Boyd 1994). The most current statement regarding the state of the field continues to reflect this theme. In closing plenary remarks at the Minnowbrook II conference, David Rosenbloom identified five steps that should be taken to make public administration a stronger and more robust field. The first step identified by Rosenbloom? *The need to aggregate knowledge in the sense of making it cumulative.* Summarizing this sentiment, Van Slyke, O'Leary, and Kim observe that in a sense, the more knowledge we create and diffuse, "the less we know, because our research is not aggregated or accumulated into substantial bodies of knowledge" (Van Slyke, O'Leary, and Kim 2010: 290).

The field of policy studies within political science has not been immune to self-critiques regarding a lack of scientific progress. Fifteen years ago, the newsletter of the Public Policy section of the American Political Science Association published a running debate between leading scholars regarding the perceived inability of the field to build cumulative knowledge or offer empirically substantiated theories of policy making (see, for example, Hill 1997; Sabatier 1997; see also Sabatier 2001). Peter DeLeon sums up this critique nicely when he states that "political scientists have spent (almost literally) countless articles and books proposing something like 'laws' or theories that, taken collectively ... have produced infinitely more confusion than clarity" (DeLeon 1998: 150).

There are at least four reasons for this collective self-doubt within public management and policy about the ability to progress via knowledge accumulation. First, a sizeable proportion of researchers in these fields reject the notion that public management and policy can produce scientifically valid and cumulative knowledge in the same way as the physical sciences (see, for example, Schram and Caterino 2006; Riccucci 2010). Second, social scientists in general may misperceive the degree of consistency of research results in the physical sciences. For example, using the tools of meta-analysis, Hedges (1987) compared the variability of findings in thirteen research areas in particle physics and thirteen research areas in psychology and found significantly more variability in physics. Perhaps the social sciences are more "scientific" than many of us believe.

A third reason why public management and policy scholars sometimes perceive little scientific progress in their fields may have something to do with the approach to original research in these fields. When reading the peer-reviewed literature, one is struck by the frequency with which scholars in effect build empirical models to test "their theory of Y." While new (or significantly revised) theories often make possible important scientific breakthroughs, this is the exception rather than the rule. To quote the eminent physicist Freeman Dyson, "the great advances in science usually result from new tools rather than from new doctrines" (Dyson 1996, 805). This approach to research is also at odds with the idea that science progresses most rapidly not by continually offering new theories or conjectures but by employing "strong inference"; that is, by devising precise tests of hypotheses, from which the results allow us to draw inferences about the value of *existing* theories (Platt 1964). Put plainly, research in public management and policy might generate more cumulative knowledge if researchers in these fields devoted more effort to testing existing theories using "strong inference" and less effort to generating and testing new theories.

Finally, knowledge accumulation in public management and policy may be unsatisfactory in part because management and policy scholars have not been using the proper tools. Meta-analysis has become the leading method through which results from original studies are aggregated. As we saw earlier, systematic and scientifically valid research syntheses, which include meta-analysis, are extremely rare in public management and policy. Researchers have been working feverishly to generate ever-higher-quality information within the first perspective on scientific advancement while virtually ignoring the second. Our hope is that more frequent use of high-quality meta-analyses will produce a clearer picture of the accumulated knowledge in public management and policy, and a clearer roadmap for where research in these fields needs to go next.

A Role for Meta-Analysis in Improving Practice

The general scientific community has recognized for better than twenty years the potential for meta-analysis to inform public policy. In the early 1990s, the National Research Council (NRC) of the National Academy of Sciences collaborated on an evaluation of the value of meta-analysis in contributing to the type of authoritative statements on the state of scientific knowledge that are the stock in trade of the NRC. This assessment concluded that meta-analysis had significant promise as a tool for informing public decision making (Wachter and Straf 1990; National Research Council 1992). The NRC has held workshops on expanding the use of meta-analysis in government-sponsored scientific assessments (Cooper 2003), and meta-analysis has figured prominently in NRC-sponsored reports in the areas of early childhood intervention (Lipsey 2009), regulatory benefit assessment (Miller, Robinson, and Lawrence 2006), and traffic safety (meta-analyses appear routinely in the Transportation Research Board publication *Transportation Research Record*). Even the journal *Science* commented favorably on the potential for meta-analysis to improve the quality of information provided to policy makers (Mann 1994).

Meta-analysis has also come to play a role in official evaluations of government programs. Hunter and Schmidt (1996) note that as early as 1994, the director of the Government Accountability Office's (GAO's) Division of Program Evaluation and Methodology spoke approvingly of the value of meta-analysis as a tool for communicating the complexity of research results to Congress. Moreover, in this position, Eleanor Chelimsky pioneered the use of meta-analysis at the GAO. Meta-analysis is now institutionalized in the GAO reference manual as a recommended technique for evaluating government programs (U.S. Government Accountability Office 2012) and commonly contributes to GAO reports (see, for example, U.S. Government Accountability Office 2009). Meta-analysis has also been used in evaluations conducted or sponsored by several other federal agencies, including the U.S. Food and Drug Administration (Berlin and Colditz 1999), Department of Justice (Lipsey, Wilson, and Cothern 2000), Department of Health and Human Services (Greenberg, Cebulla, and Bouchet 2005), and Department of Transportation (U.S. Government Accountability Office 2010). The path to greater reliance upon meta-analysis in government has had its bumps, however. In 1992 the U.S. Environmental Protection Agency (EPA) released a report linking environmental tobacco smoke (ETS, better known as "second-hand smoke") to lung cancer. The basis for this conclusion was an agency-sponsored meta-analysis of thirty-one original studies which concluded that exposure to ETS increased the risk of cancer by 20 percent. Critics quickly pointed out deficiencies in the meta-analysis, including a less-than-comprehensive coverage of the empirical literature, nontransparent criteria for identifying acceptable studies, and the use of nonstandard criteria for determining statistical significance (Cordray and Morphy 2009). Other critics pointed out that the meta-analysis found increased risks for a type of cancer that had never before been associated with tobacco smoke, suggesting that the positive results may have been an artifact of chance (Nilsson 2001). Eventually a federal district court invalidated the meta-analysis as a scientific basis for making policy recommendations.

We do not want to oversell the role of meta-analysis in practice. We are not claiming that meta-analysis is routinely used within government to evaluate public programs or to provide advice to policy makers and managers. We are simply pointing out that meta-analysis has a long history in government. We also expect that meta-analyses will become more common in the near future. This belief stems in part from the increased emphasis on evidence-based policy and management at the federal level since the passage of GPRA and reiterated by the 2010 GPRA Modernization Act. This belief is also supported by the increased use of meta-analysis in health and education policy via the efforts of the Cochrane Collaboration and What Works Clearinghouse. Finally, this belief is supported by the statements of high-level public managers. At the 2010 Conference of the National Association of Schools of Public Affairs and Administration (NASPAA), Shelley Metzenbaum (U.S. Office of Management and Budget), Naomi Goldstein (U.S. Administration for Children and Families), and Dionne Toombs (National Institute of Food and Agriculture) encouraged researchers in public management and policy to help practitioners make sense of the wide variety of research findings in areas relevant to their missions. Metzenbaum in particular implored audience members during a public address to tell public managers what the research says so that they might know what to do. Meta-analysis provides the best set of techniques for responding to these requests.

Meta-Analysis: Understanding the Basics

The Language of Meta-Analysis

Like most approaches to conducting research, meta-analysis employs a specialized vocabulary that at best poses an occasional barrier to entry for researchers new to the field and at worst leads to confusion or fundamental misunderstanding regarding the process and products of meta-analysis. In this section we provide brief descriptions of some of the key elements in the language of meta-analysis.

Original Study. *Original studies* are peer-reviewed articles, books, reports released by government agencies or private think tanks, unpublished reports, conference or working papers, or any other research product that reports the results from an empirical investigation of the research question of interest in the meta-analysis. Original studies provide the data for a meta-analysis, and meta-analysis seeks to synthesize the results from these original studies.

Focal Predictor. Most meta-analyses synthesize evidence regarding a particular treatment effect or relationship of interest. In medicine, for example, researchers may be interested in whether a new surgical procedure (X) reduces the incidence of post-operative infection (Y). In public policy, researchers may be interested in whether the use of an educational voucher (X) is associated with higher student academic achievement (Y), or whether the percentage of minority residents in communities (X) is correlated with sources of potential environmental risk in communities (Y). Meta-analysts often label the key independent variable X in these scenarios as the *focal predictor* (Becker 2009; Becker and Wu 2007). While statistical models in original studies may contain many other independent variables, meta-analysts seek to synthesize evidence only about the effect of the focal predictor.

Effect Size. The *effect size* is the unit of analysis and the fundamental quantity of interest in a meta-analysis. Without effect sizes there can be no meta-analysis. Effect sizes are standardized measures of the relationship between the focal predictor and the dependent variable in original studies. Effect sizes, symbolized using Θ_i in this book, can be compared and combined across original studies. Effect sizes possess two quantities of interest: the magnitude of the effect size Θ_i and the effect size variance $V[\Theta_i]$. Both are required for meta-analysis. Meta-analysts might calculate upward of a dozen different types of effect sizes, depending on the design characteristics of original studies, the reported results in these studies, and the measurement of the focal predictor and the dependent variable, but all effect sizes are a member of one of three families; r-based, d-based, and odds-based effect sizes. Meta-analysis in public management and policy will almost always use r-based effect sizes. Chapter 3 provides an extended treatment of the calculation of effect sizes.

Fixed and Random Effects Models. All meta-analyses combine effect sizes using either fixed effects or random effects models. These models embody different assumptions about what the effect sizes Θ_i represent and about the effect size variance $V[\Theta_i]$. *Fixed effects* models assume that there is a single, constant or "fixed" population effect size Θ and that all individual effect sizes estimate this fixed parameter: $E[\Theta_i] = \Theta$. Individual effect sizes Θ_i depart from Θ due to sampling error, so the effect size variance $V[\Theta_i]$ is completely characterized by sampling error. Readers may recognize the fixed effects assumption as identical to the assumptions about the regression population parameter β and its sample estimate b. *Random effects* models assume that the population effect size Θ is a normally distributed random variable rather than a scalar, such that $\Theta \sim N(\mu_\Theta, \tau^2)$. Individual effect sizes Θ_i estimate the mean of this distribution: $E[\Theta_i] = \mu_\Theta$. Individual effect sizes Θ_i depart from μ_Θ due to the presence of the population effect size variance τ^2 and due to sampling error. Readers may recognize the random effects assumption as akin to the assumption underlying the random parameter panel data regression model. Meta-analysis in public management and policy will almost always use the random effects model. Fixed and random effects meta-analysis are discussed at length in chapters 3, 4, and 5.

Average Effect Size. The *average effect size* $\overline{\Theta}$ is the estimate of the fixed effect population effect size Θ or the mean of the random effects population effect size distribution μ_Θ, depending on which model is being used. The average effect size is calculated as the weighted average of all individual effect sizes Θ_i extracted from original studies, where the weights are the inverse of the effect size variance. We can use the average effect size $\overline{\Theta}$ to test the null hypotheses Ho: $\Theta = 0$ and Ho: $\mu_\Theta = 0$, but this is rarely useful because the statistical power generated from combining the results of original studies means that the null hypothesis is virtually always rejected. More important, the magnitude of the average effect size—for example, the average test score gains from using educational vouchers—has far more relevance for public management and policy than does determining whether this average effect size is different from zero. Chapters 3, 4, and 5 introduce several methods for calculating unconditional and conditional average effect sizes.

Moderator Variables. *Moderator variables* are factors that are hypothesized to influence systematically the magnitude of effect sizes calculated from original studies. Some moderator variables represent design characteristics of original studies. For example, it is well-known that self-selection into treatment often inflates the estimated effects of policy interventions. We would expect, therefore, that effect sizes from original studies that control for the endogeneity of treatment would be systematically different than effect sizes from original studies that do not employ these controls. To take another example, because parameter estimates from cross-sectional regression models identify different quantities of interest than do parameter estimates from panel data models, we would expect that effect sizes from cross-sectional studies and panel data studies will differ. When coding original studies we would create moderator variables identifying effect sizes coming from original studies with these characteristics. Other often more important moderator variables represent differences in program design, outcome measures, affected populations, or implementation environments that might systematically influence effect sizes. For example, we might hypothesize that younger students benefit more from using educational vouchers than do older students. In this case we would create a moderator variable identifying effect sizes from original studies examining voucher programs in which eligibility is limited to elementary school students. In the same vein, if we believe that the benefits of educational vouchers are cumulative, we would create a moderator variable identifying the number of years students used vouchers in the models generating individual effect sizes. Moderator variables are discussed in chapter 2.

Meta-Regression. Effect sizes are increasingly being employed as dependent variables in special forms of weighted least squares regression models. These *meta-regression* models use moderator variables to explain systematic variation in effect sizes across original studies. For example, meta-regression can test whether study design characteristics such as the use of ex-post controls for endogeneity influence average effect sizes across original studies. Meta-regression can also identify publication bias (see chapter 6) by testing whether average effect sizes differ between published and unpublished original studies. Most important, meta-regression can assess whether average effect sizes vary systematically according to programmatically relevant factors. For example, in the area of environmental justice we can test whether inequities associated with more serious environmental risks (such as ambient pollution concentrations) are larger or smaller than inequities associated with less serious environmental risks (such as the location of solid waste landfills). Meta-regression can also test whether the average gains from educational vouchers are different for elementary and high school students, whether average gains from educational vouchers accumulate over time, and whether average gains from educational vouchers are different in math and reading. Meta-regression ought to be the primary focus of meta-analysis in public management and policy. The techniques of meta-regression are introduced in chapters 4 and 5, and each of the original meta-analyses in chapters 8 through 11 employs meta-regression.

Stages in Conducting a Meta-Analysis

We encourage researchers to think about conducting a meta-analysis using a six-stage process. The number of stages is somewhat arbitrary—Harris Cooper, for example, has organized the conduct of meta-analysis into five stages (Cooper 1982), six stages (Cooper 2007), and seven stages (Cooper 2010). The cumulative content of these stages and how each stage is conducted matter far more than the number of stages. In particular, at each stage of a meta-analysis researchers should strive to "meet the same rigorous methodological standards that are applied to primary research" (Cooper 2010, 3). Specifically, the rules of evidence, the values of transparency and replicability, and threats to validity are no less important in meta-analysis than in traditional research. Chapters 1 and 2, in fact, draw explicit parallels between the choices made by meta-analysts and the choices made by researchers completing original studies, while chapter 3 and (especially) chapters 4 and 5 draw these parallels with respect to data analysis.

Stage 1: Scoping. The first step in a meta-analysis is identifying a clear research topic. This topic might be problem-driven (for example, how severe are environmental inequities?), policy-driven (for example, what have been the effects from school choice?), or theory-driven (for example, does the empirical research support the theory of Ricardian equivalence?). Scoping also involves moving from a general research topic to a specific, carefully operationalized research question; identifying the key hypothesis of interest from that research question; and identifying and operationalizing the focal predictor(s) and dependent variable(s) used to test this hypothesis in original studies. The scoping process is discussed in chapter 1.

Stage 2: Literature Search. The next step in meta-analysis is to identify original studies that test empirically the key hypothesis of interest using the focal predictor(s) and dependent variable(s) identified in stage 1. The literature search defines the universe of relevant empirical research on a topic and determines the contents of the meta-analysis data set. Therefore, the literature search must be systematic, comprehensive, and replicable. Modern archives of research articles and fast and flexible electronic search engines make searching the literature far faster and easier than just ten years ago. This same convenience, however, can lead to complacency for the meta-analyst. Researchers should *never* rely solely on the peer-reviewed or "published" literature when conducting a meta-analysis. This is especially true in public management and policy, in which large numbers of relevant, high-quality empirical studies are produced by government agencies, government advisory groups, policy research firms, policy think tanks, and interest groups. The meta-analysis literature search is discussed in chapter 1.

Stage 3: Data Coding. Meta-analysts extract useable data from original studies using coding instruments. With these coding instruments, researchers essentially "interview" or "interrogate" original studies to identify the information necessary to conduct the meta-analysis. Investigators generally code three types of information from original studies: (1) information necessary to calculate effect sizes and effect size variances; (2) information on the design, specification, and execution of models in original studies; and (3) information on the outcomes measured, affected groups, and other scientifically interesting factors that might influence the magnitude of effect sizes. The construction and use of coding instruments in meta-analysis are discussed in chapter 2.

Stage 4: Calculating and Combining Effect Sizes. After entering the information collected in stage 3 into a data set, meta-analysts use these data to
calculate standardized effect sizes that measure the relationship between
the focal predictor and the dependent variable in original studies. These
effect sizes can be compared across studies to describe patterns of evidence in the empirical literature and combined to calculate average effect
sizes that estimate the population effect size characterizing the relationship of interest. Calculating effect sizes gives us the measures necessary
to answer the research question, and average effect sizes give us an initial
answer to this question. Calculating and combining effect sizes are discussed in chapter 3.

Stage 5: Explaining Differences in Effect Sizes Across Original Studies. With
increasing frequency, meta-analysis goes beyond calculating average effect
sizes and attempts to explain differences in effect sizes across original studies. Implicit in this development is the recognition that there is rarely a
single average effect size characterizing the relationship between the focal
predictor and the dependent variable. For example, the effect of vouchers
on student academic achievement might differ across subject areas, across
types of students, and across program design. Meta-regression provides a
suite of tools that allow researchers to account for variation in effect sizes
across studies. Moreover, meta-regression also allows researchers to estimate conditional average effect sizes under different scenarios that are
important to policy makers. Chapters 4 and 5 discuss meta-regression.

Stage 6: Identifying Areas for Further Research. Meta-analysis is most often
thought of as a set of tools for consolidating evidence about what we
know. But meta-analysis is also a powerful tool for highlighting what we do
not know. Comprehensive syntheses of empirical research may reveal
that there are few studies testing theoretically important hypotheses or
estimating practically important quantities of interest, and therefore can
help set the agenda or chart a course for new research. For example,
in chapter 9 Ed Gerrish and Po-Ju Wu find surprisingly little empirical
research assessing the effectiveness of performance measurement systems
outside of public safety, and also find that most evaluations of performance
measurement were released *after* high-profile assessments had judged
the performance movement as ineffective and counterproductive (see,
for example, Radin 2006). Thus the meta-analysis in chapter 9 indicates
that researchers ought to devote greater effort to evaluating performance
measurement systems across a variety of policy areas, and that summary

assessments of the effects of performance measurement were probably premature. More generally, meta-analysis can identify the most useful or highest value-added areas for future research.

Comparing Meta-Analysis and Traditional Literature Reviews

The social sciences have long recognized the value of literature reviews. Several disciplines, in fact, have created outlets for this type of synthetic research. In economics, the *Journal of Economic Literature* served this function for many years, and while *JEL* still publishes some literature reviews, many more are now being published in the *Journal of Economic Surveys*. In political science, one rationale for the creation of *Perspectives on Politics* was to provide an outlet for literature reviews that were no longer being published in the *American Political Science Review*. Moreover, both *Political Research Quarterly* and the *Review of Policy Research* explicitly devote space to reviews of the literature in political science. While meta-analysis should never supplant traditional literature reviews, meta-analyses are meaningfully distinct from these reviews in at least four respects.

The Purpose of the Review. Traditional literature reviews are written for multiple purposes. Most reviews aim to summarize the existing research on a topic, though just what is summarized can vary across reviews. Other reviews, however, aim to provide critiques of existing research, while still others seek to integrate two or more bodies of research. Meta-analysis is more single-minded in purpose, aiming to summarize the empirical evidence regarding the relationship between the focal predictor and the dependent variable in a body of original studies.

Samples and Standards of Evidence. Traditional reviews often employ convenience samples of the extant literature, and the criteria used to include or exclude studies from the review are rarely explicit or transparent. In addition, conclusions about the quality of original studies and the relative weight attributed to each study are determined solely by the judgment of the reviewer. Traditional literature reviews, then, are not replicable, nor do they meet standards of validity beyond (weak) intersubjective agreement. By contrast, meta-analyses are replicable, and the validity of meta-analyses is assessed using the same criteria used to assess traditional empirical research. These differences do not mean that traditional literature reviews are not valuable, but they do suggest that meta-analysis may provide a firmer foundation for building cumulative scientific knowledge.

Focus of the Review. Traditional literature reviews often consider multiple research questions and multiple hypotheses. This breadth is one of their virtues. Traditional literature reviews also tend to focus on statistical significance, emphasizing whether original studies reject the null hypothesis of interest. Even when traditional reviews do not focus solely on statistical significance, they are unable to make statements about the magnitude of the effects represented in the reviewed studies. By contrast, meta-analysis focuses on effect sizes rather than statistical significance and can make precise statements about the magnitude of effects present in a body of research.

Validity of Conclusions from the Review. A focus on statistical significance and the implicit "vote-counting" that characterizes many traditional reviews can lead to conclusions that are at odds with conclusions from a meta-analysis, and that are also inconsistent with the underlying relationship of interest. Consider a hypothetical example in which the author of a traditional literature review collects twenty original studies on a particular research question published in the top academic journals.[2] Assume that there is a moderately strong positive relationship between the focal predictor X and the dependent variable Y, such that $\rho_{XY} = .25$. Furthermore, assume that each of the twenty original studies estimates the sample correlation coefficient r_{XY} with statistical power $\beta = .50$, a realistic level in social science research. In this scenario, ten of the original studies would reject the null hypothesis Ho: $\rho_{XY} = 0$, but ten would not. The author of the traditional literature review would likely conclude that the empirical research is "evenly split" as to whether X is related to Y, and therefore that social science can make no authoritative statements about the presence or magnitude of this relationship. But this conclusion is wrong. The ten studies that accepted Ho: $\rho_{XY} = 0$ did so in error (a type II error) because all studies estimated the true population parameter $\rho_{XY} = .25$. By contrast, a meta-analyst examining these same twenty original studies would calculate an effect size Θ_i for each, weight these effect sizes by their precision, and calculate an average effect size $\overline{\Theta}$ that will likely be very close to the population parameter $\rho_{XY} = .25$. Not only will the conclusion from the meta-analysis differ from that of the traditional review, but the conclusion from the meta-analysis is more likely to be correct. This difference between traditional literature reviews and meta-analysis served as the basis for a major controversy regarding the effects of school expenditures on educational outcomes (Hanushek 1989, 1994, 1996; Hedges, Laine, and Greenwald 1994a, 1994b; Greenwald, Hedges, and Laine 1996a, 1996b).

Criticisms of Meta-Analysis

From the beginning, critics have raised doubts about the value of meta-analysis.[3] Hans Eysenck, in fact, famously labeled the original meta-analysis by Gene Glass an exercise in "mega-silliness" (Eysenck 1978). Many criticisms of meta-analysis have merit. Many do not. No less authority than the journal *Science* weighed in on this issue, concluding that most of the criticisms of meta-analysis were inaccurate or overblown (Wachter 1988). What is striking is that when meta-analysis penetrates new disciplines, critics in these disciplines raise many of the same objections that Eysenck articulated more than a generation ago: see, for example, the recent controversy over the use of meta-analysis in ecology (Whittaker 2010a; 2010b). In this section we describe several of the most common criticisms of meta-analysis, and other criticisms that are unique to the use of meta-analysis in the social sciences, along with responses to these criticisms.

Criticism 1: You Can't Compare Apples and Oranges. The "apples and oranges" critique questions the premise that we can meaningfully combine the results from different empirical studies. Considered carefully, there are at least four ways in which original studies might be as different as apples and oranges.

Criticism 1A: Original Studies Measure X *and* Y *on Different Scales.* This version of the apples-and-oranges critique applies to original studies that operationalize X and Y using the same indicator, but measure that indicator using different metrics. This criticism is irrelevant, as all effect sizes in meta-analysis are standardized, rendering the metrics of X and Y moot.

Criticism 1B: Original Studies Operationalize X *and* Y *Using Different Indicators.* As an example, when studying the effect of educational vouchers on student academic achievement, original studies might operationalize achievement variously as scores on standardized math tests, scores on standardized reading tests, classroom grades, graduation rates, and so on. Alternatively, original studies examining the presence of environmental inequities may operationalize the concept of minority community using the percentage of black residents, the percentage of Hispanic residents, or the percentage of nonwhite residents.

We offer three responses to criticism 1B. First, the use of multiple indicators is usually viewed as a positive attribute in social science research, and several techniques are used to combine multiple indicators into a single variable in original studies: for example, factor analysis, standardized summed indices, multidimensional scaling, and so on. As standardized weighted averages, average effect sizes fit neatly within this tradition. It is unclear why combining multiple indicators is a strength in original studies but a weakness in meta-analysis. Second, many of the theoretical constructs used in public management and policy are multifaceted (for example, job satisfaction, human capital, organizational performance, public service motivation, regulatory stringency, economic development, environmental quality, and so on). When we estimate the relationships between multidimensional constructs using one-dimensional indicators, we run the risk of drawing conclusions that are, in part, artifacts of incomplete measurement (Cook and Campbell 1979). By combining the results from original studies employing different operationalizations of the same construct, meta-analysis can provide robust tests of the theories that employ these constructs. Third, in practice meta-analyses are designed to avoid this critique by (1) narrowly defining focal predictors and dependent variables, (2) estimating separate meta-analyses for effect sizes estimated from different operationalizations, or (3) using moderator variables in a meta-regression to isolate the effect of different operationalizations of the same construct. For example, in the educational voucher meta-analysis in chapter 8, we operationalize student academic achievement using standardized test scores, and use moderator variables to distinguish between effect sizes associated with math tests, reading tests, and combined tests.

Criticism 1C. Original Studies Utilize Different Research Designs. A long-time criticism of research in public management and policy is that the more common quasi-experimental studies produce different (and less reliable) estimates of program effects than those from experimental studies (Fraker, Maynard, and Nelson 1984, LaLonde 1986; LaLonde and Maynard 1987; Barnow 1987). In addition, other design elements can influence study outcomes in these fields, including the use of ex-post controls for endogeneity, the use of lagged dependent variables, the use of cross-sectional versus panel data, and the use of treatment interactions terms. Reasonable concerns have been raised about combining results from studies with different design characteristics in a meta-analysis (Lipsey and Wilson 2001).

In response, we point out that the quality of quasi-experimental studies in public policy has improved markedly since LaLonde and others raised their concerns, due largely to the development of quasi-experimental methods of analysis modeled explicitly on Rubin's counterfactual causal framework (Holland 1986; Rubin 2005). Moreover, more recent research has shown that the differences in estimated program effects and other quantities of interest are not so great between quasi-experimental and experimental studies (see, for example, Heckman 2000; Greenberg, Michaelopoulos, and Robin 2006), even for the programs studied initially by LaLonde (Heckman and Hotz 1989; Heckman and Smith 1995). Most important, modern meta-analysis can use moderator variables to estimate and control for differences in average effect sizes driven by design elements in original studies. Therefore there are few good reasons to avoid including effect sizes from original studies using different research designs in the same meta-analysis.

Criticism 1D: Original Studies Ask Different Questions and Test Different Hypotheses. This version of the apples-and-oranges critique has merit. Even careful analysis and the use of moderator variables cannot rescue a meta-analysis that combines results from original studies asking fundamentally different questions. But this is a critique of poorly designed meta-analyses, not a problem inherent in the techniques of meta-analysis. Moreover, similar critiques can be leveled at original research when investigators combine observations from two or more different populations in an analysis. The proper response to this critique is not to avoid doing a meta-analysis, but to do meta-analysis well.

Criticism 2: Garbage In, Garbage Out. This critique articulates the concern of many observers that by combining results from high-quality and low-quality studies, meta-analysis generates results that may be untrustworthy. Kenneth Wachter (1988, 1408) gives voice to this concern by observing that while "meta-analysts worry about the many studies left in file drawers, . . . skeptics worry about too many studies not left in wastebaskets, instead crowding journals, leaving the still small voice of signal to be drowned in noise." Some meta-analysts have responded to this criticism by offering the approach of "best-evidence synthesis" (Slavin 1995) that uses information only from the highest-quality original studies. Others have offered the advice that meta-analysts ought to exclude from consideration the 90 percent of original studies that use the smallest samples (Stanley, Jarrell, and Doucouliagos 2010). Best-evidence synthesis has not been widely adopted in the meta-analysis community, and we know of no serious effort by researchers to act on Stanley's advice—which is fortunate, because as it turns out, this is very bad advice (see chapter 7).

The response of meta-analysts to the garbage-in, garbage-out critique has been twofold. First, they have noted that excluding original studies ex ante on the basis of what are often subjective quality assessments undermines three of the basic benefits of meta-analysis: objectivity, replicability, and comprehensiveness. Second, standard advice in meta-analysis is to include indicators of high-quality (or low-quality) studies as moderator variables in the meta-analysis. In this way, researchers can test the expectation that lower-quality studies generate systematically different effect sizes, rather than asserting and acting on this conclusion in the absence of evidence.

Criticism 3: Selectivity Bias. The core of the selectivity bias critique is the concern that meta-analyses may use unrepresentative samples of the existing empirical research, thereby drawing inaccurate conclusions from a synthesis of this research. In one respect, this is a concern over poorly designed meta-analysis that can also be applied to poorly designed literature reviews. The obvious solution is to conduct systematic, comprehensive, and replicable literature reviews that follow the best-practice guidelines laid out in the *Cochrane Handbook* and illustrated in chapter 1. In another respect, this is a concern about publication bias—in other words, that researchers, reviewers, and editors prefer original studies having statistically significant results, and that therefore the published literature will overestimate average effect sizes. Chapter 6 provides an extensive discussion of publication bias, and chapter 7 assesses the validity of the most common test for publication bias. The conclusion from these chapters is that when it comes to publication bias, the best defense is a good offense. That is, extensively searching for unpublished studies and other examples of "grey" literature, and including these original studies in the meta-analysis ex ante, is far more effective than attempting to control for publication bias ex post.

Criticism 4: Meta-Analysis Sacrifices Nuance and Context. Some observers have raised concerns that by distilling the content of original studies down to effect sizes and a handful of moderator variables, meta-analysis loses the nuance, context, and therefore much of the meaning of the original research. This is true. The same can be said, however, for virtually all original quantitative studies, especially those that employ regression analysis or other variants of the general linear model. The results from these models derive from conditional expectations, and therefore adequately describe only the "most typical" observations in a data set. For example, while regression models in original studies might be able to estimate whether average test scores are higher for voucher recipients or whether there are more hazardous waste incinerators in Hispanic communities, these models can tell us little about why Sally Jones scored poorly on her math test or why ChemaCorp located its hazardous waste incinerator at 1001 Washington Street in East Saint Louis, Illinois. Viewed from this perspective, criticism 4 closely resembles the time-worn arguments regarding the virtues of qualitative and quantitative research in public management and policy. Just as qualitative and quantitative original studies employ methods that deliver different types of knowledge, meta-analysis and original quantitative studies employ methods that deliver different types of knowledge. Criticism 4 is no more and no less an indictment of meta-analysis than similar critiques are indictments of original quantitative research.

Criticism 5: Meta-Analysis Cannot Be Used to Combine the Results from Multivariate Models. Criticism 5 is not a general critique of meta-analysis but rather a critique specific to the types of original studies likely to be synthesized in public management and policy research. The statistics of meta-analysis have been developed most extensively within the experimental traditions of medicine and psychology. Effect sizes in these fields are likely to be calculated from differences in observed outcomes between randomly assigned treatment and control groups. By contrast, original research in public management, public policy, and the social sciences that contributes to these fields almost always employs some version of the general linear model (for example, ordinary least squares regression, weighted least squares regression, Probit or Logit, hierarchical linear models, generalized estimating equations, fixed effects or random effects panel data models, multi-equation sample selectivity models, and so on). Effect sizes in these fields, then, are calculated from the parameter estimate b_j associated with the focal predictor X_j in these models. Three criticisms have been raised regarding the synthesis of regression and other similar coefficient estimates in meta-analysis (see Becker and Wu 2007 for one of the few explicit treatments of combining regression coefficients in meta-analysis).

Criticism 5A: Regression Parameter Estimates Are Not Directly Comparable. The substantive meaning of any regression parameter estimate b_j is conditional upon the measurement of the dependent variable Y and the focal predictor X_j. If the measurement of Y, the measurement of X_j, or the variance of Y or X_j differ across original studies 1 and 2, the respective regression parameter estimates b_{j1} and b_{j2} have different interpretations and therefore cannot be compared or combined. While this is true, meta-analysis does not combine raw regression parameter estimates, instead combining standardized effect sizes derived (in part) from these estimates. Criticism 5A, then, is irrelevant to the practice of meta-analysis.

Criticism 5B: Effect Sizes Cannot Be Calculated from Regression Coefficients. Criticism 5B is incorrect. It is an easy matter to calculate the sample partial correlation coefficient $r_{YXj.Xk}$ from multiple regression results using the formula $r_{YXj.Xk} = \sqrt{\left[t_j^2 / \left(t_j^2 + df\right)\right]}$ where t_j is the *t*-score used to test Ho: $\beta_j = 0$ in the multiple regression model (Greene 1993, 180). This formula applies regardless of the number of independent variables k included in the multiple regression model. Formulas for calculating $r_{YXj.Xk}$ using the results from other models are provided in chapter 3. Keef and Roberts (2004) show that this formula contains a slight positive bias in *k*. That is, holding the population parameter $\rho_{YXj.Xk}$ constant, the estimate of $r_{YXj.Xk}$ from any model will increase as the number of independent variables in the model increases. In chapter 3, we show that the size of this bias in practice is trivial, generally falling below rounding error in the calculation of $r_{YXj.Xk}$.

Criticism 5C: Regression Parameter Estimates from Different Models Estimate Different Population Parameters and Therefore Are Incomparable. Criticism 5C is the only accurate version of criticism 5. Assume that a team of meta-analysts is interested in synthesizing empirical results regarding the relationship between focal predictor X_1 and dependent variable Y. Furthermore, assume that the meta-analysts obtain two original studies. Study A estimates the sample regression model $Y_i = b_0 + b_1 X_{1i} + b_2 X_{2i} + b_3 X_{3i} + e_i$, while study B estimates the sample regression model $Y_i = b_0 + b_1 X_{1i} + b_2 X_{2i} + b_4 X_{4i} + e_i$. The effect size calculated from study A is $r_{YX1.X2X3}$ while the effect size calculated from study B is $r_{YX1.X2X4}$. Unless $r(X_1 X_2 X_3) = r(X_1 X_2 X_4) = 0$, $E[r_{YX1.X2X3}] \neq E[r_{YX1.X2X4}]$. Therefore, the effect sizes from study A and study B do not satisfy the fundamental assumption that all effect sizes in a meta-analysis estimate the same population effect size; that is, $E[\Theta_i] = \Theta$ in the fixed effects model and $E[\Theta_i] = \mu_\Theta$ in the random effects model.

Keef and Roberts (2004) and Becker and Wu (2007) offer methods for combining partial correlation coefficients from different model specifications in a meta-analysis. The method of Keef and Roberts, however, focuses on combining these partial effect sizes into a single average effect size. While this is often appropriate in medical research (and Keef and Roberts are medical researchers), researchers in public management and policy are rarely interested in calculating a single average effect size. The method of Becker and Wu, by contrast, focuses on combining partial effect sizes for all variables in all regression models, rather than on combining effect sizes only for the focal predictor from these models. Moreover, the

Becker and Wu approach assumes that the meta-analyst has access to the full parameter variance-covariance matrix from the original studies, which will rarely be the case in practice.

As an alternative, we recommend managing criticism 5C by creating moderator variables that identify effect sizes coming from models that include especially influential control variables. For example, in a meta-analysis of research in environmental justice, one of us included moderator variables identifying whether effect sizes came from original regression models that included control variables for property values or the size of the local manufacturing sector (Ringquist 2005). The meta-analysis of educational vouchers in chapter 8 includes a moderator variable identifying effects sizes from original models that include a pretest control variable. Including these moderator variables in a meta-regression accounts for differences in the expected value of effect sizes, thereby controlling for the effects of model specification in original studies. This approach is consistent with the meta-regression model developed by Hedges and Olkin (1985) and the conditional logistic meta-regression model of Sterne and colleagues (2002). The approach is also recognized as valid by Becker and Wu (2007). Of course, it would be unwise to include moderator variables in a meta-regression for every control variable used in any original study, just as it is unwise to include every independent variable in an original regression model that has any influence on the conditional expectation of the dependent variable Y. In meta-regression as in regular regression, researchers face the trade-off between the benefits of efficiency stemming from parsimony and the risks of excluded variable bias.

Adapting Meta-Analysis for Public Management and Policy

The context and techniques of meta-analysis are meaningfully different for public management and policy compared with medicine and psychology, and somewhat different from meta-analysis in education. While some of these differences are discussed elsewhere in the introduction, they were not identified as such. In this section we discuss how the context of meta-analysis differs for public management and policy, and how we can adapt the techniques of meta-analysis to reflect this context.

Differences in Original Studies

Original studies in public management and policy differ from the types of original studies most frequently synthesized in meta-analysis. While the characteristics of original studies identified here are not unique to research in these fields, they are unusual enough in the environment of meta-analysis to deserve comment.

Study Design. As discussed elsewhere, the statistics of meta-analysis were developed to synthesize results from experiments or clinical trials. Field and even laboratory experiments are becoming more common in public management and policy, and in the social science disciplines of economics, political science, and sociology. Nevertheless, the large majority of original studies in these fields is observational and employs quasi-experimental or correlational designs. While effect sizes can be calculated easily from these studies, heterogeneity in study design means that meta-analysts must take greater care when combining results from original studies employing different designs.

Measurement. Much of the research in psychology uses common sets of validated scales, while the measurements of treatment and outcome variables in medical research are easily comparable. Common validated scales are used less frequently in public management and policy research, and variability in the indicators used to measure outcomes and focal predictors tends to be much greater in these fields. Combining effect sizes across multiple indicators poses few problems if the goal of the meta-analysis is to test general theories of individual or collective behavior that employ complex constructs. If the aim of the meta-analysis is to estimate program effects or provide actionable input to decision makers, however, meta-analysis in policy and management must take care to account for these different measurement strategies in original studies when calculating conditional average effects.

Estimation. The large majority of original studies in public management and policy use some variant of the general linear model, but the estimated quantities of interest often differ across variants. For example, a linear regression model can be used to estimate intent to treat effects or the effect of the treatment on the treated, and these quantities should not be combined in a meta-analysis. Similarly, parameter estimates from cross-sectional and panel data regression models estimate different quantities of interest, and meta-analyses that combine results from these types of models should distinguish between them using a moderator variable.

Differences in Effect Sizes

Type of Effect Size. Most meta-analyses employ either odds-based or *d*-based effect sizes. Original studies in public management and policy, however, are far more likely to generate *r*-based effect sizes. While the statistical theory supporting the synthesis of *r*-based effect sizes is well established, researchers in public management and policy are cautioned that recent developments in the statistics of meta-analysis are rarely assessed using *r*-based effect sizes, and statistical software packages for meta-analysis handle *r*-based effect sizes only with some difficulty.

Heterogeneity in Effect Sizes. The greater variability in measurement and the use of multiple independent variables in original studies means that effect sizes in public management and policy are likely to be far more heterogeneous than effect sizes in medicine and psychology. An important implication of this heterogeneity is that the fixed effects model will rarely be appropriate for meta-analysis in these fields. Random effects meta-analysis should always be used unless there are exceptionally strong reasons to accept the assumption of fixed effects.

Number of Effect Sizes. The techniques of meta-analysis were developed under the assumption that original studies would produce a single effect size. Moreover, the statistics of meta-analysis were developed under the assumption that sample effect sizes represented independent estimates of the population effect size. Neither of these assumptions applies to meta-analysis in public management and policy. Original studies in these fields virtually always present multiple estimates of the relationship between the focal predictor and the dependent variable. These estimates might be produced by models employing different samples, different sets of control variables, or different assumptions about the model error term. In fact, these sorts of sensitivity analyses are hallmarks of high-quality research in these fields. Whereas many meta-analyses in medicine synthesize as few as ten to fifty effect sizes, meta-analyses in public management and policy will routinely work with several hundred effect sizes. Meta-analysis tools such as funnel plots, forest plots, and cumulative meta-analysis are not useful with this many effect sizes (these tools of meta-analysis are described in chapter 3). In addition, multiple effect sizes generated from the same original study are likely to be correlated. While researchers in meta-analysis have devised several methods to control for this correlation when calculating average effect sizes, similar techniques have not been developed for meta-regression. Thankfully, the field of econometrics has developed effective methods for deriving consistent and efficient regression parameter estimates from correlated observations. These techniques are adapted to meta-regression in chapter 5, and meta-regression analysis in public management and policy should use these techniques.

Differences in the Goals of Meta-Analysis

The goals of a traditional meta-analysis are to (1) describe the distribution of effect sizes across original studies, often by using a forest plot, and (2) calculate an average effect size $\overline{\Theta}$ (and its confidence interval) as an estimate of the population effect size Θ or μ_{Θ}. As mentioned earlier, forest plots and other tools for describing the distribution of effect sizes will often be unhelpful for meta-analysis in public management and policy. More important, the large heterogeneity among effect sizes from original studies in these fields means that a single average effect size will rarely be useful or informative. *The primary goal of meta-analysis in public management and policy ought to be to account for variation in effect sizes.* Sources of variation might be of scholarly interest (for example, variation in effect sizes attributable to design elements of original studies) or of practical interest (for example, variation in effect sizes attributable to affected groups or program design). Consistent with this goal, *meta-regression ought to be the primary meta-analysis technique in public management and policy.* Meta-regression can test hypotheses associated with moderator variables by leveraging both intra-study and inter-study variation in effect sizes. In addition, meta-regression can be used to estimate average effect sizes under different scenarios of interest to scholars and policy makers. This meta-regression scenario analysis is akin to the "response surface" approach to meta-analysis suggested by Rubin (1992; for an application, see Shadish, Matt, Navarro, and Phillips 2000).

Conclusion

Meta-analysis offers researchers in public management, public policy, and the social sciences a set of tools with which to improve scholarship in the sense that meta-analysis can provide more generalizable estimates of the effects from management and policy interventions, offer more robust tests of theories in public management and policy, and build cumulative knowledge in these fields. Meta-analysis also offers researchers a set of tools for generating more useful scholarship in that by synthesizing the results from multiple studies, meta-analysis can help make sense of mountains of sometimes inconsistent conclusions from original research, thereby providing clearer and more authoritative advice to management and policy professionals. Important to note, the techniques of meta-analysis have developed to the point at which, properly adapted, they can now fulfill their potential to improve the quality and relevance of research in public management and policy. Therefore we believe that the time is right for meta-analysis to play a larger role in public management and policy research.

Notes

1. The history of the development of meta-analysis presented here is selective and intentionally brief. Readers interested in a more complete account of the development of meta-analysis should consult Hunt (1997) or Lipsey and Wilson (2001).
2. We owe this example to Hunter and Schmidt (1996), though we have altered it in several respects.
3. For good summaries of these criticisms, see Sharpe (1997) and Mullen and Ramirez (2006).

PART ONE

TECHNIQUES OF META-ANALYSIS

CHAPTER ONE

CONCEPTUALIZING RESEARCH
AND GATHERING STUDIES

Evan J. Ringquist

"For many years, policy makers expressed increasing frustration with social science research. On every issue there were studies arguing for diametrically opposed conclusions. . . . In many areas meta-analysis has now provided dependable answers to the original research questions. Meta-analysis is now increasingly being used by policy makers, by textbook writers, and by theorists to provide the basic facts needed to draw both practical and explanatory conclusions"

(HUNTER AND SCHMIDT 1996, 325).

In principle, meta-analysis differs little from traditional original research, particularly quantitative research employing survey methods. First, as with original research, conducting a meta-analysis begins with identifying a research question. Good research questions for meta-analysis share characteristics with good research questions for original research; they are theoretically grounded, specific, able to be precisely operationalized, and answered by measuring a particular quantity of interest. Second, as with original research, essential elements of designing a meta-analysis include identifying units of analysis, developing a strategy for sampling those units, and executing the sampling strategy. Of course, this analogy should not be taken too far. After all, the meta-analyst surveys studies, not human subjects. Moreover, the sampling strategy of the meta-analyst aims to identify the population of relevant studies, not a random sample of these studies. Third, similar to those doing original research, the meta-analyst must develop a survey instrument and use this instrument to extract information from the sample necessary to answer the research question. In this chapter I discuss the essential elements of conceptualizing a meta-analysis and identifying the sample of original studies to be synthesized. Chapter 2 discusses the development of survey (that is, coding) instruments and their application to the original studies.

Conceptualizing a Meta-Analysis

There are two steps in conceptualizing a meta-analysis in public management, public policy, and the social sciences. First, the researcher must identify the *quantity of interest* that will be estimated by synthesizing the results from original studies. Quantities of interest for a meta-analysis may be estimates of a particular program effect; for example, the quantity of interest for the meta-analysis in chapter 8 is the effect from using educational vouchers on student standardized test scores, while the quantity of interest for the meta-analysis in chapter 10 is the effect of public housing deconcentration on the life outcomes of housing assistance recipients. Quantities of interest for a meta-analysis may also be estimates of relationships or associations; for instance, the quantity of interest for the environmental justice meta-analysis used as an example in this book is the association between the residential concentration of poor and minority residents in communities and levels of potential environmental risk in communities, while the quantity of interest for the meta-analysis in chapter 11 is the relationship between the degree of public service motivation among employees in an organization and measures of organizational performance. Whether quantities of interest represent program effects or measures of association, they can only be identified for specific research questions.

Second, *researchers must develop a conceptual model* accounting for variation in estimates of the quantity of interest across studies. A hallmark of research in public management and policy seems to be that original studies provide different and sometimes incompatible answers to the same question. That is, they provide meaningfully different estimates of the quantity of interest. These differences pose a barrier to the accumulation of knowledge and also reduce the value of research for practice. A key difference between meta-analysis in medicine and meta-analysis in public management and policy is that the former places greatest emphasis on estimating the average effect size while the latter ought to place the most emphasis on modeling variation in effect sizes across studies.

Research Topics, Research Questions, and Quantities of Interest

Quantities of interest (that is, effect sizes), can only be identified for specific research questions. Therefore, a key issue in meta-analysis (as with any empirical research) is the distinction between research *topics* and research *questions*. Research topics are subject focused, are typically vague, and implicitly suggest descriptive analysis. Examples of research topics include

- Environmental justice
- Educational vouchers
- Sustainable development
- Leadership strategies
- Housing discrimination

Research questions, however, are more precise, tend to focus on relationships between variables, and imply explanation or the measurement of effects. Examples of research questions matched to the previous research topics could include

- Are levels of environmental risk inequitably distributed with respect to race?
- Do educational vouchers work?
- Can micro-loans encourage sustainable development?
- Are different leadership strategies more effective under different circumstances?
- What accounts for housing discrimination?

Research Questions in Meta-Analysis. Meta-analysis cannot synthesize evidence regarding research topics. Meta-analysis can only synthesize evidence regarding research questions. Identifying the research question, therefore, is the first step in any meta-analysis. In this respect, designing a meta-analysis is no different from designing a piece of original research. In both instances the investigation begins by articulating a specific and well-bounded research question.

The brief examples just mentioned are simplistic in that they suggest a one-to-one relationship between research topics and research questions. In fact, any research topic can give rise to several specific research questions.

Consider the research topic of educational vouchers. We could address this topic using any of the following questions:

- Does the use of vouchers improve academic performance?
- Why do some jurisdictions adopt voucher programs and others do not?
- Does the use of vouchers affect student attitudes and behavior?
- Why do parents seek vouchers?
- Why do parents or students refuse vouchers when they are offered?
- Are vouchers a less expensive method of providing public education?
- What effects do voucher programs have on private school tuition?
- What effect does competition from vouchers have on public school performance?

Any of these questions, along with others not listed, could serve as the target for a meta-analysis. One of the most important tasks for the meta-analyst is to accurately identify the most important or meaningful research questions on a particular research topic.

Hypotheses in Meta-Analysis. Good research questions can be reconfigured as hypotheses. For example, the research question

- Does the use of educational vouchers improve academic performance?

can be transformed into the hypothesis

- Students using vouchers display higher academic performance.

Other good research questions have several hypotheses embedded within them. For example, the research question

- Why do parents seek vouchers?

becomes the set of hypotheses

- Parents seek vouchers to send their children to academically higher-performing schools.
- Parents seek vouchers to subsidize religious instruction for their children.
- Parents seek vouchers to place their children in a more homogenous school environment.

· Parents seek vouchers to send their children to schools with better athletic programs.

Meta-analysis is most commonly described as a set of techniques for combining the results from individual original studies. But meta-analysis cannot synthesize results from all studies examining a particular research question. To be combined in a meta-analysis, original studies must (1) employ quantitative data analysis and (2) test the same hypothesis or measure the same quantity of interest. Viewed from this perspective, meta-analysis is often a set of techniques for combining the results from a series of hypothesis tests. Properly identifying the most important hypotheses embedded within specific research questions, then, is as important as identifying the proper research questions in the first place.

Conceptual and Operational Definitions in Hypotheses. Research questions can be transformed into two types of hypotheses. *Conceptual hypotheses* articulate the elements of the hypothesis in terms of the theoretical concepts or constructs of interest. For example, researchers in environmental justice investigate the relationship between the residential concentration of members of groups that traditionally have received inequitable treatment and the concentration of sources of environmental risk. When assessing the value of vouchers, we are interested in the relationship between the use of the voucher and student academic achievement. The difficulty with these conceptual hypotheses, however, is that they cannot be tested because the elements of the hypotheses cannot be measured directly. Therefore, researchers take conceptual hypotheses that are formed using theoretically important constructs and transform them into *operational hypotheses*, in which the elements of the hypothesis are represented as specific, measurable indicators. This is no less true for meta-analysis than it is for original research.

Most of the important theoretical concepts in the social sciences are unnatural, or constructed, or "imaginary" in the sense that they are not directly observable in the same ways as are many of the concepts in the physical sciences. Consider, for example, the physical science concept of "temperature" and the social science concept of "achievement." Both concepts are socially constructed in the sense that physical scientists had to agree that "temperature" meant a quantity of kinetic energy or molecular motion in a sample of matter, and furthermore had to agree on a standard scale for measuring this quantity. "Achievement," however, is quite different. First, achievement is a multidimensional concept in that it can mean many things. Most social science concepts share this quality (for example, "economic development," "representation," "terrorism"). Second, unlike temperature, achievement does not exist outside of our imagination. Most social science concepts share this quality as well (for example, "organizational mission," "ideology," "equity"). Even when the physical and social sciences use the same concepts, they are often one-dimensional and directly measurable in the physical sciences but multidimensional and socially constructed in the social sciences (such as "gender").

A great challenge for social scientists, then, is developing and implementing *indicators* that can measure these multidimensional and imaginary *concepts* (Cook and Campbell 1979). This *concept-indicator* problem has two elements that are especially relevant for meta-analysis. First, there is always some question as to whether our indicators actually measure the concept of interest. For example, there is a debate in economics as to whether Gross Domestic Product is a valid measure of national economic well-being. Second, since most of our measures are one-dimensional, even if they are a valid indicator of one aspect of the concept they may do a poor job of measuring the overall concept. For example, many educators believe that standardized test scores accurately measure mastery of certain materials and skills by students, but they also believe that these scores are overly narrow and provide an incomplete measure of the concepts of "student achievement" or "educational progress."

An adequate appreciation of concept-indicator problems is essential when designing a meta-analysis. First, *the meta-analyst often defines the scope of the research by choosing to examine some indicators rather than others*. Original studies are included or excluded from a meta-analysis on the basis of whether the studies employ particular indicators of broader concepts. Table 1.1 offers examples of key concepts and their multiple indicators in environmental justice and school choice research. In the first row we see that educational vouchers are actually one operationalization (or indicator) of the broader concept of "school choice." Even within the operational definition of educational vouchers there is variation; for example, vouchers may provide direct or indirect subsidies to the parents of school-aged children, and the use of vouchers may be restricted to secular schools or allowed to be used at religious schools. Similarly, the concept of student academic achievement can be operationalized using student standardized test scores, classroom grades, graduation rates, or college admission rates. The use of vouchers may affect any of these operational definitions of "achievement." The scope of the educational voucher meta-analysis in chapter 8 is defined using these operational definitions. Specifically, we operationalize

TABLE 1.1. CONCEPTUAL AND OPERATIONAL DEFINITIONS
OF ELEMENTS OF HYPOTHESES

Conceptual Definitions (concepts)	Operational Definitions (indicators)	Sub-Indicators
School Choice	Open enrollment	Inter-district Intra-district
	Charter schools	Private Public
	Educational vouchers	Direct payment Tax credits Religious
Academic Performance	Standardized test scores	Subject test Combined test
	Graduation rates College admission rates	
Target of Inequity	Race and ethnicity	Percentage of black residents Percentage of Hispanic residents Percentage of nonwhite residents
	Class	Median household income Percentage of households below poverty line Percentage of residents with high school degree
Environmental Risk	Risky facilities	Hazardous waste facilities Solid waste landfills Polluting facilities
	Pollution levels	Air pollution Water pollution TRI releases Accidental chemical spills
	Ambient environmental risk	Cancer risk

"school choice" using "educational vouchers" and operationalize "educational vouchers" using direct subsidies. Because of these choices, the meta-analysis can say nothing about the effects of open enrollment, charter schools, or private school tax credit programs (that is, indirect voucher subsidies) on student achievement. Chapter 8 also operationalizes "academic performance" using standardized test scores, so the meta-analysis tells us nothing about the effects from using vouchers on high school graduation or college admission rates.

Second, *meta-analysts often identify important moderator variables by considering carefully the various ways key concepts are operationalized in original research*. The third and fourth rows of table 1.1 illustrate the various ways the concepts of "inequity" and "environmental risk" have been defined in environmental justice research. Unlike in the student voucher example, these operational definitions were not used to exclude original studies from the environmental justice meta-analysis that provides a running example through the book. Instead, I created *moderator variables* (defined in the next section) that identified which effect sizes represented race-based or class-based inequities and which effect sizes measured the inequitable distribution of risky facilities versus pollution levels. These moderator variables were then used in meta-regression models to explain why different studies estimated different levels of environmental inequity.

The great variety of operational hypotheses in original studies presents a double-edged sword to the meta-analyst. On the one hand, meta-analysis can combine the results from original studies that, collectively, employ multiple operationalizations (or indicators) of the same concept. Unlike researchers conducting an original study, meta-analysts rarely have to worry whether their results are an artifact of the one-dimensional indicator used to measure the multidimensional concept. In this way, the meta-analyst can conduct robust hypothesis tests that are more faithful to the conceptual theory that generated these hypotheses. On the other hand, a meta-analysis that combines results from too great a variety of operational hypotheses runs the risk of being labeled with the "apples and oranges" critique. Moreover, the results from meta-analyses that employ a wide variety of indicators are often less useful for policy makers and managers looking to meta-analysis as an input to decision making. Sensible advice is that when researchers conduct a meta-analysis in order to synthesize the evidence regarding a particular theoretical expectation, they ought to include original studies that employ a broad range of operational definitions of the theoretical construct. By contrast, when meta-analysis aims to summarize the evidence regarding a particular policy or management intervention in order to inform decision making, operational definitions ought to be bounded more narrowly.

Accounting for Variation in Effect Sizes

For most meta-analyses, the quantity of interest can be represented as a simple path diagram linking the focal predictor X and the dependent variables of interest Y as in equation 1.1.

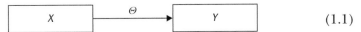

$$(1.1)$$

Meta-analysis measures the relationship between X and Y, represented by the arrow, using an effect size, represented as Θ. In the environmental justice example, X represents the percentage of minority residents in communities, Y represents potential environmental risk in communities, and Θ represents the degree of environmental inequity in the sample. In the educational voucher example, X represents the use of a voucher, Y represents student performance on standardized tests, and Θ represents the differential test score gains attributable to the use of vouchers.

If Θ was the same for all original studies, there would be no need for meta-analysis. Estimates of Θ do differ between original studies, however, sometimes dramatically, even if these studies ask the same research question and employ the same operational hypotheses. An important benefit from meta-analysis is that it can help us understand the sources of this variation in the effect size Θ, as well as help us obtain an estimate of the average effect size (or quantity of interest) across all studies. And an important aspect of designing a meta-analysis is developing a conceptual model that can help account for this variation in effect sizes.

Moderator Variables as Explanations for Effect Size Variance. The effect size Θ from path model 1.1 might vary across original studies for several reasons:

1. *Sampling Error.* All studies estimate the same population effect size Θ, but effect sizes from individual studies (Θ_i) differ from Θ because original studies employ different samples. In meta-analysis this type of variation is addressed using a fixed effects model.
2. *Non-Specific Error Variance.* All studies do not estimate a common population effect size Θ, but they estimate the same expected value μ_{Θ}. Effect sizes from original studies differ both due to sampling error and due to unobservable factors. In meta-analysis, this type of variation is addressed using a random effects model.
3. *Variation in the Measurement of* X *(different indicators, not different scales).* Studies may employ different operationalizations of the focal predictor X. For example, in the environmental justice literature, some original studies measure the proportion of minority residents in a community using the percentage of black residents, while other studies measure this quantity using the percentage of nonwhite residents.
4. *Variation in the Measurement of* Y *(different indicators, not different scales).* Studies may employ different operationalizations of the dependent variable Y. For example, in the school voucher literature, some original studies measure student academic achievement using standardized math tests, while others measure this quantity using standardized reading tests.

5. Effect sizes may differ between studies due to differences in the research design or quality of the original studies.
6. Effect sizes may differ between studies due to what Rubin (1992) calls "scientifically interesting" factors—program design, implementation context, and so on.
7. Effect sizes may differ between studies due to differences in the model specification used to generate the effect size.

The sources of effect size variance described in reasons 1 and 2 are described in detail in chapter 3. The sources of effect size variance described in reasons 3 through 7 can all be operationalized as *moderator variables*, or measurable factors that can be used to predict or explain differences in the effect sizes from original studies that examine the same research question. Developing a conceptual model to account for variation in effect sizes across original studies, then, means thinking carefully about which factors might cause this variation, and how one might measure those factors using moderator variables.

Using Moderator Variables in Meta-Analysis. Chapter 2 describes a set of procedures for creating moderator variables when coding original studies. Most commonly, moderator variables are dichotomous, indicating that a particular effect size does or does not come from an original study possessing a particular attribute. For example, a moderator variable may take on a value of 1 for effect sizes measuring the effect of educational vouchers on student math test scores (reason 4 in the previous section). A different moderator variable might take on a value of 1 for effect sizes from original studies with random assignment of subjects to treatment and control groups (reason 5 in the previous section), and a third moderator variable may take on a value of one for effect sizes from original studies in which the sample is composed only of women (reason 6 in the previous section).

Moderator variables are sometimes used to identify subgroups of effect sizes that might best be analyzed in separate meta-regressions. For example, in my 2005 meta-analysis of the environmental justice literature I conducted separate meta-analyses for effect sizes measuring race-based and class-based inequities (an example of reason 3 in the previous section; see Ringquist 2005). More commonly, however, researchers in the social sciences will use moderator variables as predictors in meta-regression models. To illustrate, if we denote the three hypothetical moderator variables described in the previous paragraph as M_1, M_2, and M_3, we might estimate the meta-regression model

$$\Theta_i = b_0 + b_1 M_{1i} + b_2 M_{2i} + b_3 M_{3i} + e_i \qquad (1.2)$$

where Θ_i is the effect size calculated from the original study. In this model, b_1 estimates how the average effect size from using vouchers is different for math scores, b_2 estimates how the average effect size from using vouchers is different in studies with experimental designs, and b_3 estimates how the average effect size from using vouchers is different for female students.

Chapters 4 and 5 discuss meta-regression in great detail. I introduce the technique here only insofar as it helps illustrate how researchers might consider conceptual models accounting for variation in effect sizes across studies. An important distinction between building empirical models in traditional analysis and building these models in meta-analysis is that while the former focuses on explaining the conditional distribution of the dependent variable Y, the latter focuses on explaining variation in the relationship between X and Y. Meta-analysts do not include moderator variables that help account for the expected value of the dependent variable Y. Instead, moderator variables are used *only if they affect in a meaningful way the relationship between the focal predictor* X *and the dependent variable of interest* Y (that is, Θ).

Moderator variables in meta-regression are akin to interaction terms in a traditional regression model. When building a conceptual model, then, a meta-analyst interested in the effects of educational vouchers on student performance does not need to identify factors that affect test scores, but rather needs to identify factors that might *moderate* the effect of vouchers on test scores. In environmental justice research, examples of moderator variables might include median household income in a community and property values in a community. Both are plausibly related to the location of polluting facilities, and both are correlated with the focal predictor. Models in original studies that include these variables, then, are likely to estimate a different relationship between the percentage of minority residents in communities and levels of potential environmental risk in communities.

When designing a meta-analysis, it is essential to think carefully about which moderator variables will be used to characterize the sources of variation in effect sizes across studies. This is especially true when using meta-regression, since it is the proper identification, operationalization, and utilization of moderator variables that allows us to combine highly heterogeneous effect sizes in a single meta-regression model. If we exclude or misspecify important moderator variables—that is, if we conceptualize and operationalize the wrong model—the results from the meta-regression will be less helpful than they might otherwise be, and potentially may be misleading. The consequences of poor model misspecification are no less important in meta-analysis than in the conduct of original studies.

Conducting a Literature Search in Meta-Analysis

A high-quality literature search is necessary for conducting a high-quality meta-analysis. The literature search identifies the original studies that will generate the effect sizes used in the meta-analysis. The design of the literature search also defines the theoretical and empirical universe that the meta-analysis characterizes. A poorly designed or poorly executed literature search, then, generates bad data and limits the theoretical and practical relevance of the research. The meta-analyst has two tasks in the literature search: finding the original studies that address the research question of interest, and judging whether those studies are acceptable for inclusion in the meta-analysis. These tasks must be completed using procedures that are systematic, transparent, and replicable.

While there have been relatively few meta-analyses in public management, public policy, or related fields, a significant proportion of the studies that have been conducted examine only the peer-reviewed or published literature (see, for example, Jarrell and Stanley 1990; Card and Krueger 1995; Stanley 1998; Stanley and Jarrell 1998; Lau, Sigelman, Heldman, and Babbitt 1999; Doucouliagos and Ulubaşoğlu 2008; but see Smith and Huang 1995). This reliance on the peer-reviewed or published literature is unfortunate for two reasons. First, the proportion of relevant original research appearing in the unpublished or grey literature is higher in the social sciences than in the medicine, psychology, and other areas where meta-analysis is more common (Grayson and Gomersall 2003; Rothstein and Hopewell 2009). While I am not aware of any systematic study of the question, the strong presence of research firms and think tanks in the fields of public management and policy makes it likely that the grey literature is probably even more important in these fields than in the social sciences writ large. Second, recent research in the statistics of meta-analysis shows that the tools for diagnosing and correcting publication bias ex post perform very poorly, and in general are untrustworthy (see chapters 6 and 7).

Meta-analysts are far better served controlling for publication bias ex ante than attempting to remedy this bias ex post. All meta-analyses in public management and policy, therefore, should employ an explicit, comprehensive, and systematic search of the grey literature.

Identifying Original Studies

Before beginning a search of the literature, you need to know what you are searching for. Therefore, a good literature review begins with the design of the meta-analysis discussed in the previous section. Literature reviews in meta-analysis need to be motivated by a specific research question, and the literature search strategy needs to be built around one or more operational research hypotheses. Investigators that have less experience in conducting systematic searches of the empirical literature might consult either *The Oxford Guide to Library Research* (Mann 2005) or the *Information Retrieval Policy Brief* (Rothstein, Turner, and Lavenberg 2004) prior to designing their literature search strategy. It is also often helpful to discuss the research plan with a good reference librarian. Many university libraries have information specialists that focus on the fields of public management and policy, and many more have specialists in the social sciences. In addition, all readers are advised to consult the *Cochrane Handbook* (Higgins and Green 2008) for the most recent advice on best practices in conducting literature searches for meta-analysis. Finally, before beginning a literature search for a meta-analysis, researchers ought to conduct a search to identify any previous meta-analyses of their research question. Because nearly all meta-analysis articles include the phase *meta-analysis* in the title or abstract, finding existing meta-analyses is usually fairly easy. One simply searches relevant databases using Boolean search terms for the keywords from the research question and the phrase *meta-analysis*. For example, in preparation for the environmental justice meta-analysis, I searched for previous meta-analyses using the Boolean combinations *environmental justice* and *meta-analysis*, *environmental racism* and *meta-analysis*, and *environmental equity* and *meta-analysis*. This strategy is not foolproof, however, so researchers should also use the search phrases *research synthesis*, *meta-analytic*, and *meta-regression* when searching for previous meta-analyses. Also, the Campbell Collaboration (www.campbellcollaboration.org) maintains an online library of meta-analyses of topics relevant to public policy.

Developing a Search Profile. The first step in conducting a literature search for a new meta-analysis is to craft a *search profile*. A search profile consists of

(1) a set of keywords for identifying relevant original studies; (2) a set of authors that will be used to identify relevant original studies; (3) a strategy for using citation searches for identifying original studies and a set of criteria bounding the literature that will be searched using these keywords, authors, and citations; and (4) a systematic process for executing the search profile.

Identifying Keywords. The large majority of the literature search will use online databases, and keywords are necessary for searching these databases. Good initial choices for keywords include words or terms that characterize the specific research question or the operational hypotheses that motivate the meta-analysis. Keywords identified in this manner are often referred to as *natural language* keywords, and natural language keywords are often combined in a literature search using "Boolean Operators." For example, scholars often use the phrases *environmental justice, environmental equity*, and *environmental racism* when considering the question of whether sources of potential environmental risk are distributed inequitably with respect to the race or class of community residents. The relative frequency with which these terms are used in original research varies across researchers and disciplines, and using only one of these terms to guide the literature search would miss a sizable portion of original studies in these fields. The environmental justice meta-analysis, then, used all three sets of keywords in searching electronic databases. In addition, we tried various other keyword combinations, including *race* and *environmental risk, class* and *environmental risk, race* and *pollution, racism* and *pollution*, and so on.

I can offer several lessons that are applicable when identifying natural language keywords for a literature search.

1. The keywords should be identified by reading several original studies that examine the research question of interest, not simply from your own imagination. Use keywords that authors of original studies use to characterize their own research.
2. The process of identifying keywords is iterative. Meta-analysts typically posit a set of keywords, then bring these keywords to the literature search engines and assess the results of the search. If the keyword search returns few relevant studies or many unexpected results, this is a sign that the keywords require revision. Alternatively, if the keyword identifies many of the important studies that examine the particular research question, this keyword is a candidate for the list of final

keywords and phrases. After reading a handful of studies and viewing the results of searches using preliminary keywords, the meta-analyst will posit a new set of keywords and repeat the process. On some occasions, the meta-analyst will identify a useful new keyword or key phrase well into the literature search process. When this happens, the meta-analyst must go back and repeat all previous literature search tasks with the new key phrase. That is, the search profile must be applied when searching all literature sources, with no exceptions.

3. Keywords should almost always be combined with the Boolean operator "and" when conducting natural language searches. For example, above we combined *race* AND *pollution* when conducting the literature search for original studies in the area of environmental justice.

4. Researchers should search for keywords and key phrases in the titles of original studies, in the abstracts of these studies, and in the full text of these studies when the search engine offers these options. One goal of the literature search is to be as comprehensive as possible, and relevant original studies might be missed by searching only study titles and abstracts.

5. In my experience an excellent literature search can be completed using relatively few keywords and key phrases. Often, six keywords and key phrases is enough—so long as the researcher is using the right keywords! One way of assessing the adequacy of the list of keywords and phrases is the number of unique records that are returned when trying out a new keyword. If new keywords do not return records that were not also discovered by previous keywords, the keyword list is probably sufficient.

6. It is vitally important to keep a comprehensive list of all keywords and key phrases that have been tried and the results from searches using these keywords. Good record keeping prevents repetition in the search for good keywords, helps to identify gaps in the types of keywords that have been tried, and encourages researchers to choose the final group of keywords and phrases on the basis of the results that they produce.

Meta-analysts can also conduct literature searches using *constructed vocabulary* as opposed to natural language. Constructed vocabulary keywords refer to the official subject categories used by research databases to organize the studies in their archives. For example, the online reference databases maintained by EBSCO (available at most university libraries) organizes entries using *Sears List of Subject Headings*. Meta-analysts may want to consult the subject headings used by various search engines, select those that match most closely the research question and operational hypotheses motivating the meta-analysis, and use these subject terms to search the databases.

Identifying Authors. A second element of designing a search profile is identifying a relatively large list of prominent authors who have conducted original studies that are relevant to your research question. The meta-analyst then contacts these authors directly in the hope that they might (1) share conference papers, working papers, or other unpublished original studies relevant to the meta-analysis; (2) identify conference papers, working papers, or other unpublished original studies completed by others; (3) identify new, relatively unknown scholars working on the same research question (these new scholars are often the Ph.D. students of the scholars you contact); or (4) identify reports or published studies that you may not have come across in your keyword searches. In conducting the educational voucher meta-analysis in chapter 8 we contacted seven leading authors in the field of educational voucher research.[1]

Leveraging Citations. The literature search profile should also identify studies using citation searches. The "ancestry" method can identify additional relevant original studies by examining the sources cited by relevant studies that have already been uncovered using either keyword searches or by contacting authors. Most readers are familiar with this tactic. In addition, the Web of Knowledge (a suite of online literature search tools available at most university and many public libraries) allows researchers to conduct a *forward citation search* that identifies all studies that cite a relevant original study that has already been identified in the literature search. For example, using the Web of Knowledge I identified twenty-four studies that cite Mohai and Saha's 2007 article examining inequities in the location of hazardous waste facilities. I can then examine these twenty-four studies to determine whether any are relevant candidates for the meta-analysis. While the ancestry method is useful for identifying older studies, the forward citation map tool is helpful for identifying the most recent relevant studies on a research question.

Bounding the Literature Search. Finally, the search profile identifies explicitly the criteria that will be used to bound the search for relevant literature. Three very common bounding criteria are time, geographic area, and language. For example, both the environmental justice meta-analysis and the educational voucher meta-analysis considered only studies that examined environmental inequities or educational vouchers in the United States (a geographic bounding criterion) and studies that were written in English (a language bounding criterion). These bounding criteria were used as a matter of convenience, since many studies have examined both the degree of environmental inequity and the effects of educational vouchers in other countries, and reported the results of these studies in languages other than English. Neither study employed temporal bounding criteria, though some meta-analyses restrict the literature search to studies written after a particular year or within a particular time frame. While the use of bounding criteria makes the literature search more tractable, it does open the meta-analyst to criticisms that her results are unrepresentative of the entire population of empirical literature examining a particular research question.

Applying the Search Profile. Once a search profile has been created, it must be applied in an identical fashion across all aspects of the literature search. For example, all keywords and key phrases must be used to search each of the electronic reference databases discussed in the next section. The meta-analyst should not use one set of keywords to search one reference database and a second set to search another. Moreover, it is a good idea to apply the keywords in the same order when searching each research archive or search engine. Similarly, all contacted authors should be asked to provide the same information—author A should not be asked to share information about her own work, while author B is asked only to provide information about the work of others. In addition, the same bounding criteria should be applied to all aspects of the literature search. By crafting a systematic literature search profile and applying this profile in the same manner in all aspects of the literature search, researchers help ensure that their review of the literature will be comprehensive, transparent, and replicable.

Developing a Search Strategy for the Published Literature. With a search profile in hand, the meta-analyst brings this profile to the published literature and uses it to identify original studies that are relevant for the meta-analysis. The distinction between "published" and "unpublished" literature is less meaningful in public management and policy than it is in many other fields. While an article that appears in *Public Administration Review*, the *Journal of Policy Analysis and Management*, or the *American Journal of Political Science* is unambiguously part of the "published" literature, what of a report issued by the Government Accountability Office or the U.S. Department of Health and Human Services? These reports are certainly "published" in that hard copies of the reports can be obtained from the U.S. Government Printing Office. From the perspective of meta-analysis, however, these government reports are part of the "unpublished" literature, since they do not appear in scholarly publication outlets. The same is true for original studies conducted by policy research firms such as Mathematica Policy Research and policy think tanks such as the Brookings Institution. Yet research from sources like these makes up an important part of the relevant empirical literature in public management and policy. In addition, online journals are beginning to make headway in public management, public policy, and the related social science disciplines (for example, *The Economist's Voice*), and it is unclear whether original studies in these outlets ought to be counted as "published" or "unpublished" studies. Rather than labeling studies found in the outlets described here as "unpublished," I use the broader and increasingly common term *grey literature*. Strategies for identifying original studies in the grey literature are discussed in the next section.

In this book I employ the traditional definition of published research as *studies published in peer-reviewed scholarly journals or books*. It is far easier to search the published literature than it was even ten years ago. A large number of comprehensive and specialty research archives are available and easily searchable online. Many of the most useful of these online research archives are listed in table 1.2. These research archives and search engines range from the general (such as EBSCO and ProQuest) to the field-specific (for example, Psych-INFO and PAIS). Some archives specialize in the most current material (such as Lexis-Nexis Academic Universe) while others restrict access to older studies (for instance, JSTOR). While most of the research archives and search engines listed in table 1.2 place a strong emphasis on domestic (U.S.) publication outlets, a few focus explicitly on providing access to international journals and books (for example, IBSS and BLDSC). Finally, some archives specialize in journal articles (such as JSTOR) while others specialize in books (for instance, WorldCat).

As recent as five years ago, the coverage of many of the research archives in table 1.2 was limited to the most recent decades. Currently, however, nearly all have extended coverage back through the 1960s, and the coverage of many extends back nearly a century. Because meta-analysis summarizes the results from original studies that employ statistical models and other quantitative techniques, the longer time frame covered by these archives is a luxury that we cannot take advantage of, since quantitative empirical research in the fields of public management and policy rarely goes back

TABLE 1.2. COMMON SOURCES FOR PUBLISHED AND GREY RESEARCH IN PUBLIC MANAGEMENT AND POLICY

Peer-Reviewed Articles	Books	Government Reports	Research Firms and Think Tanks	Working Papers	Conference Papers	Dissertations	Archives of Grey Literature
ProQuest	WorldCat	US GAO	Mathematica	NBER	Proceedings First (EBSCO)	ProQuest	SIGLE
Lexis-Nexis	IBSS	US CBO	MRDC	SSRN	Papers First (EBSCO)	WorldCat	ESRC
SSCI		US CRS	Rand	EconLit	Sociological Abstracts	Index to Theses (UK)	Evidence Network
IBSS		NTIS	IBM Business of Government	NCEE	EconLit	EconLit	C2-RIPE
JSTOR		NRC	Brookings			Sociological Abstracts	
PsychINFO		EBSCO Government Collection	AEI				

TABLE 1.2. (Continued)

Peer-Reviewed Articles	Books	Government Reports	Research Firms and Think Tanks	Working Papers	Conference Papers	Dissertations	Archives of Grey Literature
ERIC		Individual Agencies	Urban Institute				
Wilson Education Index			Heritage Foundation				
EBSCO			Resources for the Future				
PAIS International							
BLDSC							
Business Source Premier							
NCJRS							
Sociological Abstracts							
Education Abstracts							
Social Work Abstracts							
Urban Studies Abstracts							
Criminal Justice Abstracts							

more than fifty years. Readers should be aware, however, that many of the larger research archives and search engines offer differing levels of access or service (for example, EBSCO and Lexis-Nexis). This means that the results from a literature search using the same keywords may differ for researchers at institutions purchasing a lower level of access—often smaller public or liberal arts colleges—and researchers at institutions purchasing a higher level of access. Researchers are well advised to be certain of the level of access their institution provides to the online resources, and to conduct their literature searches in an environment that provides the highest level of access possible to these sources.

Finally, one research archive is notably absent from table 1.2: Google Scholar. While Google Scholar is an extraordinarily comprehensive search engine, in my experience it is of limited value to meta-analysts. Google Scholar is comprehensive because it is so undiscerning. When conducting a meta-analysis, a researcher must strike a balance between searches that are sufficiently comprehensive and searches that bury the researcher in a mountain of "false positive" results; in other words, records identified by the search that are not relevant to the meta-analysis. A meta-analyst using Google Scholar will be swamped by the number of false positive "hits" returned by any search. For example, a Google Scholar search using the key phrase *environmental justice* returns over 500,000 records published between 1990 and 2010. Searching a half million records from a single key phrase is simply not feasible in a meta-analysis. The advanced search function in Google Scholar does not improve the situation in practice. Searching for studies only in the social sciences and humanities that include the phrase *environmental justice* in the text returns over 17,000 records. If we remove the restriction to social sciences and humanities, the search returns over 20,000 records. By contrast, this same search in JSTOR returns just over 3,200 records, and a search using Academic Search Premier (EBSCO) returns 2,083 records. While searching through 3,200 records is a large task, it is far more manageable than searching through 20,000 records. Using the advanced search function, we can limit the Google Scholar search to requiring that the search phrase occurs only in the article title. Exercising this restriction reduces the number of records returned to 3,550. Requiring that the phrase *environmental justice* occur in the article title, JSTOR returns 175 records and Academic Search Premier returns 725 records. Moreover, while both JSTOR and Academic Search Premier allow one to search article abstracts, Google Scholar does not. This example gives the readers some sense of the scope of the task facing the meta-analysts in a literature review.

Developing a Search Strategy for the Grey Literature. As discussed previously, many original studies relevant to meta-analyses in public policy and management come from the grey literature. For example, a majority of the effect sizes used in the educational voucher meta-analysis in chapter 8 come from original studies that did not appear in scholarly journals or books. For the environmental justice meta-analysis, just over 20 percent of effect sizes come from studies in the grey literature. A meta-analysis in public management and policy that relies only on the published literature, then, is likely to generate erroneous or nongeneralizable conclusions. In this section I identify nearly one dozen different types of outlets that ought to be considered when searching the grey literature for original studies in public management and policy. Examples of these sources are listed in table 1.2.

- *Government Reports.* The federal government and some state governments release reports that might be considered relevant original studies for meta-analyses in public management and policy. These reports can come from dedicated governmental research entities such as the Government Accountability Office (GAO) or the Congressional Research Service (CRS), from cabinet-level departments or other large federal agencies (for example, Department of Health and Human Services, Environmental Protection Agency), or from quasi-governmental advisory organizations (for instance, National Academy of Sciences, National Academy of Public Administration, Transportation Research board).
- *Reports from Public Policy Research Firms or Think Tanks.* A remarkable number of high-quality original studies are produced by public policy research firms (such as Mathematica Policy Research, the RAND Corporation). Public policy think tanks also generate a remarkable volume of studies that are potentially relevant for meta-analyses in public management and policy. The quality of reports from think tanks is more variable than the quality of reports from policy research firms. Moreover, unlike most policy research firms, many policy think tanks are explicitly ideological (such as the Heritage Foundation), while others are more non-partisan (such as the Brookings Institution). Even the most highly partisan policy think tank, however, can produce a high-quality relevant original study. Meta-analysts should always search the websites of the policy research firms and think tanks most active in studying their research question when conducting a meta-analysis.
- *Working Papers.* The meta-analyst has access to several large archives of working papers in the fields of public management, public policy, and

related disciplines. Some of these working paper archives are sponsored and managed by the federal government (such as National Bureau of Economic Research [NBER] and National Center for Environmental Economics [NCEE]). Other working paper archives are managed by nonprofit organizations (for example, Social Science Research Network [SSRN], EconLIT).

· *Conference Papers.* Proceedings and full-text conference papers from thousands of professional conferences are available via Papers First and Proceedings First, which cover every conference and symposium archived by the British Library Document Supply Center. Access to Proceedings First and Papers First is available through many university libraries in the United States. In addition, professional organizations in some disciplines provide access to conference proceedings in their fields (for example, Sociological Abstracts). Finally, many individual professional organizations are providing access to conference programs, and even conference papers, through their websites (for example, the National Association of Schools of Public Affairs and Administration [NASPAA], the Midwest Political Science Association [MPSA]).

· *Dissertations and Theses.* It was not too long ago when researchers looking for relevant Ph.D. dissertations and master's theses had to pour through microfiche from University Microfilms International at the University of Michigan. Thankfully, the entire UMI database of dissertations and theses is searchable online through ProQuest. One can also search for dissertations online using WorldCat and other sources, and search for dissertations filed in the United Kingdom using the "Index to Theses" listed in table 1.2.

· *Archives of Grey Literature.* Rothstein and Hopewell (2009) identify a small number of online archives that focus explicitly on providing access to the grey literature. All of these archives focus on research released in Europe. These archives are included in table 1.2.

Researchers should employ the search profile when searching online repositories of grey literature in the same manner as when searching online archives of the published literature.

Judging the Acceptability of Original Studies

Classifying Studies. After employing the research profile to conduct a literature search, the next task is to judge the acceptability of the records returned from that search. That is, the meta-analyst must review the hundreds or thousands of studies identified using the techniques just described and determine which of these studies are acceptable for the meta-analysis. I find it useful to pass the records returned from the literature search through metaphorical "sieves" that employ different criteria to eliminate studies that are not acceptable for the meta-analysis. These "sieves" place records into four different categories.

1. *Hits*. "Hits" means all records returned by the literature search. These include records from the published and grey literatures and records recommended by contacted authors. The literature search for the environmental justice meta-analysis returned over 5,000 hits, while the literature search for the educational voucher meta-analysis returned 6,815 hits. These numbers illustrate that conducting a literature review for a meta-analysis is not for the faint of heart.

2. *Potentially Relevant Studies*. "Potentially relevant studies" are identified using only the titles and other bibliographic information returned in the literature search. Common criteria for excluding hits as not potentially relevant is if they are published in popular outlets (such as newspapers or magazines), are book reviews or opinion pieces, or were identified by the literature search because they contained all of the keywords in the Boolean search but in a nonsensical order. In general, researchers should use liberal or catholic criteria when placing studies into the "potentially relevant" group, because so little information is used to exclude studies at this stage. False positive decisions regarding potentially relevant studies can be corrected in a later stage of the literature search process, but false negative decisions exclude these studies permanently. The environmental justice meta-analysis identified 297 potentially relevant studies, and the educational voucher meta-analysis identified 736 potentially relevant studies.

3. *Relevant Studies*. "Relevant" studies are identified by examining the study abstract or, if available, a study summary. On some occasions determining the relevance of a study requires obtaining the full text of the study and reading the first few pages or examining the tables and figures. Potentially relevant studies are excluded from the smaller group of relevant studies if they (1) are non-analytic (that is, descriptive), (2) are nonquantitative, (3) examine dependent variables or focal predictors that are measured in a manner inconsistent with the operational hypotheses motivating the meta-analysis as defined earlier in the chapter, or (4) do not meet the bounding criteria from the

literature search profile. For example, a potentially relevant study in the area of environmental justice would be excluded if it was a case study of the siting of a solid waste landfill, or a law review article examining the potential present in current environmental statutes to remedy environmental inequities. A potentially relevant study in the area of educational vouchers would be excluded if it examined the effect of vouchers on student satisfaction, or if it examined the effects of vouchers in Chile. Relevant studies, then, are those that examine the specific research question of interest, use statistical analysis to test the operational hypotheses motivating the meta-analysis, and meet the relevant bounding criteria. Potentially relevant studies should be excluded from the relevant category only if it is clear from the abstract or study summary that the study is not relevant. If there is a question as to the relevance of the study, the meta-analysis should obtain more information (in other words, the full text of the study) or classify the study as relevant. The environmental justice meta-analysis identified 88 relevant studies, and the educational voucher meta-analysis identified 84 relevant studies.

4. *Acceptable Studies.* "Acceptable" studies are identified by examining the full text of the study. Relevant studies can be classified as unacceptable for a number of reasons. First, relevant studies might be unacceptable because they were incorrectly categorized as relevant. That is, while the study might have appeared relevant when examining only the study abstract or study summary, it is clear when reading the full text that the study does not meet one or more of the relevance criteria. Second, the study may not report sufficient statistical detail to allow the calculation of effect sizes. As we see in chapters 2 and 3, we actually need very little information to calculate effect sizes. To calculate the most useful *r*-based effect size, for example, all that is needed are the sample size and a measure of statistical significance. Still, a surprising number of original studies fail to report even this level of detail in their statistical results. Third, a study can be excluded as unacceptable if the results in that study perfectly duplicate the results in one or more other studies already deemed to be acceptable. It is not uncommon, for example, for a literature search to identify both the grey literature version of a research paper (for example, a conference paper, NBER paper, or SSRN paper) and the published version of that same paper. In many cases, the results in these two versions of the paper are identical. Researchers may employ other context-specific criteria for determining that a relevant study is unacceptable, but these

idiosyncratic reasons for excluding relevant studies should be used sparingly. The full environmental justice meta-analysis identified 49 acceptable original studies (only 48 of these studies are represented in the data set used in subsequent chapters), while the educational voucher meta-analysis identified 33 acceptable studies.

Acceptable studies are subsequently coded to extract the information necessary to calculate effect sizes and to create the necessary moderator (and mediator) variables. The process of coding acceptable original studies is covered in chapter 2, while the process of calculating effect sizes from these studies is addressed in chapter 3.

Evaluating the Reliability of Classification Decisions. It should be evident that conducting the literature search for a meta-analysis requires considerable time and effort. It should also be evident that assigning records (or original studies) to one of the four categories described in the previous section requires the researcher to exercise considerable judgment. For both of these reasons, it is best if the meta-analysis is conducted by a team of researchers. The burden of the literature review can be split among members of the team. More important, members of the team can assign studies to categories independently, and the reliability of these assignments can be assessed. Assessing the degree of intercoder reliability in identifying relevant and acceptable studies is an integral part of a meta-analysis literature search.

Social scientists have developed a handful of measures for assessing the reliability of independent assessments of events or the reliability of repeated measures of a concept. The two most common measures of intercoder reliability in meta-analysis are the *percentage agreement* and *Cohen's kappa*. Consider table 1.3, which represents the decisions of two members of a meta-analysis research team, Coder *A* and Coder *B*. Each coder must make a decision as to whether each of a hundred potentially relevant studies is relevant, or which of a hundred relevant studies is acceptable (intercoder reliability assessments are rarely conducted for identifying potentially relevant studies). Cells *A* and *D* in table 1.3 reflect studies on which Coders *A* and *B* agree, and cells *B* and *C* reflect studies on which Coders *A* and *B* disagree. The percentage agreement is calculated using $(A + D)/(A + B + C + D)$, or $70/100 = .70$.

While the percentage agreement is the most commonly reported measure of intercoder reliability in meta-analysis, this measure has been criticized for overstating intercoder reliability because it ignores the probability

TABLE 1.3. OUTCOMES OF HYPOTHETICAL LITERATURE SEARCH DECISIONS

	Coder *B* Accept	Coder *B* Reject
Coder *A* Accept	*A* [40]	*B* [10]
Coder *A* Reject	*C* [20]	*D* [30]

that the raters would agree due to chance. Cohen's kappa (κ) controls for this chance agreement. The formula for Cohen's kappa is

$$\kappa = \left(PA_o - PA_c\right) / \left(1 - PA_c\right) \qquad (1.3)$$

where PA_o is the observed relative frequency of agreement, or the standard measure of percentage agreement, and PA_c is the relative frequencies of agreement predicted due to chance. To calculate PA_c we note that Coder *A* accepted 50 percent of the studies while Coder *B* accepted 60 percent of the studies. Assuming these decisions are made independently, the probability that both Coder *A* and Coder *B* would agree to accept a study due to random chance is $(.5)(.6) = .3$, and the probability that they would agree to reject a study due to random chance is $(.5)(.4) = .2$. The overall probability of random agreement $PA_c = .3 + .2 = .5$. We would calculate Cohen's kappa as $\kappa = (.7 - .5) / (1 - .5) = .40$. By accounting for chance agreement, Cohen's kappa will always be smaller than the simple percentage agreement measure. Orwin (1994) offers the following rules of thumb for evaluating the extent of intercoder agreement using Cohen's kappa:

$.40 < \kappa < .59$	fair agreement
$.60 < \kappa < .74$	good agreement
$.74 < \kappa$	excellent agreement

Standard practice in meta-analysis is converging toward the reporting of both measures of intercoder reliability, and this is the approach we follow in chapters 8 through 11.

Summarizing the Literature Review

The *Cochrane Handbook* (Higgins and Green 2008) recommends that meta-analyses report the results from decisions made during the literature search

FIGURE 1.1. SAMPLE STUDY FLOW DIAGRAM FOR REPORTING THE RESULTS FROM THE LITERATURE SEARCH

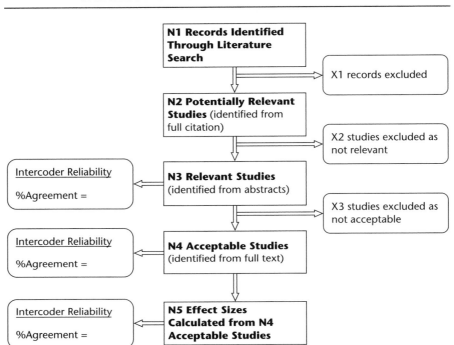

in a format that is clear and easily followed. Figure 1.1 provides one such format, the study flow diagram. Each step in the literature review is represented by one cell in the flow diagram, and the number of original studies assessed at each stage and the decisions made regarding each study are reported in these cells. In addition, measures of intercoder reliability at each stage are reported on the left-hand side of the study flow diagram. Note that the last cell in the study flow diagram reports the number of effect sizes coded from the acceptable studies. We address coding effect sizes in chapter 2.

Conclusion

Researchers experienced with conceptualizing and designing original quantitative research will find that these skills transfer directly to meta-analysis. Meta-analysts must begin their inquiry with a theoretically grounded, specific, and well-bounded research question. Meta-analysts then gather data required to estimate quantities of interest and test hypotheses that allow them to answer this research question. Meta-analysts in public management and policy, more so than their counterparts in medicine and psychology, focus on accounting for variation in the quantity of interest across original studies. As with original research, this variation provides leverage for explanation. Finally, as with original research, meta-analysts should strive to design and execute studies that are replicable. Toward that end, I strongly encourage that researchers maintain an archive of hard copies or electronic copies of all acceptable studies identified in the literature search and used in the meta-analysis (standard practice is to also include a list of these studies as an appendix in the published version of the meta-analysis). Questions that arise later in the meta-analysis, and questions from others after the completion of the meta-analysis, are much more easily addressed when these studies are close at hand.

Note

1. A list of the authors we contacted in this manner includes Joshua Cowen, Jay Greene, Alan Krueger, Jonathan Plucker, Cecelia Rouse, John Witte, and Patrick Wolf.

CHAPTER TWO

TURNING STUDIES INTO DATA

Evan J. Ringquist

"Meta-analysis has gained increasing use in recent years, and rightly so. Meta-analysis offers a powerful set of tools for extracting information from a body of related research"

(GREENWALD, HEDGES, AND LAINE 1994, 2).

"The first draft of a coding guide should never be the last"

(COOPER 2010, 86).

A systematic and exhaustive search of the published and grey literature will provide the meta-analyst with at least one dozen—and possibly several dozen—acceptable original studies. These original studies contain the data that will be synthesized in the meta-analysis. Higgins and Deeks define data for a meta-analysis as including "information about (or deriving from) a study, including details of methods, participants, settings, context, interventions, outcomes, results, publications, and investigations" (2008, 156). Once the literature search is complete, the meta-analyst turns his or her attention to extracting or coding these data from the acceptable studies.

When coding original studies, the meta-analyst is faced with two sets of decisions: (1) what to code and (2) how to organize the process of coding. I address each set of decisions in the following sections. It is important to emphasize that this chapter presents only one perspective on the process of extracting data from original studies. Coding data for a meta-analysis—like content analysis or survey construction—is context-specific, embodying as much art as science. Therefore, readers will be ill-served by relying upon this chapter alone as they prepare to code data for their own meta-analysis and ought to consult other texts that provide more extensive discussions of turning studies into data (see, for example, Lipsey and Wilson 2001; Cooper 2010).

Before discussing what to code and how to code, I will discuss different perspectives on how to organize the information coded from original studies. Meta-analysis can seek to synthesize effect sizes, studies, or reports, and the design of coding instruments and the process of coding are affected by which of these units the meta-analyst uses to organize the inquiry. *Effect sizes* represent the standardized relationship or association between the focal predictor and the dependent variable of interest. *Studies* are independent interventions, experiments, or hypothesis tests carried out by investigators when conducting original research. *Reports* are the articles, books, abstracts, white papers, or other products that report the outcomes from studies. The *Cochrane Handbook* emphasizes that meta-analyses in medicine ought to synthesize studies, not reports (Higgins and Green 2008). Lipsey and Wilson (2001) make the same recommendation. The *Handbook* offers two reasons for this emphasis on studies rather than reports. First, several different reports may include outcomes from the same study. This may occur when the investigators responsible for the study release the results in several outlets, or when separate sets of investigators release analyses of data from the same study. Second, a single report may contain the results from multiple studies.

The Cochrane Collaboration's emphasis on studies is understandable, since in medicine these studies are almost always clinical trials. Medical researchers want to know whether the outcomes of the same treatment or intervention—for example, a new surgical procedure—differ across participant groups or clinical settings. Because most of the meaningful variation in outcomes occurs across studies, meta-analysis seeks to synthesize studies and effect sizes are organized by study. By contrast, original research in public management and policy rarely reports the outcomes from clinical trials. In addition, much of the meaningful variation in social science research more broadly occurs between reports rather than between studies. For example, several evaluations of the Milwaukee school voucher program—a single "study"—have reached different conclusions about the effects of the program (see, for example, Witte 1998, 2000; Rouse 1998; Greene, Peterson, and Du 1999; Lamarche 2008). The same is true for other policy innovations, such as Head Start. A central concern for public policy researchers is why different examinations of the same program or intervention reach different conclusions. Therefore, most researchers in public management and policy will want to organize effect sizes by report rather than by study, thereby synthesizing outcomes from these reports. This is one more way in which meta-analysis in public management and policy differs from meta-analysis in medicine. When a single report includes results from several different studies—for example, when Howell and colleagues (2002) report outcomes from voucher programs in Dayton, New York City, and Washington, D.C.—effect sizes are still organized by report, and effect sizes from different studies are identified using moderator variables.

Using the language of the *Cochrane Handbook*, the description of coding effect sizes presented in this chapter organizes these effect sizes by report. However, from this point forward I will use the term *study* to refer to what the *Handbook* calls a "report," and effect sizes will be organized according to the "study" that generates these effect sizes. If scholars in public management and policy follow this convention, this choice of language will undoubtedly cause some confusion when comparing meta-analyses in these fields to meta-analyses in medicine. By the same token, this choice of language will *avoid* confusion among social scientists who are used to thinking about research products as "studies" rather than as "reports."

What to Code

Reeves and colleagues note that "every step in carrying out a systematic review is more difficult when non-randomized studies are included" (2008, 392). These difficulties begin with decisions about what information to code from original studies. In general, social scientists will want to code three types of information from original studies: search-level information, study-level information, and effect-level information.

Search-Level Information

Search-level information includes data that allow researchers, if necessary, to replicate the literature search and decisions that produced the sample of acceptable studies used in the meta-analysis. At the search level, *each potentially relevant study is assigned a unique identification number that it will maintain throughout the meta-analysis*. In practice a three-digit identification code is sufficient, as this allows coding information from up to 999 potentially relevant original studies.

A simple one-page coding form is completed for each potentially relevant study. An example of such a coding form for the environmental justice meta-analysis is provided in exhibit 2.1 (Section I) at the end of this chapter. On this form the meta-analyst records

· The first three authors of the study
· The search routine used to identify the study (the electronic search engine used, the personal contact consulted, and so on)
· A binary indicator for whether the study was classified as relevant
· The reason why the study was classified as not relevant, if classified so (reasons why potentially relevant studies might be classified as not relevant were discussed in chapter 1)

Study-Level Information

Study-level information is recorded only for original studies classified as relevant and includes three types of data. These data are recorded on a simple one- or two-page coding form. An example of such a coding form for the environmental justice meta-analysis is provided in exhibit 2.1 (section II) at the end of this chapter.

· First, for each relevant study the meta-analyst records the full bibliographic citation for the study. This information will allow the full sample of studies considered for the meta-analysis to be reconstructed in the future.
· Second, a binary indicator identifies whether the relevant study was classified as acceptable. A second field codes the reason why a relevant study was classified as unacceptable (reasons why relevant studies might be unacceptable were discussed in chapter 1).
· Third, for each relevant study information is recorded about the authors of the study, the outlet of the study, the publication date and timing of the study, and other important study-specific characteristics. These characteristics might be used later to define subsets of effect sizes for analysis, or as moderator variables in a meta-regression. Most important, coding whether the original study appeared in a peer-reviewed outlet will allow a comparison of average effect sizes between published and unpublished studies—the basis of an important test for publication bias. Study-level information has other uses as well. For example, coding the date of publication allows researchers to conduct a cumulative meta-analysis that can show how the evidence regarding a particular

research question has developed over time. Cumulative meta-analyses are discussed in chapter 3. To take another example, coding the date of the policy or management intervention can allow researchers to compare how effect sizes differ across interventions over time, which may provide evidence regarding policy learning or adaptive management. As one last example, many sociologists are interested in the relationship between gender and the conduct of and outputs from scientific inquiry. Coding the gender of the primary author allows an investigation of this topic through meta-analysis. A partial list of relevant study-level characteristics of this type includes

· Primary author gender
· Professional position of primary author (for example, academic, government, think tank)
· Primary author academic discipline
· Type of publication (peer-reviewed article, book, dissertation, government report, think tank report, conference paper, and so on)
· Academic discipline of outlet

Effect-Level Information

Coding search-level and study-level information is quite straightforward. By contrast, coding effect-level information is difficult, complicated, and time consuming. Effect-level information, however, is the heart of every meta-analysis. In general, meta-analysts will code two sorts of effect-level information. First, coders will record the information necessary to calculate effect sizes and effect size variances (effect sizes and their variances are discussed in detail in chapter 3). Second, coders will record information on moderator variables that will be used to identify subgroups of effect sizes for analysis, or be included in meta-regression models.

Meta-analysis texts offer different advice regarding the appropriate level of detail when coding effect-level information. Lipsey and Wilson (2001) encourage researchers to emphasize parsimony when coding effect-level information. By contrast, Cooper (2010) recommends that researchers recover any information that might possibly be considered relevant when coding effect-level information. Lipsey and Wilson are concerned primarily about the costs associated with using unwieldy coding instruments that, due to their comprehensive nature, will necessarily have many blank spaces when coding is complete. Cooper is concerned primarily with the high cost of recoding studies to obtain information that was not recorded during initial coding. There is merit to both positions.

Both types of costs can be minimized by developing effect-level coding instruments iteratively, a topic that is covered in the "process of coding" section of this chapter. Given the dramatic heterogeneity in research designs, data structures, and statistical techniques employed in original studies in public management and policy, however, the forms used to code effect-level information in these fields will be longer and more complicated than is typical for meta-analyses in medicine.

Virtually every acceptable study included in a meta-analysis will produce multiple effect sizes. Most commonly, multiple effect sizes arise when the authors of original studies employ different model specifications or sample restrictions to assess the robustness of their empirical results. Each model specification and sample restriction will produce a unique effect size. When original studies generate multiple effect sizes, the standard advice in meta-analysis is that the researcher should either (1) choose the "one best" effect size to include in the meta-analysis or (2) calculate an average effect size from each original study to include in the meta-analysis (Hunter and Schmidt 1990; Lipsey and Wilson 2001; Raudenbush 2009). *Meta-analysts in public management, public policy, and the social sciences should ignore this standard advice.*

The "standard advice" to use a single effect size from each original study is motivated by two concerns. First, multiple effect sizes from the same original study are likely to be correlated by virtue of being estimated by the same investigators using the same data. Because the statistical theory underpinning meta-analysis assumes independent observations, the results from a meta-analysis of correlated effect sizes may be untrustworthy. Second, results from different model specifications estimate different population parameters. For example, b_1 from the sample regression model $Y_i = b_0 + b_1 X_{1i} + b_2 X_{2i} + e_i$ estimates a different population parameter than does b_1 from the sample regression model $Y_i = b_0 + b_1 X_{1i} + b_2 X_{2i} + b_3 X_{3i} + b_4 X_{4i} + e_i$. Traditional meta-analysis, however, assumes that effect sizes from all original studies estimate the same population parameter (in the fixed effects framework), or that these effect sizes at least have the same expected value (in the random effects framework). Neither of these assumptions holds when effect sizes come from original studies employing different model specifications. In chapters 4 and 5 I introduce a set of meta-regression techniques that render both of these concerns less important, if not irrelevant. Therefore, meta-analysts in public management, public policy, and the social sciences should code information from all relevant effect sizes in each acceptable original study.

In practice, the advice offered here means that meta-analysts will complete multiple effect-level coding forms for each acceptable original study. Each effect-level coding form should receive a unique identification number (a three-digit number is generally sufficient). Each effect size, then, is identified by the combination of the unique study-level identifier and the three-digit effect size identifier. For example, in the environmental justice meta-analysis, effect size 302.009 refers to the ninth effect size coded from study #302 by Anderton, Anderson, Oakes, and Fraser (1994). An example of a simplified effect-level coding form used in the environmental justice meta-analysis is provided in exhibit 2.1 (section III) at the end of this chapter. In addition, the coding forms used for the original meta-analyses in chapters 8 through 11 are included in the appendix.

Coding Information for Effect Sizes and Effect Size Variances. Effect sizes are the fundamental metric and unit of analysis in meta-analysis. Effect sizes fall into one of three classes or families: *r*-based effect sizes, *d*-based effect sizes, and odds-based effect sizes. The large majority of effect sizes encountered in public management and policy will be *r*-based effect sizes. In some cases the choice of the research question or choice of operational hypotheses will rule out certain types of effect sizes. For example, chapter 8 reports on a meta-analysis of original studies assessing the effects of school vouchers on student academic performance. Because "academic performance" is defined as standardized test scores—a continuous variable—odds-based effect sizes are not possible in this meta-analysis. Therefore, the effect-level coding sheet does not contain fields for recording the data necessary to calculate odds-based effect sizes. In general, however, meta-analysts should be prepared to code the information required to calculate all three families of effect sizes.

To calculate effect sizes and their variances, researchers must extract three types of information from original studies: (1) a measure of the magnitude of the relationship between the focal predictor and the dependent variable, (2) a measure of the uncertainty associated with this relationship, and (3) the sample size. Each study does not always need to report explicitly all three types of information. For example, if an original study reports a correlation coefficient and the sample size, the variance (uncertainty) of the correlation coefficient can be estimated from these two pieces of information. To take another example, if an original study reports a regression parameter estimate and a *t*-score, the regression parameter estimate variance can be calculated. As a last example, if an original study reports means, standard deviations, and sample sizes for treatment and control groups, the magnitude of the relationship (that is, difference of means), its uncertainly (pooled standard deviation), and the total sample size can all be calculated using this information (see chapter 3). Code sheets for effect-level information should be designed to record all three types of information. For example, a code sheet for effect-level information might include the following elements:

- Measures of the magnitude of the relationship (recorded as absolute values)
  - Correlation coefficient
  - Regression parameter estimate
  - Logit parameter estimate
  - Probit parameter estimate
  - Difference of means
  - Mean of treatment group
  - Mean of control group
  - Number of events and non-events for treatment group
  - Number of events and non-events for control group
- Measures of uncertainty regarding the relationship
  - Parameter estimate variance
  - Parameter estimate standard deviation
  - t-score (recorded as absolute value)
  - Z-score (recorded as absolute value)
  - X^2 value
  - F-test
  - p-value associated with rejecting Ho
  - One-tailed or two-tailed hypothesis test on Ho
- Sample size information
  - Total sample size
  - Sample size for control group
  - Sample size for treatment group
  - Degrees of freedom for statistical test
  - Number of independent variables in model
- Whether the effect favors the control group (null hypothesis) or the treatment group (alternative hypothesis)

As indicated in the preceding list, to attribute meaning to the effect size we need a fourth type of information: whether the estimated effect favors the control group or the treatment group. Alternatively, we need to code whether the estimated relationship is consistent with a common null hypothesis or a common alternative hypothesis. Neither the valence of the estimated relationship nor the valence of the associated test statistic provides this information. For example, whether a positive difference of means signifies a beneficial treatment effect depends on whether this difference is calculated as (treatment-control) or (control-treatment) in the original study. Similarly, whether a positive regression parameter estimate reflects a positive association favoring rejection of the null hypothesis depends on the scale used to measure X and Y in the original study. This is why in the examples above, parameter estimates, correlation coefficients, differences of means, t-scores, and Z-scores are all recorded as absolute values when coding effect-level information for a meta-analysis. A separate field in the code form records whether the estimated effect (or outcome) favors the control group (or null hypothesis) or the treatment group (or alternative hypothesis). In my experience, this is one of the most difficult practices for coders to master, but coding the magnitude of the effect and test statistic separately from their meaning avoids many mistakes when calculating effect sizes.

Coding Scientifically Interesting Moderator Variables. Rubin (1992) emphasizes two sources of effect size heterogeneity in meta-analysis. First, this heterogeneity—in other words, differences in estimated effect sizes across original studies—could be generated by research design factors or study quality. For example, effect sizes from studies with experimental designs might differ from effect sizes in studies with quasi-experimental designs. While important to understand, these differences were termed "scientifically uninteresting" because they offer no information as to whether effect sizes truly differ across subjects or context. Far more interesting for Rubin were differences in effect sizes attributable to differences in outcomes, treatments, participants, or contexts across original studies. To illustrate this point, while it is important to understand whether the estimated effect of a medical intervention differs depending on whether the study was single-blind or double-blind, it is more useful to know whether the effect of the intervention differs for men and women. These sources of "scientifically interesting" effect size heterogeneity should be a central focus of meta-analysis in public management and policy when coding effect-level information. In particular, meta-analysts in these fields ought to code for effect level differences in the following:

· *Outcome Measures.* For example, in the environmental justice meta-analysis I code whether original studies measure potential environmental risks using the presence of noxious facilities or using levels of pollution.

To what extent levels of environmental inequities differ across types of environmental risk is a scientifically interesting question.

· *Characteristics of Participants.* For example, in the educational voucher meta-analysis we code whether samples in original studies include only black students, only Hispanic students, or students of all races and ethnicities. We also code whether samples in original studies include only elementary school students or students in all grades. To what extent the effects from using educational vouchers differ depending on the race, ethnicity, or age of students is a scientifically interesting question.

· *Type of Intervention or Measure of Focal Predictor.* For example, in the environmental justice meta-analysis I code whether original studies estimated environmental inequities using the racial and ethnic characteristics of communities or using income characteristics of communities. In addition to being scientifically interesting, this distinction is legally relevant—race is a protected class under the 1964 Civil Rights Act, while income (class) is not. Therefore, there may be legal remedies for race-based environmental inequities, but there are no legal remedies for class-based inequities.

· *Intensity of Treatment.* For example, in the educational voucher meta-analysis we code whether original studies measure the effects of vouchers after one year, two years, three years, four years, five years, or six years. Presumably the effects of vouchers are cumulative, reflecting the "intensity" of the voucher treatment, and a meta-analysis should control for this source of effect size heterogeneity across studies.

· *Design of Program or Intervention.* For example, in the educational voucher meta-analysis we code whether the use of vouchers is restricted to secular schools, and whether the voucher programs are privately or publicly funded. Whether the effects of vouchers differ between secular or religious schools, or between publicly or privately funded programs, are scientifically interesting questions.

· *Context of Intervention or Study.* The context of the intervention, study, or implementation environment may be especially important for researchers in public management and policy. For example, whether voucher programs are more effective in Cleveland or Washington, D.C., and whether environmental inequities are more severe in southern states or in midwestern states, provides valuable information to investigators. Context is more than geographic location, however; for instance, it may be important to know whether the effectiveness of a management reform differs depending on the structure of or clientele support provided to administrative agencies.

While the six general categories of moderator variables illustrated here will probably be included in most meta-analyses in public management and policy, the type and number of scientifically interesting moderator variables will be unique to each meta-analysis. Whereas Rubin emphasized "scientifically interesting" moderator variables, we lose little by substituting "policy relevant" for "scientifically interesting" in this context. That is, researchers should strive to identify program characteristics and program content that differ across original studies seeking to assess the same type of policy or management intervention. The same is true for meta-analyses of original studies that do not examine interventions. For example, it is possible that the effects of representative bureaucracy differ depending on the type of bureaucratic organization. A meta-analysis of the representative bureaucracy literature, then, ought to identify the type of organization looked at in original studies examining this question. Properly identifying and coding "scientifically interesting" characteristics places a premium on the meta-analyst having meaningful expertise regarding the substance of the particular research question, management reform, or policy intervention.

Coding Elements of Research Design and Study Quality. Effect sizes may differ across original studies—and between different models in the same original study—due to the design, estimation, and overall quality of the research reported in these studies. While Rubin (1992) may have labeled these characteristics as scientifically uninteresting, this does not mean they are unimportant. To the contrary, meta-analysts have devoted a great deal of effort to measuring the quality of original studies and to understanding the relationship between study quality and effect size. The conclusions from this work are that (1) it is essential to measure and control for the quality of original studies included in a meta-analysis, (2) quality is a multidimensional concept, and (3) single-dimensional quality scales perform poorly when one is measuring and controlling for study quality in meta-analysis (Jüni, Witschi, Bloch, and Egger 1999; Higgins and Altman 2008). Coding for study quality and design elements is especially important in public management and policy, in which original studies commonly attempt to estimate causal effects using non-experimental research designs and observational data. Even original studies that do not explicitly attempt to estimate causal effects employ a wide variety of research designs, model specifications, and estimation strategies. To combine effect sizes from these models in a meaningful way we need to identify and code these key differences. This information can then be used to identify subgroups of effect sizes for analysis, or included as moderator variables in meta-regression models.

As was true for scientifically interesting moderator variables, the types and number of moderator variables used to identify design characteristics and study quality will be specific to each meta-analysis. Furthermore, scholars might reasonably disagree over which moderator variables ought to be included in a meta-regression model. This is one more way in which the design and execution of meta-analysis is similar to the design and execution of original research.

The choice of which design elements and quality characteristics to code ought to be made with an eye toward the purposes of coding these characteristics. First, we include these moderators in meta-regression models to reduce unexplained parameter heterogeneity across studies. Unaccounted for parameter heterogeneity in a meta-regression is akin to unexplained variation in the dependent variable Y in a traditional regression model. As with traditional regression, the more parameter heterogeneity we can account for using these moderators, the more confidence we have in the results from the meta-analysis. Second, including these moderator variables in a meta-regression model allows us to calculate average effect sizes for different types of studies and thereby clearly illustrate the consequences of design and estimation choices for the outcomes from our statistical models. Third, including these moderator variables in a meta-regression allows us to estimate average effect sizes from "ideal" studies, and in a process similar to regression response surface estimation examine carefully how average effect sizes in "ideal" studies differ depending on the value of the "scientifically interesting" moderator variables discussed above (this process is discussed in detail in chapter 4).

Excluding important moderator variables may compromise all three purposes. Therefore I recommend coding several moderators measuring the design and quality of original studies. At a minimum, meta-analysts in public management, public policy, and the social sciences ought to consider coding the following design and quality characteristics from original studies:

- Statistical technique used to generate effect size
  - Least squares regression
  - Probit
  - Logit
  - Difference of means
  - ANOVA

- HLM
- GEE
- Structural equation modeling
- ARIMA
- Study research design
  - Experimental with random assignment
  - Two group pre-post quasi-experiment
  - One group pre-post quasi-experiment
  - Two group quasi-experiment posttest only
  - One group quasi-experiment posttest only
  - Multigroup pre-post quasi-experiment
  - Multigroup quasi-experiment posttest only
- Method of assignment to treatment group
  - Simple random assignment
  - Random assignment after matching
  - Nonrandom, post hoc matching
  - Nonrandom, self-selection
  - Nonrandom, other
  - Multiple methods
- Method of assignment to control group
  - Simple random assignment
  - Random assignment after matching
  - Nonrandom, post hoc matching
  - Nonrandom, self-selection
  - Nonrandom, other
  - Multiple methods
- Ex post endogeneity controls
  - Instrumental variables
  - Fixed effects
  - Matching
  - Regression discontinuity
  - Differencing
  - None
- Data structure
  - Cross-sectional
  - Time series
  - Pooled cross sections
  - True panel
- Whether, if surveys were used, the study addressed common source bias

Coding Moderator Variables from Multivariate Models. Path diagram 1.1 in chapter 1 depicted the effect size Θ estimated from the relationship between the focal predictor X and the dependent variable of interest Y. That diagram is reproduced here as path diagram 2.1.

$$(2.1)$$

Occasionally researchers in public management and policy will find original studies—typically randomized experiments—that estimate the relationship between X and Y using a simple bivariate measure of association as depicted in path diagram 2.1. More commonly, however, estimates of the relationship between X and Y in original studies come from multivariate models.[1] A multivariate model with two additional predictors is presented in path diagram 2.2.

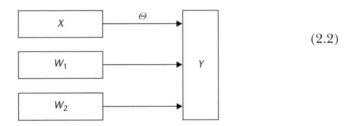

$$(2.2)$$

An original study might include variables W_1 and W_2 for two reasons. First, the study might include these variables to improve the *efficiency* of the estimated relationship between X and Y. Including W_1 and W_2 will improve the efficiency of this estimate if they are highly correlated with Y but relatively uncorrelated with X. Second, the original study might include these variables to obtain an *unbiased* or *consistent* estimate of the relationship between X and Y. Including W_1 and W_2 will generate consistent estimates of this relationship if, by doing so, the joint distribution of X and Y satisfies the properties of conditional independence and unit homogeneity (King, Keohane, and Verba 1994).

Path diagram 2.1 can be operationalized as a simple bivariate regression model $Y_i = b_0 + b_1 X_{1i} + e_i$, while the regression operationalization of path diagram 2.2 is $Y_i + b_0 + b_1 X_{1i} + b_2 W_{1i} + b_3 W_{2i} + e_i$. Because of the way effect sizes are calculated, $b_1 \neq \Theta$, though the two quantities are related. Of importance, the inclusion of W_1 and W_2 affects the effect size Θ differently than the regression parameter estimate b_1. In the regression model, $b_{1,\,2.1} = b_{1,\,2.2}$ if $b_2 = b_3 = 0$, or if $r(XY) = r(XY \mid W_1 W_2)$ (that is, if X, W_1, and W_2 are independent). By contrast, $\Theta_{2.1} = \Theta_{2.2}$ only if *both* of these conditions hold, which will be very unlikely in practice. Therefore, the presence of W_1 and/or W_2 in the regression model is likely to affect the effect size Θ, making the presence of W_1 and W_2 in original studies good candidates for moderator variables (denoted here as M_1 and M_2). M_1 and M_2 are dichotomous, taking on a value of 1 for effect sizes Θ that are calculated from models that include W_1 or W_2, and zero for effect sizes that are calculated from models that do not include these predictors.

In theory, all control variables W that occur in any model in any original study are candidates for inclusion as moderator variables M in a meta-analysis. In practice, including all of these moderator variables makes little sense, just as including all possible control variables in a traditional regression model makes little sense. Parsimony is nearly as valuable in meta-regression as it is in traditional regression. When considering moderator variables of this type, researchers should focus on those that are likely to have the largest effect on moderating the relationship between X and Y, and those that will help account for a meaningful share of the variation in effect sizes across original studies. In general, this means creating moderator variables for the presence of W only if (1) W is meaningfully correlated with both the dependent variable of interest Y and the focal predictor X, and (2) W is relatively common in original studies. By the same token, the consequences of excluding a relevant moderator variable from meta-regression are the same as the consequences of excluding an important control variable in a traditional regression model—the resulting parameter estimates are likely to be biased and contaminated by endogeneity (Wooldridge 2002).

As an illustration of these choices, I code three moderator variables of this type in the environmental justice meta-analysis: whether models in original studies include a variable measuring population density in a community, whether models in original studies include a variable measuring manufacturing employment in a community, and whether models in original studies include a variable measuring housing values in a community. Each of these variables is expected to moderate the relationship between the concentration of poor and/or minority residents in a community and the presence of potential environmental risks in a community. These expectations come from the theoretical literature on environmental inequities, and each of these variables is also a commonly used control variable in the environmental justice literature.

Coping with Missing Data. Eventually every meta-analyst must cope with the challenge of missing data due to incomplete or unclear reporting in original studies. Sometimes the data are only "partially missing," as when an original study reports a regression parameter estimate and a threshold significance level (for example, $** \leq .05$) but does not report an exact p-value or the parameter estimate standard error that would allow the calculation of an exact p-value. While we cannot calculate an exact effect size in these circumstances, we can at least calculate a lower bound for the effect size using the threshold p-value (see chapter 3).

The challenge is more difficult when data are missing completely, or missing to the degree that effect sizes and/or moderator variables cannot be extracted from the original studies. For example, some studies may report a mean difference between outcomes for the treatment and control groups, but not the uncertainty surrounding that mean difference. Alternatively, an original study might report that a parameter estimate was statistically significant, but does not report the sample size from the analysis. In these two circumstances (and many others), missing data make the calculation of effect sizes impossible. If we cannot recover these data, studies containing insufficient information to calculate effect sizes must be removed from the group of acceptable studies. Missing data can also compromise our ability to code moderator variables from original studies. For example, study narratives may not clearly specify how participants were assigned to control groups, enumerate the entire list of control variables included in the regression model, or identify important aspects of program design or implementation context.

Researchers have three options for managing missing data. First, the researcher can contact the authors of the original study and request this information. When using this tactic, it is important to make it as easy as possible for the original author to fulfill the request. One useful approach is to provide the author with the full citation to the original study, the page number or table where the missing information was expected to be found, and a brief form on which the author can place the requested information. Even taking these steps, my success rate when requesting this information is only about 50 percent. Second, researchers may be able to find the missing information in previous versions of the study or in related studies. For example, if the information is missing from a peer-reviewed article, it may be included in the conference paper, NBER study, SSRN paper, or dissertation that preceded the article. For studies published in the past few years, the missing information may be included in an online supplement maintained by the author or the publisher. Finally, if it is impossible to recover these data, meta-analysts must treat them as missing. If the missing data define moderator variables, these variables may now be measured with error. If the missing data define effect sizes, the effects must be removed from the meta-analysis. Unlike the situation with original research, it is rarely possible to recover missing effect sizes using multiple imputation or other missing data techniques (Pigott 2009).

A Word About Mediator Variables in Meta-Analysis. Original studies in public management and policy sometimes use multi-equation models with multiple endogenous variables (recursive causal models, instrumental variable models, structural equation models, and so on). A simple multi-equation model with a single intervening endogenous variable is presented in path diagram 2.3.

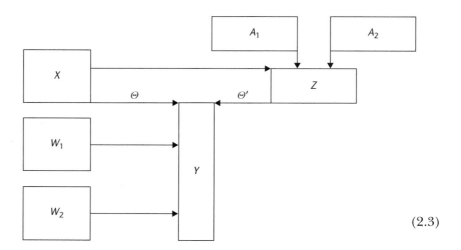

$$(2.3)$$

In this diagram, the focal predictor X has a direct effect on the dependent variable of interest Y (denoted Θ), and an indirect effect on Y through Z (denoted Θ'). In the language of meta-analysis, the intermediate endogenous variable Z is a *mediator variable* because it mediates the relationship between the focal predictor and the dependent variable of interest. As an example, consider that the location of polluting facilities [Y] may be determined in part by the political engagement of community residents [Z]. The political engagement of communities, however, is determined in part by the minority characteristics of the community [X], with minority communities being less engaged than white communities.

In most cases the meta-analyst is simply interested in estimating the magnitude of the relationship between the focal predictor and the dependent variable and explaining why this estimated relationship differs across original studies. Moderator variables are sufficient for these tasks. In rare cases, however, *the meta-analyst might be interested in explaining the mechanisms or paths through which the focal predictor is related to the dependent variable*. Mediator variables are necessary to test hypotheses about these mechanisms. There are two important differences between using mediator variables and using moderator variables in meta-analysis. First, *the effect of mediator variables can only be estimated if original studies estimate the relevant path*. Taking the example of path diagram 2.3, if an original study does not estimate both the path from X to Z and the path from Z to Y, effect sizes from this study cannot be used to assess the effect of the mediator variable in a meta-analysis. By contrast, moderators may or may not represent independent variables used in an original study. Second, *the presence of mediator variables may or may not be used as a criterion for excluding studies from a meta-analysis*. If the purpose of the meta-analysis is strictly to estimate a meta-analytic path model (see, for example, Becker 2009), the absence of mediator variables should disqualify original studies from the meta-analysis. Full-blown path meta-analyses are exceedingly rare, however, and the use of mediator variables in meta-regression is unusual as well.

The Process of Coding

The process of coding in meta-analysis is akin to interviewing or interrogating original studies. When coding data for a meta-analysis, the researcher essentially approaches the sample of acceptable studies identified in the literature review and asks the studies to reveal the information required to calculate effect sizes and code moderator variables. A successful coding process in meta-analysis, then, shares three key characteristics with original research utilizing surveys or structured interview protocols: (1) the need for clear and effective survey instruments, (2) the need to carefully train surveyors or interviewers, and (3) the need to effectively manage large amounts of data. I address all three characteristics in this section.

Developing Coding Instruments

Developing a good coding instrument is like developing a good survey questionnaire. Coding instruments also have much in common with measurement instruments in primary research in that good examples of both should embody the qualities of validity (in other words, they measure what we intend them to measure) and reliability (that is, the results are easily replicable) (Wilson 2009).

Code Books and Code Sheets. Most commonly, meta-analysts will employ two instruments when extracting information from original studies: code books and code sheets. *Code books* are longer documents that summarize the goal of the meta-analysis, identify the purpose of each of the questions or fields in the code sheet, provide complete definitions of each of the responses for each question or field in the code sheet, and provide guidelines for how to resolve common problems or ambiguities encountered when coding. The code book, then, is a reference guide for coders that both clarifies the decisions to be made when coding original studies and helps ensure that different coders make the same decisions when faced with similar circumstances.

Code sheets, however, are the forms on which coders will record information retrieved from original studies (the search-level, study-level, and effect-level information described in the previous section). An informative code book allows the code sheets themselves to be relatively short and uncluttered, containing only the fields to be recorded and the response categories for each field (code sheets should also include a place for coders to take notes or make comments about coding decisions). The use of both code books and code sheets is not universal, however. Cooper (2010) provides excellent examples of detailed code sheets that make a separate code book unnecessary. The choice to use detailed code sheets only or code sheets and code books is a matter of investigator preference and the context of the particular meta-analysis.

Unique Identifiers in Coding Instruments. All code sheets ought to include fields that provide a unique identifier for all effect sizes coded in the meta-analysis. For example, Cooper (2010) recommends a four-part identification scheme, AA.BB.CC.DD, in which AA is the report ID number, BB is the study ID number, CC is the participant or sample ID number, and DD is the outcome ID number. This complicated coding scheme is designed to allow the researcher to easily group subsets of effect sizes from different reports, studies, samples, and outcome measures. Such a scheme is useful when meta-analysts aim to extract groups of independent effect sizes from original studies or reports. The sample code sheets in exhibit 2.1 (at the end of this chapter) use a much simpler two-part identification scheme, AAA.BBB, in which AAA is the study ID number and BBB is the effect size ID number. Because meta-analysis in public management and policy will generally organize effect sizes according to studies (or what Cooper calls a "report") and use multiple correlated effect sizes from each study, this simpler identification scheme is sufficient.

In addition to providing unique identifiers for each study and effect size, code sheets should include a field identifying the coder who completed the coding. Meta-analyses are usually conducted by a research team, and measuring intercoder reliability requires that we are able to track coding decisions made by each member of the team. When using the sample coding sheets in exhibit 2.1, each coder is assigned a number, and the coder's name and assigned number are recorded in the code book. Another common practice is to have coders record their initials on the code sheet.

Finally, code sheets commonly include a field recording the date on which the study or effect size was coded, and another field recording how long it took to complete the coding. The elapsed time field is especially useful early in the coding process, as it allows the researchers to forecast how long it might take to complete the coding. This field is also useful for investigators who must bill the working hours of the research team to a grant or contract. The sample code sheets in exhibit 2.1 do not include either a date or an elapsed time field.

Preserving a Hierarchical Data Structure. Meta-analysis data are almost always structured hierarchically (for example, effect sizes nested within studies). One way in which coding instruments can be designed to preserve this structure is by using multipart identification codes described in the previous section. Each element of the code indexes a separate level of the data structure. An even more effective strategy is to craft a separate code sheet for each level of the data hierarchy. In the environmental justice example, I created a separate code sheet for each type of data collected from original studies: (1) data regarding the choices made when identifying relevant studies, (2) data characterizing important characteristics of each acceptable original study, and (3) data characterizing each effect size within a particular acceptable study. Carefully crafting coding instruments to organize data hierarchically ex ante is far more efficient and effective than trying to reconstruct this hierarchy ex post.

Developing Coding Instruments Through an Iterative Process. No researcher would take the initial draft of a survey questionnaire into the field. At a minimum, the questionnaire would be vetted by experts in the area. Standard practice is that the questionnaire would be pretested at least once. The questionnaire is then revised on the basis of feedback from the experts and lessons learned during the pretest. Coding instruments in meta-analysis, especially code sheets for effect-level information, are developed using a similarly iterative process.

After reading the theoretical and qualitative literature on a particular research question, as well as a sample of the quantitative original research, the meta-analyst should have a good understanding of the most common indicators used to measure the outcome(s) of interest and the focal predictors, the sources of disagreement regarding the results from this research, and the moderator variables that will be necessary to code both. She will also have a good understanding of the most common approaches to statistical analysis and common reporting standards used in original research studying this question. An initial set of code sheets is built using this information. These code sheets are brought to a sample of acceptable studies. The meta-analyst codes this sample of studies, paying especially close attention to (1) important information in these studies that is not represented in the draft coding sheet (such as new moderator variables), (2) sources of ambiguity in the code sheets, and (3) fields in the code sheets that do not appear with sufficient regularity in the original studies or otherwise do not perform as expected. At this initial stage, some of the most useful feedback will be whether all coders experienced the same problems, shared similar uncertainties, and completed the coded fields in the same way for each original study.

The meta-analyst takes this information and uses it to revise both the code sheets and the code book. The revised coding instruments are then brought back to a subset of acceptable studies from the original pilot test and a handful of new studies. This process is repeated until members of the research team are satisfied with the performance of the coding instruments. At this point, the coding instruments are finalized and members of the research team begin coding studies for the meta-analysis (in other words, the survey questionnaire goes into the field).

It is vitally important that every acceptable study be coded using the same coding instruments. This means that all acceptable studies coded during the pilot tests must be recoded using the final coding instruments. This also means that if the "final" coding instruments are later changed upon the discovery of important new information from some original studies, all previously coded studies must be recoded using the revised instruments.

I end this section by noting that meta-analysts face a bit of a dilemma when deciding which moderator variables will be included in the effect-level coding sheets. In an ideal world, the hypotheses tested are developed independently of the data used to test them (in other words, hypotheses of interest should come from theory). One implication of this maxim is that meta-analysts should not populate their list of moderator variables solely by considering the character and content of the original studies investigating their research question. This process is akin to "data dredging" in original studies, or deciding which hypotheses to test after examining patterns in the data that will be used in a primary analysis. Type I error rates for these hypothesis tests will always be too low. However, it makes little sense to populate a list of moderator variables with little or no knowledge of the character or content of original studies examining the research question. For one thing, important controversies in the literature are often instigated by empirical results rather than by theoretical expectations. If meta-analysis is to speak to these controversies, the meta-analyst must code moderator variables that measure the factors at the heart of the disagreements. For another, code sheets must include fields for moderator variables that actually appear in original studies. Most readers will have little trouble identifying theoretically important expectations that are rarely operationalized or tested in the empirical literature. Including fields for these moderators in a meta-analysis code sheet makes little sense. Sound advice regarding this dilemma is that meta-analysts should seek to code moderator variables on the basis of their *presence* in the original studies, not on their *performance* in these studies.

Selecting and Training Coders

Coding studies for a meta-analysis is a team sport. An effective team will have complementary strengths and be well trained. In addition, it is important to have metrics for assessing the performance of team members.

Qualifications of Coders. Coders for a meta-analysis should possess four qualities. First, coders should possess meaningful substantive expertise regarding the research question being investigated. If they do not possess this expertise, they should obtain it prior to conducting the meta-analysis by reading widely in the literature on the topic and by holding conversations with experienced scholars and practitioners in the field. Substantive expertise enables the researcher to identify critical moderator variables that might be overlooked by less experienced coders (for example, program design characteristics or important qualities of treatment groups). Substantive expertise also enables the researcher to better understand the context within which original studies are undertaken, and to recognize best practices and limitations of original studies in the area. Finally, Orwin and Vevea (2009) note that while substantive expertise will not eliminate the need for judgment in coding original studies, it will likely improve how that judgment is exercised.

Second, coders should possess a sound understanding of the purposes, techniques, and statistics of meta-analysis. One way to obtain this understanding is to read this book, or any of the several excellent books on meta-analysis. In addition to reading meta-analysis texts, coders should carefully read a handful of original meta-analyses to gain an appreciation for how the techniques are used in practice. Finally, all coders should receive explicit training in meta-analysis in general and the process of coding studies for meta-analysis in particular. I address the content of such a training program in the next section. A solid understanding of and appreciation for the techniques of meta-analysis will improve coder efficiency and the quality of the data generated by the coder.

Third, coders should have reasonably good training in descriptive and inferential statistics, and detailed familiarity with the general linear model and its extensions. A typical two-semester graduate sequence in applied social statistics or econometrics generally provides sufficient training, although occasionally more advanced quantitative skills are helpful. Coders for a meta-analysis must be able to quickly and accurately understand the information reported in a table of statistical results, and be able to identify the elements in those results that are necessary to calculate effect sizes, effect size variances, and moderator variables. All too often the level of reporting in original studies is insufficiently clear or insufficiently comprehensive to make this task easy or routine. For many original studies identifying the necessary information will require a bit of detective work, and being a good detective is easier with adequate statistical training. Furthermore, meta-analysts will frequently encounter original studies employing statistical techniques that are unfamiliar, either because they are very advanced or because they are uncommon in the coder's academic discipline. Both types of studies are present in the meta-analyses that serve as running examples in this book. For example, a small number of original studies in environmental justice employ discriminant analysis, and a few studies of school vouchers employ ANCOVA.

These techniques are uncommon in public management and policy. Two other school voucher studies estimate the Complier Average Causal Effect (CACE), a very advanced estimation routine that is also uncommon in public management and policy. Adequate training in applied statistics enables coders to understand, identify, and properly code quantities of interest from studies employing nonstandard estimation practices. Finally, it is not uncommon to discover statistical errors in original studies that influence the effect sizes that will be coded from them. Adequate training in statistics increases the probability that the coder will catch these errors.

Each member of a research team does not need to be equally skilled in all three areas. A common division of labor on a two-person coding team is for one member to be a substantive expert while the second has a high level of training in statistics. In fact, it is not unheard of for members of such a team to specialize, with the first coding the substantive aspects of original studies and the second coding the technical data from these studies (Wilson 2009). My sense is that this degree of coder specialization is unusual, and I have no firsthand experience with it. Even with coder specialization, all members of the team ought to have adequate training in meta-analysis.

Fourth, all coders are expected to possess a high degree of professionalism. One aspect of professionalism in meta-analysis is the absence of bias vis-à-vis the research question. Meta-analysts should not set out to "prove" a policy or management intervention was effective or ineffective any more than a scholar conducting primary research should set out with this aim. The absence of bias or guile may be even more important for the meta-analyst, since the techniques of meta-analysis may be able to see through the biases present in original research by policy think tanks and other researchers with a stake in the outcome of investigations in public management and policy. By the same token, meta-analysts ought to be impartial when assessing original research produced by particular investigators or by researchers in particular academic disciplines or institutions. A second aspect of professionalism in meta-analysis is diligence. The careful coding of original studies can be tedious. At times it can be drudgery. It will always be time consuming. For these reasons and others, a meta-analyst may be tempted to cut corners in coding. After all, the other members of the research team will rarely be looking over your shoulder. Resist this temptation. If the temptation becomes too strong, walk away. Lay down the coding instrument and return to the task another time when your mind, body, and conscience are fresh.

Training Coders. After the principal investigator has assembled a research team that is substantively expert, technically proficient, familiar with meta-analysis, and highly professional, it is time to train team members in coding. William Stock (1994) describes an eight-step training program that emphasizes having members of the research team practice coding small samples of original studies, both alone and collectively. This training process dovetails nicely with the iterative process used to develop the final coding instruments, since these iterations can also be used to train coders. Stock's training process is as follows (see also Wilson 2009, 173):

1. The principal investigator provides an overview of the meta-analysis and the coding process that will support the meta-analysis.
2. An initial draft of the code book is circulated and read by all coders. Initial drafts of the code sheets are distributed and each item on the code sheet and its description in the code book are read and discussed by all members of the research team.
3. The process used to complete the code sheets is described. The team discusses the organization of the code sheets with an eye toward (a) collecting together code sheet items that are typically found near each other in original studies, and (b) determining whether the organization of the code sheets will pose any difficulties for data entry.
4. A small sample of acceptable studies is chosen to test the coding instruments.
5. Each study in the sample is coded by each member of the research team. Each member of the team also records how long it took to code each study, and this information is used to estimate how long it will take to complete all coding.
6. Coded forms are compared, discrepancies are identified and resolved, and difficulties or ambiguities in coding are discussed and resolved.
7. The code book and code sheets are revised as necessary.
8. Another study is coded by each member of the research team, and steps 4 through 8 are repeated until consensus is achieved.

This description may give the impression that the eight-step process can be completed in a single afternoon session. This impression is mistaken. In practice, training coders, coding samples of studies, and revising coding instruments may take weeks. Moreover, the process of training coders often does not end until the coding is complete. During the coding phase of the meta-analysis, all members of the research team should meet regularly to share progress and discuss new difficulties or ambiguities that have cropped up during coding. These difficulties and ambiguities should be resolved, either by a majority vote of the research team or by the principal investigator, and the code book and code sheets should be revised if necessary. At a minimum, a record should be kept of the decisions that are made during these meetings so that the decisions guide practice for the remainder of the coding stage. During the coding phase of the meta-analyses in chapters 8 through 11, members of all research teams met every two to three weeks, and members of individual research teams met more frequently. Finally, open access collaborative documents, or "wikis," offer the opportunity for members of a research team to post queries regarding the coding process and to respond to the queries of others without waiting for the next team meeting. These queries can be used to set the agenda for future team meetings, and the decisions made at these meetings can be posted to the wiki so that they might guide future coding decisions.

Assessing the Performance of Coders. One important method for assessing the performance of coders in meta-analysis is to measure intercoder reliability. Chapter 1 introduced the percentage agreement and Cohen's kappa as measures of intercoder reliability during the literature search. These measures are less helpful for assessing the reliability of coding decisions because most coding decisions are not binary. For example, when coding information needed to calculate an effect size, coders will be recording the absolute value of a t-score reported in an original study, while coding a moderator variable for study quality may require the coder to choose between six different research designs that the authors of the original study may have used.

A quick and powerful way to measure intercoder reliability for these measures is to have each coder enter their coded values and unique effect size identifiers into a spreadsheet, merge these spreadsheets in a statistical software package such as Stata using the unique effect size identifier, and compute the pairwise correlation for each field in the code sheets. If the coders agree on each coding decision, the correlation coefficients will equal 1. When the correlation does not equal 1, there is a discrepancy in coding that merits investigation. When used in this fashion, the correlation coefficient is sometimes called the *intercoder correlation coefficient* (ICC, see Orwin and Vevea 2009). This is the quantity reported in the study flow diagrams for the meta-analyses in chapters 8 through 11.

The use of the ICC raises a question regarding the sample used to calculate this coefficient. For small meta-analyses, each study is often coded by two or more members of the research team (called "double coding"), and the ICC is calculated using all studies in the meta-analysis. This approach is impractical for meta-analysis in public management and policy that will often include several hundred effect sizes. For large meta-analyses, standard practice is to double code a random sample of studies and calculate the ICC for this sample. This is the approach used in chapters 8 through 11, in which the ICC is calculated using the first ten effect sizes from each study in a random sample of studies. We use a stratified sample of effect sizes, rather than a random sample of studies, because individual studies can produce a large number of effect sizes and we wanted to be sure to include a sufficient number of studies in the ICC.

The intercoder correlation coefficient provides a way of identifying coder disagreements that can be resolved ex post. There are also at least two methods for reducing coder disagreements ex ante. First, meta-analysts can design code sheets that minimize the judgment that coders need to exercise when completing these forms. These are commonly referred to as "low inference" codes in meta-analysis (Wilson 2009). To illustrate, a code sheet might assess the degree to which an original study controls for the endogeneity of treatment by asking the coder to provide a rating between 1 (weak controls) and 5 (strong controls). Most meta-analysts would view this as a high-inference code because the coder must exercise significant judgment when completing the coding. A superior low-inference approach would provide a list of ex-post endogeneity controls and ask the coder to choose the control(s) used in the model generating a particular effect size. Whenever possible, coders should be asked to employ objective, low-inference codes rather than subjective, high-inference codes.

Second, meta-analysts can combat certain types of coder bias by blinding the studies prior to coding effect-level information. Blinding studies—removing information that the coder might use to identify the author, discipline, institution, or outlet of the study—is difficult and time consuming. Moreover, experiments have shown that while blinding can improve intercoder agreement on subjective items, it has little influence on effect size data and other low-inference codes (Wilson 2009). A combination of highly professional coders and the use of low-inference codes should make study blinding unnecessary for meta-analyses in public management and policy.

Managing Coded Data

With a set of finalized coding instruments and a well-prepared research team, the meta-analyst is ready to code the acceptable studies identified from the literature search. Before coding commences, however, two remaining decisions must be made. First, the team must decide how to record information coded from original studies. Virtually all meta-analysts choose one of two options: entering coded data onto paper copies of the coding form or entering data directly into the computer using a computerized coding form. Computerized forms can be developed in many applications, including FileMaker Pro and Microsoft Access. There are strengths to each approach, some of which are summarized in table 2.1

Historically, the *Cochrane Handbook* (Higgins and Green 2008) has defined best practice in meta-analysis as recording data onto paper coding forms. The belief was that the ability to identify data entry errors from paper code sheets and the presence of a permanent record of coded data tipped the scales in favor of coding onto hard copies. Similar arguments are made in favor of retaining paper ballots in elections for public office. The most recent edition of the *Handbook*, however, does not take a position on the relative merits of coding studies on paper forms or coding studies on computer forms (Higgins and Deeks 2008). Coding studies for the meta-analyses in chapters 8 through 11 was completed using paper code sheets. Regardless of which approach is used, it is important to archive the code sheets securely.

Meta-analysts also need to choose a format for data entry and storage. One option is to enter data into a relational database such as Microsoft Access, FileMaker Pro, or MySQL. When choosing this strategy, meta-analysts can save time by merging coding and data entry into a

TABLE 2.1. STRENGTHS OF CODING STUDIES USING PAPER AND COMPUTERIZED FORMS

Strengths of Coding Using Paper Forms	Strengths of Coding Using Computerized Forms
Data coding can be conducted anywhere.	Data coding is more efficient because coding and data entry are combined.
Paper code sheets are easier to create and implement.	Data entered into computers is easier to store and retrieve.
Paper code sheets provide a permanent record of coding decisions and allow researchers to check for coding errors.	Computer coding forms can be customized to lead the coder through the form, avoiding irrelevant fields.

Source: Adapted from Higgins and Deeks 2008.

single step. Relational databases also excel at allowing researchers to extract almost unlimited subsets of effect sizes using customized queries. However, database programs often interface poorly with statistical software programs. While Stata can interface with relational databases using the ODBC facility, in my experience the learning curve for this is quite steep. Moreover, because meta-analysts in public management and policy are much less likely to calculate average effect sizes for numerous subsamples of effect sizes, this benefit of relational databases is less attractive to scholars in these fields.

A second option is to enter data directly into a dedicated software package for meta-analysis. Review Manager and Comprehensive Meta-Analysis have user friendly interfaces that allow researchers to enter data using a code-sheet-like format. Both packages also allow double entry, in which two members of a research team can enter data for the same set of studies. This simplifies the process of assessing intercoder reliability. Despite these benefits, entering and storing data in meta-analysis software packages has several meaningful drawbacks. First, these programs assume that the researcher will be using odds-based effect sizes. While r-based effect sizes are supported, the data entry interface for these data is far less user friendly. Second, RevMan and CMA require the meta-analyst to specify a hierarchical data structure a priori, and the available data structures make it difficult to handle multiple effect sizes from individual studies. Third, data files from these packages are not easily transported to other software packages. Most important, none of the dedicated meta-analysis software packages can estimate the meta-regression models introduced in chapter 5, and therefore they are of limited usefulness to researchers in public management and policy.

The third and simplest option is to enter data from code sheets as "flat files" into spreadsheet programs such as Microsoft Excel. This approach to data entry and storage has several advantages. First, spreadsheet data entry is familiar and fast for most researchers in public management, public policy, and the social sciences. Second, the flat data files exported from these spreadsheet programs are easily imported and analyzed within virtually all statistical software packages. Third, data stored in this manner are easily shared and updated. Two cautions are in order, however, when using spreadsheets to manage data for a meta-analysis. First, spreadsheets are spectacularly ill-suited for computer coding of original studies. Researchers choosing to enter and store data in spreadsheet format are virtually required to code data onto paper code sheets. Second, preserving the hierarchical structure of the meta-analysis data requires creation of a separate spreadsheet for each level of data. Data from the code sheets in exhibit 2.1 were entered into three spreadsheet flat files (or worksheets) using Microsoft Excel: one flat file records search-level information (one row for each potentially relevant study); the second records study-level information (one row for each relevant study); and the third records effect-level information (one row for each effect size). Data are matched and merged across files using the unique study ID number. The data for the meta-analyses in chapters 8 through 11 were also entered and stored as spreadsheet flat files.

Conclusion

The process of coding data from original studies in a meta-analysis must be precise, transparent, and replicable. These characteristics help distinguish meta-analysis from traditional literature reviews. Robert Orwin and Jack Vevea (2009) describe seven strategies for reducing error in coding studies that are especially useful for public management and policy scholars:

1. Contact original investigators to obtain data missing from original studies.
2. Consult other literature to obtain data missing from original studies.
3. Train coders thoroughly and carefully.
4. Pilot test the coding instruments.
5. Revise the coding instruments according to the lessons learned in the pilot test.
6. Make certain that coders have sufficient substantive expertise.
7. Strive for consensus across coders.[2]

The discussion in this chapter touches on each of these strategies. With quality data in hand, the meta-analyst is prepared to calculate the effect sizes that will lay the foundation for the meta-analysis. Calculating these effect sizes is the subject of chapter 3.

Notes

1. I use the term *multivariate* in the econometric sense to refer to models with multiple independent variables, not in the psychometric sense in which multivariate models use multiple dependent variables.
2. Two other strategies recommended by Orwin and Vevea—improving reporting standards in primary studies and using average coder ratings—are either beyond the influence or less useful for scholars in public management and policy.

ID # ____
Coder # ____

Section I: Data for Potentially Relevant Studies

1. Bibliographic Information
    a. Author 1
    b. Author 2
    c. Author 3
    d. Year

2. Search Protocol That Found Study
    (1)__ Academic Index   (2)__ Academic Universe
    (3)__ UnCover   (4)__ Web of Science
    (5)__ Dissertation abstracts   (6)__ NTIS
    (7)__ Silver Platter   (8)__ Conference proceedings
    (9)__ SUS book search   (10)__ LOC book search
    (11)__ Personal contact   (12)__ Sociological abstracts
    (13)__ Foundation or IG   (14)__ Other

3. Is Study Relevant
    a. Is study relevant?
        (1)__ Yes   (0)__ No

    b. If no, why not relevant?
        (1)__ Non-analytic   (2)__ Non-quantitative
        (3)__ Non-U.S.   (4)__ Dependent variable
        (5)__ Other

ID # ____
Coder # ____

Section II: Study Characteristics for Environmental Equity

(Complete this form only for "relevant" studies)

Bibliographic Reference (APSA Style):

1. Source
    (1)__ Peer-reviewed article   (2)__ Non-peer-reviewed article
    (3)__ Book   (4)__ Book chapter
    (5)__ Government document   (6)__ Private report
    (7)__ Dissertation   (8)__ Conference paper
    (9)__ Other unpublished source

2. Is Study Acceptable?

    (1)__ Yes   (0)__ No

3. If No, Why Unacceptable?

    (1)__ Relevance   (2)__ Data

4. Beginning/ending year of study _____

5. Discipline of publication outlet
    (1)__ Public administration   (2)__ Public policy
    (3)__ Political science   (4)__ Economics
    (5)__ Sociology   (6)__ Geography
    (7)__ Business   (8)__ Natural science
    (9)__ Interdisciplinary   (10)__ Other/Can't tell

ID # ___   **Coder** # ___
Effect # ___   **Page**# ___

Section III: Effects Measures for Environmental Equity

(Complete this form only for "acceptable" studies)

1. Page Number Where Effect Size Was Found

    _____

2. Statistical Technique
    (1)__ Difference of means   (2)__ Difference of proportions
    (3)__ Regression   (4)__ ANOVA
    (5)__ Probit   (6)__ Logit
    (7)__ Correlation   (8)__ Chi-squared
    (9)__ Discriminant analysis   (10)__ Other

3. Definition of control group
    (1)__ All non-host areas   (2)__ Limited nonhost
    (3)__ Other   (4)__ Unable to tell

4. Level of Aggregation
    (1)__ Census block group   (2)__ Census tract
    (3)__ ZIP code   (4)__ City/MSA
    (5)__ County   (6)__ State
    (7)__ GIS area unit   (8)__ Other

5. Type of Risk Vector
    (1)__ Commercial TSDF   (2)__ All TSDF
    (3)__ Superfund site   (4)__ Incinerator
    (5)__ TRI site   (6)__ Pollution levels
    (7)__ Factories   (8)__ Other

6. Effect Measured For
    (1)__ Blacks   (2)__ Latinos
    (3)__ Minorities   (4)__ Poverty
    (5)__ Income

7. Control for Population Density
    (1)__ Yes   (0)__ No

8. Control for Manufacturing Employment
    (1)__ Yes   (0)__ No

9. Control for Housing Value

    (1)__ Yes   (0)__ No

10. Host Area Sample Size
11. Nonhost Area Sample Size
12. Total Sample Size
13. Host Area Mean
14. Nonhost Area Mean
15. Mean Difference
16. Host Area Standard Deviation
17. Nonhost Area Standard Deviation
18. Pooled Standard deviation
19. Coefficient
20. Coefficient Standard Deviation
21. Type of Significance Test

    (1)__ Chi-squared   (2)__ F-value

    (3)__ T-score   (4)__ Z-score

22. Test Statistic
23. Test Statistic *df*
24. *P*-Value
25. One- or Two-Tailed Test
26. Geographic Scope

    (1)__ City/MSA   (2)__ County

    (3)__ State   (4)__ Region

    (5)__ Nation   (6)__ Other

    (7)__ Multiple geographic areas

27. Raw effect favors

    (1)__ Treatment   (0)__ Control

CHAPTER THREE

CALCULATING AND COMBINING EFFECT SIZES

Evan J. Ringquist

"Systematically reviewing and integrating . . . the literature of a field may be considered a type of research in its own right—one using a characteristic set of research techniques and methods"

(FELDMAN 1971, 86).

When conducting a meta-analysis, one of the first orders of business is to translate the empirical results from original studies into effect sizes. Effect sizes are essentially the dependent variable in meta-analysis, as we are interested in the mean value of these effect sizes and, more important, seek to account for variation in these effect sizes. There are two critical conceptual differences between an individual observation on a traditional dependent variable Y_i in an original study and an individual observed effect size Θ_i in a meta-analysis. First, Y_i represents a univariate quantity of interest; for example, a student's score on a standardized test or the level of potential environmental risk in a community. By contrast, Θ_i represents a bivariate quantity of interest; for example, the relationship between the use of an educational voucher and students' scores on standardized tests or the relationship between the concentration of minority residents in communities and levels of potential environmental risk in these communities. Second, in most original studies, including all studies employing regression analysis, Y_i is assumed to be measured without error. Therefore Y_i has no variance (though its conditional regression residual e_i does). By contrast,

Θ_i is assumed to be measured (or estimated) with error and does have variance. In fact, effect sizes have little meaning in meta-analysis without considering their associated effect size variance. In the first sections of this chapter I show how to calculate several common effect sizes and effect size variances. In latter sections I show how to combine effect sizes and their variances to provide basic descriptions of the evidence present in a set of empirical studies, and how to use these quantities to draw basic inferences from these original studies.

Calculating Effect Sizes

Effect sizes represent a standardized relationship or standardized measure of association between the focal predictor X and the dependent variable Y that is comparable across studies. Effect sizes are also the fundamental metric and the essential observation for all meta-analyses. The effect sizes commonly used in meta-analysis fall into one of three classes or families: r-based effect sizes representing correlations between the focal predictor and the dependent variable; d-based effect sizes representing standardized mean differences on Y across categories of X; and odds-based effect sizes representing the ratio or relative frequency of outcomes on Y across categories of X. Gene Glass and his colleagues originally developed an approach to meta-analysis that emphasized d-based effect sizes, and this is still the most common approach to measuring effect sizes in the field of education (Smith and Glass 1977; Glass 1978; Glass, McGraw, and Smith 1981). Meta-analysis in medicine, on the other hand, emphasizes odds-based effect sizes, and many of the recent advances in meta-analysis from medical statistics utilize these effect sizes. By contrast, r-based effect sizes receive little attention in the meta-analysis literature, though these are by far the most common type of effect size encountered in public management, public policy, and the social sciences. Standard texts in the field devote comparatively little attention to r-based effect sizes (see, for example, Borenstein, Hedges, Higgins, and Rothstein 2009; Cooper 2010; Cooper, Hedges, and Valentine 2009; Kulinskaya, Morgenthaler, and Staudte 2008; though see Hunter and Schmidt 1990 for a notable exception), and little recent research in the statistics of meta-analysis focuses on r-based effect sizes (see chapters 4 and 6). And, as we shall see, even the meta-analysis routines in the statistical software package Stata are not well equipped to use r-based effect sizes (Sterne 2009). The discussion of effect sizes in this chapter will emphasize r-based effect sizes and, secondarily, d-based effect sizes. Readers looking for a more thorough treatment of odds-based effect sizes are directed to standard treatments of the subject in the traditional meta-analysis literature (see, for example, Fleiss and Berlin 2009).

How should a researcher choose between these families of effect sizes? Borenstein and colleagues (2009) offer four criteria:

1. Effect sizes should measure similar quantities of interest across original studies.
2. Effect sizes should have good statistical properties; for example, well-understood sampling distributions.
3. Effect sizes should be computable using the information commonly reported in empirical studies examining the research question of interest.
4. Effect sizes should be substantively interpretable.

While these criteria effectively separate high-quality from low-quality effect sizes, they are less helpful in guiding the choice between the three families of effect sizes. For example, r-based, d-based, and odds-based effect sizes all satisfy criteria 2 and 4, though the statistical properties of r-based effect sizes may be understood slightly better than the others (Hunter and Schmidt 1990). Moreover, satisfying criterion 1 requires careful attention to defining the research question, selecting appropriate operationalizations of the focal predictor and dependent variable, systematic identification of acceptable studies, and other elements of designing a meta-analysis discussed at length in chapters 1 and 2. No family of effect sizes can rescue a researcher who makes poor choices in these other areas. This leaves us with criterion 3, which emphasizes context-specific feasibility rather than clear guidelines for choosing among effect sizes ex ante.

As an alternative, researchers in public management and policy ought to choose between families of effect sizes using the same criteria when choosing among alternative statistical techniques in original studies; that is, the level of information present in the data. When both the focal predictor and the dependent variable are measured using continuous indicators, meta-analysts should calculate r-based effect sizes. In fact, researchers in the social sciences ought to employ a rebuttable presumption in favor of using r-based effect sizes in all meta-analysis, since the regression models commonly used in original studies derive their parameter estimates from the correlation between independent and dependent variables. When original studies generally measure the dependent variable continuously and the focal predictor dichotomously or categorically, especially in a non-regression format, researchers should calculate d-based effect sizes. Note that the same advice does not hold if the situation is reversed. When original studies measure the dependent variable dichotomously but the focal predictor uses a continuous metric, r-based effect sizes are appropriate (though these studies estimate a point-biserial correlation coefficient rather than the more common Pearson's correlation coefficient). Finally, when both the dependent variable and the focal predictor in original studies are measured using binary indicators, researchers ought to use odds-based effect sizes. The consequences of making an incorrect choice among families of effect sizes are not grave. As we shall see, it is relatively easy to convert between families of effect sizes. Still, selecting a proper family of effect sizes ex ante is preferable to correcting or converting effect sizes ex post.

r-Based Effect Sizes

Meta-analysis texts often cite Karl Pearson's combination of correlation coefficients from different studies as an example of the first meta-analysis (Pearson 1904). This may be true, but it is also true that comparatively few modern meta-analyses follow Pearson's example by employing r-based effect sizes. One important reason for this is that correlation coefficients are often inappropriate metrics for conveying research results in the experimental traditions of medicine and psychology. By contrast, correlation coefficients and their related estimators (regression coefficients, standardized regression coefficients, Probit coefficients, factor scores, and so on) are the stock in trade for researchers in public management, public policy, and the social sciences. Meta-analyses in these fields, therefore, ought to employ r-based effect sizes. In this section I introduce the two most common r-based effect sizes, the correlation coefficient r and Fisher's Z.

The Correlation Coefficient **r.** An accurate estimate of the sample correlation coefficient r can be obtained using the t-score testing the null hypothesis that the population correlation $\rho = 0$ in the following formula:

$$r = \sqrt{\left[t^2 / \left(t^2 + df\right)\right]} \qquad (3.1)$$

This formula is appropriate for the partial correlation coefficient $rYX_j.X_k$ as well as for the traditional correlation coefficient rYX_j. An essential point is that *equation 3.1 can be used to calculate the partial correlation coefficient associated with a regression parameter estimate in any regression model.* To calculate the partial correlation coefficient $rYX_j.X_k$ we simply use the *t*-score from this model testing the null hypothesis Ho: $\beta_j = 0$. Equation 3.1 can be used regardless of the number of independent variables in the regression model (Greene 1993, 180).[1] Keef and Roberts (2004) show that the estimate of $rYX_j.X_k$ from equation 3.1 contains a small positive bias in k. That is, holding $\rho YX_j.X_k$ constant, $rYX_j.X_k$ increases as the number of independent variables k in the original regression model increases.[2] The source of this bias is in the denominator of equation 3.1. Holding the sample size n constant, increasing k will decrease the degrees of freedom df. It is also clear, however, that the magnitude of this bias will be strongly influenced by the sample size. Asymptotically this bias disappears, and in large samples this bias is likely to be trivial. As an illustration, consider an original study in which $t_j = 2.0$, $n = 100$ and $k = 4$. The estimated partial correlation coefficient $rYX_j.X_k = .2$. If we increase k to 8, we calculate $rYX_j.X_k = .204$. Doubling the number of independent variables leads to less than a 2 percent increase in the calculated effect size. Substituting $n = 1,000$ in the same scenario, $rYX_j.X_k = .06325$ where $k = 4$ and $rYX_j.X_k = .06337$ when $k = 8$. With the larger sample size of $n = 1,000$, doubling the number of independent variables inflates the effect size by less than 0.2 percent. In most cases faced by meta-analysts in practice, then, the bias in effect sizes from using equation 3.1 will be ignorable.

Equation 3.1 also applies whether X and Y are both measured continuously or whether either X or Y is binary. In the latter circumstance r represents the *point biserial correlation coefficient* rather than the *product–moment correlation coefficient*. If either X or Y is dichotomized artificially in original studies (for example, if $X = 1$ for communities where the percentage of minority residents is above the national average and $X = 0$ for communities where the percentage of minorities is below the national average), the point biserial correlation coefficient will underestimate the true product moment correlation. While this bias is generally quite small, Hunter and Schmidt (1990) offer corrections for this and other sources of attenuation in r-based effect sizes. Virtually all of these corrections require access to information that is generally unavailable to researchers in public management and policy (such as reliability of measures or degree of range restriction for measures used in the original studies). Therefore, it is unlikely that readers will be able to employ these corrections in practice. The variance of the correlation coefficient is calculated as

$$V[r] = \left(1 - r^2\right)^2 / (n - 1) \qquad (3.2)$$

I select one of the effect sizes in the environmental justice data set (effect #1 from study 369, Downey 1998) to illustrate calculating a correlation coefficient using the results from a regression model in an original study. Downey's study estimates a regression model predicting pollution emissions (Y) in a sample of 116 communities ($n = 116$) using the percentage of minority residents in a community (X_1) and two control variables ($k = 3$, $df = 112$ ($n - k - 1$)). Downey is able to reject the null hypothesis of no relationship with a t-score of 3.38 ($p < .001$). From these results we can calculate the partial correlation between the percentage of minority residents in communities and pollution emissions in communities $[r(YX_1|X_2X_3)]$ as $r = \sqrt{[3.38^2/(3.38^2 + 112)]} = .30$ with variance $V[r] = (1 - .30^2)^2 / (116 - 1) = .0072$.

The partial correlation associated with a given t-score drops as the sample size (or degrees of freedom) increases. I illustrate this using effect #53 from study 282 (Ringquist 1997). Study 282 estimates a regression model predicting the release of Toxics Release Inventory (TRI) pollutants (Y) in a sample of 29,214 communities ($n = 29214$), using the percentage of minority residents in a community (X_1) and ten control variables ($k = 11$, $df = 29202$ ($n - k - 1$)). In this study I was able to reject the null hypothesis of no relationship with a t-score of 3.09 ($p < .001$). The t-score and p-value from this study are nearly identical to those from the Downey study, but the sample size in the Ringquist study is nearly 250 times larger. From these results we calculate the partial correlation between the percentage of minority residents in communities and TRI releases in communities as $r = \sqrt{[3.09^2/(3.09^2 + 29202)]} = .018$ with variance $V[r] = (1 - .018^2)^2 / (29214 - 1) = .000034$. Nearly identical t-scores produce very different estimates of the partial correlation coefficient depending on the sample size, reflecting the fact that t-scores embody both the magnitude of the underlying effect and the precision with which this effect is estimated. Also note that the variance is much smaller for the effect size from the larger study.

Not all statistical techniques used in the fields of public management and policy test hypotheses using t-scores. Moreover, conventions for reporting the results from statistical analysis in the social sciences are not well developed and seldom enforced (as anyone with experience in meta-analysis can attest!). When encountering a study that does not report a t-statistic for the relationship of interest, meta-analysts have the following options:

1. What if the original study estimates models using maximum likelihood?

$$r = \sqrt{[Z^2/n]} \tag{3.3}$$

2. What if the original study tests hypotheses using Wald tests?

$$r = \sqrt{\left[X_1^2/n\right]} \qquad (3.4)$$

3. What if the original study does not report t-scores, but reports parameter estimates and standard errors?

$$t = b_j/s_{bj} \qquad (3.5)$$
$$r = \sqrt{\left[t^2/\left(t^2 + df\right)\right]}$$

4. What if the original study only reports parameter estimates and identifies statistically significant parameter estimates using asterisks or other symbols?
    ·   In these situations researchers should set the t-score equal to the value of t at the symbol threshold and given degrees of freedom. For example, if an original study reports $b_j = 1.50**$ where $n = 54$, $k = 3$, and $**p < .05$, then $t = 2.009$; that is, $p|t_{50} > 2.009| = .05$. Readers should be aware that partial correlation coefficients calculated using these values of t represent *lower bounds*. The actual partial correlation coefficient will be larger, but we cannot tell how much larger without additional information. If a large proportion of effect sizes are calculated using this method, meta-analysts should caution their readers that average effect sizes also represent lower bound estimates and that the true population effect size may be slightly larger. The truncation in this estimate of the partial correlation coefficient provides a strong argument for more complete reporting of statistical results in original research.

5. What if an original study only reports that a parameter of interest is not statistically significant?
    ·   In these situations researchers have two options: (1) they can exclude the effect size from the data set, or (2) they can set $t = 0$ and calculate $r = 0$. The first option assumes that we have no information about the effect size, which is not true, or that the estimated effect size does not exist in the literature, which also is not true. Excluding these effect sizes will almost certainly inflate average effect sizes from the meta-analysis. The second option assumes that the effect size is zero. An inability to reject Ho:$\beta_j = 0$ does not mean $E[b_j] = 0$. Still, setting $r = 0$ in these situations does make use of the best information available regarding the magnitude of the effect size. As with the previous

example, setting $t = 0$ places a lower bound on the effect size. If a large proportion of effect sizes are calculated this way, average effect sizes may underestimate the true population effect size. However, the conservative posture reflected in this choice is consistent with the skepticism regarding true effects that underlies null hypothesis testing and scientific inquiry in general.

6. What if an original study reports standardized regression coefficient estimates?

$$r = \beta_j \tag{3.6}$$

7. What if an original study reports the correlation coefficient but not its t-score?

$$r = r \tag{3.7}$$

Fisher's Z. Using one of the formulas in the preceding section, researchers should be able to calculate partial correlation coefficients (and their variances) from most if not all of the acceptable original studies they encounter when conducting a meta-analysis. While r is easy to calculate, is comparable across studies, and can be aggregated in linear combinations, it does suffer from three shortcomings. First, r contains a very small downward bias as an estimate of the population parameter ρ. Second, r is bounded by $-1 \leq r \leq 1$, meaning that r is both truncated and censored. In rare cases, this may make the partial correlation coefficient a poor choice as a dependent variable in a meta-regression analysis. Third, the variance of r depends strongly on its value (see equation 3.2). To remedy these shortcomings, the correlation coefficient r is typically transformed into the r-based effect size Fisher's Z, denoted Z_r, prior to conducting a meta-analysis

$$Z_r = 0.5 \ ln \left[(1 + r) / (1 - r) \right] \tag{3.8}$$

with variance

$$V\left[Z_r \right] = 1 / (n - 3) \tag{3.9}$$

Schmidt, Hunter, and Raju (1988) and Hunter and Schmidt (1990) provide evidence that Z_r itself may contain a small positive bias as an estimate of the population parameter ρ, and these authors express a preference for using r rather than Z_r in meta-analyses of r-based effect sizes. In practice, any bias in r and Z_r is very small, and the difference between r and

Z_r is typically less than two significant digits (that is, within rounding error) over the range of partial correlations common in regression analysis (for example, $|r| < .4$). Convention in meta-analysis is to use Z_r, and we employ this effect size throughout the book.

d-Based Effect Sizes

When Gene Glass coined the term *meta-analysis*, his example was calculating and combining a set of standardized mean differences, or d-based effect sizes, across a set of original studies. To understand the intuition behind the d-based effect size, consider a single original study that compares the average outcome of interest for one group (μ_1, estimated using $\overline{Y}_1$) with the average outcome of interest for a second group (μ_2, estimated using $\overline{Y}_2$). If we make the common assumption that the variances and standard deviations of the outcome of interest are the same for each group ($\sigma_1 = \sigma_2 = \sigma$), we can calculate a standardized mean difference across groups using the formula

$$\delta = \left(\mu_1 - \mu_2\right)/\sigma \tag{3.10}$$

While Glass estimated σ using the control group sample standard deviation s, nearly all modern meta-analysts estimate σ using the pooled sample standard deviation. This effect size, described further on, is often referred to as "Cohen's d."

Hedges and Olkin (1985) offer two rationales for why δ can be considered comparable across studies, First, if the outcome variables in all studies are linear transformations of one another, the standardized mean difference can be viewed as the value we would obtain if outcome measures in all studies were transformed to have within-groups standard deviations $\sigma = 1$. For readers who view this linear combination requirement as too restrictive, standardized mean differences can also be viewed as a measure of the degree to which distributions on the outcome measure for the two groups overlap. Where $\delta = 0$, the overlap is perfect. As δ increases, the distributions become more distinct. Using this rationale, the assumption that each study measures identical outcomes is unnecessary.

d-based effect sizes will sometimes be appropriate for meta-analysis in public management and policy, especially when original studies employ difference of means tests or Analysis of Variance (ANOVA); that is, when the dependent variable Y is continuous and the focal predictor X is dichotomous. In this section I describe the two most common d-based effect sizes, Cohen's d and Hedges's g.

The Standardized Mean Difference: Cohen's d. The method for calculating the sample standardized mean difference d (which estimates the population effect size δ) differs depending on whether the outcome of interest is obtained from independent groups or from groups that are correlated in some manner. Independent groups, such as treatment and control groups constructed using random assignment, are more typical. Correlated groups are often produced by comparing pretest and posttest measures for the same set of subjects, or by comparing outcomes across matched pairs, and are less common in original studies in public management and policy. d-based effect sizes *need not be calculated* for original studies that employ regression discontinuity designs or propensity score matching, so long as data generated from the latter are analyzed using regression-like models. While members of treatment and control groups are matched prior to analysis when using these designs, in nearly all cases these designs will generate r-based effect sizes calculated from the t-scores on the resulting regression parameter estimates. Finally, unlike correlation coefficients, there is no common metric for assessing the magnitude of d-based effect sizes. Cohen (1988) suggests that values of d below .25 represent small effects, values of d approaching .5 should be considered moderate effects, and values of d near or above .8 might be considered large effects. These are only rules of thumb, however, and the importance of the effect size magnitude should be judged within the context of each meta-analysis.

Estimating d *from Independent Groups.* We estimate the standardized mean difference from studies that use independent groups using equation 3.11:

$$d = \left(\overline{Y}_1 - \overline{Y}_2\right) / S_{\text{Pooled}} \tag{3.11}$$

where $\overline{Y}_1$ and $\overline{Y}_2$ represent group sample means and S_{Pooled} represents the pooled within group sample standard deviation:

$$S_{\text{Pooled}} = \sqrt{\left[\left(\left(n_1 - 1\right) s_1^2 + \left(n_2 - 1\right) s_2^2\right) / \left(n_1 + n_2 - 2\right)\right]} \tag{3.12}$$

Occasionally original studies will not report values of $\overline{Y}_1$ or $\overline{Y}_2$, but instead report whether the difference $\left(\overline{Y}_1 - \overline{Y}_2\right)$ is statistically significant. In these situations d can be calculated as

$$d = t\sqrt{\left[\left(n_1 + n_2\right)/n_1 n_2\right]} \qquad (3.13)$$

or

$$d = Z\sqrt{\left[\left(n_1 + n_2\right)/n_1 n_2\right]} \qquad (3.14)$$

or

$$d = \sqrt{\left[F\left(n_1 + n_2\right)/n_1 n_2\right]} \qquad (3.15)$$

In circumstances in which original studies report the two-tailed p-value associated with the difference $\left(\overline{Y}_1 - \overline{Y}_2\right)$ rather than the test statistic for this difference, d can be calculated using

$$d = +/- t^{-1}\left(p/2\right)\sqrt{\left[\left(n_1 + n_2\right)/n_1 n_2\right]} \qquad (3.16)$$

where $t^{-1}(p/2)$ represents the inverse of the cumulative t-distribution with degrees of freedom $(n_1 + n_2 - 2)$. That is, $t^{-1}(p/2)$ is simply the value of $t_{n_1+n_2-2}$ associated with $p/2$ where p is the p-value for the null hypothesis test reported in the original study. The variance of d is given by

$$V[d] = \left(\left(n_1 + n_2\right)/n_1 n_2\right) + \left(d^2/2\left(n_1 + n_2\right)\right) \qquad (3.17)$$

To illustrate the calculation of Cohen's d, I selected an effect size from the educational voucher meta-analysis in chapter 8: effect size #1 from study 22,171 (Metcalf, West, Legan, Paul, and Boone 2003). In this study, the average standardized test score for 275 students using vouchers is 534.63 with a standard deviation of 26.72 ($n_1 = 275$, $\overline{Y}_1 = 534.63$, $s_1 = 26.72$). The average standardized test score for a control group of 239 students who did not receive vouchers is 525.33 with a standard deviation of 29.07 ($n_2 = 239$, $\overline{Y}_2 = 525.33$, $s_2 = 29.07$). I calculate S_{Pooled} as $\sqrt{\left[\left(275 - 1\right)26.72^2 + \left(239 - 1\right)29.07^2\right)/\left(275 + 239 - 2\right)\right]} = 27.84$. Using this value for S_{Pooled} I calculate $d = \left(534.63 - 525.33\right)/27.84 = .334$. This value of d indicates that for the sample of students used in this one model in this one study, vouchers have had a small to moderate positive effect on student academic achievement. The variance of this standardized mean difference $V[d] = \left(\left(275 + 239\right)/275*239\right) + \left(.334^2/2\left(275 + 239\right)\right) = .00796$.

Estimating d *from Correlated Groups.* When original studies calculate differences in outcomes across independent groups, they are likely to report the standard deviations for outcomes within each group as in the preceding example. When original studies calculate differences in outcomes using matched pairs or pretest-posttest scores for the same group, however, the studies are likely to report the standard deviation of the difference, rather than the standard deviation of outcomes within each group (Borenstein 2009). To calculate d we need to recover or impute within-group standard deviations from the reported standard deviation of differences using

$$S_{\text{Within}} = S_{\text{Difference}}/\sqrt{[2(1-r)]} \tag{3.18}$$

where r is the correlation between matched pairs or the correlation between pretest and posttest scores. If r is not reported in the original study (a common occurrence), it can be estimated from other similar studies, but finding these studies in public management and policy research will be difficult. More commonly, researchers in these fields will need to posit a range of plausible values for r and assess the sensitivity of d as r changes.

We calculate the standardized mean difference across paired observations using

$$d = \left(\overline{Y}_1 - \overline{Y}_2\right)/S_{\text{Within}} \tag{3.19}$$

which has variance

$$V[d] = \left[(1/n) + \left(d^2/2n\right)\right]2(1-r) \tag{3.20}$$

Alternative formulas for calculating the correlated observations version of d under different reporting scenarios in original studies are provided in table 3.2, further on in this chapter.

The Corrected Standardized Mean Difference: Hedges's g. Cohen's d contains a slight positive bias, overestimating the population effect size δ in small samples. Hedges (1981) provides a correction factor J:

$$J = 1 - \left(3/\left(4df - 1\right)\right) \tag{3.21}$$

When applied to d, this correction factor produces the most common d-based effect size used in meta-analysis: Hedges's g:

$$g = J * d \tag{3.22}$$

Hedges's g has variance

$$V[g] = J^2 * V[d] \qquad (3.23)$$

The correction factor J will always be less than one, so Hedges's g will always be slightly smaller than Cohen's d, eliminating the upward bias in the latter measure. Using our sample effect size $d = .334$ calculated earlier, we would calculate $J = 1 - (3/((4*512) - 1)) = .99853$, $g = J(d) = .333$, and $V[g] = J^2 \, V[d] = .00794$. Note that both g and $V[g]$ are slightly smaller than their counterparts d and $V[d]$.

Odds-Based Effect Sizes

When both the focal predictor and the dependent variable are measured using binary indicators, odds-based effect sizes are appropriate. This situation is common in medical research in which investigators are often interested in the frequencies of a dichotomous outcome (for example, heart attacks) between treatment and control groups defined by administering a new drug or a placebo. While odds-based effect sizes are probably the most commonly used effect sizes in meta-analysis, they are generally inappropriate for public management and policy because original studies in these fields rarely employ experimental designs in which both treatment and outcomes are dichotomous. Moreover, when policy and management scholars do encounter binary focal predictors and outcome measures in original studies, the relationship between the two is most commonly estimated using a dummy variable X in a Logit or Probit model. r-based effect sizes can be calculated directly from the Z-scores or X_1^2 values used to test the null hypothesis that $b_j = 0$ in these models. In these cases r estimates the *tetrachoric correlation coefficient*, which is an estimate of the correlation coefficient we would obtain if X and Y were measured on continuous scales (Pearson 1900).

Five odds-based effect sizes are commonly used in meta-analysis. To understand the differences between these measures, it is useful to think of the outcomes of an experiment arranged as in table 3.1.

The *risk ratio* (also commonly called the *rate ratio*) effect size RR is calculated as

$$RR = (A/n_1) / (C/n_2) \qquad (3.24)$$

RR represents the relative risk of an event, occurring in the treatment group compared to the control group. A second common odds-based

TABLE 3.1. OUTCOMES OF A HYPOTHETICAL EXPERIMENT WITH BINARY TREATMENT AND OUTCOMES

	Event Occurs ($Y = 1$)	Event Does Not Occur ($Y = 0$)	Sample Size
Treatment Group ($X = 1$)	A	B	n_1
Control Group ($X = 0$)	C	D	n_2

effect size, the *odds ratio OR*, is calculated as

$$OR = AD/BC \qquad (3.25)$$

OR represents the relative odds of an event occurring in the treatment groups compared to the control group. Both RR and OR generally enter meta-analysis in their logged forms

$$L_r = \ln [RR] \qquad (3.26)$$

and

$$L_o = \ln [OR] \qquad (3.27)$$

Many readers may recognize the log of the odds ratio L_o as the quantity of interest estimated by the Logit model frequently employed by social scientists, though these quantities are only comparable when X_j in the Logit model is dichotomous. While the *log risk ratio* L_r has a more intuitive meaning, the *log odds ratio* L_o has superior statistical properties (Borenstein, Hedges, Higgins, and Rothstein 2009; Fleiss and Berlin 2009), and L_o is used more frequently in meta-analysis. The variance of L_o is calculated as

$$V[L_o] = (1/A) + (1/B) + (1/C) + (1/D) \qquad (3.28)$$

While RR, OR, L_r, and L_o are measures of relative risk, the *risk difference* effect size RD is a measure of absolute risk, and is sometimes more meaningful in clinical settings. RD is calculated as

$$RD = (A/n_1) - (C/n_2) \qquad (3.29)$$

The treatment of odds-based effect sizes in this section is intentionally brief. Standard meta-analysis texts such as those by Borenstein and colleagues (2009) and Cooper, Hedges, and Valentine (2009) provide more extensive discussions of this family of effect sizes.

Summarizing the Calculation of Effect Sizes

Formulas 3.1 through 3.29 should equip readers to calculate proper effect sizes from most original studies encountered when conducting a meta-analysis. Table 3.2 collects the most common formulas for r-based and d-based effect sizes and their variances.

Converting Between Effect Sizes. When conducting a meta-analysis, it is common for original studies to generate different types of effect sizes. For example, most of the original studies in the educational voucher meta-analysis presented in chapter 8 used regression techniques, so we were able to calculate r-based effect sizes. Some original studies, however, presented differences in conditional and unconditional means for treatment and control groups. For these studies we were only able to calculate d-based effect sizes. Moreover, a few original studies directly reported d-based effect sizes rather than group means. To conduct a meta-analysis,

TABLE 3.2. FORMULAS FOR r-BASED AND d-BASED EFFECT SIZES AND VARIANCES

r-Based Effect Sizes	d-Based Effect Sizes (Independent)	d-Based Effect Sizes (Matched or Correlated)
$r = \sqrt{[t^2/(t^2 + df)]}$	$d = (\overline{Y}_1 - \overline{Y}_2)/S_{\text{pooled}}$	$d = (\overline{Y}_1 - \overline{Y}_2)/S_{\text{within}}$
$r = \sqrt{[Z^2/n]}$	$d = t\sqrt{[(n_1 + n_2)/(n_1 n_2)]}$	$d = t\sqrt{[2(1-r)/n]}$
$r = \sqrt{[X_1^2/n]}$	$d = +/- t^{-1}(p/2)$ $\sqrt{[(n_1 + n_2)/(n_1 n_2)]}$	$d = +/-$ $t^{-1}(p/2)\sqrt{[2(1-r)/n]}$
$V[r] = (1-r^2)^2/(n-1)$	$V[d] = [((n_1 + n_2)/(n_1 n_2)) + (d^2/2(n_1 + n_2))]$	$V[d] = (1/n + d^2/2n)$ $2(1-r)$
$Z_r = 0.5\ \ln[(1+r)/(1-r)]$	$g = [1 - (3/(4df-1))]*d$	$g = [1 - (3/(4df-1))]*d$
$V[Z_r] = 1/(n-3)$	$V[g] = [1 - (3/(4df-1))]^2 *V[d]$	$V[g] = [1 - (3/(4df-1))]^2 *V[d]$

all effect sizes must represent the same quantity. That is, all effect sizes must be of the same type. Thankfully, it is a fairly easy matter to convert between effect sizes. Figures 3.1 and 3.2 present the formulas for these conversions. Most meta-analyses in public management and policy will use r-based effect sizes, and all r-based effect sizes should be converted to Fisher's Z (Z_r) prior to conducting the analysis (though see Hunter and Schmidt 1990 for a different perspective). This is the approach we take in chapters 8 through 11, converting all d-based effect sizes to the

FIGURE 3.1. FORMULAS FOR CONVERTING BETWEEN EFFECT SIZES IN META-ANALYSIS

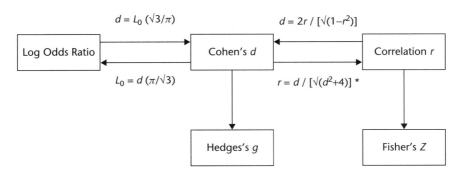

* 4 in this equation is an approximation for $(n_1 + n_2)^2 / (n_1 n_2)$.

FIGURE 3.2. FORMULAS FOR CONVERTING BETWEEN EFFECT SIZE VARIANCES IN META-ANALYSIS

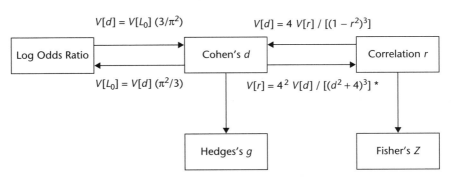

* 4 in this equation is an approximation for $(n_1 + n_2)^2 / (n_1 n_2)$.

correlation coefficient r, and then converting r to Z_r. In some situations a majority of original studies may produce d-based effect sizes. In these cases all other effect sizes should be converted to Cohen's d, and then these effect sizes should be adjusted to Hedges's g. Log odds effect sizes require no adjustment.

As discussed, each effect size has an associated variance. Therefore when converting between r-based, d-based, and odds-based effect sizes, the effect size variances must be converted as well. Figure 3.2 provides a diagram and the associated formulas for converting between effect size variances in meta-analysis.

Fixed Effects and Random Effects Meta-Analysis

Before analyzing effect sizes, we need to decide what the individual effect sizes calculated in the previous section represent, and what conclusions we want to be able to draw when analyzing them. Answering these questions requires us to choose between a *fixed effects* model and a *random effects* model (I use the terms *model*, *framework*, and *approach* interchangeably when discussing fixed and random effects meta-analysis). Social scientists familiar with analyzing pooled or panel data should not be misled by these terms. Fixed and random effects models in meta-analysis are fundamentally different from these same models in panel data analysis. In virtually all cases meta-analysis in public management, public policy, and the social sciences will be conducted using the random effects framework. Meta-analysis was developed within the fixed effects framework, however, and this approach is still common in many other fields. Moreover, understanding the differences between the fixed and random effects approaches helps to develop a better intuition of what meta-analysis does when synthesizing the results from original studies. Therefore, I cover both approaches here.

The Fixed Effects Approach to Meta-Analysis

The fixed effects model assumes that each individual effect size Θ_i estimated from an original study is a single realization of a common population effect size Θ that is identical across all studies. The notion that there is a single "fixed" effect size characterizing the relationship between the focal predictor X and the dependent variable Y gives rise to the "fixed effects" label, though Borenstein and colleagues (2009) point out that "common effect model" might be more appropriate. The fixed effects approach assumes that individual effect sizes Θ_i vary across studies solely because of sampling error. That is,

$$\Theta_i = \Theta + e_i \tag{3.30}$$

This is why variances of effect sizes in meta-analysis are only a function of their sample sizes (see table 3.2). Moreover, the sampling error associated with Θ_i is assumed to be normal, so that

$$e_i \sim N\left(0, v_i\right) \tag{3.31}$$

where v_i is the effect size variance from table 3.2. Since each original study estimates the same underlying common or "true" effect, if all original studies used infinitely large samples (or were estimated with infinite precision), all original studies would estimate the same effect size; in other words, $\Theta_i = \Theta_j = \Theta_k = \Theta$. In the context of our continuing examples, the fixed effects approach assumes that the effect of educational vouchers on student academic achievement is the same for all students regardless of location (Cleveland, New York City, Washington, D.C., and so on) and regardless of student characteristics (race, ethnicity, gender, age, and so on). By the same token, the fixed effects approach assumes that the degree of environmental inequity is the same regardless of location or the source of potential environmental risk.

The assumptions underlying fixed-effects meta-analysis may strike many social scientists as implausible. These assumptions are less implausible within the fields of medicine and psychology, however, in which the fixed effects approach is common. For example, it is not implausible to assume that a drug or psychotherapy treatment has the same effect on individuals across randomized trials. Moreover, upon reflection social scientists will recognize the fixed effects assumption as analogous to the assumption of parameter stability that undergirds the common least squares regression model. That is, the regression parameter estimate b representing the relationship between focal predictor X and dependent variable Y estimates a population parameter β that is the same for all observations in the sample. In theory, $b = \beta + e$, where $e \sim N(0, \sigma^2)$ and the variance of b is the product of sampling error.[3] If the regression equation could be estimated with an infinitely large sample (or with infinite precision), $b = \beta$. Because the effect size Θ_i is analogous to observation Y_i in regression analysis, from this vantage point the assumption motivating fixed effects meta-analysis appears less unusual.

The assumption embodied in equation 3.30 defines the meaning of the fixed effect size Θ_i. This assumption also conditions the inferences we can make from these effect sizes. Specifically, any conclusions we draw when comparing or combining effect sizes in the fixed effects framework *apply only to the studies in the current data set*. The conclusions or inferences we draw from these effect sizes cannot be applied to existing studies that are not included in the current sample, nor can they be projected to future studies examining the same research questions. The external validity of fixed effects meta-analysis is very limited.

The Random Effects Approach to Meta-Analysis

In contrast to the fixed effects approach, random effects meta-analysis does not assume a single common effect size for all studies, nor does it assume that the relationship between the focal predictor X and the dependent variable Y is identical for all samples in all circumstances. Rather than conceiving of the population effect size Θ as a constant, Θ is conceived of as a normally distributed random variable

$$\Theta \sim N\left(\mu_\Theta, \tau^2\right) \tag{3.32}$$

where μ_Θ is the population effect size mean and τ^2 is the *random effects variance component tau squared*. Tau squared is commonly referred to as a measure of *effect size heterogeneity*. In this way effect sizes in random effects meta-analysis are akin to parameters in random coefficient (not random effects) panel data regression models (Hsiao 1986) or to level effects in hierarchical linear models (Gelman and Hill 2007). In the random effects framework, individual effect size estimates Θ_i have the following components:

$$\Theta_i = \mu_\Theta + \tau^2 + e_i \tag{3.33}$$

Each observed effect size estimates Θ_i the mean of the distribution of effect sizes μ_Θ. This estimate departs from the population mean for two reasons. First, Θ_i contains the same type of sampling error found in the fixed effects model (v_i). Second, the value of Θ_i is affected by the random effects variance component τ^2. Note that τ^2 is a scalar common to all effect sizes.

While the effect size estimates Θ_i take on the same value in the fixed effects and random effects frameworks, they represent distinct quantities of interest. The conclusions we draw when comparing or combining effect sizes in the random effects framework differ as well. Specifically, the random effects model assumes that the studies in our data set represent a random sample from the population of all studies of interest. The observed effect sizes, then, represent a random sample from the population of effect sizes of interest. Therefore, any conclusions we draw from this sample apply to the entire population of effect sizes; in other words, to effect sizes from similar studies not included in our sample, and to future studies examining the same research question. Conclusions drawn from random effects meta-analysis have far greater external validity than conclusions from the fixed effects model.

Before moving on it is worthwhile to point out that effect sizes can vary across studies for two reasons (that is, the random effects variance component τ^2 itself has two elements). First, effect sizes may vary systematically across studies (or across models within any particular study) due to factors that are observable to the meta-analyst. Generically, effect sizes may vary depending on the composition of treatment and control groups, the intensity or duration of treatment, or the instrument used to measure treatment outcomes. In our continuing examples, the effects of educational vouchers on academic achievement may vary across types of students or according to the design of voucher programs. Similarly, the severity of environmental inequities may differ across racial and ethnic communities, or according to the source of potential environmental risk. These observable factors can be coded as moderator variables by the meta-analyst (see chapter 2) and be included in meta-regression models that account for variation in effect sizes within and across original studies (see chapters 4 and 5). Second, effect sizes may vary across studies according to factors that are unobservable to the meta-analyst and unrelated to sample size.

Assessing Effect Size Heterogeneity: Fixed or Random Effects?

The methods for combining effect sizes presented later in this chapter and the methods for accounting for effect size heterogeneity presented in chapters 4 and 5 differ depending on whether we employ a fixed or random effects framework. Therefore, we need to be able to identify when each approach to meta-analysis is most appropriate. In this section I describe the most common approaches to testing for random effects, for quantifying the relative magnitude of the random effects variance, and for measuring the absolute magnitude of the random effects variance component.

Testing for Random Effects: The **Q** *Test.* Before describing the most common test for random effects in meta-analysis, it is useful to conceive of random effects as *variance in observed effect sizes over and above what we would expect due to sampling error alone.* From table 3.2 we know the variance associated with each individual effect size Θ_i due to sampling error. For example, the variance for effect size Z_r is $1/(N-3)$. For any individual effect size Θ_i, then, we can identify whether its value is unusual by comparing its squared deviation $[(\Theta_i - \overline{\Theta})^2]$ with its expected variance $[v_i]$ using the formula

$$\left[(\Theta_i - \overline{\Theta})^2 / v_i\right] \qquad (3.34)$$

where $\overline{\Theta}$ is simply the arithmetic mean of all effect sizes in the sample. By extension, we can obtain an estimate of the total variability in the sample of effect sizes, or an indication of how unusual the values of Θ_i are in aggregate, by summing equation 3.34 across all effect sizes ($i = 1$ to m, where m equals the meta-sample size). In meta-analysis, this quantity is called Q.

$$Q = \Sigma \left[(\Theta_i - \overline{\Theta})^2 / v_i\right] \qquad (3.35)$$

An equivalent representation of equation 3.35 is

$$Q = \Sigma \left[(\Theta_i - \overline{\Theta}) / s_i\right]^2 \qquad (3.36)$$

where s_i is the standard error (or square root of the variance) of effect size Θ_i. Many readers will recognize equation 3.36 as the sum of squared standardized deviations. Since e_i in equation 3.31, and therefore Θ_i in the fixed effects model, is expected to be distributed normally, Q is actually the sum of a set of squared standardized normal random variables, which is distributed as X^2 with expectation equal to its degrees of freedom $m - 1$, where m is the number of effect sizes in the sample (in other words, the meta-sample size). That is, $Q \sim X^2_{m-1}$. An obvious test for excess variation in effect sizes is the extent to which $Q > df$, or $Q > (m - 1)$. *Equations* 3.35 *and* 3.36, *then, illustrate the Q-test for random effects in meta-analysis* (sometimes referred to as Cochrane's Q). The null hypothesis for this test is that variation in effect sizes is no greater than what we would expect due to sampling error ($Q = (m - 1)$). That is, the fixed effects model is appropriate. The alternative hypothesis is that there is variation among the effect sizes that cannot be accounted for by sampling error alone, and that the random effects model is appropriate. The p-value associated with the calculated value of Q is the probability of incorrectly rejecting the true null hypothesis that the fixed effects model is correct. An alternative conceptualization of Q is that Ho: $\tau^2 = 0$ and Ha: $\tau^2 > 0$. This is true only conceptually, however, not literally, since Q does not utilize any measure of sampling variability for τ^2. While the Q-test is useful, it has low power. Therefore, an inability to reject the null hypothesis should not be interpreted as strong evidence that the fixed effects model is appropriate (Borenstein, Hedges, Higgins, and Rothstein 2009; Shadish and Haddock 2009). In fact, researchers are advised to choose between the fixed and random effects models on the basis of theoretical criteria rather than on the basis of the Q-test. This is especially true for scholars in public management and policy who will be working with highly heterogeneous sets of effects sizes for which the fixed effects model will rarely be appropriate.

Later in this chapter I illustrate how to combine effect sizes using inverse variance weights w_i where $w_i = 1/v_i$. Using these weights leads to two additional formulas for Q,

$$Q = \Sigma w_i \left(\Theta_i - \overline{\Theta} \right)^2 \tag{3.37}$$

$$Q = \Sigma \left(w_i \Theta_i \right)^2 - \left[\left(\Sigma w_i \Theta_i \right)^2 / \Sigma w_i \right] \tag{3.38}$$

where all summations occur across i ($i = 1$ to m).

The I^2 Statistic. The Q statistic provides a (low power) test for identifying excess variance (that is, random effects) in a sample of effect sizes. The Q statistic by itself, however, does not offer an indication of the magnitude of the random effects variance component. By contrast, the I^2 statistic offers a measure of the variability in Θ_i that is not attributable to sampling error:

$$I^2 = \left[\left((Q - df) / Q \right) * 100 \right] \tag{3.39}$$

If total variability in our sample of Θ_i is equal to what we would expect due to sampling error, the numerator in equation 3.39 and the value of I^2 become zero. As excess variability in Θ_i increases, so does I^2. Where total variability in the sample of effect sizes is three times what would be expected due to sampling error alone, $I^2 = .67$. I^2 is like R^2 from least squares regression in that it is bounded by 0 and 1 and it provides a metric for assessing variation rather than a test-statistic (Higgins, Thompson, Deeks, and Altman 2003).

Estimating the Random Effects Variance Component. While the I^2 statistic gives us a measure of the relative magnitude of the (average) fixed effects and random effects variance components, it does not provide a specific value for the random effects variance component τ^2 that we can use to calculate the total variance associated with each effect size.

$$V_i^r = \tau^2 + v_i \tag{3.40}$$

DerSimonian and Laird (1986) offer the following method of moments formula for calculating the random effects variance component:

$$\tau^2 = (Q - df)/c \tag{3.41}$$

where

$$c = \Sigma w_i - \left(\Sigma w_i^2 / \Sigma w_i\right)$$

and

$$w_i = 1/v_i$$

W_i in equation 3.41 is an *inverse variance weight*, a commonly used quantity in meta-analysis. Using this formula, τ^2 is measured in the same (squared) metric as the effect size Θ_i (for example, Z_r, g, and so on), and can therefore be used to calculate the total variance for Θ_i in the random effects model.

Combining Effect Sizes

After calculating a set of *r*-based, *d*-based, or odds-based effect sizes and converting them all into the same type of effect size, we can begin to analyze effect sizes by combining them in a basic meta-analysis. We combine effect sizes from different original models and studies for three purposes. First, we combine effect sizes so that we might calculate an average effect size $\overline{\Theta}$ across all original studies. It is only a slight exaggeration to say that calculating average effect sizes was the original purpose of meta-analysis. This average effect size is our estimate of the population effect size Θ in the fixed effects model, and our estimate of the expected population effect size μ_Θ in the random effects model. Second, we combine effect sizes so that we might assess the statistical and substantive significance of the estimated population effect size. Third, we combine effect sizes so that we might provide a clearer description of how they vary across studies or over time.

Weighting Effect Sizes

Before we can undertake any of the tasks described in the previous paragraph we must weight the effect sizes. Unlike basic techniques in descriptive and inferential statistics, meta-analysis does not treat all observations equally by giving them identical weight. Rather, all meta-analysis techniques work with weighted effect sizes where the weights are the precision with which the effect size is estimated. More precisely estimated effect sizes are given greater weight. Precision is defined as the inverse of the effect size variance, which is simply the weight w_i in equation 3.41.

Fixed and Random Effects Inverse Variance Weights. The fixed effect variance v_i for many common effect sizes can be calculated using the formulas in table 3.2. For example, the fixed effects variance v_i for the Fisher's Z effect size Z_r is $1/(n-3)$. Therefore the fixed effects inverse variance weight $w_i = 1/v_i$ is $w_i = 1/(1/(n-3)) = n-3$. We weight each effect size by forming the product $w_i\Theta_i$, so when using Fisher's Z we form the product $(n-3) * (Z_r)$. Using the example of Z_r it is easy to see how precision weighting gives greater weight to effect sizes estimated from larger samples.

Using inverse variance weights is only slightly more complicated using the random effects model. Recall that the random effects variance contains two components: $v_i^r = \tau^2 + v_i$. The random effects weight w_i^r is simply the inverse of this random effects variance $w_i^r = 1/v_i^r$. We weight each effect size in the random effects model by forming the product $w_i^r\Theta_i$. Combining effects in the random effects framework requires the extra step of calculating the random effects variance component τ^2.

There are two key differences when using fixed effects versus random effects inverse variance weights. First, the random effects variance is always larger, meaning that there is greater uncertainty about the true value of the effect size estimated by Θ_i. Therefore there is greater uncertainty associated with random effects estimates of the population values Θ and μ_Θ. Second, effect sizes are weighted more equally in the random effects model. While more precise effect sizes estimated from larger studies still receive greater weight, the differences in weights between large and small sample studies is reduced when using random effects.

Inverse Variance Weights in Practice. Table 3.3 provides an example of using fixed and random effects inverse variance weights in practice, and the differences attributable to the choice of fixed or random effects (recall

TABLE 3.3. EXAMPLES OF WEIGHTING EFFECT SIZES FROM LARGE AND SMALL SAMPLE STUDIES USING FIXED EFFECTS AND RANDOM EFFECTS

	Fixed Effects Ringquist 1997	Fixed Effects Stretesky and Lynch 1999	Random Effects Ringquist 1997	Random Effects Stretesky and Lynch 1999
n	29,214	164	29,214	164
r	.018	.250	.018	.250
Z_r	.018	.256	.018	.256
v_i	.000034	.0062	.000034	.0062
τ^2	0	0	.0016	.0016
w_i	29211	161	612	128
$w_i Z_r$	526	41.2	11.0	32.8

that the random effects approach will be most appropriate in virtually all situations faced by researchers in public management and policy). For this illustration I chose two effect sizes from the sample environmental justice data set, one from a study using a large sample (Ringquist 1997, $n = 29{,}214$) and a second from a study using a small sample (Stretesky and Lynch 1999, $n = 164$). Both studies generate positive effect size estimates, indicating that both studies find evidence of environmental inequity in their respective samples. Note, however, that the effect size estimate from the Stretesky and Lynch study ($r = .25$, $Z_r = .26$) is more than ten times the size of the effect size from the Ringquist study ($r = .018$, $Z_r = .018$). From the perspective of meta-analysis, we ought to have greater confidence in the effect size estimate from the study using the larger sample, and therefore give it greater weight when combining effect sizes. The second and third columns of table 3.3 illustrate the fixed effects approach. We account for precision in the fixed effects model by multiplying the effect size Z_r by the inverse variance weight w_i, which equals 29,211 for the Ringquist study and 161 for the study by Stretesky and Lynch. Precision weighting attributes greater influence to the effect size from the Ringquist study ($w_i \Theta_i \approx 526$) than to the effect size from the Stretesky and Lynch study ($w_i \Theta_i \approx 41$). Fixed effects meta-analysis combines these weighted effect sizes, rather than their raw counterparts.

The fourth and fifth columns of table 3.3 demonstrate the difference when weighting using random effects. We obtain an estimate of the random effects variance component ($\tau^2 = .0016$) using the *metan* command in Stata. This is simpler and often more accurate than calculating τ^2 using equation 3.41. We then use this value to form the random effects variance for each effect size using $v_i^r = \tau^2 + v_i$ and the respective random effects variance weight $w_i^r = 1/v_i^r$. Table 3.3 shows that the random effects variance weights are smaller than the fixed effects weights for each effect size (reflecting larger total variances), but that the difference is much larger for the effect size from the Ringquist study (reflecting that the relative differences in weights are smaller when using random effects). Using random effects, the weighted effect size from the Stretesky and Lynch study $\left(w_i^r \Theta_i = 32.8 \right)$ is larger than the weighted effect size from the Ringquist study $\left(w_i^r \Theta_i = 11.0 \right)$, though this difference is much smaller than the difference between the respective unweighted values of Z_r. While effect sizes from smaller studies always receive relatively larger weights when using random effects, in this particular example the weighted effect size from the smaller study ends up being larger than the comparable effect size from the larger study, but this is not a general result. Random effects meta-analysis combines these weighted effect sizes, rather than their raw counterparts.

Calculating Average Effect Sizes

A fundamental purpose of meta-analysis is to draw generalizable conclusions using information from disparate and sometimes conflicting original studies. Calculating an average effect size $\overline{\Theta}$ from a set of individual effect sizes Θ_i is clearly relevant to this purpose. In addition to calculating average effect sizes, meta-analysis can estimate confidence intervals for these effects and test the hypothesis that the average effect size is equal to zero. An important caveat is that calculating average effect sizes embodies the assumption that the individual effect sizes Θ_i all represent quantities that are similar enough so that their average value conveys meaningful information. This criterion is often easy to satisfy when combining effect sizes from experimental studies that estimate the effect of a common intervention. This criterion is generally more difficult to satisfy in the social sciences, in which original studies embody different operationalizations of key concepts, employ different research designs, and specify different regression models. Because of these differences, meta-analysis in public management and policy should focus on explaining why different studies produce different effect sizes, and on estimating conditional average effect sizes under a variety of scenarios using meta-regression (see chapters 4 and 5), rather than estimating a single unconditional average effect size and assuming that this value adequately summarizes the relevant literature. That said, calculating average effect sizes is an important first step in any meta-analysis.

Average Effect Sizes Using Fixed and Random Effects. Meta-analysis does not calculate average effect sizes using simple arithmetic means. Rather, all average effect sizes in meta-analysis are weighted means where the weights are the inverse fixed effects or random effects variances described in the previous section. The value of weighting becomes evident when we consider that each individual effect size Θ_i is an estimate of the population effect size of interest; Θ in the fixed effects case, and μ_Θ in the random effects case. *Ceteris paribus*, values of Θ_i estimated with greater precision will be closer to the relevant population value, and therefore ought to be given more weight when we seek to estimate these population values.

The formula for calculating an average effect size is the same regardless of the specific effect size we use (*r*-based, *d*-based, or odds-based) or the variance framework we employ (fixed or random effects). The average effect size $\overline{\Theta}$ is calculated as

$$\overline{\Theta} = \Sigma w_i \Theta_i / \Sigma w_i \qquad (3.42)$$

Θ_i in equation 3.42 can be replaced by any effect size from table 3.2. Using fixed effects, $w_i = 1/v_i$, so w_i can be replaced by the inverse of any fixed effects variance from table 3.2. Using random effects, $w_i = 1/v_i^r$ where v_i^r is defined as above. In the fixed effects framework, $\overline{\Theta}$ represents our estimate of the population parameter Θ. In the random effects framework, $\overline{\Theta}$ estimates the population mean of the distribution of effect sizes μ_Θ.

Assessing the Significance of Average Effect Sizes. Determining whether the average effect sizes calculated using equation 3.42 are important or significant requires a measure of uncertainty. The variance of any average effect size $\overline{\Theta}$ is estimated as

$$V\left[\overline{\Theta}\right] = 1/\Sigma w_i \qquad (3.43)$$

where w_i is either a fixed or random effects inverse variance weight, summed across all observations $i = 1$ to m. Using equations 3.42 and 3.43 we can test the null hypothesis that the population effect size is zero using

$$Z = \overline{\Theta}/\sqrt{V\left[\overline{\Theta}\right]} \qquad (3.44)$$

where Z is a standard normal deviate. The *p*-value associated with Z represents the probability of making a type I error by incorrectly rejecting a true null hypothesis. Under fixed effects, this null hypothesis is Ho: $\Theta = 0$. Precisely speaking, in the fixed effects case failing to reject Ho: means that we believe all effect sizes Θ_i are not different from zero.[4] Under random effects, this null hypothesis is Ho: $\mu_\Theta = 0$.

Placing confidence bands around the estimated average effect size is generally more useful than testing whether this average effect size is something other than zero. We can place a $(1 - \alpha)$ confidence interval around $\overline{\Theta}$ using equation 3.45:

$$\overline{\Theta} + / - Z_{a/2} \left(\sqrt{V\left[\overline{\Theta}\right]} \right) \tag{3.45}$$

where Z represents a standard normal deviate and the standard deviation of the average effect size $\sqrt{V\left[\overline{\Theta}\right]}$ is defined as in equation 3.43.

Calculating Average Effect Sizes Using Stata. Using table 3.2 and equation 3.42, readers will be able to calculate an average effect size in virtually any circumstance they encounter. Adding the information in equations 3.43, 3.44, and 3.45 will also allow readers to test the null hypothesis that the population effect size is zero and to place a confidence interval around $\overline{\Theta}$. Using Stata greatly simplifies these tasks. The *metan* command in Stata calculates average effect sizes using fixed and random effects variances, tests the null hypothesis that the population effect size is zero, and calculates a 95 percent confidence interval around $\overline{\Theta}$ (confidence intervals of other sizes can be obtained using one of the options in *metan*).

While *metan* will calculate *d*-based and odds-based effect sizes and their variances using information coded from original studies, it will not calculate *r*-based effect sizes or their variances. Therefore, prior to using *metan* researchers must calculate *r*-based effect sizes and effect size variances using the formulas from table 3.2. These quantities can be calculated directly in the spreadsheet containing the data coded from original studies. Effect sizes and variances calculated in the spreadsheet can then be imported into Stata. I do not recommend this strategy. As a general proposition, it is inadvisable to manipulate data stored in an original data set, as one risks contaminating the original data or damaging the data file. Instead, I recommend importing the original data and calculating effect sizes and effect size variances (and standard deviations) using a Stata command file. For example, the following Stata commands calculate *r*-based effect sizes from *t*-scores using equations 3.1 and 3.8, standard deviations, and inverse variance weights using the data from the environmental justice meta-analysis:

```
insheet using C:\meta_analysis\ej\ejmetaanalysisdata.csv,
clear
gen weight1 = n-3
gen eff = sqrt(tstat^2/(tstat^2+df))
gen effect = eff if favors == 1
replace effect = -1 * eff if effect == .
gen fishersz = .5*(ln((1+effect)/(1-effect)))
gen sterr1 = sqrt(1/weight1)
```

The *r*-based effect size *fishersz* and effect size standard deviation *sterr1* are then used in Stata by employing the *theta, se_theta* option in the *metan* command. It is important to note that when using this option, *metan* expects researchers to import fixed effects standard errors, $\sqrt{v_i}$, rather than fixed effects variance v_i. It is also important to note that *metan* will calculate the proper random effects variances if these are requested. Researchers need not calculate the random effects variances independently. (Researchers *will* have to calculate proper random effects variances when estimating the random effects meta-regression models in chapters 4 and 5).

I used the following Stata code to calculate an average effect size from the 680 individual effect sizes in the environmental justice data set using both a fixed effects and random effects model.

```
metan fishersz sterr1, fixed
metan fishersz sterr1, random
```

Assuming fixed effects, $\overline{\Theta} = .017$ with a 95 percent confidence interval of $[.016 - .018]$. We can reject the null hypothesis that $\Theta = 0$ at $p < .0001$ ($Z = 39.28$). Because this meta-analysis calculates effect sizes, using Z_r, $\overline{\Theta}$ can be interpreted as the average correlation between the percentage of minority residents in communities and the level of potential environmental risk in these communities. Therefore, this synthesis of the relevant literature estimates a significant but substantively very small degree of environmental inequity in these studies. The fixed effects model is almost certainly inappropriate for these data, however, an expectation that is confirmed by the Q-statistic ($Q = 9,285$, $E[Q] = 679$, $p < .0001$) and I^2 statistic of 92.7 percent. The I^2 statistic tells us that over 92 percent of the variance in our sample of 680 effect sizes cannot be attributed to sampling variability across original studies. The *metan* command estimates a random effects variance component of $\tau^2 = .0016$. The more appropriate random effects meta-analysis estimates $\overline{\Theta} = .043$ with a 95 percent confidence interval of $[.039 - .047]$. We can reject the null hypothesis that $\mu_\Theta = 0$ at $p < .0001$ ($Z = 22.29$). While the random effects estimate of $\overline{\Theta}$ is positive, significant, and more than twice the size of the fixed effects estimate, the estimated degree of environmental inequity is still substantively small.

Describing Effects Sizes

Meta-analysis commonly describes effect sizes using two tools. A *forest plot* is a visual device for describing the distribution of effect sizes across studies and the contribution made by each effect size to the calculated average effect size. A *cumulative meta-analysis* is a visual device for describing how the magnitude of the average effect size and our confidence in this estimate has changed over time.

Forest Plots. The unit of analysis in a typical forest plot is the individual weighted effect size (forest plots can describe effect sizes using either the fixed or random effects model). A sample fixed effects forest plot is provided in figure 3.3, and a sample random effects forest plot is provided in figure 3.4. A forest plot conveys several pieces of information. Each effect size is summarized in a single row in the forest plot. The value of each effect size Θ_i is represented by a dot, and the 95 percent confidence interval for this effect size is represented by the lines extending on either side of this dot (the scale of Θ_i is found on the horizontal axis at the bottom of the forest plot). Each dot representing the value of Θ_i is surrounded by a shaded box, and the volume of this box represents the relative contribution of each effect size to the calculated average effect size. The effect size Θ_i, its 95 percent confidence interval, and its contribution to the average effect size are also reported on the right side border of the forest plot. Finally, the estimated average effect size and its 95 percent confidence interval are represented by the diamond in the last row of the forest plot. Note that the relative contributions of individual effect sizes to the average effect size are much more evenly distributed when using random effects. Note also that the confidence interval around the average effect size is much larger when using random effects.

The forest plots in figures 3.3 and 3.4 were created using the same *metan* commands provided earlier (in other words, forest plots are part of the normal output from *metan*). *Metan* offers several options for customizing forest plots, including options for identifying the authors and dates of

FIGURE 3.3. FIXED EFFECTS FOREST PLOT FOR A 5 PERCENT SAMPLE OF Z_r EFFECT SIZES FROM THE ENVIRONMENTAL JUSTICE DATA SET

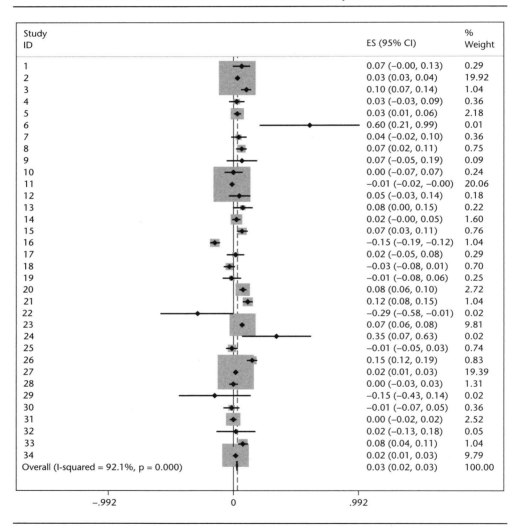

FIGURE 3.4. RANDOM EFFECTS FOREST PLOT FOR A 5 PERCENT SAMPLE OF Z_r EFFECT SIZES FROM THE ENVIRONMENTAL JUSTICE DATA SET

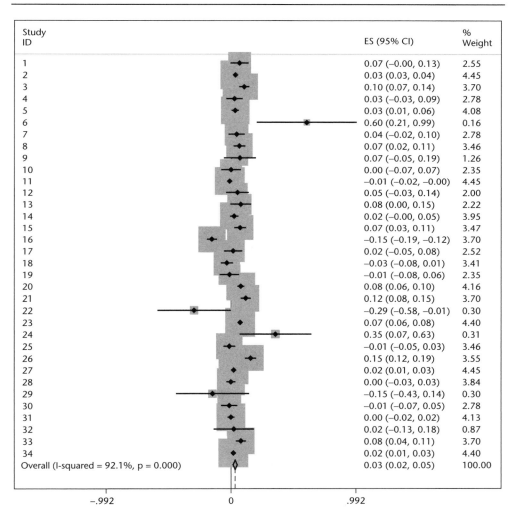

Study ID	ES (95% CI)	% Weight
1	0.07 (−0.00, 0.13)	2.55
2	0.03 (0.03, 0.04)	4.45
3	0.10 (0.07, 0.14)	3.70
4	0.03 (−0.03, 0.09)	2.78
5	0.03 (0.01, 0.06)	4.08
6	0.60 (0.21, 0.99)	0.16
7	0.04 (−0.02, 0.10)	2.78
8	0.07 (0.02, 0.11)	3.46
9	0.07 (−0.05, 0.19)	1.26
10	0.00 (−0.07, 0.07)	2.35
11	−0.01 (−0.02, −0.00)	4.45
12	0.05 (−0.03, 0.14)	2.00
13	0.08 (0.00, 0.15)	2.22
14	0.02 (−0.00, 0.05)	3.95
15	0.07 (0.03, 0.11)	3.47
16	−0.15 (−0.19, −0.12)	3.70
17	0.02 (−0.05, 0.08)	2.52
18	−0.03 (−0.08, 0.01)	3.41
19	−0.01 (−0.08, 0.06)	2.35
20	0.08 (0.06, 0.10)	4.16
21	0.12 (0.08, 0.15)	3.70
22	−0.29 (−0.58, −0.01)	0.30
23	0.07 (0.06, 0.08)	4.40
24	0.35 (0.07, 0.63)	0.31
25	−0.01 (−0.05, 0.03)	3.46
26	0.15 (0.12, 0.19)	3.55
27	0.02 (0.01, 0.03)	4.45
28	0.00 (−0.03, 0.03)	3.84
29	−0.15 (−0.43, 0.14)	0.30
30	−0.01 (−0.07, 0.05)	2.78
31	0.00 (−0.02, 0.02)	4.13
32	0.02 (−0.13, 0.18)	0.87
33	0.08 (0.04, 0.11)	3.70
34	0.02 (0.01, 0.03)	4.40
Overall (I-squared = 92.1%, p = 0.000)	0.03 (0.02, 0.05)	100.00

−.992   0   .992

Note: Weights are from random effects analysis

studies associated with each effect size (Sterne 2009). Figures 3.3 and 3.4 represent the default options for forest plots using *metan*. I offer two cautions to researchers crafting forest plots in a meta-analysis. First, *metan* is not designed for the type of data used by researchers in public management and policy. This means that, as described earlier, *metan* will calculate neither *r*-based effect sizes nor their variances. Researchers must calculate these quantities independently and import them into *metan* as effect sizes and effect size standard deviations, as illustrated above. Second, forest plots were developed for the typical situation in medicine and psychology in which each original study produces a single effect size. This historical development has two implications. The first is that the average effect sizes and their 95 percent confidence intervals from forest plots assume that all effect sizes are independent. This assumption will rarely apply in public management and policy research, which means that the average effect sizes and variances from *metan* will be incorrect. The second, more important implication is that forest plots are useful only for meta-analyses using small numbers of effect sizes. Figures 3.3 and 3.4 are generated using a 5 percent random sample of effect sizes from the environmental justice data set. Imagine a forest plot that used all 680 effect sizes in this data set. Such a plot would be uninterpretable. Forest plots are valuable for their clarity and simplicity, and both qualities are lost as the plots become crowded with large numbers of effect sizes. In my experience, forest plots become difficult to interpret with more than 60 effect sizes. Therefore, forest plots will rarely be useful for meta-analysis in public management and policy, for which effect sizes will routinely number in the hundreds.

Cumulative Meta-Analysis. A second descriptive tool is the cumulative meta-analysis, a visual device that organizes effect sizes in chronological order and provides estimates of the average effect size (and its 95 percent confidence interval) as more effect sizes—and more evidence—enter the literature on a particular research question. A cumulative meta-analysis, then, can provide a picture of how the evidence regarding a research question has developed over time. Cumulative meta-analysis is conducted in Stata using the *metacum* command. Like *metan*, *metacum* will not calculate *r*-based effect sizes or their variances. Therefore, researchers wanting to conduct a cumulative meta-analysis must calculate these quantities independently using Excel, Stata, or some other software package, and import these quantities into *metacum*. Like *metan*, *metacum* expects that these quantities will be imported as effect sizes and fixed effects standard deviations, rather than as variances.

The *metacum* display is nearly identical to the *metan* forest plot output in that the unit of analysis is the individual effect size and each effect size is summarized in a single row of the graph. The differences between the *metan* and *metacum* displays are (1) *metacum* lists effect sizes chronologically, and (2) each dot and boxplot in the *metacum* display represents the average effect size and variance from all studies completed by that date. Given the similarities between the *metan* and *metacum* displays, *metacum* is also best suited to meta-analyses with small numbers of effect sizes. It would be nearly impossible to interpret a cumulative meta-analysis graph of the 680 effect sizes in the environmental justice data set. More important, conducting this analysis would make little sense. Each original study in the environmental justice data set produces multiple effect sizes. By contrast, like *metan*, *metacum* assumes that each original study generates a single effect size. A cumulative meta-analysis re-estimates the average effect size after incorporating each new effect size encountered in the data set. When each original study generates a single effect size, the cumulative meta-analysis shows how the average effect size is influenced by each new study. When original studies generate multiple effect sizes, however, this intuitive understanding of the cumulative meta-analysis is lost. Therefore, researchers in public management and policy who want to conduct a cumulative meta-analysis are advised to first calculate a single average effect size (and average effect size variance) for each original study in their data set. Then, these study-level average values can be entered into *metacum* so that the resulting cumulative meta-analysis shows how the aggregate empirical evidence regarding a research question changes with each new study.

Figure 3.5 reports a year-level cumulative meta-analysis using *metacum* and the environmental justice data set. To create this cumulative meta-analysis I first obtained the random effects variance component from *metan* and used this to calculate the proper random effects variance weight for each effect size (see equation 3.40) and weighted all effect sizes by the inverse of this variance. Second, I calculated an average (weighted) effect size and average random effects variance for all effect sizes present in all studies occurring in each year. That is, rather than calculate study-level average effects, I calculated year-level average effects. Combining effect sizes for multiple studies in each year reduces the number of average effect sizes for the cumulative meta-analysis, but this tactic has the benefit of producing a cleaner temporal narrative for changes in average effect sizes over time. Finally, I imported these year-level average effect sizes and their respective standard deviations into *metacum*. The cumulative meta-analysis in figure 3.5 was calculated using the fixed effects option

FIGURE 3.5. RANDOM EFFECTS
CUMULATIVE META-ANALYSIS USING
YEAR-LEVEL AVERAGE EFFECT SIZES FROM
THE ENVIRONMENTAL JUSTICE DATA SET

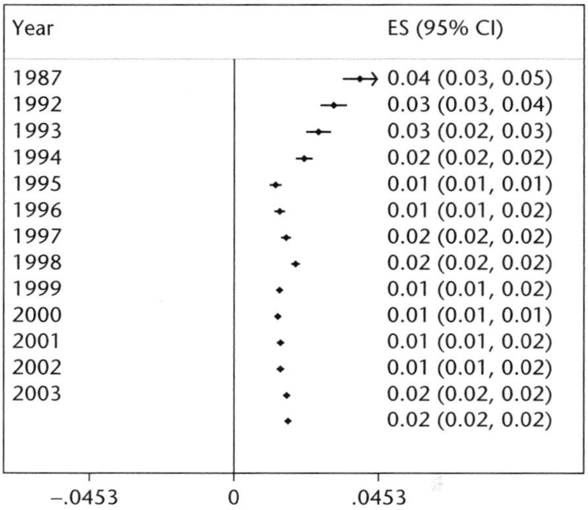

Year		ES (95% CI)
1987		0.04 (0.03, 0.05)
1992		0.03 (0.03, 0.04)
1993		0.03 (0.02, 0.03)
1994		0.02 (0.02, 0.02)
1995		0.01 (0.01, 0.01)
1996		0.01 (0.01, 0.02)
1997		0.02 (0.02, 0.02)
1998		0.02 (0.02, 0.02)
1999		0.01 (0.01, 0.02)
2000		0.01 (0.01, 0.01)
2001		0.01 (0.01, 0.02)
2002		0.01 (0.01, 0.02)
2003		0.02 (0.02, 0.02)
		0.02 (0.02, 0.02)

| −.0453 | 0 | .0453 |

in *metacum*. Using this option, *metacum* does not add a random effects variance component to the imported effect size variances. Adding this component is unnecessary because I had already calculated the appropriate random effects variance before importing the data into *metacum* (τ^2 needs to be calculated from the entire sample of effect sizes, $m = 680$, rather than from the 13 average effect sizes included in this example of *metacum*). The Stata code used to conduct this study-averaged cumulative meta-analysis is provided here:

```
gen revar = 1/((n-3)+(.0016))
gen reweight = 1/revar
gen refishersz = fishersz * reweight
collapse (sum) refishersz reweight, by (idnumber)
gen avgrefishersz = refishersz/reweight
gen avgsterr = sqrt(1/reweight)
sort year
metacum avgrefishersz avgsterr, fixed lcols(year)
```

Figure 3.5 shows that early studies estimated relatively large and positive environmental inequities. As studies accumulated over time, the evidence still supports the conclusion that environmental inequities exist, but the estimated magnitude of these inequities was reduced. Beginning about 1994, research in this area settled around an estimated average effect size of .02. While the cumulative meta-analysis in figure 3.5 provides a useful picture of how evidence of environmental equities has changed over time, readers should remember that the specific values in this analysis combine effect sizes within studies and within groups of studies that were released during the same year. The individual effect sizes in the environmental justice data set are very heterogeneous (recall the I^2 statistic of 92.7 percent), calling into question the wisdom of combining them into study-level or year-level averages. Therefore, the cumulative meta-analysis in figure 3.5 should be viewed as having pedagogical value, rather than presenting precise estimates of meaningful average effect sizes over time.

Conclusion

The material in this chapter should allow readers to calculate proper effect sizes from original studies, weight these effect sizes using the appropriate fixed effects or random effects model, and combine these effect sizes in ways that are useful for both description and inference. I conclude this chapter with two pieces of advice for researchers setting out to calculate and combine effect sizes.

First, the sign of calculated effect sizes is context specific. An effect size less than zero does not mean that there is a negative association between the concepts of interest any more than a negative t-score in a regression model indicates a negative association between concepts. The sign of r-based effect sizes depends entirely on the measurement of X and Y in original studies. To illustrate, consider two original studies that examine the effect of campaign contributions (X) on the votes of members of Congress (MOCs) on environmental legislation (Y). Study A codes whether MOCs vote in favor of environmental legislation, whereas study B measures whether MOCs vote against environmental legislation. Assume that campaign contributions from groups opposed to stringent environmental policy are negatively correlated with pro-environmental votes on legislation. In study A, this relationship produces a negative coefficient estimate, while in study B this relationship produces a positive coefficient estimate. The effect of campaign contributions on environmental voting is the same in each study, but the coefficient on the campaign contribution variable takes on different signs. Similarly, the sign of d-based effect sizes depends on the definition of the groups constituting $\overline{Y}_1$ and $\overline{Y}_2$. Consider two original studies estimating the effects of vouchers on academic achievement. Both studies estimate this difference using $\overline{Y}_1 - \overline{Y}_2$, but in the first study $\overline{Y}_1$ measures the average test score of voucher recipients whereas in the second, $\overline{Y}_1$ measures the average test score of nonvoucher recipients. If vouchers have a positive effect, d (or g) will be positive in the first study but negative in the second. Combining effect sizes will give an average effect size close to zero, even though vouchers had meaningful positive effects in both studies.

To avoid this mistake I recommend strongly that researchers calculate effect sizes in three steps. First, when coding the characteristics of original studies, *researchers should code a field identifying whether the outcome from the study favors the treatment or control group, or alternatively, whether the outcome of the study is in the direction of an alternative hypothesis that is common to all studies* (for example, whether the outcome of the study is consistent with the presence of environmental inequities—see chapter 2). Second, *researchers should record the absolute value of t, Z, $\left(\overline{Y}_1 - \overline{Y}_2\right)$, or whatever metric is reported in the original study, and use this metric to calculate an absolute r-based or d-based effect size.* Third, *researchers should assign a sign to the absolute value of the effect size using the field coding for whether the result in the original study favors the treatment group or the common alternative hypothesis.* This is the approach I used in the earlier example of how to calculate r-based effect sizes in Stata.

The second piece of advice is that, while calculating effect sizes is a purely technical matter, determining whether these effect sizes are comparable and combinable requires exercising considerable judgment. Researchers should always take care to avoid the "apples and oranges" critique of meta-analysis. One good strategy toward this end is to decide a priori whether to place effect sizes from original studies into one of four categories.

1. Effect sizes that estimate comparable quantities of interest and there-fore can be combined to form unconditional average effect sizes
2. Effect sizes that estimate related quantities of interest and therefore can be analyzed in the same meta-analysis, but which cannot be combined to estimate a single unconditional average effect size
3. Effect sizes that estimate quantities of interest that are relevant to the particular research question being addressed, but that are different enough to require separate meta-analyses

4. Effect sizes that do not estimate quantities of interest relevant to the particular research question being addressed

Effect sizes in category 4 should be excluded ex ante through the design of the meta-analysis and the identification of acceptable original studies. For example, the educational voucher meta-analysis in chapter 8 excludes effect sizes measuring the effect of vouchers on parent or student satisfaction with schools. In the environmental justice meta-analysis, I was interested in both race- and class-based inequities and calculated effect sizes for both types. I felt, however, that these inequities were different enough conceptually and theoretically to require separate individual meta-analyses, and the two types of effect sizes were never combined in any analysis (this is an example of effect sizes fitting category 3). Finally, considering only the race-based environmental inequities, I had to decide whether all race-based effect sizes could be aggregated to calculate a single average effect size. I decided against this strategy and instead coded moderator variables identifying (for example) whether these effect sizes were associated with polluting facilities, levels of pollution, or levels of ambient risk. These moderator variables were then included in a meta-regression model that allowed the calculation of separate conditional average effect sizes for each category of potential environmental risk (category 2).

Decisions regarding the comparability of effect sizes should be based on theory or on a sound and compelling substantive argument. In this respect, justifying the comparability of effect sizes in a meta-analysis is similar to justifying measurement and sampling choices in original empirical studies.

Notes

1. Formula 3.1 has been the standard for calculating r-based effect sizes in meta-analysis for thirty years. However, Ariel Aloe and Betsy Jane Becker (n.d.) offer an alternative formula: $r = t_f \sqrt{\left(R_Y^2 - R_f^2 \right)}$, where t_f is the t-score for the null hypothesis on the focal predictor of interest from the original regression model, $R^2{}_Y$ is the R^2 from the original regression model, and $R^2{}_f$ is the R^2 from the original regression model that omits the focal predictor. This formula for the semi-partial correlation coefficient r can also be written as $r = [(t_f \sqrt{(1 - R_Y^2)} / \sqrt{(n - p - 1)})$. Only time will tell whether this new formula for calculating r-based effect sizes from original regression studies will be widely adopted in meta-analysis.

2.   Peterson and Brown (2005) show that the relationship between the standardized regression parameter estimate β and the partial correlation coefficient is unaffected by the number of independent variables k.

3.   Here e is the error in estimating β, not the error in estimating Y from the regression equation.

4.   This version of the null hypothesis can be tested more directly using any member of a family of "meta-significance tests," including Stouffer's sum of Zs, Fisher's sum of logs, and George's cumulative logit (see Borenstein, Hedges, Higgins, and Rothstein 2009). The alternative hypothesis associated with these combined significance tests—that at least one effect size is different from zero—is hardly very interesting, particularly in public management and policy research in which analysts may work with hundreds of effect sizes.

CHAPTER FOUR

META-REGRESSION ANALYSIS

Evan J. Ringquist

"The quantification of effect size and exploration of the pattern of variation in effect size among studies is a far more important goal of meta-analysis than the construction of powerful tests of null hypotheses"

(OSENBERG, SARNELLE, COOPER, AND HOLT 1999, 1105).

Chapter 3 introduced methods for calculating effect sizes from original studies and for combining these effect sizes in order to estimate a single average effect size and confidence interval that characterize the results from research on a particular question. Combining effect sizes in this manner can provide a single answer to simple questions such as What is the average effect of a policy intervention? What is the average size of a relationship of interest for public management?

In most management and policy research, however, a more interesting question is *What accounts for variation in effect sizes across studies?* In some instances our interest in accounting for variation in effect sizes may be purely academic; for example, we may be interested in why different studies reach different conclusions regarding the effectiveness of educational vouchers or the existence of environmental inequities. In other instances, understanding variability in effect sizes may have direct implications for practice. For example, discovering that the impact of educational vouchers varies across types of students may help to better target voucher programs or to design them more effectively, while discovering that environmental inequities differ depending on the level of civic engagement in communities may help environmental managers and community organizers prevent these inequities.

Explaining variation in social, economic, and political phenomena may be the most common purpose of quantitative research in the social sciences, and regression analysis is the most commonly used technique for this task. Regression techniques have been adapted for meta-analysis, and *meta-regression* has rapidly become the most commonly used tool for explaining variability in effect sizes. In this chapter I introduce the standard fixed effects and random effects meta-regression models. A discussion of advanced approaches to meta-regression that make the technique more useful to social scientists is reserved for chapter 5. I begin, however, with a brief discussion of the development of meta-regression.

Historical Development of Meta-Regression

While many observers view meta-regression as a newer development, the technique has a history nearly as long as meta-analysis itself. Glass (1978) and Smith and Glass (1977) recommended using ordinary least squares regression to predict effect sizes from different studies using independent variables and coding for the design characteristics of these studies. The statistical theory and methods for fixed effects meta-regression were developed by Hedges (1982) and Hedges and Olkin (1985) (for an early application, see Li and Begg 1994), and development of the random effects meta-regression model is generally attributed to Berkely and colleagues (1995). While the random effects model in particular was originally developed to account for variation in odds-based effect sizes, techniques of meta-regression have been extended to all types of effect sizes. Somewhat later, Thompson and Higgins (2002) demonstrated that if effect sizes vary systematically, meta-regression is a superior method for accounting for this variation compared with the traditional practice of conducting separate subgroup meta-analyses, as this latter approach is both less powerful and unable to explicitly test for differences in effect sizes across groups.

Meta-regression is now firmly established in the toolkit of the meta-analyst. While early textbooks in meta-analysis did not include discussions of meta-regression (see, for example, Cook et al. 1992; Cooper and Hedges 1994b; Hunter and Schmidt 1990; Lipsey and Wilson 2001), nearly all current texts devote at least one chapter to the topic (for example, Borenstein, Hedges, Higgins, and Rothstein 2009; Cooper, Hedges, and

Valentine 2009; Kulinskaya, Morgenthaler, and Staudte 2008), though none consider the special challenges of meta-regression in the social sciences. Meta-regression is also being used with increasing frequency to study questions related to policy and management, including business administration (Farley, Lehmann, and Sawyer 1995), the effects of inducements on survey response rates (Gelman, Stevens, and Chan 2003), the behavioral consequences of college diversity experiences (Bowman 2010a, 2010b), estimating the quality of agricultural products (Paul, Lipps, and Madden 2006), gender differences in mathematics performance (Schram 1996), the effects of climate change on wildlife (Root et al. 2003), the efficiency gains from privatizing public service delivery (Bel, Fageda, and Warnerd 2010), and the effect of democratic institutions and freedoms on economic growth (Doucouliagos and Ulubaşoğlu 2008).

As a final piece of evidence regarding the growing importance of meta-regression, consider figure 4.1. The top line in the graph illustrates the total number of publications referenced by Google Scholar using the term *meta-regression* between 1990 (7 publications) and 2011 (4,280 publications), with most of this growth occurring since 2002. The bottom line in figure 4.1 reports this same metric restricted to business, the social

FIGURE 4.1. NUMBER OF PUBLICATIONS USING THE TERM
***META-REGRESSION* REFERENCED BY GOOGLE SCHOLAR**
BETWEEN 1990 AND 2011

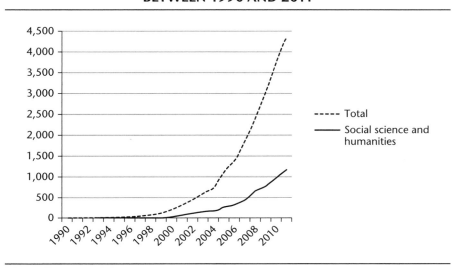

sciences, and the humanities, in which publications increased from 2 in 1990 to 1,150 in 2011. Only a tiny fraction of these publications occur in outlets for management and policy research, despite the tremendous potential of meta-regression to provide valuable information for scholars and practitioners in these fields.

Designing a Meta-Regression

Meta-regression models have much in common with the familiar multiple regression model. While the terminology, estimation, and interpretation of the meta-regression model are slightly different, readers familiar with weighted least squares regression should have no trouble following the presentation here. The basic meta-regression model includes a single dependent variable and one or more independent or predictor variables. Meta analysts commonly recognize two types of independent variables, *moderator* variables and *mediating* variables. The differences between moderator and mediator variables were introduced in chapter 2 and are discussed in the following sections. Similar to traditional regression analysis, parameter estimates from meta-regression models can be used to test hypotheses, to predict average conditional effect sizes, or for decision making.

Developing the Meta-Regression Model

Dependent Variable. The dependent variable in a meta-regression model is one of the unweighted effect sizes from chapter 3. It is important to keep in mind that the dependent variable in a meta-regression is a measure of the relationship between the focal predictor and the outcome of interest in the original studies. If the original study is a randomized controlled trial, the dependent variable in a meta-regression represents the causal effect of the focal predictor (or the treatment) on the outcome of interest. If the original study uses a more typical observational design, the dependent variable in the meta-regression model represents the association between the focal predictor and the outcome of interest. The dependent variable in a meta-regression model *does not* represent the expected value of the outcome of interest (Y) in the original studies.

Consistent with our focus on research in public management and policy, the presentation and examples in this chapter will use the r-based effect size Z_r (that is, Fisher's Z) with fixed effects variance $1/(n-3)$. d-based and odds-based effect sizes may also serve as dependent variables in a meta-regression. All meta-regression is based on large-sample distribution theory, with the result that if the data in original studies are multivariate normal, Z_r is normally distributed around its population parameter. Therefore, meta-regression models using Z_r are very accurate (Hedges and Pigott 2004; Hedges 2009). Since d-based and odds-based effect sizes are only approximately normal in large samples, there is a slight preference for using r-based effect sizes in meta-regression.

Moderator Variables. Moderator variables in a meta-regression are factors that influence the conditional expectation of the effect size. Mathematically, the interpretation of the parameter estimate on a moderator variable in meta-regression is the same as for a parameter estimate from a traditional regression; that is, it represents the average change in Θ associated with a one-unit change in the moderator. The substantive interpretation for the parameter estimate on a moderator variable is somewhat different. Because the dependent variable Θ represents the relationship between the focal predictor and the outcome of interest, the meta-regression parameter should be interpreted akin to an interaction term in traditional regression. That is, the moderator changes (or moderates) the relationship between the focal predictor and the outcome of interest, rather than shifting the conditional expectation of the outcome of interest itself. Moderator variables are often grouped into two categories: those that generate genuine effect size heterogeneity, and those that represent design elements of the original studies.

Moderators Generating Genuine Heterogeneity. First and most important, moderators may represent factors that genuinely affect the magnitude of the relationship between the focal predictor and the outcome of interest. That is, they may generate "genuine" heterogeneity in effect sizes. Moderator variables representing genuine heterogenity in the relationship between the focal predictor and the outcome of interest are often considered the most scientifically interesting or meaningful moderators (Rubin 1992; Vanhonacker 1996; Glasziou and Sanders 2002). Consider the following examples. First, the relationship between the racial composition of a community and the exposure of that community to environmental risk may be different for risks posed by abandoned hazardous waste dumps than for risks posed by air pollution. Similarly, the effect of school vouchers on student academic achievement may differ across math and reading. In these examples, the moderator represents differences in outcome measures. While the effect of this moderator may be parameterized by including it as an independent variable in a meta-regression, more commonly moderators of this type are addressed by estimating separate meta-regression models for each outcome measure. This approach has the added benefit of helping to avoid the "apples and oranges" critique of meta-analysis. Moderators may also generate genuine effect size heterogeneity through a different process. For example, the degree of environmental inequity may differ between black and Hispanic communities, or the effects of vouchers on student achievement may differ between black and Hispanic students. In this case, effect size heterogeneity is driven by the composition of treatment and control groups, and this difference is parameterized by including moderating variables in the meta-regression that identify whether the effect is defined using members of these groups. In both cases, variation in effect sizes is generated by real differences in the causal processes linking focal predictors to outcomes of interest in original studies. Finally, moderators may capture genuine effect size heterogeneity generated by differences in the design or implementation environment of public programs. For example, the effect of educational vouchers on student academic achievement may differ depending on whether vouchers can be used to attend parochial schools.

Moderators Representing Design Elements of Original Studies. A second class of moderators represent design elements of original studies that may affect the effect sizes coded from these studies. Three examples may help illustrate this class of moderators. First, estimates of an effect size may differ depending on whether the original study used cross-sectional, time series, or panel data. Parameter estimates from these studies will be identified using different variance components; for instance, parameter estimates from panel data models represent a weighted average of cross-sectional and temporal effects. Therefore we may want to include a variable in the meta-regression model identifying whether the original study used panel data. Second, the population parameter estimated by b_j in an original study is conditional upon the other variables included in the original regression model. For instance, estimates of the relationship between the racial composition of communities and environmental risk in those communities are influenced strongly by whether the statistical models in the original studies include controls for community property values and the political activism of community residents (Hamilton 1995; Ringquist 2005). Similarly, the estimated effect of educational vouchers on student test scores differs depending on whether one includes baseline test scores in the regression model (Krueger and Zhu 2003). Simply stated, the control variables included in original studies will affect $E[b_j]$, and meta-regression models ought to include independent variables identifying whether Θ_i comes from models that include key control variables. Finally, the quality of original studies may influence the estimated relationship between the focal predictor and the outcome of interest in original studies. Even in medicine, the quality of randomized controlled trials is associated with the magnitude of treatment effects estimated from these trials (Jüni, Witschi, Bloch, and Egger 1999). In policy and management research, an obvious indicator of quality is the degree to which the original studies control for potential endogeneity of treatment when estimating the effect of an intervention. There are multiple indicators of research quality. Therefore, best practice in meta-regression is to use multiple variables to characterize the quality of original studies, rather than relying on a single composite indicator of study quality (Jüni, Witschi, Bloch, and Egger 1999; Greenland and O'Rourke 2001).

Mediating Variables. Mediating variables in a meta-regression are different from moderator variables in that they are hypothesized to affect the causal structure producing heterogeneity in effect sizes, rather than simply affecting the conditional expectation of the effect size. Mediating variables may enter a meta-regression model in two ways. First, mediators may enter the model as interaction terms. For example, in the meta-regression model $\Theta_i = b_0 + b_1 X_{1i} + b_2 X_{2i} + b_3 (X_{1i} X_{2i}) + e_i$, X_2 may be considered a mediating variable (in this model, b_3 would be akin to a three-way interaction term in an original study). An illustration of this example would be if school vouchers have a larger effect on the test scores of black students ($X_1 = 1$) from poorly performing schools ($X_2 = 1$) than on the test scores of black students ($X_1 = 1$) from high-performing schools ($X_2 = 0$). Second, mediating variables may enter the model as intervening endogenous variables in a recursive causal model framework. For example, in the two-equation recursive system $\Theta_i = b_0 + b_1 X_{1i} + b_2 X_{2i} + b_3 X_{3i} + e_i$ and $X_{2i} = a_0 + a_1 X_{4i} + a_2 X_{5i} + v_i$, X_2 would be considered a mediating variable.

Complications in the Meta-Regression Model

Researchers face two major complications when estimating meta-regression models; effect size heterogeneity and non-independence of observations. We address effect size heterogeneity in this chapter. While we discuss the sources of non-independence here, we reserve a complete treatment of the problem for chapter 5.

Effect Size Heterogeneity. As discussed in chapter 3, classical meta-analysis assumes the fixed effects framework in which $\Theta_i \sim N\left(\Theta, v_i\right)$ and v_i is a known variance that is a function of the sample size used in the original study. In the fixed effects framework, Θ_i from each original study is an estimate of a common population effect size Θ. Using one of our continuing examples, the fixed effects framework assumes that there is a single treatment effect associated with the use of educational vouchers, and that different studies produce different estimates of this effect simply because they employ different samples. The more generalizable and often more appropriate random effects framework assumes the distribution $\Theta_i \sim N\left(\Theta, v_i + \tau^2\right)$ where τ^2 is a constant between-effect variance component. In traditional meta-analysis, effect size heterogeneity is estimated using τ^2.

Meta-regression extends traditional meta-analysis by decomposing the random effects variance τ^2 into two components: a systematic component that can be described (and parameterized) using moderator variables, and a stochastic or irreducible component. If the systematic component of τ^2 dominates in the limit, then effect size heterogeneity can be completely accounted for using moderator variables in a meta-regression: for example,

$$\Theta_i = b_0 + b_1 X_{1i} + b_2 X_{2i} + b_3 X_{3i} + e_i \text{ where } e_i \sim N\left(0, v_i\right) \quad (4.1)$$

where v_i is the known fixed effects variance. This equation represents the basic *fixed effects meta-regression model*. Readers should note that the standard random effects meta-analysis model $\Theta_i \sim N\left(\Theta, v_i + \tau^2\right)$ is equivalent to the fixed effects meta regression model with covariates $\Theta_i \sim N\left(\mu\Theta | X_1 X_2 X_3, v_i\right)$. While the fixed effects meta-regression model is useful for pedagogical purposes, its assumptions are unreasonable, and this model has been shown to perform poorly in practice (Thompson and Higgins 2002, Higgins and Thompson 2004).

A more realistic perspective is that while covariates may help to identify and account for some systematic variation in τ^2, some unexplainable effect size heterogeneity remains after including these covariates. This gives us the *random effects meta-regression model*

$$\Theta_i = b_0 + b_1 X_{1i} + b_2 X_{2i} + b_3 X_{3i} + e_i \text{ where } e_i \sim N\left(0, v_i + \tau^2\right) \quad (4.2)$$

where τ^2 can be considered akin to the error term in a traditional regression in that it embodies the effects of excluded variables and other unmeasured or unobservable factors that generate variation in e_i (and Θ_i). The random effects meta-regression model is sometimes referred to as a *mixed effects model* because τ^2 is accounted for by systematic (that is, conditional fixed) and stochastic (random) components. Much of the statistical work developing the random effects regression model has focused on developing valid estimates of τ^2 and assessing the consequences of not accounting for remaining variability represented by τ^2.

Non-Independence of Observations. Meta-regression rests on many of the same statistical assumptions as traditional regression analysis (for an excellent presentation of the assumptions of least squares regression, see Gujarati and Porter 2009, chapter 3). Among the most important of these assumptions for meta-regression is that the observations (that is, the effect sizes from original studies) are independent. There are at least four ways in which this assumption may be violated.

Dependence Across Observations: Multiple Treatment Studies. In medicine and psychology randomized controlled trials sometimes have multiple treatment groups (or treatment arms) that are exposed to different interventions. For example, in a medical trial examining the prevention of heart attacks one treatment group may be required to exercise for thirty minutes per day while a second group may be required to take a cholesterol-lowering drug. In psychology, treatment groups may be subjected to different psychotherapeutic procedures. In both cases the outcome of interest in each treatment group is compared to a common control group, and this shared control group may produce a positive correlation between effect sizes from the different arms of the trial. Therefore, including effect sizes from all treatment groups in the same meta-regression model may violate the independence of observations assumption. There are well-established procedures for controlling this type of dependence among effect sizes (Gleser and Olkin 2009). Multiple treatment studies are uncommon in public management and policy research, so they will not be discussed further.

Dependence Across Observations: Common Data Sets. One or more original studies may use the same data set. For example, several research teams have estimated the effects of school vouchers using common data sets from Milwaukee (Rouse 1998; Witte 1998; Greene, Peterson, and Du 1999; Lamarche 2008) and New York City (Mayer, Peterson, Myers, Tuttle, and

Howell 2002; Barnard, Frangakis, Hill, and Rubin 2003; Krueger and Zhu 2003, 2004). Effect sizes calculated from these different studies may be correlated by virtue of sharing a common sample of students and a data set where measurement errors and other unobserved factors are identical. Hedges (1994) provides an excellent summary of methods that are useful for correcting shared variation due to common data sets (see also Hunter and Schmidt 1990). Most of these techniques require knowledge of the reliability of indicators from these data sets, covariances among the indicators in these data sets, or other information not commonly available in public management and policy research.

Dependence Across Observations: Common Research Teams. Norms of academic specialization and the pressure to publish in multiple outlets make for a situation where the same researcher or research team often publishes multiple original studies addressing the same research question. For example, Douglas Anderton and his colleagues have published several studies examining whether the racial, ethnic, and class composition of communities are correlated with the concentration of hazardous waste treatment, storage, and disposal facilities in these communities (Anderton, Anderson, Oakes, and Fraser 1994; Davidson and Anderton 2000; Oakes, Anderton, and Anderson 1996), while a team led by Paul Peterson at Harvard University has produced more than a dozen assessments of the effectiveness of different educational voucher programs (see chapter 8). Idiosyncratic choices within research teams regarding sample selection, model specification, and the interpretation of statistical results may produce a correlation among the effect sizes calculated from the studies produced by these teams. Therefore, using all of these effect sizes in the same meta-regression model may violate the independence of observations assumption. Correlations among effect sizes from the same research team can be handled in the same way as correlations among effect sizes produced by common data sets (Hedges 1994; Stevens and Taylor 2009), but they are also commonly handled by parameterizing these effects by including moderator variables in the meta-regression that identify effect sizes produced by the same research teams.

Dependence Across Observations: Multiple Effect Sizes Per Study. The norm in meta-analysis is that each original study produces a single effect size (see, for example, Cooper 2010). In the medical sciences this norm is consistent with scientific practice, since few randomized controlled trials produce multiple treatment effects (though see the discussion of multiple treatment studies above). As discussed at length in the introduction and chapter 2, however, original studies in public management, public policy, and the social sciences almost always produce multiple effect sizes. Indeed, the multiple measures, multiple models, and sensitivity analyses that generate multiple effect sizes are seen as hallmarks of high-quality research in these fields. When faced with original studies having multiple effect sizes, standard advice within meta-analysis has been to choose the "one best" effect size or to calculate a single average effect size from each original study (Cooper and Hedges 1994b; Lipsey and Wilson 2001; Stanley 2001). In addition to discarding enormous amounts of information, this advice prevents the meta-analyst from estimating the effects of moderator variables within studies, even though this is generally preferable to estimating these effects between studies (Glasziou and Sanders 2002). Consider, for example, one original study of the effectiveness of educational vouchers in Milwaukee (Rouse 1998). In this study, Rouse estimates separate models for the effects of vouchers on standardized math and reading scores, separate models for the effects from intent to treat as well as treatment on the treated, separate models in which endogeneity is addressed through instrumental variables and through the use of fixed effects, and separate models in which control groups are chosen through random assignment and by post-assignment matching. The multiple effect sizes in this study provide excellent leverage for estimating the effect of these moderator variables, holding constant other elements of research design, model specification, and data that might differ across studies. Choosing a single effect size from this study, or calculating a single average effect size would negate these advantages. Therefore, I recommend using all effect sizes coded from original studies as observations in meta-analyses in public management and policy (see chapters 2 and 3). One important consequence of this choice is that effect sizes from the same study are likely to be strongly correlated, for the same reason that effect sizes from the same research teams or the same data sets are correlated, therefore violating the independence of observations assumption. I offer several methods for addressing this complication in chapter 5.

Fixed Effects Meta-Regression

Estimating the Fixed Effects Model

In the traditional ordinary least squares (OLS) regression model $Y_i = b_0 + \Sigma b_k X_{ki} + e_i$, the regression parameter vector $\boldsymbol{b}$ is estimated as $E[\boldsymbol{b}] = \beta = (\boldsymbol{X'X})^{-1} \boldsymbol{X'Y}$ with variance $\text{var}[b] = \sigma^2 (\boldsymbol{X'X})^{-1}$. A key assumption of these least squares estimators is that the error term e_i is homoskedastic (that is, $e_i \sim N(0, \sigma^2)$). In meta-regression, however, we know that the homoskedasticity assumption does not hold because the effect sizes Θ_i are estimated from studies employing different sample sizes. That is, in the fixed effects framework $\Theta_i \sim N(\Theta, v_i)$, not $\Theta_i \sim N(\Theta, v)$. Therefore, the error term from a fixed effects meta-regression departs from the traditional least squares error term in two respects. First, the fixed effects error variance is assumed to be known (v_i), rather than estimated (in least squares regression, σ^2 is generally estimated using s^2). Second, the error term from the fixed effects meta-regression will be heteroskedastic. Both of these characteristics influence how we go about estimating meta-regression models.

Generalized Least Squares Regression. Traditional regression analysis addresses heteroskedasticity using generalized least squares (GLS), and GLS estimation serves as the foundation for estimating the fixed effect meta-regression model. In OLS, the error variance-covariance matrix takes the form $ee' = \sigma^2 I$ (where I is the identity matrix). By contrast, the GLS error variance-covariance matrix under heteroskedasticity takes the form $ee' = \sigma^2 \Omega$ where Ω is (typically) a diagonal matrix with elements h_1 to h_n representing the proportional error variance across observations.

$$\Omega = \begin{pmatrix} h_1 & 0 & 0 & 0 \\ 0 & h_2 & 0 & 0 \\ . & . & . & . \\ 0 & 0 & 0 & h_n \end{pmatrix} \quad \text{and} \quad \Omega^{-1} = \begin{pmatrix} 1/h_1 & 0 & 0 & 0 \\ 0 & 1/h_2 & 0 & 0 \\ . & . & . & . \\ 0 & 0 & 0 & 1/h_n \end{pmatrix}$$

Therefore, the GLS estimator of the parameter vector b becomes

$$E\left[b_{\text{gls}}\right] = \beta_{\text{gls}} = \left(X'\Omega^{-1}X\right)^{-1} X'\Omega^{-1}Y \tag{4.3}$$

with variance

$$\text{var}\left[b_{\text{gls}}\right] = \sigma^2 \left(X'\Omega^{-1}X\right)^{-1} \tag{4.4}$$

Weighted Least Squares Regression. While the GLS parameter variances can be estimated by manipulating the error variance-covariance matrix, it is often simpler to manipulate X and Y directly. Specifically, if a researcher is able to identify the source of the nonconstant error variance, this information can be used to transform or *weight* the original observations X_i and

Y_i. The key in the weighted least squares (WLS) approach is to find a weight matrix W so that $W'W = \Omega^{-1}$. That is,

$$W = \begin{matrix} 1/\sqrt{h_1} & 0 & 0 & 0 \\ 0 & 1/\sqrt{h_2} & 0 & 0 \\ \cdot & \cdot & \cdot & \cdot \\ 0 & 0 & 0 & 1/\sqrt{h_n} \end{matrix}$$

Using the weight matrix W,

$$E\left[b_{\text{wls}}\right] = \beta_{\text{wls}} = \left(X'W'WX\right)^{-1} X'W'WY \tag{4.5}$$

and

$$\text{var}\left[b_{\text{wls}}\right] = \sigma^2 \left(X'W'WX\right)^{-1} \tag{4.6}$$

Assuming that the researcher has correctly identified the sources of heteroskedasticity and that the proper weights can be identified, WLS estimates and their standard errors can be derived from the elements of W by transforming the original data so that $Y_i^* = Y_i/\sqrt{h_i}$ and $X_i^* = X_i/\sqrt{h_i}$. After this transformation, $E[b_{\text{wls}}] = \beta_{\text{wls}} = (X^{*\prime}X^*)^{-1} X^{*\prime}Y^*$ with variance $\text{var}[b_{\text{wls}}] = \sigma^2(X^{*\prime}X^*)^{-1}$, and these estimates are unbiased and (most important) efficient. Readers of a certain age may recognize this WLS model as an early approach to controlling for heteroskedasticity. Using this approach, researchers generally assume that the heteroskedasticity in the error term is proportional to either (1) the number of observations used to calculate Y_i and X_i, or (2) the magnitude of one of the independent variables X_j. In these examples, h_i becomes n_i or X_{ji}, respectively, and researchers weight Y_i and X_i by $\sqrt{n_i}$ or $\sqrt{X_j}$. The WLS approach is well-suited to meta-regression because meta-analysis assumes that the source of heteroskedasticity—that is, the effect size variance—is known. While this traditional approach to addressing heteroskedasticity has been almost completely replaced by the robust parameter standard errors made possible by White's (1980) heteroskedasticity consistent covariance matrix, the WLS approach serves as the foundation for the fixed effects (and random effects) meta-regression model.

Weights in Fixed Effects Meta-Regression. Fixed effects meta-regression (FEMR) models are estimated using the weighted least squares approach summarized in the previous section. For the specific examples used in this book, the effect size Θ_i is Fisher's Z (Z_r) with variance $1/(n_i - 3)$. Therefore, the diagonal elements of W are $1/\sqrt{(n-3)}$ and the elements of Θ and X are divided by these weights (for example, $\Theta_i^* = \Theta_i/\left(1/\sqrt{(n_i - 3)}\right)$). Larger, more precisely estimated effect sizes receive greater weight in the meta-regression model just as they do in a standard meta-analysis (see chapter 3).

Traditional weighted least squares may be estimated in any statistical software package, and can be used to estimate a fixed effect meta-regression model using effect size Θ_i and its associated variance v_i. While the regression parameter vector b_{femr} will be estimated properly using this approach, parameter standard errors will be incorrect. To see why this is so, consider again the difference between the error variance-covariance matrix from the FEMR model and the WLS model, reproduced here:

$$ee'_{\text{femr}} = \begin{matrix} v_1 & 0 & 0 & 0 \\ 0 & v_2 & 0 & 0 \\ . & . & . & . \\ 0 & 0 & 0 & v_n \end{matrix} \quad \text{and} \quad ee'_{\text{wls}} = \sigma^2 \begin{matrix} h_1 & 0 & 0 & 0 \\ 0 & h_2 & 0 & 0 \\ . & . & . & . \\ 0 & 0 & 0 & h_n \end{matrix}$$

The key difference is that the weight used in traditional WLS is a *proportional* inverse variance weight $\left(1/\sqrt{h_i}\right)$, while the weight in a fixed effects meta-regression is an *actual* inverse variance weight $\left(1/\sqrt{v_i}\right)$. That is, the weights in the FEMR model reflect the entire error variance, while the weights in WLS reflect only the relative difference in error variance across observations. To make the parameter standard errors from WLS equivalent to the parameter standard errors from a fixed effects meta-regression, the WLS parameter standard errors must be divided by the root mean squared error from the regression. That is, $s_{bk,\,\text{femr}} = s_{bk,\,\text{gls}}/\text{RMSE}_{\text{gls}}$.

Hypothesis Testing

Testing for Residual Heterogeneity. We begin by assessing the adequacy of the fixed effects meta-regression model. Because the fixed effects model assumes that the random effects variance component τ^2 is completely accounted for by the covariates $X_1 - X_k$ (see equation 4.1), an appropriate test is whether $\tau^2 = 0$ in the meta-regression model after controlling for these covariates. Unfortunately, this test does not exist in the meta-analysis literature. We can, however, evaluate the equivalent test that Θ_i is exactly determined by Xb; that is, that the remaining error variance in the FEMR model is no larger than what we would expect due to sampling error in the original studies. Readers may recall that this is the basis for the Q-test from chapter 3: $Q = \Sigma \left[\Theta_i - \overline{\Theta} \right]^2 / v_i] \sim X^2_{m-1}$ where m is the number of effect sizes.

If we replace the unconditional mean $\overline{\Theta}$ with the conditional mean Xb from the FEMR model, the formula for Q is equivalent to the standardized summed squared error from the FEMR model: $SSE_{femr} = \sum \left[\Theta^*_i - X^*b \right]$ where Θ^*_i and X^* denote weighting by $1/\sqrt{v_i}$. Because the sum of squared standardized random variables has an X^2 distribution, $SSE_{femr} \sim X^2_{m-k-1}$, and the test for residual heterogeneity becomes Ho: $SSE_{femr} \leq m - k - 1$ and Ha: $SSE_{femr} > m - k - 1$. Using SSE from the FEMR model, we can test for the appropriateness of this model at any type I error level. The intuition behind this test is that if the residual variation from the fixed effects meta-regression model is larger than what we would expect due to fixed effects, there must be remaining between-study variance in effect sizes that is unaccounted for by the covariates in the model.

While testing for residual heterogeneity has pedagogical value, this test should not be used to choose between the fixed effects and random effects meta-regression models. Theoretically, the assumptions of the FEMR model are nearly always untenable; that we can construct an empirical model that completely accounts for systematic between-study differences in effect sizes. Statistically, this test has low power (Thompson and Higgins 2002), which means that we may conclude that residual heterogeneity is not present when it is. Fixed effects meta-regression produces unacceptably large type I error rates when between-study effect size heterogeneity is present (Higgins and Thompson 2004). Therefore, it is sensible to use random effects meta-regression whenever possible.

Hypothesis Tests on Individual Parameters. As with traditional regression, fixed effects meta-regression can be used to test the standard null hypothesis that $b_j = 0$. In meta-regression, this null hypothesis asserts that the moderator variable is independent from the effect sizes calculated from original studies, and therefore that this moderator variable cannot help account for variation in effect sizes across studies. Effect sizes are assumed to be distributed normally, and meta-regression relies upon asymptotic properties of estimators. Therefore, b_j/s_{bj} should be distributed as a standard normal variable (where s_{bj} is the parameter standard error calculated using the proper inverse variance weight), and the null hypothesis Ho: $b_j = 0$ can be evaluated using a Z-test on b_j. When meta-regression models are estimated by maximum likelihood methods, this is equivalent to a Wald test. Note that this approach to null hypothesis testing is different from the traditional regression model, which uses t_{n-k-1} rather than Z.

While the ratio b_j / s_{bj} is asymptotically normal, in practice using Z to test Ho: $b_j = 0$ produces unacceptably large type I errors. One simple correction is to test this null hypothesis using the t-distribution with $m - k - 1$ degrees of freedom as is done in least squares regression (Hartung and Knapp 2001). One benefit of estimating fixed effects meta-regression using the WLS approach described here is that hypothesis tests on individual parameters are automatically conducted using t_{m-k-1}.

Another meaningful difference between hypothesis tests in traditional regression and meta-regression is the importance of the intercept in the latter. The constant term is rarely of much consequence in traditional regression, and is commonly viewed as a necessary if uninteresting component of the model that allows the researcher to estimate an unbiased slope parameter. Moreover, in most regression models estimating the constant term requires extrapolation well beyond the data in hand (that is, it is uncommon that data sets contain observations that are jointly zero on all independent variables). In these cases, the regression intercept describes a world that does not exist in practice. None of these qualities of the intercept apply in meta-regression. Since the values of moderator variables are set by the researcher, observations in which all moderators are jointly zero are both possible and possibly interesting. In many cases, the meta-regression intercept can be viewed as a type of "baseline" effect size in which the baseline is set such that all moderator variables take on values of zero. For example, using equation 4.1, if Θ_i represents the effect of educational vouchers on academic achievement, X_1 represents models examining outcomes for black students, X_2 represents models examining outcomes for female students, and X_3 represents models examining outcomes in high-performing schools, then the meta-regression intercept b_0 estimates the average effect of educational vouchers on the academic achievement of nonblack boys in poorly performing schools. Alternatively, in meta-regression moderator variables are sometimes transformed to represent deviations from their mean values. In these cases, b_0 represents the effect size with all moderators held at their respective means. Using this approach, the meta-regression intercept has the virtue of representing something like a true "average" effect size in which "average" is defined as the expected value of the effect size under the most typical conditions. The value of b_0 is also less subjective than under the "baseline" approach, since the meaning of "baseline" depends on how the researcher codes the moderator variables. Alternatively, the "average" effect size estimated when de-meaning moderator variables may not represent a situation that exists in practice nor can be easily interpreted, whereas b_0 using the baseline approach can be defined to estimate a meaningful quantity of interest.

Compound Hypothesis Tests. In addition to conducting hypothesis tests on individual regression parameters, researchers often want to test the joint significance of several parameters. In traditional regression analysis, this hypothesis test is conducted by way of an F-test. A joint significance test on all parameters in the meta-regression model leverages the difference between the summed squared errors from a meta-regression model with an intercept ($\text{SSE}_{\text{femr}} | b_0$, or the restricted model) and the summed squared errors from a model containing all of the model parameters ($\text{SSE}_{\text{femr}} | b_0 \ldots b_k$, or the unrestricted model). Specifically, ($\text{SSE}_{\text{restricted}} - \text{SSE}_{\text{unrestricted}}) \sim X_k^2$, so the expectation where Ho: $b_1 \ldots b_k = 0$ is true is that $X_k^2 = k$. A simpler and equivalent test leverages the fact that when the null hypothesis is true, in the fixed effects meta-regression the summed squared regression SSR $\sim X_{k-1}^2$ where k is the number of parameters estimated in the regression model. If SSR $\leq k - 1$ can be rejected at some type I error rate α, we conclude that $b_1 \ldots b_k$ are not jointly zero. More generally, for some subset of parameters r in parameter vector $\boldsymbol{b}$, we can test the null hypothesis Ho: $\boldsymbol{b}_r = 0$ (that is, the joint significance of this subset) using the expectation that under the null hypothesis $(\text{SSE}_{\text{restricted}} - \text{SSE}_{\text{unrestricted}}) \sim X_r^2$.

The parallels between joint hypothesis tests in meta-regression and the same tests in least squares regression are obvious. Notice, however, that unlike a traditional F-test or Chow test in least squares regression, there is no need to divide SSE by its degrees of freedom to conduct these tests in meta-regression. This is because the difference between Θ_i and $\boldsymbol{Xb}$ has been normalized with a variance of 1, so the sum of the squared errors is distributed as an X^2. In this way, compound hypothesis tests in the FEMR are similar to likelihood ratio tests.

Prediction and Power

While ubiquitous, the outcomes of standard null hypothesis tests are sometimes the least interesting and least important results from least squares regression. This is particularly true in meta-regression, in which the parameter estimates represent the average conditional effect size across all studies (that is, b_0) or the difference in effect sizes attributable to moderating variables (such as b_j). In either case, stating with some degree of certainty that these quantities are different from zero is less informative than estimating the magnitude of the effect size or estimating the probability that there is no effect.

Prediction and Meta-Regression. Meta-regression parameters serve as point estimates for conditional average effect sizes. *For meta-regression in which the effect size Θ_i is estimated using Fisher's Z (in other words, for most meta-analyses in public management and policy), regression parameters must be transformed back into correlation coefficients using the formula*

$$\rho = \left[\left(e^{2*Zr} - 1 \right) / \left(e^{2*Zr} + 1 \right) \right] \qquad (4.7)$$

though this transformation often makes little practical difference in the interpretation of these coefficients unless ρ is very large. Among the most important of these point estimates is the meta-regression intercept, b_0, which identifies the average effect size when all moderator and mediating variables take on values of 0. As discussed, the value and therefore the meaning of the meta-regression intercept depend on whether the variables in X are centered at their mean. In this case, the intercept represents a multivariate conditional average effect size. Point estimates for the effects of moderator variables are simply the regression parameter estimates for these variables (b_j). Confidence intervals for point estimates of effect size are calculated in the standard manner, as are regression-based prediction intervals (see, for example, Gujarati and Porter 2009).

Rubin (1992) offers a different perspective on predicting effect sizes from meta-analyses. To lay the foundation for Rubin's approach, consider again that systematic variability in effect sizes Θ_i can be decomposed into variability that is the product of scientifically interesting moderating factors X (parameterized using b) and scientifically uninteresting factors Z (parameterized using a) that produce nuisance variance from study design characteristics. From this perspective, the most useful predictions from a meta-analysis are those that estimate the effects of Xb on Θ_i while eliminating the effects of Za. One natural candidate for estimating such optimized effect size predictions is response surface regression. If one could identify two key moderating factors in X and extrapolate all studies to have optimal values on Z (in other words, effect sizes all come from hypothetical ideal studies), then one could estimate the quadratic response surface $\Theta_i = b_0 + b_1 X_{1i} + b_2 X_{1i}^2 + b_3 X_{2i} + b_2 X_{2i}^2 + b_5 X_{1i} X_{2i}$ and manipulate or simulate values of X_1 and X_2 that maximize and minimize the conditional average effect size. For instance, we could simulate conditions that maximize the effectiveness of education vouchers or minimize the magnitude of environmental inequities. Knowing the conditions leading to these maxima and minima are of obvious interest for policy and management.

The response surface approach has some appeal, but its application in practice faces several significant challenges. Rubin himself only sketched out the approach, making no effort to derive the estimators necessary to extrapolate effect sizes to their theoretical optimum vis-à-vis **Z**. While Vanhonacker (1996) has offered one such estimator, it has not been used by practicing meta-analysts. The response surface approach faces practical challenges as well. For example, most moderator variables in meta-regression are dichotomous, and therefore poor candidates for quadratic response surface estimation.

One can approximate the spirit of the response surface approach by estimating a meta-regression model, setting the values of all variables in **Z** at their theoretical optimum and then predicting Θ_i for different values of scientific variables **X**. For example, assume that we are interested in predicting the conditional average effect size of educational vouchers on student academic achievement (Θ_i). Assume further that this effect size is determined partially by the racial and ethnic characteristics of students receiving vouchers, measured as $X_1 = 1$ for black students and 0 otherwise, and $X_2 = 1$ for Hispanic students, 0 otherwise. Also assume that the estimated effects of vouchers are affected by the characteristics of the original studies, measured as $Z_1 = 1$ for randomized controlled trials and 0 otherwise, and $Z_2 = 1$ for studies that included baseline test scores and 0 otherwise. If we estimate the meta-regression model $\Theta_i = b_0 + b_1 X_{1i} + b_2 X_{2i} + a_1 Z_{1i} + a_2 Z_{2i} + e_i$, we can estimate the average effect of educational vouchers on academic achievement for black students in ideal studies ($b_0 + b_1 + a_1 + a_2$) and the average effect of educational vouchers on academic achievement for Hispanic students from hypothetical "ideal" studies ($b_0 + b_2 + a_1 + a_2$). When Shadish and colleagues (2000) used this approach in the field of mental health, they found no significant difference between the average effect sizes from meta-analyses of "ideal" studies and the effect sizes derived from large clinical trials. I recommend that meta-analysts use this analog to response surface estimation to predict average effect sizes from hypothetical ideal studies using meta-regression.

Power Analysis in Meta-Regression. While predicting the magnitude of an effect size from a meta-regression model is useful, it is also useful to be able to make statements with some certainty that there is no evidence of a treatment effect from original studies (in other words, that $b_0 = 0$ or that $b_j = 0$). An inability to reject the null hypothesis of independence tells us little about whether the average effect size is actually zero. As the saying goes, absence of evidence is not evidence of absence. To answer this question we need to assess the power of the hypothesis tests in our meta regressions, or the ability of these tests to identify and reject a true null hypothesis.

Power analysis is particularly important in meta-regression. First, moderator variables in meta-regression posit the presence of interaction effects in original studies, and tests of interaction effects are less powerful than tests of main effects. Second, moderator variables are often used to test hypotheses that average effect sizes (or treatment effects) differ across groups. A finding of no difference can have real consequences if this result is used for decision making (Hedges and Pigott 2004). For example, educational vouchers are offered as an effective tool to reduce gaps in educational achievement across different racial and ethnic groups (Howell, Wolf, Campbell, and Peterson 2002). In the previous section we offered a hypothetical meta-regression model capable of assessing this hypothesized effect. If this meta-regression is unable to reject the null hypothesis that $b_1 = 0$ and $b_2 = 0$, we would conclude that the effects of educational vouchers do not differ between black, Hispanic, and white students. The implications of this conclusion are that vouchers are not an effective tool for reducing black-white and Hispanic-white test score gaps, which might significantly undermine one important justification for expanding educational voucher programs. Given the potential consequences of this conclusion, it is important to conduct a power analysis of the hypothesis tests on b_1 and b_2.

Power analysis is most commonly conducted prospectively to determine the minimum sample size required to detect an effect size of a particular magnitude. Power analysis may also be conducted retrospectively to estimate the power of a hypothesis test from a particular statistical model. The retrospective approach assumes that the estimated effect size from the model is equal to the population effect size (note that this is the same assumption that underlies all regression parameters: $E[b_j] = \beta_j$). For this and other reasons, retrospective power analysis is sometimes controversial (Ellis 2010). While neither sort of power analysis is common in meta-analysis, when power analyses are conducted they are almost always retrospective.

Hedges and Pigott (2004) offer a straightforward approach for retrospective power analysis in meta-regression. The power of a one-sided hypothesis test on meta-regression parameter b_j is equal to

$$1 - \Phi\left(c_\alpha - \left(b_j/s_{bj}\right)\right) \tag{4.8}$$

where c_α is the critical value of the standard normal distribution at a chosen type I error rate α (this formula shows explicitly the trade-off between type I and type II errors). In a hypothetical example where $\alpha = .05$, $c_\alpha = 1.645$, and $b_j/s_{bj} = 2.00$, the power of a null hypothesis test $b_j = 0$ is 0.639. That is, assuming $b_j = \beta_j$, in repeated trials this test will reject a true null hypothesis 64 percent of the time, for a type II error rate of 36 percent. The power of a two-tailed null hypothesis test on b_j is equal to

$$1 - \Phi\left(c_{\alpha/2} - \left(b_j/s_{bj}\right)\right) + \Phi\left(-c_{\alpha/2} - \left(b_j/s_{bj}\right)\right) \tag{4.9}$$

In a hypothetical example where $\alpha = .05$, $c_\alpha = 1.96$, and $b_j/s_{bj} = 2.00$, the power of a null hypothesis test $b_j = 0$ is 0.515. That is, assuming $b_j = \beta_j$, this test will reject a true null hypothesis 52 percent of the time, for a type II error rate of 48 percent.

There are no hard-and-fast rules about what level of statistical power is acceptable, though a value of .80 is a common convention (Ellis 2010). An acceptable level of statistical power is more properly assessed by considering the research context and the consequences of failing to reject a true null hypothesis. In medicine, a type II error often means concluding that a healthy patient is sick. At a large scale this error will increase the cost of medical care, but is generally preferable to the alternative. In policy and management, a type II error may mean concluding that a management innovation was ineffective when in fact it was effective, or that policy effects do not vary across treatment groups when in fact they do. Whether the consequences of these type II errors are as grave as those in medicine, and therefore determining the desirable power of a statistical test, is a decision that should be made on a case-by-case basis.

Goodness of Fit

The goodness of fit of any fixed effects meta-regression model is determined by two factors: (1) the predictive power of the moderator variables in X, and (2) the adequacy of the fixed effects assumption that the conditional random effects variance component $\tau^2 = 0$. Goodness of fit is most commonly measured using one of three metrics: the Birge ratio, the I^2 statistic, and the Pseudo-R^2.

The Birge Ratio. The Birge ratio (R_B) measures excess residual variation in the errors from a meta-regression; that is, error variation over and above what is expected due to sampling error. The Birge ratio is calculated as

$$\left(R_B\right) = SSE_{femr}/m - k - 1 \tag{4.10}$$

or alternatively as $Q/m - k - 1$ where Q is defined as above (Konstantopoulos and Hedges 2009). If the nonsampling variation in Θ_i is perfectly characterized by Xb, the Birge ratio will equal 1. Like the R^2 in OLS regression, the Birge ratio is a descriptive metric, not a test statistic. Unlike R^2, the Birge ratio has no theoretical upper bound. Birge ratios greater than 1 indicate that the conditional variation in the error term is greater than can be accounted for by sampling variability. The larger the Birge ratio, the lower the goodness of fit of the meta-regression model.

The I² Statistic. The I^2 statistic measures the percentage of the variation in the meta-regression error variance that is not accounted for by sampling variability (that is, unaccounted for by fixed effects). Stated differently, I^2 is the percentage of variation attributable to unexplained effect size heterogeneity. The statistic is calculated as

$$I^2 = 100 * \left[\left(Q - (m - k - 1)\right)/Q\right] \tag{4.11}$$

(Higgins, Thompson, Deeks, and Altman 2003). Negative values of I^2 are set to zero so that I^2 is bounded by 0 percent and 100 percent. Since $Q = SSE_{femr}$, an alternative calculation is $I^2 = 100 * [(SSE_{femr} - (m - k - 1))/SSE_{femr}]$. Like the Birge ratio, I^2 is a descriptive metric rather than a test statistic. Higgins and colleagues (2003) suggest that I^2 values below 50 percent indicate low levels of remaining heterogeneity (and strong goodness of fit), I^2 values between 50 percent and 75 percent indicate moderate remaining heterogeneity, and I^2 values above 75 percent indicate high remaining heterogeneity in effect sizes.

The Pseudo-R². The meta-regression pseudo-R^2 (denoted P^2) is the least common of the three measures of goodness of fit for meta-regression models, but it will be the most familiar to scholars in public management and public policy. Intuitively P^2 measures the proportion of effect size heterogeneity accounted for by the moderator variables in X. Recall that some fraction of the variation in Θ_i is due to sampling error in the original studies (in other words, it is irreducible). Unlike least squares regression, then, P^2 cannot be calculated using the total sum of squares. Only the variance component τ^2 can be accounted for by X. Therefore, the pseudo-R^2 is calculated as

$$P^2 = [(\text{SSE}_{\text{restricted}} - (m - 1)) - (\text{SSE}_{\text{unrestricted}} - (m - k - 1))/$$
$$(\text{SSE}_{\text{restricted}} - (m - 1))] \tag{4.12}$$

The elements $(m - 1)$ and $(m - k - 1)$ subtract the fixed effects portion of the summed squared errors from the meta-regression model, leaving only the error variance attributable to τ^2 and therefore explainable by X in the unrestricted model. Like the R^2 from least squares regression, P^2 is bounded by 0 and 1. $P^2 = 0$ if Xb accounts for none of the nonsampling variability in Θ_i, and $P^2 = 1$ if Xb accounts for all of this variability. If we have estimates of τ^2, we can use these to calculate P^2 more simply as

$$P^2 = 1 - \left[(\tau^2_{\text{restricted}} - \tau^2_{\text{unrestricted}})/\tau^2_{\text{restricted}} \right] \tag{4.13}$$

(Borenstein, Hedges, Higgins, and Rothstein 2009; Konstantopoulos and Hedges 2009).

Fixed Effects Meta-Regression in Stata

A handful of dedicated meta-analysis statistical software packages will estimate fixed effects meta-regression models, including Comprehensive Meta-Analysis (CMA), Review Manager (RevMan), and MetaWin. None of these packages, however, is designed for the type of data useful for meta-analysis in public management and policy. For example, many of these packages handle r-based effect sizes only with some difficulty, and none is well equipped to utilize data sets in which single studies generate large numbers of effect sizes. Moreover, public management and policy scholars are generally unfamiliar with these packages. To present the FEMR model in a familiar computing environment, I illustrate how to estimate and interpret these models using Stata, among the most commonly used statistical packages in the social sciences. The focus here is on estimating the FEMR model, assessing the adequacy of this model, and providing a basic treatment of hypothesis testing and goodness of fit. I reserve a full treatment of these topics, and examples of prediction and power analysis, for the more appropriate random effects meta-regression model discussed in the next section.

Neither the commercial version of Stata nor the ado programs written by members of the Stata users group support fixed effects meta-regression, but FEMR models can be estimated easily in Stata. Moreover, estimating these models without the benefit of a prepackaged routine supports the pedagogical purpose of learning meta-regression through the familiar WLS framework.

The Sample Regression Model. I illustrate fixed effects meta-regression using the environmental equity data set introduced in chapter 3 and used in Ringquist 2005. This data set contains 680 Fisher's Z effect sizes from forty-eight original studies representing the relationship between the proportion of racial and ethnic minority residents in a community and indicators of potential environmental risk in those communities. I account for variation in these effect sizes using seven moderator variables. Two moderators can be considered "scientifically interesting" in that they are used to test whether average effect sizes differ depending on the source of potential environmental risk: whether the original study examines inequities in the location of Superfund sites (X_1) or inequities in the emission of pollutants (X_2). Two moderators are used to test whether average levels of environmental inequity differ depending on the spatial definition of community: whether communities are defined using residential ZIP codes (X_3) or using census tracts (X_4). Three moderators might be considered "scientifically uninteresting" in that they code for design characteristics of the original studies that might affect estimated effect sizes: whether original studies employ a geographically limited control group (X_5); whether models in these studies use a full complement of key control variables (X_6); and whether the sample of communities was chosen by selecting on the dependent variable (X_7). These last three moderators are all aspects of the quality of the original models. The sample fixed effects meta-regression model is

$$\Theta_i = b_0 + b_1 X_{1i} + b_2 X_{2i} + b_3 X_{3i} + b_4 X_{4i} + b_5 X_{5i} + b_6 X_{6i} + b_7 X_{7i} + e_i, e_i \sim N\left(0, v_i\right) \tag{4.14}$$

FIGURE 4.2. OLS REGRESSION OF FIXED EFFECTS
META-REGRESSION MODEL IN STATA

```
. reg fishersz superfund pollution zipcode census limited controls selection
```

Source	SS	df	MS		Number of obs =	680
					F(7, 672) =	7.47
Model	.941972307	7	.134567472		Prob > F =	0.0000
Residual	12.1030175	672	.018010443		R-squared =	0.0722
					Adj R-squared =	0.0625
Total	13.0449898	679	.019212062		Root MSE =	.1342

fishersz	Coef.	Std. Err.	t	P>|t|	[95% Conf. Interval]	
superfund	.0325039	.0219854	1.48	0.140	−.0106645	.0756723
pollution	−.02609	.0117264	−2.22	0.026	−.0491148	−.0030652
zipcode	−.0088284	.0086056	−1.03	0.305	−.0257256	.0080687
census	.0021603	.0082973	0.26	0.795	−.0141314	.0184521
limited	.0553847	.0190076	2.91	0.004	.0180633	.092706
controls	−.0540345	.0142907	−3.78	0.000	−.0820943	−.0259747
selection	−.1546814	.0256551	−6.03	0.000	−.2050551	−.1043076
_cons	.0886455	.008503	10.43	0.000	.0719499	.1053412

Model Estimation. As a point of reference I estimate a standard OLS regression model and present the results from this model in figure 4.2. We know that the OLS parameter estimates are incorrect because they do not consider the varying levels of confidence we have in the elements of Θ, and we know that the OLS parameter variances are incorrect because they do not consider the heteroskedasticity in Θ_i (and e_i) generated by sampling variability.

Manually Weighted Least Squares in Stata. Next I estimate the proper WLS model by manually transforming each observation using the proper inverse variance. For the Z_r effect sizes used here I divide the elements of Θ and X (including the vector of ones used to estimate the constant term) by $1/\sqrt{(n-3)}$, the standard error of the effect size. The results from this model are presented in figure 4.3. The order of the independent variables in figure 4.3 the same as in figure 4.2 (that is, X_1 = superfund, X_0 = constant term, and so on). The WLS parameter estimates in figure 4.3 are correct, but the parameter standard errors are not. To recover the correct meta-regression parameter standard errors we need to divide the WLS standard errors by the root mean squared error from the WLS model. When we do this, the standard error for b_0 (the average effect size when all moderator variables are zero) becomes (.0042834 / 3.5601) = .0012, and the test statistic for the null hypothesis that $b_0 = 0$ becomes (.02704 / .0012) = 22.53 with $p < .00001$. Notice that the inferences we draw from the incorrect OLS

FIGURE 4.3. MANUALLY WEIGHTED WLS FIXED EFFECTS META-REGRESSION MODEL IN STATA

```
. reg Yw x1 x2 x3 x4 x5 x6 x7 x0, noc
```

Source	SS	df	MS		Number of obs =	680
					F(8, 672) =	22.79
Model	2310.61148	8	288.826435		Prob > F =	0.0000
Residual	8517.18655	672	12.6743847		R-squared =	0.2134
					Adj R-squared =	0.2040
Total	10827.798	680	15.9232324		Root MSE =	3.5601

Yw	Coef.	Std. Err.	t	P>|t|	[95 %Conf. Interval]	
x1	−.0093292	.006622	−1.41	0.159	−.0223314	.003673
x2	−.0027425	.0038743	−0.71	0.479	−.0103496	.0048646
x3	.0009998	.0043933	0.23	0.820	−.0076264	.0096259
x4	−.0076312	.0040489	−1.88	0.060	−.0155812	.0003188
x5	.0013055	.0072815	0.18	0.858	−.0129916	.0156027
x6	.0034307	.0041634	0.82	0.410	−.0047441	.0116056
x7	−.0172156	.0086964	−1.98	0.048	−.034291	−.0001403
x0	.0270401	.0042834	6.31	0.000	.0186296	.0354506

model in figure 4.2 are fundamentally different from the inferences drawn from the correct WLS model. The results in figure 4.3 are produced using the following Stata command statements:

```
gen sterr1 = sqrt(1/weight1)
gen x0= 1/sterr1
gen x1= superfund/sterr1
gen x2= pollution/sterr1
gen x3= zipcode/sterr1
gen x4= census/sterr1
gen x5= limited/sterr1
gen x6= controls/sterr1
gen x7= selection/sterr1
gen Yw = fishersz/sterr1
reg Yw x1 x2 x3 x4 x5 x6 x7 x0, noc
```

Standard Weighted Least Squares in Stata. One might question why I go to the trouble of weighting the observations manually rather than simply using the weight function in Stata. The regression program in Stata offers researchers the choice of four weights: frequency weights, sampling weights, analytic weights, and importance weights. Discussing the differences among these weights is beyond the scope of this book, but analytic weights are most appropriate for meta-regression because they represent proportional inverse variances. If we estimate the WLS model in Stata using analytic weights, we obtain parameter estimates and standard

FIGURE 4.4. WLS FIXED EFFECTS META-REGRESSION MODEL USING ANALYTIC WEIGHTS IN STATA

```
. reg fishersz superfund pollution zipcode census limited controls
selection [w=weight1]
(analytic weights assumed)
(sum of wgt is 5.4762e+06)
```

Source	SS	df	MS		Number of obs =	680
					F(7, 672) =	8.65
Model	.095347157	7	.013621022		Prob > F =	0.0000
Residual	1.05761999	672	.001573839		R-squared =	0.0827
					Adj R-squared =	0.0731
Total	1.15296715	679	.001698037		Root MSE =	.03967

fishersz	Coef.	Std. Err.	t	P>|t|	[95 %Conf.	Interval]
superfund	−.0093292	.006622	−1.41	0.159	−.0223314	.003673
pollution	−.0027425	.0038743	−0.71	0.479	−.0103496	.0048646
zipcode	.0009998	.0043933	0.23	0.820	−.0076264	.0096259
census	−.0076312	.0040489	−1.88	0.060	−.0155812	.0003188
limited	.0013055	.0072815	0.18	0.858	−.0129916	.0156027
controls	.0034307	.0041634	0.82	0.410	−.0047441	.0116056
selection	−.0172156	.0086964	−1.98	0.048	−.034291	−.0001403
_cons	.0270401	.0042834	6.31	0.000	.0186296	.0354506

errors that are identical to those obtained using the manual weighting approach (see figure 4.4). Because of the way Stata analytic weights enter the estimation, however, the root mean squared error (RMSE) from the Stata WLS model cannot be used to adjust the parameter standard errors (notice the difference between the RMSE in figure 4.3 and in figure 4.4). Therefore, proper estimation of the FEMR model requires that we use manual WLS rather than analytic weights in Stata.

The Stata VWLS Command. The best approach for estimating a FEMR model in Stata is to use the variance weighted least squares (VWLS) command. VWLS differs from regular WLS in that it requires that the conditional variance of Y_i (or Θ_i) be calculated prior to estimating the regression. Moreover, unlike WLS with analytic weights, the VWLS weights are treated as true variances rather than as proportional variances (though as with normal WLS, these variances enter estimation as standard errors, or $1/\sqrt{(n-3)}$ where Θ_i is measured as Z_r). Therefore we do not have to adjust parameter standard errors from FEMR models estimated using VWLS. Results from the VWLS FEMR are presented in figure 4.5. Note that the parameter estimates from the VWLS model are identical to those from the manual WLS model and the WLS model employing Stata analytic weights. This should give readers confidence in using manual WLS to estimate meta-regression models. The parameter standard errors,

FIGURE 4.5. VWLS FIXED EFFECTS META-REGRESSION MODEL IN STATA

```
. vwls fishersz superfund pollution zipcode census limited controls
selection, sd(sterr1)
```

Variance-weighted least-squares regression					Number of obs =	680
Goodness-of-fit chi2(672)	= 8517.19				Model chi2(7) =	767.85
Prob > chi2	= 0.0000				Prob > chi2 =	0.0000

fishersz	Coef.	Std. Err.	z	P>|z|	[95 % Conf. Interval]	
superfund	−.0093292	.00186	−5.02	0.000	−.0129748	−.0056836
pollution	−.0027425	.0010882	−2.52	0.012	−.0048754	−.0006096
zipcode	.0009998	.001234	0.81	0.418	−.0014189	.0034184
census	−.0076312	.0011373	−6.71	0.000	−.0098602	−.0054021
limited	.0013055	.0020453	0.64	0.523	−.0027032	.0053143
controls	.0034307	.0011695	2.93	0.003	.0011387	.0057228
selection	−.0172156	.0024427	−7.05	0.000	−.0220033	−.012428
_cons	.0270401	.0012032	22.47	0.000	.024682	.0293983

however, are identical to the corrected standard errors from the manual WLS model. Note also that the VWLS results do not contain an analysis of variance table or traditional measures of goodness of fit. These alterations stem from the fact that VWLS treats the conditional variance in Θ_i as determined a priori without error. The results in figure 4.5 are produced using the following Stata command statement:

```
vwls fishersz superfund pollution zipcode census limited
controls selection, sd(sterr1)
```

Interpreting the Results from Fixed Effects Regression in Stata.

Parameter Interpretation. Parameter estimates from the VWLS model in figure 4.5 are measured on the scale of Z_r, and therefore should be interpreted as the average change in effect size associated with a one-unit increase in the moderator variable. Since all moderator variables in this model are dichotomous, the parameter estimates represent the effect on Θ_i of the presence of the condition indexed by the moderator variable. For example, effect sizes from models that choose their samples on the basis of the value of the dependent variable are .0172 units smaller than average effect sizes from models that do not select on the dependent variable. We can transform these regression parameters back into correlation coefficients using equation 4.7. This transformation leaves the value of the parameter estimate on the "selection" variable unchanged to four significant digits, so that the average correlation between the percentage of minority residents in a community and the level of potential environmental risk in a community is .017 smaller in studies that select on the dependent variables. Looking at the other parameter estimates in figure 4.5 we see that the correlation between minority status and potential environmental risk is lower for Superfund sites and pollution emissions than for other potential sources of environmental risk, and lower when communities are defined using census tracts. By the same token, the correlation between minority concentration and sources of potential environmental risk is larger in higher-quality studies that include key control variables. None of these correlation coefficients are substantively large.

The intercept or constant term is an especially useful parameter in meta-regression models, as it represents the baseline effect size where all moderator variables take on a value of zero. In figure 4.5, we might interpret the intercept as an estimate of the baseline level of environmental inequity across all 680 effect sizes. This estimate is positive, but small, indicating a correlation of roughly .03 between the percentage of minority residents in communities and potential sources of environmental risk in those communities.

Hypothesis Tests. Using VWLS, hypothesis tests on individual meta-regression parameters employ the standard normal distribution (see figure 4.5). Using this criterion and the conventional type I error rate of .05, we would conclude that environmental inequities are significantly smaller (in a statistical sense) in studies that examine Superfund sites and pollution emissions, in studies that define community using census tracts, and in studies that choose their samples by selecting on the dependent variable. By contrast, estimated environmental inequities are significantly larger in higher-quality studies that employ a key set of control variables. Finally, we can conclude that the baseline level of environmental inequity across all 680 effect sizes is significantly larger than zero. In small samples the assumption that b_j/s_{bj} is normally distributed often does not hold, leading to overly liberal hypothesis tests and inflated type I error rates (Hartung and Knapp 2001). To guard against these artifacts we could assume that b_j/s_{bj} is distributed as t_{m-k-1}, but where $m = 680$ and $k = 7$, this change has no meaningful effect on the results of our hypothesis tests.

We test the hypothesis that $b_1 \ldots b_k$ are jointly zero using the Model X^2 from the VWLS results in figure 4.5. This model X^2 is equal to the summed squared regression (SSR) from the previous theoretical discussion of goodness of fit in fixed effects meta-regression. With $X^2_7 = 767.85$, we can reject the null hypothesis that all regression coefficients are jointly zero at $p < .0001$. Alternatively, the goodness of fit X^2 from the VWLS model (8517.19) is equivalent to the unrestricted SSE discussed earlier (see equations 4.10 and 4.12). The sum of the goodness of fit X^2 (8517.19) and the VWLS model X^2 (767.85) is equal to the restricted SSE discussed in that section. Therefore, we can test the null hypothesis that all regression parameters are jointly zero using $(9285.04 - 8517.19) \sim X^2_7$, which of course gives us the same result as using the model X^2 from the VWLS table. The corresponding test in the manual WLS framework is the F-test, $F = 22.79$, $p = .0000$, from figure 4.3.

Goodness of Fit. While not strictly a measure of goodness of fit, Cochrane's Q (see chapter 3 and the previous section) does assess whether the FEMR model fits the assumptions of the fixed effects framework. The goodness of fit X^2 from the VWLS model is equivalent to Cochrane's Q; therefore the Q-test for effect size heterogeneity is $X^2_{672} = 8517.19$, so we can reject the null hypothesis that the fixed effects model is appropriate at $p < .0001$.

Recall that the Birge ratio is calculated as $\text{SSE}_{\text{femr}} / m - k - 1$, so using the results from the VWLS model we can calculate the Birge ratio as the goodness of fit $X^2 / m - k - 1$, or $8517.19 / (672) = 12.67$. If FEMR is strictly appropriate, meaning that Xb accounts for all of the systematic variation in Θ_i, the Birge ratio should equal 1.0. Clearly there is excess variation in effect sizes not accounted for by the moderator variables in the FEMR model in figure 4.5, and it is likely that the fixed effects model is inappropriate for these data. We can obtain a more precise estimate of the percentage of unaccounted for variation in Θ_i using the I^2 statistic. Using the SSE_{femr} or goodness-of-fit X^2 from the VWLS model, the I^2 statistic is $100 *$ $[(8517.19 - 672)/8517.19] = 92$ percent, which means that 92 percent of the remaining variation in e_i cannot be attributed to sampling variability in the original studies. According to Higgins and colleagues (2003) this is a very high level of residual effect size heterogeneity.

Finally, we can use P^2 to measure the degree of systematic variation or heterogeneity in Θ_i that is accounted for by the meta-regression model. $\text{SSE}_{\text{restricted}}$ from the VWLS model is the sum of the goodness-of-fit X^2 and the model X^2, or $8517.19 + 767.85 = 9285.04$. P^2, then, is equal to $[((9285.04\text{-}679) - (8517.19\text{-}672)) / (9285.04 - 679)] = .088$, which means that the moderator variables in the fixed effects meta-regression model account for roughly 9 percent of the nonsampling variance in Θ_i. Note that this figure is much smaller than the adjusted R^2 of .20 from the manual WLS FEMR model in figure 4.3.

Random Effects Meta-Regression

Earlier I stated that while the FEMR model is useful pedagogically, the random effects meta-regression (REMR) model is almost always preferable in practice. There are at least five reasons to prefer the REMR to the FEMR. First, the Q-test for the appropriateness of the FEMR has low power. Therefore an inability to reject the null hypothesis Ho: $\tau^2 = 0$ does not provide strong evidence that τ^2 is actually zero. If we estimate a FEMR when a REMR is more appropriate, we obtain biased parameter estimates, unreliable parameter variances, and inflated type-I errors (Higgins and Thompson 2004).

Second, most analysts find untenable the FEMR assumption that effect size heterogeneity is completely accounted for by the moderator variables in the model. This requirement is akin to estimating a standard OLS regression model where $R^2 = 1.0$. The possibility of constructing such a model is highly suspect, and even if it were possible the model would violate norms of parsimony in model construction.

Third, public management and policy scholars will in general calculate effect sizes using the parameter estimates on focal predictors from multivariate models in original studies. The population parameters estimated in these studies are conditional upon the control variables used in the models. Coefficients from models employing different control variables estimate different quantities. Therefore the effect sizes calculated from these coefficients will also differ, generating significant effect size heterogeneity that is inconsistent with the assumptions of the FEMR model.

Fourth, the external validity of results differs meaningfully between FEMR and REMR models. Strictly speaking, the results from fixed effects models apply only to the original studies in the data set used to estimate the model, and not to new studies or to existing studies that are not included in this sample. By contrast, the results from random effects models generalize to all other studies sharing the characteristics of the studies included in the data set, and to any random sample of those studies (Cooper and Hedges 1994a). Therefore, REMR models have greater external validity.

Fifth, FEMR assumes a common population effect size, conditional upon the moderating variables included in the model. In medicine, this assumption implies, for example, that the effect of a drug is the same for all patients. In policy and management, this assumption might imply that the effect of educational vouchers on student achievement is the same for all students (or for all black students, or for all high school students, depending on the moderator variables used), or that racial inequities regarding the distribution of pollution are the same in all jurisdictions. By contrast, the random effects framework assumes that effect sizes conditional upon moderating variables are distributed normally—in other words, that the effects of drugs, vouchers, and minority status may differ across units—and that the REMR estimates the central tendency in these distributions.

Readers familiar with the Stable Unit Value Treatment Assumption (SUVTA) from Rubin's potential outcomes framework commonly used in policy analysis may not find this FEMR assumption inappropriate (Holland 1986). A critical difference between SUVTA and FEMR, however, is that while both assume a common effect of treatment among units within any particular study, only FEMR assumes a (conditional) common treatment effect *for all units across all studies*. This broader assumption is less tenable.

Estimating the Random Effects Variance Component

The FEMR is estimated using either WLS or VWLS where the elements of the weight matrix W consist of the square root of the sampling variability $\sqrt{v_i}$ associated with Θ_i. It stands to reason, then, that the REMR might be estimated using WLS where the elements of the weight matrix consist of the square root of the total variability in Θ_i, or $\sqrt{(v_i + \tau^2)}$. The difficulty with this approach is that while v_i is known, τ^2 is unknown and must be estimated from the data. Estimation of τ^2 is one of the central challenges of random effects meta-regression, and one of two approaches is generally employed.

Restricted Maximum Likelihood Estimation of τ^2. The random effects variance component is most commonly estimated using restricted maximum likelihood (REML), which is based on maximizing the likelihood of the residual e_i. REML estimation of τ^2 is the default method in Stata and most dedicated meta-regression statistical software packages, and is derived by maximizing the residual log likelihood

$$L_e\left(\tau^2\right) = -.5 * \Sigma \left[\ln\left(v_i + \tau^2\right) + \left(e_i^2 / \left(v_i + \tau^2\right) - .5\right) * |\ln X' v^{-1} X|\right]$$
$$(4.15)$$

where e_i is the residual from an initial REML model and v is the main diagonal from the random effects error variance-covariance matrix ee' (these elements will be equal to $(v_i + \tau^2)$. Since estimation of τ^2 requires a starting value of τ^2, REML is clearly an iterative process. One common starting value is $\tau^2 = 0$, which means that e_i and the elements of v in the REML equation will come from the fixed effects meta-regression model. The process is then iterated until the change in τ^2 is lower than some predetermined threshold. When estimating REMR models, Stata uses a starting value equal to the method of moments estimate of τ^2, discussed in the next section, to speed convergence.

Method of Moments Estimation of τ^2. While the REML estimate of τ^2 is asymptotically unbiased and efficient, it does have three shortcomings. First, the benefits of the REML approach only occur in large samples. In small samples, other methods of estimating τ^2 are preferred. Second, REML provides an iterative rather than an analytical solution to estimating τ^2. Third, REML assumes that we know the full distribution of the random effects (the REML formula above assumes that these effects are normally distributed). As an alternative to REML, we can use the older method of moments (MOM) estimator that was derived as an extension to the random effects estimator of DerSimonian and Laird (1986). The MOM estimator performs relatively well in small samples, offers an analytic solution for estimating τ^2, and only requires that we make assumptions about the first two moments of the distribution of the random effects. The full MOM estimator is rather cumbersome and is estimated in two steps:

1. Derive the FEMR estimates and SSE_{femr}
2. Estimate $\tau^2 = (\text{SSE}_{\text{femr}} - (m - k - 1)) / tr(\boldsymbol{M})$ where

$$tr(\boldsymbol{M}) = \Sigma v_i^{-1} - tr\left[\left(\Sigma v_i^{-1} \boldsymbol{X}\boldsymbol{X}'\right)^{-1} \left(\Sigma v_i^{-2} \boldsymbol{X}\boldsymbol{X}'\right)\right] \qquad (4.16)$$

Raudenbush (1994) offers two much simpler approximations to the full MOM estimator:

$$\tau^2 = \left[\text{SSE}_{\text{ols}} / (m - k - 1)\right] - v_{\text{bar}} \qquad (4.17)$$

where

· SSE_{ols} is the summed squared error from the meta-regression model estimated with ordinary least squares
· v_{bar} is the average fixed effects variance $\Sigma v_i / k$

and

$$\tau^2 = m \left[\left(Q/m - k - 1\right) - 1\right] / \Sigma w_i \qquad (4.18)$$

where

· Q is from the FEMR model
· w_i is the inverse variance weight from the FEMR model

Alternative Estimators for τ^2. There are a handful of alternative estimators for the random effects variance component, including a full maximum likelihood estimator (FEML) that maximizes the likelihood associated with both the regression parameters and the model residual, and an Empirical Bayes estimate of τ^2 based on the work of Morris (1983). The FEML estimator is theoretically more efficient in large samples, but Thompson and Sharp (1999) found that REML often outperforms FEML in practice, largely because REML accounts for the additional uncertainty produced by estimating the regression parameters $b_1 \ldots b_k$ (Raudenbush 2009). Simulations by Thompson and Sharpe conclude that use of the Empirical Bayes estimator should be limited to meta-analyses using small samples. Therefore, this estimator is unlikely to be used by meta-analysts in public management, public policy, and the social sciences.

Estimating the Random Effects Model

The random effects meta-regression model

$$\Theta_i = b_0 + b_1 X_{1i} + b_2 X_{2i} + b_3 X_{3i} + e_i \ \text{ where } \ e_i \sim N\left(0, v_i + \tau^2\right) \ \ (4.19)$$

can be estimated using GLS, WLS, or restricted maximum likelihood. The error variance-covariance matrix from this model takes the form

$$ee'_{\text{remr}} = \begin{pmatrix} \left(v_1 + \tau^2\right) & 0 & 0 & 0 \\ 0 & \left(v_2 + \tau^2\right) & 0 & 0 \\ \cdot & \cdot & \cdot & \cdot \\ 0 & 0 & 0 & \left(v_n + \tau^2\right) \end{pmatrix}$$

so the weights in WLS must be equal to the square root of the total conditional variance in Θ_i, or $1/\sqrt{\left(v_i + \tau^2\right)}$, where τ^2 is estimated using one of the methods described above. With an appropriate weight matrix W, the REMR parameters can be estimated by GLS using $\beta_{\text{remr}} = (X'W'WX)^{-1} X'W'W\Theta$ with variance $\text{var}[b_{\text{remr}}] = \sigma^2 (X'W'WX)^{-1}$. Alternatively, the researcher can simply weight each element of Θ and X by $1/\sqrt{\left(v_i + \tau^2\right)}$ and estimate as with manual WLS FEMR.

Hypothesis Testing

Testing for Residual Heterogeneity. Since we are using the random effects model there is no need to test the adequacy of the fixed effects model.

Hypothesis Tests on Individual Parameters. Hypothesis tests on individual parameters can be conducted using the Z or t_{m-k-1} distributions as is done with the FEMR. Simulations by Knapp and Hartung (2003), however, show that even the t_{m-k-1} distribution often produces inflated type I errors when testing hypotheses on individual parameters in REMR. These authors offer an improvement that multiplies the parameter variance by a quadratic factor that incorporates the random effects variance component τ^2, then uses the student t_{m-k-1} distribution for calculating confidence intervals and completing hypothesis tests. This variance estimator is the default for hypothesis tests on regression parameters when using the Stata *metareg* command. In my experience, there is often little difference between the results of hypothesis tests using this estimator versus using the standard parameter variance estimator, so long as t_{m-k-1} is used to conduct these tests.

Higgins and Thompson (2004) note that even hypothesis tests using the Knapp and Hartung (2003) approach may be too liberal in that they can produce unacceptably large type I errors. Incorrectly rejecting a true null hypothesis in meta-regression is especially likely if researchers conduct hypothesis tests for several moderator variables sequentially (k is large) using effect sizes from a relatively small number of studies (m is small). To avoid results that capitalize on chance when k is large and m is small, these authors offer a permutation-based t-test in which groups of covariates X_k are randomly allocated to outcomes Θ_i, and t-tests are calculated for each reallocation. Using a process akin to bootstrapping, an empirical t-distribution is created from the models using permuted data sets. The exact p-value for the null hypothesis Ho: $b_j = 0$ is the proportion of permuted t-scores that exceed the t-score from the original meta-regression. The permutation approach to testing regression parameters is especially useful with small numbers of effect sizes, but this means it is of limited value for meta-regression in public management and policy where m will be large. Not surprisingly, all approaches to hypothesis tests on b_j converge in very large samples.

Compound Hypothesis Tests. Conducting joint hypothesis tests in the REMR model is identical to conducting these tests using the FEMR model. Specifically, one tests the null hypothesis that all REMR regression parameters are zero using $(\text{SSE}_{\text{restricted}} - \text{SSE}_{\text{unrestricted}}) \sim X_k^2$, so the expectation where Ho: $b_1 \ldots b_k = 0$ is true is that $X_k^2 = k$. A simpler and equivalent test leverages the fact that when the null hypothesis is true, in the random effects meta-regression the summed squared regression SSR $\sim X_{k-1}^2$ where k is the number of parameters estimated in the regression model. More generally, for some subset of parameters r in parameter vector b, we can test the null hypothesis Ho: $b_r = 0$ (that is, the joint significance of this subset) using the expectation that under the null hypothesis $(\text{SSE}_{\text{restricted}} - \text{SSE}_{\text{unrestricted}}) \sim X_r^2$. The *metareg* command in Stata, discussed further on, offers an alternative method of conducting joint hypothesis tests.

Prediction and Power

As in the FEMR model, regression parameters serve as point estimates for conditional average effect sizes in REMR. For REMR models where the effect size Θ_i is measured using Fisher's Z, regression parameters must be transformed back into correlation coefficients using equation 4.7, though this transformation makes little difference in practice unless ρ is very large. In addition, the process for approximating a regression response surface and for assessing the power of hypothesis tests in REMR is identical to that for FEMR.

Goodness of Fit

Since the REMR assumes that there is heterogeneity in Θ_i over and above what can be accounted for by sampling variability, the Birge ratio is inappropriate as a measure of goodness of fit for REMR models. We can still quantify the degree of heterogeneity in REMR models using the I^2 statistic. I^2 in REMR is calculated in the same way as in FEMR: $I^2 = 100 * [(Q - (m - k - 1)) / Q]$ or $I^2 = 100 * [(\text{SSE}_{\text{remr}} - (m - k - 1)) / \text{SSE}_{\text{remr}}]$. Two versions of the psuedo-R^2 can be calculated for the REMR model. First, as in the fixed effects model, P^2 can be calculated as $P^2 = [(\text{SSE}_{\text{restricted}} - (m - 1)) - (\text{SSE}_{\text{unrestricted}} - (m - k - 1)) / (\text{SSE}_{\text{restricted}} - (m - 1))]$. With REMR, however, we can use the estimate of the random effects variance component τ^2 to obtain a second estimate of the pseudo-R^2. If we denote τ_0^2 as the random effects variance component from a model with no covariates and denote τ_k^2 as the random effects variance component from a REMR model with k predictors, we can calculate an adjusted R^2 value using equation 4.13 (that is, $R_{adj}^2 = (\tau_0^2 - \tau_k^2) / \tau_0^2$

(Raudenbush 2009). If **Xb** accounts for none of the nonsampling heterogeneity in Θ_i, $R^2_{adj} = 0$, while if the moderating variables in the REMR model account for all of the heterogenity in Θ_i, $R^2_{adj} = 1$. Note that in the latter case, the FEMR model is appropriate.

Random Effects Meta-Regression in Stata

Dedicated meta-analysis software packages are no better equipped to estimate the types of random effects meta-regression models used in public management and policy than they are to estimate the FEMR model. While random effects meta-regression is not supported by the commercial version of Stata, members of the Stata Users Group have crafted an ado file "*metareg*" command that allows researchers to estimate these models easily (Harbord and Higgins 2008; Sterne 2009). As with most meta-analysis packages, *metareg* is designed to be used with odds-based effect sizes or *d*-based effect sizes. However, *metareg* can estimate REMR models using *r*-based effect sizes such as Fisher's *Z* as long as these effect sizes (and their standard errors) are calculated outside of *metareg*. Unfortunately, *metareg* cannot estimate the types of REMR models most useful to researchers in public management, public policy, and the social sciences. Therefore, I also illustrate how to estimate REMR models in Stata without the use of *metareg*. The ability to estimate REMR models in Stata without *metareg* will prove very useful when estimating the more advanced models introduced in chapter 5.

The Sample Regression Model. To illustrate random effects meta-regression in Stata I return to the environmental equity data set and the sample random effects regression model:

$$\Theta_i = b_0 + b_1 X_{1i} + b_2 X_{2i} + b_3 X_{3i} + b_4 X_{4i} + b_5 X_{5i} + b_6 X_{6i} + b_7 X_{7i} + e_i, e_i$$
$$\sim N\left(0, v_i + \tau^2\right) \tag{4.20}$$

where Θ_i is an effect size measuring race-based environmental inequities, X_1 indexes whether these inequities are estimated using the location of Superfund sites, X_2 indexes whether these inequities are estimated using pollution emissions, X_3 and X_4 identify effect sizes from models in which community is defined using residential ZIP codes and census tracts, respectively, and X_5, X_6, and X_7 are measures of the quality of the original studies.

Metareg *in Stata Using Restricted Maximum Likelihood.* The default method for estimating REMR models using *metareg* is to estimate τ^2 using restricted maximum likelihood, estimating parameter variances using the quadratic variance inflation factor of Knapp and Hartung (2003), and testing Ho: $b_j = 0$ using a *t*-distribution with $m - k - 1$ degrees of freedom. Figure 4.6 presents the results of estimating the environmental equity meta-regression model using these default options. Figures 4.7 and 4.8, respectively, report the results of REMR estimated with *metareg* where hypothesis tests on regression parameters are conducted using the standard normal distribution and the permutation approach of Higgins and Thompson (2004). The results in figure 4.6 are produced using the following Stata command statement:

```
metareg fishersz superfund pollution zipcode census limited
controls selection, wsse(sterr1)
```

Interpreting the Results from **Metareg.**

Interpreting Regression Parameters. Because Θ_i is measured as Z_r, parameter estimates in figure 4.6 can be interpreted as partial correlation coefficients. The constant term indicates that in models in which all moderator variables are zero, the average correlation between the percentage of minority residents and levels of potential environmental risk across communities is .068.

FIGURE 4.6. RANDOM EFFECTS META-REGRESSION MODEL USING STATA *METAREG* WITH DEFAULT OPTIONS

```
. metareg fishersz superfund pollution zipcode census limited controls
selection, wsse(sterr1)

Meta-regression                                   Number of obs  =      680
REML estimate of between-study variance           tau2           = .005708
% residual variation due to heterogeneity         I-squared_res  =  92.11%
Proportion of between-study variance explained    Adj R-squared  =  10.73%
Joint test for all covariates                     Model F(7,672) =     7.56
With Knapp-Hartung modification                   Prob > F       =  0.0000
```

fishersz	Coef.	Std. Err.	t	P>|t|	[95% Conf. Interval]	
superfund	.0062388	.0150539	0.41	0.679	−.0233195	.0357971
pollution	−.0199238	.0084974	−2.34	0.019	−.0366084	−.0032393
zipcode	−.0076215	.0061185	−1.25	0.213	−.0196351	.0043922
census	.0106787	.005865	1.82	0.069	−.0008372	.0221946
limited	−.0060321	.0156759	−0.38	0.701	−.0368117	.0247475
controls	−.0364036	.0097337	−3.74	0.000	−.0555158	−.0172914
selection	−.0776066	.0189497	−4.10	0.000	−.1148144	−.0403988
_cons	.0678888	.0060924	11.14	0.000	.0559263	.0798513

FIGURE 4.7. RANDOM EFFECTS META-REGRESSION MODEL USING STATA *METAREG* WITH *Z*-SCORE OPTION

```
. metareg fishersz superfund pollution zipcode census limited controls
selection, wsse(sterr1) z

Meta-regression                                      Number of obs   =      680
REML estimate of between-study variance              tau2            =  .005708
% residual variation due to heterogeneity            I-squared_res   =   92.11%
Proportion of between-study variance explained       Adj R-squared   =   10.73%
Joint test for all covariates                        Model chi2(7)   =    66.13
Without Knapp-Hartung modification                   Prob > chi2     =   0.0000
```

fishersz	Coef.	Std. Err.	z	P>|z|	[95% Conf. Interval]	
superfund	.0062388	.013463	0.46	0.643	−.0201481	.0326257
pollution	−.0199238	.0075993	−2.62	0.009	−.0348183	−.0050294
zipcode	−.0076215	.0054719	−1.39	0.164	−.0183461	.0031032
census	.0106787	.0052452	2.04	0.042	.0003984	.020959
limited	−.0060321	.0140192	−0.43	0.667	−.0335093	.0214451
controls	−.0364036	.008705	−4.18	0.000	−.0534652	−.019342
selection	−.0776066	.0169471	−4.58	0.000	−.1108223	−.0443909
_cons	.0678888	.0054486	12.46	0.000	.0572098	.0785678

FIGURE 4.8. RANDOM EFFECTS META-REGRESSION HYPOTHESIS TESTS USING PERMUTATION OPTION IN STATA *METAREG*

```
. metareg fishersz superfund pollution zipcode census limited controls
selection, wsse(sterr1) permute(10000)

Monte Carlo permutation test for meta-regression

Moment-based estimate of between-study variance
Without Knapp & Hartung modification to standard errors

P-values unadjusted and adjusted for multiple testing

                    Number of obs   =      680
                    Permutations    =    10000
```

fishersz	Unadjusted	P Adjusted
superfund	0.843	1.000
pollution	0.007	0.053
zipcode	0.149	0.614
census	0.024	0.136
limited	0.314	0.906
controls	0.001	0.003
selection	0.000	0.001

```
largest Monte Carlo SE(P) = 0.0049
```

This estimate is more than twice as large as that obtained using the fixed effects model, and this difference is attributable to the different weights used in FEMR and REMR (REMR places greater weight on effect sizes from studies using smaller samples). Moreover, the meaning of this parameter is different as well. In FEMR, regression parameters estimate a single population effect, while in REMR these parameters estimate the mean of a normal distribution of conditional effects. Other parameters can be interpreted in a similar fashion. For example, the average correlation between the concentration of minority residents and levels of potential environmental risk is .0199 lower in studies that measure this risk using pollution levels, and .0776 lower in studies that draw their samples by selecting on the dependent variable.

We can also use the results from the REMR model to predict the expected level of environmental inequity from "ideal" studies. In the current context, an "ideal" study is one that does not employ a limited control group ($X_5 = 0$), one that includes all key control variables ($X_6 = 1$), and one that does not select on the dependent variable ($X_7 = 0$). Therefore, the baseline level of environmental inequity in the ideal study is .0679 (b_0) $-$ .0364 (b_6) $=$ .0315. This baseline measure of inequity is larger in ideal studies examining the concentration of superfund sites across census tracts ($b_0 - b_6 + b_1 + b_4 = .0484$) and smaller in ideally designed studies examining pollution emissions across residential ZIP codes ($b_0 - b_6 - b_2 - b_3 = .004$). While all of these estimated effects are positive, they are substantively small.

Hypothesis Tests. Hypothesis tests on individual regression parameters are conducted using the standard method. Using $\alpha = .05$ to define an acceptable type I error rate, figure 4.6 shows that we are able to reject the null hypothesis that $b_j = 0$ for the constant term and for the parameter estimates on the variables identifying the use of pollution emissions, the use of appropriate control variables, and the practice of selecting on the dependent variable. If we relax the criterion to $\alpha = .10$, we can also reject the null hypothesis that average effect sizes are no different from studies that define community using census tracts. The compound hypothesis that all regression coefficients are jointly zero can be rejected at $p < .0001$ ($F_{7, 672} = 7.56$).

In addition to determining the probability of making a type I error, we can conduct a retrospective power analysis to identify the probability of making a type II error. Using the formulas provided by Hedges and Pigott (2004), the type II error rate for incorrectly accepting a false null hypothesis on the constant term is $p < .0001$ (power $> .9999$). The type II error rate for the hypothesis test on the superfund coefficient is $p = .144$ (power $= .856$), while the type II error rate for the hypothesis test on the census tract coefficient is $p = .395$ (power $= .605$). Given this calculation, if we conclude that there really is no difference between the average effect size from studies that define community using census tracts and the average effect size from studies that define community using some other level of aggregation, we may be wrong roughly 40 percent of the time.

Goodness of Fit. Metareg estimates that the random effects variance component τ^2 is equal to $.005708$. *Metareg* also provides two direct measures of goodness of fit. $I^2 = 92.11$ percent, which tells us that 92 percent of the variation in Θ_i cannot be attributed to sampling variability. You will notice that this figure is identical to the I^2 statistic that we calculated using results from the FEMR model. I^2 in FEMR and REMR estimate the same quantity. *Metareg* also calculates an adjusted R^2 value of $.1073$, which means that the moderator variables in the regression model account for roughly 11 percent of the nonsampling variability in Θ_i. This figure is slightly larger than the P^2 value of $.088$ calculated for the FEMR model. The main reason for this discrepancy is that P^2 in FEMR is calculated using the summed squared errors, while R^2 in the REMR model is calculated using conditional and unconditional estimates of τ^2 (see above). The latter method is generally viewed as being more accurate (Raudenbush 2009).

Alternative Methods for Conducting Hypothesis Tests in Metareg. *Metareg*
also gives researchers the option of conducting hypothesis tests by (1) utilizing a standard normal distribution for b_j / s_{bj} and (2) utilizing the nonparametric permutation based approach of Higgins and Thompson (2004) (the permutation approach uses the method of moments estimate for τ^2). The former is consistent with the asymptotic assumptions underlying meta-regression, but is less conservative than the default approach of Knapp and Hartung (2003). The permutation approach abandons the distributional assumptions regarding b_j, and is more conservative than the default approach. Also, the permutation approach has the drawback of not providing adjusted p-values for hypothesis tests on the constant term. Given the importance of the constant term in meta-regression, this is a meaningful limitation. The Z-score-based approach is strictly appropriate only in very large samples, while the permutation approach is generally preferred when the ratio k/m is large. *Metareg* output using both of these alternatives is provided in figures 4.7 and 4.8, respectively. For the permutation-based approach I chose to draw 10,000 random permutations

of X_i. Given the relatively large sample of 680 effect sizes and the relatively small ratio of k to m (7/680), the outcomes of the hypothesis tests are quite similar from all three strategies. The permutation-based approach, however, also provides a correction for multiple hypothesis testing in the spirit of Bonferonni adjustments (Higgins and Thompson 2004). Because our moderator variables were identified a priori, because we did not choose among these moderators using the results from preliminary meta-regressions, and because our k / m ratio is very low, there is little to recommend the adjusted p-values over the unadjusted p-values for this particular meta-regression model.

Other Approaches to Estimating REMR in Stata Using Restricted Maximum Likelihood. While *metareg* is an extraordinarily useful command for conducting standard random effects meta-regression, it is not especially flexible, and is often ill-suited to estimate the type of meta-regression models that are most useful in public management and policy research. Thankfully, other commands in Stata may be used to estimate random effects meta-regression.

Estimation Using Manual WLS. First, the most flexible method is to estimate a REMR model using manually weighted least squares. As with FEMR, in this approach we weight all observations by the square root of the total variance in Θ_i (that is, $v_i + \tau^2$), obtaining the estimate of τ^2 from *metareg* or some other method. We then estimate a least squares regression on these transformed data. The results from estimating a REMR model using manual WLS are presented in figure 4.9. These results were produced using the following Stata command statements:

```
gen totalvarml= var + .005708
gen resterrml = sqrt(totalvarml)
gen weight1re = (1/totalvarml)
gen x0ml= 1/resterrml
gen x1ml= superfund/ resterrml
gen x2ml= pollution/ resterrml
gen x3ml= zipcode/ resterrml
gen x4ml= census/ resterrml
gen x5ml= limited/ resterrml
gen x6ml= controls/ resterrml
gen x7ml= selection/ resterrml
gen Ywml = fishersz/ resterrml
reg Ywml x1ml x2ml x3ml x4ml x5ml x6ml x7ml x0ml, noc
```

A comparison of figures 4.6 and 4.9 shows that the parameter estimates, parameter standard errors, and outcomes of hypothesis tests are identical

FIGURE 4.9. MANUAL WLS RANDOM EFFECTS META-REGRESSION USING RESTRICTED MAXIMUM LIKELIHOOD

```
. reg Ywml x1ml x2ml x3ml x4ml x5ml x6ml x7ml x0ml, noc
```

Source	SS	df	MS		Number of obs =	680
					F(8, 672) =	28.87
Model	288.814243	8	36.1017804		Prob > F =	0.0000
Residual	840.206859	672	1.25030783		R-squared =	0.2558
					Adj R-squared =	0.2470
Total	1129.0211	680	1.66032515		Root MSE =	1.1182

Ywml	Coef.	Std. Err.	t	P>|t|	[95% Conf.	Interval]
x1ml	.0062388	.0150539	0.41	0.679	−.0233195	.0357971
x2ml	−.0199238	.0084974	−2.34	0.019	−.0366084	−.0032393
x3ml	−.0076215	.0061185	−1.25	0.213	−.0196351	.0043922
x4ml	.0106787	.005865	1.82	0.069	−.0008372	.0221946
x5ml	−.0060322	.0156759	−0.38	0.701	−.0368117	.0247474
x6ml	−.0364036	.0097337	−3.74	0.000	−.0555157	−.0172914
x7ml	−.0776066	.0189497	−4.10	0.000	−.1148144	−.0403988
x0ml	.0678888	.0060924	11.14	0.000	.0559263	.0798512

when using manual WLS or *metareg*. While in FEMR we had to correct manual WLS parameter standard errors by dividing them by the RMSE of the WLS model, this correction is unnecessary for the REMR model. While the values of the *F*-test are different for *metareg* and manual WLS, the outcome of these tests is identical: we are able to reject the null hypothesis that all regression parameters are jointly zero at $p < .0001$. The only meaningful difference between the results from *metareg* and the results from manual WLS is that the adjusted R^2 from manual WLS is twice as large as that from *metareg*. There is no systematic comparison of these measures of goodness of fit in the statistical literature on meta-analysis, so there is little basis on which to choose between them.

Estimation Using VWLS. Using the same estimate of total variation in Θ_i from the previous section, we can also estimate a REMR model using the Stata VWLS command. The results from estimating the REMR model using VWLS are presented in figure 4.10. These results are produced using the following Stata command statement:

```
vwls fishersz superfund pollution zipcode census limited
controls selection, sd(resterrml)
```

Comparing figures 4.9 and 4.10, we see that the regression parameter estimates are identical and that the results of parameter hypothesis tests are nearly identical. Parameter standard errors from VWLS are different than those from manual WLS. After multiplying the manual

FIGURE 4.10. VWLS RANDOM EFFECTS META-REGRESSION USING RESTRICTED MAXIMUM LIKELIHOOD

```
. vwls fishersz superfund pollution zipcode census limited controls
selection, sd(resterrml)

Variance-weighted least-squares regression          Number of obs =      680
Goodness-of-fit chi2(672)   =   840.21              Model chi2(7) =    66.13
Prob > chi2                 =   0.0000              Prob > chi2   =   0.0000
```

fishersz	Coef.	Std. Err.	z	P>|z|	[95 % Conf. Interval]	
superfund	.0062388	.0134629	0.46	0.643	−.020148	.0326257
pollution	−.0199238	.0075993	−2.62	0.009	−.0348183	−.0050294
zipcode	−.0076215	.0054719	−1.39	0.164	−.0183461	.0031032
census	.0106787	.0052452	2.04	0.042	.0003984	.020959
limited	−.0060322	.0140192	−0.43	0.667	−.0335093	.021445
controls	−.0364036	.008705	−4.18	0.000	−.0534651	−.019342
selection	−.0776066	.0169471	−4.58	0.000	−.1108222	−.0443909
_cons	.0678888	.0054486	12.46	0.000	.0572098	.0785677

WLS parameter standard errors by the RMSE, however, they are equivalent. For example, the corrected WLS parameter standard error for the constant term is (.0060924 / 1.1182) = .005448, or exactly the value we get from VWLS. This indicates that the quadratic variance inflation factor proposed by Knapp and Hartung (2003) and implemented in *metareg* simply reverses the correction of dividing manual WLS parameter standard errors by the RMSE. We can see further evidence of this by noting that the parameter standard errors in VWLS are equal to those obtained from *metareg* using the Z-score option (see figure 4.7). The results from estimating REMR models using VWLS, then, are equivalent to the results obtained when estimating REMR using *metareg* with the Z-score option for conducting hypothesis tests—with one exception. The P^2 calculated from VWLS [((903.34 − 679) − (840.21 − 672) / (906.34 − 679)) = 0.26] is equal to the R^2 from manual WLS estimation (.2558). Recall that both of these figures are substantially larger than the adjusted R^2 reported by *metareg*, and that the statistical literature provides little or no guidance in choosing between these measures of goodness of fit.

Random Effects Meta-Regression in Stata Using Method of Moments.

Method of Moments Estimation Using Metareg. The Stata *metareg* command can also be used to estimate a REMR model where τ^2 is calculated using the method of moments. Results from this model are reported in figure 4.11. The first item of note from these results is that the MOM estimate of

FIGURE 4.11. RANDOM EFFECTS META-REGRESSION MODEL USING STATA *METAREG* WITH METHOD OF MOMENTS

```
. metareg fishersz superfund pollution zipcode census limited controls
selection, wsse(sterr1) mm
Meta-regression                                          Number of obs  =     680
Method of moments estimate of between-study variance tau2  = .001512
% residual variation due to heterogeneity                I-squared_res  =  92.11%
Proportion of between-study variance explained           Adj R-squared  =   4.51%
Joint test for all covariates                            Model F(7,672)  =    8.62
With Knapp-Hartung modification                          Prob > F       =  0.0000
```

fishersz	Coef.	Std. Err.	t	P>|t|	[95% Conf. Interval]	
superfund	.0023461	.0126195	0.19	0.853	−.0224322	.0271245
pollution	−.0188715	.0073802	−2.56	0.011	−.0333625	−.0043805
zipcode	−.0077151	.0054955	−1.40	0.161	−.0185055	.0030754
census	.011469	.0051905	2.21	0.027	.0012776	.0216605
limited	−.0134085	.0139238	−0.96	0.336	−.040748	.013931
controls	−.0290914	.0083607	−3.48	0.001	−.0455077	−.0126752
selection	−.0633161	.0163374	−3.88	0.000	−.0953945	−.0312377
_cons	.0604128	.0054029	11.18	0.000	.0498042	.0710215

$\tau^2 = .001512$ is much smaller than the restricted maximum likelihood estimate of $\tau^2 = .005708$. An important consequence is that the total variance of Θ_i under MOM is smaller than under REML. Therefore the weights used in estimating the REMR model will be different in that MOM places less weight on the results from studies using smaller sample sizes. Comparing figures 4.11 and 4.6, we see that both the parameter estimates and parameter standard errors differ when using MOM. The inferences we draw from the MOM and REML results are broadly similar, however, since the parameter estimates are not that dissimilar and the outcomes of the hypothesis tests are the same. Turning our attention to goodness of fit, because the I^2 statistic relies on Q (or SSE) rather than on τ, I^2 is identical in the MOM and REML models. The adjusted R^2 does rely on the estimate of τ^2, however, and this measure of goodness of fit is much smaller in the MOM model than in the REML model. With a large meta-sample of $m = 680$, the REML approach is preferred to MOM in this example.

Other Approaches to Estimating Random Effects Meta Regression Using MOM. Occasionally researchers may want to complete a random effects meta regression without relying on (or without access to) the *metareg* command. In these instances, the REMR model can still be estimated using manual WLS and an estimate of τ^2 derived from the MOM approximation just described. Figure 4.12 reports the results from estimating this model where $\tau^2 = .0137$. The results in figure 4.12 are produced using the following Stata command statements:

```
summarize var, meanonly
scalar meanvar=r(mean)
display meanvar
reg fishersz superfund pollution zipcode census limited
controls selection
scalar revar=e(rmse)^2-meanvar
display revar
gen totalvarmm = var+revar
gen resterrmm = sqrt(totalvarmm)
gen weight1re=(1/(totalvarmm))
gen x0mm= 1/resterrmm
gen x1mm= superfund/ resterrmm
gen x2mm= pollution/ resterrmm
gen x3mm= zipcode/ resterrmm
gen x4mm= census/ resterrmm
gen x5mm= limited/ resterrmm
gen x6mm= controls/ resterrmm
gen x7mm= selection/ resterrmm
gen Ywmm = fishersz/ resterrmm
reg Ywmm x1mm x2mm x3mm x4mm x5mm x6mm x7mm x0mm, noc
```

Note that τ^2 from the MOM approximation is much larger than τ^2 calculated using the MOM option in *metareg*. Comparing figures 4.12 and 4.9

FIGURE 4.12. RANDOM EFFECTS META-REGRESSION MODEL USING MANUAL WLS WITH METHOD OF MOMENTS

```
. reg Ywmm x1mm x2mm x3mm x4mm x5mm x6mm x7mm x0mm, noc
```

Source	SS	df	MS		
Model	159.371876	8	19.9214844	Number of obs =	680
Residual	487.065746	672	.724800217	F(8, 672) =	27.49
				Prob > F =	0.0000
				R-squared =	0.2465
				Adj R-squared =	0.2376
Total	646.437622	680	.950643561	Root MSE =	.85135

Ywmm	Coef.	Std. Err.	t	P>|t|	[95% Conf. Interval]	
x1mm	.0117938	.0168771	0.70	0.485	−.0213443	.0449319
x2mm	−.0198142	.0093497	−2.12	0.034	−.0381723	−.001456
x3mm	−.0074463	.0067063	−1.11	0.267	−.0206142	.0057216
x4mm	.0087214	.0064545	1.35	0.177	−.0039521	.0213949
x5mm	.0059664	.0169174	0.35	0.724	−.027251	.0391838
x6mm	−.0413007	.0108537	−3.81	0.000	−.062612	−.0199894
x7mm	−.0933794	.0209078	−4.47	0.000	−.134432	−.0523269
x0mm	.0729195	.0066928	10.90	0.000	.0597783	.0860607

we can see that the manual WLS results using MOM and restricted maximum likelihood are very similar. Parameter estimates, parameter standard errors, and goodness of fit measures are comparable, and the outcomes of hypothesis tests are virtually identical. While REML estimates should be used whenever they are available, it is reassuring to know that manual WLS using a MOM approximation will not lead us far astray if restricted maximum likelihood is unavailable.

Finally, we can use VWLS to estimate a REMR model with τ^2 estimated using the MOM approximation. Results from this model are reported in figure 4.13. While there is little to recommend this model in practice, we can see that the results from REMR estimation using VWLS with MOM are broadly consistent with the results obtained using the preferred *metareg* and manual WLS results.

Threats to Inference in Random Effects Meta-Regression

Collinearity and Micronumerisity. Meta-regression faces many of the same threats to inference as does traditional regression. First, much of the research developing meta-regression highlights the risks posed by *micronumerisity* (in other words, a small meta-sample size m). In meta-analyses where original studies produce a single effect size, micronumerisity can be a problem. In policy and management research, however, original studies generally produce several effect sizes, rendering this concern less relevant. Of greater concern is *collinearity* among the moderator variables, which will have the same effects on efficiency as does micronumerisity.

FIGURE 4.13. RANDOM EFFECTS META-REGRESSION MODEL USING VWLS IN STATA WITH METHOD OF MOMENTS

```
. vwls fishersz superfund pollution zipcode census limited controls
selection, sd(resterrmm)
Variance-weighted least-squares regression        Number of obs =      680
Goodness-of-fit chi2(672)    =    487.07            Model chi2(7) =    34.89
Prob > chi2                  =     1.0000            Prob > chi2   =   0.0000
```

fishersz	Coef.	Std. Err.	z	P>|z|	[95 % Conf. Interval]	
superfund	.0117938	.0198238	0.59	0.552	−.0270602	.0506478
pollution	−.0198142	.0109822	−1.80	0.071	−.0413389	.0017106
zipcode	−.0074463	.0078773	−0.95	0.345	−.0228855	.0079929
census	.0087214	.0075815	1.15	0.250	−.0061381	.0235809
limited	.0059664	.0198713	0.30	0.764	−.0329806	.0449133
controls	−.0413007	.0127488	−3.24	0.001	−.0662879	−.0163135
selection	−.0933795	.0245584	−3.80	0.000	−.141513	−.0452459
_cons	.0729195	.0078613	9.28	0.000	.0575116	.0883274

Most moderator variables in meta-regression are dichotomous, and dichotomous variables can quickly exhibit high levels of collinearity even with very large sample sizes. This nature of the moderators places a premium on well-specified but parsimonious meta-regression models.

Measurement Error in the Endogenous Variable. Researchers conducting meta-regression also must be aware of the threat posed by *measurement error in the endogenous variable* Θ_i. Recall that Θ_i represents an effect size characterizing a specific theoretical relationship between X and Y or a particular treatment effect in the original studies. While the theoretical constructs motivating X and Y may be very broad (for example, the racial characteristics of a community and potential environmental risk, respectively, in environmental justice research), the actual operationalization and measurement of X and Y are likely to be far narrower in any particular study. One of the virtues of meta-analysis is that by combining effect sizes across studies that operationalize X and Y differently we can get a more robust test of the broader relationship between these constructs. However, if our criteria for identifying relevant studies are imprecise, we may end up including original studies in which the effect sizes measure quite different theoretical properties or quantities of interest. In these cases, Θ_i will be contaminated with nonrandom measurement error with all of the attendant problems for inference (see Berry and Feldman 1985). As with traditional regression, the best defense against this threat is the careful specification of *what* will be measured and *how* it will be measured, and high levels of intercoder reliability in identifying acceptable studies.

Endogeneity. The most serious threat to inference in meta-regression may come from *endogeneity*. The quantity estimated by effect size Θ_i is conditional upon the independent variables used in the original models. Unless, for example, models 1, 2, and 3 employ identical control variables, it is very unlikely that $E[\Theta_1] = E[\Theta_2] = E[\Theta_3]$. The random effects meta-regression model addresses this heterogeneity in two ways; by allowing for a random effects variance component τ^2, and by predicting differences in these conditional expectations using moderator variables that identify whether key control variables are included in the original models.

Given the great variety in model specifications used by researchers, the list of control variables included in any original model is likely to be quite long. It would be inconvenient to include an exhaustive design matrix X of moderator variables that identified which original models included which control variables (if a total of thirty control variables were used across all original models, the meta-regression model would need to include thirty moderator variables in X). Given the collinearity concerns described previously, including this exhaustive list of moderator variables would also be unwise. Of course, any systematic variation in Θ_i that is not captured by the moderator variables in X will be passed through to the meta-regression error term. If the potential moderator variables excluded from the meta-regression model are uncorrelated with moderators included in X, the only consequences of this are losses in efficiency and power. If, however, the potential moderator variables excluded from the meta-regression are correlated with the moderators included in X, the resulting endogeneity may bias the meta-regression parameter estimates and compromise the inferences we might draw from them.

Most readers will quickly recognize that meta-regression is no different on this account than traditional regression. With both techniques researchers must take care to specify a regression model that faithfully represents the underlying theoretical model. In traditional regression this theoretical model accounts for the conditional expectation on Y_i, while in meta-regression this theoretical model accounts for the conditional expectation on the effect size Θ_i. Guarding against excluded variable bias may be somewhat easier in meta-regression than in traditional regression. In traditional regression, many of the excluded independent variables that might affect $E[Y_i]$ are unmeasured or even unknown. In meta-regression, however, these variables are both known (that is, they are the excluded moderator variables identifying the control variables used in the original models) and measurable. In addition, the random effects meta-regression model contains the variance component τ^2 accounting for variation in Θ_i (but not in its conditional expectation) produced by unmeasured factors. The critical task for the meta-analyst, then, is to specify a parsimonious meta-regression model that does not fall prey to endogeneity produced by excluded moderator variables.

Conclusion

Random effects meta-regression is a powerful and underutilized tool in public management and policy research. Meta-regression can help us understand why different studies reach different conclusions, determine whether the effects of management and policy interventions differ across targets and contexts, and identify whether policy-relevant relationships differ across individuals and environments. Given these strengths, some researchers may be tempted to stretch the meaning of meta-regression results too far. For example, the parameters from a meta-regression model simply represent correlations, not causal effects. Therefore, if a meta-regression model finds that environmental inequities are larger in Hispanic communities than in black communities, we cannot say that ethnicity caused this difference. This is true even if the effect sizes used in the meta-regression come from randomized controlled trials. For example, if we find that the benefits of educational vouchers are larger for children in classrooms with experienced teachers, we cannot conclude that teacher experience caused these larger effects. Moreover, meta-regression faces the same threats to inference as does traditional regression, including measurement error, collinearity and micronumerisity, and endogeneity stemming from excluded variable bias. Therefore, proper specification of the meta-regression model—specifying a sample model that faithfully represents the theoretical or population model—is essential if the meta-regression results are to be trustworthy.

CHAPTER FIVE

ADVANCED META-REGRESSION FOR PUBLIC MANAGEMENT AND POLICY

Evan J. Ringquist

"Meta-Analytic techniques developed to date have not addressed the problem of combining information on second-order effects, such as partial regression coefficients. Consequently, meta-analysis has not been very useful in the synthesis of evidence from causal/explanatory research"

(BECKER 1992, 342).

The meta-regression models in chapter 4 (and the techniques for combining effect sizes in chapter 3) assume that the effect sizes are distributed independently. This assumption is generally of little consequence in medicine and psychology, where randomized controlled experiments typically produce a single estimated treatment effect. On those occasions when experiments do generate more than one effect size—for example, experiments with multiple treatment arms, experiments with multiple outcome measures, or block-randomized experiments conducted in several locations—meta-analysts have developed techniques for combining these effect sizes by adjusting for the correlations among them (Hunter and Schmidt 1990; Hedges 2007; Ishak, Platt, Joseph, and Hanley 2007; Gleser and Olkin 2009; Riley 2009).

The assumption that effect sizes are independent poses a much greater challenge for researchers in public management and policy. Best practices for research in the social sciences virtually guarantee that individual original studies will produce more than one relevant effect size. Best practice considerations often motivate researchers to employ multiple measures of the outcome variable and of the focal predictor (Shadish, Cook, and Campbell 2002). Best practice considerations also motivate researchers to conduct sensitivity analyses with respect to model specification (for example, including different control variables) and sampling frames. These best practices help ensure that conclusions from the analysis are robust and not artifacts of particular measurement, specification, or sampling choices. By the same token, these practices create a situation wherein a single study will generate multiple effect sizes defined by the permutations of measurement, specification, and sampling choices. For example, a single study in a meta-analysis of environmental equity research produced 117 effect sizes (Ringquist 2005). In the sample environmental justice data set used here, all but one of the forty-eight studies generates multiple effect sizes. Since these effect sizes are generated by the same researcher using the same data sets, it is unlikely that they are independent.

When faced with multiple correlated effect sizes from original studies, the standard advice for meta-analysts has been to either choose the "one best" effect size from each study (Cooper and Hedges 1994b, Lipsey and Wilson 2001; Stanley 2005) or calculate a single average effect size for each study to be included in a second-stage meta-analysis (Hunter and Schmidt 1994; Lipsey and Wilson 2001). While these tactics will ensure that the effect sizes in the meta-analysis satisfy the independence assumption, the drawbacks of this approach clearly outweigh the benefits.

As an alternative, there are at least four reasons why researchers in the social sciences should include all effect sizes coded from original studies in their meta-analyses. First, this approach is consistent with the original intent of meta-analysis as a method for drawing broad generalizations from varying results across multiple studies. Indeed, Gene Glass recommended that meta-analysts include all effect sizes calculated from original studies, believing that choosing some subset of these effect sizes introduced an unacceptable degree of subjectivity and potential bias (Glass 1978). Second, using a single effect size from each original study tosses away a majority of the information present in these studies, effectively reducing both the efficiency of the statistical estimates from meta-analysis and their power. Third, many moderating variables, especially those identifying design characteristics or control variables used in models, exhibit meaningful within-study variation. Including a single effect size from each original study makes it difficult or impossible to test hypotheses associated with these moderators. Moreover, if moderator variables exhibit variation both within and between studies, the within-study variation provides the best evidence of their effects (Glasziou and Sanders 2002). Finally, there is a long tradition in econometrics of developing estimators that are efficient in the presence of non-independent observations. Rather than throw away the information contained in multiple effect sizes, a better strategy is to use the information contained in these effect sizes while controlling for their dependence.

Using multiple correlated effect sizes from original studies poses three challenges for meta-regression in particular. First, it is useful to think of multiple effect sizes as "clustered" within original studies. Since the effect sizes will likely be correlated within these clusters, they violate the independence of observation assumption that underlies regression analysis.[1] Second, including multiple effect sizes from each study creates the potential for study-level heteroskedasticity in the meta-regression error term. Third, if the distribution of effect sizes is unbalanced across clusters, a small number of studies may contribute a large majority of the effect sizes. The first two challenges pose threats to inference, as both will affect the variance of the meta-regression parameter estimates. The third challenge poses no statistical threat, but does pose a threat to external validity. If a small number of studies dominate the data set, then the meta-regression will describe the results from these studies rather than presenting a (presumably) more balanced story that summarizes all of the studies on a particular topic. The remainder of this chapter offers advice and techniques for meeting all three challenges.

Clustered Robust Estimation in Meta-Regression

Problems of Inference with Clustered Observations

To begin the discussion it will be useful to consider a standard ordinary least squares regression model estimated using clustered data:

$$Y_{ig} = b_0 + b_k X_{kig} + e_{ig} \tag{5.1}$$

where i indexes observations on individual units, g indexes the groups within which these units are clustered, and k indexes independent variables in the model. A common example is to think of students (i)

clustered within classrooms (g). The problem for inference is that by assuming independence across i, the standard OLS estimator exaggerates the unique information contained in each observation. Because units are correlated within groups, some of the information contained in these observations is common to all units in the same group. Believing that we have more information than we do, OLS overstate the certainty (and underestimate the variance) associated with the regression parameter estimates.

The degree to which clustering causes us to over-estimate the information in our data is measured using the intra-class correlation coefficient. To estimate this quantity we begin by decomposing the error term into its two constituent parts, $e_{ig} = u_g + w_{ig}$, where u_g is the error component common to each group and w_{ig} is the residual component unique to each unit.[2] The intra-class correlation coefficient is calculated as

$$\rho_e = \sigma^2 u_g / \left(\sigma^2 u_g + \sigma^2 w_{ig} \right) \tag{5.2}$$

If $\rho_e = 1$, a single unit contains all of the information for all of the units in each group, and the effective sample size for the regression model is G, not N. This is the assumption implicit in the standard advice to use only one effect size when studies contain multiple effect sizes. If $\rho_e = 0$, observations are independent within each group. We can use ρ_e to calculate the observed correlation between observations within a group: $r(e_{ig}e_{jg}) = \rho_e\sigma_e^2$.

Moulton (1990) offers a method whereby we can use the intra-class correlation coefficient to correct the underestimated parameter variances from the OLS regression model. Specifically, the ratio of the OLS parameter variance ($V[b_{ols}]$) to the correct clustered parameter variance ($V[b_c]$) is equal to

$$V\left[b_c\right] / V\left[b_{ols}\right] = 1 + (n - 1)\rho_e \tag{5.3}$$

So $V[b_c] = V[b_{ols}] * [1 + (n-1)\rho_e]$. If $\rho_e = 0$ and observations within units are independent, then the clustered parameter variances and the OLS parameter variances are equal. As ρ_e becomes large and positive, the clustered parameter variances become larger than the OLS parameter variances. Of course if ρ_e is negative, the OLS parameter variances will be smaller, but this seldom happens in practice.

The Problem of Inference in Matrix Form

Clustered Robust Variance Estimation. As an alternative approach to the challenges posed by clustered observations, consider the regression error variance-covariance matrix under clustering:

$$
\mathbf{ee'} =
\begin{matrix}
\sigma_1^2 & \rho_1 & 0 & \cdot & & \cdot & & \cdot & \cdot & & \cdot & & \cdot & & 0 \\
\rho_1 & \sigma_1^2 & \cdot & & & & & & & & & & & & \cdot \\
0 & \cdot & \sigma_2^2 & \rho_2 & \rho_2 & \rho_2 & & & & & & & & & \cdot \\
\cdot & & \rho_2 & \sigma_2^2 & \rho_2 & \rho_2 & & & & & & & & & \cdot \\
\cdot & & \rho_2 & \rho_2 & \sigma_2^2 & \rho_2 & & & & & & & & & \cdot \\
\cdot & & \rho_2 & \rho_2 & \rho_2 & \sigma_2^2 & & & & & & & & & \cdot \\
\cdot & & & & & & \cdot & & & & & & & & \cdot \\
\cdot & & & & & & & \cdot & & & & & & & 0 \\
\cdot & & & & & & & & & & \sigma_g^2 & \rho_g & \rho_g \\
\cdot & & & & & & & & & & \rho_g & \sigma_g^2 & \rho_g \\
0 & \cdot & & \cdot & & \cdot & & \cdot & \cdot & 0 & \rho_g & \rho_g & \sigma_g^2
\end{matrix}
$$

This matrix is block diagonal where $\sigma_1^2 \ldots \sigma_g^2$ represents the group specific error variance and $\rho_1 \ldots \rho_g$ represents the intra-class correlation coefficient for each cluster. This matrix will be familiar to many readers, but I note in passing that the block off-diagonal elements ρ address the first challenge posed by using multiple effect sizes from individual studies in meta-regression (that is, non-independence), while the diagonal elements σ^2 address the second (cluster heteroskedasticity). Because observations are assumed to be correlated within groups but independent across groups, all diagonal elements of the off-diagonal blocks of the matrix are equal to zero. Note that *ee'* with clustered observations is very different from *ee'* in either the fixed effects or random effects meta-regression models from chapter 4. In fact, this matrix does not exist in the meta-analysis literature, though it does exist in the econometrics literature—it is simply the heteroskedasticity-consistent error matrix used by White (1980) and adjusted for clustering. If we collapse this matrix within groups we can use it to obtain the clustered robust parameter variance-covariance matrix (Liang and Zeger 1986; Arellano 1987)

$$
V\left[b_c\right] = \left(X'X\right)^{-1} \left(\Sigma X_g \left(e_g e_g'\right) X_g\right) \left(X'X\right)^{-1} \tag{5.4}
$$

where X_g is a matrix of group averages for independent variables. Clustered robust parameter standard errors are simply the square root of the diagonal elements of this matrix.

Clustered Robust Standard Errors in Meta-Regression. The standard clustered robust variance estimator (CRVE) in equation 5.4 cannot be applied to random effects meta-regression without adaptation. To see why, consider again the clustered error variance-covariance matrix presented earlier (note that to reflect the situation faced in nearly every meta-regression, there are unequal numbers of units in each cluster). This matrix is inconsistent with the assumptions of meta-regression. In particular, ee' in clustered OLS does not incorporate either the fixed effect or the random effect variance component required in meta-regression. A fully specified error variance-covariance matrix for random effects meta-regression using clustered observations would take the following form:

$$
ee' =
\begin{pmatrix}
(\tau^2 + v_{11} & \rho_1 & 0 & \cdot & \cdot & \cdot & \cdots & \cdot & \cdot & 0 \\
\;\;\;+\sigma_1^2) & & & & & & & & & \\
\rho_1 & (\tau^2 + v_{21} & \cdot & & & & & & & \cdot \\
 & \;\;\;+\sigma_1^2) & & & & & & & & \\
0 & \cdot & \sigma_2^2** & \rho_2 & \rho_2 & \rho_2 & & & & \cdot \\
\cdot & & \rho_2 & \sigma_2^2** & \rho_2 & \rho_2 & & & & \cdot \\
\cdot & & \rho_2 & \rho_2 & \sigma_2^2** & \rho_2 & & & & \cdot \\
\cdot & & \rho_2 & \rho_2 & \rho_2 & \sigma_2^2** & & & & \cdot \\
\cdot & & & & & & \cdot & & & \cdot \\
\cdot & & & & & & & \cdot & & \cdot \\
\cdot & & & & & & & & \cdot & 0 \\
\cdot & & & & & & & \sigma_g^2** & \rho_g & \rho_g \\
\cdot & & & & & & & \rho_g & \sigma_g^2** & \rho_g \\
0 & \cdot & \cdot & \cdot & \cdot & \cdot & \cdots 0 & \rho_g & \rho_g & \sigma_g^2**
\end{pmatrix}
$$

where τ^2 is the random effects variance component common across all studies, v_{ig} is the effect-size specific fixed effects variance component, and σ_g^2 and ρ_g are defined as above (σ_g^{2**} is a shorthand designation for the additive error term $(\tau^2 + v_{ig} + \sigma_g^2)$). This error model does not exist in the meta-analysis literature, and the associated meta-regression model cannot be estimated in any meta-analysis software package, including Stata. Moreover, this is not the model that underlies the calculation of CRVE. In the next section I show how to estimate this error model using Stata.

The use of CRVE in meta-regression is uncommon, but not unheard of. Sterne and colleagues (2002) may have been the first to employ this technique in meta-analysis, and other examples are provided by Ringquist (2005) and Bel, Fageda, and Warnerd (2010). The latter study, however, does not estimate a random effects meta-regression model. Rather, it estimates the simpler (and questionable) Meta Regression Analysis (MRA) model common in economics. I evaluate the MRA approach to meta-analysis in detail in chapter 7. While the most comprehensive meta-analysis textbook now also includes a brief treatment of the use of cluster robust standard errors in random effects meta-regression (Raudenbush 2009), other treatments of correlated observations in the meta-analysis literature do not mention this method of addressing the problem (Ishak, Platt, Joseph, and Hanley 2007; Riley 2009). Given its utility for deriving efficient estimates from clustered observations, the use of CRVE deserves to become standard practice in meta-regression for public management and policy.

Random Effects Meta-Regression with Clustered Standard Errors in Stata

None of the specialized meta-analysis statistical software packages can estimate a CRVE random effects meta-regression model, nor can this model be estimated using the *metareg* command in Stata. This limitation is not surprising, since these packages were not designed for the type of data commonly used in management and policy research. We saw in chapter 4, however, that we can estimate a random effects meta-regression model in Stata using manually weighted least squares that produce parameter estimates and statistical inferences identical to those from *metareg* (see figures 4.6 and 4.9). Using this approach we can use τ^2 and v_{ig} to weight the effect sizes and model these transformed effect sizes using the standard regression commands in Stata. We can use the same strategy to prepare our effect sizes for incorporation into a regression model that employs CRVE. We then estimate the random effects meta-regression model with clustered standard errors by simply including the robust (cluster) option when we estimate the manual weighted least squares model in Stata. I re-estimate the environmental equity random effects meta-regression model from chapter 4 using this option and present the results in figure 5.1. This model was estimated using the following Stata command statements:

```
gen constant = 1
gen var= 1/(n-3)
gen totalvar2 = var + .005708
gen resterr1 = sqrt(totalvar)
gen weight1re = (1/totalvar)
gen x0b= 1/resterr1
```

```
gen x1b= superfund/ resterr1
gen x2b= pollution/ resterr1
gen x3b= zipcode/ resterr1
gen x4b= census/ resterr1
gen x5b= limited/ resterr1
gen x6b= controls/ resterr1
gen x7b= selection/ resterr1
gen Ywb = fishersz/ resterr1
reg Ywb x1b x2b x3b x4b x5b x6b x7b x0b, noc vce (cluster
idnumber)
```

The first thing to note when comparing figure 5.1 to figure 4.9 (and figure 4.6) is that the parameter estimates from the meta-regression models are identical. This is because while clustered observations bias parameter variance estimates, the parameters themselves remain consistent. This is true in meta-regression as well as traditional regression. The second item to note is that the parameter standard errors are larger in figure 5.1, as expected. These larger standard errors—coupled with the fact that with the cluster option Stata tests hypotheses using t_{G-1} rather than t_{n-k-1}—mean that moderator variables that had a statistically significant relationship with effect sizes in figure 4.9 are no longer statistically significant in figure 5.1. Specifically, after controlling for correlated observations and group heteroskedasticity, conditional average effect sizes are no longer significantly smaller for studies examining pollution levels (variable x2b)

FIGURE 5.1. MANUAL WLS RANDOM EFFECTS META-REGRESSION IN STATA WITH CLUSTERED ROBUST STANDARD ERRORS

```
. reg Ywb x1b x2b x3b x4b x5b x6b x7b x0b, noc vce (cluster idnumber)
Linear regression
                                              Number of obs =      680
                                              F( 8, 47)     =    11.55
                                              Prob > F      =   0.0000
                                              R-squared     =   0.2558
                                              Root MSE      =   1.1182

                   (Std. Err. adjusted for 48 clusters in idnumber)
```

Ywb	Coef.	Robust Std. Err.	t	P>|t|	[95% Conf. Interval]	
x1b	.0062388	.0157284	0.40	0.693	−.0254026	.0378802
x2b	−.0199238	.0145964	−1.36	0.179	−.049288	.0094404
x3b	−.0076215	.0108089	−0.71	0.484	−.0293661	.0141232
x4b	.0106787	.010212	1.05	0.301	−.0098652	.0312227
x5b	−.0060322	.0338206	−0.18	0.859	−.0740704	.0620061
x6b	−.0364036	.0118211	−3.08	0.003	−.0601846	−.0126226
x7b	−.0776066	.0324537	−2.39	0.021	−.142895	−.0123181
x0b	.0678888	.011047	6.15	0.000	.0456652	.0901124

or significantly larger in studies defining communities using census tracts (variable x4b). Conditional average effect sizes are still smaller in studies that employ a set of key control variables (variable x6b) and in studies that select on the dependent variable (variable x7b). Most important, perhaps, is that the meta-regression constant term (x0b) in figure 5.1 is significantly different from zero, which means that the empirical research contains significant evidence of environmental inequities even after controlling for correlated observations and cluster heteroskedasticity. Prediction and power analyses using results with clustered standard errors proceed in a manner identical to the examples provided in chapter 4. Finally, while results from clustered robust estimation in Stata do not include an analysis of variance table, we can still conduct compound hypothesis tests using the F-statistic and assess model goodness of fit using the adjusted R^2 from this model.

Limitations of Cluster Robust Standard Errors. There are two meaningful limitations associated with cluster robust standard errors, both having to do with their asymptotic properties. White's (1980) original covariance matrix is only consistent, not unbiased, which means that we can have confidence in parameter standard errors from this matrix only in large samples. The asymptotic properties of CRVE occur in G, not N. Therefore, with small numbers of groups or clusters, parameter standard errors and the inferences that we draw using them may be incorrect.

The first limitation relates to the estimated error variance s_e^2. This sample statistic converges to the population variance σ_e^2 only asymptotically in G. In data sets with a small number of clusters, s_e^2 will underestimate σ_e^2. Several small sample adjustments to the sample variance have been proposed, both in the economics literature (Mancl and DeRouen 2001; Bell and McCaffrey 2002; Stock and Watson 2008) and in the meta-analysis literature (Fay, Graubard, Freedman, and Midthune 1998; Fay and Graubard 2001). The Stata statistical software package uses the small sample correction $\sqrt{(G/(G-1)/((N-1)/(N-k))} * e_g$, where the first term is roughly equal to $\sqrt{(G/(G-1))}$.

The second limitation relates to the assumption that under Ho: $b_j = 0$, the ratio $b_j / s_{b_j} \sim N(0, 1)$, and therefore that Wald tests for Ho will be distributed as a Z-score. While this is true asymptotically, with small numbers of clusters this assumption does not hold, and hypothesis tests using Z-scores will return inflated type I errors (Cameron, Gelbach, and Miller 2008). Two corrections for this problem have been proposed. The first uses a different theoretical probability distribution to test Ho: $b_j = 0$, such as the t or the F distribution (see Pan and Wall 2002 for an example of this approach in meta-analysis). In application, when the cluster robust option is chosen in Stata, hypothesis tests on b_j are conducted using t_{G-1} rather than Z. The second correction builds an empirical distribution to test Ho: $b_j = 0$ using the bootstrap. I address this approach in the next section.

The Wild Cluster Bootstrap

Returning for the moment to the traditional regression framework, even with the adjustments described above, with small numbers of groups, hypothesis tests on b_j using CRVE routinely over-reject the null hypothesis. Cameron, Gelbach, and Miller (2008) report Monte Carlo results showing that in the best case scenario of homoskedasticity and observations equally balanced across groups, when $G = 5$ the type I error rate for clustered robust standard errors is .20, four times the nominal level of $\alpha = .05$. Where $G = 10$ the type I error rate falls to .13, and where $G = 30$ the type I error rate $= .07$, 40 percent above its expected level. Introducing cluster-specific heteroskedasticity and clusters of unequal size further degrades the performance of clustered robust standard errors: where $G = 10$, $\alpha = .18$. Cameron, Gelbach, and Miller (2008) offer an approach to inference using clustered observations that is based on the "wild cluster bootstrap" (WCB). The WCB outperforms standard CRVE in all scenarios, producing type I errors at the desired rate of $\alpha = .05$ with as few as five groups.

The Basics of Bootstrapping. Those unfamiliar with bootstrapping will find an excellent introduction in Mooney and Duval (1993), while Field and Welsh (2007) offer a more technical treatment of bootstrapping clustered data. Traditional hypothesis testing relies on theoretical probability distributions (for example, the regression parameter estimate b_j is assumed to be distributed normally), but the assumptions justifying reliance upon these distributions may not always hold in practice. By contrast, bootstrapping conducts hypothesis tests by building empirical probability distributions for statistics of interest (for example, b_j, t, μ) and drawing inferences from these distributions. Empirical probability distributions are generated by drawing a "pseudo-sample" or resample of size n with replacement from the parent data set N, calculating the test statistic of interest, and repeating the process R times.

For example, consider the problem of estimating the population mean μ from a sample of 500 observations. Relying on the central limit theorem we would estimate μ using the sample mean $\overline{X}$ and assume that $\overline{X}$ was distributed normally with a standard deviation of $\overline{X}/\sqrt{n}$. By contrast, to bootstrap this sample mean we would draw a sample of (for example) $n = 250$ observations with replacement from our sample of 500 and calculate the sample mean $\overline{X}_1$. We would then draw a second sample of 250 with replacement and calculate a second sample mean $\overline{X}_2$. We would do this R times. The mean of the R resampled means $\overline{X}_r$ would be our estimate of μ, and the standard deviation of the vector of sample means $\overline{X}_r$ would be the estimate of the standard error of the distribution of sample means. Most commonly $n = N$ in bootstrapping (in other words, the size of the resample is equal to the original sample size). Generally, $R = 1,000$ is sufficient for most statistics (Mooney and Duval 1993). Researchers have at least four important decisions to make when conducting a bootstrap: (1) what to bootstrap, (2) which statistics to calculate, (3) whether to seek asymptotic refinement, and (4) whether to impose the null hypothesis.

What to Bootstrap. In regression analysis, researchers can resample observations (called a "pairs" bootstrap by Cameron, Gelbach, and Miller [2008]) or resample residuals. When resampling observations, researchers draw R pseudo-samples of size n from the joint distribution of Y and X and estimate R regression models, one from each pseudo-sample. When resampling residuals, researchers estimate a single regression equation using the parent sample N, then draw R pseudo-samples from the error vector e. The proper approach is context specific, though Mooney and Duval (1993) favor resampling observations as the default choice.

Which Statistics to Calculate. Bootstrapping may be used to calculate any statistic of interest. In regression, the choices are generally restricted to calculating the regression parameter b_j, its standard error s_{bj}, or t, the test statistic associated with Ho: $b_j = 0$. The choices of what to bootstrap and which statistics to calculate are not independent. If you want to bootstrap the regression parameter b_j you must resample observations, not residuals. Which statistics are calculated will determine how hypothesis tests are conducted. For example, to test Ho: $b_j \leq 0$, one could calculate a thousand estimates of b_j from a thousand pseudo-samples, then use the mean of this empirical distribution as the estimate of the population parameter β_j and its standard error to estimate s_{bj}. The ratio (mean b_j)$/s_{bj}$ is then used to test the null hypothesis. Cameron, Gelbach, and Miller (2008) call this the "bootstrap-*se*." Alternatively, one could calculate b_j from a regression model using the parent sample N, resample the residuals R times, add these resampled residuals to the expectation $\boldsymbol{Xb}$ to generate Y^* and calculate R values of t_{bj}^* for each Y^*. This empirical distribution of t_{bj}^* is used to draw inferences about the test statistic t_{bj} from the original regression model. Cameron, Gelbach, and Miller call this the "bootstrap-t," while Mooney and Duval (1993) call it the "percentile-t."

Whether to Seek Asymptotic Refinement. Asymptotic refinement essentially means choosing a bootstrapping approach in which the outcomes of the hypothesis test converge to α (the desired type I error rate) more quickly as a function of N than do hypothesis tests employing the relevant theoretical probability distribution. According to Cameron, Gelbach, and Miller (2008), bootstrap-t's produce asymptotic refinement while bootstrap-se's do not. Therefore the WCB calculates t from the pseudo-samples, not b_j or s_{bj}.

Whether to Impose the Null Hypothesis. When bootstrapping a regression model, imposing the null hypothesis means that in order to test Ho: $b_j = 0$, you resample residuals from a model that imposes the restriction that $b_j = 0$. To illustrate, assume that we have the unrestricted regression model $Y_{ig} = b_0 + b_1 X_{1ig} + b_2 X_{2ig} + e_{ig}$ and we would like to use the bootstrap to test Ho: $b_1 = 0$. We would first estimate the restricted model $Y_{ig} = b_0 + b_2 X_{2ig} + e_{ig}$ (that is, a model that imposes the null hypothesis). Next we would resample the residuals from this restricted model and add them to the restricted prediction $\boldsymbol{Xb} + e_{ig}^*$ to generate the pseudo-dependent variable Y_{ig}^*. Finally, we would estimate the unrestricted model R times using R pseudo-variables Y_{ig}^*. Following the advice of Davidson and MacKinnon (1999), the WCB of Cameron, Gelbach, and Miller (2008) imposes the null hypothesis.

Implementing the Wild Cluster Bootstrap in Random Effects Meta-Regression.

The wild cluster bootstrap is not an option in any statistical software package, and to the best of my knowledge it has not been adapted for use in meta-regression nor been used to estimate a meta-regression model. The technique is not difficult to program, however, and can easily be adapted for random effects meta-regression. Stata code for using the WCB to estimate the random effects meta-regression model is provided on the companion website. Implementing the WCB in random effects meta-regression consists of eight steps. For the purposes of this illustration, assume the random effects meta-regression model with covariates $\Theta_{ig} = b_0 + b_1 X_{1ig} + b_2 X_{2ig} + e_{ig}, e_{ig} \sim (0, v_{ig} + \tau^2)$.

1. Estimate the random effects meta-regression model using the Stata *metareg* command to obtain a restricted maximum likelihood estimate of τ^2.

2. Weight each observation in Θ and X, including the intercept, by the inverse of the total variance of the effect size $(\tau^2 + v_{ig})$. For Fisher's Z, this weight is $1/\sqrt{((n-3) * \tau^2)}$. Save the weighted observations as $\Theta*$ and $X*$.

3. Use OLS with CRVE to estimate the unrestricted regression model $\Theta^*_{ig} = b_0 + b_1 X^*_{1ig} + b_2 X^*_{2ig} + e^*_{ig}$.
   A. Save t_0, the t-score testing Ho: $b_0 = 0$.

4. Use OLS with CRVE to estimate the restricted regression model $\Theta^*_{ig} = b_1^r X^*_{1ig} + b_2^r X^*_{2ig} + e^r_{ig}$ (that is, impose the null hypothesis $b_0 = 0$).
   A. Save e^r_{ig}.
   B. Save the restricted prediction $X*b^r$.

5. For each cluster g, create $e^{r*}_{ig} = \left(e^r_{ig} * 1 \right)$ with probability .5 and $e^{r*}_{ig} = \left(e^r_{ig} * -1 \right)$ with probability .5 (this is the "wild" element of the WCB). It is critical that the assignment of $(1, -1)$ be at the cluster level. Generate $\Theta^{**}_{ig} = X* * b^r + e^{r*}_{ig}$; that is, add the wild cluster residual to the prediction from the restricted model to generate the pseudo-variable Θ^{**}_{ig}.

6. Draw a random sample of G clusters with replacement from the joint distribution of Θ^{**}_{ig} and $X*$. Use OLS with CRVE to estimate the unrestricted regression model $\Theta^{**}_{ig} = b_0 + b_1 X^*_{1ig} + b_2 X^*_{2ig} + e^{**}_{ig}$.
   A. Save t_0^*, the t-score testing Ho: $b_0 = 0$.

7. Repeat steps 5 and 6 R times ($R \geq 500$) and build an empirical distribution for t_0^*. The p-value associated with incorrectly rejecting Ho: $b_0 = 0$ is the percentage of values of $t_0^* \geq |t_0|$. That is, you compare the t-score from the original unrestricted random effects meta-regression using CRVE (step 3) with the empirical distribution of t-scores produced by the WCB. For the one-tailed hypothesis Ho: $b_0 \leq 0$, the relevant p-value is the percentage of values of $t_0^* > t_0$.

8. Repeat steps 4 through 7 for each meta-regression parameter of interest.

The wild cluster bootstrap should prove to be a powerful tool for estimating random effects meta-regression models with clustered effect sizes. But as with any tool, it should not be used in a rote manner. First, the WCB is only intended for data sets with effect sizes from a small number of studies. With a large number of studies, say $G \geq 30$, the CRVE standard errors perform quite well. In this vein, it is worth remembering that the WCB only corrects for excessive type I errors associated with CRVE in small samples. CRVE controls both for non-independence of observations and for cluster-specific heteroskedasticity whether or not the WCB is used. Second, if some moderator variables differ across only a few studies—that is, if only a small number of studies display a particular design characteristic—parameters on these variables may be estimated imprecisely, or not at all, when using the WCB. This is because a large percentage of resamples may select no study (that is, group) providing variation on these moderators.

Implementing the Wild Cluster Bootstrap in Stata. To illustrate the use of the wild cluster bootstrap in Stata I return to the random effects meta-regression model for environmental justice research. Strictly speaking, the environmental equity database is not a good candidate for estimation with the WCB, since it contains effect sizes from a relatively large number of studies ($G = 48$). In cases like this, CRVE standard errors are more appropriate. Therefore, for the purposes of this illustration I drew a sample of nineteen studies from the original forty-eight and re-estimated a more limited version of the environmental justice random effects meta-regression model

$$\Theta_{ig} = b_0 + b_2 X_{2ig} + b_4 X_{4ig} + b_6 X_{6ig} + e_{ig}, e \sim \left(0, v_{ig} + \tau^2\right) \quad (5.5)$$

where X_2, X_4, and X_6 are defined as in chapter 4 (in other words, X_2 identifies effect sizes from models examining pollution levels, X_4 identifies effect sizes from models defining communities using census tracts, and X_6 identifies effect sizes from models that include a full complement of key control variables). I chose these three independent variables for this illustration because they each generated statistically significant parameters in the original random effects meta-regression model (see figure 4.9). While simple to implement, the WCB is somewhat tedious in that hypothesis tests for each regression parameter of interest must be bootstrapped independently. Moreover, because the WCB guards against incorrectly rejecting a true null hypothesis, it makes little sense to use this technique to re-estimate hypothesis tests on parameters that are not statistically significant in the original random effects meta-regression model.

The results from this more limited model using CRVE standard errors are presented in figure 5.2. We can see from this figure that using $\alpha = .05$ we can reject the null hypothesis that $b_0 = 0$ and $b_6 = 0$, whereas using $\alpha \approx .10$ we can reject the null hypothesis that $b_2 = 0$.

The results from the wild cluster bootstrap estimation ($R = 1,000$) are provided in table 5.1.

The WCB leaves CRVE meta-regression parameters and their t-scores unchanged. All that changes is the probability distribution for assessing whether these t-scores are unusual enough to allow the researcher to reject the null hypothesis with confidence α. The fourth column in table 5.1

FIGURE 5.2. RESTRICTED MANUAL WLS RANDOM EFFECTS META-REGRESSION IN STATA WITH CLUSTERED ROBUST STANDARD ERRORS

```
. reg Ywb x2b x4b x6b x0b, noc vce (cluster idnumber)
Linear regression                          Number of obs =     398
                                           F( 4, 18)     =   13.37
                                           Prob > F      =  0.0000
                                           R-squared     =  0.2215
                                           Root MSE      =  1.1649

                    (Std. Err. adjusted for 19 clusters in idnumber)
```

Ywb	Coef.	Robust Std. Err.	t	P>|t|	[95% Conf. Interval]	
x2b	−.0315042	.0183577	−1.72	0.103	−.0700723	.0070639
x4b	.0062989	.0061101	1.03	0.316	−.0065379	.0191358
x6b	−.0356105	.013345	−2.67	0.016	−.0636472	−.0075737
x0b	.0642313	.013158	4.88	0.000	.0365874	.0918751

TABLE 5.1. RESULTS FROM HYPOTHESIS TESTS IN RANDOM EFFECTS META-REGRESSION MODELS USING CLUSTERED ROBUST STANDARD ERRORS AND THE WILD CLUSTER BOOTSTRAP

Predictor	Parameter Value	t-Score	p-Value CRVE[a]	p-Value WCB[b]
Constant (x0b)	0.0642	4.88	.000	≈.01
Pollution Level (x2b)	−0.0315	−1.72	.103	≈.30
Census Tracts (x4b)	.0063	1.03	.316	≈.65
Use of Control Variables (x6b)	−0.0356	−2.67	.016	≈.15

Notes: [a] p-values from standard clustered robust standard errors.

[b] p-values from clustered robust standard errors using wild cluster bootstrap.

reports the p-value associated with this t-score when using CRVE. The null hypotheses that $b_0 = 0$ and $b_6 = 0$ can be easily rejected at $\alpha = .05$ (note that these p-values are the same as those in figure 5.2). The fifth column in table 5.1 reports the p-values associated with the t-scores using the wild cluster bootstrap. While we are still able to reject the null hypothesis that the constant term is equal to zero at $\alpha = .01$, we are no longer able to reject the null hypothesis that the other parameters are equal to zero at any standard confidence level. That is, using the wild cluster bootstrap, we would conclude that average effect sizes are no different in models that examine pollution levels, and no different in models that include a full complement of key control variables.

Multi-Level Clustering in Meta-Regression

Thus far the discussion of CRVE implicitly assumes that effect sizes are clustered on only one dimension; that is, effect sizes clustered within studies. In many applications common in the social sciences, however, researchers may work with data that are clustered on multiple dimensions. Threats to inference posed by clustered observations are magnified in the presence of multi-way clustering (Pepper 2002; Wooldridge 2003). In this section, I consider the relevance for meta-regression of recent developments in estimating models with multi-way clustering.

Multi-way clustered data structures are commonly nested, as when students are clustered within classrooms and classrooms are clustered within schools. In this situation, researchers are advised to cluster on the highest level of aggregation (Cameron, Gelbach, and Miller 2011) or to use the hierarchical linear modeling approach discussed in the next section (Raudenbush and Bryk 2002). Just as commonly, however, multi-way clusters will not be nested. In economic development studies, investment may be clustered by industry and by region. In public management research, workers may be clustered by civil service grade and by government agency. More generally, in panel data observations are clustered spatially (for example, individuals, states, or countries) and within time periods. Efficient estimation in the presence of non-nested multi-way clustering is less straightforward. The standard approach has been to estimate multi-way error components models, but these impose a set of restrictive assumptions, including conditional homoskedasticity and the equal correlation of observations across all clusters.

Recently, Cameron, Gelbach, and Miller (2011) introduced a less restrictive robust approach to controlling for multi-way clustering (see also

Acemoglu and Pischke 2003; Petersen 2009). To illustrate their approach, consider the standard multiple regression model $Y_{igc} = \Sigma b_k X_{igck} + e_{igc}$ where i indexes individuals ($i = 1$ through N) and these individuals are clustered in dimension g ($g = 1$ through G) and clustered in separate dimension c ($c = 1$ through C) (k indexes independent variables in X). Cameron, Gelbach, and Miller propose estimating three separate CRVE models—one for dimension G, one for dimension C, and one for the intersection GC. If we call the parameter variance-covariance matrix for b_k in the first model V_G, the second V_C, and the third V_{GC}, then the two-way clustered robust parameter variance-covariance matrix is $V_M = V_G + V_C - V_{GC}$. The standard errors for the elements of b_k are simply the square roots of the diagonal elements in V_M. In addition to being intuitive, this approach to robust inference with multi-way clustering is easily implemented in any standard statistical software package that estimates CRVE, including Stata.

Virtually any data set is a potential candidate for multi-way clustering. In meta-regression, effect sizes might be viewed as being clustered by study and by author or research team, particularly if these teams produce several studies that address similar relevant research questions. Alternatively, effect sizes might be seen as being clustered by study and by the academic discipline of the authors. Multi-way clustering probably has little applicability in meta-regression. In the examples offered here, while effect sizes may be clustered on more than one dimension, this cluster structure is nested rather than non-nested. Second, for authors, research teams, or disciplines producing a single study, observations in the two clustering dimensions will be identical. Furthermore, the estimates from the multi-way clustering approach are consistent only in the dimension with the fewest number of units. If there are few clusters in one of the dimensions, multi-way clustering is not advised. While meta-regression will typically be a poor candidate for multi-way clustering, this approach may be valuable in specialized circumstances.

Alternatives for Addressing Dependence in Meta-Regression

Clustered robust variance estimation is only one method of controlling for non-independence of observations in meta-regression. At least two other methods—hierarchical linear models (HLM) and generalized estimating equations (GEE) are common in the social sciences, and each has been used to estimate the random effects meta-regression model. In addition, the "delta-splitting" method of Stevens and Taylor (2009) has been developed specifically to address non-independence within the meta-regression framework. In this section I address each of these alternatives and provide an explicit assessment of their applicability to meta-regression.

Hierarchical Linear Models

Management and policy scholars often answer questions using "nested" data. For example, when studying the effect of school reforms, researchers may have performance data for students nested within classrooms. Similarly, public management scholars may have performance data for civil servants nested within government agencies. These data are generally considered to have a hierarchical structure, with students and civil servants at the lowest level of the hierarchy.

Hierarchical (or multilevel) data pose two important challenges. First, they pose a challenge to the causal structure implicit in traditional regression models. Traditional regression models produce a single parameter estimate characterizing the relationship between X and Y for all observations in the data set. Multilevel data, however, allow the researcher to relax this assumption and consider causal heterogeneity across higher-level units. Continuing with the earlier example, the effect of organizational leadership on the performance of civil servants may vary across government agencies. If this type of causal heterogeneity exists, maintaining the traditional regression assumption of a homogeneous relationship between X and Y across all units creates serious specification error and the attendant biases. Second, subjects nested within higher-level groups (for example, students within the same classroom) are exposed to common unmeasured factors that often produce correlations among observations for members of the same group. Ignoring this non-independence within groups leads to the same problems of inference associated with clustered observations (Moulton 1990). Hierarchical linear models (HLM) are the most common approach for estimating models with multilevel data (Raudenbush and Bryk 2002).[3] A key strength of HLM is that they can accommodate both causal heterogeneity and non-independence of observations (Steenbergen and Jones 2002).

To fix ideas, consider a situation in which we are interested in the academic performance of elementary school students (denoted Y), and we believe that this performance is influenced by the quality of the teacher (denoted W), and by whether or not a student has received an educational voucher (denoted X). Furthermore, assume that we have observations on students (level 1 units denoted i where $i = 1$ though N) nested within classrooms (level 2 units denoted j where $j = 1$ through J). A standard regression equation would take the form

$$Y_{ij} = b_0 + b_1 X_{ij} + b_2 W_j + e_{ij} \tag{5.6}$$

Because OLS regression ignores the dependence of observations between students in the same classrooms, estimation of equation 5.6 would produce invalid inferences. And, because OLS regression assumes parameter constancy, estimating equation 5.6 does not allow us to determine whether the effect of teacher quality or educational vouchers varies across classrooms. Moreover, this model does not allow us to assess whether the effect of vouchers is conditional upon teacher quality.[4]

In contrast to the OLS regression model, the comparable hierarchical linear model is structured as

$$\text{Level 1 Model:} \qquad Y_{ij} = b_{0j} + b_1 X_{ij} + e_{ij} \tag{5.7}$$

$$\text{Level 2 Model:} \qquad b_{0j} = \alpha_{00} + \alpha_{01} W_j + u_{0j} \tag{5.8}$$
$$b_{1j} = \alpha_{10} + \alpha_{11} W_j + u_{1j}$$

$$\text{Combined Model:} \qquad Y_{it} = \alpha_{00} + \alpha_{01} W_j + \alpha_{10} X_{ij} + \alpha_{11} W_j X_{ij} + u_{0j}$$
$$+ u_{1j} X_{ij} + e_{ij} \tag{5.9}$$

where

α_{00} is the grand (conditional) mean of educational achievement (Y_{ij}).

u_{0j} is the classroom-specific component of Y_{ij}.

α_{01} is the average effect of teacher quality on Y_{ij}.

α_{10} is the average effect of vouchers on Y_{ij}.

α_{11} is the differential effect of vouchers on Y_{it} conditional upon teacher quality.

u_{1j} is the classroom-specific effect of vouchers on Y_{it}.

e_{ij} is the idiosyncratic error term specific to each student.

The HLM method is generally estimated using restricted maximum likelihood. The statistical software package HLM is designed specifically to estimate hierarchical linear models (and the many variants of models that are nested within equation 5.9). In addition, most general statistical software packages can estimate HLM, including the PROC MIXED command in SAS and the *xtmixed* command in Stata.

HLM in Meta-Regression. Raudenbush and Bryk (1985) were the first to recognize that a random effects meta-regression model could be estimated within the HLM framework. Therefore, the HLM approach to the REMR model actually predates the more standard approach to estimating REMR. From the perspective of HLM, data in meta-regression can be viewed as having a natural hierarchical structure in that research subjects are nested within original studies. An HLM approach to meta-regression faces four challenges:

1. Because meta-analysis makes use of model results from original studies, the meta-analyst does not have data on level 1 subjects.
2. Because observations on the dependent variable in meta-regression (that is, effect sizes) come from different studies, outcomes are measured differently across level 2 units.
3. Because original studies employ different research designs or model specifications, observations on the dependent variable in meta-regression estimate different quantities.
4. In meta-regression, the study-specific variance component is assumed known, while in traditional HLM this variance component is estimated.

Using HLM, challenge 1 is met by fitting a level 1 model without covariates (see below). Challenge 2 is met using standard tools of meta-analysis; that is, by transforming results from original studies into commonly recognized effect sizes. Challenges 3 and 4 are met using standard tools of meta-regression; that is, by including study-level covariates in HLM meta-regression and by estimating these models using variance-weighted least squares. Meeting these four challenges produces the following two-level hierarchical linear meta-regression model:

$$\text{Level 1 Model:} \quad \Theta_j = b_{0j} + v_j \tag{5.10}$$

$$\text{Level 2 Model:} \quad b_{0j} = \alpha_0 + \alpha_1 W_{1j} + \alpha_2 W_{2j} + \ldots + u_j \tag{5.11}$$

$$\text{Combined Model:} \quad \Theta_j = \alpha_0 + \Sigma \alpha_k W_{kj} + u_j + v_j \tag{5.12}$$

where

Θ_j is the meta-analysis effect size from original study j.

α_0 is the grand (conditional) mean effect size (Θ_j).

u_j is the study-specific component of Θ_j.

α_k is the average effect of study-level moderator variables on Θ_j.

v_j is the fixed effects error component specific to each effect size.

If we consider ε_j as the composite random effects error $\varepsilon_j = u_j + v_j$, then $\varepsilon_j \sim N(0, \tau^2 + v_j)$. The HLM random effects meta-regression model then becomes the familiar REMR model from chapter 4. In fact, the HLM meta-regression model is often estimated in the same manner as the REMR model: τ^2 is estimated using restricted maximum likelihood, and the vector α_k and its variance are estimated using weighted least squares (Raudenbush and Bryk 2002, chapter 7).

An additional benefit of HLM is that the results from the combined models allow the researcher to calculate a "shrunken" estimate of Θ_j that Raudenbush and Bryk (2002) compare to the best empirical estimate of the population effect size estimated by study j. Specifically, the Empirical Bayes estimate of each population effect size Θ_j^* can be estimated as

$$\Theta_j^* = \lambda_j \Theta_j + \left(1 - \lambda_j\right)\left(\alpha_0 + \Sigma \alpha_k W_{kj}\right) \qquad (5.13)$$

where $\lambda_j = \tau^2 / (\tau^2 + v_j)$. A close look at the formula for lambda shows that the Empirical Bayes estimator "shrinks" effect sizes with large sampling variances v_j. In this way, the shrinkage factor acts much like the weights attached to individual effect sizes when calculating average effect sizes in traditional meta-analysis (see chapter 3).

HLM Meta-Regression and Non-Independence of Observations. While standard two-level hierarchical linear models control for the non-independence of observations when applied to individual level data in original studies, two-level HLM meta-regression does not. When using HLM meta-regression we do not have observations on level 1 subjects, only summary statistics. We see this when comparing equation 5.10 (the level 1 model for HLM meta-regression) to equation 5.7 (the level 1 equation for a traditional HLM). Θ in equation 5.10 has only one subscript, j, whereas in the traditional level 1 HLM equation Y has subscripts i and j. Stated plainly, two-level HLM meta-regression contains no level 1 observations that might be correlated. In fact, *a central assumption of HLM meta-regression is that the effect sizes* Θ_j *represent independent observations* (Raudenbush and Bryk 2002; Raudenbush 2009). This is another way in which HLM meta-regression is identical to the REMR model presented in chapter 4.

Extensions of HLM Meta-Regression. The HLM method has been adapted for one situation in which single original studies produce multiple effect sizes—multiple outcome studies. If each original study reports multiple and identical outcomes (for example, each original study reports the effects of vouchers for math and reading scores), then the meta-analyst can estimate a multivariate (in the sense of multiple dependent variables) HLM meta-regression. More typically, original studies report multiple outcomes, but reported outcomes are not identical across studies. HLM meta-regression treats this as a situation of incomplete multivariate data (Kalaian and Raudenbush 1996) and parameterizes the average effect size for different outcome measures using dummy variables in the level 1 model (see also Li and Begg 1994). An example might help illustrate this procedure. Consider a situation in which you have ten original studies that estimate the effect of a particular intervention on a total of four outcome indicators, Y_1, Y_2, Y_3, and Y_4. Studies one through five estimate the effect of the intervention on Y_1, Y_2, and Y_4, while studies six through ten estimate the effect of the intervention on Y_1 and Y_3. These ten studies will produce twenty-five effect sizes Θ_{js} where j indexes the outcome measure and s indexes the study. An incomplete multivariate hierarchical linear model would estimate the following level 1 model:

$$\text{Level 1:} \qquad \boldsymbol{\Theta}_{js} = \boldsymbol{\gamma}_{js}\boldsymbol{X}_{js} + v_{js} \qquad\qquad (5.14)$$

where X is a 10×4 design matrix identifying which studies estimate which outcome measures, and γ is a 1×4 parameter vector estimating the average effect size for each outcome measure. In this example, the elements of X for study one would be [1 1 0 1] and the elements of X for study six would be [1 0 1 0]. Notably, the error v_{js} is assumed to have a known variance *and a known covariance* (formulas for calculating these covariances for different effect sizes are found in Hedges and Olkin 1985).

HLM meta-regression has been advanced in other ways by researchers in statistics. For example, both Silliman (1997) and Lee and Nelder (2006) extend the general HLM method in a manner that controls for non-specific heteroskedasticity across effect sizes.[5] Silliman goes even further, integrating both weighting and data augmentation schemes for remedying publication bias using HLM meta-regression (Chapter 6 addresses the issue of publication bias in meta-analysis). Finally, Goldstein and colleagues (2000) move beyond the standard two-level hierarchical linear model to a three-level hierarchical linear model for meta-regression. Further discussion of these advanced HLM techniques is beyond the scope of this book.

Examples of HLM Meta-Regression in Practice. The most comprehensive textbook in meta-analysis introduces the random effects meta-regression model using the HLM framework (Raudenbush 2009), and currently HLM may be the most popular method of estimating the REMR model. Examples of the HLM framework in practice can be found in the fields of medicine and public health (Gmel, Gutjahr, and Rehm 2003; Tengs and Lin 2003), education (Bowman 2010a, 2010b; Raudenbush and Bryk 1986; Swanborn and de Glopper 1999; Swanson and Jerman 2006), clinical psychology (Lissek et al. 2005), social work (Kim 2008), and organizational behavior (LePine, Erez, and Johnson 2002).

The majority of researchers follow the advice of Raudenbush and Bryk (2002) and include only a single effect size from each study at level 1, thereby guaranteeing that observations used to estimate the regression model will be independent. When data sets include multiple effect sizes from individual studies, researchers have used one of five methods to address this dependence within the HLM framework. First, a few scholars do not recognize the dependence among their effect sizes and make no effort to control for it (for example, Swanborn and de Glopper 1999). Second, many researchers follow the standard meta-regression advice offered by Hunter and Schmidt (1990) and Lipsey and Wilson (2001), calculating a single average effect size from each study, or choosing one effect size per study at random (for example, LePine, Erez, and Johnson 2002; Kim 2008). Third, for other researchers multiple effect sizes represent different outcome measures derived from relatively independent samples. In these cases, the observations are treated as independent at level 1 (for example, Frost, Clarke, and Beacon 1999; Gmel, Gutjahr, and Rehm 2003). Fourth, still other researchers treat effect sizes measuring multiple outcomes using the incomplete multivariate data approach described above (Bowman 2010a, 2010b). Finally, a large number of researchers recognize the dependence among effect sizes and explicitly rely upon the level 1 variance component estimate in HLM to control for this correlation (for example, Bateman and Jones 2003; Tengs and Lin 2003; Swanson and Jerman 2006).

Choosing Between HLM and CRVE in Meta-Regression. Hierarchical linear models and clustered robust estimation are often considered alternative methods of addressing the problem of non-independent observations in traditional social science research. Good standard practice in applied statistics is to choose among alternative estimators on the basis of theory and the structure of your data. That said, the most recent advice from political science is that there are good reasons to prefer CRVE to HLM if the goal is simply to control for non-independence (Primo, Jacobsmeier, and Milyo 2007). First, CRVE requires fewer assumptions than HLM. For example, the HLM method assumes that the components of level 1 and level 2 variances are properly specified. If this assumption is not met in practice, the resulting maximum likelihood estimates of α will be biased. By contrast, parameter estimates remain unchanged (and unbiased) when using CRVE. Second, the HLM method does not perform well with small numbers of clusters. While the same is true for CRVE, there are remedies for small numbers of clusters in CRVE that are unavailable when using HLM. Third, the HLM approach often experiences convergence problems, especially when there are large numbers of observations and when the model contains large numbers of cross-level interactions (Steenbergen and Jones 2002).

The HLM approach to meta-regression is far more common than CRVE, and the HLM meta-regression model is easier to estimate with standard statistical software packages. Despite the popularity of the HLM approach, there are good reasons to prefer clustered robust estimation to HLM for meta-regression in public management and policy, but these reasons are mostly different from those offered by Steenbergen and Jones (2002) and Primo, Jacobsmeier, and Milyo (2007) in the case of analyses using original data.

HLM Is an Untested and Less Robust Method of Controlling for Non-Independence. As developed by its originators, the HLM approach to estimating the random effects meta-regression model assumes that effect sizes are independent. While researchers routinely ignore this quality and use the level 1 variance component in HLM to address non-independence, I am aware of no formal assessment of this approach in the statistics literature. Even if this evidence were available, there are at least two reasons for concern when using HLM to control for correlated effect sizes in meta-regression. First, the HLM approach assumes that level 1 variances are conditionally homoskedastic—that is, the level 1 predictors completely account for differences across studies in the variability of effect sizes within studies. This assumption may be plausible when level 1 observations are, for example, students clustered within schools, but it is less plausible when level 1 observations are effect sizes from multivariate models with varying specifications. By contrast, CRVE allows for non-specific study-level heteroskedasticity. Second, the HLM method assumes a common correlation among all nested observations, rather than allowing the degree of correlation among observations to vary between studies. CRVE allows the correlation among observations to vary between studies.

HLM Meta-Regression Has No Advantage for Modeling Causal Heterogeneity. A great strength of HLM is that they allow the researcher to model causal heterogeneity of level 1 covariates across level 2 units. While this strength has undeniable advantages when compared to the traditional regression model, it does not apply to the meta-regression model.[6] A key difference between traditional regression and meta-regression is that the former attempts to predict the conditional expectation of the univariate random variable Y while the second attempts to predict the conditional expectation of the bivariate relationship represented by Θ. Because of this, hypothesis tests for moderator variables in meta-regression are akin to tests of interaction effects in traditional regression (see chapter 4). Consider equation 5.9, where the parameter α_{11} provides an estimate of the differential effect of vouchers on student performance conditional upon teacher quality. This type of cross-level interaction effect is what gives HLM the ability to account for causal heterogeneity. In the HLM meta-regression equation 5.12, Θ_j represents the effect of vouchers on student academic achievement in each original study. If we assume that the variable W_1 in equation 5.11 (and equation 5.12) identifies whether original studies include teacher quality as a control variable, then the parameter α_1 in equation 5.11 (and equation 5.12) tests whether the effect of vouchers differs conditional upon teacher quality. That is, parameters for moderator variables in meta-regression account for the same sort of causal heterogeneity as do cross-level effects in HLM. Since the HLM approach is identical to the standard random effects meta-regression model regarding its ability to model causal heterogeneity, there is no reason to prefer HLM to REMR estimated with CRVE.

Incomplete Multivariate Data Are Uncommon in Management and Policy Research. While promising for some applications, the incomplete multivariate HLM framework of Kalaian and Raudenbush (1996) is of little use for public management and policy research. First, this model assumes that each study produces a single effect size estimate for multiple outcome measures, whereas original studies in public management and policy often produce multiple effect size estimates for a single outcome measure. Second, incomplete multivariate hierarchical linear models assume that the correlation among effect sizes is solely a function of the correlation among the outcome measures, whereas in public management and policy research, this correlation stems from modeling choices in the original studies. In the latter case, the assumption that the covariance among effect sizes is known is untenable. Instead, we need to estimate this covariance. Clustered robust estimation does this, while incomplete multivariate HLM do not.

HLM Estimates Conditional Models While CRVE Estimates Marginal Models. Consider a simple clustered regression model $Y_{ig} = b_0 + b_1 X_{ig} + u_g + e_{ig}$ where u_g is a cluster-specific component of the variance of Y_{ig}. Standard OLS regression ignores u_g, estimating instead $Y_{ig} = b_0 + b_1 X_{ig} + e_{ig}$, where b_1 represents the average effect on Y of a one-unit change in X across the entire joint distribution of X and Y. In this way OLS is a *marginal* or *population averaged* model where b_1 represents the marginal effect of X on Y for the entire sample. But this model is incorrect in the presence of u_g, and we need to account for u_g in our estimate of b_1. Traditional fixed effects and random effects regression models account for u_g in a similar fashion: fixed effects by using G parameters (one for each group) and random effects by using two parameters (the mean and variance of u_g). Both approaches to parameterizing u_g, however, change the interpretation of b_1. Fixed and random effects models are *conditional* or *subject-specific* models where b_1 represents the effect of a one-unit change in X on Y within a cluster, averaged across all clusters (Burton, Gurrin, and Sly 1998; Zorn 2001; Ghisletta and Spini 2004). By way of illustration, in an original study of the effectiveness of school vouchers in which students are nested within classrooms and the assignment of vouchers varies within classrooms, *marginal* models estimate the effect of vouchers by comparing average academic achievement of all voucher and nonvoucher recipients in the entire sample, while *conditional* models estimate this effect by comparing the averages of voucher and nonvoucher recipients within the same classroom. The benefit of conditional models is that they allow for a more precise estimate of causal effects from clustered data. The drawbacks are that conditional models have more difficulty handling independent variables that do not vary within clusters, and, strictly speaking, parameter estimates from conditional models lose the "all other things equal" generalizability of parameter estimates from marginal models.

By using random effects to account for clustering, the HLM framework is a conditional or subject-specific model.[7] By contrast, because CRVE accounts for clustering solely by adjusting the parameter variance-covariance matrix—leaving the original OLS parameter estimates unchanged—CRVE models (and the GEE models discussed in the next section) are marginal or population averaged models. In practice the differences between conditional and marginal parameter estimates is small, with the former generally being larger than the latter. Still, the purpose of meta-regression is to draw conclusions about the entirety of a body of research on a particular question. Furthermore, parameter estimates from meta-regression lack a causal interpretation, rather being considered general measures of association between moderator variables and effect sizes. The effect of moderators is interpreted as operating over all effect sizes, not simply within clusters of effect sizes from a particular study. For these reasons, parameter estimates from marginal models (such as CRVE) seem better suited to the purpose of meta-regression than are parameter estimates from conditional models (such as HLM).

General Difficulties with HLM Compared with Clustered Robust Estimation. We might overcome the inability of HLM meta-regression to account for clustered observations by simply adding a third layer to the HLM framework: in other words, we might organize our data set so that we have effect sizes Θ_{js} where unobserved subjects produce each effect size (level 1), there are j correlated effect sizes from a particular original study (level 2) and these j effect sizes are nested within s original studies (level 3). Indeed, this specification is the natural extension of the traditional two-level HLM meta-regression model as employed by Bateman and Jones (2003), Tengs and Lin (2003), and Swanson and Jerman (2006). While the three-level HLM model is well established for original research (Raudenbush and Bryk 2002, chapter 8), its performance in meta-regression has not been assessed (though see Goldstein, Yang, Omar, Turner, and Thompson 2000). More important, like traditional two-level HLM, a three-level HLM model would be estimated using maximum likelihood rather than WLS, so all of the reasons to prefer CRVE to HLM offered by Steenbergen and Jones (2002) and Primo, Jacobsmeier, and Milyo (2007) become relevant for three-level HLM meta-regression.

Generalized Estimating Equations

Pioneered by Liang and Zeger (1986), generalized estimating equations (GEE) have become increasingly popular among researchers in medicine and the social sciences as a method of addressing the problem of non-independent observations. GEE have also occasionally been used to estimate the random effects meta-regression model (see, for example, Janiszewski, Noel, and Sawyer 2003; Boudville et al. 2006; Garg et al. 2006). Compared with the HLM approach, however, the use of GEE in meta-regression is uncommon. This is unfortunate, since many aspects of GEE make them well suited to estimating the random effects meta-regression model with correlated effect sizes. As more researchers recognize the advantages of GEE for meta-analysis, the use of this technique ought to grow. My treatment of GEE here is necessarily brief. Interested readers might consult the original work by Liang and Zeger (1986; see also Zeger and Liang 1986), and less technical (but nonetheless excellent) introductions to GEE by Burton, Gurrin, and Sly (1998), Zorn (2001); Hanley, Negassa, Edwardes, and Forrester (2003); and Ghisletta and Spini (2004). A complete textbook treatment is provided by Hardin and Hilbe (2003).

A Simple Introduction to GEE. Three key assumptions of traditional regression are that (1) $E[Y] = Xb$, (2) Y_i is normally distributed conditional upon X, and (3) ee' is defined by $\sigma^2 I$. GEE offer a very general framework that relaxes all three of these assumptions. First, GEE replace the expectation and conditional normality assumption (assumptions 1 and 2) with the less restrictive assumption that Y can be conditionally distributed according to a large number of theoretical probability distributions and that the expected value of Y is related to X through a *linkage function* so that

$$E[Y] = h(Xb) \tag{5.15}$$

where the inverse of h is the linkage. For traditional regression, Y is distributed normally and the linkage is an identity so that $E[Y] = Xb$. For Logit and Probit models, the conditional distribution is the Bernoulli and the linkage is the logit or probit, respectively. Models employing the poisson, negative binomial, and gamma distributions can be used in a similar fashion. Second, GEE replace the OLS error variance assumption (assumption 3) with

$$V[Y_i|X_i] = \sigma_i^2 = g([\mu_i]/\varphi \tag{5.16}$$

where g is a function linking the expected value of Y_i to its variance and φ is a scale parameter. Note that GEE only make assumptions about the mean of Y (μ) and its variance (σ^2 is a function of μ). Therefore, GEE models are members of the large class of quasi-likelihood models.

GEE Estimates of μ. GEE calculate the expected value of Y using an optimal weighted average where the weights are a function of the correlations among observations. In the simple example used here, $E[Y] = \mu$, but the intuition is easily extended to the regression case where $E[Y] = Xb$. In the regression case, the weights assigned by GEE influence the regression parameter vector b.

Consider a simple scenario in which we have three observations on Y from two clusters: Y_{11}, Y_{21}, and Y_{22}. If we assume that the observations are independent, the expected value of Y is

$$\mu = (1/3) \, Y_{11} + (1/3) \, Y_{21} + (1/3) \, Y_{22} \tag{5.17}$$

If observations from cluster 2 are not independent, then μ from equation 5.17 and its associated variance are estimated believing we possess more information than we actually do. In this situation Y_{21} and Y_{22} contain less information than does Y_{11}, and therefore ought to have less influence when we calculate $E[Y]$ and its variance. In fact, if observations in cluster 2 are perfectly correlated, we can drop Y_{21} (or Y_{22}) without loss of information, giving us

$$\mu = (1/2) \, Y_{11} + (1/2) \, Y_{22} \tag{5.18}$$

If observations in cluster 2 are positively but imperfectly correlated, equation 5.18 wastes information by dropping observation Y_{21}. We would be better off estimating something like

$$\mu = (1/2) \, Y_{11} + (1/4) \, Y_{21} + (1/4) \, Y_{22} \tag{5.19}$$

It is worth pointing out that the estimate in equation 5.17 reflects the assumption made when estimating the meta-regression models in chapter 4 and in figures 5.1 and 5.2. By contrast, the estimates in equations 5.18 and 5.19 reflect the standard advice offered to researchers faced with original studies generating multiple effect sizes; that is, choose a single effect size from each study (equation 5.18) or calculate an average effect size from each original study (equation 5.19) for inclusion in the meta-regression. Hanley and colleagues (2003) point out that all three estimates of μ in equations 5.17, 5.18, and 5.19 are consistent, but they have different variances.[8] If the intra-class correlation coefficient $\rho = 0$, the estimator in equation 5.17 is most efficient, while when $\rho = .5$ the estimator in equation 5.19 has the smallest variance. The variance of μ then depends on ρ, and ideally we could derive an optimal expectation on Y that uses weights accounting for ρ. This is the GEE estimator. Hanley and colleagues show that in the illustration used here, the GEE estimator is

$$\mu = \left[((1 + \rho) / (3 + \rho)) \, Y_{11} \right] + \left[(1 / (3 + \rho)) \, Y_{21} \right] + \left[(1 / (3 + \rho)) \, Y_{22} \right]$$
$$(5.20)$$

This estimator also has minimum variance across all values of ρ.

Extending this discussion to meta-regression simply requires substituting the effect size Θ for Y and the conditional expectation Xb for the unconditional expectation μ. From this illustration we can see that unlike CRVE, controlling for non-independence of observations using GEE changes our regression parameter estimates as well as their variances. Using GEE, correlated observations contribute less to our estimates of b than do independent observations. The GEE model is the only method considered in this chapter that adjusts meta-regression parameter estimates to reflect the fact that large numbers of correlated effect sizes may come from a small number of studies.

GEE Estimates of σ^2. GEE handle correlated observations through what is commonly referred to as a "working correlation matrix," denoted R (Liang and Zeger 1986). The working correlation matrix posits a block diagonal structure for ee' with values of 1 on the diagonal and values of ρ on the off-diagonal elements of diagonal blocks. Because GEE, like CRVE, assume that observations are correlated within clusters but independent across clusters, the elements of the off-diagonal blocks of ee' are assumed to be zero. The key issue for variance estimation in GEE, then, is the values of ρ. There are many theoretical working correlation matrices. Following are four of the most common:

- *Independent*: $\rho = 0$ for all cells. Observations are independent.
- *Exchangeable*: ρ is a scalar, meaning that the correlation between observations is identical within and across clusters.
- *Autoregressive*: ρ is an exponential decay function ρ^{L-1} as is commonly used in GLS models (here L is the lag length).
- *Unstructured*: ρ can take on any value $-1 \leq \rho \leq 1$ for all off-diagonal elements in a cluster.

Once a working correlation matrix is selected, the variance of Y then becomes

$$\sigma^2 = (A)^{1/2} \, R \, (A)^{1/2} \tag{5.21}$$

where A is a diagonal matrix with values μ_i on the diagonal.

A strength of GEE is that regression parameters in b are consistent even if the researcher posits an incorrect working correlation matrix; that is, if we model $R =$ independent when $R =$ exchangeable (to see why this is true, consider again the illustration in the previous section where all estimates of μ in equations 5.17 through 5.20 are consistent).[9] As a consistency property, however, this applies only asymptotically. With sample sizes commonly encountered by researchers in practice, b does differ depending on the specification of R (Zorn 2001; Ghisletta and Spini 2004). Parameter variances are not insensitive to the choice of R. Given the implications that the specification of R can have for inference, it is useful to have some guidelines for choosing R. In general, an exchangeable R is best suited for observations that have no logical ordering within clusters. Specifying R as autoregressive is most appropriate with panel or time series data, and an unstructured R is a good candidate when you have a large number of balanced clusters with few observations in each cluster (Ghisletta and Spini 2004).

The specifications of R described above produce what are typically referred to as "model" parameter variances. Because these parameter variances are sensitive to misspecification in R, however, in practice GEE models generally estimate parameter variances using a version of the familiar robust variance matrix of White (1980) adjusted for clustering by Liang and Zeger (1986). These are typically referred to as "empirical" variance estimates. In practice, then, GEE use the CRVE for parameter variances. When using clustered robust variance estimation, GEE results differ from traditional CRVE results because the former employ the optimal weighting scheme discussed above when calculating regression parameter estimates, whereas the latter derive parameter estimates using OLS that implicitly weights all observations equally when calculating the elements of b.

Estimating GEE Models. Estimation of GEE is most easily explained by considering the iterative approach to deriving quasi-maximum likelihood estimates of β and σ.

1. Estimate a naïve structural model for Y assuming independent observations to obtain starting values for the regression parameters b and the regression error vector e.

2. Use e to estimate the elements of the working correlation matrix $\boldsymbol{R}$.
3. Re-estimate the structural model with weights derived from the estimated values of ρ in $\boldsymbol{R}$.
4. Iterate steps 2 and 3 to convergence.

GEE Meta-Regression in Stata. GEE models can be estimated with most standard statistical software packages. Stata estimates GEE models using the "*xtgee*" command. Using *xtgee*, the user specifies the structural model, the conditional distribution of the dependent variable, the linkage function, the working correlation matrix, and the method of estimating parameter variances. For meta-regression, the conditional distribution of effect sizes Θ_i is assumed to be normal (this is true for Fisher's Z as well as for d-based and most odds-based effect sizes) with an identity linkage function (that is, $E[\boldsymbol{\Theta}] = \boldsymbol{Xb}$). The GEE approach to meta-regression is too new to have established standards of practice, but the exchangeable correlation structure is appropriate in most circumstances likely to be faced by researchers. Finally, parameter variances should be taken from the empirical robust variance-covariance matrix.

At least three items are worth pointing out when estimating meta-regression models using *xtgee*. First, it is important to note that *xtgee* is not designed for meta-regression. Therefore, GEE estimates do not take into account either the known fixed-effects variance component of Θ_i nor its random effects component. When using *xtgee* for random effects meta-regression, the dependent variable should be the manually weighted version of Θ_i, not the raw effect size Fisher's Z. Second, recall that GEE was developed in the context in which observations are clustered within units over time. In meta-regression, effect sizes are clustered within studies and therefore do not have a temporal element. In these situations, users may only specify $\boldsymbol{R}$ as exchangeable or as independent when using *xtgee*. Third, it is important to remember that specifying the working correlation matrix $\boldsymbol{R}$ has a separate and different effect on GEE results than does specifying the model or empirical variance estimator. The specification of $\boldsymbol{R}$ determines how weights derived from ρ affect regression parameter estimates $\boldsymbol{b}$, while specifying the model or empirical variances affects only var$[\boldsymbol{b}]$, not the values of $\boldsymbol{b}$. Stated more plainly, *xtgee* using *model* variance estimates uses the elements of $\boldsymbol{R}$ to adjust both parameter estimates in $\boldsymbol{b}$ and the variance of these estimates, var$[\boldsymbol{b}]$. By contrast, *xtgee* using *empirical* variance estimates uses the elements of $\boldsymbol{R}$ to adjust parameter estimates in $\boldsymbol{b}$, but adjusts var$[\boldsymbol{b}]$ using CRVE, not the elements of $\boldsymbol{R}$. Two examples might help to further explain these differences. First, using *xtgee* you can adjust parameter variances without adjusting parameter estimates. Specifying an *xtgee* model where R = independent and using *model* variances will produce different results than using *xtgee* where R = independent and using *empirical* variance estimates. In the first instance the researcher will receive results equivalent to OLS assuming $ee' = \sigma^2 I$ while in the second the researcher will receive results equivalent to OLS with CRVE. In the first instance independence of observations is assumed when calculating both b and var$[b]$, while in the second independence is assumed when calculating b while independence is *not* assumed when calculating var$[b]$. Second, controlling for non-independence using R and controlling for non-independence by specifying *empirical* variance estimates are not substitutes. Specifying *xtgee* where R = exchangeable and using *model* variances will produce different results than specifying *xtgee* where R = independent and using *empirical* variance estimates. In the first instance *xtgee* weights the parameter estimates in b using estimates of ρ from R and calculates parameter variances using R, while in the second *xtgee* only adjusts the variances of elements of b using CRVE, not the parameter estimates themselves. *In most situations, random effects meta-regression models using* xtgee *should specify* $\mathbf{R}$ = *exchangeable and* σ^2 *containing empirical robust variance estimates (CRVE).*

I illustrate the use of GEE to estimate the REMR using the environmental justice data set. First I specify a GEE model where R = independent and using empirical robust variance estimates. These results, presented in figure 5.3, are virtually identical to those from figure 5.1 using OLS with CRVE (the slight differences in parameter variances stem from the fact that Stata uses a different finite population correction factor in *xtgee*). I estimate this model using the following Stata command statements:

```
xtgee Ywb x1b x2b x3b x4b x5b x6b x7b x0b, nocon
family(normal) link(identity) corr(independent) vce(robust)
```

New information in figure 5.3 shows us that there is great heterogeneity in the number of effect sizes produced by different studies, from a minimum of 1 to a maximum of 80, with an average of 14.2 effect sizes per study. Next, I estimate this same model specifying GEE where R = exchangeable and using empirical robust variance estimates. I estimate this model using the following Stata command statements:

```
xtset idnumber
xtgee Ywb x1b x2b x3b x4b x5b x6b x7b x0b, nocon
family(normal) link(identity) corr(exchangeable) vce(robust)
```

FIGURE 5.3. GEE ESTIMATES OF RANDOM EFFECT META-REGRESSION WITH INDEPENDENT CORRELATION MATRIX AND EMPIRICAL VARIANCE ESTIMATES

```
. xtgee Ywb x1b x2b x3b x4b x5b x6b x7b x0b, nocon family(normal) link
(identity) corr(independent)  vce(robust)

Iteration 1: tolerance    = 4.418e-16

GEE population-averaged model            Number of obs      =        680
Group variable:              idnumber    Number of groups   =         48
Link:                        identity    Obs per group: min =          1
Family:                      Gaussian                   avg =       14.2
Correlation:              independent                   max =         80
                                         Wald chi2(8)       =      93.35
Scale parameter:             1.235598    Prob > chi2        =     0.0000

Pearson chi2(680):             840.21    Deviance           =     840.21
Dispersion (Pearson):        1.235598    Dispersion         =   1.235598

                          (Std. Err. adjusted for clustering on idnumber)
```

Ywb	Coef.	Semi-robust Std. Err.	z	P>|z|	[95% Conf.	Interval]
x1b	.0062388	.0156471	0.40	0.690	−.0244289	.0369066
x2b	−.0199238	.014521	−1.37	0.170	−.0483844	.0085368
x3b	−.0076215	.010753	−0.71	0.478	−.028697	.0134541
x4b	.0106787	.0101592	1.05	0.293	−.009233	.0305905
x5b	−.0060322	.0336458	−0.18	0.858	−.0719767	.0599124
x6b	−.0364036	.01176	−3.10	0.002	−.0594528	−.0133543
x7b	−.0776066	.032286	−2.40	0.016	−.1408859	−.0143272
x0b	.0678888	.0109899	6.18	0.000	.046349	.0894285

This model adjusts parameter estimates by placing less emphasis on effect sizes from studies that generate multiple effect sizes. These GEE estimates help guard against a few studies dominating the results of the meta-regression. The implicit assumption when using this model is that effect sizes from the same original study contain less information than if these same effect sizes came from different studies. Results from this model are presented in figure 5.4. The meta-regression results in figures 5.3 and 5.4 are very similar, suggesting that a few large studies do not inordinately influence the results from our meta-regression. Most important, the story told in figure 5.4 is identical to the story told in figures 5.3 and 5.1; in other words, the existing research supports the conclusion that there is a statistically significant but substantively small degree of baseline environmental inequity in the United States (correlation $\approx$ .07), and estimates of these inequities are smaller in higher-quality studies that include key control variables (see the parameter estimate on x6*b*) and smaller in lower-quality studies that select on the dependent variable (see the parameter estimate on x7*b*). This robustness to different estimation strategies gives us greater confidence in these meta-regression results.

FIGURE 5.4. GEE ESTIMATES OF RANDOM EFFECT META-REGRESSION WITH EXCHANGEABLE CORRELATION MATRIX AND EMPIRICAL VARIANCE ESTIMATES

```
. xtgee Ywb x1b x2b x3b x4b x5b x6b x7b x0b, nocon family(normal) link
(identity) corr(exchangeable)  vce(robust)

Iteration 1: tolerance    = .01321375
Iteration 2: tolerance    = .00170971
Iteration 3: tolerance    = .00024699
Iteration 4: tolerance    = .00003655
Iteration 5: tolerance    = 5.422e-06
Iteration 6: tolerance    = 8.045e-07

GEE population-averaged model            Number of obs      =        680
Group variable:                idnumber  Number of groups   =         48
Link:                          identity  Obs per group: min =          1
Family:                        Gaussian                 avg =       14.2
Correlation:                exchangeable                 max =         80
                                         Wald chi2(8)       =      71.49
Scale parameter:               1.250865  Prob > chi2        =     0.0000

                        (Std. Err. adjusted for clustering on idnumber)
```

| | | Semi-robust | | | | |
Ywb	Coef.	Std. Err.	z	P>|z|	[95% Conf.	Interval]
x1b	.0014946	.0117036	0.13	0.898	−.0214441	.0244332
x2b	−.0149066	.0144263	−1.03	0.301	−.0431817	.0133685
x3b	.0076981	.0092475	0.83	0.405	−.0104266	.0258228
x4b	−.0010263	.0101983	−0.10	0.920	−.0210146	.018962
x5b	.0040849	.0200722	0.20	0.839	−.0352559	.0434257
x6b	−.0413722	.0148734	−2.78	0.005	−.0705235	−.0122209
x7b	−.072211	.0206248	−3.50	0.000	−.1126349	−.0317872
x0b	.0674127	.0114158	5.91	0.000	.0450381	.0897872

Choosing Between GEE and CRVE. While there are good reasons to prefer CRVE to HLM when estimating a random effects meta-regression model with correlated effect sizes, the decision is less clear-cut when choosing between GEE and CRVE. In practice, the parameter standard errors produced by CRVE and GEE are very similar as long as GEE use empirical variance estimates (Burton, Gurrin, and Sly 1998; Zorn 2006). In addition, both GEE and CRVE estimate population-averaged or marginal models rather than cluster-specific or conditional models, and marginal models are more consistent with the motivation behind meta-analysis. Finally, both GEE and CRVE can account for the fixed effects and random effects variance components unique to meta-analysis through manually weighting the effect size Θ_i.

GEE do have some advantages over CRVE for meta-regression. For example, only GEE parameter estimates account for the fact that some studies produce more effect sizes than others, thereby providing some protection against a few large studies dominating the results. In the environmental justice model this difference was of little consequence, even though the ratio of large to small effect sizes within studies reached 80 to 1. More generally, this benefit of GEE depends on how we conceive of the information present in effect sizes from the same study. CRVE assumes that the *unexplained* element of shared effect sizes, e_i from Θ_i, has a common component within original studies. When this correlation is positive, treating the Θ_i as independent will underestimate parameter variances. However, CRVE assumes that the *systematic* element of Θ_i explained by X is equally valuable whether Θ_i comes from the same study or from different studies. By contrast, GEE assume that the systematic information in Θ_i from the same study is less useful for estimating *both* parameters and their variances than are the same effect sizes coming from different studies. While the second assumption is well grounded in statistical theory, the first is less so. Recall from equations 5.17 through 5.20 that we prefer the GEE estimate of $E[Y_i]$ not because it is less biased, but because it is more efficient. Therefore, the decision as to whether observations Y_{21} and Y_{22} (or effect sizes Θ_{21} and Θ_{22}) contain less valuable information than do observations Y_{11} and Y_{21} (or effect sizes Θ_{11} and Θ_{21}) has as much to do with the research context and epistemological perspective as it does with statistical theory. Finally, even if we believe that effect sizes from the same study contain less systematic information than independent effect sizes, the ability of GEE to leverage this belief is somewhat limited, since the exchangeable working correlation matrix assigns the same intra-class correlation coefficient ρ to all pairs of observations within and across clusters. That is, using $R = $ exchangeable, all correlated effect sizes receive the same weight whether they come from studies generating ten effect sizes or a hundred (this helps explain the small differences in parameter estimates in figures 5.3 and 5.4).

CRVE may also have some limited advantages over GEE for meta-regression. First, GEE models are much more complex, and therefore experience convergence problems more frequently than do CRVE models (Zorn 2006). Second, both parameter estimates and their variances can be sensitive to the structure of the working correlation matrix. Unless we conduct sensitivity analyses by using alternative specifications of R, there is some chance that the inferences we draw from GEE models may be an artifact of model specification. Finally, GEE and CRVE variance estimates are consistent in G, the number of groups or clusters. When the number of clusters is small, parameter variances may be seriously underestimated. Good small sample corrections are available for CRVE (for example, the wild cluster bootstrap), but not for GEE (though see Pan and Wall 2002).

Delta-Splitting

Recently, John Stevens and Alan Taylor proposed an alternative method for addressing the non-independence of effect sizes in meta-regression, dubbed "delta-splitting" (Stevens and Taylor 2009). I begin the discussion of delta-splitting with a slightly different presentation of the standard random effects meta-regression model:

$$\boldsymbol{\Theta} = \boldsymbol{Xb} + \boldsymbol{\delta} + \varepsilon \tag{5.22}$$

where $\boldsymbol{\Theta}$ is a vector of effect sizes, $\boldsymbol{X}$ and $\boldsymbol{b}$ are a matrix of moderator variables and the vector of parameter estimates associated with these variables, respectively. In equation 5.22, ε is the error component vector associated with sampling variability, and $\boldsymbol{\delta}$ is the error component vector associated with nonsampling variability. The assumptions of meta-regression require that the elements of ε and $\boldsymbol{\delta}$ be independent. The conditions under which the elements of ε violate this assumption are well known and well studied. For example, clinical trials may estimate the effect from different treatments in separate arms of the trial by using a common control group. Alternatively, observational studies may estimate the effect of an intervention on several related outcome measures. Finally, effect sizes may come from different studies that use the same data set. In each of these cases, the standard fixed effects variance component v_i will be biased. Stevens and Taylor (2009) offer a method of controlling for this *sampling dependence* across studies that is in the tradition of Hedges and Olkin (1985) and Hunter and Schmidt (1990), but that does not rely as heavily on large sample distribution theory as these earlier approaches. Because sampling dependence is a less serious and a less tractable problem for the type of data used in meta-regression in public management and policy, I will not discuss it further.

More relevant for our purposes is that Stevens and Taylor (2009) also address the relatively understudied variance component $\boldsymbol{\delta}$. Under the assumption of independence, $\boldsymbol{\delta} \sim N(0, \boldsymbol{\tau})$ where $\boldsymbol{\tau}$ is $\tau^2 \boldsymbol{I}$; that is, it is simply the familiar random effects variance. When the independence assumption is violated (in other words, when effect sizes from the same study, or effect sizes produced by the same research team, are correlated) $\boldsymbol{\tau} \neq \tau^2 \boldsymbol{I}$. These authors "split" $\boldsymbol{\delta}$ into two components; the random effects variance τ^2 and the covariance component ς representing the correlation among effect sizes within the same cluster. Two methods are offered for estimating ς; an iterative restricted maximum likelihood approach derived from the standard random effects variance estimator of DerSimonian and Laird (1986), and a hierarchical Bayes approach derived from the work of DuMouchel and Normand (2000). Using either approach (and ignoring the estimator for sampling dependence ε), the delta-splitting method estimates the following REMR error variance-covariance matrix:

$$ee' = \begin{pmatrix}
(\tau^2 + v_{11}) & \varsigma & 0 & \cdot & \cdot & \cdot & \cdot\cdot\cdot & \cdot & \cdot & 0 \\
\zeta & (\tau^2 + v_{21}) & \cdot & & & & & & & \cdot \\
0 & \cdot & \sigma_2^2** & \varsigma & \varsigma & \varsigma & & & & \cdot \\
\cdot & & \varsigma & \sigma_2^2** & \varsigma & \varsigma & & & & \cdot \\
\cdot & & \varsigma & \varsigma & \sigma_2^2** & \varsigma & & & & \cdot \\
\cdot & & \varsigma & \varsigma & \varsigma & \sigma_2^2** & & \cdot & & \cdot \\
\cdot & & & & & & \cdot & & & \cdot \\
\cdot & & & & & & & \cdot & & \cdot \\
\cdot & & & & & & & & \cdot & 0 \\
\cdot & & & & & & & \sigma_g^2** & \varsigma & \varsigma \\
\cdot & & & & & & & \varsigma & \sigma_g^2** & \varsigma \\
0 & \cdot & & \cdot & \cdot & \cdot & \cdot\cdot 0 & \varsigma & \varsigma & \sigma_g^2**
\end{pmatrix}$$

Like ee' under CRVE and unlike two-level HLM meta-regression, the delta-splitting approach explicitly controls for non-independence of observations due to clustering. Unlike CRVE, however, this method imposes a common correlation among all nested observations, rather than allowing this correlation to vary across clusters. In this way, the delta-splitting method is akin to GEE models with exchangeable correlation structures. The primary advantage of delta-splitting over GEE is that the former incorporates the fixed and random effects variance components unique to meta-regression directly while the latter incorporates these effects only by manually transforming θ_i. The primary disadvantage of delta-splitting vis-à-vis GEE is that the latter models are easily estimated using standard statistical software packages, while the former are available only as specialized algorithms written in programming languages R and S+. In addition, unlike CRVE, delta-splitting does not allow for study-level heteroskedasticity in effect sizes (for example, the σ_g^2 component of ee' in clustered robust estimation is not present in ee' from delta-splitting). The delta-splitting method should be of great value for meta-regression in fields in which sampling dependence among effect sizes is known or easily estimated (for example, medicine, psychology, and education) and in which we do not expect cluster-specific heteroskedasticity or cluster-specific intra-class correlations. For meta-regression in public management and policy research, however, researchers are advised to use CRVE or GEE rather than delta-splitting.

Conclusion

A central concern in meta-analysis is that using multiple and potentially correlated effect sizes from the same original study may compromise our ability to draw accurate inferences from meta-regression. This concern has led many meta-analysts to recommend using only one effect size per study when estimating meta-regression models (Hunter and Schmidt 1990; Lipsey and Wilson 2001; Stanley 2005). While methods for addressing these types of correlated effect sizes have been slow to develop in the meta-analysis community (though see Stevens and Taylor 2009), researchers in econometrics and biostatistics have developed a handful of tools for addressing correlated observations in original research, including CRVE, HLM, and GEE. With modification, all of these approaches can be used to estimate the random effects meta-regression model. To this point, HLM are the dominant alternative in this respect. As we have seen, however, as originally conceived the HLM meta-regression model does nothing to control for correlated effect sizes nested within original studies. While the HLM meta-regression model has been extended to the correlated observations environment, its performance in this environment has not been rigorously evaluated. Moreover, there are reasons to expect that the HLM approach to estimating meta-regression models with correlated effect sizes possesses less desirable properties than CRVE or GEE. These include estimating cluster-specific rather than population-averaged effects, an inability to control for cluster-specific heteroskedasticity, and more frequent problems with convergence when estimating HLM. These qualities *do not* mean that HLM cannot be used to estimate random effects meta-regression models. Indeed, there is often little difference between HLM and GEE in practice when used in original research (Burton, Gurrin, and Sly 1998), and the same may be true in the meta-regression environment. Rather, the conclusion from this chapter is that while CRVE, HLM, and GEE are all superior alternatives to the traditional random effects meta-regression model with correlated effect sizes, for the types of questions and data commonly confronted by management and policy scholars, CRVE and GEE should be preferred in most instances to HLM.

Notes

1. Technically the assumption is that the error term e_i is distributed i.i.d., meaning that observations are conditionally independent.
2. In econometrics this decomposition is often referred to as the random effects model. I do not use that term here to avoid any confusion with the random effects meta-regression model.
3. An extended treatment of HLM is beyond the scope of this book. Interested readers are referred to Raudenbush and Bryk (2002) and Gelman and Hill (2007).
4. These limitations can be overcome by including a large and probably cumbersome number of interaction terms.
5. While Lee and Nelder (2006) did not develop their technique specifically for meta-analysis, it can be easily adapted to HLM meta-regression.
6. Bateman and Jones (2003) claim advantages for HLM estimation of meta-regression models over traditional techniques, but they compare HLM to regular OLS regression of non-standardized effect sizes—a common approach in the field of economics—so their analysis simply demonstrates the superiority of random effects meta-regression to OLS, not the added value of HLM.
7. Random effects in HLM should not be confused with random effects variance components in meta-analysis. These latter random effects are attached to individual effect sizes, not to groups of effect sizes.
8. This consistency assumption is true only for the unconditional expectation μ in this simple example. If $Y_i = \Theta_i$ and Θ_i is produced using different regression models—that is, if Θ_i is a conditional rather than an unconditional expectation—the assertion of consistency holds only for the multiple conditional expectations of Θ_i, not for the unconditional expectation μ.
9. Strictly speaking β is consistent only under the original GEE1 model described here. A discussion of GEE2 and GEE3 models are beyond the scope of this book.

CHAPTER SIX

PUBLICATION BIAS

Evan J. Ringquist

"(P)ublication bias is leading to a new formulation of Gresham's law—like bad money, bad research drives out good"

(BLAND 1988, 450).

"There are no single statistical tests that can document or exclude bias in meta-analysis with certainty. In most meta-analyses in current practice, the applied statistical tests are either inappropriate or meaningless or both and they should either not be used at all or applied with full appreciation and acknowledgement of their limitations"

(IOANNIDIS 2008, 955–956).

As discussed in the Introduction, meta-analysis has become the most common method for accumulating scientific knowledge in medicine, psychology, and education, and the use of these techniques is increasing in the core social science disciplines that contribute to research in public management and public policy. Much of the stock of scientific knowledge is contained in the peer-reviewed literature, and many meta-analyses summarize only the results from peer-reviewed research. If peer-reviewed research is contaminated by *publication bias*—that is, the tendency for a greater proportion of statistically significant or positive results to be published, and a corresponding smaller likelihood that nonsignificant results will be published—then systematic reviews of this research will portray inaccurately the state of scientific knowledge on a particular question. Most commonly, publication bias will lead systematic reviews to overestimate the degree of scientific consensus on a particular question, and to overestimate the average effect size of interest.

Publication bias (also known as "positive outcome bias" or "selectivity bias") has been called the "Achilles' Heel" of meta-analysis and is widely accepted as a major threat to the validity of systematic reviews in health care, psychology, and education (Torgerson 2006). Hopewell, Clarke, and Mallett (2005) point out that the potential for publication bias is greater in the social sciences than in medicine, largely because of the greater variety of peer-reviewed publication outlets in these disciplines. This enhanced potential for publication bias is exacerbated in management and policy because a much larger proportion of this research appears in non-peer-reviewed outlets (books, government reports, working papers from research centers and policy think tanks, and so on). Despite the greater potential for publication bias in the social sciences, empirical evidence of publication bias in this area is limited, and research on this topic is relatively underdeveloped compared to medicine and psychology (Hopewell, Clarke and Mallett 2005).

Sources and Consequences of Publication Bias

Types of Publication Bias

Publication bias can be directional or nondirectional. With directional publication bias, results from original studies that are inconsistent with well-established theory are unlikely to be published. For example, the peer-reviewed literature in biology contains few studies demonstrating the genetic transfer of learned behavioral traits, and the peer-reviewed literature in economics contains few studies demonstrating negative price elasticities. A more relevant and problematic example of directional publication bias is when original studies challenging the dominant ideological perspective or "received wisdom" within a scholarly community are less likely to be published. Following are some examples:

· Research finding that levels of economic freedom are unrelated to levels of economic growth might be less likely to be published in the field of economics.

· Research finding that voter mobilization campaigns do not increase voter turnout may be less likely to be published in the field of political science.

· Research finding that privatization does not reduce the cost or improve the efficiency of public service delivery may be less likely to be published in the field of public policy.

· Research finding that rich and supportive stakeholder networks do not improve managerial effectiveness may be less likely to be published in the field of public management.

Publication bias may also be nondirectional; in other words, original studies that are able to reject the null hypothesis of independence are more likely to be published than are studies that are unable to reject this hypothesis, regardless of the direction of the outcome. Previous research indicates that directional publication bias is more common in medicine—that is, publication bias works to the advantage of original studies demonstrating a positive effect from some medical intervention (Torgerson 2006; Sutton 2005). While publication bias has received less attention in the social sciences, it appears as if nondirectional publication bias may be relatively more common in these fields (De Long and Lang 1992; Sterling, Rosenbaum, and Weinkam 1995).

Sources of Publication Bias

Publication bias may arise from the decisions of reviewers and editors, or from the decisions of researchers.

Decisions of Reviewers and Editors. Much of the early research into the sources of publication bias focused on the decisions of peer reviewers and editors. If these research gatekeepers have a strong preference for studies that reject the null hypothesis or estimate an effect in a particular direction, these preferences will generate systematic biases in the results from peer-reviewed research. Under ideal conditions, neither reviewers nor editors are supposed to be influenced by these sorts of predispositions. Upon honest reflection, however, many of us who routinely serve as reviewers, editors, or other gatekeepers in the publication process may recognize these tendencies in ourselves or (more commonly) in others. Indeed, the common aphorism in peer review that "extraordinary claims require extraordinary evidence" likely contributes to directional publication bias.

In one of the earliest studies examining potential sources of publication bias, Greenwald (1975) surveyed peer reviewers and found that they were much more likely to give a positive recommendation for manuscripts that were able to reject the null hypothesis. Similar results have been found in the field of medicine for both reviewers and editors (Dickersin, Chan, Chalmers, Sacks and Smith 1987). Moreover, cohort studies that followed clinical trials from their date of registration have found that trials generating statistically significant effects are more than twice as likely to be published as are trials that generate null results (Dickersin and Chalmers 2010; see also Turner, Matthews, Linardatos, Tell, and Rosenthal 2008). Most convincingly, there have been a handful of experimental studies in which researchers submitted manuscripts for peer review to different journals where the manuscripts differed only with respect to the reported significance levels for the null hypothesis tests. Each of these studies found that the statistical significance of the reported results had a dramatic effect on the probability that the manuscript received positive reviews, and on the eventual decision to publish the research (Mahoney 1977; Epstein 1990; Emerson et al. 2010).

Decisions of Researchers. Publication bias may also be driven by the decisions of researchers. One such decision has been dubbed the "file drawer" problem in which research that is unable to reject the null hypothesis remains in the author's file drawer and is never submitted for peer review (Iyengar and Greenhouse 1988). Greenwald (1975) found that scholars are eight times more likely to submit for peer review research that rejects the null hypothesis. This "file drawer" decision may be strategic (in that scholars recognize that null results will be difficult to publish) or sincere (in that scholars find these null results genuinely uninteresting). In either case, the file drawer problem will lead to published results composing a biased sample of all research conducted on the question. In their summary of the evidence from clinical trials research, Dickersin and Chalmers (2010) conclude that the failure to publish null results is largely produced by the decisions of investigators (that is, the file drawer problem) rather than by the decisions of reviewers or editors. The extent to which these results can be generalized to research in policy, management, and the social sciences is unknown.

Publication bias might also be produced when researchers engage in selective reporting of research results. In the social sciences in particular, researchers commonly consider alternative measures of key independent and dependent variables and try out alternative model specifications (for example, different functional forms or different control variables). If (as seems likely) the probability of reporting the results from alternative models is positively related to whether they allow the rejection of a key null hypothesis, this will generate publication bias. Specification searches and selective reporting are not unique to the social sciences. When studying a set of registered clinical trials, Sutton and Pigott (2005) noted that the published reports of these trials often differed from the research plan in the trial registry, and that the characteristics of the research protocols that were altered (such as the use of different outcome measures) were more likely to be associated with statistically significant results.[1]

Consequences of Publication Bias

Consequences for Scientific Consensus in the Published Literature. One consequence of publication bias is that the published literature may inflate the degree of scientific consensus surrounding research questions. Sterling (1959) may have been the first to highlight this danger, pointing out that over 90 percent of published articles in leading psychology journals contained statistically significant results. A reanalysis of this question by Sterling and his colleagues (1995) found that the frequency of statistically significant results in the published psychology literature had not changed meaningfully in thirty years. Extraordinarily high percentages of peer-reviewed research containing statistically significant results have also been found in social psychology (Greenwald 1975), educational interventions (Lipsey and Wilson 1993), and economics (De Long and Lang 1992).

We should be careful when interpreting these findings. The fact that most (or nearly all) original research is able to reject the null hypothesis can only be viewed as evidence of publication bias if we know a priori the proper proportion of true null hypotheses in this research. This proportion is unknowable, and there are other plausible explanations for these results. If researchers are exceptionally skilled at identifying effective therapies, policy instruments, managerial innovations, or other treatments or interventions, research examining the consequences of these interventions will generally conclude that they have an effect (see, for example, Lipsey and Wilson 1993). Similarly, if social scientists are skilled in developing insightful theories of human and institutional behavior, then tests of the key hypotheses from these theories ought to frequently reject the null hypothesis of independence. A less comforting explanation for the preponderance of positive results may be that virtually any treatment or intervention (that is, departure from the status quo) is likely to generate some effect, even if it is only a placebo effect. Alternatively, perhaps the traditional null hypothesis of independence employed in regression analysis is so weak as to be easily rejected in even moderately sized samples (Leamer 1978; McCloskey 1985). If any combination of these perspectives accurately characterizes a meaningful fraction of scholarship, then published research contains a predominance of statistically significant results not because of publication bias, but because most null hypotheses are in fact false. De Long and Lang (1992) formalize this idea, and in an extensive review of the economics literature they estimate that *virtually no unrejected null hypotheses in the peer-reviewed literature are false*. At most, one third of unrejected null hypotheses may be true. While De Long and Lang identify publication bias as the most likely source of this result, they interpret publication "bias" as the ability of editors and reviewers to weed out manuscripts that incorrectly fail to reject a false null hypothesis.

Consequences for Estimates of Effect Sizes. The outcome of a null hypothesis test is often the least interesting and least useful bit of information from scholarly research. Far more meaningful is the magnitude of the estimated effect, especially in management and policy research (in other words, what are the gains in student achievement from school vouchers? What are the cost savings from privatization?). Publication selection biases the estimates of average effect sizes in meta-analysis.

A well-known result in the statistics of meta-analysis is that publication bias in general will inflate average effect sizes, and that the relative magnitude of this bias is an inverse function of the population effect size (that is, the bias is largest when the actual effect size is smallest; see Sutton 2009). The inflation of average effect sizes often occurs regardless of whether publication bias is directional or nondirectional. This inflation stems from the fact that under publication bias, the average effect size in a meta-analysis is calculated from a censored distribution of effect sizes (see Greene 1993 for an excellent treatment of estimates from censored distributions). For example, if we assume that the population of effect sizes from original research is distributed normally so that $\Theta \sim N(\mu, \sigma^2)$, and if the observed realization of Θ is truncated at p-value P (that is, if values below P are not observed), then $E[\Theta_i \mid \Theta_i > P] = \mu + \delta(\alpha)\sigma$ where $\alpha = (P - \mu)/\sigma$ and $\delta(\alpha) = \varphi(\alpha)/(1 - (\Phi(\alpha)))$. From the standard normal density, $\delta(\alpha)$ will always be greater than zero, so the expected value of Θ_i will always be inflated.

While it may be obvious why directional publication bias inflates average effect sizes, the similar effect for nondirectional publication bias may require additional explanation. Recall that under nondirectional publication bias, manuscripts that reject the null hypothesis are more likely to be published regardless of the direction of the hypothesis test. Under these conditions, censoring is on the absolute value of the effect size, $|\Theta_i|$, conditional upon its variance. Since small values of Θ_i will be unobserved in the published literature, the mean absolute value of the observed effect size will increase. Moreover, since this censoring of small effect sizes will be symmetric only if $E[\Theta_i] = 0$—an unlikely occurrence—nondirectional publication bias will produce bias in average effect sizes similar to that produced by directional bias, though of smaller magnitude (for example, if $E[\Theta_i] > 0$, then nondirectional publication bias will overestimate the average effect size). With nondirectional publication bias, the magnitude of the bias is an inverse function of the sample size and the "true" effect size (Hedges 1984, 1992; Begg and Berlin 1988).

Meta-analyses have uncovered exactly this type of upward bias in average effect sizes in the published literature. For example, Smart (1964) found that average effect sizes from published articles in psychology were significantly larger than average effect sizes from unpublished conference papers or dissertations. Smart also found that dissertations with larger effect sizes were more likely to be published. When examining meta-analyses in education and the social sciences, Smith (1980) found that average effect sizes in published articles were one-third larger than average effect sizes from the unpublished literature. More recent research has concluded that effect sizes in published research are larger than effect sizes from unpublished research in the fields of behavioral treatments (Lipsey and Wilson 1993), education (Kulik and Kulik 1989), and medicine (Dickersin 2002; Egger, Jüni, Bartlett, Holenstein, and Sterne 2003, Turner 2008).

An alternative method for identifying the effect of publication bias in meta-analysis in the medical literature is to compare the average effect size from meta-analyses of small studies with the effect size calculated from large randomized trials. This approach gained prominence when it was discovered that while meta-analyses estimated that administering magnesium and nitrates to patients significantly reduced the mortality rate from heart attacks, later large-scale randomized controlled trials found no beneficial effect from these treatments (Cappelleri et al. 1996). In a systematic study of over sixty meta-analyses in the medical field, these authors found that conclusions regarding treatment effects from meta-analyses and large randomized controlled trials (RCTs) were in agreement in between 82 and 90 percent of cases, depending on how one defined a "large" RCT. When the results from meta-analyses and large RCTs disagree, however, estimated effect sizes from meta-analyses are nearly always larger (Cappelleri et al. 1996; see also Sutton 2005). Many researchers view these discrepancies as evidence of publication bias in the studies used in the meta-analyses.

While the effects of publication bias on average effect sizes are well understood, far less research has assessed the effect of publication bias on effect size variance. These effects from publication bias may be particularly noteworthy for random effects meta-regression where the between-study variance component is calculated using the sample of studies included in the meta-analysis. If this sample of studies constitutes a nonrandom sample of all studies conditional upon the magnitude of effect sizes, the random effects variance component will be estimated with error. Jackson (2006) asserts that it is impossible to make generalizations about how we should revise estimates of effect size variance in the presence of publication bias. In his later work, Jackson (2007) offers some advice regarding how one might adjust effect size variances to address publication bias, but these techniques are beyond the scope of this book.

Identifying Publication Bias

Funnel Plots and Radial Plots

Given its important implications for meta-analysis, researchers have devised several methods for identifying publication bias in a set of published studies. One of the earliest tools for identifying publication bias, and still among the most popular, is the funnel plot.

Imagine a relationship of interest in a population between variables Y and X. This relationship may be the correlation coefficient ρ_{XY}, the regression coefficient β, the difference in the average values of Y given various values of X, or the odds of a particular outcome in Y (for example, success or failure) given a particular state of X (for example, treatment or control). As we saw in chapter 3, common effect sizes for these relationships are Fisher's Z, Hedges's g, and the log odds ratio. Now imagine that a researcher draws a sample of N observations from the population and uses this sample to calculate the sample effect size $[\Theta_i]$. In repeated samples Θ_i will have variance σ_i^2 and standard error s_i. One simple way of testing the null hypothesis Ho: $\Theta = 0$ is using the standard normal deviate $Z = \Theta_i / s_i$, (or its small sample analog $t = \Theta_i / s_i$). Assuming unbiased sampling, the value of the sample estimate Θ_i will be unaffected by the sample size N, so that $E[\Theta_i] = \Theta$ for all N. This is not true for the precision of the sample estimate Θ_i, generally operationalized as the inverse of the standard error $(1/s_i)$. Since the variance of Θ_i is inversely proportional to N, the precision of Θ_i will be directly proportional to N. Under repeated samples (that is, across multiple studies using multiple samples), estimates of Θ_i will be normally distributed around Θ, and the variance of this distribution will be proportional to N.

Light and Pillemer (1984) were among the first to conceive of statistical results from a set of original studies examining a particular relationship of interest as analogous to estimates of Θ_i from repeated samples. If this sample of original studies was uncensored, a plot of Θ_i (on the horizontal axis) against s_i (on the vertical axis) ought to take the shape of an inverted funnel. That is, the distribution of effect sizes from original studies with large samples ought to be tightly clustered near the top of the funnel (where precision is high), and this distribution ought to spread out for original studies using smaller samples that estimate Θ_i with less precision. Moreover, this funnel ought to be symmetric around the population effect size Θ. Figure 6.1 shows an example of a symmetric funnel plot summarizing effect sizes from two hundred simulated studies with sample sizes ranging from 10 to 1,000 and an average effect size of .10. This plot was generated using the Stata command statement *metafunnel fishersz sterr* where the effect size Fisher's Z and its standard error were calculated as in chapter 3.

A visual examination of the funnel plot can provide two important pieces of information. First, since the funnel plot will be symmetric around Θ, it gives some information about the validity of the null hypothesis Ho: $\Theta = 0$ (that is, if the funnel plot is symmetric around some value of Θ other than zero, the null hypothesis is unlikely to be true). Second, and more important, if researchers, peer reviewers, or editors act in a way that censors nonsignificant research findings, the funnel plot will not be symmetric. For example, if original studies concluding that increases in the minimum wage do not increase unemployment are less likely to make it into the published literature, values of $\Theta_i = 0$ or $\Theta_i < 0$ will be "missing" from the funnel plot of these studies, especially in small samples (see, for example, Card and Krueger 1995). Figure 6.2 shows an example of an asymmetric funnel plot in which studies showing negative effects or small positive effects ($\Theta_i <$ .10) from small samples ($N < 200$) are excluded from the meta-analysis. These restrictions eliminated twenty-three of the two hundred effect sizes from figure 6.1, and the result is that figure 6.2 is clearly asymmetric, with effect sizes "missing" from the lower left quadrant of the funnel plot.

FIGURE 6.1. SYMMETRIC FUNNEL PLOT OF EFFECT SIZE AGAINST EFFECT SIZE STANDARD ERROR

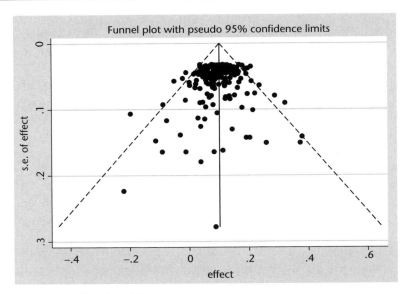

Note: Average effect size = .10.

Figure 6.3 illustrates a contour funnel plot for the same simulated effects sizes in figure 6.1. This funnel plot was generated with the Stata command statement *confunnel fishersz sterr* where the effect size Fisher's Z and its standard error were calculated as in chapter 3. Contour funnel plots include shaded bands representing values of Θ_i and s_i that allow the rejection of the null hypothesis $\Theta = 0$. If observed effect sizes are significantly more common just above the line demarking standard significance levels (in other words, if the published literature contains many more studies with results that are "barely" significant), this is often viewed as evidence of publication bias (see Moreno et al. 2009). This interpretation of contour funnel plots is problematic for meta-analysis in public management and policy. Many researchers in the social sciences do not report their regression results in sufficient detail to allow the meta-analyst to calculate an exact *p*-value. That is, many social scientists simply report the magnitude of the regression parameter estimates and identify the significance level of these estimates using asterisks. In these

FIGURE 6.2. ASYMMETRIC FUNNEL PLOT OF EFFECT SIZE AGAINST EFFECT SIZE STANDARD ERROR

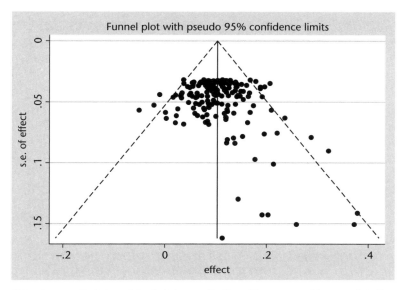

Notes: Average effect size = .10; effect sizes smaller than .10 are censored from small studies (*N* < 200).

cases, the meta-analyst can only calculate effect sizes that represent lower bounds; that is, the effect size associated with the particular number of asterisks reported in the original table. In virtually all cases, this effect size will underestimate the true sample effect size from the original study because the exact (unreported) *p*-value will be smaller than the reported *p*-value (see chapter 3). This reporting convention in the social sciences will also produce a large number of effect sizes that are "barely significant" at any standard *p*-value used to denote the number of asterisks commonly used in statistical tables (for example, $p < .05$, $p < .01$). Therefore, this reporting convention will produce many effect sizes that lie near the boundaries of the contour funnel plot. An unsuspecting meta-analyst following the advice of Moreno and colleagues might conclude that this pattern of effect sizes reflects potential publication bias, when in fact this pattern is an artifact of reporting conventions in the social sciences. The contour funnel plot in figure 6.3 using simulated data shows no evidence of publication bias.

**FIGURE 6.3. SYMMETRIC CONTOUR FUNNEL PLOT WITH
SIGNIFICANCE BANDS AT $p < .05$, $p < .01$, AND $p < .001$**

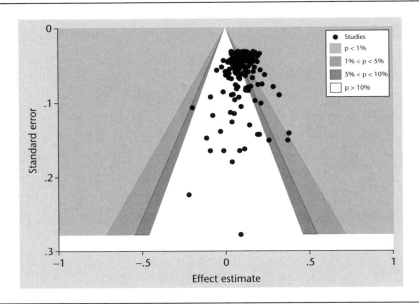

While the funnel plot was a useful first step, conclusions from a simple visual examination of these plots are neither precise nor unambiguous. Galbraith (1988, 1994) adapted the funnel plot by (1) replacing measures of Θ_i and s_i with measures of the standardized effect size Z and precision $1/s_i$, and (2) rotating the axes so that Z was now on the vertical axis and precision was measured on the horizontal axis. The resulting *radial plot* (also called a Galbraith plot) has a distinct advantage over the funnel plot in that the slope of a least squares regression line through the origin of the radial plot is an unbiased estimate of Θ from the sample of original studies (though this is true only in the fixed effects meta-analysis framework). Thus a significance test on b_1 from the radial plot regression

$$Z_i = b_1 \left(1/s_i\right) \tag{6.1}$$

allows us to test the null hypothesis that $\Theta = 0$. Figure 6.4 presents the data from figure 6.1 as a radial plot, which shows both the regression line b_1 and the 95 percent confidence bands around this regression line. Figure 6.5

FIGURE 6.4. RADIAL PLOT OF PRECISION AGAINST STANDARDIZED EFFECT SIZE

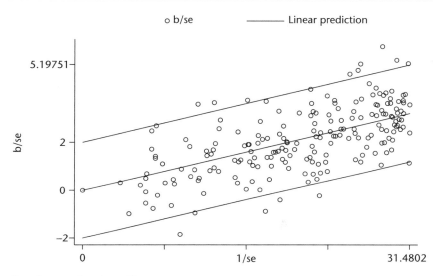

Note: Average effect size = .10.

presents the data from figure 6.2 as a radial plot. The radial plots in figures 6.4 and 6.5 were created using the Stata command statement *galbr fishersz sterr* where the Fisher's *Z* effect size and its standard error are calculated as in chapter 3. Note that like the funnel plot in figure 6.2, the radial plot in figure 6.5 shows a group of "missing" studies in the lower left quadrant (that is, where effect sizes are negative or small and the precision of the effect size estimate is low).

Tests for Funnel Asymmetry

Mathias Egger and his colleagues were among the first to recognize that the radial plot, properly amended, could provide a statistical test for publication bias (Egger, Smith, Schneider, and Minder 1997; see also Copas and Lozada-Can 2009). Specifically, if one relaxes the assumption that the radial plot regression line runs through the origin and estimates the model

$$Z_i = b_0 + b_1 \left(1/s_i \right) + e \tag{6.2}$$

FIGURE 6.5. RADIAL PLOT OF PRECISION AGAINST STANDARDIZED EFFECT SIZE

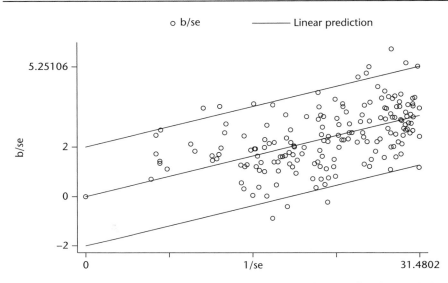

Notes: Average effect size = .10; effect sizes smaller than .10 are censored from small studies ($N < 200$).

using least squares, a hypothesis test on the intercept b_0 can be viewed as a test for publication bias in the sample of original studies. To see why this is so, consider the standard interpretation of a regression intercept as the average value of the dependent variable where all independent variables take on a value of zero. In the Egger test, the dependent variable is the standardized effect size and the independent variable is the estimate of the precision with which the effect size is estimated. When the measure of precision is equal to zero—that is, when Θ_i in an original study is estimated with infinite imprecision—the standardized effect size ought to be equal to zero (that is, $\Theta_i/\infty = 0$ regardless of the value of Θ_i). Therefore, if b_0 is something other than zero, this is evidence of censoring in the distribution of effect sizes from original studies.

Figure 6.6 reports the results from the Egger test for funnel plot asymmetry using the simulated effect size data from figures 6.2 and 6.4. Figure 6.6 was generated using the Stata command statement *metabias fishersz sterr1, egger* where the effect size Fisher's Z and its standard error are calculated as in chapter 3. The reader should recognize that the

FIGURE 6.6. EGGER TEST FOR FUNNEL PLOT ASYMMETRY; PRECISION IS PLOTTED AGAINST STANDARDIZED EFFECT SIZE

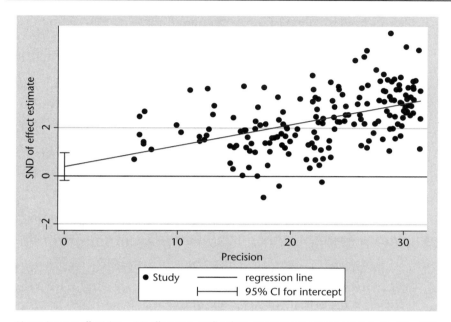

Notes: Average effect size = .10; effect sizes smaller than .10 are censored from small studies ($N < 200$); Ho: b_0 is rejected at $\alpha = .10$.

Egger test plot is identical to the radial plot in all respects, except that the regression line is no longer constrained to pass through the origin. The estimated value of b_0 in figure 6.5 is .34, and we can reject the null hypothesis that $b_0 = 0$ at $\alpha = .10$ (the standard significance level for the Egger test). We cannot reject Ho: $b_0 = 0$ at $\alpha = .05$.

Criticisms of the Egger Test for Publication Bias

The Egger test is routinely used in meta-analyses in the natural sciences, medicine, psychology, and education, and maintains its position as the default test for publication bias in meta-analysis computer software packages (such as Stata, Comprehensive Meta-Analysis, and RevMan). In fact, the original paper by Egger and colleagues is one of the most widely cited papers ever published in the *British Medical Journal*. (In January

2012, Google Scholar reported nearly five thousand citations for this paper.) Moreover, best practice standards of the Cochrane Collaboration (QUORUM) and the MOOSE group (Meta-analysis for Observation Studies in Epidemiology) both recommend using the funnel plot to diagnose publication bias. Despite this popularity, researchers in statistical science have identified a number of significant shortcomings of the Egger test.

Lack of Power. From the beginning, researchers have highlighted the low power of the Egger test; that is, the test often does not identify publication bias even when it is known to be present. Egger and his colleagues identified this shortcoming in their original article, and subsequent researchers have characterized the low power of the test through extensive Monte Carlo simulations (see, for example, Macaskill, Walter, and Irwig 2001; Peters, Sutton, Jones, Abrams, and Rushton 2006). Standard advice for practitioners is that they ought to counteract the low power of the test by using a more liberal α level (such as .10) when testing for publication bias (Egger, Smith, Schneider, and Minder 1997; Sterne et al. 2011).

Excessive Type I Error Rates. In addition to a lack of power, the Egger test has been shown to suffer from exaggerated type I error rates, over-rejecting the null hypothesis of no publication bias. That is, the Egger test often concludes that publication bias is present when it is not. Researchers have identified at least three reasons for these inflated type I errors: design elements in the original studies, statistical artifacts produced by the Egger test, and effect size heterogeneity.

Design Elements in Original Studies. Under the ideal conditions identified by Light and Pillemer (1984), in the absence of publication bias a graph of effect sizes plotted against their standard errors will take the shape of a funnel symmetric around the true effect size (see figure 6.1). Stated differently, under the assumptions that underlie the funnel plot and any tests for publication bias that employ the funnel plot, the magnitude of the (understandardized) effect size should be unrelated to its precision, variance, or sample size (in other words, the expected value of the effect size should be the same for all studies regardless of their sample size). If the average effect size is larger for studies using small samples, the funnel plot will be asymmetric, and the Egger test will reject the null hypothesis that $b_0 = 0$ from equation 6.2. In practice, rejecting the Egger test for funnel plot symmetry is almost invariably interpreted as evidence of publication bias (see figure 6.5). Egger and others, however, take care to point out that there are many reasons why small studies might produce larger effect sizes, including the following:

- Smaller studies allow for more effective monitoring of treatment compliance and more effective safeguards against attrition, so that smaller studies show larger treatment effects.
- The treatment may be especially effective for a small group of high-risk individuals, and these individuals may make up a larger proportion of the treatment group in small studies.
- Smaller experimental studies may be of inferior quality, and smaller observational studies may include fewer control variables. Both of these factors may lead to larger effect sizes in smaller studies.

The first two explanations for larger small-study effects will ring true for public policy scholars familiar with the problems experienced when "scaling up" policy innovations; in other words, the estimated effects from policy interventions in small-scale pilot programs frequently are significantly larger than those experienced in full-scale program implementation. Research in program evaluation often refers to this as the difference between the "treatment on the treated" and the "average treatment effect" (Wooldridge 2002). Any of the situations described above will produce a correlation between study size (that is, precision) and effect size, and the Egger test will interpret this correlation as evidence of publication bias. For these reasons, many scholars emphasize that the Egger test is more properly viewed as a test for small study effects, rather than as a test for publication bias (Sutton 2009).

Statistical Artifacts. Research in statistical science illustrates four ways in which evidence for publication bias from the Egger test may be artifactual. First, the standard Egger test violates the regression assumption that all variables are measured without error. Measurement error in predictor variables (X) is especially problematic because, unlike measurement error in the dependent variable (Y), measurement error in X can generate biased regression parameter estimates. The key predictor variable in the Egger test, $1/s_i$, is estimated from original studies and therefore contains sampling error (measurement error). In the simple bivariate Egger test in equation 6.2 this bias will generate an underestimate of b_1 and a corresponding overestimate of b_0, increasing the probability that the test will reject the null hypothesis that $b_0 = 0$. In the multivariate case (where the Egger test contains additional predictors of Z), b_1 may be biased up or down, depending on the magnitude of the measurement error in $1/s_i$ and the variance-covariance matrix $X'X$ (Berry and Feldman 1985). In either case, b_0 will also be biased, increasing the probability that the Egger test will reject the null hypothesis of no publication bias. Copas and Lozada-Can (2009) demonstrate that bias stemming from sampling error in the estimation of s_i generates serious bias in hypothesis tests in b_0 in the Egger test.

Second, most meta-analyses in medicine and psychology employ odds-based effect sizes, most commonly the log of the odds ratio comparing the treatment outcome in the experiment and control groups. It is well known that the variance of an odds ratio is proportional to its magnitude, which generates a correlation between the log of the odds ratio and its precision (Draper and Smith 1981). This correlation leads to asymmetry in the funnel plot of standardized effect sizes and means that Egger tests are more likely to incorrectly find publication bias among original studies with large effect sizes. Moreover, the magnitude of this correlation increases with the effect size, leading to the unfortunate situation where invalid tests for publication bias will lead researchers to have less confidence in meta-analyses where the true average effect size is large. Monte Carlo simulations show that for even moderate effect sizes (for example, log odds ratios of 1.5), the Egger test rejects a true null hypothesis of no publication bias up to 20 percent of the time (Macaskill, Walter, and Irwig 2001; Peters, Sutton, Jones, Abrams, and Rushton 2006; Copas and Lozada-Can 2009).

Third, Monte Carlo simulations also show that null hypothesis rejection rates for the Egger test are affected by the meta-sample size (that is, the number of effect sizes or studies included in the meta-analysis). Specifically, the probability that the Egger test incorrectly rejects a true null hypothesis increases with meta-sample size. Larger and presumably better (more comprehensive) meta-analyses are more likely to incorrectly conclude that original studies are contaminated by publication bias (Schwarzer, Antes, and Schumacher 2002; Peters, Sutton, Jones, Abrams, and Rushton 2006). Type I error rates also increase with the variability of sample sizes across original studies (Copas and Lozada-Can 2009). This is unfortunate, because this variability in sample sizes from original studies is what gives the Egger tests leverage to test the null hypothesis that the average effect size is zero (in other words, the hypothesis test on b_1 in equation 6.2).

Fourth, the appearance of funnel plot asymmetry, and the results of the Egger test, can be affected by the metric used to measure effect sizes (binary or continuous measures of effect size), and the metric used to measure precision (inverse variance, inverse standard error, sample size, or square root of the sample size) (Sutton 2009).

Effect Size Heterogeneity. A key assumption underlying the use of the funnel plot to detect publication bias is that all original studies attempt to measure the same population effect size Θ; in other words, that effect sizes from different studies (Θ_i) constitute a sample from a single population of effect sizes, and that effect sizes differ across studies due only to sampling variability (Light and Pillemer 1984). Strictly speaking, then, the funnel plot and any statistical test based on the funnel plot are appropriate only for fixed effects meta-analysis, though these tests can be employed in the random effects framework if effect sizes are standardized by the appropriate random effects variance. Indeed, in their original article, Egger and his colleagues cautioned that their test for publication bias was only appropriate for homogenous effect sizes (Egger, Smith, Schneider, and Minder 1997). Despite this warning, researchers routinely employ the Egger test for publication bias under conditions of significant effect size heterogeneity (see, for example, Lau, Ioannidis, Terrin, Schmid, and Olkin 2006).

Monte Carlo simulations clearly show that the Egger test generates unacceptably high type I error rates in the presence of effect size heterogeneity (Terrin, Schmid, Lau, and Olkin 2003; Sterne et al. 2011), and Peters and colleagues (2006) show that type I error rates can approach 100 percent under conditions of large heterogeneity in effect sizes and large meta-sample sizes. That is, in large meta-analyses of heterogeneous effect sizes, researchers may identify significant publication bias up to 100 percent of the time when no publication bias is present. Sterne and colleagues conclude that tests for funnel plot asymmetry are inappropriate for meta-analyses with heterogeneous effect sizes.

Researchers in meta-analysis identify three sources of effect size heterogeneity (Peters et al. 2010). *Clinical heterogeneity* arises when the effect of a treatment or policy intervention genuinely varies across categories of subjects in treatment groups (for example, by age, race, or gender), and the prevalence of these groups varies across studies. *Explained heterogeneity* is produced by measurement or design choices in the original studies. For example, Study A may estimate treatment effects after two years while Study B estimates treatment effects after four years, or Study A may estimate an effect from a cross-sectional regression model while Study B estimates an effect using a panel data model. In these cases it is possible to amend the basic Egger test to control for these design elements. In the first example, the meta-analyst could create a continuous moderator variable that measures the time elapsed since the treatment. In the second example, the meta-analyst could create a dichotomous moderator variable coded 1 for effect sizes from cross-sectional designs and coded 0 for effect sizes from panel designs. If we call these new variables M, the meta-analyst can estimate an augmented Egger test using the equation

$$Z_i = b_0 + b_1 \left(1/s_i\right) + b_2 M_i + e \qquad (6.3)$$

In the augmented Egger test, publication bias is still assessed using a hypothesis test on b_0. Borenstein and colleagues (2009) recommend using augmented Egger tests in almost all circumstances (see also Sutton 2009). Sterne and Egger (2005) illustrate the use of augmented Egger tests to control for parameter heterogeneity in traditional meta-analysis, though surprisingly these authors do not report the size of these augmented tests for identifying publication bias. Finally, *residual heterogeneity* is variability in effect sizes unexplained by clinical heterogeneity, study characteristics, or sample sizes from original studies (that is, fixed effects). Residual heterogeneity is generally measured using the random effects variance component τ^2.

Overall Recommendations. The shortcomings of the Egger test have led several researchers to offer alternative tests for publication bias. To avoid artifacts generated by measurement error in the independent variable, Macaskill, Walter, and Irwig (2001) recommend using n_i or $1/n_i$ rather than $1/s_i$ as the measure of precision in the Egger test. Subsequent research has shown that the Macaskill method has even lower power than the original Egger test, and few researchers in meta-analysis employ this test (Peters, Sutton, Jones, Abrams, and Rushton 2006). To avoid artifacts generated by the correlation between the magnitude of the odds ratio and its variance, Harbord, Egger and Sterne (2006) and Peters and colleagues offer alternative tests for publication bias for effect sizes calculated from binary outcomes. The Harbord and Peters tests are more powerful than the Egger test, and they avoid some of the latter's problems with inflated type I error rates. Unfortunately, these tests are appropriate only in the case of binary outcomes, and therefore can be used only with odds-based effect sizes. This restriction makes these tests of little use for researchers in public management and policy. Moreover, Peters and colleagues (2006) and Peters and others (2010) evaluate the performance of several augmented regression-based tests for publication bias, including several versions of the Egger test and the Harbord and Peters tests, and conclude that all have very low power to detect publication bias.

The shortcomings of regression-based tests for publication bias have led several researchers to recommend abandoning this approach, or to dramatically reduce our reliance upon it. For example, a group of the most prominent scholars in meta-analysis concluded that "even ignoring statistical concerns of power and choice of metric and weights, it is still unclear if funnel plots really diagnose publication bias" (Lau, Ioannidis, Terrin, Schmid, Ingram, and Olkin 2006, p. 599). In the most recent review of research regarding the Egger test, Sterne and his colleagues (2011) conclude that tests for funnel plot asymmetry should be used only in a minority of carefully chosen meta-analyses. One key piece of evidence supporting this recommendation is a study in which John Ioannadis and Thomas Trikalinos (2007) examined nearly seven thousand meta-analyses archived in the Cochrane Collaboration database and found that only 5 percent were characterized by low levels of unexplained parameter heterogeneity, relatively large meta-sample sizes, and meaningful differences in sample sizes across original studies. That is, few meta-analyses in practice possess the characteristics that serve as the foundation for the validity of funnel-plot tests of publication bias.

Testing for Publication Bias in Stata

Figures 6.1 to 6.6 illustrate publication bias using simulated data. In this section I use the meta-analysis ado files in Stata to test for publication bias in the sample data set summarizing original research in the area of environmental justice.[2] This example uses 680 effect sizes measuring the correlation between potential environmental risk in communities and the percentage of racial and ethnic minority residents in communities coded from forty-eight original studies.

Figure 6.7 shows the funnel plot for these effect sizes produced using the *metafunnel* command in Stata. Note that figure 6.7 seems to indicate an asymmetric funnel plot, with small studies showing negative correlations being absent from the funnel. Figure 6.8 shows the contour funnel plot for these effect sizes using the *confunnel* command in Stata. Figure 6.8 reinforces the impression of asymmetry, suggesting that the literature on environment justice may be contaminated with publication bias or small-study effects.

Because visual inspections of funnel plots are notoriously unreliable, I turn to two common statistical tests for publication bias. First I use the

FIGURE 6.7. FUNNEL PLOT OF 680 EFFECT SIZES CODED FROM THE ENVIRONMENTAL JUSTICE LITERATURE

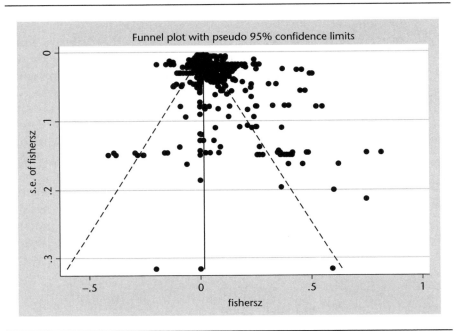

metabias command in Stata to conduct an Egger test. The intercept estimate from this test is 1.73 with a standard error of 0.18. Therefore I can reject the null hypothesis of funnel symmetry (which is typically interpreted as no publication bias) at $p < .001$ ($t = 9.43$). *Metabias* also calculates a second common test for publication bias, the Begg test based on rank order correlations between effect sizes and their variances (Begg and Mazumdar 1994). The standard normal statistic for the Begg test is 5.45, meaning that this test allows us to reject the null hypothesis of no publication bias at $p < .001$.[3]

All four indicators of funnel plot asymmetry suggest that the conclusions from original research in environmental justice may be contaminated by publication bias. While we cannot reject these results out of hand, we also need to remember that (1) both the Egger test and the Begg test suffer from low power, (2) the Egger test in particular is prone to false-positive

FIGURE 6.8. CONTOUR FUNNEL PLOT OF 680 EFFECT SIZES CODED FROM THE ENVIRONMENTAL JUSTICE LITERATURE

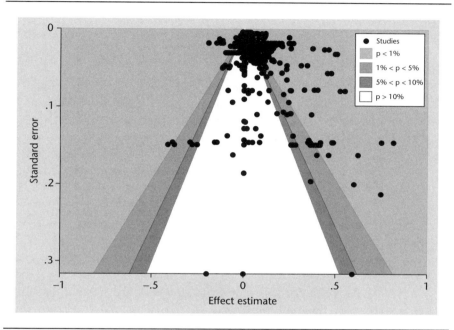

results in the presence of effect size heterogeneity, and (3) there are many sources of funnel plot asymmetry beyond publication bias. I return to the question of the accuracy of these tests at the end of the chapter.

Remedying and Preventing Publication Bias

Quantifying Threats from Unpublished Studies

The oldest approaches to remedying publication bias are not "remedies" so much as they are methods of measuring the severity of the threat posed by publication bias if it exists.

The Fail-Safe N. Rosenthal (1979) asks a simple question: assuming that a meta-analysis of m effect sizes is able to reject the null hypothesis that the average (or population) effect size $[\Theta]$ is zero, *how many effect sizes of zero would need to exist in the unpublished literature to reverse the conclusions from this hypothesis test?* Rosenthal called this number, N, the "fail-safe N."

The method for calculating the fail-safe N begins with the Stouffer sum of Z's meta-significance test. The formula for this test is

$$Z_s = \left[\sum_{i=1}^{m} Z_i \right] / \sqrt{m} \tag{6.4}$$

where m equals the number of effect sizes in the meta-analysis and Z represents the standard normal deviate (Z-score) associated with the p-value from a one-tailed hypothesis test on the null hypothesis that $\Theta = 0$ in the original study. The value Z_s can be compared to a standardized normal distribution to test the null hypothesis that all effect sizes $\Theta_1 = \Theta_2 = \ldots = \Theta_m = 0$ (for example, if $Z_s = 1.96$, we can reject the null hypothesis that all sample effect sizes equal zero at $\alpha = 0.05$).

Rosenthal then asks what value of N would satisfy the following formula:

$$\left[\sum_{i=1}^{m} Z_i \right] / \sqrt{(m = N)} < Z_\alpha \tag{6.5}$$

where Z_a is the critical value from the standard normal distribution associated with the null hypothesis in the meta-analysis. From this formula Rosenthal calculates

$$N = \left[\left(\sum Z_i \right) / Z_\alpha \right]^2 - m \tag{6.6}$$

N, the fail-safe N, represents the number of effect sizes where $\Theta_i = 0$ (or, more properly, the number of effect sizes where the average effect size equals zero) that would need to be included in the meta-analysis to be unable to reject the null hypothesis associated with the Stouffer test. Rosenthal conceived of this as the number of null results in the unpublished literature, or in the "file drawers" of researchers, required to invalidate the results from the Stouffer test. As a rule of thumb, Rosenthal suggested that if $N > (5*m) + 10$, the results from the meta-analysis are insensitive to publication bias.

The fail-safe N is commonly reported, especially in older meta-analyses. Current best practice, however, recommends against relying on the fail-safe N as a method of assessing the threat posed by publication bias (Becker 2005). First, since the fail-safe N employs the assumption that average effect sizes in the unpublished literature are equal to zero, it only assesses threats from nondirectional publication bias. With directional publication bias, the average of unpublished effect sizes would be larger or smaller than zero. Second, the fail-safe N is distribution free and does not rest on any statistical model. Therefore it is best viewed as a guidepost or heuristic, rather than as a precise test for the threat posed by publication bias. Finally, the fail-safe N assumes a fixed effects meta-regression and does not afford for adjustments using covariates or random effects variance components. This last limitation makes the fail-safe N particularly ill-suited for meta-analysis in public management and policy research.

Orwin's N_{es}. Orwin (1983) attempted to improve the utility of the fail-safe N approach by emphasizing the magnitude of effect sizes from original studies, rather than the p-values associated with null hypothesis tests from these studies. Specifically, Orwin asks the researcher to choose a minimum value Θ_{fs} where the effect size ceases to be substantively meaningful. Orwin's approach then asks, given the average effect size Θ_o from the observed sample of m effect sizes in the meta-analysis, how many effect sizes of value Θ_c must exist in the unpublished literature for the population average effect size to be below the minimum meaningful value Θ_{fs}? Orwin offers the following formula:

$$N_{es} = \left[\left(m \left(\Theta_0 - \Theta_c \right) / \left(\Theta_c - \Theta_{fs} \right) \right) \right] \tag{6.7}$$

For example, if a researcher concludes that effect sizes below 0.10 are not meaningful for a particular policy intervention, and a meta-analysis of 100 effect sizes from original studies produces an average calculated effect size of 0.25, Orwin's formula allows us to calculate that for the true average effect size to be below 0.10, at least 150 effect sizes equal to zero (that is, $\Theta_c = 0$) must be present in the unpublished literature. This formula is very flexible in that it can be used for odds-based, d-based, or r-based effect sizes.

Gleser and Olkin's $N^\wedge$. Gleser and Olkin (1996) offer the following formula for estimating the number of unpublished effect sizes that exist ($N^\wedge$) given a set of m observed effect sizes in a particular meta-analysis:

$$N^\wedge = \left[\left(m \left(1 - p_{max} \right) - 1 \right) / p_{max} \right] \tag{6.8}$$

where p_{max} represents the largest one-sided p-value from the null hypothesis test that $\Theta = 0$ in any original study. A critical limitation of $N^\wedge$ is that it assumes that the null hypothesis is true—that is, it assumes that the population effect size $\Theta = 0$. To illustrate this method, if the largest p-value associated with a sample of 100 effect sizes is .4, the Gleser and Olkin approach suggests that there are 148 effect sizes in unpublished studies. $N^\wedge$ is like the fail-safe N in that if it is implausibly large, this suggests that the results of the meta-analysis are robust to publication bias.

Trim-and-Fill Methods

In a pair of pathbreaking articles, Sue Duval and Richard Tweedie offered a suite of related methods that simultaneously estimate the degree of publication bias present in a set of effect sizes and adjust estimates of average effect sizes in the presence of publication bias (Duval and Tweedie 2000a; 2000b). The use of these "trim-and-fill" methods has become common practice in meta-analysis, and some version of trim-and-fill is available in all meta-analysis software packages, including Comprehensive Meta-Analysis, RevMan, and Stata.

Unfortunately, the assumptions underlying trim-and-fill, and recent assessments of its performance, generally make this suite of tools unsuited for meta-analysis in public management and policy, and in the social sciences more generally. First, the trim-and-fill method, described below, assumes that publication bias is directional—in other words, that effect sizes estimating either positive or negative effects are systematically excluded from the published literature. While directional publication bias is common in health care research, nondirectional publication bias may be more common in the social sciences. More important, recent assessments demonstrate that trim-and-fill methods perform poorly in the presence of effect size heterogeneity. Terrin and colleagues (2003) find that when effect sizes are heterogeneous, trim-and-fill methods identify and adjust for publication bias where none exists. That is, in the presence of effect size heterogeneity, trim-and-fill methods suffer from the same inflated type 1 errors as the Egger test. Peters and colleagues (2007) conclude that there is great variability across the related trim-and-fill methods, so that conclusions from these methods may contain significant error. In addition, these authors find that in the presence of meaningful effect size heterogeneity, trim-and-fill methods significantly underestimate the magnitude of average effect sizes (see also Moreno et al. 2009, Peters et al. 2010). For these reasons, trim-and-fill methods are not recommended for researchers in public management and policy, and the brief description of these methods provided here is for informational purposes only.

To introduce the method of trim-and-fill, it is worth revisiting the symmetric funnel plot in figure 6.1 and the asymmetric funnel plot produced by directional publication bias in figure 6.2. The central idea behind trim-and-fill is to (1) identify the number of censored studies in the bottom left quadrant of figure 6.2 (compared with figure 6.1); (2) "trim off" an equal number of studies from the bottom right quadrant of figure 6.2 and use the remaining effect sizes to calculate an unbiased estimate of the population effect size Θ; (3) estimate the magnitude of the censored effect sizes; and (4) use these estimated "pseudo" effect sizes to "fill in" the funnel plot in figure 6.2 so that one might calculate an unbiased estimate of effect size variance.

Recall that figure 6.2 presents an asymmetric funnel plot of 177 effect sizes. Denote each of these effect sizes as Θ_i. From figure 6.2 we can calculate an estimate of the population effect size Θ, denoted $\Theta^\wedge$.

- The first step in trim-and-fill requires calculating an effect size deviation $D_i = \Theta_i - \Theta^\wedge$ and rank ordering D_i.
- The second step in trim-and-fill requires identifying γ, the length of the run of the largest values of D_i from the right side of the funnel plot in figure 6.2 (that is, the length of the run of the largest positive deviations). Using the assumption that in the absence of publication bias funnel plots will be symmetric, we can estimate the number of censored effect sizes in figure 6.2 as $N = \gamma - 1$ (this is the simplest of three estimates of N provided by Duval and Tweedie).
- In the third step, the largest N effect sizes are removed from the lower right quadrant of figure 6.2 (that is, these studies are "trimmed"), and a new estimate $\Theta^\wedge$ is calculated from this trimmed sample of effect sizes. In practice, the first three steps are iterated until the value of $\Theta^\wedge$ converges.
- The fourth step in trim-and-fill is estimating the magnitude of the unobserved (censored) effect sizes. This is done by taking the value of each of the N trimmed effect sizes, multiplying this value by (-1), and placing these new N pseudo-effect sizes into the lower left quadrant of the funnel plot in figure 6.2. That is, these estimated pseudo-effect sizes are used to "fill in" the asymmetric funnel plot (the variances of the N trimmed effect sizes are attached to these new pseudo-effect sizes).
- The fifth step in trim-and-fill is to re-estimate $\Theta^\wedge$ (and its variance) using the full sample of original and pseudo-effect sizes.

Figure 6.9 is produced using the Stata command statement *metatrim fishersz sterr, funnel* where the effect size Fisher's Z and its standard error

FIGURE 6.9. FUNNEL PLOT FOR "TRIMMED AND FILLED" EFFECT SIZES PLOTTED AGAINST EFFECT SIZE STANDARD ERRORS

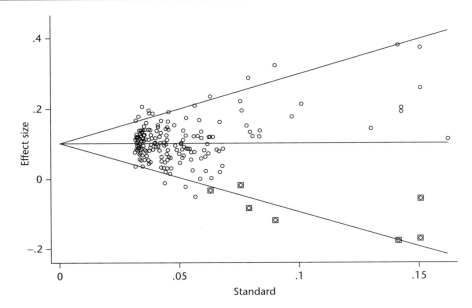

Note: Funnel plot for "trimmed and filled" effect sizes (vertical axis) plotted against effect size standard errors (horizontal axis). Filled effect sizes are represented by squares.

are calculated as in chapter 3. This *metatrim* command implements the trim-and-fill method on the 177 simulated effect sizes from figure 6.2. *Metatrim* correctly diagnoses significant funnel asymmetry among these 177 effect sizes, and correctly identifies that there is little heterogeneity across effect sizes beyond that attributable to differences in sample size (in other words, average effect sizes can be estimated using a fixed effects model). In this example the trim-and-fill method is a bit underpowered, since the estimate of N (the number of censored effect sizes) is only 7, whereas 23 effect sizes are censored in figure 6.2. The "filled" funnel plot is presented in figure 6.9, with the original effect sizes represented with circles and the pseudo-effect sizes represented using squares (note that the output from the *metatrim* command reverses the funnel plot axes). The average effect size calculated from this filled sample of 184 effect sizes is 0.102, which is nearly identical to the value of 0.10 used to generate the simulated effect sizes.

Selection Bias Models

The second most common approach to remedying publication bias is to calculate corrected estimates of average effect sizes using models that explicitly incorporate publication selection. Selection bias models have two major advantages over the far easier trim-and-fill method. First, researchers are able to use covariates when estimating effect sizes in selection bias models, whereas trim-and-fill cannot accommodate covariates. Second, selection bias models of effect size can be designed to avoid the excessive type I errors regarding publication bias that plague trim-and-fill in the presence of effect size heterogeneity.[4]

The Selection Bias Model Approach. Correcting estimates of effect size through selection bias modeling requires two equations. The *effect size equation* describes the distribution of effect sizes in the absence of publication bias. This equation can take one of four familiar forms:

1. A fixed effects model with no covariates: $\Theta_i \sim N\left(\Theta, \sigma_i^2\right)$
2. A random effects model with no covariates: $\Theta_i \sim N\left(\mu_\Theta, \sigma_i^2 + \tau^2\right)$
3. A fixed effects model with covariates: $\Theta_i = \beta_0 + \sum \beta_k X_k + \varepsilon_i, \varepsilon_i \sim N\left(0, \sigma_i^2\right)$
4. A random effects model with covariates: : $\Theta_i = \beta_0 + \sum \beta_k X_k + \varepsilon_i, \varepsilon_i \sim N\left(0, \sigma_i^2 + \tau^2\right)$

Average effect sizes from models 1 and 2 are estimated using the techniques described in chapter 3, while average effect sizes from models 3 and 4 are estimated using the techniques described in chapter 4.

The *selection equation* defines how the observed effect sizes Θ_i^* are affected by publication bias. As we saw above, in the absence of publication bias $E\left[\Theta_i^*\right] = E\left[\Theta_i\right] = \Theta$, and $\Theta_i^* \sim \Theta_i$. In the presence of publication bias, neither of these identities holds, and the selection equation specifies how Θ_i^* can be transformed into Θ_i. If the selection mechanism were known, we could derive Θ_i from Θ_i^* by simply inverting this mechanism and calculating a weight (ω_i) for each value of Θ_i^* so that $\omega_i\left(\Theta_i^*\right) = \Theta_i$. Since the selection process is never known, however, the parameters of the selection equation must be estimated from the data or set a priori. When the parameters of the selection equation are estimated, we can use them to transform Θ_i^* into an approximation of Θ_i. When the parameters of the selection equation are set a priori, however, we can only use them to conduct a sensitivity analysis to estimate the expected value of Θ_i under the hypothetical conditions defined by the parameters selected a priori.

There are two general selection bias models in the meta-analysis literature. The oldest approach is to model selection (or publication) conditional only upon P, the p-value associated with the key null hypothesis test in the original study (see Hedges 1984; Iyengar and Greenhouse 1988; Hedges 1992; Hedges and Vevea 1996, 2005; Copas and Malley 2008). Consistent with the discussion earlier, the probability that an effect size Θ_i appears in the published literature increases as $P(t_i)$ decreases (for directional publication bias) or as $P(|t_i|)$ decreases (for nondirectional publication bias), where t_i is the t-score associated with the key null hypothesis test. An alternative approach is to model selection conditional upon both Θ_i and σ_i, with the probability of publication an increasing function of the first and a decreasing function of the second (Copas 1999; Copas and Shi 2000, 2001). For simplicity, I will refer to these two selection bias models as the Hedges method and the Copas method, respectively. While neither method is commonly used in the meta-analysis literature, in practice the Hedges method is more often used to correct effect sizes for publication bias, while the Copas method is generally restricted to conducting sensitivity analyses. The Copas method is also more difficult to estimate in practice.

Selection Bias Model Estimation: The Hedges Method. While the function linking publication to p-values is almost certainly continuous, the Hedges method approximates this continuous function with a step function. That is, the meta-analyst chooses a set of categories or ranges of $P(t_i)$ and estimates or selects a common weight ω that is applied to all Θ_i^* with p-values in that range. For example, assume that the probability of selection or publication (the inverse probability of censoring) is directional as a function of $P(t_i)$ so that effect sizes Θ_i with smaller p-values are more likely to be published. A simple three-category step function might look like this:

$$\omega\left(p\right) = \begin{array}{lll} \omega_1 = 1 & \text{if} & 0 \le p_i \le 0.05 \\ \omega_2, & \text{if} & 0.05 < p_i \le 0.50 \\ \omega_3, & \text{if} & 0.50 < p_i \le 1.00 \end{array} \qquad (6.9)$$

where the ω are the parameters of the selection equation. This step function says that there are three probabilities that any effect size Θ_i will be published. Since we assume that the probability of publication increases as $P(t_i)$ decreases, $\omega_1 > \omega_2 > \omega_3$. Because the population size for Θ_i is unknowable (we do not know how many effect sizes exist in the population), ω

cannot be operationalized as an absolute weight, but only as a relative weight. Therefore, we lose nothing by normalizing one of the ω (in this case ω_1) to 1, and ω_2 and ω_3 are some positive fraction of ω_1. Using these weights we can recover the estimated effect sizes Θ_i in the absence of publication bias using $\omega\left(\Theta_i^*\right)$. We can then use these publication bias corrected effect sizes to calculate an average effect size (corrected for publication bias), or estimate a meta-regression model where these publication bias corrected effect sizes are used as the dependent variable.

The weights ω in the step function are the parameters of the selection equation. These parameters can be estimated from the observed Θ_i^* using maximum likelihood. While the specifics of this estimation are quite technical, and beyond the scope of this book, interested readers can find excellent presentations of this approach in Hedges (1992) and Hedges and Vevea (1996, 2005). Alternatively, these parameters can be posited a priori, and the sensitivity of meta-analysis results to publication bias can be assessed by positing different sets of values for ω (Vevea and Woods 2005). One final benefit of the Hedges method is that the selection-weighted models can be used to test for publication bias, as well as correct for this bias. In the absence of publication bias, MLE estimates of the selection model parameters ought to be equal. In our case, in the absence of publication bias $\omega_1 = \omega_2 = \omega_3$. The null hypothesis Ho: $\omega_1 = \omega_2 = \omega_3$ can be evaluated using a likelihood ratio test on the estimated parameters ω. The test statistic is distributed as a X^2 with degrees of freedom equal to $j - 1$ (or 2 in the present example).

One important strength of the selection bias modeling approach is its flexibility. Weight functions can be estimated or posited for r-based, d-based, and odds-based effect sizes, and these weights can be used to correct or assess the sensitivity of any of these effect sizes in the presence of publication bias. In fact, Hedges (1992) and Hedges and Vevea (2005) are two of the few examples where r-based effect sizes are used to illustrate the development of new statistical tools in meta-analysis. In addition, this approach can be used to model directional or nondirectional publication bias, and can be used when estimating average effect sizes with or without covariates.

Selection Bias Model Estimation: The Copas Method. The Copas method uses the same effect size equations as the Hedges method (in other words, effect sizes are predicted using fixed or random effects models with or without covariates). But whereas the Hedges method assumes that publication is strictly a function of the p-value associated with the key null hypothesis in original studies, the Copas method assumes that the probability of publication is a function of both the magnitude of the estimated effect size Θ_i and its standard error s_i (Copas 1999; Copas and Shi 2000, 2001). Specifically, the Copas method assumes that publication selection can be modeled as a Probit equation of the form

$$Z_i = a + b/s_i + \delta_i, \delta_i \sim N(0, 1) \qquad (6.10)$$

where a represents the baseline probability that an effect size will be published and b is a positive parameter denoting the increased probability of publication as the precision of the effect size increases.

Two aspects of the Copas selection equation are especially noteworthy. First, Θ_i is observed (that is, the effect size is published) only when $Z_i > 0$. Second, e_i from the effect size equation and δ_i from the selection equation share a bivariate normal distribution with correlation coefficient ρ. With the Copas method, meta-analysts can calculate effect sizes corrected for publication bias using the following formula:

$$E\left[\Theta_i | Z_i > 0, s_i\right] = \Theta^* + \rho\sigma_i\lambda\left(a + b/s_i\right) \qquad (6.11)$$

where λ is the Mills Ratio $[\varphi\,(a + b/s_i)]/[\Phi\,(a + b/s_i)]$.

The Copas selection model and the approach to estimating publication-bias corrected effect sizes should be familiar to many social scientists as the Heckman (1979) method for estimating treatment effects under conditions of partial observability. There are two key differences between the Copas method and the Heckman method. First, Copas models selection using the Mills ratio, while Heckman models observability using the inverse Mills ratio. That is, Copas corrects for the nonrandom process of inclusion whereas Heckman corrects for the nonrandom process of exclusion. This difference has no effect on the corrected estimates of effect sizes or treatment effects. Second, and more important, when using the Heckman approach researchers believe they understand the selection process and parameterize this process by including independent variables in the selection model. By contrast, the Copas method makes no claim about knowledge of the selection process, which means that the parameters a and b in the Copas selection equation 6.10 cannot be estimated, but must be set a priori. In practice, researchers posit a range of values for both a and b that reflect more or less severe publication selection, then estimate corrected effect sizes using various values of a and b.[5] If these "corrected" effect sizes from equation 6.11 differ markedly from the observed effect sizes Θ^* in the published literature, the researcher concludes that Θ^* are biased by publication selection.

Limits of the Selection Model Approach. Despite the potential embodied in selection bias modeling, both the Hedges and Copas methods have meaningful limitations for researchers in practice. First, the validity of the results from selection modeling rests heavily upon properly specified equations. Proper specification of the effect size equation is especially important. Misspecification of this equation can lead to excessive effect size heterogeneity, and such heterogeneity can invalidate likelihood ratio tests for publication bias (in other words, these tests will produce inflated type I errors, much like the Eggert test) and produce "corrected" effect size estimates that are far from correct (Hedges and Vevea 2005). Second, methods for estimating weighted selection models are generally difficult to implement. Estimating selection model parameters using maximum likelihood is quite complicated, and these algorithms are not included in any of the most popular software packages for meta-analysis (such as RevMan, Comprehensive Meta-Analysis, or Stata). Moreover, estimation of these models often fails, especially with small samples (Vevea and Woods 2005; Stanley 2008; Rucker, Carpenter, and Schwarzer 2011). Using these methods for sensitivity analysis, where the researchers posit values of ω a priori, is much more tractable. Finally, both the Hedges method and the Copas method assume that each study in the meta-analysis generates a single effect size. That is, the likelihood functions underlying estimation of these methods assume that the observations in the meta-analysis are independent. We saw in chapters 4 and 5, however, that this assumption is virtually always false for meta-analyses in public management, in public policy, and for the social sciences in general. Moreover, the techniques for robust cluster estimation that are often essential for the conduct of meta-regression in these fields are generally incompatible with the type of weighting schemes used in selection bias modeling. Therefore, while these approaches are intriguing, they cannot be recommended until their performance with social science data is better understood and until they are adapted for situations in which effect sizes are not independent.

Weighted Regression Models

Recently, Rucker and her colleagues (Rucker 2010; Rucker, Schwarzer, Carpenter, Binder, and Schumacher 2010; Rucker, Carpenter, and Schwarzer 2011) have proposed a new approach to controlling for publication bias that does not make use of a separate selection equation. In effect, the Rucker method treats publication bias and other types of small-study effects as a special form of between-study heterogeneity. The fundamental equation for the Rucker method is

$$\Theta_i^{\#} = \Theta^{\wedge} + \sqrt{(\sigma_i^2 + \tau^2) * (\alpha + \varepsilon_i)} \tag{6.12}$$

where $\Theta_i^{\#}$ is the estimated sample effect size corrected for publication bias, $\Theta^{\wedge}$ is the estimate of the population effect size corrected for publication bias, and α is the estimate of small study effects for publication bias. When $\alpha = 0$, this formula reduces to the familiar random effects meta-analysis without covariates.

Estimation of $\Theta_i^{\#}$ requires that we obtain estimates of σ_i^2, τ^2, $\Theta^{\wedge}$ and α. The first two are simply the familiar fixed effects and random effects variance components, which can be estimated from the data. $\Theta^{\wedge}$ and α are the slope and intercept (b_1 and b_0) from the Egger test for publication bias (equation 6.2), estimated via maximum likelihood.

In addition to $\Theta_i^{\#}$, Rucker offers what she calls the "limit effect size," $\Theta_{\infty i}$, which is the estimated sample effect size that one would obtain if the original study generating that effect size had used a sample of infinite size. That is:

$$\Theta_{\infty i} = \Theta^{\wedge} + \sqrt{[\tau^2 / (s_i^2 + \tau^2)] * (\Theta_i - \Theta^{\wedge})}, \tag{6.13}$$

and

$$E[\Theta_{\infty i}] = \Theta^{\wedge} + \tau \alpha \tag{6.14}$$

$\Theta_i^{\#}$ and $\Theta_{\infty i}$ are offered as two alternative estimates of effect sizes corrected for publication bias. These two estimates can be combined using the methods described in chapter 3 to calculate estimates of average effect sizes from samples of effect sizes contaminated with publication bias. Presumably, these corrected estimates of effect sizes could also be used as vectors of dependent variables in a meta-regression model, though Rucker does not use them in this manner.

Rucker offers this method as an improvement over the selection modeling approaches of Hedges and Copas, since the method neither relies upon the untestable assumptions of Hedges's and Copas's selection models, nor interprets small sample effects as being driven solely by selection bias. While both assertions are accurate, at the present time researchers in public management and policy should avoid using the regression weighting approach to correct for publication bias. First, the approach is quite new, and its performance has not been studied extensively, particularly when using the types of data common in meta-analyses in the social sciences. Second, and more important, the Rucker method corrects for small sample effects using estimates from the Egger test for publication bias. Earlier in this chapter we saw that estimates of b_0 from the Egger test can be exceptionally poor estimates of publication bias. It is unknown how well b_0 estimates other sources of small sample effects, or what meaning we might read into these values of b_0. Second, recent simulation studies have found that the slope parameter b_1 from the Egger test is a poor estimate of effect sizes corrected for publication bias. In particular, the performance of b_1 as a publication-bias corrected estimate of average effect size deteriorates markedly as the true effect size increases, as the meta-sample size decreases, and as effect size heterogeneity increases (Moreno et al. 2009).

Preventing Publication Bias

Despite significant progress in developing statistical techniques that test for publication bias and control for the effects of publication bias when it is present, the tools for addressing publication bias are still plagued with serious deficiencies. An obvious alternative to attempting to manage threats from publication bias ex post is to try to prevent these threats ex ante. More than a decade ago, Sterne, Egger, and Smith (2001) suggested that the best advice for addressing publication bias is that prevention is better than a cure, and this advice has not changed (Sterne et al. 2011). Lau and his colleagues concur, stating that "the prevention of publication bias is much more desirable than any diagnostic or corrective analysis" (Lau, Ioannidis, Terrin, Schmid, Ingram, and Olkin 2006, 600).

The most obvious method for avoiding the threats posed by publication bias is to is to try to include as much of the unpublished or grey literature as possible when conducting a meta-analysis. This is the approach recommended in chapter 1. By carefully searching the unpublished literature and coding effect sizes from unpublished studies, the meta-analyst can simultaneously test for publication bias and control for its effects by including a dichotomous moderator variable in a meta-regression model that identifies effect sizes from unpublished studies. The null hypothesis test on the parameter for this variable tests for the presence of publication bias, while its magnitude provides an estimate of the importance of this bias. While managing publication bias ex ante through sampling design and data gathering requires more time and effort than diagnosing and controlling for it ex post, it is far more effective. From this perspective, controlling threats to inference in meta-analysis is really no different than controlling threats to inference in most of social science research: design trumps analysis (Rubin 2008).

To illustrate this method of managing publication bias, I turn again to the sample data set of 680 effect sizes from the environmental justice literature. In chapter 5 I estimated a CRVE random effects meta-regression using this data set. When coding these effects I also coded whether they came from published or unpublished studies. For this example I re-estimate the CRVE random effects meta-regression and include a moderator variable identifying whether the effect size came from an unpublished study. The parameter estimate for this variable is $b = -0.02$ with a standard error of 0.013. The intercept for this model is 0.066, which represents the average conditional effect size from published studies. Therefore, the parameter estimate for the moderator variable suggests that on average, effect sizes from unpublished studies are 30 percent smaller than effect sizes found in the peer-reviewed literature, though we cannot reject the null hypothesis that this unpublished study effect is zero ($t = -1.53$, $p = 0.133$). These results contradict the results from the funnel plots, Egger test, and Begg test described earlier. Using this preferred method, then, there is limited evidence that effect sizes in the environmental justice literature are contaminated by publication bias.

Conclusion

Decades of research into the process of peer review have led to concerns about the possibility of publication bias in the scientific literature. If the peer-reviewed literature represents a biased sample of all research completed on a particular question, then any systematic review of this literature will produce an inaccurate picture of scientific knowledge regarding this question. It is not an exaggeration to state that the potential for publication bias causes some researchers to question the value of meta-analyses, though I would hasten to point out that these same concerns should apply to any review of the published literature on a topic.

Several tests for publication bias have been offered, though as discussed, recent research has cast doubt on both the size and the power of these tests. And, as I show in chapter 7, the most common test for publication bias in the social sciences is unreliable in almost all circumstances faced by researchers in practice. Similarly, several methods for controlling or remedying publication bias have been offered. Some of these methods, such as trim-and-fill, are of little value to researchers in public management and policy. Other approaches, such as selection bias models, are difficult to execute in practice and not particularly robust. Therefore, they are best thought of as sensitivity tests for the likely consequences of varying degrees of publication bias, if in fact publication bias is present (which is generally unknowable). While the new regression-based approaches to controlling for publication bias have promise, their performance under conditions commonly faced by researchers in management, public policy, and the social sciences has not been adequately assessed. Therefore, the best advice for researchers hoping to conduct a meta-analysis in public management and policy is to (1) take care to gather as much of the unpublished or grey literature as possible and (2) use meta-regression analysis to parameterize any differences between average effect sizes in the published and unpublished literature.

Notes

1. Denton (1985) demonstrates that the effects of publication bias may arise even when individual researchers do not engage in this type of "data mining." Specifically, the probability that a set of researchers acting independently but using a common data set will produce results that incorrectly reject a true null hypothesis increases with the number of hypotheses tested and with the number of researchers using the data set.
2. All Stata commands necessary to replicate this analysis are provided on the companion website.
3. The *metabias* and *metafunnel* commands in Stata also support Harbord's and Peters's tests for publication bias. These tests are only appropriate for original studies with binary outcomes, so they are not illustrated here.
4. A third benefit is that selection models can be used to assess and correct for publication bias when sample sizes in original studies are chosen on the basis of formal power analysis. In these situations, there is often a strong inverse relationship between effect size and sample size that is not due to publication bias (Hedges and Vevea 2005). While sample size based on power analysis is increasingly common in medicine and psychology, this technique is still uncommon in public management and policy research.
5. P_s, the marginal probability that an effect size will be published, is estimated using $P_s = \Phi(a + b/s_{es})$. Evaluating this equation at the minimum and maximum observed values of s_{es} will give the minimum and maximum probability that an effect size $(\Theta_i|\,S_i)$ will be observed.

CHAPTER SEVEN

META-ANALYSIS IN ECONOMICS

Evan J. Ringquist

"Furthermore, it is hoped that empirical surveys in general, and submissions to the Journal of Economic Surveys *in particular, will soon feature MRA methods—adopted as the rule, rather than as the exception"*

(ROBERTS 2005, 297).

"In spite of their widespread use in Economics, methods for summarizing regression slopes have received less attention in the statistical literature . . . and analytical approaches [have] been proposed in the methods sections of substantive syntheses without much attention to the statistical behavior of the estimators and tests involved"

(BECKER AND WU 2007, 415).

The approach to meta-analysis and meta-regression illustrated in this book relies on the techniques developed substantively in the disciplines of psychology, medicine, and education, and developed technically in the fields of statistics and biostatistics. A distinct approach to meta-analysis has developed independently in the discipline of economics. This approach, pioneered and developed by Tom Stanley and his collaborators, has come to be known as "FAT-MST-PET-MRA," a compound acronym for "Funnel Asymmetry Test-Meta Significance Test-Precision Effect Test-Meta Regression Analysis" (Stanley 2005; Callot and Paldam 2011). To be sure, research in economics contains assessments of publication bias (Card and Krueger 1995; Ashenfelter, Harmon, and Oosterbeek 1999) and meta-analyses of policy-relevant effects (see, for example, Smith and Kaoru 1990; Smith and Huang 1995) that do not use FAT-MST-PET-MRA. These examples notwithstanding, the FAT-MST-PET-MRA is by far the most common approach to meta-analysis in economics. A Google Scholar search in January 2012 found 724 citations to the key expository articles for FAT-MST-PET-MRA (Stanley and Jarrell 1989; Stanley 2001; Stanley 2005), and the *Journal of Economic Surveys* (a publication of the American Economics Association) devoted a special issue to illustrating this approach to meta-analysis and advocating greater utilization of it. By contrast, FAT-MST-PET-MRA is all but invisible in the traditional meta-analysis community, as none of the standard books in this field reference Stanley's contributions (see Lipsey and Wilson 2001; Rothstein, Sutton, and Borenstein 2005; Cooper 2010; Kulinskaya, Morgenthaler, and Staudte 2008; Borenstein, Hedges, Higgins, and Rothstein 2009; Cooper, Hedges, and Valentine 2009). Becker and Wu (2007) have noted that FAT-MST-PET-MRA is less explicitly grounded in statistical theory than is the traditional approach to meta-analysis. Despite its popularity, the performance of FAT-MST-PET-MRA has not been rigorously assessed. In this chapter I introduce the FAT-MST-PET-MRA approach and provide one of the first comprehensive assessments of its components.

The FAT-MST-PET-MRA Approach to Meta-Regression

To oversimplify, original research using statistical analysis has two goals: estimation and inference. These goals are related but distinct. Estimation focuses on measuring the magnitude of associations or the effects from treatments or interventions, and these estimates are often used in decision making. In regression analysis, the quantity of interest for estimation is generally the parameter estimate b_j. Inference (or hypothesis testing), by contrast, focuses on the ability to distinguish estimated effects from zero. Results from hypothesis tests are often used to test implications or expectations from theories of behavior. In regression analysis, the quantity of interest for hypothesis testing is the p-value for the test statistic on the parameter estimate b_j. While standard null hypothesis testing has its critics (see, for example, Gill 1999; Parkhurst 2001; McCloskey and Ziliak 2008), it is likely to remain a staple of quantitative empirical research for the foreseeable future.

Meta-analysis can also emphasize the goals of estimation and inference. By utilizing effect sizes and focusing on the measurement of average aggregate effects, the traditional approach to meta-analysis emphasizes estimation. By contrast, in utilizing *t*-scores and focusing on statistical significance, the FAT-MST-PET-MRA approach to meta-analysis emphasizes inference. Specifically, FAT-MST-PET-MRA has three elements: (1) identifying publication bias through hypothesis testing (the FAT); (2) identifying the presence of "true" effects (that is, effects purged of publication bias) through hypothesis testing (the MST); and (3) estimating the magnitude of "true" effects (the PET). The two approaches converge to a meaningful degree in meta-regression in that both traditional meta-analysis and FAT-MST-PET-MRA use this technique to help account for why original studies reach different conclusions when examining a common research question.

Testing for Publication Bias Using the FAT

Testing for publication bias using the FAT begins with the familiar observation from chapter 6 that in the absence of publication bias, observed estimates of some effect Θ_i should vary randomly around the true population value Θ regardless of the precision with which Θ_i is estimated. That is,

$$\Theta_i = b_1 + b_0 \left(se_i\right) + e_i \qquad (7.1)$$

where b_1 is the consistent estimate of the population effect size Θ and se_i is the precision with which Θ_i is estimated. I use Θ_i in this illustration to preserve consistency with the presentation of effect sizes in other chapters. *An essential difference for FAT-MST-PET-MRA compared with traditional meta-analysis is that Θ_i is actually the parameter estimate associated with the key variable of interest (the focal predictor) from a regression model in an original study, rather than an effect size.* se_i is the standard error of this parameter estimate. In the context of our continuing examples, Θ_i would be the parameter estimate b_j for the variable X_j identifying voucher recipients in an original study of the effectiveness of school vouchers (with $se_i = s_{bj}$), and Θ_i would be the parameter estimate b_j for the variable X_j measuring the proportion of minority households in a community in an original study of environmental inequities (with $se_i = s_{bj}$). Bias stemming from publication selection regarding Θ_i will be proportional to ($b_0^* se_i$). More important, in the absence of publication bias b_0 in equation 7.1 ought to be zero because, assuming random sampling, even when regression parameters are estimated imprecisely these estimates are still consistent. Therefore, the precision of the parameter estimate (se_i) does not affect its expectation. A simple test for publication bias, then, is a null hypothesis test on b_0 from equation 7.1. The problem with this approach is that e_i in equation 7.1 is heteroskedastic. The source of this heteroskedasticity is the varying precision in the estimate of Θ_i. Therefore, if we divide all elements of the data matrix by the standard error of Θ_i, the error from the resulting equation will be homoskedastic:

$$t_i = b_0 + b_1 \left(1/se_i \right) + e_i \qquad (7.2)$$

where $t_i = \Theta_i / se_i$, or the t-score associated with the regression parameter on the focal predictor in the original study. In the absence of publication bias, the intercept in equation 7.2 ought to be zero. This is so because when a regression parameter is estimated with infinite imprecision (that is, $se_i = \infty$ and $1/se_i = 0$), the expected value of t_i will be zero regardless of the value of the parameter estimate itself. Therefore the test for the presence of publication bias (the FAT) is a null hypothesis test on b_0 in equation 7.2.[1] Many readers will recognize the FAT as equivalent to the more standard Egger test for publication bias introduced in chapter 6 (Egger, Smith, Schneider, and Minder 1997). There are two differences between the FAT and the Egger test: (1) the Egger test measures effects using standard r-based, d-based, or odds-based effect sizes, while the FAT measures effects using the regression parameter b_j, and (2) the effect size variance in the Egger test is affected only by the magnitude of the effect and the sample size (see chapter 3) while the variance of b_j in the FAT is affected by many other factors.

Testing for "True" Effects Using MST

In the absence of publication bias—in other words, when observations on Θ_i are drawn at random from the distribution of all $\Theta_i s$—the value of t_i ought to be related to its degrees of freedom, and linearly related to $\sqrt{df}$. More precisely, in the equation

$$ln\left[t_i\right] = \alpha_0 + \alpha_1 \ ln\sqrt{df} + e_i \qquad (7.3)$$

where ln is the natural log, $\alpha_1 = 0.5$ if Θ_i represents a "true" effect in the absence of publication bias. Similarly, $\alpha_1 = 0$ in the absence of a "true" effect. Publication bias will attenuate the relationship between t_i and its degrees of freedom, so if Θ_i represents a "true" effect but the sample of observed $\Theta_i s$ is contaminated with publication bias, $0 < \alpha_1 < 0.5$. Therefore, the test for the presence of a "true" effect is a null hypothesis test on α_1 from equation 7.3. This is the Meta Significance Test (MST).[2]

Estimating the Magnitude of the "True" Effect Using PET

Stanley (2001; 2005) suggests that Θ_i can be corrected for publication bias by estimating equation 7.2 using the absolute value of t_i and then "shrinking" $|t_i|$ by $b_0 se_i$. More important, Stanley also notes that b_1 from equation 7.2 may be considered an average effect size corrected for publication bias. That is, b_1 is the estimated average "true" effect from the empirical literature. In this way, equation 7.2 provides both a test for publication bias and an estimate of the average (or baseline) effect size. A null hypothesis test on b_1 from equation 7.2 is the Precision Effect Test (PET).

Assessing the FAT as a Test for Publication Bias

Sterne, Becker, and Egger (2005) point out that funnel plots are used less frequently in the social sciences than in medicine, and that the performance of funnel plots is rarely the topic of research in the social sciences. As the use of meta-regression has increased in the social sciences, however, so has the use of the FAT to test for publication bias. Using the FAT and related FAT-like tools, economists in particular routinely find evidence of publication bias in the peer-reviewed literature (see, for example, Card and Krueger 1995; Ashenfelter, Harmon, Oosterbeck 1999; Doucouliagos, Laroche, and Stanley 2005; Nijkamp and Poot 2004; Rose and Stanley 2005; Bel, Fageda, and Warnerd 2010). In a summary of research employing FAT-like tests, Stanley (2005; 313) concludes that "thus far, nearly all economic applications of meta-analytic methods that detect publication bias have found evidence of it." In fact, evidence regarding the pervasiveness of publication bias based on the FAT is so overwhelming that Stanley, Jarrell, and Doucouliagos (2010) recommend that researchers (and meta-analysts) ought to ignore or discard results from the 90 percent of original studies employing the smallest samples! Since virtually all published literature is contaminated by publication bias, these authors argue, we can have little confidence that small sample studies contain any useful information regarding true effect sizes.

Critiques of the Egger Test Applied to the FAT

Chapter 6 includes a thorough presentation of criticisms of the Egger test as a measure of publication bias in meta-analysis. To what extent do the limitations of the Egger test apply to the FAT? Answering this question begins by reiterating that the Egger test and the FAT are mathematically equivalent. Ceteris paribus, the limitations of the Egger test ought to also apply to the FAT. The key differences are in application, and three of these differences are worth exploring in detail. First, meta-analyses in medicine and psychology typically employ odds-based effect sizes, while education researchers generally employ d-based effect sizes. By contrast, in using t-scores from regression models, the FAT uses a type of r-based effect size. All of the Monte Carlo simulations discussed in chapter 6 assess the performance of the Egger test as applied to odds-based effect sizes, and these researchers are uncertain as to whether their results apply to other types of effect sizes (Peters, Sutton, Jones, Abrams, and Rushton 2006). There are no Monte Carlo assessments of the performance of the Egger test as applied to r-based effect sizes in the statistics, psychology, or medical literature.

Second, the measures of effect size precision in traditional meta-analyses depend only on the study sample size and the magnitude of the effect. For example, the variance for the most commonly used r-based effect size, Fisher's Z, is simply $1/(N-3)$, and the variance for the most commonly used d-based effect size, Hedges's g, is $\{[(n_1 + n_2)/(n_1 n_2)]/[g^2/2(n_1 + n_2 - 2)]\}$. The variance for the odds ratio is $[(1/n_{11}) + (1/n_{12}) + (1/n_{21}) + (1/n_{22})]$ (see chapter 3). By contrast, the variance of the regression parameter b—the measure of effect size precision used in the FAT—is $\sigma^2_e (X'X)^{-1}$, where σ^2_e is the variance of the error term from the regression model in the original study and $(X'X)^{-1}$ is the variance-covariance matrix for the independent variables from that regression model. Therefore, whereas the measures of effect size precision used in traditional meta-analysis are affected only by the sample size and the magnitude of the effect, the measure of effect size precision used in the FAT is influenced by

- The sample size in the original study (through σ^2_e and $X'X$)
- The magnitude of the effect (through σ^2_e)
- Measurement error in Y in the original study (through σ^2_e)
- The degree of collinearity among the predictors in the original study (through $(X'X)$)

We know that for the odds ratio, bias in the Egger test is a function of the components of the precision estimate (in other words, the magnitude of the effect size and the sample size). Therefore, the components used to estimate the precision of b_j may affect bias in the FAT.

Third, there is far greater heterogeneity in the effect sizes used in the FAT than in the effect sizes traditionally used in the Egger test. Most commonly, scholars using the Egger test are examining effect sizes from individual studies that employ experimental designs. These original studies typically produce a single effect size characterizing the difference in outcomes between the treatment and control groups. Less commonly, these experiments produce a small number of effect sizes, each characterizing the difference in outcomes between treatment and control groups in different arms of the experiment. By contrast, scholars using the FAT examine effect sizes from multiple regression models that employ observational data and correlational or quasi-experimental designs. In these studies the effect size is the X-standardized partial correlation of X_j on Y; that is, the regression parameter b_j. This effect size is conditional upon the other exogenous variables in the regression model. Models that employ different control variables therefore estimate different effect sizes (see chapters 3 and 4 for a more complete discussion of this perspective). For example, study 1 may use b_j to estimate $\beta_j \mid X_k X_1 X_m$, whereas study 2 uses b_j to estimate $\beta_j \mid X_n X_o X_p$ and study 3 uses b_j to estimate $\beta_j \mid X_k X_m X_p$ (these three models may also be estimated in the same original study). Because each model uses different control variables, each b_j estimates a fundamentally different effect size β_j. Therefore, contrary to the assumptions that underlie the funnel plot and funnel-plot-based tests for publication bias, the vector of effect sizes b_j from studies 1, 2, and 3 will contain significant effect size heterogeneity. Moreover, heterogeneity in the underlying population effect sizes will be greater than anything encountered in medicine, psychology, or other fields in which the Egger test for publication bias is used routinely. Since we know that the size of the Egger test is sensitive to this type of heterogeneity, greater heterogeneity among the effect sizes used in the FAT should give us even more cause for concern. These differences between the use of the Egger test and the FAT test in practice suggest that the FAT may be even more prone to type I errors than is the Egger test.

Assessing the Performance of the FAT

The performance of any statistical test is characterized by two elements, size and power. In this section I assess the performance of the FAT by examining the type I error rate in the absence of publication bias; that is, performance is measured by the frequency with which the FAT concludes that publication bias is present when it is not. This is referred to as the size of the test. The complementary measure of performance—the power of the FAT, or the frequency with which the FAT correctly identifies publication bias when it is present—is of less concern, since the low power of the comparable Egger test is well established. I examine the size of the FAT when manipulating three sets of factors:

1. Factors that previous researchers have found affect the size of the Egger test when applied to odds-ratio effect sizes: in other words, the magnitude of the effect, sample sizes in original studies, and the meta-sample size.
2. Factors affecting the precision of b_j that do not affect the precision of other measures of effect size: that is, measurement error in Y and collinearity among the predictors in the original studies $(X'X)^{-1}$.
3. Heterogeneity of effect sizes stemming from different model specifications in the original studies.

Previous Assessments of the FAT. Stanley (2008) used simulations to assess the performance of the FAT, the MST, and the PET. While the majority of the simulations examine the MST and the PET, Stanley does show that the FAT rejects a true null hypothesis of no publication bias only 5 percent of the time with meta-sample sizes of 20 and 80. These meta-sample sizes are chosen on the basis of the recommendation that researchers ought to select a single effect size from original studies when conducting a meta-analysis (Stanley 2005). The perspective adopted in this book, however, is that meta-analysis in public management, public policy, and the social sciences ought to use all effect sizes from original studies, rather than selecting a single effect size from each study. If followed, this advice will produce meta-sample sizes that are easily an order of magnitude larger than those used in Stanley's (2008) simulations. In addition, these simulations do not assess the performance of the FAT in the face of measurement error in Y, the magnitude of the effect size, collinearity among the predictors in the original studies, or effect size heterogeneity driven by model specification. Therefore the relevance of these simulations for meta-regression in practice is uncertain. Stanley (2008) does show that the FAT has low power, just like the Egger test.

Callot and Paldam (2011) conduct the most comprehensive assessment of the performance of the FAT. Using a series of Monte Carlo simulations, these authors find that the rejection rate of the FAT varies systematically and dramatically across different scenarios. The discussion here will focus on two scenarios in which the FAT fairs poorly. First, when there is strong dependence in the data sets used in the original studies (that is, when the original studies use common data sets that expand by only a small number of observations over time, for example, macroeconomic time series) over-rejection rates for the FAT are substantial. In these cases, the rejection rate of the FAT ranges from 0.20 to 0.60 (increasing with the meta-sample size) when there are no structural breaks in the data, and rejection rates reach 1.00 (in other words, the FAT always concludes that publication bias exists when it does not) when the data series used in the original studies contain a structural break. The lesson here is that researchers should not use the FAT when original studies use a common data set with temporal dependence (though meta-regression of these data might be conducted using the delta-splitting method of Stevens and Taylor 2009).

Second, Callot and Paldam (2011) examine the performance of the FAT under conditions of effect size heterogeneity generated by alternative model specifications in the original studies. Specifically, these authors simulate the performance of the FAT when the population data generating process is $Y_i = b_0 + b_1 X_{1i} + b_2 X_{2i} + e_i$ but half of the original studies included in the meta-analysis estimate the misspecified model $Y_i = b_0 + b_1 X_{1i} + e_i$. In these circumstances, the rejection rate of the FAT increases dramatically, quickly approaching 1.0 in nearly all simulations. That is, effect size heterogeneity produced by alternative model specifications in original studies leads the FAT to consistently reject a true null hypothesis of no publication bias. Callot and Paldam go on to estimate an augmented FAT akin to the augmented Egger test discussed in chapter 6. They estimate the augmented FAT $t_i = b_0 + b_1(1/s_{b1i}) + b_2 X_{2i} + e$ where X_{2i} is defined as "an appropriate control" (p. 27). Callot and Paldam refer to this as the MRA(k) model (further on I refer to this model as an *intercept augmented FAT*), and the measurement of X_{2i} is not specified. In Callot and Paldam's simulations, specifying an MRA(k) model eliminates the excessive type I error rates for the FAT under conditions of effect size heterogeneity. The results of these simulations may be suspect, however, because these authors fix N in all simulations, meaning that variations in precision are strictly a function of model specification. In all real-world situations, effect sizes will come from original studies that vary according to sample size, specification, and collinearity among the predictors. A second reason to interpret these simulations with caution is that Callot and Paldam's MRA(k) model produces far fewer type I errors than expected given statistical theory. Whereas we would expect the MRA(k) simulations to produce type I error rates of 0.05, in fact type I error rates fall well below 0.05 in all simulations, and fall well below 0.01 in half of the simulations. This departure between observed and expected results is not discussed by the authors.

Simulation Structure. Assessing the performance of the FAT requires two levels of simulations. First, we need to simulate original studies that produce the effect sizes for the meta-analysis. Second, we need to simulate the meta-analyses that make use of these effect sizes. I describe the basic structure of these simulations here. Details regarding how the simulation structure is varied to assess FAT performance under different conditions are described in subsequent sections.

- All first-level simulations assume a population model for original studies of $Y_i = \beta_0 + \beta_1 X_{1i} + \beta_2 X_{2i} + \beta_{3i} X_{3i} + \varepsilon_i$. The key relationship of interest from this model is β_1, and is measured using the parameter estimate b_1 from the first-level simulations. The t-score on b_1 (t_{b1}) provides the standardized effect size used in the FAT test, while the inverse of the standard error of b_1 provides the measure of the precision of this effect size.
- The means of the exogenous variables in the population model are characterized by the vector $\boldsymbol{\mu}$ [μ_{X1}, μ_{X2}, μ_{X3}]. In the simulations reported here $\boldsymbol{\mu} = [0, 0, 0]$, but the results from the simulations are invariant to the values in this vector.
- The standard deviations of the exogenous variables in the population model are characterized by the vector $\boldsymbol{\sigma}$ [σ_{X1}, σ_{X2}, σ_{X3}]. In the simulations reported here $\boldsymbol{\sigma} = [1, 1, 1]$, but the results from the simulations are invariant to the values in this vector.
- X_1, X_2, and X_3 come from a multivariate normal distribution characterized by $\boldsymbol{\mu}$, $\boldsymbol{\sigma}$, and $\boldsymbol{C_{XX}}$, the covariance matrix. The elements of $\boldsymbol{C_{XX}}$ are operationalized as correlation coefficients. Values on $\boldsymbol{X}$ are fixed across simulations. Simulations incorporate different levels of collinearity among the predictors in the original studies by varying the values for the elements $c_{Xj,Xk}$ in $\boldsymbol{C_{XX}}$.
- $e \sim N(0,1)$ except in simulation 2 where $e \sim N(0, \sigma_i)$ and σ_i is varied to incorporate different levels of measurement error.
- Y_i is generated from the population regression model $Y_i = \beta_0 + \beta_1 X_{1i} + \beta_2 X_{2i} + \beta_2 X_{3i} + \varepsilon_i$. Simulations incorporate different magnitudes of effect sizes in the original studies by varying the values for β_1 and β_2.
- First-level simulations generate a population of 9,999 simulated original studies, and these simulated studies generate 9,999 values of b_1 and t_{b1}.

The sample size used to generate each b_1 is denoted N, and N varies across simulations.

· Second-level simulations generate 1,000 simulated meta-analyses that employ bootstrapped resamples of the 9,999 effect sizes and precision estimates from the first-level simulations. The number of effect sizes used in each meta-analysis is referred to as the meta-sample size and is denoted M. M varies across simulations. The performance of the FAT is assessed using the proportion of these 1,000 simulated meta-analyses that reject a true null hypothesis of no publication bias at $\alpha = .05$.

Performance of the FAT Under Ideal Conditions. The first set of simulations assesses the performance of the FAT in an ideal world characterized by identical sample sizes across all original studies ($N = 100$ in all first-level simulations), no collinearity (all elements $c_{Xj,Xk}$ are zero), and no effect size heterogeneity. I estimate the standard FAT where $t_{b1} = b_0 + b_1$ $(1/se_{b1}) + e$. I set $\beta_1 = 0.7$ in simulations assuming large effect sizes, while $\beta_1 = 0.2$ in simulations assuming small effect sizes in the original studies. The meta-sample size is $M = 25, 100, 1,000$, or $9,999$ depending on the simulation. I allow β and M to vary because assessments of the performance of the Egger test indicate that type I error rates increase with both of these factors when employing odds-based effect sizes. It will be useful to know whether we observe the same effect for the FAT. The results of the baseline simulation are presented in table 7.1.

In virtually all simulations the two-tailed rejection rate for the FAT is very close to the expected value of 0.05. The FAT substantially over-rejects Ho: $b_0 = 0$ when M and effect sizes are large, and the average t-test for the FAT is 1.43, far larger than its expected value of zero. While this is consistent with the results from assessments of the performance of the Egger test, the magnitude of this effect for the FAT is smaller. We can conclude that the FAT performs well in this ideal case.

Performance of the FAT as N, Measurement Error, and Collinearity Vary. The second set of simulations assesses the performance of the FAT when we maintain most of the characteristics of the baseline simulation, varying only N (the sample size in the original studies) and measurement error in Y. Since the precision of the effect size estimate is affected by N, the performance of the FAT may be affected by N as well, and Callot and Paldam (2011) find some evidence of this effect. In these simulations, $N = 25, 100$, and $1,000$ in an equal number of original studies (that is, 3,333). The results from this simulation are presented in the top

TABLE 7.1. BASELINE SIMULATIONS ESTIMATING SIZE OF FAT

$\beta_1, \beta_2, \beta_3$	Meta-M	Mean t-Score	Type I Error $\|t\| > 1.96$
0.7, 0.3, 0.3	25	0.04	.053
	100	0.18	.054
	500	0.28	.060
	9,999	1.43	.304
0.2, 0.1, 0.1	25	−0.04	.065
	100	0.05	.058
	500	0.02	.069
	9,999	0.13	.055

Notes: Sample size in original studies = 100; number of original studies = 9,999; number of bootstrap replications = 1,000; no measurement error; $r(X_i, X_j) = 0$.

panel of table 7.2. In addition, I allow for varying measurement error in Y. Standard regression theory assumes that all variables are measured without error, but this assumption rarely holds in practice, and we know that the parameter variances in regression models are strongly affected by measurement error in Y (though $E[b_j]$ remains unaffected). Since measurement error in Y affects parameter variances in the original studies, both the precision of the key independent variable in the FAT, $1/se_{b1}$ and the covariance between t_{b1} and se_{b1} will be affected. Consequently, b_1 from the standard FAT regression $t_{b1} = b_0 + b_1 (1/se_{b1}) + e$ may be affected, which in turn will affect b_0. If measurement error in Y indirectly affects b_0 through this effect on b_1, it may also affect rejection rates for the FAT. In these simulations measurement error in Y (error[Y]) $\sim N(0, \sigma_i)$ where $\sigma_i = 0.5$, 1.0 and 2.0. Therefore measurement error produces heteroskedasticity. The results from this simulation are presented in the bottom panel of table 7.2.

The top panel of table 7.2 shows that in almost all cases the two-tailed rejection rate for the FAT continues to be very close to the expected value of .05. Asymptotically, however, the increased variation in the measure of effect size precision creates a tendency for the FAT to over-reject a true null hypothesis when M gets very large—the rejection rate of .186 when effect sizes are large is nearly four times its expected value. The bottom panel of table 7.2 tells a slightly different story. Measurement error in Y does not measurably affect the performance of the FAT. Rejection rates for the true null hypothesis of no publication bias remain very close to the nominal level of .05 except when M is very large and the effect size

TABLE 7.2. SIZE OF FAT, VARYING SAMPLE SIZES AND MEASUREMENT ERROR IN *Y*

$\beta_1, \beta_2, \beta_3$	Meta-*M*	Mean *t*-Score	Type I Error $\|t\| > 1.96$
Varying *N*, No Measurement Error			
	25	−0.04	.068
	100	−0.06	.049
0.7, 0.3, 0.3	500	−0.25	.052
	9,999	−1.09	.186
	25	0.04	.064
	100	0.07	.059
0.2, 0.1, 0.1	500	0.03	.048
	9,999	0.32	.065
Varying *N*, Measurement Error			
	25	0.00	.067
	100	0.00	.042
0.7, .03, 0.3	500	0.07	.064
	9,999	0.18	.045
	25	0.07	.049
	100	0.02	.054
0.2, 0.1, 0.1	500	0.16	.051
	9,999	0.60	.105

Notes: Sample size in original studies = 25 (3,333), 100 (3,333), 1,000 (3,333); $e[Y] \sim (0,.5)$; $e[Y] \sim (0,1.0)$; $e[Y] \sim (0,2.0)$ in 3,333 original studies each; number of original studies = 9,999; number of bootstrap replications = 1,000; $r(X_i, X_j) = 0$.

is very small. In most situations faced by researchers in practice, then, the performance of the FAT is quite good in the face of variation in sample sizes and measurement error in original studies. For meta-analyses with large numbers of effect sizes, however, the FAT is increasingly likely to conclude that publication bias exists when it does not.

A unique quality of the FAT, compared with the Egger test, is that the precision of effect size estimates in the FAT is affected by collinearity among independent variables used in regression models in the original studies. Therefore, it is important to assess whether collinearity among predictors affects the performance of the FAT. This fourth simulation employs all of the conditions from the second simulation reported in the top panel of table 7.2. Of importance, in this fourth simulation I reinstate the assumption that Y in the original studies is measured without error. Instead, we replace the assumption from the baseline simulation that $c_{XjXk} = 0$ with the condition that $c_{XjXk} = .2$ (the low collinearity case), $c_{XjXk} = .6$ (the moderate collinearity case), and $c_{XjXk} = .8$ (the high collinearity case). I choose these values because where $c_{XjXk} = .2$ nearly all of the variation in X_j is unique (96 percent), whereas at $c_{XjXk} = .6$ roughly two-thirds of the variation in X_j is unique and at $c_{XjXk} = .8$ roughly one-third of the variation in X_j is unique. The results from these simulations are presented in table 7.3.

In nearly all simulations the two-tailed rejection rate for the FAT is very close to the expected value of .05. Once again, however, at very large values of M, the FAT is often likely to over-reject a true null hypothesis of no publication bias. This asymptotic bias in M is particularly noteworthy in situations in which the effect size from original studies is small. In these situations, type I error rates from the FAT rise to .477, nearly ten times the expected value of .05. We can conclude that in most situations faced by meta-analysts, collinearity among predictors in the original model has little effect on the FAT. For very large meta-analyses, however, the FAT is likely to mislead researchers into concluding that publication bias is present when it is not.

Performance of the FAT Under Effect Size Heterogeneity. Though informative, simulations 1 through 4 are highly artificial. While they allow for effect sizes in original studies to be estimated with varying precision, all assume that original studies seek to estimate a common underlying effect size. That is, they assume all original studies estimate identical regression models, and that this common sample regression model perfectly represents the population regression model.

In practice, original studies examining the same core hypothesis rarely employ the same empirical model. For example, much of the literature on environmental justice examines the common hypothesis of interest that levels of potential environmental risk in a community (Y) are related to the proportion of minority residents in that community (X_1). This common hypothesis of interest is reflected in the basic bivariate population regression model $Y_i = \beta_0 + \beta_1 X_{1i} + \varepsilon_i$, and the effect size of interest is estimated by b_1 in the sample regression model $Y_i = b_0 + b_1 X_{1i} + e_i$. When testing the common hypothesis of interest, the author of one study might control for average income in the community (X_2), levels of unemployment in the community (X_3), and voter turnout in the community (X_4), leading to the

TABLE 7.3. SIZE OF FAT, VARYING COLLINEARITY

$\beta_1, \beta_2, \beta_3$	Corr(X_j, X_k)	Meta-M	Mean t-Score	Type I Error $|t| > 1.96$
		25	−0.03	.062
		100	0.06	.050
	0.20	500	0.17	.048
		9,999	0.70	.114
		25	−0.08	.063
		100	−0.03	.053
0.7, 0.3, 0.3	0.60	500	−0.12	.052
		9,999	−0.43	.074
		25	0.03	.063
		100	0.00	.052
	0.80	500	−0.04	.056
		9,999	−0.34	.061
		25	0.04	.050
		100	0.13	.057
	0.20	500	0.22	.049
		9,999	0.99	.180
		25	−0.03	.056
		100	−0.05	.059
0.2, 0.1, 0.1	0.60	500	−0.11	.042
		9,999	−0.28	.052
		25	0.10	.055
		100	0.14	.063
	0.80	500	0.47	.072
		9,999	1.87	.477

Notes: Sample size in original studies = 25, 100, and 1,000 in 3,333 original studies each; number of original studies = 9,999; number of bootstrap replications = 1,000; no measurement error.

sample regression equation $Y_i = b_0 + b_1 X_{1i} + b_2 X_{2i} + b_3 X_{3i} + b_4 X_{4i} + e_i$. The author of a second study may control for income (X_2), land values (X_5), and levels of home ownership (X_6), leading to the sample regression equation $Y_i = b_0 + b_1 X_{1i} + b_2 X_{2i} + b_3 X_{5i} + b_4 X_{6i} + e_i$. Clearly b_1 in these two studies estimates a very different parameter, leading to heterogeneity in effect sizes across original studies. Model specification may also lead to effect size heterogeneity *within* studies in the common situation in which original studies estimate more than one regression model (and therefore contribute more than one effect size).

In simulation 5 I assess the performance of the FAT under these conditions. Specifically, I assume a common population regression model across all original studies $[Y = \beta_0 + \beta_1 X_1 + \beta_2 X_2 + \beta_3 X_3 + \varepsilon]$ where X_1, X_2, and X_3 are drawn from a multivariate normal distribution $(\boldsymbol{\mu}, \boldsymbol{\sigma}, \mathbf{C_{XX}})$ as defined above, and ε is the pure product of sampling variability (that is, there is no measurement error in Y). In simulation 5, one-third of the original studies estimate the sample version of this population model $[Y = b_0 + b_1 X_1 + b_2 X_2 + b_3 X_3 + e]$, one-third of the original studies estimate the alternative model $[Y = b_0 + b_1 X_1 + b_2 X_2 + e]$, and one-third of the original studies estimate the alternative model $[Y = b_0 + b_1 X_1 + e]$. Simulation 5 keeps all other conditions from simulation 4. The results from this simulation are presented in table 7.4.

Table 7.4 shows that like the Egger test, the FAT performs poorly under conditions of effect size heterogeneity, and this performance is strongly affected by the magnitude of the effect size, by levels of collinearity among the predictor variables in the original studies, and by the meta-sample size M. With low levels of collinearity and values of M up to 100, type I error rates are close to the expected value of .05. When the relationship between Y and X_1 is large, type I error rates climb sharply as a function of C_{XjXk}, approaching or reaching 1.00 when M is as small as 100 in the high-collinearity case, and reaching 1.00 asymptotically in all cases except where $M = 25$. That is, in these cases every FAT reaches the wrong conclusion, finding significant publication bias where none exists. Moreover, when collinearity is high, the rejection rate for the FAT is several times the expected value of 0.05 even when M is as small as 25. The performance of the FAT is only marginally better when the relationship between X_1 and Y is small. Asymptotically, type I error rates reach 1.00 with moderate and severe collinearity, and exceed the expected value of .05 by a large margin in nearly all cases. The only scenario in which the FAT performs well is when effect sizes and levels of collinearity are both small. The takeaway from table 7.4 is that under conditions of effect size heterogeneity the traditional FAT is unreliable, as it is more a measure of collinearity and specification differences in original studies than it is a test of publication bias. Using the FAT under common conditions, meta-analysts are likely to conclude that publication bias is present when it is not.

Why Does the FAT Perform So Poorly Under Effect Size Heterogeneity? The statistical theory underlying the FAT is predicated on two assumptions: (1) all models in original studies seek to estimate a common population effect

TABLE 7.4. SIZE OF FAT WITH EFFECT SIZE HETEROGENEITY IN ORIGINAL STUDIES

$\beta_1, \beta_2, \beta_3$	Corr(X_j, X_k)	Meta-M	Mean t-Score	Unaugmented FAT Type I Error $\|t\| > 1.96$
		25	−0.20	.034
		100	−0.28	.035
	0.20	500	−0.65	.084
		9,999	−2.91	.879
		25	−0.68	.065
		100	−1.54	.268
0.7, 0.3, 0.3	0.60	500	−3.56	.981
		9,999	−15.87	1.00
		25	−1.42	.278
		100	−3.24	.961
	0.80	500	−7.40	1.00
		9,999	−33.19	1.00
		25	−0.07	.055
		100	−0.07	.044
	0.20	500	−0.26	.046
		9,999	−1.11	.179
		25	−0.56	.076
		100	−1.23	.211
0.2, 0.1, 0.1	0.60	500	−2.70	.806
		9,999	−12.31	1.00
		25	−1.16	.208
		100	−2.56	.746
	0.80	500	−5.73	1.00
		9,999	−25.79	1.00

Notes: Sample size in original studies = 25, 100, and 1,000 in 3,333 original studies each; models in original studies: $Y = b_0 + b_1X_1 + e$ in 3,333 original studies; $Y = b_0 + b_1X_1 + b_2X_2 + e$ in 3,333 original studies; $Y = b_0 + b_1X_1 + b_2X_2 + b_3X_3 + e$ in 3,333 original studies; number of original studies = 9,999; number of bootstrap replications = 1,000; no measurement error.

size Θ (in other words, Θ is fixed), and (2) the precision with which Θ is estimated is strictly a function of sample size. Therefore, if Θ is fixed (or as in random effects meta-analysis, it varies normally around an expectation that is constant across all studies), the standardized effect size will vary only as a function of sample size N (or more accurately, the degrees of freedom associated with the hypothesis test on Θ).

Neither of these assumptions holds true where Θ is estimated using b_j from a multiple regression model and precision is measured using se_{bj}. As we have seen, $b_j s$ from sample regression models that include different control variables estimate different population parameters. Therefore, neither β_j nor its expectation are fixed. Furthermore, the precision of the effect size estimate b_j is affected by the correlations among independent variables in the original models and by the magnitude of the effect itself, as well as by the sample size. Since neither condition underlying the FAT as a test for publication bias is likely to hold in practice, its poor performance in the simulations should not be surprising.

I conduct two simulations to illustrate the consequences of violating the statistical assumptions underlying the FAT. Both simulations posit the population regression model $Y_i = \beta_0 + \beta_1 X_{1i} + \beta_2 X_{2i} + \beta_3 X_{3i} + \varepsilon_i$ where the effect of interest $\beta_1 = 0.7$. Figure 7.1 plots the t-scores and

FIGURE 7.1. PLOT OF 333 SIMULATED STANDARDIZED EFFECT SIZES VERSUS EFFECT SIZE PRECISION FROM MODELS WITH UNCORRELATED PREDICTORS AND NO SPECIFICATION ERROR

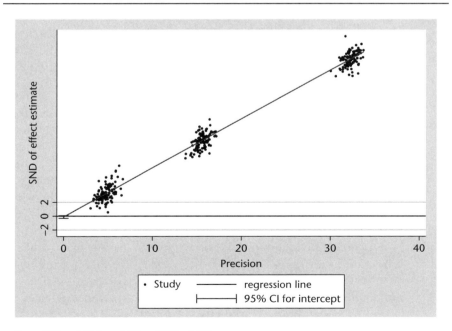

Notes: FAT = −0.12 (t = −1.22) and PET = 0.712.

precision estimates from 333 original regression models estimating the sample regression model $Y_i = b_0 + b_1 X_{1i} + b_2 X_{2i} + b_3 X_{3i} + e_i$ where $\rho_{XjXk} = 0$. That is, figure 7.1 preserves both of the assumptions underlying the validity of the FAT as a test for publication bias. One hundred and eleven models use $N = 25$, and b_1 from these studies is estimated with low precision. Effects from these models are clustered in the lower left corner of figure 7.1. Another 111 models are estimated using $N = 250$ and $N = 1,000$, respectively, and effect sizes from these models are estimated with increasing precision as evidenced by their clustering along the precision dimension. The line in figure 7.1 represents the least squares regression from equation 7.2. Consistent with the statistical theory undergirding the FAT, the standardized effect size (t_i) increases with the precision of the effect size estimate $(1/se_i)$. The intercept of the least squares regression line through these 333 effect sizes is -0.12 with a t-score of -1.22. Therefore, the FAT finds no evidence of publication bias among these effects. Moreover, the slope of this regression line—the PET—is 0.712, very close to the population parameter $\beta_1 = 0.7$.

The second simulation incorporates two important changes. First, I incorporate an additional 333 effect sizes from the sample regression model $Y_i = b_0 + b_1 X_{1i} + b_2 X_{2i} + e_i$ and another 333 effect sizes from the sample regression model $Y_i = b_0 + b_1 X_{1i} + e_i$. The effect size heterogeneity introduced by these different specifications violates the assumption that $E[b_1]$ is the same for all models. Second, severe collinearity is introduced by setting $\rho_{XjXk} = 0.9$ so that now the precision of the effect size is not strictly a function of sample size. While this high level of collinearity helps create the clear separation of subgroups of observations in figure 7.2, bias in the FAT occurs at much lower levels of collinearity. Figure 7.2 reports the results from the second simulation. The outcome from the FAT ($b_0 = -2.81$ with $t = -22.50$), leads us to reject the true null hypothesis of no publication bias at $p < .000001$. Moreover, the estimated value of b_1 from the PET—1.290—is nearly twice the true value of $\beta_1 = 0.7$. In the presence of effect size heterogeneity and strong collinearity, both the FAT and the PET fail.

A careful look at figure 7.2 shows several distinct groups of effect sizes. The three clusters identified using circles are effect sizes from models where $N = 1,000$. The group estimated with the greatest precision at the top right corner comes from the sample regression model $Y_i = b_0 + b_1 X_{1i} + e_i$. As additional predictors X_2 and X_3 are added to this model, the precision with which b_1 is estimated declines. The three clusters of observations identified using rectangles highlight effect sizes from models

FIGURE 7.2. PLOT OF 999 SIMULATED STANDARDIZED EFFECT SIZES VERSUS EFFECT SIZE PRECISION FROM MODELS WITH STRONGLY CORRELATED PREDICTORS AND VARYING SPECIFICATIONS IN THE ORIGINAL MODELS

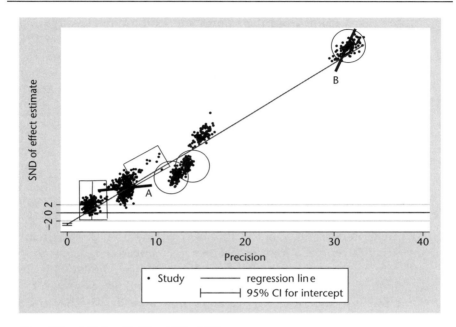

Notes: FAT = −2.81 (*t* = −22.50) and PET = 1.290.

where $N = 25$. The other groups of effect sizes come from models where $N = 250$. The statistical theory motivating the FAT assumes that the expected values of the standardized effect size will be constant, holding the sample size N constant. Figure 7.2 shows that this may not be true in practice, as holding N constant, the value of t_i (measured on the vertical axis) varies dramatically as a function of model specification and as a function of collinearity among the predictors in the original models.

Two additional items are worthy of note when considering these clusters. First, collinearity can dominate sample size in determining effect size precision. In many cases, effect sizes from small samples are estimated with greater precision than effect sizes using larger samples. In the most extreme cases, b_1 is estimated nearly as precisely when $N = 25$ as when $N = 1,000$. Second, the relationship between precision and the standardized effect size is meaningfully different across groups of observations. The line segments labeled A and B represent the slope estimates characterizing the relationship between t_i and $1/se_i$ (that is, b_1 from equation 7.2, or the PET). Segment A ($b_1 = 0.19$) represents this relationship from the sample regression equation $Y_i = b_0 + b_1 X_{1i} + b_2 X_{2i} + b_3 X_{3i} + e_i$ with $N = 250$, while segment B ($b_1 = 1.18$) represents this relationship from the sample regression equation $Y_i = b_0 + b_1 X_{1i} + e_i$ when $N = 1,000$. By estimating a single regression line through these various clusters of observations, the FAT and the PET actually report a complex weighted average of the regression lines characterizing different groups of observations defined by the combination of model specification, sample size, and collinearity in the original models. Under these conditions, without sound statistical theory it is uncertain just what quantities the FAT and the PET estimate.

Assessing the Performance of the Augmented FAT. Like simulations 1 through 4, simulation 5 employs the basic version of the FAT from equation 7.2. This version cannot account for varying model specifications in original studies that generate effect size heterogeneity. As discussed in chapters 4 and 5, however, meta-regression analysis regularly includes variables representing these design elements, recognizing that the effect sizes may be conditional upon these factors. Similarly, as discussed in chapter 6, the Egger test for publication bias is routinely expanded to include dichotomous variables that identify whether the effect size comes from an original study that includes a particular control variable. Both Stanley (2008) and Callot and Paldam (2011) augment the FAT in this fashion. These *augmented* funnel asymmetry tests are used with increasing frequency, and Borenstein and colleagues (2009) recommend that researchers always utilize an augmented funnel asymmetry test for publication bias. An augmented FAT for the simulations used here requires estimating the following equation:

$$t_i = b_0 + b_1 \left(1/se_i\right) + b_2 \bmod X_{2i} + b_3 \bmod X_{3i} + e_i \qquad (7.4)$$

where $\bmod X_2$ and $\bmod X_3$ are dichotomous moderator variables taking on values of 1 for effect sizes from models that include X_2 or X_3 as independent variables and zero otherwise. I call this the "intercept augmented FAT" because including the moderator variables shifts the conditional expected value of t_i, or the intercept of the FAT equation, by b_2 and b_3 respectively. This is the standard approach to augmenting the Egger test, and it allows the average value of the standardized effect size to vary depending on the specification of the original model.

To fully appreciate the implications of the intercept augmented FAT it is worth returning to figure 7.2. First, note that adding $\text{mod}X_2$ and $\text{mod}X_3$ to the basic FAT equation means that the FAT intercept b_0 now represents the average t-score (or standardized effect size) from original sample regression equations that are estimated with infinite precision (where se_i equals zero) and that only include X_1 among the predictors (where both $\text{mod}X_2$ and $\text{mod}X_3$ equal zero). One implication of this change is that b_0 is estimated well beyond the scope of the data, and is therefore suspect (this is also true of the basic FAT). Another implication is that *the augmented FAT is now a test for publication bias only in original studies in which models contain the single predictor X_1*. Second, adding dichotomous moderator variables to the basic FAT equation will shift the intercept of the regression line in figure 7.2, but not its slope. Yet it is clear that the *slopes of regression lines through each cluster of effect sizes are different*. This must be so, because if X_2 and X_3 are correlated with X_1, including them in a regression equation with X_1 will change the expected value of the parameter estimate b_1 as well as its variance. The traditional intercept-augmented FAT is unlikely to perform well in this situation, since under all conditions where $C_{XjXk} \neq 0$, the inclusion of control variables in the original model will affect not only the *precision* of the effect size but its *magnitude* as well.

A more appropriate method of augmenting the FAT is to interact the dichotomous moderator variables with the measure of effect size precision, effectively estimating different regression slopes for each group of effect sizes defined by the combination of independent variables used in the original model. In the simulations used here, the *slope augmented FAT* takes the form

$$t_i = b_0 + b_1 \left(1/se_i \right) + b_2 \left(\text{mod}X_{2i} * 1/se_i \right) + b_3 \left(\text{mod}X_{3i} * 1/se_i \right) + e_i \quad (7.5)$$

Table 7.5 reports the results from simulations using both the intercept augmented FAT and this slope augmented FAT.

Instead of correcting the over-rejection bias of the FAT, the intercept augmented FAT exacerbates this bias. Under all scenarios in table 7.5, type I error rates for the intercept augmented FAT reach 1.00 asymptotically. More important, in all scenarios but one (small effect sizes, low collinearity, and small meta-sample sizes), rejection rates for a true null hypothesis are four or more times their expected value of 0.05. In virtually all situations faced by researchers in practice, the intercept-augmented FAT is likely to conclude that publication bias is present in the original studies when it is

TABLE 7.5. SIZE OF AUGMENTED FAT WITH EFFECT SIZE HETEROGENEITY

$\beta_1, \beta_2, \beta_3$	Corr(X_j, X_k)	Meta-M	Mean t-Score	Intercept Augmented FAT Type I Error $\|t\| > 1.96$	Mean t-Score	Slope Augmented FAT Type I Error $\|t\| > 1.96$
		25	1.37	.264	−0.42	.068
		100	3.02	.838	−0.65	.110
	0.20	500	6.75	1.00	−1.47	.319
		9,999	30.26	1.00	−6.63	1.00
		25	2.52	.687	−0.31	.071
		100	5.22	1.00	−0.48	.097
	0.50	500	11.83	1.00	−1.22	.234
0.7, 0.3, 0.3		9,999	52.86	1.00	−5.50	1.00
		25	2.81	.800	0.26	.080
		100	5.40	1.00	0.44	.072
	0.80	500	11.83	1.00	1.07	.171
		9,999	52.86	1.00	4.65	.996
		25	0.61	.107	−0.04	.069
		100	1.29	.224	−0.03	.042
	0.20	500	2.91	.846	−0.17	.056
		9,999	13.08	1.00	−0.68	.093
		25	1.39	.272	−0.04	.054
		100	2.84	.810	−0.06	.044
	0.50	500	6.52	1.00	−0.02	.045
0.2, 0.1, 0.1		9,999	29.23	1.00	−0.28	.069
		25	1.50	.325	0.06	.064
		100	2.90	.837	0.05	.058
	0.80	500	6.59	1.00	0.26	.059
		9,999	29.46	1.00	1.16	.208

Notes: Sample size in original studies = 25, 100, and 1,000 in 3,333 original studies each; models in original studies: $Y = b_0 + b_1 X_1 + e$ in 3,333 original studies; $Y = b_0 + b_1 X_1 + b_2 X_2 + e$ in 3,333 original studies; $Y = b_0 + b_1 X_1 + b_2 X_2 + b_3 X_3 + e$ in 3,333 original studies; number of original studies = 9,999; number of bootstrap replications = 1,000; no measurement error.

not. By contrast, the performance of the slope-augmented FAT is somewhat better, especially in data sets in which the average effect size is small. In these simulations, the type I error rate for this test is near its expected value of 0.05 except when both collinearity and the meta-sample size are very large. When effect sizes are large, type I error rates are less than two times their expected value when the meta-sample size is 100 or lower, but this error rate climbs sharply as $M > 500$. While the performance of the slope augmented FAT is meaningfully better than the intercept augmented FAT, I cannot recommend either as a valid test for publication bias in public management and policy. The lesson from this chapter is the same as the lesson from chapter 6: controlling for publication bias ex ante using a thorough search of the grey literature is a far better strategy than identifying and attempting to control for publication bias ex post.

Identifying "True" Effects Using the MST

Clearly the FAT does not perform well as a test for publication bias under conditions commonly faced by public management and policy scholars in practice. The economics approach to meta-analysis, however, also offers methods of testing the null hypothesis that the average effect size is zero (the MST) and a method of measuring the magnitude of this average effect (the PET). Perhaps the MST and the PET elements of the FAT-MST-PET-MRA perform better than does the FAT element.

On the basis of large sample theory in which observed effect sizes represent a random sample of all effect sizes—that is, where there is no publication bias—α_1 in equation 7.3 (the MST) should take on a value of 0.5 when the true (absolute) average effect size is greater than zero. In the absence of any true empirical effect, α_1 in equation 7.3 will take on a value of 0. Values of α_1 that are statistically different from zero but meaningfully less than 0.5 provide indirect evidence of publication bias.

In table 7.6, I assess the performance of the MST in the same six simulation environments used to assess the FAT in tables 7.4 and 7.5: using meta-analysis data sets containing effect size heterogeneity produced by model specification in the original studies; large and small effect sizes; and low, moderate, and severe levels of collinearity among predictors in the original studies. The meta-sample size M is fixed at its maximum value of 9,999 in all simulations, but this choice has no meaningful effect on the results.

Assessing the performance of the MST is less straightforward than assessing the FAT. The MST is not a statistical test for the presence of a "true" effect; therefore we cannot speak meaningfully about the "size" or error rate of the MST. Rather, it provides a benchmark for the presence of such an effect ($\alpha_1 = 0.5$). In all six simulations, the value of the MST falls between 0.45 and 0.56 in data sets with no publication bias and in

TABLE 7.6. PERFORMANCE OF THE MST UNDER CONDITIONS OF EFFECT SIZE HETEROGENEITY

$\beta_1, \beta_2, \beta_3$	$Corr(X_j, X_k)$	MST (Estimate of α_1)	95% Confidence Interval for MST
0.7, 0.3, 0.3	0.20	0.5212	0.5178 − 0.5245
	0.60	0.4809	0.4769 − 0.4848
	0.80	0.4573	0.4497 − 0.4648
0.2, 0.1, 0.1	0.20	0.5542	0.5454 − 0.5630
	0.60	0.5195	0.5099 − 0.5290
	0.80	0.4612	0.4501 − 0.4723

which a "true" effect is present. In my subjective assessment, these figures are close enough to the benchmark of $\alpha_1 = 0.5$ to conclude that the MST performs well in these simulations. Sticklers for statistical significance might point out that the 95 percent confidence interval for α_1 does not contain 0.5 in any of the six simulation scenarios. Thus, while estimates of α_1 are significantly different from 0 (the value of α_1 when there is no "true" effect, t-scores not shown), these estimates are also significantly different from the asymptotic expectation of 0.5. Clearly estimates of α_1 are much closer to 0.5 than they are to zero, however, which leads me to conclude that the MST performs well as an indicator of the presence of true effects under effect size heterogeneity and collinearity.

Estimating the Magnitude of "True" Effects Using the PET

While the MST performs well in these simulations, it is the weakest element of the FAT-MST-PET-MRA approach to meta-analysis in that it provides a benchmark against which to compare the results from the MST, rather than a test for the presence of "true" effects. Moreover, there are no accepted guidelines for concluding how close is "close enough" when comparing α_1 to its asymptotic expectation of 0.5. Most important, while the MST gives us some subjective evidence of the presence of a "true" effect, it delivers no information about the *magnitude* of this effect. One of the great strengths of meta-analysis is that it allows us to make statements about the magnitude of average effects with a degree of power or certainty that cannot be matched by single original studies (Hunter and Schmidt 1990). Policy and management scholars in particular are typically more interested in the substantive importance of interventions and associations than in whether these effects or relationships are identifiably different from zero.

Stanley (2005) offers the Precision Effect Test as a measure of the magnitude of the "true" effect present in a set of effect sizes after they have been purged of publication bias. Recall that the estimated magnitude of this "true" effect is the value of parameter estimate b_1 from equation 7.2, while a test for whether this "true" effect is significantly different from zero is a null hypothesis test on b_1.

There are two reasons why we might expect the PET to provide a poor estimate of the average effect size estimated by a set of original studies. First, while Copas and Malley (2008) demonstrate that b_1 from the PET can be interpreted as an estimate of the average treatment effect in the presence of publication bias, these authors are clear that the validity of b_1 and the PET are restricted to the case of a fixed effects meta-regression. As we have seen, the fixed effects approach is nearly always inappropriate for meta-analyses in the social sciences. While Copas and Malley offer an alternative estimator for random effects meta-analysis, this estimator is not developed for random effects meta-regression with covariates. In summary, then, Copas and Malley illustrate that the Stanley (2001; 2005) approach to estimating "true" effects purged of publication bias is inappropriate in nearly all situations faced by researchers in public management and policy.[3] The intuition underlying the failure of the PET in these circumstances becomes clear when we recall that b_1 represents the relationship between the standard error of the regression parameter estimate and the t-score associated with the null hypothesis test for that parameter estimate in an original study. This relationship is conditioned by (1) the number of independent variables included in the original regression models, (2) the degree of collinearity among these independent variables, and (3) the sample size in the original study. Different combinations of predictors, degrees of collinearity, and sample sizes lead to different values of b_1 across groups of effect sizes that share these characteristics (see again figure 7.2). Estimating equation 7.2 using effect sizes from models with different specifications, varying levels of collinearity, and varying sample sizes will produce an estimate of b_1 where the metric is some unknown weighted average of the various $b_1 s$ associated with each cluster of effect sizes having similar specifications, collinearity, and sample sizes. Under these conditions it is unlikely that b_1 will accurately estimate the "true" effect size estimated by these original studies. Indeed, the bias in b_1 under these conditions contributes to the bias in the FAT (or b_0 from equation 7.2) that we see in tables 7.4 and 7.5.

Second, interpreting b_1 from equation 7.2 as an estimate of the "true" effect requires that Y and the focal predictor X be measured on the same scale across all studies. To illustrate this assumption, change b_0 and b_1 from equation 7.2 into γ_0 and γ_1 so that γ_1 now estimates the average "true" effect using the PET. Furthermore, use b_{ji} to refer to the regression parameter estimate on the focal predictor X_j from original study i. Now we have the set of equations

$$E\left[t_{ji}\right] = \gamma_0 + \gamma_1\left(1/se_{ji}\right) \qquad (7.6)$$
$$E\left[b_{ji}/se_{ji}\right] = \gamma_0 + \gamma_1/se_{ji}$$
$$b_{ji} \approx \gamma_1$$

where $\approx$ reflects the metric of b_{ji} and γ_1 rather than their values. Of course, the value of b_{ji} in any original study is determined by the measurement and scale of Y and X_j. If either the measurement of Y or X_j or the scale of this measurement differ across original studies, γ_1 is measured on some unknown compound metric of X_j and Y, and therefore becomes uninterpretable. For example, assume that we want to conduct a meta-analysis using forty studies examining the effect of educational vouchers on student academic achievement where ten studies measure achievement using point gains on the Iowa Test of Basic Skills (ITBS), ten studies measure achievement using percentile increases in the ITBS, ten studies measure achievement using point gains on the Stanford Achievement Test (SAT), and ten studies measure achievement using percentile increases in the SAT. The magnitude of the "true" effect γ_1 would be interpreted as some combination of point and percentile gains on the ITBS and the SAT. This example is fairly benign, as only the measurement of Y differs across studies and the scale of the ITBS and the SAT are somewhat comparable. We could complicate the example by assuming that these forty original studies estimate the effect of educational expenditures (X_j) on student test scores (Y), and that expenditures are measured using per pupil dollars in some studies and per pupil thousands of dollars in other studies, and furthermore allowing some studies to log both expenditures and test scores (in other words, some studies estimate elasticities). In this situation, b_1 from equation 7.2 (or γ_1 from equation 7.6) becomes completely uninterpretable, and therefore of little use as a measure of the "true" effect or average effect size from these original studies. *In essence, the PET ignores the fundamental reason why raw regression coefficients cannot be combined in a meta-analysis*—and by extension, why t-scores are poor choices for standardized effect sizes in meta-regression.

Performance of the PET with Identical Measurement of *Y* and *X*

I assessed the performance of the FAT by measuring the frequency with which the test rejected the true null hypothesis of no publication bias under various scenarios. While the PET can also be used in this fashion—testing the null hypothesis that the "true" effect size is zero—the central value of the PET is that it provides an estimate of the magnitude of the "true" effect. In this way the PET better reflects the original purpose of meta-analysis than does either the FAT or the MST. This quality also means that we must assess the PET differently from the FAT. Specifically, the simulations here compare the mean value and 90 percent confidence interval for b_1 in bootstrapped replications of equation 7.2 with the known value of the population parameter β_1 as set in the simulation environment. The performance of the PET is assessed by comparing how close the estimated value of b_1 comes to the known population parameter β_1. In the first simulations all original studies operationalize the dependent variable *Y* and independent variables *X* (including the focal predictor X_1) using identical measures and identical scales.

To provide a more useful context for assessing the PET, I conduct a matched set of simulations in which I use the random effects meta-regression (REMR) model to estimate the "true" effect size from a set of original studies. The "true" effect from the REMR model differs from the "true" effect in the PET model in two important ways. First, the PET estimates "true" effects using the scale of b_j in the original studies. As with any regression coefficient, the meaning of this "true" effect can only be interpreted if we know the scales used to measure *X* and *Y* in the original studies. By contrast, when using *r*-based effect sizes the REMR estimates "true" effects using partial correlation coefficients. Therefore, the metric of the PET and the metric of the REMR will differ. Second, while the benchmark for evaluating the PET is unaffected by the sample size or the degree of collinearity among predictors in the original models, the benchmark for evaluating the REMR is affected by both. For example, if we simulate a set of original studies using the population regression model $Y_i = \beta_0 + \beta_1 X_{1i} + \beta_2 X_{2i} + \varepsilon_i$, the PET should recover β_1 regardless of $\rho(X_1 X_2)$. By contrast, the partial correlation $\rho(Y, X_1 . X_2)$ associated with β_1 in this model will differ depending on $\rho(X_1 X_2)$. When $\rho(X_1 X_2)$ is large and positive, $\rho(Y, X_1 . X_2)$ will be smaller than when $\rho(X_1 X_2)$ is small and positive. To see why this is so, recall the formula for calculating a partial correlation coefficient from the results of a multiple regression model presented in chapter 3: $\rho\left(Y, X_j.X_k\right) = \sqrt{\left(t_j^2 / \left(t_j^2 + df\right)\right)}$. Holding β_j fixed, as $\rho(X_jX_k)$ increases, t_j declines, reducing the partial correlation coefficient $\rho(Y, X_j.X_k)$. Therefore, the benchmark for evaluating the performance of the REMR will differ across simulations that hold β_j constant.

I use an identical format to assess the performance of the REMR and the PET in that I compare the mean value and 90 percent confidence interval for the REMR constant term with the "known" value of the partial correlation coefficient in the simulation environment. To determine whether the REMR model can recover the population partial correlation coefficient used to simulate original studies, the dependent variable in the REMR models is the partial correlation r-based effect size, rather than its normalized version Z_r. Because the meta-sample size is large ($M = 500$) and because all original studies are generated independently, these simulations employ the standard REMR model rather than the CRVE or GEE models from chapter 5.

Performance of the PET with Homogeneous Effect Sizes. I begin the first set of PET simulations using the following environment:

- All first-level simulations assume a population model for original studies of $Y_i = \beta_0 + \beta_1 X_{1i} + \beta_2 X_{2i} + \beta_3 X_{3i} + \varepsilon_i$. The key relationship of interest from this model is β_1, and is measured using the parameter estimate b_1 from the first-level simulations. The t-score on b_1 (t_{b1}) provides the standardized effect size used in the PET test, while the inverse of the standard error of b_1 provides the measure of the precision of this effect size.
- The means of the exogenous variables in the population model are characterized by the vector $\boldsymbol{\mu}$ [μ_{X1}, μ_{X2}, μ_{X3}]. In the simulations reported here $\boldsymbol{\mu} = [0, 0, 0]$, but the results from the simulations are invariant to the values in this vector.
- The standard deviations of the exogenous variables in the population model are characterized by the vector $\boldsymbol{\sigma}$ [σ_{X1}, σ_{X2}, σ_{X3}]. In the simulations reported here $\boldsymbol{\sigma} = [1, 1, 1]$, but the results from the simulations are invariant to the values in this vector.
- X_1, X_2, and X_3 come from a multivariate normal distribution characterized by $\boldsymbol{\mu}, \boldsymbol{\sigma}$, and $\boldsymbol{C_{XX}}$, the covariance matrix. The elements of $\boldsymbol{C_{XX}}$ are operationalized as correlation coefficients. Values of $\boldsymbol{X}$ are

fixed across simulations. Simulations incorporate different levels of collinearity among the predictors in the original studies by varying the values for the elements $c_{Xj,Xk}$ in $\mathbf{C_{XX}}$.

- $\varepsilon \sim N(0,1)$.
- Y is generated from the population regression model $Y_i = \beta_0 + \beta_1 X_{1i} + \beta_2 X_{2i} + \beta_2 X_{3i} + \varepsilon_i$. Simulations incorporate different magnitudes of effect sizes in the original studies by varying the values for β_1 and β_2.
- First-level simulations generate a population of 9,999 simulated original studies, and these simulated studies generate 9,999 values of b_1 and t_{b1}. The sample size used to generate each b_1 is denoted N, and N varies across simulations.
- A partial correlation coefficient (an r-based effect size) is calculated using t_{b1} and the degrees of freedom from each of the 9,999 first-level sample regression equations.
- For the PET assessment, second-level simulations generate 1,000 simulated meta-regressions that employ bootstrapped resamples of the 9,999 effect sizes and precision estimates from the first-level simulations. The number of effect sizes used in each meta-analysis (the meta-sample size) is $M = 500$ in all simulations. The performance of the PET is assessed by comparing the mean value and 90 percent confidence interval for b_1 from the second-level bootstrapped PET meta-regressions without covariates ($t_i = b_0 + b_1 (1/se_i + e_i)$) to the known value of β_1 used in the first-level simulations.
- For the REMR assessment, second-level simulations generate 1,000 simulated meta-regressions that employ bootstrapped resamples of 9,999 r-based effect sizes. The average fixed effects variance is calculated for each bootstrapped resample using the formula from chapter 3. The random effects variance component is set at twice the size of the average fixed effects variance, generating a plausible I^2 statistic of 0.667 for the second-level REMR models. The performance of the REMR is assessed by comparing the mean value and 90 percent confidence interval for b_0 from the second-level bootstrapped REMR meta-regressions without covariates ($\Theta_i = b_0$) to the known partial correlation coefficient from the first-level simulations.

This simulation environment is identical to that used in table 7.3, except that the meta-sample size is fixed at a plausible $M = 500$. While table 7.3 focuses on the intercept from the meta-regression equation 7.2 (the FAT), the current simulations focus on the estimate of b_1 from this equation (the

TABLE 7.7. PERFORMANCE OF THE PET AND REMR WHERE *X* AND *Y* ARE MEASURED IDENTICALLY ACROSS ORIGINAL STUDIES AND ALL ORIGINAL STUDIES ESTIMATE THE SAME SAMPLE REGRESSION MODEL

Corr (X_j, X_k)	PET Population Parameter $[\beta_1]$	PET (b_1) Estimate and 90% CI	REMR Population Parameter $[\rho(Y, X_1 . X_2 X_3)]$	REMR (b_0) Estimate and 90% CI
.20	.7000	.6933 (.6929 − .7054)	.5297	.5665 (.5614 − .5714)
.60	.7000	.7000 (.6911 − .7085)	.4311	.4758 (.4696 − .4820)
.80	.7000	.7011 (.6892 − .7133)	.3284	.3626 (.3562 − .3694)
.20	.2000	.1998 (.1937 − .2065)	.1726	.2013 (.1952 − .2077)
.60	.2000	.1988 (.1904 − .2072)	.1356	.1636 (.1574 − .1697)
.80	.2000	.1978 (.1857 − .2097)	.1010	.1316 (.1253 − .1377)

PET). Recall that the intercept from the REMR model (equation 4.19) estimates the average effect size, or the "baseline" effect size when covariates are included in the model. Therefore, b_0 is the quantity of interest when comparing the REMR to the PET.

Simulation results are reported in table 7.7. Column 1 reports the level of collinearity among predictors in the first-level simulations. Columns 2 and 4 in table 7.7 report the population parameter estimated by the PET and the REMR (that is, the partial regression coefficient from original studies or the partial correlation coefficient from original studies, respectively) from the first-level simulations. These numbers are set a priori. The first number in columns 3 and 5 reports the mean value of the 1,000 bootstrapped replications of the PET and REMR in the second-level simulations that seek to estimate this population parameter (b_1 from the PET and b_0 from the REMR). The second set of numbers in columns 3 and 5 reports the 90 percent confidence interval for the 1,000 bootstrapped estimates of b_1 (PET) and b_0 (REMR).

In all scenarios in table 7.7 the PET provides a remarkably good estimate of the population regression parameter, or "true" effect. The mean estimate from the PET never departs from the population parameter by more than 5 percent, and the 90 percent confidence interval for PET estimates always includes the population parameter. By contrast, the REMR estimates of "true" effects are biased upward, exceeding the population partial correlation coefficients by between 8 percent and 30 percent, depending on the simulation environment. This bias is especially large when effect sizes are small and collinearity is high. The lesson from this first set of simulations is that when all original studies measure X and Y using the same indicator and the same scale, when all original studies estimate the same sample regression model, and when this sample regression model is identical to the population regression model, the PET provides an unbiased estimate of the "true" effect size, whereas the REMR model sometimes does not.

Performance of the PET with Heterogeneous Effect Sizes. The second set of simulations introduces effect size heterogeneity generated by model specification. In these simulations, one-third of the original studies estimate the sample version of the population model [$Y_i = b_0 + b_1 X_{1i} + b_2 X_{2i} + b_3 X_{3i} + e_i$], one-third of the original studies estimate the alternative model [$Y_i = b_0 + b_1 X_{1i} + b_2 X_{2i} + e_i$], and one-third of the original studies estimate the alternative model [$Y_i = b_0 + b_1 X_{1i} + e_i$]. All other elements of the simulation environment remain the same. The PET and REMR regression equations account for this parameter heterogeneity by including moderator variables identifying effect sizes coming from original models that include X_2 or X_3 as recommended by Stanley (2005) and Raudenbush (2009). The PET model becomes $t_i = b_0 + b_1 (1/se_i) + b_2 \text{mod} X_{2i} + b_3 \text{mod} X_{3i} + e_i$ (that is, equation 7.4), and the REMR model becomes

$$\Theta_i = b_0 + b_1 \text{ mod } X_{2i} + b_2 \text{ mod } X_{3i} + e_i \tag{7.7}$$

This simulation environment is identical to that used in table 7.4, and the results from these simulations are reported in table 7.8.

According to Stanley (2001; 2005) and Collot and Paldam (2011), the estimand from the PET does not change in the presence of specification differences in the original studies. That is, the intercept augmented PET (equation 7.4) is still expected to recover the parameter β_1 (for the focal predictor) from the population regression model even if some original

TABLE 7.8. PERFORMANCE OF THE PET AND REMR WHERE *X* AND *Y* ARE MEASURED IDENTICALLY ACROSS ORIGINAL STUDIES, BUT WITH EFFECT SIZE HETEROGENEITY FROM SPECIFICATION CHOICES IN ORIGINAL STUDIES

Corr (X_j,X_k)	PET Population Parameter $[\beta_1]$	PET (b_1) Estimate and 90% CI	REMR Population Parameter $[\rho(Y,X1)]$	REMR (b_0) Estimate and 90% CI
.20	.7000	.7572 (.7489 − .7654)	.5766	.5928 (.5837 − .6011)
.60	.7000	.8960 (.8790 − .9131)	.6808	.7000 (.6937 − .7057)
.80	.7000	1.0097 (.9889 − 1.0305)	.7233	.7749 (.7692 − .7807)
.20	.2000	.2190 (.2126 − .2261)	.2103	.2348 (.2239 − .2448)
.60	.2000	.2684 (.2594 − .2774)	.2788	.3060 (.2954 − .3166)
.80	.2000	.3064 (.2952 − .3173)	.3119	.3600 (.3493 − .3714)

studies estimate sample regression equations with different specifications. In the simulations here, this means that the parameter estimate b_1 from the PET should recover the population parameters $\beta_1 = .7$ and $\beta_1 = .2$ from the population regression model in the original studies as defined in the simulation environment.

By contrast, *the intercept from the REMR model in equation 7.7 is supposed to recover the partial correlation between X_1 and Y from original models that do not contain X_2 and X_3* (that is, where the two moderator variables in the REMR take on values of 0). So, while b_0 from the REMR model without covariates in table 7.7 is supposed to recover the partial correlation coefficient associated with β_1 from the population regression model, b_0 from the REMR model with covariates in table 7.8 is supposed to recover the partial correlation coefficient associated with β_1 from the population regression model $Y_i = \beta_0 + \beta_1 X_{1i} + \varepsilon_i$ as estimated by the misspecified original sample regression model $Y_i = b_0 + b_1 X_{1i} + e_i$. This means that the simulation target for the REMR changes in the presence of effect size heterogeneity, but the simulation target for the PET does not. Because the simulations are constructed with a positive correlation among the predictors $[\rho(X_1, X_2, X_3) > 0]$, the estimation target for the REMR grows larger as the degree of collinearity increases (in other words, β_1 from the bivariate population regression model is larger than β_1 from the multivariate population model due to the exclusion of predictors X_2 and X_3 that are positively correlated with X_1).

What if we want to recover an estimate of the partial correlation coefficient associated with the "true" effect β_1 from the properly specified regression model $Y_i = \beta_0 + \beta_1 X_{1i} + \beta_2 X_{2i} + \beta_3 X_{3i} + \varepsilon_i$, rather than from the misspecified regression model $Y_i = \beta_0 + \beta_1 X_{1i} + \varepsilon_i$? The REMR model in equation 7.7 can recover this estimate as well by combining b_0 and the parameter estimates from the moderator variables in the REMR. That is, we recover the partial correlation coefficient associated with β_1 in $Y_i = \beta_0 + \beta_1 X_{1i} + \beta_2 X_{2i} + \beta_3 X_{3i} + \varepsilon_i$ using $b_0 + b_1 + b_2$ from the REMR model.

Table 7.8 compares the ability of the PET to recover β_1 (estimated using b_1 from equation 7.4) with the ability of REMR to recover the partial correlation coefficient from the original regression model $Y_i = \beta_0 + \beta_1 X_{1i} + \varepsilon_i$ (estimated using b_0 from equation 7.7). Column 1 in table 7.8 reports the level of collinearity among predictors in the first-level simulations. Columns 2 and 4 report the population parameter estimated by the PET and the REMR (that is, the partial regression coefficient from original studies or the partial correlation coefficient from original studies, respectively) from the first-level simulations. These numbers are set a priori. The first number in columns 3 and 5 reports the mean value of the 1,000 bootstrapped replications of the PET and REMR in the second-level simulations that seek to estimate this population parameter. The second set of numbers in columns 3 and 5 reports the 90 percent confidence interval for the 1,000 bootstrapped estimates of b_1 (PET) and b_0 (REMR).

The performance of the PET degrades noticeably in the presence of effect size heterogeneity. Estimates of "true" effects using the PET are biased upward, and the degree of bias ranges from 10 percent (large and small effects with low collinearity) to around 50 percent (large and small effects with high collinearity). Similar to what we observed with the FAT, the performance of the PET is affected by the degree of collinearity among predictors in the original models. Estimates of "true" effects from the REMR models are also biased upward, but the degree of bias in REMR estimates is far smaller, never exceeding 8 percent in models with large "true" effects and only reaching 15 percent in models with small "true" effects. In the more common situation in which original studies employ regression models with varying specifications, the PET performs poorly as a method for estimating "true" effects. In these circumstances, researchers would be better served using the random effects meta-regression model.

Table 7.8 illustrates that the REMR does a better job recapturing the relevant population parameter from original studies than does the PET. Recall, however, that b_0 from the REMR recaptures an estimate of the correlation coefficient $\rho(Y, X_1)$ from the incorrect population regression model $Y_i = \beta_0 + \beta_1 X_{1i} + \varepsilon_i$. In many instances, meta-analysts will be interested in recapturing the partial correlation coefficient associated with β_1 from the correct population regression model $Y_i = \beta_0 + \beta_1 X_{1i} + \beta_2 X_{2i} + \beta_3 X_{3i} + \varepsilon_i$. In the previous paragraph I stated that the REMR can recapture this parameter by combining the coefficient estimates on the moderating variables with the coefficient estimate for b_0. I demonstrate this procedure in table 7.9. Some readers may wonder if the same procedure can be applied to the PET to recover the regression parameter β_1 from the properly specified population regression model. This is not possible when using the PET. To see why, recall that the dependent variable in the PET is the t-score from the hypothesis test on the focal predictor from original studies. Because the moderator variables in equation 7.4 are dichotomous, parameter estimates on these variables (b_2 and b_3 in equation 7.4) are measured using the metric of t-scores. By contrast, because X_1 in equation 7.4 is measured using the parameter standard errors rather than values of 0 and 1, b_1 in equation 7.4 is measured according to the metrics of X and Y in the original studies (recall that this is why b_1 from the PET can be interpreted as a measure of the "true" effect present in the original studies). Because b_1, b_2, and b_3 from equation 7.4 are measured on different metrics, they cannot be combined in any meaningful fashion, and the moderator variables used in the PET cannot be used to recover a better estimate of β_1 from the properly specified first-stage population regression model. Table 7.9 illustrates this point.

Columns 1 and 2 in table 7.9 report the degree of collinearity among predictors in the original studies and the type of meta-regression model estimated, respectively. Column 3 reports the value of the population parameter of interest from the properly specified population regression model $Y_i = \beta_0 + \beta_1 X_{1i} + \beta_2 X_{2i} + \beta_3 X_{3i} + \varepsilon_i$. This value comes from table 7.7. Column 4 reports the relevant estimate of this population parameter from each meta-regression model in the presence of effect size heterogeneity. These values come from table 7.8. Columns 5 and 6 report the parameter estimates associated with the moderator variables in the meta-regression equations 7.4 and 7.7. Finally, column 7 reports the predicted value of the population parameter of interest obtained by

TABLE 7.9. ABILITY OF REMR AND PET TO RECOVER POPULATION PARAMETER OF INTEREST IN THE PRESENCE OF EFFECT SIZE HETEROGENEITY FROM SPECIFICATION CHOICES IN ORIGINAL STUDIES

Corr (X_j, X_k)	Model	Population Parameter of Interest	Estimate of b_0(REMR) b_1(PET)	Parameter Estimate for Moderator Variable X_2	Parameter Estimate for Moderator Variable X_3	Predicted Value of Population Parameter of Interest
.20	REMR	.5297	.5928	−.0169	−.0090	.5669
	PET	.7000	.7572	−1.0310	−.6436	−.9174
.60	REMR	.4311	.7000	−.1598	−.0643	.4759
	PET	.7000	.8960	−3.5050	−1.1406	−3.7496
.80	REMR	.3284	.7749	−.3254	−.0879	.3616
	PET	.7000	1.0097	−4.5077	−.9136	−4.4116
.20	REMR	.1726	.2348	−.0223	−.0123	.2002
	PET	.2000	.2190	−.3736	−.2102	−.3648
.60	REMR	.1356	.3060	−.1077	−.0302	.1681
	PET	.2000	.2684	−1.2124	−.3724	−1.3164
.80	REMR	.1010	.3600	−.2009	−.0278	.1313
	PET	.2000	.3064	−1.4920	−.3002	−1.4858

combining the relevant parameter estimates from the meta-regression models. In all cases the predicted value for the population parameter of interest from the REMR models is close to its expected value. Indeed, the predicted value for the population partial correlation coefficient in the presence of effect size heterogeneity in table 7.8 is very near the REMR estimate of the partial correlation coefficient in the absence of effect size heterogeneity from table 7.6. This is as it should be. By contrast, the predicted value of the relevant population parameter from the PET bears no resemblance to its actual value as set in the first-level simulations. This nonsensical result arises because the PET combines parameter estimates that are measured using different metrics, as described above. In the presence of effect size heterogeneity, then, the PET provides a seriously biased estimate of the "true" effect present in the original studies (see table 7.8), but it is unable to recover a reasonable estimate of this true effect when using moderator variables in equation 7.4. If researchers are interested in using meta-regression techniques to estimate average "true" effects of focal predictors in original studies, they are well advised to avoid relying upon the PET.

Performance of the PET with Varying Measurement of Y and X

Thus far I have evaluated the PET in the highly artificial environment in which all original studies operationalize the dependent variable Y and the focal predictor X using the same indicator measured on the same scale. In nearly all situations faced in practice, however, meta-analysts in public management, public policy, and the social sciences are likely to encounter variation across studies in the indicators used to operationalize Y and X and in the scales used to measure these variables. To take a simple example, consider the controversy regarding the relationship between educational expenditures and student outcomes described in the introduction to this book. Some original studies examining this relationship (denoted here as Group A) measured the focal predictor "expenditures" in dollars $[X_{1A}]$, while other studies (Group B) measured expenditures in thousands of dollars $[X_{1B} = (X_{1A}/1000)]$, and still other original studies (Group C) measured expenditures using the natural log of dollars $(X_{1C} = ln(X_{1A}))$. Clearly we cannot combine regression coefficients b_{1A}, b_{1B}, and b_{1C} in any meaningful sense, even if student outcomes (Y) are measured identically across all original studies. Yet this is just what the PET does. By using t-scores from the null hypothesis tests on b_{1A}, b_{1B}, and b_{1C}, the PET estimate of the "true" effect (estimated using b_1 from equation 7.3 or 7.4) is measured on a scale that is some unknown weighted average of the scales used to measure X_{1A}, X_{1B}, and X_{1C}. The estimate of the "true" effect from the PET becomes even more uninterpretable if the measurement of Y varies across original studies as well. By contrast, traditional meta-analysis remedies this problem by calculating effect sizes that are comparable and combinable across studies regardless of the measurement of X and Y (so long as X and Y represent the same concepts in all original studies). Therefore, unlike the PET, the random effects meta-regression model ought to be able to recover the population partial correlation coefficient if the measurement of X and Y varies across original studies.

I evaluate the performance of the REMR model in the presence of varying sample sizes, effect size heterogeneity, and varying measurement for X and Y using the following simulation environment:

· All first-level simulations assume a population model for original studies of $Y_i = \beta_0 + \beta_1 X_{1i} + \beta_2 X_{2i} + \beta_3 X_{3i} + \varepsilon_i$. The key relationship of interest from this model is the partial correlation coefficient associated with β_1, which is measured using the r-based effect size from b_1 in the first-level simulations.

- The means of the exogenous variables in the population model are characterized by the vector $\boldsymbol{\mu}$ [μ_{X1}, μ_{X2}, μ_{X3}]. In the simulations reported here $\boldsymbol{\mu} = [100, 60, 25]$, but the results from the simulations are invariant to the values in this vector.

- The standard deviations of the exogenous variables in the population model are characterized by the vector $\boldsymbol{\sigma}$ [$\sigma_{X1}, \sigma_{X2}, \sigma_{X3}$]. In the simulations reported here $\boldsymbol{\sigma} = [20, 20, 2]$, but the results from the simulations are invariant to the values in this vector.

- X_{1A}, X_2, and X_3 come from a multivariate normal distribution characterized by $\boldsymbol{\mu}$, $\boldsymbol{\sigma}$, and $\boldsymbol{C_{XX}}$, the covariance matrix. The elements of $\boldsymbol{C_{XX}}$ are operationalized as correlation coefficients. The subscript $_A$ is used to designate that the focal predictor X_1 comes from the original draw from the multivariate normal distribution. Values of $\boldsymbol{X}$ are fixed across simulations. Simulations incorporate different levels of collinearity among the predictors in the original studies by varying the values for the elements $c_{Xj,Xk}$ in $\boldsymbol{C_{XX}}$.

- Y is generated from the population regression model $Y_{Ai} = \beta_0 + \beta_1 X_{1Ai} + \beta_2 X_{2i} + \beta_2 X_{3i} + \varepsilon_i$. Simulations incorporate different magnitudes of effect sizes in the original studies by varying the values for β_1 and β_2. The subscript $_A$ is used to designate that the dependent variable Y is generated using predictors coming from the original draw from the multivariate normal distribution. $\varepsilon \sim N(0,30)$.

- Variation in the measurement of the focal predictor X_{1A} is produced by generating $X_{1B} = (X_{1A} * 1,000)$ and by generating $X_{1C} = ln(X_{1A})$. Variation in the dependent variable Y_A is produced by generating $Y_B = (Y_A * 1,000)$ and by generating $Y_C = ln(Y_A)$.

- First-level simulations generate a population of 10,800 simulated original studies (200 simulated studies for each of the nine combinations of Y_A, Y_B, Y_C, X_{1A}, X_{1B}, and X_{1C}. These simulated studies generate 10,800 values of b_1 and t_{b1}. The sample size used to generate each b_1 is denoted N, and N varies across simulations. One-half of the simulations are of $N = 50$ and one-half of the simulations are of $N = 500$.

- A partial correlation coefficient (an r-based effect size) is calculated using t_{b1} from each of the 10,800 first-level sample regression equations.

- For the REMR assessment, second-level simulations generate 1,000 simulated meta-regressions that employ bootstrapped resamples of 500 r-based effect sizes. The average fixed effects variance is calculated using the formula from chapter 3. The random effects variance component is set at twice the size of the average fixed effects variance, generating a plausible I^2 statistic of 0.667 for the second-level REMR models. The performance of the REMR is assessed by comparing the mean value for b_0 from the second-level bootstrapped REMR meta-regressions (equation 7.7) to the known partial correlation coefficient from the first-level simulation environment.

The results from these simulations are reported in table 7.10. In effect, this last set of simulations takes the simulation environment from table 7.9 and introduces the added complication that original studies may measure the dependent variable Y and focal predictor X_1 in one of three ways. Allowing the metric of Y and X_1 to vary in this way makes the simulation more tedious. For example, the data generating the results in each row of table 7.9 come from three sample regression models: $Y_i = b_0 + b_1 X_{1i} + e_i$; $Y_i = b_0 + b_1 X_{1i} + b_2 X_{2i} + e_i$; and $Y_i = b_0 + b_1 X_{1i} + b_2 X_{2i} + b_3 X_{3i} + e_i$, each estimated using sample sizes of 25, 100, and 1,000. By contrast, the data generating comparable results in table 7.10 come from the same three sample regression models estimated for each combination of the measurement of Y and the measurement of X_1, each estimated using sample sizes of 50 and 500. Therefore, each row in table 7.10 represents $3^3 * 2 = 54$ sets of simulated original studies. To compensate for this added complexity, the simulations in table 7.10 are limited to the most plausible scenarios faced by researchers in practice: sample sizes in original studies are set at 50 and 500; collinearity among predictors is set at $\rho(X_j X_k) = .6$; and the meta-sample size is set at $M = 500$. The population partial regression coefficient in the first row of table 7.10 is generated using $\beta_1 = .7$ in the population

TABLE 7.10. ABILITY OF REMR TO RECOVER POPULATION PARAMETER OF INTEREST IN THE PRESENCE OF EFFECT SIZE HETEROGENEITY AND VARIATION IN THE MEASUREMENT OF X AND Y IN ORIGINAL STUDIES

Corr (X_j, X_k)	Population Parameter of Interest	Estimate of b_0	Parameter Estimate for Moderator Variable X_2	Parameter Estimate for Moderator Variable X_3	Predicted Value of Population Parameter of Interest
.60	.3234	.5008	−.1648	−.0253	.3107
.60	.0950	.1644	−.0552	−.0065	.1027

regression model, while the population partial regression coefficient in the second row is generated using $\beta_1 = .2$.

Table 7.10 shows that even with varying sample sizes in original studies, effect size heterogeneity generated by specification differences in original studies, and large variation in the measurement of Y and X in original studies, the REMR model is still able to recapture the population partial correlation coefficient with a high degree of accuracy. With small effects, the difference between the value of partial correlation coefficient estimated by the REMR (.1027) and the population value set in the simulation (.0950) is 8 percent. With large effects, the REMR estimate is even more precise; a 4 percent difference. Comparable figures for the PET are impossible to obtain, because the coefficient for the PET is some uninterpretable combination of the various metrics used to measure Y and X_1.

Conclusion

Meta-analysis in the discipline of economics is dominated by the FAT-MST-PET-MRA approach to meta-regression. The simulations in this chapter show that most elements of this approach perform poorly in environments commonly encountered by researchers in public management, public policy, and the social sciences. Specifically, type I error rates for the FAT rise dramatically as a function of collinearity among predictors in the original models, and as a function of effect size heterogeneity introduced by differences in model specification across original studies. It is little wonder, therefore, that economists who have used the FAT to test for publication bias have found it virtually everywhere they have looked (Stanley 2005). The poor performance of the FAT is not completely unexpected, given the criticisms of the equivalent Egger test in the medical statistics literature over the past decade (see chapter 6). Similarly, in conditions commonly faced by social scientists in practice—collinearity among predictors and effect size heterogeneity in original studies—the PET provides a poor estimate of "true" underlying effect sizes in these studies. Moreover, when the dependent variable and focal predictors are measured using different indicators or different scales in original studies, the PET becomes uninterpretable. By contrast, the average effect sizes estimated by the random effects meta-regression model are remarkably close to the population parameters set in the simulation environment. Researchers in public management and policy are well advised to avoid relying on the

FAT-MST-PET-MRA, and instead to use the standard meta-analysis and meta-regression techniques presented in chapters 3 through 5.

Notes

1. Technically the hypothesis test on b_0 from equation 7.2 only tests for directional publication bias. Testing for nondirectional publication bias requires replacing t_i in equation 7.2 with its absolute value $|t_i|$.
2. Stanley (2005) offers additional specifications of the MST. Because they are functionally equivalent I do not address them.
3. There is no evidence that Stanley or Copas and Malley are aware of the work of the other, as neither author cites the other. While Copas and Malley never identify the PET by name, the method illustrated by these researchers is mathematically identical to the PET.

PART TWO

META-ANALYSIS IN PUBLIC MANAGEMENT AND POLICY RESEARCH

CHAPTER EIGHT

EVALUATING THE EFFECTIVENESS OF EDUCATIONAL VOUCHERS

Mary R. Anderson, Tatyana Guzman and Evan J. Ringquist

"Extensive research has been conducted on the academic success of students enrolled in school choice programs nationwide. Rigorous studies show strong gains for voucher and scholarship tax credit recipients . . . "

(ALLIANCE FOR SCHOOL CHOICE 2011).

"The reason that vouchers had subsided as a point of advocacy is because they don't work"

(RANDI WEINGARTEN, PRESIDENT, AMERICAN FEDERATION OF TEACHERS; QUOTED IN ASSOCIATED PRESS 2011).

"Few contemporary questions in American education have produced such wide-spread controversy as that regarding the potential of school vouchers to reduce inequality in student outcomes. This potential has been studied by many scholars . . . these efforts notwithstanding, answers to the voucher question still appear uncertain"

(COWEN 2008, 301).

Education produces positive externalities in that those not party to an educational transaction nevertheless benefit through a more able and efficient workforce, a better-functioning democracy, and the like. Under these conditions, the quantity of education supplied by a free market will be suboptimal, justifying government intervention to increase the supply of (and require attendance at) educational institutions. For at least 150 years, governments in the United States have addressed this issue using the direct production and delivery of educational services through public schools. Simply because government intervention in education can be justified using the tenets of welfare economics, however, does not mean that government production is the most effective or efficient means of intervention. Fifty years ago Milton Friedman argued that a system of publically funded vouchers that citizens could redeem for educational services at private schools would be a more efficient method of maximizing social welfare with respect to education (Friedman 1962).

Educational voucher programs have been introduced in nearly a dozen U.S. cities and in a handful of U.S. states. Unfortunately, research on the effects of these voucher systems is characterized by a distressingly familiar situation of disparate studies producing contradictory conclusions. Reducing the uncertainty surrounding the effects of educational vouchers has important scientific and practical consequences. First, the efficiency and performance gains expected from voucher programs arise squarely from core behavioral theories in economics, political science, and public administration. Generalizable conclusions regarding the effects of voucher programs, then, speak directly to the validity of these theories in the area of education. Second, policy makers from presidents on down have expressed a desire for expanding the use of educational vouchers, and since 2010 there has been renewed interest in educational vouchers by policy makers at all levels of government (Associated Press 2011).

In this chapter we synthesize the research regarding the effects of educational vouchers on student achievement, and offer evidence regarding the conditions under which these vouchers are most and least likely to improve student achievement. While politicians rarely base their support for policy options solely on evidence that these options will be effective, continued public and private support for expanded use of educational vouchers clearly hinges in part on estimates of their effectiveness, as does the rationale for increasing or decreasing public funding for educational voucher programs.

School Choice and Educational Vouchers

Educational Vouchers as One Element of School Choice

Over the past twenty-five years, widespread dissatisfaction with the public education system on the part of certain groups has brought the option of school choice to the foreground of policy debates surrounding education. Educational vouchers are one option among a broader suite of choice alternatives. These alternatives include the following:

· *Open enrollment* is a system in which public school students are free to attend any public school of their choice. Minnesota has had a mandatory statewide open enrollment system since 1990. State school funding follows students across school district lines.
· *Magnet schools* are public schools that use specialized curricula (math, science, arts, humanities, or others) or distinctive teaching approaches. As is similar to the open enrollment alternative, students attending magnet schools are not limited by neighborhood boundaries and can attend a magnet school of their choice outside the school district lines. In contrast to open enrollment, magnet schools often require students to pass entry tests.
· *Charter schools* are alternative public schools that can utilize their own curriculum (rather than a state-mandated curriculum), are freer to use innovative teaching methods, and are bound by fewer state educational rules and requirements. As of 2009, forty-one states and the District of Columbia had charter schools (Lake 2010).
· *Educational vouchers* are essentially subsidies or scholarships that allow selected public school students to attend private schools. These subsidies may be direct, in that state funds are used to pay for some portion (up to 100 percent) of private school tuition for voucher recipients. These subsidies may also be indirect, when parents are offered a state income tax credit for the costs of private school tuition and fees (see following). States use different criteria to determine eligibility to receive a voucher, including means testing, attendance at a failing public school, or having disabilities or special needs. Table 8.1 provides a summary of current publically funded voucher programs for non-special-needs students.
· *Tuition tax credits* become a popular alternative to vouchers. With this option taxpayers (individuals or organizations) receive a state income tax relief (in the form of income tax deductions or credits) toward education-related expenses.

Linking Vouchers to Student Achievement. Proponents and opponents of educational vouchers both offer plausible causal stories about their likely effects. Proponents argue that educational vouchers will improve student educational performance and improve parental and student satisfaction with schools, all at lower cost than the current system of public schools. Proponents offer two causal stories linking vouchers to student

TABLE 8.1. EDUCATIONAL VOUCHER PROGRAMS IN THE UNITED STATES, 2011

State	Program Name	Year Enacted	Eligibility	Enrollment
Colorado	Choice Scholarships (Douglas County Only)	2011	All public school students	500
Indiana	Choice Scholarship Program	2011	Means tested	Unlimited (7,500 first year)
Louisiana	Student Scholarships for Educational Excellence (New Orleans Only)	2008	Means tested and failing schools	1,697
Ohio	Cleveland Scholarship Tuitioning Program	1995	Means tested	5,624
Ohio	Educational Choice Scholarships	2005	Failing schools	13,195
Wisconsin	Milwaukee Parental Choice Program	1990	Means tested	20,189
Washington, D.C.	DC Opportunity Scholarship Program	2004	Means tested	1,012

Source: Campanella, Glenn, and Perry 2011; Center on Education Policy 2011.

achievement; the "competition effect" and the "private school effect." The competition effect perspective embodies the idea that public school monopolies are no different from other monopolies in that they will seek rents by producing goods and services of inferior quality at higher prices. Both tendencies are exacerbated by X-inefficiencies (Weimer and Vining 2009). Vouchers create a more competitive market-like environment for traditional public schools, and successful schools will respond by improving the quality and reducing the cost of educational services. In this respect, the long-term effect of vouchers will be to raise the performance of voucher recipients and nonrecipients alike. The private school effect rests upon the widespread notion that private schools do a better job of educating students than do public schools (which, some researchers show, may not necessarily be the case). See for example, Lubienski, Lubienski, NAEP, and NCSPE 2006 and Lubienski, Lubienski, and Crane 2008. This private school advantage may stem from organizational characteristics—that is, private schools have fewer regulations regarding student discipline, teacher hiring, and retention, and less administrative overhead. This greater flexibility and efficiency leads to higher student academic achievement (see, for example, Chubb and Moe 1990). The private school advantage may also stem from peer effects. Private school students and their parents are hypothesized to be more motivated by educational quality, which creates a peer environment of educational excellence at private schools. Programs in which vouchers may be used for private school tuition may increase student achievement by exposing voucher recipients to both types of private school benefits.

Opponents argue that vouchers will transfer resources from strapped public schools to private schools, "cream" the best students from the public schools, and allow parents to send their students to private schools in pursuit of religious education or a more homogeneous racial or cultural environment, rather than in pursuit of a higher-quality education (see, for example, Meier and Smith 1995).

Public Support for School Choice and Vouchers. According to a recent survey by the Pew Charitable Trusts, large majorities of American citizens feel that Congress should do more to improve the educational system in the United States. In fact, reforming K–12 education ranks second only to defending the United States from terrorist attacks as a policy priority for survey respondents (Public Agenda 2011). Public confidence in U.S. public schools has declined markedly since the 1970s (along with confidence in most other public institutions), and half of all survey respondents are dissatisfied with the quality of K–12 education in the United States (Public Agenda 2011).

While large majorities of U.S. citizens are in favor of reforming public education, public opinion regarding educational vouchers is less consensual. A 2004 survey by the Annenberg School found the public evenly divided over vouchers, with 36 percent in favor of publically funded voucher programs, 34 percent opposed, and 30 percent having no opinion (Gelman 2009). The Program on Education Policy and Governance at Harvard University has tracked public support for vouchers over several years. Between 2007 and 2010, support for publically funded educational voucher programs dropped from 45 percent to 31 percent, while opposition to these programs rose from 34 percent to 43 percent. The most recent data from 2011 show greater balance: 39 percent of survey respondents favor voucher programs while 38 percent oppose them (Howell, Peterson, and West 2011). Support for voucher programs is not homogeneous, however. In general, racial and ethnic minorities are more supportive of educational vouchers than are whites, largely because students from these groups are more likely to attend low-performing public schools (Howell, Wolf, Campbell, and Peterson 2002). The effect of income is more complex. For example, Andrew Gelman found a positive correlation between income and support for vouchers among white citizens, but a negative correlation between income and support for vouchers among racial and ethnic minorities (Gelman 2009). Thus, while proponents and opponents of vouchers may claim that public opinion is "on their side," the reality is that the public is evenly divided on the issue.

A Brief History of Educational Vouchers in the United States

While Maine and Vermont have had voucher-like "town tuitioning" programs for more than one hundred years, the first broadly recognized, publically funded educational voucher program began in Milwaukee, Wisconsin, in 1990. The initial Milwaukee Parental Choice Program was very small. Only students in the Milwaukee Public School system were eligible for vouchers, the number of vouchers was capped at 900, and students were prohibited from using these vouchers to attend religious schools. In 1998 the Wisconsin Supreme Court ruled in *Jackson v. Benson* that religious schools could receive public revenue through educational vouchers, and participation in the Milwaukee Parental Choice Program increased by more than 400 percent (Kisida, Jensen, Wolf, and SCDP 2011). Beginning in 2005, all students participating in the Milwaukee Parental Choice Program were required to take the same standardized tests required of public school students. The cap on vouchers has been raised several times over the years, and in 2010 20,996 students received vouchers under this program at a cost of $131 million. In 2011, the Wisconsin State Legislature liberalized eligibility requirements for this program and expanded educational vouchers to students in the Racine school district (Campanella, Glenn, and Perry 2011). The Milwaukee Parental Choice Program is still the largest operating educational voucher program in the country.

In 1996, Cleveland, Ohio, introduced the Cleveland Scholarship and Tuitioning Program, a publically funded voucher program for elementary school students. Unlike in the Milwaukee program, from the outset voucher recipients in Cleveland could send their children to private religious schools. This characteristic of the Cleveland program spawned a legal challenge that was not resolved until the U.S. Supreme Court (2002) ruled in *Zelman v. Simmons-Harris* that publically funded vouchers given to parents who then redeem these vouchers at religious schools does not violate the anti-establishment clause of the U.S. Constitution. This landmark 5–4 decision reversed the ruling from the Sixth Circuit Court of Appeals and opened the door for a large expansion of publically funded voucher programs. While state constitutions might bar using public funds for tuition scholarships at religious schools, the U.S. Constitution no longer served as a barrier to this practice. In 2010, 5,264 students were enrolled in the Cleveland program at a cost of $17.6 million (Campanella, Glenn, and Perry 2011). In 2005, after *Zelman v. Simmons-Harris*, Ohio created the statewide Educational Choice Scholarship Program, which offered educational vouchers to students in chronically failing public schools. In 2010, 13,195 students received vouchers through this program at a cost of $58 million. In 2011 Ohio quadrupled the cap on these voucher programs from 14,000 to 60,000 students (Associated Press 2011).

Throughout the 1990s, several cities experimented with small, privately funded voucher programs, including Charlotte, North Carolina; Dayton, Ohio; New York; San Antonio, Texas; San Francisco; and Washington, D.C. The next major development in publically funded voucher programs occurred in 2004 when the U.S. Congress created the Opportunity Scholarship Program in Washington, D.C., which provided federally funded vouchers to nearly 4,000 students a year between 2005 and 2009 at a cost of roughly $14 million per year. The Opportunity Scholarship Program was terminated in 2009, but Congressional Republicans resurrected the program as part of the 2010 budget negotiations. The program is authorized through the 2015–16 academic year, and currently 1,000 students receive vouchers through this program.

In 2011, Indiana enacted the most extensive state-supported educational voucher system to date. Though participation in the program is limited to 7,500 students in the first year and 15,000 students in the second year, there is no cap on student enrollment when the program is fully implemented after three years, and students may use vouchers to attend secular or religious schools. The Indiana program is also among the most generous in the nation: the value of the voucher is $4,500, and families with incomes up to $61,000 per year are eligible to receive vouchers (Center on Education Policy 2011).

Despite the growth of voucher programs, the history of educational vouchers in the U.S. contains some notable setbacks. In 1999 the state of Florida established the nation's first statewide educational voucher program. The Florida Opportunity Scholarship Program offered K–12 students in persistently failing public schools a voucher to attend any public or private school of their choice, so long as this school received a grade of "C" or better on the state school assessment. By 2005 nearly 4,000 students were taking advantage of this program. In 2006, however, the Florida Supreme Court ruled in *Bush v. Holmes* that the Florida Constitution prohibited state-funded vouchers from being used to attend private schools (Supreme Court of Florida 2006). The public school option still exists, and in 2010 just over 1,000 students used this option to attend a higher-performing public school (Center on Education Policy 2011). In 2004, the Colorado Supreme Court also struck down a pilot state-wide voucher program targeted at poor children in low-performing school districts. In *Owens v. Colorado Congress of Parents* the court ruled that the program violated the state constitutional requirement that local school districts maintain control over locally generated revenue (Center on Education Policy 2011). In addition, each time the creation of a state-wide voucher program has been voted on directly by citizens, voters have rejected these programs (for example, California and Michigan in 2000, Utah in 2007).

Both public controversy and policy activity regarding vouchers ebbed during the past several years. The elections of 2010, however, and the large gains made by Republicans in Congress and state legislatures served to reinvigorate vouchers as a policy issue. More state governments than ever considered school vouchers in 2011. Legislators in at least thirty states have introduced bills to create voucher programs, and twenty-eight states have considered or are considering state tax credits for private school tuition (in other words, indirect voucher subsidies). Six states have passed legislation creating new voucher programs or new tax credits. By contrast, only nine voucher bills were introduced in state legislatures in 2009, and only one passed (the creation of a voucher program for special needs students in Oklahoma) (Associated Press 2011). These developments make solid evidence regarding the effectiveness of vouchers especially timely.

The Effectiveness of Educational Vouchers

The question "Do vouchers work?" is too simplistic. When defining our research question regarding the effects of educational vouchers we need to consider (1) effects on *whom*, (2) effects on *what*, and (3) the *types of treatment effects*. In this section we address effects on whom (students, as compared to parents or schools) and effects on what (student academic achievement). We address types of treatment effects in a later section.

Defining Voucher Effects

Educational vouchers are hypothesized to have a number of consequences. First and most important, vouchers are expected to increase student academic achievement (sometimes referred to as student performance). That is, vouchers are expected to help students "learn more" and "learn better," and these improvements are supposed to be evident through metrics such as grades and standardized test scores. Second, vouchers are hypothesized to improve student academic attainment. Attainment is measured using indicators such as high school graduation and admission to college. Third, voucher programs and the competition, transfer of resources, and increased scrutiny that comes with these programs are hypothesized to affect schools and other educational organizations. Voucher proponents expect that these organizational effects will be positive, and will include greater efficiency, greater retention of students and teachers, and stronger organizational morale (Campanella, Glenn, and Perry 2011). Voucher opponents expect that these organizational effects will be negative, and will include creaming of the best students, reductions in already scarce resources, and weaker organizational morale. Finally, vouchers are expected to increase both student and parental satisfaction regarding school quality and the overall educational experience. While we recognize the importance of all of these hypothesized effects of vouchers, *in this meta-analysis we define voucher effects using only student academic achievement*. Historically, academic achievement has been the primary justification given for the creation of voucher programs, and these effects are at the center of disagreements over the wisdom of voucher programs. Despite this history, most recently the rhetoric used to support voucher programs has shifted from an emphasis on student achievement to an emphasis on parental satisfaction, graduation rates, and the intrinsic virtues of educational choice (Center on Education Policy 2011).

Reviewing the Effects of Vouchers on Educational Achievement

The Milwaukee Parental Choice Program. At the end of a five-year evaluation, John Witte concluded that Milwaukee students who received vouchers and attended private schools performed no better on standardized math or reading tests than did comparable students who remained in the Milwaukee public school system (Witte 1998; an earlier preliminary study by the Wisconsin Legislative Audit Bureau [1995] reached similar conclusions). After conducting a reanalysis of the Milwaukee data, Greene, Peterson, and Du (1999) concluded that Milwaukee voucher recipients had indeed outperformed nonvoucher recipients on both standardized math and reading tests. The most significant difference between these studies is that Witte used a control group of matched Milwaukee Public School District students, while Greene and colleagues used a control group made up of students who applied for vouchers but did not receive them. (Witte chose not to use this control group because of high levels of attrition.) In yet another analysis of these same data, Cecilia Rouse split the difference between the Witte and Greene studies. Using both types of control groups, Rouse concluded that voucher recipients outperformed nonrecipients on standardized math tests, but not reading tests (Rouse 1998). In his final evaluation of the Milwaukee program, Witte (2000) concludes that any effect of voucher use on student test scores is highly sensitive to the composition of the treatment and control groups, to the control variables used in empirical models, and to the statistical tests used to identify treatment effects. Most recently, using quantile regression, Lamarche (2008) estimated small positive gains in math scores for voucher users in Milwaukee (2.2 point test score gains), but found that these gains were much larger for low-achieving students (3.5–4 point gains) and smaller for high-achieving students (0–1.5 point gains). Using this same approach, Lamarche found no significant voucher effects on student reading scores.

The Cleveland Scholarship and Tutoring Program. The official evaluation of the Cleveland Scholarship and Tutoring Program compared the educational performance of voucher recipients with the performance of students that applied for but did not receive a voucher, and with the performance of a comparison group of Cleveland public school students. The initial evaluation of the Cleveland program concluded that voucher recipients and nonrecipients performed equally well on five different standardized achievement tests (Metcalf, Boone, et al. 1998). In a reanalysis of these same data, Peterson, Greene, and Howell (1998) concluded that while voucher and nonvoucher recipients performed equally well in reading, math, and social studies, voucher recipients performed significantly better on the science and language exams. A later, more comprehensive analysis by Metcalf, Muller, and colleagues (1998) did little to clarify the matter. In this second-year report, voucher students attending established private schools outperformed a comparison group of public school students on science and language exams, but not on reading, math, and social studies exams. However, voucher students who attended new private schools scored significantly worse than their public school peers on all five subject exams. The final report evaluating the Cleveland program concluded that by the end of a five-year period there was no difference in reading scores, math scores, science scores, or overall composite test scores between students who used vouchers and students who did not use vouchers. However, test score gains in language and social science were 2 percent higher after five years for voucher users compared to students who received vouchers but did not use them (Plucker, Muller, Hansen, Ravert, and Makel 2006).

The Washington, D.C., Opportunity Scholarship Program. The U.S. Congress required annual evaluations of the DC Opportunity Scholarship Program that used "the strongest possible research design to determine the effectiveness of the program" (U.S. Government Accountability Office 2007). The first-year evaluation of the DC program concluded that voucher recipients performed no better than nonvoucher recipients in reading or math, and that there were no meaningful differences in test score performance among high-priority subgroups of voucher recipients (that is, vouchers did not differentially improve the performance of low-performing students or for students who had attended low-performing schools prior to receiving a voucher) (Wolf et al. 2008). The final evaluation of the DC program concluded that after three years, "there is no conclusive evidence that the OSP affected student achievement" (Wolf et al. 2010, 5). That is, reading and math test scores were not significantly different between students who were offered vouchers and students who were not offered vouchers. The absence of a significant effect was consistent when all voucher recipients were considered and when subgroups of voucher recipients were examined as defined by race, gender, or at-risk status.

Privately Funded Municipal Voucher Programs. The strongest evidence that vouchers improve student academic achievement come from evaluations of privately funded voucher programs such as those in Charlotte, North Carolina; Dayton, Ohio; New York; San Antonio, Texas; San Francisco; and Washington, D.C. (the privately funded D.C. program is different from the Congressionally mandated DC Opportunity Scholarship Program discussed above). Most evaluations of these programs have been completed by researchers affiliated with the Program on Educational Policy and Governance (PEPG) at Harvard University. In Charlotte, Greene (2000) found that voucher recipients scored better on both math and reading exams than did nonrecipients. A more recent assessment of the Charlotte program replicates these positive results for intent to treat and treatment on the treated effects, but finds that vouchers have no effect on academic achievement when a Complier Average Causal Effect is estimated (Cowen 2008). (We discuss the difference between treatment on the treated [TT], intent to treat [ITT], and Complier Average Causal Effects [CACE] in a later section). In Dayton, the use of vouchers has been associated with increased reading scores for African American students, but vouchers have had no effect on African American math scores or on test scores from other student groups (West, Peterson, and Campbell 2001). In Washington, D.C., African American voucher recipients outperformed their control group counterparts on standardized math and reading exams, but the effect of vouchers could not be established for any other group (Wolf, Peterson, and West 2001). A summary assessment of the Dayton, Washington, D.C., and New York voucher programs concluded that the use of vouchers had no effect on average student math scores, reading scores, or combined test scores (Howell, Wolf, Campbell, and Peterson 2002). This same assessment, however, found that vouchers did significantly improve math score gains for African American students in New York (4.2 points), Dayton (6.5 points), and Washington, D.C. (9.2 points).

The results from the New York City voucher program have been particularly contentious. As we just saw, Howell and colleagues (2002) concluded that this program meaningfully improved the math performance of African American students. Mayer and colleagues (2002) also conclude that African American voucher recipients outperformed their control group peers on standardized math and reading tests, but that Latino voucher recipients scored no better than nonrecipients, and there were no positive test effects of vouchers across the population of voucher recipients. Krueger and Zhu (2003; 2004) have taken issue with these results, claiming that they are an artifact of sampling and the definition "African American." For example, when estimating voucher effects, Howell and colleagues include only those students for whom they have baseline test scores and use the treatment on the treated estimator. Krueger and Zhu (2003) show that if you include students who do not have baseline test scores and estimate an intent to treat effect, vouchers provide no benefit to African American students. Moreover, Krueger and Zhu (2004) show that if one defines African American students using either the race of the mother or the father, rather than simply using the race of the mother (as Howell and colleagues do), the positive effect of vouchers for African American students evaporates. However, using a Bayesian principal stratification approach, Barnard and colleagues (2003) conclude that vouchers are associated with greater gains in math scores for

African American students and students from lower-performing schools, but that vouchers provide no benefits for any students on reading tests. In summary, despite providing some evidence that vouchers may have positive effects on academic achievement, overall the evaluation of these privately funded programs do little to clarify the picture regarding the educational benefits of vouchers.

Overall Assessments of Voucher Programs. The literature reviews on voucher programs are aimed at different audiences, academic and general public. But even reviews written for the same audience reach twofold conclusions. One subset of reviews finds no or ambiguous effect of vouchers on student achievement. For example, a report by the research arm of the American Federation of Teachers finds that "although voucher proponents claim that vouchers will improve student achievement, especially among low-income youngsters, evaluations of voucher programs have found no or only modest achievement gains among voucher students relative to comparable public school students" (American Federation of Teachers 2002, 1). Another overall assessment of research on this topic concluded that "the jury is still out on whether vouchers are an effective policy for improving education and what effects they have on student achievement" (Kober 2000, 7). Similarly, Zimmer and Bettinger in their review of voucher literature conclude that "in sum, researchers have failed to come to consensus on efficacy of vouchers as a reform effort" (Zimmer and Bettinger 2008, 458). In the most recent summaries of the topic, the Center on Education Policy finds that "additional research has demonstrated that vouchers do not have a strong effect on student's academic achievement" (2011, 3). Finally, a contemporary peer-reviewed summary of the literature comparing public and private school performance (which the author seeks to generalize to the voucher debate) concludes that "results among numerous studies suggest no difference or only a slight advantage for private schools over public schools in student achievement for a given student" (Levin 1998, 373).

The other subset of reviews, in their summaries of the literature on the topic, typically finds school vouchers to be more effective in improving students' scores. For example, Jay Greene in a review titled "The Surprising Consensus on School Choice" claims "what is striking about the recent research on school choice is not just its quality but that it consistently reveals positive benefits from school choice" (Greene 2001, 20). The Alliance for School Choice (2011) concludes that the existing research shows strong achievement gains for voucher recipients. Paul Teske and

Mark Schneider in the review titled "What Research Can Tell Policymakers About School Choice" (2001) conclude that there are test score improvements for some groups of students, but not for all.

Such inconsistency in the findings serves as further evidence that an objective, nonpartisan analysis of the issue of the impact of school vouchers on academic achievement is long overdue.

Designing a Meta-Analysis of Voucher Effects

Chapter 1 makes plain that meta-analysts face the same choices regarding research design, modeling, and measurement as do researchers conducting more traditional types of original research. In particular, meta-analysts much choose a dependent variable, identify key hypotheses associated with systematic variation in the dependent variable, devise a method of measuring these variables, and select the scope within which to measure these variables. We have already chosen the outcome concept of interest for the meta-analysis: the effects of vouchers on student academic achievement. In this section we discuss how we will measure that concept and the variables we will use to account for systematic variation in the effectiveness of vouchers.

Choosing a Measure of Academic Achievement

Student academic achievement in voucher studies is invariably assessed using performance on standardized tests. However, the same standardized test is not used in each original study. More important, students in each original study take between two and five standardized tests in different subject areas, and the estimated effects of vouchers are rarely consistent across these subject tests. Consequently, voucher proponents may emphasize those subject tests that demonstrate a positive effect for vouchers, while opponents may emphasize those subject tests that demonstrate no such difference. Why private schools might be more effective in educating students in the area of math, for example, than in the area of reading is unclear. Nevertheless, one reason that conclusions regarding the effectiveness of educational vouchers vary across studies may be that these conclusions emphasize the results from different subject tests. Since the effect of vouchers is unlikely to be constant across subject tests, *we include moderator variables in our meta-regression models identifying effect sizes based on student performance on standardized math tests, student performance on standardized reading tests, student performance on all other subject tests, and student composite test scores.*

Choosing a Type of Treatment Effect

When evaluating the consequences of a policy or management intervention, researchers may choose among a handful of possible treatment effects (see, for example, Heckman and Hotz 1989; Rubin 1986, 2005). Two of these treatment effects are most relevant for studying the effects of vouchers. First, researchers may estimate the effect of the *treatment on the treated* (TT). In the context of educational vouchers, TT is estimated by comparing the test scores of students that used a voucher with the test scores of a control group of students who did not use a voucher. The key problem here is creating a control group that is identical to voucher users in all other respects. Random assignment of vouchers is the easiest and (usually) the surest method of creating a control group with these characteristics, though there are other methods. TT is a policy-relevant effect because it estimates the average effect of vouchers on students who use them. Most early research investigating the effects of vouchers estimated these effects using TT, and this treatment effect is still in common use.

Over the past decade or so, doubts have surfaced about the validity of TT estimates of treatment effects. These concerns center around the effect that noncompliance with treatment has on estimates of TT. In the context of educational vouchers, many students who are chosen to receive vouchers do not use them. In the privately funded voucher programs described earlier, voucher "uptake" (compliance with treatment) often was as low as 50 percent—in other words, half of the students who received a voucher did not use one (Howell, Wolf, Campbell, and Peterson 2002). For the purposes of estimating TT, students who receive but do not use a voucher are placed in the control group. If students who receive and use a voucher are systematically different from students who receive but do not use a voucher, the estimate of TT may be biased. If, as is likely, students who would benefit least from the voucher are less likely to use it, estimates of TT will be biased upward and voucher programs will appear to be more effective than they really are. For these reasons, many researchers prefer to estimate the effect of the *intent to treat* (ITT). ITT is estimated by comparing the test scores of students that received a voucher with the test scores of a control group of students that did not receive a voucher. Critics of this approach emphasize that ITT identifies the effect of vouchers using students that do not actually use the vouchers. Advocates of this approach counter that TT estimates may be biased and that ITT estimates can be corrected by using instrumental variables to predict voucher use. In addition, advocates assert that ITT is a policy-relevant effect because it estimates the average effect of vouchers in a real-world situation in which not everyone eligible for a voucher will actually use it. That is, while TT might be an upper-bound of the expected benefits of vouchers, ITT is probably a better estimate of the effects of vouchers in practice. Much of the most recent research investigating the effects of vouchers estimates these effects using ITT.

Most recently, researchers have tried to recapture the intuitive benefits of TT (estimating the effects of vouchers by examining only those students who use them) while avoiding the pitfalls of TT (that is, controlling for the nonrandom nature of voucher use). The resulting treatment effect estimate is referred to as the *Complier Average Causal Effect* (CACE; see Barnard, Frangakis, Hill, and Rubin 2003, Cowen 2008). In the context of educational vouchers, CACE is estimated by comparing the test scores of students who comply with the treatment (that is, voucher users) with the test scores of a control group who comply with the control (that is, students who do not receive a voucher and who remain in the public schools). Estimates from both groups are adjusted for the nonrandom nature of compliance (CACE is better known in the literature as "local average treatment effect," or LATE). Relatively few studies have estimated the effects of vouchers using CACE. *The current meta-analysis measures voucher effects using TT or CACE estimates from original studies. We do not use ITT estimates because early research does not estimate ITT and because ITT estimates a fundamentally different effect than does TT and CACE.*

Accounting for Variability in Voucher Effects

"Do vouchers improve student academic achievement?" is not the most relevant policy question. This question is also inconsistent with the proper purpose of meta-analysis in public management and policy research. As stated in chapter 5, the goal of meta-analysis should rarely be to estimate a single average effect size associated with some policy or management intervention. While meta-regression allows us to estimate this (conditional) average effect size, the primary benefit of meta-regression is that it allows researchers to identify sources of systematic variation in effect sizes and to test hypotheses about which factors generate this variation. That is, meta-regression allows the researcher to identify conditions under which educational vouchers produce larger or smaller effect sizes—a much more interesting and useful policy question. We examine four categories of moderator variables that are hypothesized to influence estimates of voucher treatment effects: the characteristics of outcome measures, the characteristics of students, the characteristics of voucher programs, and the characteristics of the original studies.

Characteristics of Outcome Measures. Earlier we stated that original studies commonly use dependent variables measuring the performance on different subject tests. Specifically, depending on the voucher program and the study, subject tests in math, reading, language, science, social studies, or combined test scores are used to evaluate the effectiveness of educational vouchers, with math and reading tests being used far more commonly than the other subject-specific tests. Therefore, we created three moderator variables identifying effect sizes from math tests, effect sizes from reading tests, and effect sizes from all other subject-specific tests. In the meta-regression models that follow, effect sizes from combined standardized tests represent the excluded category.

Characteristics of Students. While proponents hope that educational vouchers might improve the performance of all students, there is a clear expectation—and some empirical evidence—that vouchers may benefit some students more than others. One of the most powerful normative arguments for vouchers is that they might disproportionately benefit students that traditionally perform poorly in public schools, such as racial and ethnic minorities. Indeed, some researchers offer vouchers as an effective tool for reducing the "achievement gap" for minority students (Howell, Wolf, Campbell, and Peterson 2002). Many educational voucher studies disaggregate student test scores by the racial and ethnic status of the student. Those studies that report separate test scores by race and ethnicity often find that the effect of vouchers on student performance varies across these groups. No study has yet offered a convincing causal argument explaining these racial and ethnic differences. However, the race and ethnicity of students is clearly a factor to be explored when considering variation in voucher effects. Therefore we create one moderator variable identifying effect sizes from studies examining African American students and a second moderator variable identifying effect sizes from studies examining Hispanic students.

There is good evidence of gender differences in performance on standardized test scores (Becker 1989), and the effect of vouchers on test score gains may vary by gender as well. Unfortunately, too few studies employ gender-specific samples to allow us to test the hypothesis that voucher effects differ by gender.

Characteristics of Voucher Programs. A key question for policy makers and other interested stakeholders is whether the effectiveness of educational vouchers is influenced by the design of voucher programs. We measure the characteristics of voucher programs using four variables. First, the full effect of any social experiment, including vouchers, is unlikely to be realized in the short term. We know that students who change schools regularly tend to do poorly on standardized tests, and students accepting vouchers will require time to adjust to their new schools. Moreover, the advantages of private schools—if they exist—are undoubtedly cumulative, which means that the effect of vouchers on student achievement will be proportionate to the length of time students use vouchers. A cursory examination of existing voucher studies supports this notion. The estimates of voucher effects in both New York City and Cleveland became larger and more stable in later years of the voucher programs (Mayer, Peterson, Myers, Tuttle, and Howell 2002; Metcalf, Muller, et al. 1998). Thus we create a moderator variable identifying the number of years students had used vouchers prior to the assessment of voucher effects. The scale of this variable begins at two years of treatment, so that the intercept in the meta-regression models represents voucher effects after one year of treatment.

Second, some voucher programs restrict recipients to attend secular schools (for example, the early Milwaukee program), while other programs allow recipients to attend parochial schools. There is at least some evidence that parochial school students outperform students in secular schools (Levin 1998). While we do not take a position on whether this evidence is conclusive, we believe that the existence of this evidence is enough to test whether vouchers are more effective for students attending religious schools. Therefore, we create a moderator variable identifying whether effect sizes come from programs that allow students to attend parochial schools.

Third, voucher programs vary according to their source of funding, and this may influence the effectiveness of the programs. Therefore, we code whether effect sizes come from voucher programs that are privately funded (such as the Dayton program). Publically funded programs (such as the Cleveland program) serve as the reference category.

Finally, voucher programs vary regarding student eligibility. Most important for our analysis, some voucher programs target elementary school students, while others allow middle school and high school students to receive vouchers. There is some evidence that younger students are more responsive to educational interventions than are older students (Karoly et al. 1998). A handful of original studies estimate separate treatment effects for vouchers conditional upon the grade level of the student. Therefore, we create a moderator variable identifying effect sizes from studies that examine the effects of vouchers only for elementary school students. Depending on the program, eligibility for vouchers is determined by other factors. For example, while most voucher programs are means tested, the eligibility threshold varies markedly across programs (for example, the New York City program offered vouchers only to students from the poorest families, while the Indiana program offers vouchers to families earning over $60,000 per year). Other programs allow virtually all students from "failing" or poorly performing public schools to apply for vouchers (such as the Ohio Educational Choice program), while still others restrict eligibility to students with special needs (for example, the Florida McKay scholarship program). While these other eligibility criteria may influence the effects of vouchers, we do not include control for these factors in our meta-regression models.

Characteristics of Original Studies. Researchers are virtually unanimous in their recommendation that meta-regression include variables measuring the characteristics of original studies (Thompson and Higgins 2002; Konstantopoulos and Hedges 2009; Raudenbush 2009). One of the most important characteristics of original studies is their quality. Since study quality is a multifaceted concept, we use four indicators of study quality in our meta-regressions.

First, perhaps no characteristic of educational voucher studies has produced as much acrimony as the designation of control groups. In nearly all voucher programs, the number of parents seeking vouchers for their children far exceeds the number of vouchers available. In these situations, vouchers are allocated among applicants through a random lottery. This means that treatment groups are generated via random assignment. Under lottery conditions, voucher applicants who did not receive a voucher can be considered a control group in a randomized controlled trial, since they entered the control group through random assignment. Generation of treatment and control groups through randomization is sometimes referred to as the "gold standard" of evaluation designs (see, for example, Howell, Wolf, Campbell, and Peterson 2002). Greene, Peterson, and Du (1999) claim that their conclusions about the Milwaukee, Dayton, New York, and Washington, D.C., voucher programs differ from those of Witte (1998) largely because they use this experimental control group of voucher nonrecipients whereas Witte uses a nonrandom control group consisting of Milwaukee public school students. Witte (1998) counters that differential attrition between the randomly generated treatment and control groups in Milwaukee significantly undermines their utility. Regardless of the value of randomization in the Milwaukee case, control groups generated through randomization are generally perceived as generating higher-quality studies than groups generated using some other criteria. Hence, the estimated effects of voucher programs may vary depending on whether the control groups were constructed via randomization. Specifically, we create two moderating variables identifying the method of assignment to treatment groups: one identifying effect sizes when treatment groups were created through nonrandom matching, and a second identifying effect sizes when treatment groups were created through some ex post, nonmatching process (for example, when the control group consists of a sample of public school students). The excluded category is control groups generated using random assignment.

Second, endogeneity of treatment poses a serious threat to any estimate of voucher effects. While random assignment to treatment and control groups is one method of controlling for endogeneity, it is not the only method. Therefore, we create a moderating variable identifying whether original studies include an ex post control for endogeneity (fixed effects, instrumental variables, or some other method).

Third, researchers disagree whether estimates of voucher effects ought to control for the baseline test scores of voucher recipients and nonrecipients. In theory, under random assignment, estimates of treatment effects from models that do not include baseline test scores will be consistent (see, for example, Greene, Peterson, and Du 1999; Krueger and Zhu 2003). In practice, however, many factors may compromise the consistency of effect estimates from randomized controlled field trials (Cook and Campbell 1979). Including baseline test scores in models of student achievement is an effective method of controlling for preexisting differences between treatment and control groups that might otherwise masquerade as a voucher treatment effect. Therefore, we code whether effect sizes come from models that include baseline test scores among their predictors.

Finally, all original studies employing experimental designs and most original studies employing quasi-experimental designs employ a pretest-posttest design in which voucher effects are estimated by comparing test score gains for voucher and nonvoucher recipients. A handful of quasi-experimental studies, however, assess the effectiveness of vouchers using a posttest-only design—that is, by comparing test scores for the treatment and control groups only after treatment. These design choices may have a meaningful influence on estimates of voucher effects. Therefore, we create one moderator variable identifying effect sizes from quasi-experimental pretest-posttest designs and a second moderator variable identifying effect sizes from quasi-experimental posttest-only designs.

Searching the Literature

The literature search for this chapter proceeded in two steps. The research in this chapter began in 2001, and an initial draft of the paper was presented at the 2002 Midwest Political Science Association Annual Meeting. At that time we identified eighteen studies as acceptable and estimated a total of 294 effect sizes from these studies. We felt, however, that the study count was not large enough for the meta-analysis, especially taking into account that nine of these eighteen studies were coauthored by the same researcher, Paul Peterson, which could potentially bias the results. When the work resumed in 2011, we identified twenty-one additional acceptable studies and eliminated seven acceptable studies from the earlier list because they (1) examined a different outcome variable (student satisfaction), (2) estimated ITT effects rather than TT effects, or (3) had been published subsequent to the original analysis.

We began the literature search by identifying eight types of studies that might contain the results of quantitative analysis necessary for a meta-analysis: (1) peer-reviewed articles, (2) non-peer-reviewed articles, (3) books and book chapters, (4) government documents and reports, (5) private reports issued by interest groups or think tanks, (6) Ph.D. dissertations, (7) conference papers, and (8) other unpublished sources. We employed four tactics in conducting a comprehensive search for published and unpublished studies in these eight categories: (1) we conducted computer-aided searches of a large number of online archives of published research; (2) we conducted computer-aided searches for unpublished research archived in on-line conference proceedings, archives of government reports and documents, Ph.D. dissertations and master's theses, papers produced by NGOs, think tanks, and other research organizations, and papers produced by individual scholars; (3) we contacted one dozen of the most prominent researchers on the topic of school vouchers and asked them to identify and share any important new or unpublished research on this topic; and (4) we conducted ancestry searches of the relevant articles identified using tactics 1 through 3. A list of the literature sources used in our literature search is provided in table 8.2.

TABLE 8.2. LIST OF SEARCH ENGINES, ORGANIZATIONS, AND SITES SEARCHED FOR SCHOOL VOUCHER STUDIES

Government Publications Government Accountability Office (GAO) U.S. Department of Education databases	**Academic Search Engines** ERIC EBSCO Academic Search Premier JSTOR ProQuest Dissertations Search ISI Web of Knowledge Worldcat
Think Tanks and NGOs Friedmans' Foundation RAND Corporation Mathematica Policy Research Inc. National Center for the Study of 　　Privatization in Education	
	Working Papers SSRN NBER Econlit
Conference Proceedings	
Association for Public Policy Analysis and 　　Management (APPAM) American Educational Research 　　Association (AERA) Association for Budgeting and Financial 　　Management (ABFM) National Tax Association (NTA)	

We searched each of the sources in table 8.2 using the keywords *school voucher, education voucher, educational voucher*, and *student voucher*. These searches, coupled with the ancestry searches and directly contacting researchers in the field, produced 6,815 "hits," or returned records. We used three successively more restrictive criteria to identify the small subset of studies that were suitable for a meta-analysis. First, we identified a set of "potentially relevant studies" from the thousands of publications produced by our keyword searches. Potentially relevant studies were identified solely through their bibliographic references. We took a catholic approach to what constituted a potentially relevant study, excluding only publications from popular outlets (such as newspapers and news magazines), publications that obviously made it into the database because they contained all of the searched keywords but in a nonsensical order, book reviews, and publications that did not focus on our research questions. All remaining studies were placed in the category of potentially relevant, and were coded on the first section of our coding form (the complete coding form is provided in Appendix A1). We identified 736 potentially relevant studies, and assigned each potentially relevant study a unique study ID number that it would keep through all subsequent coding and analysis.

We examined each potentially relevant study in more detail by obtaining the study abstract or a study summary through a more in-depth bibliographic search. Occasionally we read the introductory sections of the study. The goal of this examination was to separate "relevant" studies from the much larger class of potentially relevant studies. Potentially relevant studies were excluded from the class of relevant studies if they were (1) non-analytic (that is, descriptive), (2) non-quantitative, (3) non-U.S., or (4) examining a dependent variable other than standardized test scores. A small number of potentially relevant studies were excluded due to other criteria. Relevant studies, then, were those that were analytic in nature, used statistical techniques to test hypotheses, and focused on the effects of voucher programs on student standardized test scores in the United States. Eighty-four relevant studies met all of these criteria. To make sure that all members of the research team were using the same criteria to identify relevant studies, we took a random sample of fifty potentially relevant studies and had each member of the research team code the relevance of each study. Intercoder agreement in this exercise was 88 percent, with a Cohen's kappa of 0.63.

Next we obtained the full text of each relevant study and coded the characteristics of each study using the second section of the meta-analysis coding form. Our first goal after gathering the full text of each study was to determine if the study was "acceptable" for the meta-analysis. Relevant studies could be deemed unacceptable if (1) a mistake was made in concluding that the study was relevant, (2) the study was relevant, but contained insufficient statistical detail in the reporting of results to be included in the meta-analysis, (3) the study reported ITT estimates of voucher effects and no TT effects of voucher effects, or (4) statistical results in the study perfectly duplicated results in other relevant studies. This last criterion was particularly relevant for studies produced by the PEPG research group at Harvard University, as many of the studies produced by this group were duplicative. We identified thirty-two acceptable studies using these criteria. Again, we conducted an intercoder reliability assessment for identifying acceptable studies from the broader class of relevant studies. Intercoder agreement in this exercise was 86 percent with a Cohen's kappa of 0.65.

Finally, from each acceptable study we extracted the data necessary to calculate effect sizes and data for moderator variables used in the meta-regression models, recording these data on the third section of the meta-analysis coding form in Appendix A1. All acceptable studies produced more than one effect. The reasons for this are numerous. All studies examined more than one dependent variable or outcome measure.

A few studies examined outcomes using variously defined control groups. Many studies evaluated the effects of voucher programs for several subgroups of students (blacks, Hispanics, and so on), and across several years. Finally, many studies offered numerous multivariate models with various statistical controls. Each permutation of type of outcome, control group, student subgroup, time of treatment, and modeling choice generated a separate effect measure. We calculated a total of 611 effect sizes from the thirty-two acceptable studies. Effects within each study were assigned a unique identification number, so that each effect could be identified through a combination of the study ID and effect ID numbers. We conducted a final intercoder reliability assessment of a sample of 50 effect sizes from five acceptable studies, and the level of intercoder agreement was 99 percent. A flow diagram summarizing the literature search process is provided in figure 8.1.

FIGURE 8.1. FLOWCHART OF LITERATURE SEARCH PROCESS AND INTERCODER RELIABILITY

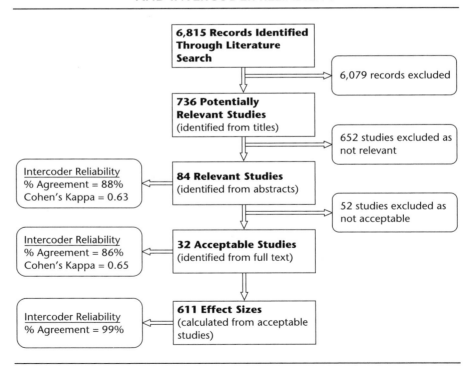

Data Analysis: Synthesis

Average Effect Sizes for the Effects of Educational Vouchers

Our 611 effect sizes are not evenly distributed across studies, ranging from a minimum of 2 effect sizes (Lamarche 2008, Wille 2010) to a maximum of 84 effect sizes (Plucker, Muller, Hansen, Ravert, and Makel 2006). A fixed effects meta-analysis of the 611 effect sizes produces an estimated average effect size of .019 with a 95 percent confidence interval of [.016 − .022]. While we can reject the null hypothesis that this average effect size is equal to zero ($Z = 14.09$, $p < .000$), the Q-statistic of 1250.2 ($p < .000$) indicates that a fixed effects meta-analysis is inappropriate for these data, and the I^2 statistic of 51.2 percent indicates that roughly 51 percent of the variation in effect sizes cannot be accounted for by sampling error. More important, the fixed effects framework is theoretically inappropriate when effect sizes come from multiple regression models and other types of original studies generating meaningful heterogeneity in effect sizes. The average effect size from the random effects meta-analysis is .020 with a 95 percent confidence interval of [.016 − .024] (the random effects variance component $\tau^2 = .0012$). This average effect size can be interpreted as the average partial point biserial correlation between the use of a voucher and student performance on standardized tests. Transformed to a d-based effect size, this effect indicates a standardized mean difference in test scores between voucher users and nonvoucher users of 0.04. While this effect is distinguishable from zero ($Z = 9.33$, $p = .000$), the magnitude of the effect is very small, suggesting that vouchers have a very small positive effect on student academic achievement. This unconditional estimate of the effects of vouchers, however, masks important variation in effect size estimates across studies that will be investigated using meta-regression.

To determine whether evidence regarding the effectiveness of vouchers has changed over time we conduct a cumulative meta-analysis. A forest plot of 611 effect sizes would be uninterpretable. Therefore, as a first step we calculate the average effect size for each of the thirty-two acceptable studies in our data set. We then arrange these studies in chronological order. The results of the study-level cumulative meta-analysis are reported in figure 8.2 and illustrate that while early studies varied widely in their effect estimates for vouchers, by 2002 the literature had settled around an estimated average effect size of .03 (95 percent confidence interval [.02 − .04]). This average effect size has not changed in the past decade. The cumulative meta-analysis tells the same story as the traditional

FIGURE 8.2. STUDY-LEVEL CUMULATIVE META-ANALYSIS OF EFFECTS OF EDUCATIONAL VOUCHERS ON STUDENT ACADEMIC ACHIEVEMENT, EFFECT SIZE = Z_r

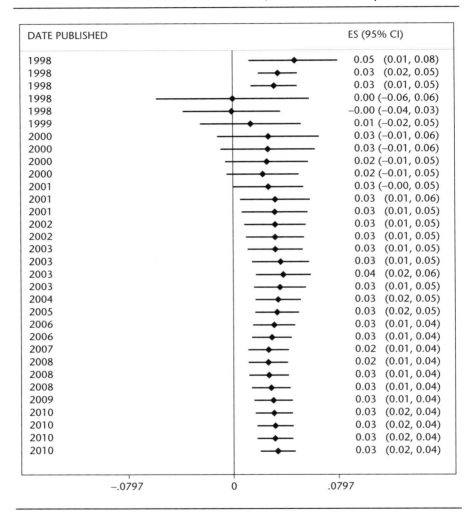

meta-analysis: vouchers have had a positive and significant but substantively trivial effect on student academic achievement. It is important to note that that the cumulative meta-analysis weights all studies equally, regardless of the number of effect sizes a study generates. Since the thirty-two acceptable studies in our data set generate between 2 and 84 effect sizes, the consequences of this weighting scheme might be substantial (one obvious consequence is that the average effect size from the cumulative meta-analysis, while very small, is 50 percent larger than the average effect size from the standard random effects meta-analysis). Moreover, the cumulative meta-analysis does not account for heterogeneity in effect sizes, and therefore is subject to the "apples and oranges" critique often leveled at meta-analysis.

A First Look at Publication Bias

Figure 8.3 displays a contour enhanced funnel plot for the 611 effect sizes using fixed effects variance weights, and figure 8.4 displays the same plot using random effects variance weights. Chapters 6 and 7 confirm that funnel plots by themselves are poor tools for diagnosing publication bias, but the funnel plot still provides a useful tool for examining the

FIGURE 8.3. FIXED EFFECTS CONTOUR ENHANCED FUNNEL PLOT FOR EFFECT SIZES FOR MEASURING EFFECTS OF SCHOOL VOUCHERS ON STUDENT STANDARDIZED TEST SCORES

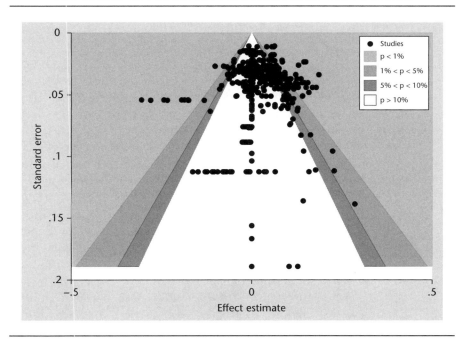

FIGURE 8.4. RANDOM EFFECTS CONTOUR ENHANCED FUNNEL PLOT FOR EFFECT SIZES FOR MEASURING EFFECTS OF SCHOOL VOUCHERS ON STUDENT STANDARDIZED TEST SCORES

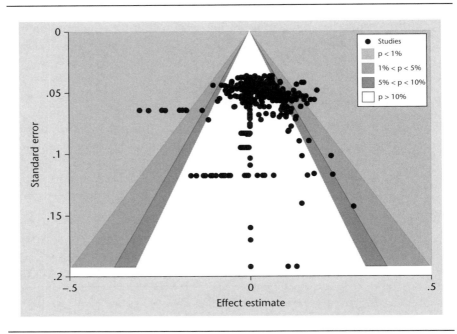

variation in effect sizes across models. Consistent with the results from the standard meta-analysis, effect sizes in both funnel plots are centered on 0, with a slight preponderance of positive effect sizes. Both funnel plots may be slightly asymmetric, with a few more positive effect sizes than expected in relatively low precision models. Egger tests do not confirm this impression for the random effects model, as the intercept for the Egger test regression (or equivalently, the FAT regression) leads us to accept the null hypothesis of no publication bias ($b_0 = -.15$, $t = -0.91$, $p = .36$). Readers should recall that like the funnel plot, the Egger and FAT tests are poor instruments for identifying publication bias. At best—in the absence of effect size heterogeneity—the Egger test ought to be viewed as an indicator of small-study effects.

To further investigate possible differences between published and unpublished studies, we conducted separate meta-analyses for each group of effect sizes. The majority of effect sizes (341) come from unpublished or non-peer-reviewed studies. Only 44 percent of our effect sizes (270) come from peer-reviewed studies. This distribution reinforces the importance of searching the grey literature when conducting meta-analyses in public management and policy, as many of the relevant studies are unpublished. On average, peer-reviewed studies do use larger samples (average N = 1,319 for peer-reviewed studies, average N = 681 for non-peer-reviewed studies). A random effect meta-analysis also finds that the average effect size from non-peer-reviewed studies (.022, Z = 7.10, p = .000, [.016 – .024]) is virtually identical to the average effect size from peer-reviewed studies (.018, Z = 5.49, p < .000, [.011 – .024]). These results do not indicate that the estimated effects of vouchers differ between published and unpublished studies. This result is not definitive, as accurately identifying potential publication bias requires comparing average effect sizes between published and unpublished studies while holding other study characteristics constant. This is a job for meta-regression.

Meta-Regression Analysis

Accounting for Variation in Effect Sizes

Earlier we offered four explanations for why effect sizes might differ systematically across models in original studies. In this section we operationalize these differences as moderator variables to be included in the meta-regression models.

Characteristics of Outcome Measures. The effects of vouchers may differ depending on the subject test administered to students. While the causal mechanisms behind these differences are unclear, there is some evidence that students who receive vouchers may perform better on some subject tests than on others (Howell, Wolf, Campbell, and Peterson 2002, Metcalf, West, Legan, Paul, and Boone 2003). We include three moderator variables identifying different types of subject tests in our meta-regression models:

· A moderator variable coded 1 if the effect size comes from a standardized math test and zero otherwise
· A moderator variable coded 1 if the effect size comes from a standardized reading test and zero otherwise
· A moderator variable coded 1 if the effect size comes from a standardized language, science, social science, or other nonmath, nonreading test, and zero otherwise

The excluded category for outcome measures is effect sizes that come from combined standardized tests. One hundred and eleven effect sizes measure the effect of vouchers on combined test scores.

Characteristics of Students. Educational vouchers have been identified as one method through which race- and ethnicity-based test score gaps might be reduced (Mayer, Peterson, Myers, Tuttle, and Howell 2002), and surveys regularly show that racial and ethnic minorities are more supportive of school vouchers than are whites (Gelman 2009). An important policy question, then, is whether the effects of vouchers differ across types of students. We include three moderator variables in our meta-regression models identifying effect sizes estimated using different groups of students:

- A moderator variable coded 1 if the effect size is estimated from a sample including only black students and zero otherwise
- A moderator variable coded 1 if the effect size is estimated from a sample including only Hispanic students and zero otherwise
- A moderator variable coded 1 if the effect size is estimated from a sample including only students of other specific racial or ethnic groups, only male students, only female students, or any other specific group of students

The excluded category for student characteristics is effect sizes estimated from samples that include all types of students. Three hundred and sixty-three effect sizes measure the effect of vouchers from samples including all types of students.

Design of Voucher Programs. Policy makers and public managers are often keenly interested in whether the design of programs influences their effectiveness. One virtue of research synthesis is that compared with individual original studies, meta-analysis is able to better investigate the effects of program design on outcomes. Policy makers might then use this information to design more effective programs. We include four moderator variables identifying design elements of voucher programs in our meta-regression models:

- A moderator variable coded 1 for effect sizes from programs in which vouchers can be used to attend religious schools and zero otherwise.
- A moderator variable coded 1 for effect sizes from voucher programs that are privately funded and zero otherwise.

- A moderator variable coded 1 for effect sizes from voucher programs in which eligibility is restricted to elementary school students and zero otherwise.
- A moderator variable that ranges from 0 to 4 and where the variable value represents the number of years students in the original study used vouchers, minus one. This variable represents the time or intensity of treatment. We subtract the value 1 from the time of treatment so that the baseline category for the meta-regression intercept represents effect sizes associated with using vouchers for one year.

Characteristics and Quality of Original Studies. Effect sizes may also vary because of the design elements or quality characteristics of the models producing these effects. Rubin (1992) might consider these "scientifically uninteresting" factors that need to be controlled for in order to obtain unbiased estimates of the baseline average treatment effect and unbiased coefficient estimates for the moderator variables measuring scientifically interesting factors. We include eight moderator variables in our meta-regression models identifying design elements or quality characteristics of the original studies generating our 611 effect sizes:

- A moderator variable coded 1 for effect sizes from models that include an ex post control for endogeneity of treatment (for example, fixed effects or instrumental variables) and zero otherwise
- A moderator variable coded 1 for effect sizes from models that construct control groups using matching rather than through random assignment and zero otherwise
- A moderator variable coded 1 for effect sizes from models that construct control groups using neither random assignment nor matching and zero otherwise
- A moderator variable coded 1 for effect sizes from models using pretest-posttest quasi-experimental designs and zero otherwise
- A moderator variable coded 1 for effect sizes from models using posttest-only quasi-experimental designs and zero otherwise
- A moderator variable coded 1 for effect sizes from models that include baseline test scores when predicting student gains from using vouchers and zero otherwise
- A moderator variable coded 1 for effect sizes from models that estimate compound treatment effects using regression interaction terms and zero otherwise

· A moderator variable coded 1 for effect sizes from models appearing in the peer-reviewed published literature and zero otherwise

Characteristics of the Baseline Scenario. Chapters 4 and 5 emphasize the special importance of the parameter estimates for the intercept in meta-regression models. Typically, moderator variables are constructed so that this intercept term—the average effect size when all moderator variables take on values of zero—describes a meaningful and interesting baseline scenario. In the meta-regression models estimated here, the intercept represents the average effect size measuring the consequences of using vouchers for one year on combined standardized test scores for students in publically funded voucher programs that allow students in all grades to attend secular schools. This baseline average effect size is estimated from models employing experimental designs with random assignment to treatment and control groups, that do not utilize ex post endogeneity controls, pretest controls, or interaction effects. That is, the meta-regression intercept estimates the average effect of vouchers on combined test scores for all school students from field experiments.

Estimating the Meta-Regression Models

The meta-regression models are estimated using all 611 effect sizes from the thirty-two acceptable studies. These data clearly violate the assumption of independent observations, and we account for this dependence in two ways. First, consistent with the recommendations from chapter 5, we estimate a random effects meta-regression model with clustered robust parameter variances (the CRVE model). Because our effect sizes come from a reasonably large sample of studies, we do not need to employ the wild cluster bootstrap version of the CRVE. Recall, however, that the CRVE model only controls for the effect of correlated effect sizes on inference, not their effect on estimation. Using CRVE, the meta-regression parameter estimates (but not their variances) weight all effect sizes equally. With our data, this means that the five largest studies (generating 273 effect sizes) exercise nearly as much influence over the meta-regression parameter estimates as do the twenty-seven smallest studies (338 effect sizes). With such large variation in the number of effect sizes generated by each study, prudent practice dictates the use of generalized estimating equations (GEE) to estimate the random effects meta-regression model (see chapter 5). Using GEE, dependence among effect sizes conditions regression parameter estimates as well as their variances, which reduces (but does not equalize) the influence of studies generating large numbers of effect sizes. Therefore, we estimate a second random effects meta-regression model using GEE with an identity link function, an exchangeable error correlation matrix, and a robust parameter covariance matrix. Results from the CRVE and GEE meta-regression models are presented in table 8.3.

The summary statistics for the meta-regression model are encouraging. Recall that the I^2 value from the unconditional random effects meta-regression was 51.2 percent. The I^2 value from the conditional random effects meta-regression model is 25.01 percent. Therefore, the moderator variables in the meta-regression model have reduced systematic variation in effect sizes by 51 percent ($(51.2 - 25.01) / 51.2$), which is an alternative measure of the adjusted R^2 in table 8.3. The pseudo-R^2 estimated using the Stata *metareg* command is even larger at .68. Consistent with standard practice in meta-regression, our discussion of the effects of individual moderator variables will emphasize parameter estimates and their confidence intervals rather than emphasizing tests of significance.

Average Effects of Vouchers in the Baseline Scenario. The intercept from the CRVE model shows that the average point biserial correlation between the use of vouchers and performance on standardized tests is .11 with a 95 percent confidence interval of [.06 – .16). That is, field experiments estimate that vouchers have a small, positive, and significant effect on combined test scores for students in nonreligious schools. While this effect is small (the corresponding *d*-based effect size is .22), it is several times larger than the unconditional average effect size from the random effects meta-analysis (.02) or the study-level average effect size of .03. If experimental studies are higher-quality studies, this suggests that better studies estimate larger positive effects from vouchers. The GEE model tells a similar story. Fully controlling for correlated effect sizes, the average point biserial correlation between the use of vouchers and performance on standardized tests is .083 ($d = .17$) with a 95 percent confidence interval of [.03 – .14]. Using GEE we conclude that vouchers have a small positive effect on student academic performance in the baseline scenario. Given the dramatic differences in the number of effect sizes generated by original studies, there is good reason to prefer the GEE estimates to the CRVE estimates when evaluating the effects of vouchers.

Effects of Outcome Measures on Effect Sizes. We find no significant difference between the effects of vouchers on combined test scores and their effects on math scores, reading scores, or scores on other subject-specific

TABLE 8.3. RANDOM EFFECTS META-REGRESSION RESULTS USING CRVE AND GEE; DEPENDENT VARIABLE IS EFFECT SIZE OF EDUCATION VOUCHERS ON STUDENT STANDARDIZED TEST SCORES

Independent Variables	CRVE Parameter Estimates (St. Err.)	CRVE 95% CI		GEE Parameter Estimates (St. Err.)	GEE 95% CI	
Math Test	−0.0017 (0.0074)	−0.0169	0.0134	0.0006 (0.0060)	−0.0125	0.0112
Reading Test	−0.0092 (0.0071)	−0.0238	0.0054	−0.0076 (0.0057)	−0.0088	0.0036
Other Test	0.0041 (0.0106)	−0.0176	0.0258	0.0069 (0.0095)	−0.0117	0.0255
Black Student	0.0296** (0.0130)	0.0030	0.0562	0.0370*** (0.0116)	0.0143	0.0598
Hispanic Student	−0.0470*** (0.0103)	−0.0680	−0.0259	−0.0413*** (0.0084)	−0.0577	−0.0248
Other Student	0.0005 (0.0115)	−0.0240	0.0230	0.0005 (0.0100)	−0.0191	0.0201
Treatment Exposure	0.0025 (0.0020)	−0.0067	0.0016	−0.0004 (0.0020)	−0.0042	0.0035
Religious Schools	−0.0312 (0.0187)	−0.0693	0.0069	0.0180 (0.0201)	−0.0574	0.0213
Private Funding	0.0034 (0.0190)	−0.0352	0.0421	−0.0078 (0.0199)	−0.0468	0.0312
Elementary Students	−0.0082 (0.0120)	−0.0328	0.0163	0.0025 (0.0144)	−0.0256	0.0307
Endogeneity Controls	0.0031 (0.0109)	−0.0191	0.0254	0.0054 (0.0092)	−0.0126	0.0233
Matched Control Groups	−0.0097 (0.0064)	−0.0226	0.0033	−0.0069* (0.0040)	−0.0148	0.0009
Convenience Control Groups	−0.0073 (0.0085)	−0.0246	0.0101	−0.0082 (0.0082)	−0.0243	0.0078
Pre-Post Quasi-Experiment	−0.0524*** (0.0151)	−0.0833	−0.0215	−0.0511*** (0.0166)	−0.0837	−0.0186
Post-Only Quasi-Experiment	−0.0650*** (0.0143)	−0.0940	−0.0359	−0.0716*** (0.0183)	−0.1074	−0.0358
Pretest Included	−0.0326*** (0.0115)	−0.0560	−0.0092	−0.0228* (0.0120)	−0.0464	0.0008

TABLE 8.3. (Continued)

Independent Variables	CRVE Parameter Estimates (St. Err.)	CRVE 95% CI		GEE Parameter Estimates (St. Err.)	GEE 95% CI	
Treatment Interaction	0.0033 (0.0111)	−0.0193	0.0259	−0.0003 (0.0076)	−0.0151	0.0145
Peer Reviewed	−0.0080 (0.0070)	−0.0223	0.0064	0.0063 (0.0111)	−0.0280	0.0154
Intercept (Baseline Effect Size)	0.1097*** (0.0257)	0.0573	0.1620	0.0830*** (0.0299)	−0.0243	0.1416
Adjusted R^{2a}	.44			na		
Pseudo-R^{2a}	.68			na		
I^{2a}	25.01%			na		
Sample Size	611			611		

Notes: *$p < .10$, **$p < .05$, ***$p < .01$.

[a] Calculated from unclustered random effects meta-regression model.

standardized tests. All parameter estimates in the CRVE and GEE models are very small ($< .01$), and all 95 percent confidence intervals cover 0. This result is somewhat surprising, given that a few original studies have concluded that vouchers have a larger effect on math test scores (Howell, Wolf, Campbell, and Peterson 2002, Barnard, Frangakis, Hill, and Rubin 2003). The meta-regression results illustrate that this effect is not generalizable across voucher programs.

Effects of Student Characteristics on Effect Sizes. While the average effect of vouchers on student academic achievement does not vary across outcome measures, this effect does vary appreciably across types of students. Both the CRVE and GEE models show that average gains from vouchers are larger for black students than for students overall. While these effects are substantively small ($b = .03$ and $b = .037$), they are different from zero, and relatively large given the estimated effects in the baseline case. For example, in the CRVE model, average voucher effects are 27 percent larger for black students than for students overall. By the same token, both the CRVE and GEE models show that average gains from vouchers are *smaller* for Hispanic students than for students overall. In the CRVE model, average gains for Hispanic students are still positive, but the magnitude of the effect has been reduced by nearly half (.1097 − .0470 = .0637). The GEE model also predicts that on average Hispanic students who use vouchers benefit only half as much as do other students who use vouchers; that is, .0830 − .0413 = .0417.

Effects of Voucher Program Design on Effect Sizes. In a finding that may disappoint many policy scholars (and policy makers), our meta-regression models show that the design of voucher programs has virtually no influence on their effectiveness. The CRVE model estimates that gains from voucher use are smaller when vouchers are restricted to elementary school students and when they are used at religious schools, but the GEE model estimates that these gains are larger when voucher programs are restricted to elementary students. The CRVE model also estimates that gains from voucher use are larger in privately funded programs, but the GEE model estimates that these gains are smaller for privately funded programs. Finally, the length of voucher treatment has a very small positive relationship with average voucher effects. In the CRVE model, the difference in the effects sizes associated with using a voucher for one year and using a voucher for seven years is .015. In the GEE model this effect is negative and larger at −.024. Inconsistencies like these arise naturally when true effects lie near zero, and should not be interpreted as meaningful uncertainty generated by the choice of CRVE or GEE when estimating meta-regression models.

Effects of Study Design and Quality on Effect Sizes. Design characteristics and the quality of original studies exert the largest influence over effect sizes. For example, average effect sizes are markedly smaller from original studies employing posttest-only quasi-experimental designs in both the CRVE ($b = -.0650$) and GEE models ($-.0716$). These effects are large enough to render the average effect size near zero in the GEE model. Posttest-only designs are inferior to experimental designs when estimating program effects (Cook and Campbell 1979; Rossi and Freeman 1993). In fact, all of the moderator variables identifying departures from experimental designs—matched control groups, convenience control groups, and both types of quasi-experimental designs—have negative parameter estimates in the CRVE and GEE models. If we can assume that, *ceteris paribus*, studies with these characteristics are lower quality studies, these results tell us that lower-quality studies estimate smaller average effect sizes.

We conclude our discussion of study quality with two observations. First, original studies that include baseline test scores in their models generate smaller effect sizes than do models that do not include this control. Strictly speaking, this control is unnecessary when using random assignment to treatment and control groups. In practice, the use of these controls contributes to higher-quality studies. In this instance, higher-quality studies produce smaller rather than larger effect sizes, and the magnitude of this effect is non-ignorable (CRVE $b = -.0260$, GEE $b = -.0228$). Finally, we note that the meta-regression models find no meaningful or significant difference between effect sizes from the peer-reviewed literature and effect sizes from studies that have not undergone peer review. That is, the meta-regression model provides no evidence that the literature examining the effects of vouchers on student achievement is contaminated by publication bias. Differences in average effect sizes between published and unpublished studies are fully accounted for by the moderator variables in the meta-regression models.

Estimated Effect Sizes Under Various Scenarios. Some readers may find the dense matrix of regression results in table 8.3 difficult to interpret. Meta-regression results can often be presented more usefully by using these results to estimate average effect sizes under various scenarios. Toward that end, table 8.4 reports average r-based effect sizes (Fisher's Z) and average d-based effect sizes (Hedges's g) from the CRVE and GEE models under seven different scenarios. The first row of table 8.4 reports average effect sizes under the meta-regression baseline scenario. The second and third rows report average effect sizes for math tests and reading tests under the baseline scenario, respectively. The fourth and fifth rows report average effect sizes under the baseline scenario for black students and for Hispanic students. Finally, rows six and seven report average effect sizes estimated from the lowest-quality and highest-quality original studies. In defining the lowest-quality original studies we make the following changes to the baseline scenario: quasi-experimental posttest-only designs; nonrandom, nonmatched control groups; no ex post controls for endogeneity; no baseline predictors in the models; and not peer reviewed. In defining the highest-quality original studies we make the following changes to the baseline scenario: the use of pretest controls and publication in a peer-reviewed outlet.

Average effect sizes are positive under all scenarios using results from the CRVE and the GEE models. The largest average effect size is associated with the effect of vouchers for black students ($Z_r = .1393$, $d = .28$) in the CRVE model, while the smallest average effect size comes from the lowest-quality studies ($Z_r = .0.32$, $d = .006$) in the GEE model . The highest-quality studies generate an average r-based effect size of .0691 in the CRVE model

TABLE 8.4. AVERAGE EFFECT SIZES FOR THE EFFECT OF VOUCHERS ON STUDENT STANDARDIZED TEST SCORES UNDER DIFFERENT SCENARIOS, AS PREDICTED FROM CRVE AND GEE RANDOM EFFECTS META-REGRESSION MODELS

Scenario	Effect Size Type	CRVE Estimate	GEE Estimate
Baseline	r-based	.1097	.0830
	d-based	.2207	.1666
Baseline Math Test	r-based	.1080	.0824
	d-based	.2173	.1654
Baseline Reading Test	r-based	.1005	.0754
	d-based	.2020	.1512
Baseline Black Students	r-based	.1393	.1200
	d-based	.2813	.2417
Baseline Hispanic Students	r-based	.0627	.0417
	d-based	.1256	.0835
Lowest-Quality Studies	r-based	.0374	.0032
	d-based	.0749	.0064
Highest-Quality Studies	r-based	.0691	.0534
	d-based	.1385	.1080

and $Z_r = .0534$ in the GEE model. Both estimates are roughly 40 percent smaller than the average effect in the baseline scenario.

Conclusion

Our meta-analysis suggests that vouchers have had a very small but positive effect on student academic achievement as measured by standardized test scores. These effects range from a correlation of .02 in the random effects meta-analysis to a correlation of .11 in the baseline scenario of the CRVE random effects meta-regression model. Effects from vouchers are larger for black students ($Z_r = .12$, $d = .24$ in the GEE model) and smaller for Hispanic students ($Z_r = .04$, $d = .08$ in the GEE model). The best estimates from our meta-analyses, however, suggest that the true effect of vouchers may be somewhat smaller. For example, the highest-quality studies produce an average effect size of .07 in the CRVE model and .05 in the GEE model. Moreover, there is little evidence that voucher programs might be redesigned to increase their effectiveness, at least using the design criteria investigated here. While the estimated effects from vouchers are small, they are positive. Moreover, students using vouchers may derive other benefits, such as increased satisfaction with their school, increased graduation rates, or improved life outcomes. Our results do mean that the case for continued or expanded public support for educational vouchers will have to be made on grounds other than dramatic improvements in the academic performance of students.

Studies Coded for Meta-Analysis

Barnard, John, Constantine E. Frangakis, Jennifer L. Hill, and Donald B. Rubin. Principal Stratification Approach to Broken Randomized Experiments: A Case Study of School Choice Vouchers in New York City. *Journal of the American Statistical Association* 98, no. 462, (2003): 299–311.

Belfield, Clive R. *The Evidence on Education Vouchers: An Application to the Cleveland Scholarship and Tutoring Program.* (2006). Retrieved from http://www.ncspe.org/publications _files/OP112.pdf.

Cowen, Joshua M. "School Choice as a Latent Variable: Estimating the 'Complier Average Causal Effect' of Vouchers in Charlotte." *Policy Studies Journal* 36, no. 2 (2008): 301–315. doi: 10.1111/j.1541-0072.2008.00268.x.

Cowen, Joshua. "Who Chooses, Who Refuses? Learning More from Students Who Decline Private School Vouchers." *American Journal of Education* 117, no. 1 (2010): 1–24.

Greene, Jay. *The Effect of School Choice: An Evaluation of the Charlotte Children's Scholarship Fund Program.* New York: Manhattan Institute for Policy Research, 2000.

Greene, Jay, Paul Peterson, and Jiangtao Du. "Effectiveness of School Choice: The Milwaukee Experiment." *Education and Urban Society* 31, no. 2 (1999): 190–213.

Howell, William G., Patrick Wolf, Paul Peterson, and David Campbell. "Effects of School Vouchers on Student Test Scores." In *Charters, Vouchers, and Public Education*, edited by Paul E. Peterson and David E. Campbell. Washington, D.C.: Brookings Institution, 2001.

Krueger, Alan B., and Pei Zhu. "Another Look at the New York City School Voucher Experiment." *American Behavioral Scientist* 47, no. 5 (2004): 658–698. doi: 10.1177/0002764203260152.

Lamarche, Carlos. "Private School Vouchers and Student Achievement: A Fixed Effects Quantile Regression Evaluation." *Labour Economics* 15, no. 4 (2008): 575–590. doi: 10.1016/j.labeco.2008.04.007.

Metcalf, Kim, William Boone, Frances Stage, Todd Chilton, Patty Muller, and Polly Tait. *A Comparative Evaluation of the Cleveland Scholarship and Tutoring Grant Program, Year One: 1996– 97.* Paper prepared by the School of Education and the Smith Research Center, Indiana University, Bloomington, Indiana, 1998.

Metcalf, Kim, Patricia Muller, William Boone, Polly Tait, Frances Stage, and Nicole Stacey. *Evaluation of the Cleveland Scholarship Program: Second-Year Report (1997– 98).* Bloomington: Indiana Center for Evaluation, Indiana University, 1998.

Metcalf, Kim, Stephen D. West, Natalie A. Legan, Kelli M. Paul, and William J. Boone. *Evaluation of the Cleveland Scholarship and Tutoring Program: Student Characteristics and Academic*

Achievement. Technical Report 1998–2002. Bloomington: Indiana University, Indiana Center for Evaluation, 2003.

Mayer, Daniel P., Paul E. Peterson, David E. Myers, Christina Clark Tuttle, and William G. Howell. *School Choice in New York City After Three Years: An Evaluation of the School Choice Scholarships Program: Mathematica Policy Research, Inc., and the Program on Education Policy and Governance,* Cambridge, MA: Harvard University, 2002.

Myers, David, Paul Peterson, Daniel Mayer, Julia Chou, and William Howell. *School Choice in New York City After Two Years: An Evaluation of the School Choice Scholarships Program.* Princeton, NJ: Mathematica Policy Research, 2000.

Peterson, Paul, Jay Greene, and William Howell. *New Findings from the Cleveland Scholarship Program: A Reanalysis of Data from the Indiana University School of Education Evaluation.* Paper prepared under the auspices of the Program on Education Policy and Governance, Harvard University, Cambridge, Massachusetts, 1998.

Peterson, Paul E., William G. Howell. *Exploring Explanations for Ethnic Differences in Voucher Impacts on Student Test Scores.* Cambridge, MA: Kennedy School of Government, 2001.

Peterson, Paul E., William G. Howell, and Harvard University, Kennedy School of Government. *Efficiency, Bias, and Classification Schemes: Estimating Private-School Impacts on Test Scores in the New York City Voucher Experiment.* Cambridge, MA: Kennedy School of Government, 2003.

Peterson, Paul E., Patrick J. Wolf, William G. Howell, David E. Campbell, and Harvard University, Kennedy School of Government. *School Vouchers: Results from Randomized Experiments.* Cambridge, MA: Kennedy School of Government, 2002.

Plucker, Jonathan A., Matthew C. Makel, John A. Hansen, and Patricia A. Muller. "Achievement Effects of the Cleveland Voucher Program on High Ability Elementary School Students." *Journal of School Choice* 1, no. 4 (2007): 77–88.

Plucker, Jonathan, Patricia Muller, John Hansen, and Russ Ravert. *Evaluation of the Cleveland Scholarship and Tutoring Program, Technical Report 1998–2005.* Bloomington: Center for Evaluation and Education Policy, Indiana University, 2006.

Rouse, Cecilia Elena. "Private School Vouchers and Student Achievement: An Evaluation of the Milwaukee Parental Choice Program." *The Quarterly Journal of Economics* 113, no. 2 (1998): 553–602.

Wille, Michael Patrick. *School Vouchers Source/Amount of Funds and Effects on Math/Reading Scores.* (M.P.P.), Georgetown University, 2010. Retrieved from http://worldcat.org/oclc/664008028/viewonline.

Witte, John F. "The Milwaukee Voucher Experiment." *Educational Evaluation and Policy Analysis 20,* no. 4 (1998): 229–251. doi: 10.3102/01623737020004229.

Witte, John F. *The Market Approach to Education: An Analysis of America's First Voucher Program.* Princeton, NJ: Princeton University Press, 2000.

Wolf, Patrick J. *Looking Inside the Black Box: What School Factors Explain Voucher Gains in Washington, D.C.?* Paper presented at the Annual Meeting of the American Political Science Association, Philadelphia, August 27, 2003.

Wolf, Patrick J. "School Vouchers in Washington, DC: Achievement Impacts and Their Implications for Social Justice." *Educational Research and Evaluation* 16, no. 2 (2010): 131–150.

Wolf, Patrick, Babette Gutmann, Michael Puma, Brian Kisida, Lou Rizzo, and Nada Eissa. *Evaluation of the DC Opportunity Scholarship Program: Impacts After Two Years.* NCEE 2008–4023. Washington, DC: National Center for Education Evaluation and Regional Assistance, 2008.

Wolf, Patrick, Babette Gutmann, Michael Puma, Brian Kisida, Lou Rizzo, and Nada Eissa. *Evaluation of the DC Opportunity Scholarship Program: Impacts After Three Years*. NCEE 2009–4050. Washington, DC: National Center for Education Evaluation and Regional Assistance, 2009.

Wolf, Patrick, Babette Gutmann, Michael Puma, Brian Kisida, Lou Rizzo, and Nada Eissa. *Evaluation of the DC Opportunity Scholarship Program: Final Report*. NCEE 2010–4018. Washington, DC: National Center for Education Evaluation and Regional Assistance, 2010.

Wolf, Patrick, William Howell, and Paul Peterson. *School Choice in Washington*, DC: *An Evaluation After One Year*. Paper presented at the Conference on Vouchers, Charters and Public Education, sponsored by the Program on Education Policy and Governance, Harvard University, Cambridge, Massachusetts, 2000.

Wolf, Patrick, Paul Peterson, and Martin West. "Results of a School Voucher Experiment: The Case of Washington, DC." *After Two Years*. Paper presented at the The American Political Science Association, San Francisco, 2001.

Yau, Y. C. P. *Analyzing the Impact of School Vouchers and Private Schooling*. Ph.D. dissertation. Philadelphia, PA: University of Pennsylvania, 2005. http://repository.upenn.edu/dissertations/AAI3179842.

◆ ◆ ◆

Tatyana Guzman *is a Ph.D. candidate in public affairs in the School of Public and Environmental Affairs at Indiana University. Ms. Guzman specializes in public finance and policy analysis, with research interests in education finance, municipal securities markets, and the personal income tax.*

CHAPTER NINE

PERFORMANCE MANAGEMENT IN THE PUBLIC SECTOR

Ed Gerrish and Po-Ju Wu

"The Government is very keen on amassing statistics. They collect them, add them, raise them to the nth power, take the cube root and prepare wonderful diagrams. But you must never forget that every one of these figures comes in the first instance from the village watchman, who just puts down what he pleases"

(ATTRIBUTED TO SIR JOSIAH STAMP AS QUOTED IN SMITH [1989, 129]).

"It is only a slight exaggeration to say that we are betting the future of governance on the use of performance information"

(MOYNIHAN 2008, 4–5).

"Performance management is here to stay" asserts one scholar (Julnes 2009, 8). Yet performance management (PM) has numerous outspoken critics of its use, implementation, and assumptions (Frederickson and Frederickson 2006; Radin 1998). Even supporters acknowledge that performance management systems can be used as "symbolic tools to express frustration with bureaucracy" (Moynihan 2008, 11). Despite criticism, performance management remains intuitively appealing to elected officials, public managers, and the general public resulting from a desire to improve public bureaucracies and to hold them accountable. This attraction has led to the adoption and readoption of performance management under different guises. On the basis of decades of experience, it seems that performance management will persevere in public organizations.

Performance management comprises a variety of management practices. Moynihan (2008) defines performance management as "a system that generates *performance information* through *strategic planning* and *performance measurement* routines and that connects this information to *decision venues*, where, ideally, the information influences a range of possible decisions" (p. 9, italics added). This definition lacks functional clarity largely because performance management incorporates many management practices, such as strategic planning and performance measurement, that themselves require definition. These practices alone, however, do not constitute performance management. As Smith (2009, 500) notes, "Measuring performance is a necessary but not sufficient condition for performance management."

Rather than attempt to create a single functional definition of performance management that includes all PM activities, we instead offer a number of characteristics many PM systems share. These characteristics include

- Setting performance goals through fiat, negotiations, or models
- Using incentives to achieve performance goals, including monetary rewards and performance-based contracts
- Grading, categorizing, or recognizing superior or inferior performance relative to expectations
- Systematically collecting data on organizational activities and target outcomes designed for use in strategic planning
- Benchmarking current performance to previous performance or performance of other entities, both within and outside of the agency
- Linking agency or departmental budgets implicitly or explicitly to achievement of performance goals
- Publishing performance targets and results publicly for managers, employees, stakeholders, and the public to view

At least one of these characteristics is found in all of the managerial reforms that are often associated with the PM movement, including Pay-for-Performance, Management by Objectives, Total Quality Management, and Performance Budgeting. None of these reforms use all of the characteristics described above, and some pay-for-performance programs rely only on setting targets and providing cash incentives. As we progress through this analysis, we will implicitly refer to performance management as systems that utilize two or more characteristics described above, especially if they also incorporate planning and benchmarking along with performance incentives. This tends to eliminate much of the performance contracting and pay-for-performance literature that does not discuss the use of other PM characteristics.

This chapter is organized as follows. In the upcoming section we examine the origins of performance management and why it has become popular in public bureaucracies. Next, we examine two controversies surrounding performance management: (1) Does it further the appropriate values? and (2) Does it work? We also summarize findings from the literature and describe the outcome variables used in this analysis and our testable hypotheses. In the section after that, we detail the literature search process used to determine acceptable studies and report intercoder reliability results. Then we present descriptive statistics and figures of our research findings, including forest plots and tests for publication bias. We next present the results of our meta-regressions and interpret the findings as they relate to policy makers and scholars. Finally, we discuss the importance of the findings and identify areas for future research.

Origin of Performance Management

The origin of performance management mirrors the scientific management movement attributed to Max Weber and Woodrow Wilson, who popularized the notion that public bureaucracies should be run by professionals employing scientific methods. Their works (along with others) transformed and created the field of public administration. The first organization purported to have used performance management to improve performance was the New York Bureau of Municipal Research in 1906. The agency collected statistics on inputs, outputs, and results, using every technique from reviewing employee timecards to auditing the use of cement by counting sacks (Williams 2003).

The modern incarnation of performance management is often attributed to the reinventing government movement of the early 1990s (Osborne and Plastrik 1997; Osborne and Gaebler 1992). The authors of *Reinventing Government* argued that governments should make a number of market-oriented reforms including introducing market forces (contracting) to break up the government monopoly, focusing on preventing problems not just delivering services, and introducing managerial practices adopted from business (Osborne and Gaebler 1992). The ideas behind *Reinventing Government* created renewed focus on performance management in the Clinton Administration with the National Performance Review (NPR), which tasked government with cutting red tape and empowering employees, and the Government Performance and Results Act (GPRA), which created a process for reviewing the strategic plans and performance of federal agencies.

However, performance management in one form or another has existed at the state and local levels well before the federal government was "reinvented." In particular, organizations such as the Urban Institute and International City/County Management Association (lCMA) have been recognized for their efforts to spread the adoption of performance measurement since the 1970s (Williams 2003). Other PM systems, often coopted from business, have simultaneously arisen at the state and local levels under labels such as Management-by-Objectives and Total Quality Management (Moynihan 2008). In the 1970s a performance budgeting system, Zero-Based Budgeting, was transplanted from Georgia to the federal government by President Carter. Later, the National Performance Review and GPRA were introduced under President Clinton, and President George W. Bush replaced GPRA with a PM system of his own, the Performance Assessment and Ratings Tool (PART). As a result of efforts by officials all over the country, PM systems are now ubiquitous at all levels of government.

To highlight this prevalence, table 9.1 lists some of the performance management systems found at different levels of government and policy areas. This list is not intended to be an exhaustive list of all PM systems in public organizations; instead it reflects areas in which scholars have confirmed the use of performance management in public organizations. It also contains the PM systems uncovered during our literature search for empirical evidence of performance management.

Performance Management Systems in the Public Sector

To give some context as to how performance management is used in public organizations, we now describe two very different PM systems: the Compstat policing program originating from the New York Police Department and the Government Performance and Results Act (GPRA) and its successor, the Program Assessment and Ratings Tool (PART). These management systems have inspired volumes of books, journal articles, and newsprint. Instead of breaking new ground, our intent is to illustrate how both represent performance management in very different ways.

TABLE 9.1. USE OF PERFORMANCE MANAGEMENT SYSTEMS IN POLICY AREAS

Policy Area	Examples of Output or Outcome Measures	Examples of PM System Types or Names
General, Federal	Number of new drugs approved	Government Performance and Results Act (GPRA)
	Number of cases of waterborne illnesses	Performance Assessment Ratings Tool (PART)
General, State, and Local	Fire department response time	Citistat
	Number of home helps for the elderly	Performance Budgeting Management by Objectives Total Quality Management
Education	Standardized test scores	No Child Left Behind
Crime or Policing	Crimes reported in a geographic area	Compstat Operational Performance Reviews (OPRs)
	Number of cases cleared	
Transportation	Time to completion	Performance Contracting
	Miles of road repaired	
Job Training	Job placement rate	Job Training Partnership Act (JTPA)
	Earnings at new employment	
	Increase in earnings from previous employment	Workforce Investment Act (WIA)
Food Stamps	Food stamp payment error rate	Unnamed
Housing	Number of housing placements	Performance Contracting
Public Health	Beta-blocker at patient arrival	Hospital Quality Incentive Demonstration (HQID)
	Antibiotic received within one hour prior to surgical incision	Health Employer Data and Information Set (HEDIS) Pressure Ulcer Expert Panels

Compstat Policing Program. The New York Police Department's Compstat program was launched in 1994 under then Police Commissioner William Bratton and Mayor Rudy Giuliani. The launch was immediately followed by a 12 percent decline in violent crime after only one year of implementation, a fact that Bratton and Giuliani were quick to claim as evidence of its success (Smith and Bratton 2001).

There were two central components to Compstat (a portmanteau of computer and statistics). First, crime statistics were tracked in real time, as opposed to collecting crime data over a period of months and reviewing the data as they came available. Second, semi-weekly meetings were held to link top executives with precinct managers to discuss successes and challenges, and devise strategies to combat crime trends (Smith and Bratton 2001). The founding theory behind the Compstat model was "broken windows," a theory of crime forwarded by George Kelling and James Q. Wilson (1982) which argued that indicators of minor crimes, such as broken windows in neighborhoods, were harbingers of major crimes. As a PM system, Compstat and its successors combine three main elements. First, performance information is collected rapidly. Second, the performance information is included in the strategic planning and decision making process during the semi-weekly meetings. Third, previous performance provides a clear benchmark for future performance goals.

We would be remiss to omit that Compstat has recently attracted scrutiny for the practice of down-coding: coding crimes as less serious to make crime statistics appear more favorable. In a 2010 survey, approximately one-quarter of retired police captains reported observing an alteration of crime data in response to Compstat and that the change was "highly unethical." These actions reflect a tendency to "game" performance indicators, a concept we cover in more detail later. A majority of respondents, however, also believed Compstat was "a valuable management innovation" (Eterno and Silverman 2010). In the chapter Addendum, we examine the meta-analytic impact of Compstat-like programs on crime rates.

GPRA and PART. Implemented in the nation's largest police department, Compstat had a singular goal of reducing crime. By comparison, the federal government's performance programs GPRA and PART were implemented in the nation's largest bureaucracy and encountered a variety of diverse program goals (Radin 1998). Enacted in 1994 (but implemented in 1997), GPRA required federal agencies to develop strategic plans, including a comprehensive mission statement, delineation of measurable objectives, and a process by which those objectives would be achieved. The Office of Management and Budget (OMB) was then tasked to evaluate programmatic and agency performance. In practice, both the OMB and the Government Accountability Office (GAO) evaluated performance plans and results.

Whereas GPRA was a measure initiated by Congress, the Program Assessments and Rating Tool (PART) was a tool created in 2002 by the OMB in the George W. Bush White House to improve GPRA. The Bush administration considered GPRA to be the beginning of a comprehensive performance management portfolio (Moynihan 2008) and created PART as a complement to the regular executive budgeting process through the OMB. PART was implemented as a performance budgeting initiative, promising to provide funding to high-performance programs and cut funding to underperformers. PART ranked federal programs from "effective" to "results not demonstrated" using extensive questionnaires based on seven program typologies. A rating of "effective" was given to programs that set ambitious goals, achieved them, and improved efficiency. A rating of "results not demonstrated" was given to programs that were unable to create measurable objectives or show improvement in their objectives.

Some scholars have critiqued PART's rating system. Agencies such as the Department of Health and Human Services (HHS) have had difficulty crafting measurable objectives in some programs, particularly those targeting vulnerable populations or programs that are designed to prevent harm rather than provide services. For instance, Frederickson and Frederickson write, "Even the most determined effort on the part of [Health Resources and Services Administration] might not produce measurable improvements in health outcomes. Is it reasonable under such circumstances to hold HRSA accountable for health outcomes?" (2006, p. 68).

Research has demonstrated that PART scores are correlated with changes in presidential budgets. However, there is also evidence to suggest that PART scores in the Bush Administration were highly political; PART scores were lower for agencies supported by Democratic leaders and programs supported by the administration's opponents encountered greater proposed cuts compared to programs supported by the Bush Administration with equivalent PART scores (Posner and Walker 2004). In addition, the impact of performance scores on proposed budgets was vastly overshadowed in magnitude by political considerations, including program purpose and historical political support, contradicting the claim that PART would reward high-performing programs (Gilmour and Lewis 2006). These concerns, along with their high profile as federal reforms, make GPRA and PART some of the most frequently critiqued performance management efforts in the United States (Frederickson and Frederickson 2006; Moynihan 2008; Radin 2006; 1998).

In response to these criticisms, the Obama Administration discontinued the use of PART but has reinforced the commitment to performance management at the federal level. So far their efforts have avoided both significant investigation and a four-letter abbreviation (Joyce 2011; Moynihan 2010).

It is easy to see that both Compstat and GPRA-PART were created with similar goals, improving the performance of public bureaucracies. The two PM systems share similar elements in that they measure performance relative to previous benchmarks and involve creating targets or goals. Yet their implementation and focus are quite different. For example, the unit responsible for success in Compstat is a small group of police officers while in GPRA and PART the responsible unit was an entire program. This heterogeneity of implementation is part of what makes performance management so difficult to discuss in broad generalities.

Performance Management in the Literature

This section discusses the important questions surrounding performance management as a tool of reform in the public sector, as well as why our primary research question, "Does performance management work?" is not as simple as it appears. It also summarizes the literature in performance management, both theoretical and empirical.

Performance Management as Reform Tool

Scholars of public administration and policy are interested in performance management for two main reasons. The first is that implementation of PM mirrors a larger debate surrounding the central values of governance. In that debate, PM implicitly values efficiency and rationality at the expense of due process, equality, and democratic governance. Second, this research is important to both scholars and practitioners because they want to know whether performance management "works." While the second question appears to be an empirical one, it is intrinsically interwoven with the first. The next three sections will introduce the foundations of support for performance management, the debate surrounding values and governance, and begin to address the question which is central to this meta-analysis—does performance management work?

Foundations of Performance Management. The widespread use of performance management draws its support from two sources. The first view is typified by supporters of the reinventing government movement (Osborne and Plastrik 1997; Osborne and Gaebler 1992), who support a more market-oriented approach and urge governments to focus on consumer satisfaction and prevent problems rather than provide services. Some argue that this view advocates running government like a business, but Osborne, Gaebler, and others argue that market orientation is only part of the answer. The second group of advocates draw support from theories of scientific management pioneered by John Taylor (Nelson 1980). Taylorism emphasizes the use of scientific methods in management rather than rules of thumb and a focus on efficiency and output maximization.

The two groups of supporters are similar in that they are interested in rational management and maximizing productivity. In addition, both views are drawn from the private sector and were modified for the particular challenges of the public sector. However, modern scientific management scholars are less interested in a market-oriented philosophy but see a role for rational, scientific management techniques for improving governance and organizational performance.

Both avenues of support have contributed to the spread of PM in the United States and abroad. To organize the current and sometimes contradictory support for recent efforts of performance management, Moynihan (2008, 27) lists five assumptions underlying PM, which he calls the performance management doctrine:

· Government is inefficient.
· Government can transform itself to become more efficient.
· The poor performance of government is of major consequence in terms of fiscal health and public trust in government.
· Government can and should make more rational decisions.
· Performance information will improve decisions and can be used to foster accountability.

Moynihan argues that these assumptions rest at the heart of most management reforms in the past three decades; specifically the call from elected officials for increased accountability. While Moynihan examines both the successes and failures of performance management (finding success in prison management in Vermont but not Alabama), he argues that crafting performance management systems based on these five assumptions does not lead to success.

He also contends that one of the reasons PM implementation is unsuccessful is that it is adopted for symbolic rather than instrumental reasons. Symbolic reforms are reforms that are primarily used as a signal to the electorate. After the reform is adopted, elected officials pay little attention to results. Instrumental reforms are reforms that are a means to an end; advocates are more concerned about the results than the signal. Instrumental and symbolic motivations are not mutually exclusive; elected officials may chiefly value the symbolic benefits, while managers value instrumental benefits. The tension arises, Radin (2006) observes, when elected officials implement PM systems both for symbolic reasons and to centralize control over decision making rather than promote managerial autonomy. This combination tends to produce failures (Moynihan 2008).

Performance Management and Values of Governance. Both symbolic and instrumental motivations for performance management intrinsically value efficiency, rationality, and productivity. Radin (2006) argues that as a result, PM tends to undermine principles such as democratic governance, due process, and attention to vulnerable populations. For instance, Radin (1998) points to the inability of agencies under the National Performance Review and later GPRA to both measure and evaluate the performance of programs serving underprivileged communities because of GPRA's requirements that program goals be "objective, quantifiable, and in measurable form (Radin 1998, 308)." She also notes that PM systems tend to concentrate responsibility in the executive, another abrogation of democratic principles. For example, the OMB is chiefly in charge of creating PART scores, reducing the power of Congress both by allowing the OMB to direct programs toward performance goals they deem acceptable and by increasing the information overload of the legislative branch.

This debate over whether performance management works rests on the assumption that trading these values for increases in organizational performance is acceptable. For some, it is not. Thus the question of whether PM improves organizational performance is largely tangential. However, these scholars are also interested in whether performance management works; if not, then performance management is a failure on two fronts.

Does Performance Management Work?. The question of whether performance management works is essential in part because, as the introductory quote suggests, so many governments have implemented performance management with an aim to improving performance that we have essentially bet the future of government on PM (Moynihan 2008). It is also critical because PM systems rely on theories from public administration and economics about how organizational performance is related to public sector employee motivation, managerial strategies, the value of information, and optimal incentive structures. If PM systems in public organizations do not improve organizational performance, then theories about organizational behavior must be reassessed.

On the question of whether PM improves performance, critics generally argue that it is not effective for two reasons. First they argue that performance management has failed to create improvements in measurable objectives. For example, Radin (2006) argues that the No Child Left Behind (NCLB) Act has failed to even modestly improve standardized test scores over the period in which it has been in effect. This appraisal of performance management, like much of the criticism, is based on qualitative assessments. These assessments have the richness of case studies and personal experience working for federal agencies burdened with implementing PM systems (Frederickson and Frederickson 2006), but are not methodical. Some critics of PM have also acknowledged perceived success stories at the local level. Radin, for example, positively references the New York Police Department and its use of the Compstat program.

Second, Radin (2006) argues that performance measures are exposed to multiple interpretations. Numbers are subjective measures of performance and devoid of meaning without their interpretation from political actors. In other words, success is in the eye of the beholder. Supporting this claim is an investigation conducted by Moynihan (2006) using graduate students to reevaluate PART scores assigned by the OMB using the same data used by OMB staff. Students scored programs differently than the OMB in many instances and for a number of reasons. For example, when program functions were inherently difficult to measure, students found that the OMB was more likely to rate programs "results not demonstrated."

Among economists, one of the critical questions of performance management is whether staff "game" performance targets to their advantage but to the detriment of the organization. For example, Courty and Marschke (2004) find that job training agencies engage in a number of strategic behaviors to achieve minimum performance benchmarks such as delaying performance reporting to the next accounting period. Their evidence also suggests that this has a real detrimental impact on the effectiveness of the job training programs. It is thus important that measured outputs are strongly correlated with desired outcomes. This phenomenon, grounded in principal-agent theory, can be best summarized by the line, "What gets measured gets done" (Berman 2002). Of course, it is also true that what does not get measured does not get done. This behavior could create situations in which organizations achieve measured objectives but fail organizational missions; a problem described as the performance paradox.

We attempt to address these concerns in our meta-analysis. First, we are able to combine quantitative analyses of performance management at different levels of government to test whether effectiveness varies between federal programs such as NCLB and local initiatives such as Compstat.

Second, we are able to code studies in which authors express concern about gaming behavior and hypothesize that performance measures in these situations will demonstrate larger gains, even if those gains are illusory. Finally, coding for research design characteristics allow us to test whether performance management systems are more or less effective even when controlling for a rigorous design.

Review of Empirical Literature

Because PM systems are being used at all levels of government both in the United States and abroad, there has been a significant amount of literature written on the subject. A simple search in Google Scholar for the phrase *performance management* nets about 157,000 hits—8,000 hits in the title alone.[1] However, the overwhelming frequency of the literature of performance management remains in qualitative and case-study form (Yang and Hsieh 2007). Generally speaking, the PM literature can be divided into four areas. First is the theoretical and case study literature of PM systems, which includes important recent works by Moynihan (2008), Radin (2006), Frederickson and Frederickson (2006), Heinrich and Marschke (2010), and many others. This literature is largely summarized in the previous sections, and it focuses on why performance management should improve governmental performance and critiques of performance management from different perspectives. Second, there exists a large "how-to" literature that contains best practices and lessons learned from experience in implementing performance management systems. Think tank members such as the Urban Institute's Harry Hatry are leaders in this literature (Hatry 2006), as well as many others (Behn 2003; Folz 2004; Poister 2003). This literature is not reviewed in this analysis as it largely draws upon the theoretical literature but is written for a practitioner audience. Third is a small but excellent survey literature described in the following section, and fourth is a "hard" empirical literature using data from public organizations.

Survey Literature. There is a small survey literature that examines the adoption, implementation, and perceived effectiveness of performance management systems (Cavalluzzo and Ittner 2003; Ho 2006; Julnes 2009; Julnes and Holzer 2001; Moynihan and Pandey 2010; Yang and Hsieh 2007). This survey data is particularly useful for generating testable hypotheses. A number of findings appear to be consistent among the surveys. First, support for performance management among managers, both at middle and higher levels, is associated with greater adoption and implementation of PM (Cavalluzzo and Ittner 2003) and is both directly and indirectly related to perceived effectiveness (Yang and Hsieh 2007). Second, stakeholder support improves PM effectiveness both directly and indirectly, but is not associated with its initial adoption (Yang and Hsieh 2007). Third, training in preparation for PM implementation is associated with greater perceived effectiveness (Cavalluzzo and Ittner 2003; Julnes and Holzer 2001). Finally, mission-orientation activities such as the establishment and reevaluation of mission goals is correlated with the implementation of PM, but evidence on mission orientation is lacking for perceived effectiveness (Wang and Berman 2001).

Although survey data are useful for understanding the foundations of performance management use and why managers think performance management effective, they are less useful at assessing whether PM systems change measurable performance. We have excluded surveys from the meta-analysis because there may be some incentive for managers to report that performance management is more effective than it is, intentional or not. As a case in point, Tat-Kei Ho (2006) found that Midwestern mayors who were most familiar with PM systems were more likely to believe that performance measurement was associated with cost-effectiveness and improving strategic planning. This may be expected of mayors who have made performance measurement a priority.

"Hard" Empirical Literature. The final set of literature of performance management is the empirical literature that assesses the impact of organizational performance systems using "hard" measures of performance, in which a hard measure of performance might be a reduction in poverty in a target population or any other measure that does not rely on the self-report of an employee or manager. Some authors claim that the empirical research on performance management is sparse (Heinrich and Marschke 2010; Yang and Hsieh 2007). We do not agree with that assessment. However, we recognize that the empirical literature assessing the impact of PM systems is divided among various policy areas. As a result, much of the empirical literature used in this meta-analysis was not found in a typical ancestry search or searches using the keywords *performance management*. For example, there are a number of studies assessing the relationship between the implementation of Compstat-like policing programs and reported crime. While Compstat is generally considered a PM system (both by Moynihan 2008 and Radin 2006), empirical evidence of its performance does not cite nor address the broader PM literature; Compstat studies situate themselves within theories of policing. Lynn, Heinrich, and Hill make the same observation about research on governance more generally (2001). This fact has contributed to the misperception that the empirical literature on performance management is sparse. Through our literature search we have identified "hard" empirical research on PM systems in the fields of policing, job training, education, and public health using the search strategies described in the literature search section. In total, we collected thirty empirical studies on the effectiveness of performance management for this study.

A non-meta-analytic review of the empirical literature suggests that the impact of PM systems is mixed. In the crime field, for example, implementing a Compstat-like policing program is correlated with a reduction of some minor crime rates, but typically not major crimes. Important to note, it does not seem to be systematically associated with reductions in minor crimes, which are supposed to be the targets of "broken window" policing. Other studies find that the use of Compstat-like programs is correlated with a higher crime clearance rate, but not statistically associated with decreases in crime rates, and one study notes that use of Compstat-like procedures is correlated with an increase in reported crime rates, most likely due to self-selection issues (Garicano and Heaton 2010).

Similarly, economists studying job training programs have found that while some Service Delivery Areas (SDAs) successfully attain performance goals, there is only a weak correlation between these short-term performance goals and the long-term labor market success of participants (Heckman, Heinrich, and Smith 1997). One reason economists have for this finding is that employees (agents) are focusing on short-term performance goals to the detriment of the larger organization (the principal). Heinrich and Marschke (2010) conduct a review of the economic literature on performance management through the lens of principal-agent theory. They examine the precursor to the Worker Investment Act (1998 onward), the Job Training Partnership Act (1982–1998), and Wisconsin's Welfare to Work program (first implemented in the late 1980s and continued through national welfare reform). Heinrich and Marschke cite examples of both successful and unsuccessful attempts to manage the performance of agents who are continually adapting to changing performance incentives; the Welfare to Work program altered its performance measures every year for four years citing concerns of performance target manipulation by private contractors. They conclude that identifying successful performance incentive systems is difficult without considering the "evolutionary dynamic" of potential principle-agent problems.

Finally, we should note that not all fields we searched produced enough empirical evidence on performance management to summarize in a literature review. Fields in which this was most apparent were highway and public works construction, nutritional assistance programs (for example, food stamps), housing assistance programs, and prison management.[2] The scholarly literature and our literature search determined that performance management is in use in all of the areas identified in table 9.1. Adoption of PM systems, however, does not appear to bear any relationship to the existence of empirical evidence on its effectiveness. This result could occur either because this evidence does not exist, or the search terms and methods used to find them were inadequate.

Outcome Measures and Key Hypotheses

This section discusses the use of outcome measures in empirical examinations of performance management systems in policy areas as well as some of the key hypotheses we hope to test using meta-analytic techniques.

Outcome Measures in Performance Management. Measures of organizational performance are as varied as the performance management systems themselves. Authors studying job training programs identify outcome measures from welfare-to-work programs as employment ratios, earnings at new jobs, or earnings improvement from previous employment (Courty and Marschke 2007; Heckman, Heinrich, and Smith 1997; Heinrich 2002). In the field of policing, authors such as Mazerolle, McBroom, and Rombouts (2011) use reported crime rates in assault, robbery, and unlawful entry. Other authors use clearance rates (Garicano and Heaton 2010). In education studies, the typical performance indicator is standardized test scores (Boyne and Chen 2007).

We recognize that the dependent variables in the original studies we use are very different even though they all intend to measure the same underlying construct—organizational performance. In meta-analysis, this creates concerns about apples-to-oranges comparisons in which studies are too different to be combined meaningfully (Borenstein, Hedges, Higgins, and Rothstein 2009). Recognizing this potential problem, we attempt to control for some of the background variation in outcome measures using two sets of control variables. First, the outcome measures are classified by their type as identified in the program evaluation literature (Langbein and Felbinger 2006); dependent variables are coded as output, outcome, or efficiency measures. We hypothesize that dependent variables which closely reflect an organization's mission (outcome variables) may be more difficult to achieve through PM than output measures. Second, we use a set of controls for the source of the dependent variable: health outcome records, geographic information data, or financial information. We also considered controlling for the broad issue area but severe multicollinearity between policy areas and the previous two sets of control variables seems to suggest that we have captured much of the available variation along this dimension.

Testable Hypotheses. Using these measures of organizational performance, we test four specific hypotheses. These hypotheses are directly derived from the previous discussion of the theoretical, survey, and empirical literature. We believe that these hypotheses are of interest to both scholars studying the rise of performance management in government and the practitioners using PM systems. The first hypothesis is the basic hypothesis regarding the relationship between performance management and organizational performance in the public sector.

H1: Performance management is positively correlated with improved organizational performance.

Hypothesis 2 examines the type of measure that is being used as a performance target. We believe that "high quality" measures, measures that are more closely aligned to organizational goals (outcomes or impacts), will show a weaker relationship to organizational performance than lower-quality measures such as employee activities (outputs). This hypothesis comes from two fields of research. First, the program evaluation literature suggests that outcome measures have much greater background variation and are thus less amenable to change (for example, job training impacts may be dominated by business cycle effects). Second, the economic literature suggests that the more closely aligned the performance measures are with an organization mission, the less likely it is that performance management will create large changes due to gaming responses. Taken together, this suggests hypothesis 2.

H2: The use of "higher quality" outcome variables will be more weakly associated with organizational performance than output measures.

Hypothesis 3 is derived from Moynihan's observation that public managers are more likely to implement performance management for instrumental rather than symbolic reasons (Moynihan 2008) and that instrumental reforms are more likely to be successful. Because we cannot assess the motivations for PM adoption, we instead proxy for this motivation by noting whether the reform originated from legislatures and executives (top down) or managers and staff (bottom up).

> H3: Performance management is more effective when performance management adoption derives from managers rather than when imposed by legislators or executives.

Finally, as mentioned earlier, Radin (1998), Frederickson and Frederickson (2006), and others are critical of the implementation of performance management at the federal level. However, there seems to be less skepticism of performance management at the local level, likely due to the issues of control and the size of the bureaucracy. Lacking reliable data from our studies on issues of organizational control and size, we use the more general hypothesis.

> H4: Performance management is more effective at the state and local levels than at the federal level.

Literature Search

This section discusses the process by which we conducted our search for empirical literature on the impact of performance management on organizational performance. It also reports our efforts to measure the inter-rater reliability of the two authors.

Literature Search Method

We conducted a broad literature search that reflects the scattered nature of PM systems among various policy areas. Our search methodology covered all permutations using three search criteria: (1) a search engine or website, (2) a substantive issue area, and (3) a performance-management-related search term.

We examined approximately twenty-six academic search engines, conference proceedings, working paper directories, or organizational websites (including both government and nongovernmental organizations). Readers can find a list of all of the sources we searched in table 9.2.

TABLE 9.2. LIST OF SEARCH ENGINES, ORGANIZATIONS, AND SITES SEARCHED FOR PERFORMANCE MANAGEMENT STUDIES

Academic Search Engines
 Academic Search Premier (EBSCO)
 Business Source Premier (EBSCO)
 JSTOR
 ProQuest
 ISI Web of Knowledge
 Google Scholar (First 100 hits)
 Eric
 WorldCat
 IUCAT (Indiana University's Library
  System)
 British Library Document Supply
  Centre (BLDSC)
 PsycINFO

Working Papers
 SSRN[a]
 NBER[b]
 Econlit[c]

Substantive Issue Areas Search Terms
 Child Support AND Enforcement
 food stamp
 food assistance
 nutrition assistance
 SCHIP[j] (spelled and abbrev.)
 Medicaid
 Compstat
 Citistat
 Police AND Crime
 Prison
 No Child Left Behind
 Transportation Construction
 Welfare-to-Work
 Job Training Partnership Act
 Government Performance and
  Results Act
 Performance Assessment Ratings
  Tool

Conference Proceedings
 ASPA[d]
 APPAM[e]
 Political Research Online

Government Publications
 GAO[f]
 OMB[g]
 CBO[h]

Think Tanks and NGOs
 Urban Institute
 Brookings Institution
 American Enterprise Institute
 The Performance Institute
 RAND[i]
 National Academy of Public
  Administration

Performance-Related Search Terms
 Performance Management
 Performance Measurement
 Performance Information
 Performance Standard
 Performance System
 Performance Goal
 Performance Benchmark

---

[a] http://www.ssrn.com/
[b] http://www.nber.org/
[c] http://www.aeaweb.org/econlit/
[d] http://www.aspanet.org
[e] http://www.appam.org/
[f] http://www.gao.gov/
[g] http://www.whitehouse.gov/omb/
[h] http://www.cbo.gov/
[i] http://www.rand.org/
[j] State Children's Health Insurance Program.

We searched the following substantive issue areas: child support enforcement, education, food stamps and nutrition assistance, GPRA and PART, incarceration and prisons, job training programs, policing and crime, public health, transportation and construction, and welfare-to-work programs. We arrived at these issue areas by synthesizing the literature on performance management that discussed preexisting performance management systems in these areas. They are not intended to be an exhaustive search of performance management, but this decision made searching through the 157,000 hits found in a cursory Google Scholar search more amenable.

The performance-related search terms included one of the following exact phrases: *performance information, performance management, performance measurement, performance standard*, and *performance system*. The initial search criteria included the phrases *performance benchmarking* and *performance goal*, but substantive duplication suggested that these additional search terms were unnecessary and were omitted. The full list of the search engines, and the exact phrasing used in the policy area searches can be found in table 9.2.

There was a four-tiered process for deciding whether a study should be deemed "acceptable" and therefore included in the meta-analysis. The first step was to take all "hits" returned from a search and read each title in order to identify studies that were "potentially relevant." Potentially relevant documents were then assessed for "relevance" by reading only the title, keywords, citation, and abstract and was marked "relevant" or "not relevant" using our coding document. Studies coded as relevant were then assessed for "acceptability" by reading the entire document and searching for appropriate outcome and treatment variables. Determining whether a study was acceptable was based on four criteria:

1. For a study to be included in the analysis, the outcome variable had to be a "hard" figure, where we previously defined *hard* as a *measure* of organizational performance and excluded survey responses regarding the *perceived* effectiveness of performance management. We made this decision because survey respondents may feel obliged to report success in PM efforts, particularly if they are responsible for performance management in their organization.

2. The independent variable had to be a measure of performance management. Recalling the introductory discussion regarding the characteristics of PM systems, the performance management *systems* need to include at least two characteristics of the systems described. As a result,

we filtered out a number of pay-for-performance and performance-contracting studies for lacking multiple elements of a PM system.

3. The study had to be done within a public organization or in organizations that relied primarily on public sources of funding. For instance, we used studies that examined PM systems in nursing homes with patients' fees paid by Medicare or Medicaid.

4. Finally, the analysis had to be quantitative in nature and to conduct an appropriate statistical test to derive an effect size and confidence interval.

Figure 9.1 illustrates the number of hits and acceptable documents found in each issue area and the way the acceptable documents were identified in parentheses. Potentially relevant and relevant documents are excluded from this figure.

FIGURE 9.1. FLOWCHART OF LITERATURE SEARCH PROCESS AND INTERCODER RELIABILITY

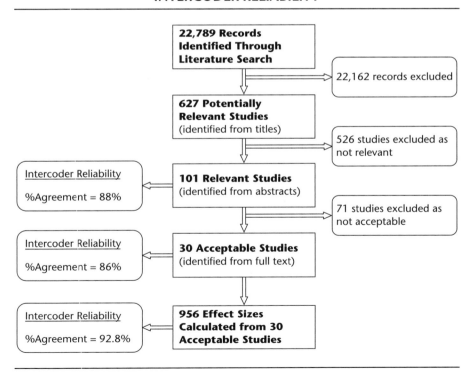

Intercoder Reliability Assessments

Integral to our literature search process was ensuring that both authors were coding documents similarly. Therefore we conducted three sets of intercoder reliability assessments as we assessed relevance and acceptability. The first intercoder reliability assessment measured whether the authors were similarly marking studies as relevant. In that reliability assessment there was 88 percent agreement between the two authors with a Cohen's kappa of .74 ($n = 50$).[3] The second intercoder reliability, which assessed the reliability of coders marking relevant documents as acceptable, had a similar percentage agreement of 86 percent and a Cohen's kappa of .71 ($n = 50$). Finally, the authors assessed levels of agreement in coding effect sizes and a number of other important details of coding effect sizes such as sample size, degrees of freedom, and the test statistic, among others. In this portion we used a percentage agreement measure, as the two-by-two matrix structure used for the first two intercoder reliability assessments was not appropriate. The authors had a percentage agreement of 93 percent ($n = 1120$).[4] In each of these assessments, the intercoder reliability between the authors proved acceptable using rules of thumb for intercoder reliability assessments which suggest that a Cohen's kappa score of .9 or above is excellent, .8 to .9 is good, and .7 to .8 is acceptable. None of our intercoder reliability assessments would be considered excellent. Figure 9.1 highlights the results of these intercoder reliability assessments as well as their location in the coding process. It also demonstrates the number of documents filtered out at each stage of the process. Duplicative hits were counted in the cumulative hit count.

Data Analysis: Synthesis

This section outlines the structure of the meta-analytic data and goes over some of the descriptive statistics. First we describe the effect sizes we use in this analysis, including the distribution of effect sizes. Second, we examine forest plots for mean effect sizes by issue area, and finally we examine tests for publication bias and results.

Effect Sizes

For this study, we utilize the r-based effect size, Fisher's Z. These effect sizes are roughly analogous to Pearson's correlation coefficient in that they range between -1 and 1 with 0 indicating no correlation and 1 indicating perfect positive correlation. Values of $+/- 0.2$ are considered weak correlation and $+/- 0.7$ strong correlation. All regression coefficients (or any other measures of association) are first transformed into an r-based measure to allow for comparison across studies and sample sizes. We then make a correction for small sample biases transforming the effect sizes into Fisher's Z. Technically, Fisher's Z does not range from -1 to 1, particularly at extreme r values (greater than $+/- 0.7$). However, this is not a concern for this analysis for two reasons. First, because few effect sizes have values that large, and second because we transform our results back to conform to the range of Pearson's r. See chapter 3 for a detailed discussion of effect sizes and their use in meta-analysis.

This meta-analysis utilizes 956 total effect sizes from 30 studies. The median study has 11 effect sizes, with the smallest study containing only 2. The largest study contains 337 effect sizes.[5] The effect sizes have an unweighted mean of 0.054, a median of 0.045, and a standard deviation of 0.15. The effect sizes have a wide range in values from -0.74 to 0.69, a consequence of some small samples with large positive and negative effect sizes. The mean number of observations in the models that created the effect sizes is 1,357 and the median is 185. The largest models had nearly 30,000 observations, and the smallest only 16. In our meta-regressions, the effect size becomes the dependent variable and we use independent variables to explain variation in Fisher's Z.

Descriptive Analysis

Test for Random Effects. Throughout the remainder of this analysis, we examine the mean effect size or meta-regression results using the assumption of either a fixed effects or a random effects framework. Fixed and random effects have the unfortunate coincidence of sharing names with both the panel data and mixed-model terminology, though the concepts are different. In meta-analysis, the fixed effects model assumes that there is a *true* single effect size and the effect sizes we have coded vary only by sampling error. Random effects, in contrast, assumes that there is a *distribution* of effect sizes and each study is attempting to uncover an original effect size. In other words, we are trying to uncover a distribution of effect sizes that also contain sampling error. As a consequence, random effects estimates give more weight to smaller studies and have larger confidence intervals. We generally assume that fixed effects estimates are more appropriate for experimental scientific studies and medical trials and random effects estimates are more appropriate for social sciences. However, we conduct a test of the appropriateness of the fixed effects model.

The diagnostics calculated using the meta-analysis package for Stata demonstrate that the correct specification is a random effects model. Specifically, the I^2 statistic, which is the measure of what percentage of the variance cannot be attributable to sampling error, is 80.2 percent. Put another way, 80.2 percent of the effect size variance is attributable to variation in study effect sizes. This variance is significantly different from zero at the $p < .001$ level using a chi-squared test.[6] Therefore when we report results from forest plots and meta-regression, we employ a random effects specification.

Forest Plots. We present forest plots that examine mean effect sizes by study in four areas: job training programs (ten studies), policing and public safety studies (nine studies), public health studies (seven studies), and miscellaneous (five studies). The five miscellaneous studies contain three studies on education, one on child support enforcement, and one general study on performance management among local governments in the United Kingdom. These forest plots are presented in figures 9.2 through 9.5.

The four forest plot figures show that the mean effect size is roughly zero for both job training programs and Compstat and Citistat programs, somewhat positive though not substantively significant (less than 0.2) for both public health and other studies. Variation between studies in the job training programs hover around zero and are quite consistent, largely because much of the research comes from the same JTPA data but analyzed using different empirical methods and specifications. The mean effect size for the Compstat and Citistat programs is also roughly zero although the variation between studies is quite large.

Performance management in public health is positive but the variation between studies is large and the mean effect size of 0.07 is not substantively meaningful. Each of the studies in the miscellaneous category demonstrates positive mean effect sizes, most strongly for the study on child support enforcement incentives to the states and one on generic PM systems in the United Kingdom. The mean effect size in these other policy areas, 0.16, is the closest group to being substantively different from zero, which suggests, oddly, that the least examined policy areas show the greatest potential for effective PM systems. In addition, the strong research designs in these five other studies are the most robust to confounding effects, though future research may soften this conclusion.

FIGURE 9.2. FOREST PLOT OF RESEARCH ON JOB TRAINING PROGRAMS

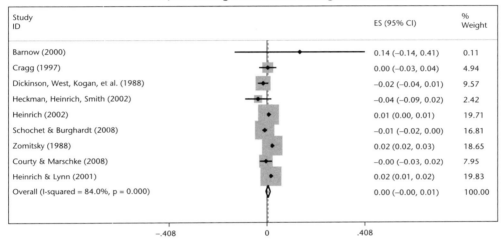

Forest Plot of Job Training Performance Management Studies

Study ID		ES (95% CI)	% Weight
Barnow (2000)		0.14 (−0.14, 0.41)	0.11
Cragg (1997)		0.00 (−0.03, 0.04)	4.94
Dickinson, West, Kogan, et al. (1988)		−0.02 (−0.04, 0.01)	9.57
Heckman, Heinrich, Smith (2002)		−0.04 (−0.09, 0.02)	2.42
Heinrich (2002)		0.01 (0.00, 0.01)	19.71
Schochet & Burghardt (2008)		−0.01 (−0.02, 0.00)	16.81
Zomitsky (1988)		0.02 (0.02, 0.03)	18.65
Courty & Marschke (2008)		−0.00 (−0.03, 0.02)	7.95
Heinrich & Lynn (2001)		0.02 (0.01, 0.02)	19.83
Overall (I-squared = 84.0%, p = 0.000)		0.00 (−0.00, 0.01)	100.00

−.408   0   .408

Note: Weights are from random effects analysis.

FIGURE 9.3. FOREST PLOT OF RESEARCH IN POLICING AND PUBLIC SAFETY

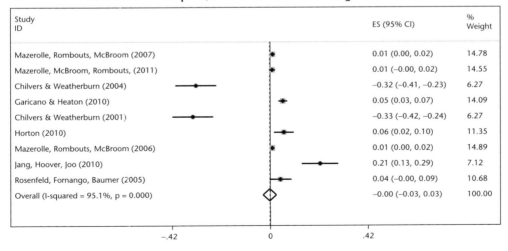

Forest Plot of Compstat/Citistat Performance Management Studies

Study ID		ES (95% CI)	% Weight
Mazerolle, Rombouts, McBroom (2007)		0.01 (0.00, 0.02)	14.78
Mazerolle, McBroom, Rombouts, (2011)		0.01 (−0.00, 0.02)	14.55
Chilvers & Weatherburn (2004)		−0.32 (−0.41, −0.23)	6.27
Garicano & Heaton (2010)		0.05 (0.03, 0.07)	14.09
Chilvers & Weatherburn (2001)		−0.33 (−0.42, −0.24)	6.27
Horton (2010)		0.06 (0.02, 0.10)	11.35
Mazerolle, Rombouts, McBroom (2006)		0.01 (0.00, 0.02)	14.89
Jang, Hoover, Joo (2010)		0.21 (0.13, 0.29)	7.12
Rosenfeld, Fornango, Baumer (2005)		0.04 (−0.00, 0.09)	10.68
Overall (I-squared = 95.1%, p = 0.000)		−0.00 (−0.03, 0.03)	100.00

−.42   0   .42

Note: Weights are from random effects analysis.

FIGURE 9.4. FOREST PLOT OF RESEARCH IN PUBLIC HEALTH

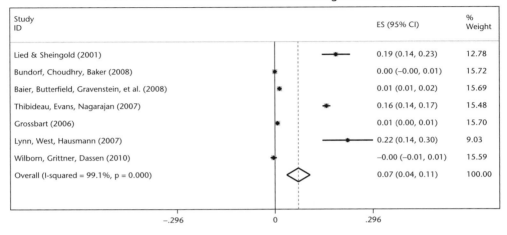

Forest Plot of Public Health Performance Management Studies

Study ID	ES (95% CI)	% Weight
Lied & Sheingold (2001)	0.19 (0.14, 0.23)	12.78
Bundorf, Choudhry, Baker (2008)	0.00 (–0.00, 0.01)	15.72
Baier, Butterfield, Gravenstein, et al. (2008)	0.01 (0.01, 0.02)	15.69
Thibideau, Evans, Nagarajan (2007)	0.16 (0.14, 0.17)	15.48
Grossbart (2006)	0.01 (0.00, 0.01)	15.70
Lynn, West, Hausmann (2007)	0.22 (0.14, 0.30)	9.03
Wilborn, Grittner, Dassen (2010)	–0.00 (–0.01, 0.01)	15.59
Overall (I-squared = 99.1%, p = 0.000)	0.07 (0.04, 0.11)	100.00

–.296 0 .296

Note: Weights are from random effects analysis.

FIGURE 9.5. FOREST PLOT OF RESEARCH IN MISCELLANEOUS FIELDS

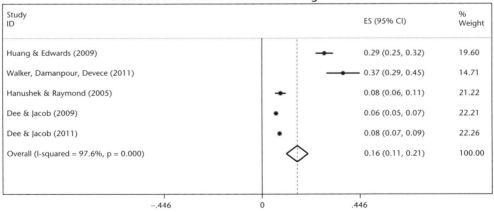

Forest Plot of of Other Peformance Management Studies

Study ID	ES (95% CI)	% Weight
Huang & Edwards (2009)	0.29 (0.25, 0.32)	19.60
Walker, Damanpour, Devece (2011)	0.37 (0.29, 0.45)	14.71
Hanushek & Raymond (2005)	0.08 (0.06, 0.11)	21.22
Dee & Jacob (2009)	0.06 (0.05, 0.07)	22.21
Dee & Jacob (2011)	0.08 (0.07, 0.09)	22.26
Overall (I-squared = 97.6%, p = 0.000)	0.16 (0.11, 0.21)	100.00

–.446 0 .446

Note: Weights are from random effects analysis.

Simple Hypothesis Tests

Test for Zero Mean Effect Size. A naïve analysis of the mean effect size weighted by sample size finds an average effect size of 0.05 with confidence intervals of 0.045 to 0.055.[7] This mean effect size tests hypothesis 1: whether performance management is correlated with organizational performance. We find that, on average, it is. However, the coefficient of 0.05 is not very large. When we omit the two largest studies containing 568 effect sizes from the Dee and Jacob NCLB studies (2009; 2011) to check the robustness of our findings to these sample size outliers, the mean effect size is reduced to 0.035 with confidence intervals of $+/-$ 0.006; the large Dee and Jacob studies change the mean effect size, but not the conclusion.

Tests for Publication Bias. The tests we conduct for publication bias return conflicting results. Publication bias tests are important for understanding whether there are studies that appear to be systematically "missing" from our sample. Studies can be missing for two reasons. First, studies that present results which are counter to expectations (particularly negative results) can be systematically rejected by journal editors and peer reviewers. Second, authors may not even seek to publish results that conflict with their own (or their field's) a priori expectations. The latter problem is called the file drawer problem.

The logic of publication bias tests is that we ought to observe effect sizes roughly equally distributed on the left and right side of our mean effect size with the interval narrowing as the sample size increases and estimates become more efficient. See the contour funnel plot in figure 9.6 for a graphical illustration of this idea. If there appears to be no systemically missing effect sizes, then we tentatively conclude that there is no bias resulting from either journal filtering or the file drawer problem.

The Begg test removes parametric assumptions and examines the rank correlation of both the effect size and standard error of the effect size. A significant finding suggests that the effect sizes are asymmetric. The Begg test shows no correlation statistically different from zero. The Egger test, which is a parametric test that retains information about effect size and standard errors does show publication bias. However, simulation results presented in chapter 6 of this book show that the Egger test performs poorly under even lenient assumptions. The final, and perhaps most robust publication bias test, which is a meta-regression with a dichotomous variable indicating whether the study appeared in a peer-reviewed outlet, is not statistically significant using the wild cluster bootstrap method described in further detail

FIGURE 9.6. CONTOUR FUNNEL PLOT

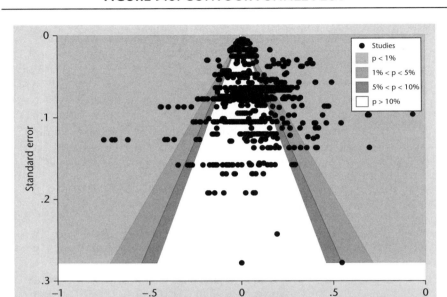

below. Table 9.3 displays the results of the three publication bias tests. As a result of these three tests, we do not consider any corrections for publication bias aside from including an indicator variable for peer review in our meta-regression models.

Figure 9.6 displays a contour funnel that plots the standard error on the y axis (the standard error is a direct function of the sample size) and the effect size on the x axis. An eye test of the contour funnel plot in figure 9.6

TABLE 9.3. RESULTS OF TESTS FOR PUBLICATION BIAS

	Begg Test	Egger Test	Meta-Regression Using Wild Cluster Bootstrap Errors
Coefficient	0.48	0.85	0.035
Significance Level	$p > 0.629$	$p < .001$	$p > 0.158$
Conclusion	No publication bias	Publication bias	No publication bias

indicates that there may be some empty space in the lower left quadrant of the plot. However, the effect does not appear to be systematic.

Meta-Analytic Regression Analysis

In this section, we describe the meta-regression techniques we use in this analysis as well as the independent variables and the results of our meta-regressions. Meta-regression models compose the core of this meta-analysis. The simple test for mean effect size different from zero is the analytic equivalent to a regression model that contains only the constant. Meta-regression tests a richer conditional model that allows us to understand why effect sizes vary between studies and allows us to test the four hypotheses enumerated earlier.

Estimation Techniques

In this meta-analysis, we use four analytic techniques. These techniques build upon one another to address two violations of ordinary least squares assumptions that cause standard errors to be calculated incorrectly. First, estimates will be heteroskedastic; as the sample size increases, the variability of the r-based effect size decreases due to reduction in sampling error. Since we know the structure of the heteroskedastic disturbance, we can apply a weight matrix of the inverse of the sample size to derive consistent and efficient estimates.

Second, because each study has more than one effect size, our observations are non-independent. Coefficient estimates remain unbiased, but standard errors will be calculated incorrectly due to within-study effect size correlation. One potential solution to this problem is to aggregate these effect sizes into a single study-level effect. However, this option eliminates within-study variation, which is essential to reaching conclusions about our hypotheses. The general solution is to use standard errors clustered by study (referred to as CRVE in previous chapters).

Unfortunately, clustered standard errors have their own limitations. Simulation results (Cameron, Gelbach, and Miller 2008) find that clustered standard errors inflate alpha rejection rates (type I error) both for a small number of groups and for variation in the number of observations within groups. In our case, even with thirty groups, we still have unequal cluster sizes, and alpha rejection rates we believe to be around 5 percent will be closer to 10 percent.

This problem necessitates the use of bootstrapping techniques to empirically derive a consistent distribution of t statistics. We estimate a distribution of t statistics using a technique called the wild cluster bootstrap (WCB) (Cameron, Gelbach, and Miller 2008). A more detailed review of how this process works and the theory behind it can be found in chapter 5. In general, wild cluster bootstrapping tends to widen the distribution of t statistics. In our case, this eliminates much of the perceived statistical significance in the clustered standard error models by replacing t statistics with consistent ones.

Another potential method for alleviating this problem is to employ generalized estimating equations (GEE). GEE employ a flexible working variance-covariance matrix, and the error structure is defined as exchangeable, where the correlations for all pairs of observations within each cluster is constant, but independent across clusters. Observations essentially are weighted to give preference to independent observations. The imposition of a constant within-cluster correlation may still be too strict, however, which is one reason we report results from both the WCB and GEE. A brief introduction to GEE can be found in chapter 5 of this volume. The estimation problems discussed above suggest four correction procedures reported below: weighted least squares (WLS), WLS with clustered standard errors, WLS with clustered standard errors using the WCB technique, and GEE.

We also have two studies that account for most of the effect sizes in our sample. We test the robustness of our model with and without these studies. The largest single study, which examines the impact of No Child Left Behind (NCLB), has 337 unique effect sizes. This is a working paper that was subsequently published with additional unique effects (Dee and Jacob 2009; 2011). Together these two papers contain 568 effects sizes, or about 60 percent of our sample. Results of these robustness-check meta-regressions using the three specifications described above can be found in table 9.6. Parameter estimates between the original models and with the Dee and Jacob papers omitted are quite robust; none of the estimates change in sign or in magnitude by more than 25 percent. The largest single change comes in the unconditional mean (a model with only the constant) because the Dee and Jacob papers find a positive effect of NCLB. In that case, we observe a change in the coefficient from 0.054 to 0.035 (the same result as in the mean effect size, above), but neither coefficient is substantively large.

Finally, we examine six meta-regression models by including only indicator variables for policy area. Results for those models, both with and without the Dee and Jacob studies, are reported in table 9.7. We test this specification only to make the general argument that performance management varies by policy area. This result implies that the best specification is probably to stratify meta-regression by issue area, but we have too few studies in most issue areas to allow for stratification.

Independent Variables

We categorize our twelve right-hand-side (RHS) variables (plus the constant) into six broad categories. The first two categories describe the outcome measures in the original studies as part of our strategy to control for apples-to-oranges differences between policy areas. The first two *variables* control for the type of outcome variable as it would be defined in the PM literature; outcome measures and efficiency measures with the reference case being outputs. These two variables are also interesting in their own right; we hypothesize previously that these higher-quality measures of organizational performance will not be as strongly associated with organizational performance. Second, we include three binary variables: outcomes measured in dollars, GIS or information technology records,[8] and health outcomes with the reference case being standardized test scores in order to control for the inherent variability in the outcome measure.

Another category contains two variables that identify the genesis of performance management adoption. The first is adoption coming from elected political officials (with the reference case being public managers), and the second is whether the PM system is imposed from other officials or is developed internally.[9] We hypothesize above that adoption by managers ought to be correlated with improved effectiveness of PM systems.

We also code whether the PM system is adopted at the state or local level with the reference case being the national or federal level and whether the organization utilized benchmarking in its PM system. Also, to test for elements of gaming as identified in the economics literature, we include a variable that identifies whether the original authors identified that the outcome variable of interest may be susceptible to gaming behavior.

Finally we include two variables that are indicators of study quality. Again invoking the program evaluation literature, we code whether the original researchers used a pre-post quasi-experimental design with a comparison group. Since none of the studies we examined used experimental designs, the two-group quasi-experimental design was the strongest design we came across. All other research designs are the reference case. We also code whether the study was published in a peer-reviewed outlet. Table 9.4

TABLE 9.4. SUMMARY STATISTICS OF INDEPENDENT VARIABLES

Variable	Full Sample			Excluding Dee and Jacob (2009, 2011)		
	0	1	Total	0	1	Total
Outcome Type (Reference Case: Output Measure)						
Outcome Measure	120	836	956	120	268	388
Efficiency	919	37	956	351	37	388
Dependent Variable Characteristic (Reference: Test Scores)						
Dollars	779	177	956	211	177	388
Administrative Record (for example, GIS/IT report)	850	106	956	282	106	388
Health Outcomes	883	73	956	315	73	388
Breadth of PM Adoption (Reference: National)						
State and Local	848	108	956	280	108	388
Origin of PM Adoption						
Origin Is Political Actors: Yes = 1, No = 0	171	785	956	171	217	388
Nonrandom Selection, Imposed by Other Entity	103	853	956	103	285	388
Evidence of Use of Benchmarking						
Yes	230	726	956	230	158	388
Validity of Outcome Measure (Reference: Valid or No Indication)						
Not Valid Due to Gaming	901	55	956	333	55	388
Indicators of Quality						
Research Design: Two Group Quasi-Experimental with Pre-Post Observations	798	167	956	221	167	388
Peer Reviewed	360	596	956	129	259	388

shows the number of observations that are coded either 1 or 0 in the full sample and in the sample that excludes the Dee and Jacob papers (2009; 2011).

Results

Before analyzing the results of the meta-regressions, it is important to note that because all of the variables on the RHS are binary variables, there is a much greater chance of perfect multicollinearity during the wild cluster bootstrap resampling procedure. This problem is especially salient for this chapter compared to others in the volume as we have less intrastudy variation due to the diversity of issue areas and lack of a cohesive theoretical research base for performance management. Therefore instead of relying on intrastudy characteristics such as key control variables we often rely on characteristics that are constant within studies but vary across them. As a result, the WCB procedure has significantly widened the empirical t distribution, and only one variable remains statistically significant at the 10 percent level. The other estimation methods do supply statistically significant results, but with some assumptions of constant within-cluster correlation (or, in the case of random effect meta-regression independent observations), which may not be met. Therefore, we interpret the coefficients in the WCB model with some caution, relying on the signs and magnitude of coefficients as a reference. The GEE framework (model 5) largely mirrors the results from the model employing cluster robust standard errors (model 3); therefore we report statistical deviations between these two models and the WCB model. Table 9.5 displays the results of our meta-regression specifications.

First, the unconditional random effects meta-regression confirms the naïve mean effect size hypothesis test conducted above; use of performance management is associated with increases in organizational performance. However, the result of 0.054 is weak and not substantively different from zero. So our first hypothesis is confirmed only in part.

As predicted by our second hypothesis, higher-quality study dependent variables such as outcome measures or measures of efficiency are associated with significantly lower effect sizes than output measures that have a significantly larger average effect size. In our case, the more easily manipulable output measures are associated with larger effect sizes of organizational performance of 0.14 and 0.16 points than outcome of efficiency measures, respectively. This result is quite large given the mean effect size of 0.054. This finding (in the *outcome* indicator variable) is one of the few that remains robust in the WCB model. This result is likely explained by the fact that outcome or efficiency measures are harder to affect due to greater background variation or that they may be less susceptible to yet unidentified gaming behavior. Thus we find considerable support for our second hypothesis.

Our third hypothesis is that PM adoption by elected officials will be more negatively associated with organizational performance as compared to adoption by public managers. However, we find that adoption by elected officials is slightly positively associated with organizational performance

TABLE 9.5. META-REGRESSION OF THE IMPACT OF PERFORMANCE MANAGEMENT SYSTEMS ON ORGANIZATIONAL PERFORMANCE

	Expected Sign	Unconditional Meta-Regression (Model 1)	Random Effects Meta-Regression (Model 2)	Clustered Standard Errors (Model 3)	Wild Cluster Bootstrap (Model 4)	Generalized Estimating Equations (Model 5)
Constant	(+)	0.054***	0.157***	0.157**	0.157	0.136**
		(0.004)	(0.053)	(0.071)	(0.071)	(0.067)
Outcome Type (Reference case: Output Measure)						
Outcome Measure	(−)		−0.148***	−0.148***	−0.148*	−0.130***
			(0.028)	(0.039)		(0.035)
Efficiency	(−)		−0.160***	−0.160	−0.160	−0.127
			(0.046)	(0.101)		(0.099)
Dependent Variable Characteristic (Reference: Test Scores)						
Dollars	(+/−)		0.130***	0.130***	0.130	0.119**
			(0.031)	(0.048)		(0.046)
Administrative Record (for example, GIS/IT report)	(+/−)		−0.091*	−0.091	−0.091	−0.095
			(0.050)	(0.083)		(0.078)
Health Outcomes	(+/−)		−0.067	−0.067	−0.067	−0.063
			(0.041)	(0.083)		(0.077)
Breadth of PM Adoption (Reference: National)						
State and Local	(+)		0.067	0.067	0.067	0.074
			(0.061)	(0.093)		(0.088)

		(1)	(2)	(3)	(4)
Origin of PM Adoption					
Origin Is Political Actors: Yes = 1, No = 0	(−)	0.056**	0.056	0.056	0.070
		(0.028)	(0.054)		(0.051)
Nonrandom Selection, Imposed by Other Entity	(−)	−0.102***	−0.102***	−0.102	−0.110***
		(0.019)	(0.029)		(0.030)
Evidence of Use of Benchmarking					
Yes	(+)	0.091***	0.091***	0.091	0.086***
		(0.023)	(0.029)		(0.026)
Validity of Outcome Measure (Reference: Valid or No Indication)					
Not Valid Due to Gaming	(+)	−0.073***	−0.073*	−0.073	−0.067*
		(0.025)	(0.038)		(0.037)
Indicators of Quality					
Research Design: Two Group Quasi-Experimental with Pre-Post Observations	(+/−)	−0.087***	−0.087***	−0.087	−0.093***
		(0.020)	(0.033)		(0.033)
Peer Reviewed	(+/−)	0.027***	0.027**	0.027	0.043*
		(0.009)	(0.011)		(0.024)
Adjusted R^2		n.a.	0.120	n.a.	n.a.
N		956	956	956	956
F		n.a.	5.916	n.a.	n.a.

Note: *** $p < 0.01$, ** $p < 0.05$, * $p < 0.1$

but note that the interpretation of this effect is conditional on another variable, that performance management was not imposed on the organization. A model that included an interaction effect between the two variables (not shown due to collinearity with other results) demonstrates that the interaction effect of adoption imposed by elected public officials is negatively associated with organizational performance, a result that comports with ex ante expectations. In addition, imposing PM systems is negatively associated with organizational performance. Taken together (and interacted), these two variables lend support to the hypothesis that self-selection of PM by managers is more efficacious than imposition by elected officials. However, once again this support is tempered by wide confidence intervals in the WCB model.

Finally, we find little support for the fourth hypothesis. Origination of PM at the state and local levels is slightly more likely to be associated with successful PM implementation with an increase in mean effect sizes of about 0.07. This tentatively supports prior expectations from scholars that PM at the state and local levels ought to be more effective than at the federal level. However, this result is small in comparison to other estimates, and confidence intervals are large and contain zero in all of the models; thus we conclude that there is little support in our data for this hypothesis.

Counter to our expectations, when the authors who conducted the original studies used in our meta-analysis acknowledged that their results may be susceptible to gaming by public managers, the PM systems are *negatively* associated with organizational performance. We had expected that when agents use strategic behavior to secure performance bonuses there should be a strong and positive correlation between performance management and measured organizational performance, even if that performance is illusory. This result, however, has two limitations. First, we only coded studies in which the original authors discussed the possibility of gaming behavior; a number of studies did not consider gaming to be a potential problem even if it probably was, as Eterno and Silverman (2010) have argued about the Compstat program. We deferred to the judgment of the experts in their fields, though in this case that would result in too conservative results. Second, there is some collinearity between our coding of output measures versus outcome measures, as output measures are inherently easier to manipulate. As a result, we find little support in our data for the principle-agent hypothesis even if we suspect that it may exist.

To get an idea about the difference between the "best" and "worst" implementation of PM systems, we estimate mean effect sizes using best practices suggested by the literature to derive a response surface estimate

TABLE 9.6. META-REGRESSION RESULTS: ROBUSTNESS OF FINDINGS EXCLUDING DEE AND JACOB STUDIES (2009, 2011)

	Expected Sign	Unconditional Meta-Regression (Model 1)	Random Effects Meta-Regression (Model 2)	Clustered Standard Errors (Model 3)	Wild Cluster Bootstrap (Model 4)	Generalized Estimating Equations (Model 5)
Constant	(+)	0.039*** (0.007)	0.156** (0.063)	0.156** (0.068)	0.156	0.018 (0.095)
Outcome Type (Reference case: Output Measure)						
Outcome Measure	(−)		−0.145*** (0.029)	−0.145*** (0.038)	−0.145**	−0.058 (0.037)
Efficiency	(−)		−0.164*** (0.050)	−0.164 (0.105)	−0.164	0.035 (0.071)
Dependent Variable Characteristic (Reference: Test Scores)						
Dollars	(+/−)		0.122*** (0.035)	0.122** (0.048)	0.122	0.095** (0.047)
Administrative Record (for example, GIS/IT report)	(+/−)		−0.091* (0.052)	−0.091 (0.081)	−0.091	−0.078 (0.066)
Health Outcomes	(+/−)		−0.080* (0.047)	−0.080 (0.070)	−0.080	−0.027 (0.066)
Breadth of PM Adoption (Reference: National)						
State and Local	(+)		0.057 (0.065)	0.057 (0.086)	0.057	0.117 (0.076)

TABLE 9.6. (Continued)

	Expected Sign	Unconditional Meta-Regression (Model 1)	Random Effects Meta-Regression (Model 2)	Clustered Standard Errors (Model 3)	Wild Cluster Bootstrap (Model 4)	Generalized Estimating Equations (Model 5)
Origin of PM Adoption						
Origin Is Political Actors: Yes = 1, No = 0	(−)		0.058** (0.029)	0.058 (0.050)	0.058	0.105** (0.049)
Nonrandom Selection, Imposed by Other Entity	(−)		−0.098*** (0.020)	−0.098*** (0.029)	−0.098	−0.141*** (0.033)
Evidence of Use of Benchmarking						
Yes	(+)		0.093*** (0.023)	0.093*** (0.028)	0.093	0.065** (0.033)
Validity of Outcome Measure (Reference: Valid or no indication)						
Not Valid Due to Gaming	(+)		−0.081*** (0.026)	−0.081** (0.040)	−0.081	−0.046 (0.028)
Indicators of Quality						
Research Design: two Group Quasi-Experimental with Pre-Post Observations	(+/−)		−0.094*** (0.022)	−0.094** (0.040)	−0.094	−0.066** (0.031)
Peer Reviewed	(+/−)		0.040*** (0.015)	0.040 (0.030)	0.040	0.086* (0.047)
Adjusted R^2		n.a.	n.a.	0.218	n.a.	n.a.
N		388	388	388	388	388
F		n.a.	10.003	5.462	n.a.	n.a.

Note: *** $p < 0.01$, ** $p < 0.05$, * $p < 0.1$

TABLE 9.7. META-REGRESSION EXAMINING DIFFERENCES BY POLICY AREA

Policy Area	Full Sample				Excludes Dee and Jacob (2009, 2011)			
	Random Effects	CRVE	WCB	GEE	Random Effects	CRVE	WCB	GEE
Education	.060***	.060***	.060*	.065***	.075**	.075***	.075	.080***
	(.011)	(.009)		(.009)	(.030)	(.007)		(.006)
Crime and Policing	−.007	−.007	−.007	−.007	−.007	−.007	−.007	−.007
	(.015)	(.025)		(.026)	(.016)	(.024)		(.032)
Public Health	.079***	.079*	.079	.078*	.078***	.078*	.078	.067*
	(.015)	(.042)		(.041)	(.015)	(.042)		(.035)
Child Support Enforcement	.277***	.277***	.277	.278***	.276***	.276***	.276	.281***
	(.043)	(.007)		(.007)	(.045)	(.007)		(.006)
Other	.362***	.362***	.362	.363***	.362***	.362***	.362	.366***
	(.062)	(.007)		(.007)	(.065)	(.007)		(.006)
Job Training	.008	.008	.008	.007	.009	.009	.009	.004
	(.009)	(.007)		(.007)	(.009)	(.007)		(.006)
Adj. R^2	.183	.104	n.a.	n.a.	n.a.	.188	n.a.	n.a.
N	956	956	956	956	388	388	388	388
F	23.17	n.a.	n.a.	n.a.	18.90	n.a.	n.a.	n.a.

Notes: *** $p < 0.01$, ** $p < 0.05$, * $p < 0.1$

CRVE = clustered robust variance estimator

WCB = wild cluster bootstrap

GEE = generalized estimating equations

of the best case PM scenario using the estimates from the WCB model. Best practices suggest using outcome measures rather than output variables, using benchmarking, and adopting performance management through self-selection by public managers. The literature also suggests that PM is more successful at the state and local levels, but that is not a variable that managers can manipulate. Our meta-regression of PM systems predicts that best practice approaches result in an effect-size point estimate of 0.080 for Fisher's Z, our *r*-based measure of association. In contrast, a worst practices approach predicts an association between PM systems and organizational performance of 0.043. This difference reflects (1) that the difference between best practices and worst practices is not substantive, and (2) the confidence intervals (not reported) are wide and insignificant, suggesting that the difference may be trivial. Similarly, estimating best and worst practices at the local level generates estimates of 0.147 and 0.110, respectively. Once again, neither result is statistically different, although a best practices approach at the local level approaches what would be considered weak positive correlation (+0.2).

Results reported in table 9.5 also confirm what we report in the forest plots; the effect of performance management varies by issue area. It is difficult to ascertain why these policy areas differ without stratified meta-regressions. However, in most issue areas, we have too few studies to run stratified meta-regressions with standard errors clustered by study. An exception to this is the eight studies using Compstat or Compstat-like programs. This stratified meta-regression is discussed further in the chapter Addendum.[10]

Conclusion

Significance of Findings

In general, we find tentative support for all of our hypotheses. We find that performance management is statistically associated with improved organizational performance but that improvement is very slight, 0.039 to 0.054 depending on the sample, which falls below typical rules of weak association. The only result we find to be both substantively and statistically significant in the WCB model is that outcome measures are negatively associated with the effectiveness of PM systems. We conclude that using high-quality measures of performance is a necessary condition to further the organization's mission and avoid gaming behavior. In contrast, in our models employing cluster robust standard errors, we find statistically significant results in most of our hypotheses, though parameters remain unchanged from WCB. Finally, our models suggest that best practices of performance management at the state and local levels show the most potential for gains in organizational performance attributable to PM systems. We believe that scholars should continue to explore ways to improve and measure improvement in this area.

These results, along with the other results of the model suggest that the PM systems that have been examined thus far are not systematically effective at improving organizational performance. Even using best practices as identified by the literature only modestly improves the estimated effectiveness of PM systems. The evidence supplied in this chapter suggests that performance management has not been particularly successful at improving performance in public organizations.

Areas for Future Research

Our meta-analysis of the scholarly literature of performance management has allowed us to reflect on the content and direction of the PM literature. We arrive at four general conclusions about the current state of the research and observations about the direction of future research.

First, we note that much of the research in performance management is quite recent; over half of the studies used in this meta-analysis have been published in the past five years. This optimistically suggests that the body of empirical literature is growing rapidly. We are able to suggest some fruitful areas for which PM is purportedly in use but for which we uncovered no empirical research. These areas include poverty and social welfare programs (such as nutrition assistance, welfare-to-work programs, and low-income housing), transportation and infrastructure funding, and performance-based budgeting. We found only three examples in the field of education, which was surprising given its recent prominence with NCLB. Taken together with the fact that our research suggests (in table 9.5) that the effectiveness of performance management and organizational performance varies by policy area, we believe it is important that performance management be studied in areas where it is in use.

Second, we note that very few researchers consider the impact of PM on organizational *efficiency*. That is, few studies include a model employing a measure of impacts over inputs as their dependent variable; only two studies in our meta-analysis examined efficiency and in only a handful of models. Performance management, of course, is not a costless exercise. So while it is important that PM improve performance, it is just as important that PM systems improve efficiency; higher performance at an even higher cost may result in a net loss. We hope that future researchers consider efficiency measures for at least some of their measures of organizational performance.

One of the great advantages of meta-analytic techniques is that we were able to take variation between studies to try to open the "black box" and understand the process of improving organizational performance. However, we were somewhat stymied in this effort by fuzzy descriptions of how some PM systems were supposed to have worked in practice. We hope that future authors who write explicitly in the area of performance management consider variations in implementation as leverage for uncovering why PM systems in some areas are more effective than in others. For example, Heinrich (2002) uses a hierarchical model to examine whether management practices at different service-delivery areas altered the effectiveness of job training programs. This type of research will help to solidify the best practices literature and will be a benefit to agencies who have already adopted performance management.

Finally, it would be beneficial to authors who examine PM systems to be aware of gaming behaviors resulting from measuring and rewarding performance. We hope that more authors use methods such as the general gaming test suggested by Courty and Marschke (2008), or a test similar to the one employed by Hanushek and Raymond (2005) who examine whether special education placements increased after state school accountability programs were adopted. These checks provide greater assurance that we are measuring real performance improvements, not illusory gains through gaming behavior.

Notes

1. This search was conducted on October 13, 2011.
2. As noted earlier, the analysis is restricted to studies that included more than just pay-for-performance, for which a meta-analysis already exists (Weibel, Rost, and Osterloh 2010) and performance-based contracting, which involves only one characteristic of performance management. These limitations may have excluded some studies from the fields listed.
3. Cohen's kappa is a measure of intercoder reliability that adjusts the probability using an expectation of agreement from a random draw.
4. N of 1,120 is derived from a total of 112 effect sizes for which we measured 10 characteristics.
5. This study was a working paper for a paper that eventually was published and contains 231 additional effect sizes (Dee and Jacob 2009; 2011). These two studies contain 60 percent of all effect sizes used in our analysis and as discussed further on, we run all meta-regression without them for robustness. The results are substantively the same as shown in table 9.6.
6. The chi-squared test is actually on a related statistic, the Q statistic. However, the Q statistic is directly related to I^2.
7. *Naïve* in this context means that it ignores problems of non-independence of observations as well as any conditional expectations (regression parameters).
8. GIS/IT measures are overwhelmingly from Compstat programs—they track crime over time in specific geographic areas.
9. These two variables have significant overlap, with 90 percent of observations in agreement. We also test a model with these two origin terms interacted. A discussion of those results can be found further on.
10. Job training programs have enough studies, but too little variation between studies, as most of the studies use the JTPA data set.

Studies Coded for Meta-Analysis

Baier, R. R., K. Butterfield, S. Gravenstein, and Y. Harris. "Aiming for Star Performance: The Relationship Between Setting Targets and Improved Nursing Home Quality of Care." *Journal of the American Medical Directors Association* 9, no. 8 (2008): 594–598.

Barnow, Burt S. "Exploring the Relationship Between Performance Management and Program Impact: A Case Study of the Job Training Partnership Act." *Journal of Policy Analysis and Management* 19, no. 1 (2000): 118–141.

Bundorf, M. Kate, Kavita Choudhry, and Laurence Baker. "Health Plan Performance Measurement: Does It Affect Quality of Care for Medicare Managed Care Enrollees?" *Inquiry* 45, no. 2 (2008): 168–183.

Chilvers, M., and D. Weatherburn. "Do Targeted Arrests Reduce Crime?" *Contemporary Issues in Crime and Justice* 63 (2001): 1–15.

Chilvers, M., and D. Weatherburn. "The New South Wales 'Compstat' Process: Its Impact on Crime." *The Australian & New Zealand Journal of Criminology* 37 (2004): 22–48.

Courty, P., and G. Marschke. "A General Test for Distortions in Performance Measures." *The Review of Economics and Statistics* 90, no. 3 (2008): 428–441.

Cragg, Michael. "Performance Incentives in the Public Sector: Evidence from the Job Training Partnership Act." *Journal of Law, Economics, & Organization* 13, no. 1 (1997): 147–168.

Dee, Thomas, and Brian Jacob. *The Impact of No Child Left Behind on Student Achievement.* National Bureau of Economic Research Working Paper Series No. 15531, 2009.

Dee, Thomas, and Brian Jacob. "The Impact of No Child Left Behind on Student Achievement." *Journal of Policy Analysis and Management* 30, no. 3 (2011): 418–446.

Dickinson, Katherine, and others. *Evaluation of the Effects of JTPA Performance Standards on Clients, Services, and Costs: Final Report.* National Commission for Employment Policy Research Report no. 88–16 (2011).

Garicano, L., and P. Heaton. "Information Technology, Organization, and Productivity in the Public Sector: Evidence from Police Departments." *Journal of Labor Economics* 28, no. 1 (2010): 167–201.

Grossbart, Stephen. "What's the Return? Assessing the Effect of Pay-for-Performance: Initiatives on the Quality of Care Delivery." *Medical Care Research and Review* 63, Supplement (2006).

Hanushek, E. A., and M. E. Raymond. "Does School Accountability Lead to Improved Student Performance?" *Journal of Policy Analysis and Management* 24, no. 2 (2005): 297–327.

Heckman, James J., Carolyn Heinrich, and Jeffrey Smith. "The Performance of Performance Standards." *The Journal of Human Resources* 37, no. 4 (2002): 778–811.

Heinrich, Carolyn J. "Outcomes-Based Performance Management in the Public Sector: Implications for Government Accountability and Effectiveness." *Public Administration Review* 62, no. 6 (2002): 712–725.

Heinrich, Carolyn J., and Laurence E. Lynn. "Means and Ends: A Comparative Study of Empirical Methods for Investigating Governance and Performance." *Journal of Public Administration Research and Theory* 11, no. 1 (2001): 109–138.

Horton, James. "An Examination of the Applicability of the Citistat Performance Management System to Municipal Fire Departments." Thesis, School of Public Affairs, Urban University of Texas at Arlington, 2010.

Huang, Chien-Chung, and Richard L. Edwards. "The Relationship Between State Efforts and Child Support Performance." *Children and Youth Services Review* 31, no. 2 (2009): 243–248.

Jang, H., L. T. Hoover, and H. J. Joo. "An Evaluation of Compstat's Effect on Crime: The Fort Worth Experience." *Police Quarterly* 13, no. 4 (2010): 387–412.

Lied, T. R., and S. Sheingold. "HEDIS Performance Trends in Medicare Managed Care." *Health Care Financing Review* 23, no. 1 (2001): 149–160.

Lynn, J., and others. "Collaborative Clinical Quality Improvement for Pressure Ulcers in Nursing Homes." *Journal of the American Geriatrics Society* 55, no. 10 (2007): 1663–1669.

Mazerolle, Lorraine, James McBroom, and Sacha Rombouts. "Compstat in Australia: An Analysis of the Spatial and Temporal Impact." *Journal of Criminal Justice* 39, no. 2 (2011): 128–136.

Mazerolle, Lorraine, Sacha Rombouts, and James McBroom. The Impact of Operational Performance Reviews on Reported Crime in Queensland. Canberra: Australian Institute of Criminology, 2006.

Mazerolle, Lorraine, Sacha Rombouts, and James McBroom. "The Impact of Compstat on Reported Crime in Queensland." *Policing* 30, no. 2 (2007): 237–256.

Rosenfeld, Richard, Robert Fornango, and Eric Baumer. "Did Ceasefire, Compstat, and Exile Reduce Homicide?" *Criminology & Public Policy* 4, no. 3 (2005): 419–449.

Schochet, P. Z., and J. A. Burghardt. "Do Job Corps Performance Measures Track Program Impacts?" *Journal of Policy Analysis and Management* 27, no. 3 (2008): 556–576.

Thibodeau, Nicole, John H. Evans III, Nandu J. Nagarajan, and Jeff Whittle. "Value Creation in Public Enterprises: An Empirical Analysis of Coordinated Organizational Changes in the Veterans Health Administration." *Accounting Review* 82, no. 2 (2007): 483–520.

Walker, Richard M., Fariborz Damanpour, and Carlos A. Devece. "Management Innovation and Organizational Performance: The Mediating Effect of Performance Management." *Journal of Public Administration Research & Theory* 21, no. 2 (2011): 367–386.

Wilborn, D., U. Grittner, T. Dassen, and J. Kottner. "The National Expert Standard Pressure Ulcer Prevention in Nursing and Pressure Ulcer Prevalence in German Health Care Facilities: A Multilevel Analysis." *Journal of Clinical Nursing* 19, nos. 23–24 (2010): 3364–3371.

Zornitsky, Jeffrey, and Mary Rubin. *Establishing a Performance Management System for Targeted Welfare Programs*. National Commission for Employment Policy Research, 1988.

Addendum: Stratified Meta-Regression of Compstat and Compstat-Like Programs

This addendum presents a stratified meta-regression using the eight studies that examined the impact of the Compstat policing strategy program and programs which are largely similar to the Compstat program implemented outside of New York City. See our brief description earlier for more information on how Compstat works and its organizing principles.

Scholars have pointed out that police chiefs and elected officials quickly claimed credit for the drop in crime starting in the mid-1990s, which (they argue) followed the implementation of the Compstat policing strategy (Smith and Bratton 2001). As Rosenfeld and colleagues ask, "How could they resist" attributing the drop in crime to their new policing strategy? (Rosenfeld, Fornango, and Baumer 2005). In the intervening years, rival explanations for the drop in crime emerged, including reductions of lead in water, as lead is linked to violent behavior (Reyes 2007); psycho-pharmaceutical drugs and mental health treatment (Marcotte and Markowitz 2011); and the legalization of abortion, which created a decrease in youth at risk of criminal activity (Donohue and Levitt 2001).

In our search process we found eight quantitative studies examining the impact of Compstat (and Compstat-like programs) on crime. There were a handful of other studies that examined the impact of measured arrests for minor crimes (a key element of the broken windows philosophy) on major crimes. However, we were unable to use these studies in our meta-analysis because researchers did not report the increase in minor crime arrests after the Compstat program began. As a result, we rely largely on indicator variables of Compstat implementation in interrupted time series designs or interrupted time series with comparison groups.

Our meta-regressions of Compstat include only six independent variables (including the constant) because clustered standard errors require that the number of regressors not exceed the number of groups (in this case, studies). The independent variables include the type of dependent variable: outcome measures with output measures as a reference group. Second, we include the country of study origin. There are two countries where our studies originate: the United States and Australia. Implementation of Compstat originated in the United States in the early 1990s at about the same time as a decrease in crime occurred. In Australia, Compstat-like programs started in the early 2000s, almost a decade later and against a different environment in crime trends (Chilvers and Weatherburn 2004; Mazerolle, McBroom, and Rombouts 2011). If U.S. implementation of Compstat simply coincided with larger trends, we would hypothesize that Australia's experience with Compstat-like programs would be less encouraging than that in the United States.

Another moderating variable is whether the dependent variable is a measure of violent crime. One of the defining elements of Compstat-like programs is that by preventing minor crimes, property crimes other then violent crimes will also be reduced. We would expect the sign of the coefficient to be negative as the reference case is nonviolent crime, indicating that there ought to be less reduction in violent crimes than property (and other nonviolent) crimes. We also examine whether the origin of Compstat is with the top-level managers rather than elected officials or the legislature, and hypothesize that greater autonomy and self-selection would beget more effective implementation. Finally we include a control variable that indicates whether the original authors employed an interaction term in the

TABLE 9.8. META-REGRESSIONS OF PERFORMANCE MANAGEMENT SYSTEMS IN COMPSTAT AND COMPSTAT-LIKE PROGRAMS

	Unconditional Meta-Regression (Model 1)	Random Effects Meta-Regression (Model 2)	Clustered Standard Errors (Model 3)	Wild Cluster Bootstrap (Model 4)	Generalized Estimating Equations (Model 5)
Dependent Variable Is Outcome Measure		−0.000 (0.058)	−0.000 (0.023)	−0.000	0.023 (0.015)
Compstat-Like Programs in Australia		−0.128** (0.052)	−0.128** (0.064)	−0.128	−0.118** (0.059)
Origin Is Public Managers		0.079 (0.060)	0.079 (0.054)	0.079	0.044 (0.049)
Dependent Variable Is Violent		−0.027 (0.022)	−0.027* (0.014)	−0.027	−0.026* (0.014)
Interaction Effect in Original Model		−0.053*** (0.018)	−0.053* (0.030)	−0.053	−0.038** (0.016)
Constant	0.005 (0.012)	0.063 (0.046)	0.063*** (0.012)	0.063	0.051*** (0.007)
Adjusted R^2	n.a.	0.136	0.165	n.a.	n.a.
Number of Observations	80	80	80	80	80
F	n.a.	4.303	n.a.	n.a.	n.a.

Note: *** $p < 0.01$, ** $p < 0.05$, * $p < 0.1$

original study. Interaction terms in the original models would change the interpretation of the base effectiveness of Compstat-like programs.

Table 9.8 displays the results of the meta-regression of Compstat programs. Models 1 and 2 are random effects meta-regressions. Model 1 is an unconditional model containing only the constant and is the mean effect size. The results show that Compstat and Compstat-like programs are not associated with improvements in measures of crime or crime clearance (the two dependent variables in the studies examined) when we do not consider any other factors. This effect, .005, is very close to zero and is neither substantively nor statistically significant.

Models 2 through 5 present conditional models. Model 2 uses standard meta-regression, which relies on the false assumption that observations are independent as effect sizes within studies are likely to be correlated. Model 3 uses standard errors clustered by study, which, as reported in the main text, has a problem in that clustered standard errors tend to reject the null hypothesis far too often when the number of groups is small and group size varies. Here we have only eight groups with widely divergent effect sizes nested within studies. As a result, we use wild cluster bootstrapped t statistics to empirically derive a distribution of t statistics. As with the main results of this chapter, wild cluster bootstrapping demonstrates that the clustered standard errors were far too small; none of the coefficients estimated are significant at the alpha 10 percent level, which is indicated by the absence of stars in model 4. Model 5 is the GEE estimates which again roughly track model 3, cluster robust errors.

There are a few surprising results in models 2 thru 5 given the signs and magnitude of the coefficients alone. First, as expected, Compstat programs in Australia seem to be less effective than in the United States, likely because they missed the wave of crime reduction that U.S. Compstat programs may have accidentally caught. This is a rather large effect compared to the other effects and the unconditional mean in model 1. Second, also as expected, violent crime showed a modestly lower impact than measures of nonviolent crimes. Third, public managers initiating the Compstat program are also modestly associated with more effective programs; self-selection seems to be correlated with improved results in this instance. Finally, whether the reported measure was a crime rate or a crime clearance rate is not associated with any change in the r-based effect size. These results suggest that, while we cannot say why crime has declined in recent years, this meta-analysis of the Compstat literature provides additional evidence to support the notion that it was not the adoption of Compstat or Compstat-like programs. These conclusions should be interpreted cautiously, however, as they are derived from findings that are robust to the empirically estimated confidence intervals derived from the WCB model.

Ed Gerrish is a doctoral student in public affairs at Indiana University's School of Public Environmental Affairs.

Po-Ju Wu is a doctoral student in inquiry methodology at Indiana University's School of Education.

CHAPTER TEN

THE EFFECTS OF FEDERAL POVERTY DECONCENTRATION EFFORTS ON ECONOMIC SELF-SUFFICIENCY AND PROBLEMATIC BEHAVIORS

Joe Bolinger and Lanlan Xu

"The concentration of affordable rental housing in pockets of poverty isolates residences from social and economic opportunities. A growing body of social science research indicates that living in a distressed, high-poverty neighborhood undermines the long-term life chances of families and children. By helping families relocate from high-poverty to low-poverty neighborhoods, the housing voucher program has the potential to lead to significant improvements in families' well-being and long-term life chances"

(KATZ AND TURNER 2008, 330).

"Policies that relocate the poor outside of high-poverty neighborhoods usually fail to improve their economic situation or health and often disrupt their social support system, creating new difficulties to overcome. It is difficult to know whether to blame the failure on the policy's implementation, its translation from social science diagnosis to policy, its underlying theory, or the political dynamics of recent years"

(GOETZ AND CHAPPLE 2010, 229).

In recent decades, U.S. housing policy has been moving away from government-owned-and-operated public housing projects and toward policy instruments that encourage recipients to live in mixed-income communities. This approach was motivated in part by a widely held belief among policy makers and the public that large-scale public housing developments, particularly high-rise projects, harmed residents' life chances by exposing them to high *concentrations* of poverty in their neighborhoods. Federal housing policy began to shift toward the use of vouchers and mixed-income developments to help ensure that recipients of housing subsidies could live in neighborhoods with lower concentrations of poverty. The most powerful image of this new approach is the demolition of stark and dilapidated high-rise public housing projects in crime-ridden neighborhoods. Social experiments such as Gautreaux and Moving to Opportunity, and public housing programs such as the Housing Choice Voucher Program (aka Section 8) and Hope VI mixed-income housing developments, have been greeted with enthusiasm from the general public and academics alike. All of these programs have been motivated at least in part by the goal of spatially deconcentrating inner-city, assisted housing tenants, integrating those tenants into suburban, middle-class communities, and enabling them to exercise more choice in their housing decisions.

After almost two decades of the most ambitious urban redevelopment efforts in the nation's history, Congress, HUD, housing groups, local elected officials, resident advocates, the media, and policy analysts are asking challenging questions about what these investments have accomplished, and about what unintended consequences these housing policies might be producing. Are these policies really producing the improvements in individual tenants' lives that their supporters predicted? This chapter uses meta-analysis to synthesize the findings of the literature so far and shed light on important housing policy questions.

History of Poverty Deconcentration Programs in the United States

From the Housing Act of 1937 until the mid-1970s, the federal government's main form of low-income rental assistance was the funding of government-owned-and-operated housing units, usually referred to by the term *public housing*. Public housing projects are only available to low-income residents, so by definition, they lead to geographic concentrations of low-income persons. Good-faith efforts over the years to reserve public housing for only the most impoverished populations ended up exacerbating this concentration. The tendency of public housing to concentrate poverty was especially true for very large public housing projects, which often constitute a large percentage of a neighborhood's population.

Concerns about the role of public housing in concentrating poverty have led to a variety of efforts by the U.S. Department of Housing and Urban Development (HUD) to geographically disperse the recipients of housing subsidies. Section 8 of the United States Housing Act of 1937 (commonly referred to as Section 8) was amended in 1974 to authorize the payment of rental housing assistance to private landlords on behalf of low-income households. Although not a major component of the initial motivation for the policy, over time, policy makers have come to see the Section 8 family of programs as a useful tool in the battle to deconcentrate poverty. By allowing recipients of housing subsidies to find private rental housing, Section 8 offers poor families the chance to move into less poor neighborhoods. It has now exceeded the public housing program in size and has become the largest public housing program in the United States. Currently, the largest Section 8 program is the "tenant-based" voucher program, under which recipients are free to live anywhere, as long as landlords are willing to accept the voucher and meet HUD's basic qualifications. In the somewhat smaller "project-based" Section 8 program, the voucher is limited to a specific site, where the owner reserves some or all of the units for low-income tenants. In both programs, the federal government pays the difference between the tenant's contribution (30 percent of their monthly income) and the rent specified in the owner's contract with the government.

In addition to these programs, there have been two large housing experiments conducted in U.S. cities to address poverty concentration. These two experiments, Moving to Opportunity and Gautreaux, both placed participants in low-poverty neighborhoods and required them to stay for at least one year. In 1976, a court order required the Chicago Housing Authority to desegregate its public housing. Their response, called the Gautreaux program, placed participants in low-poverty, racially integrated neighborhoods, accompanied by fairly intensive housing counseling services. Because the Gautreaux program appeared to show positive impacts, HUD authorized a much larger five-city study called Moving to Opportunity (MTO) in the early 1990s. Unlike Gautreaux, which placed residents in economically *and* racially integrated neighborhoods, MTO only required residents to live in non-poor neighborhoods. The MTO experiment has now had three waves of follow-up and has been subject to a wide variety of ex-post analyses by a number of research teams across the country.

HUD's latest policy initiative to deconcentrate poverty is called HOPE VI (Housing Opportunities for People Everywhere). HOPE VI is a major HUD plan to revitalize the worst public housing projects into mixed-income multifamily dwellings. The public housing units in the nation's largest cities have long been seen as substandard and even dangerous living environments. This was particularly true of the high-rise public housing projects that emerged in large cities such as Chicago and New York. Many critics argued that these living environments were detrimental to those trapped within them, and the concentrated poverty and crime were seen as having negative effects on both the public housing tenants and the surrounding communities. The HOPE VI program began in 1992 and includes a variety of grant programs including Revitalization, Demolition, and the Main Street grant programs. Over the course of fifteen years HOPE VI grants were used to demolish 96,200 public housing units and produce 107,800 new or renovated public housing units, of which 56,800 were to be affordable to the lowest-income households (U.S. Department of Housing and Urban Development 2010). Residents who were not rehoused in these mixed-income developments were granted Section 8 vouchers to use in the private rental market.

Racial segregation has been a delicate but important undercurrent in U.S. housing subsidies since their inception. While the Gautreaux program is the only one of these poverty dispersal programs that explicitly focuses on racial integration, race is an important undercurrent in the others as well. Race has long been a major factor in the geographical dispersion of poverty in U.S. cities and in the development of federal low-income housing policy, particularly in the site selection of public housing projects (Hirsch 1983; Massey and Denton 1993; Dreier, Mollenkopf, and Swanstrom 2004). Many scholars have argued that the negative effects of concentrated poverty interact particularly perniciously with high levels of racial segregation in U.S. cities (Wilson 1987; Massey and Denton 1993). Race may be contributing to the these negative effects in a number of ways, such as increased likelihood of discrimination on the part of potential employers, lack of access to levers of political power, increased likelihood of bureaucratic neglect, and the development of "oppositional" cultural characteristics as a result of experiencing sustained, hostile discrimination by whites (Massey and Denton 1993; Wilson 1996; Anderson 1999). In short, the impact of living in concentrated poverty may be worse for racial minorities living in racially segregated neighborhoods. While race is not used as an explicit criterion for participation in any program besides Gautreaux, policy makers can address racial segregation by default through poverty deconcentration policies, since public housing projects are populated by a disproportionate share of racial minorities. Explicit discussions of racial integration may have been too politically sensitive to commit to paper, but it is likely that they played a role in motivating this suite of poverty dispersal policies.

These policies in recent years have all attempted to deconcentrate poverty and promote mixed-income or more racially integrated neighborhoods. Whether or not they have succeeded in their goal of deconcentrating poverty, and whether, if so, that deconcentration has actually improved the life outcomes of those receiving public housing subsidies, is an empirical question on which there appears to be little consensus in the scholarly community. Although there is an extensive literature on different kinds of housing dispersal programs, the findings are often inconsistent and contradictory. By synthesizing the literature using meta-analysis, we might help answer these questions about neighborhood effects and provide guidance for future policy innovations.

Theoretical Foundations of Poverty Deconcentration Policies

Poverty deconcentration policies are based in part on a body of scholarly research that links life outcomes to the characteristics of an individual's neighborhood of residence. This work often goes by the shorthand term of "neighborhood effects." The research on neighborhood effects has been a vital area of social science research across a variety of disciplines because it touches on a question that is central to scholars of many stripes.

Scholars have long sought to explain the mechanisms underlying the reproduction of social class across generations. Though not mutually exclusive, explanations have divided into several camps, broadly speaking: structural explanations, cultural and familial background explanations, and human or social capital explanations (Corcoran 1995; Wilson 2010). In each of these families of theories (described further on), a person's neighborhood of residence may play an important role in transferring poverty and its consequences across generations.

One of the key variables in the neighborhood effects literature is the degree of poverty concentration that residents face. In 2000, 3.5 million poor people across the United States lived in neighborhoods with poverty rates in excess of 40 percent (Jargowsky 2003). Because poor families tend to be grouped together in poor neighborhoods in cities rather than spread out, scholars have wondered, Do living and growing up in a poor *neighborhood* make it even harder for a person to escape poverty than it would be from simply being poor? A growing social science literature suggests that poverty *concentration* has a variety of detrimental effects on the residents of these areas, in terms of both their current well-being and their future opportunities (Wilson 1987, 1996; Jencks and Mayer 1990; Brooks-Gunn, Duncan, Klebanov, and Sealand 1993). Extremely poor neighborhoods are often home to higher crime rates, higher rates of juvenile delinquency, underperforming public schools, poor housing and health conditions, limited access to public services, and limited access to job opportunities (Kneebone, Berube, and Brookings Institution 2008). These conditions are thought to build on each other such that the neighborhood problems are greater than simply the sum total of the constituent residents' problems. For instance, if large numbers of poor people cluster together, perhaps fewer businesses will locate in that area, leading to fewer jobs available to residents, whereas if the same number of poor people were dispersed across middle-class neighborhoods, they would enjoy closer physical proximity to available jobs. The deleterious effects of high-poverty areas are thought to be especially severe for children, whose behavior and prospects may be particularly susceptible to neighborhood impacts. Children raised in poor, disadvantaged neighborhoods are at greater risk for developing anti-social behaviors (Catalano and Hawkins 1996). Disorganized neighborhoods may have weak social control networks that allow criminal activities to go unmonitored and unnoticed (Sampson and Lauritsen 1994). Numerous studies have identified links between deviant peer group influences and adolescents' test scores (Darling and Steinberg 1997) and mental health (Simon et al, 1996), as well as antisocial behavior and substance abuse (Case and Katz, 1991; Dubow, Edwards, and Ippolito 1997; Gonzales, Cauce, and Mason 1996).

For the neighborhood effects literature to be of any interest, one must first establish that poverty is indeed "transferred" across generations. Evidence does suggest the presence of substantial reproduction of social class over time in the United States. Despite early research that found a relatively high degree of economic mobility across generations (Blau and Duncan 1967; Becker and Tomes 1986), in recent years, scholars using new data have found a relatively low degree of mobility in the United States compared to other industrialized countries (Solon 1999; Mazumder 2005), and that the level of mobility has declined over time. One method of measuring economic mobility across generations is to look for simple correlations of parental incomes to their children's adult incomes. Recent estimates of income elasticity across generations range between .4 and .6, as opposed to early findings of .2, suggesting that parental income is more strongly predictive of children's future income today than in the past. Most notably, mobility of families starting near the bottom of the income distribution has worsened over time (Bradbury and Katz, 2009). Being a child of poor parents is associated with worse adult life outcomes, on average, than one would predict if ability were randomly distributed and opportunity were evenly distributed across the population. While these studies focus on the population as a whole, others that focus on poor children specifically find considerable evidence that growing up poor reduces a person's future income (Corcoran 1995). The possibility of upward mobility is also divided along racial lines. Bradbury and Katz (2009), for example, find that the mobility of black families is markedly lower than that of white families, both on average and conditional on starting out poor or near the bottom of the income distribution. In 2008, the poverty rate for African Americans was 25 percent and for Latinos it was 24 percent, compared to 11 percent for whites (DeNavas-Walt, Proctor, and Smith 2008). In 2004, the incarceration rate for African American males was about 14 percent, compared to 2 percent for white males. These figures are even more stark for high school dropout rates: blacks and whites at 34 percent and 7 percent, respectively (Western and Wildeman 2009). Over their lifetimes, 27 percent of black men born between 1975 and 1979 will spend at least some time in federal prisons, compared to 5 percent for whites (Western and Pettit 2010).

Structural theories of poverty transfer focus on exogenous factors, such as changes in the economy and the impact of racial discrimination, as being most explanatory of poverty transfer. Under this structural approach, a person's neighborhood of residence is enormously important for understanding his or her life outcomes, because it determines what sorts of jobs, social networks, and services that person can access physically. W. J. Wilson's work (1987; 1996) has focused on structural changes in the economies of central cities, with high-quality manufacturing jobs, stores and banks, and middle-class residents fleeing to suburbs, leaving behind a core of poor and minority individuals who lack physical access to high-quality jobs for people with low skill levels and who lack the social connections with affluent people that may help them secure a job in the first place. This concept that the jobs and the people who need them are in different physical locations has been called "spatial mismatch." Wilson (1987), Jargowsky and Bane (1991), and Danziger and Gottschalk (1987) documented large and growing spatial concentrations of poverty in American cities and pointed out that concentrated poverty has strong racial overtones. Poor people of color are many times more likely to live in concentrated poverty than are their white counterparts. Massey and Denton (1993) have further augmented this spatial mismatch explanation by describing how racial discrimination in real estate practices, housing policies, and zoning laws have exacerbated patterns of racial segregation in urban neighborhoods. Partially, this process of low-income and racial concentration was furthered by the intentional and discriminatory location of large-scale public housing projects in poor, minority neighborhoods (Hirsch 1983).

Cultural theories of poverty posit that poverty transfer is driven by the beliefs, values, behaviors, frames, social skills, and other components of culture that are transmitted across generations by families and communities. The connection to the neighborhood effects debate is the idea that communities, not simply families, are important for transferring culture across generations. Oscar Lewis's (1966) concept of a "culture of poverty," for instance, argued that poor communities across the world were characterized by similar sets of values, such as an emphasis on machismo, a "present time orientation," and anti-intellectualism. While Lewis traced the development of these cultural characteristics to macro-economic conditions, his overall approach of examining the role of culture in transferring poverty across generations fell out of favor with the scholarly community. These types of theories were eschewed by many U.S. sociologists and anti-poverty scholars for some time for (perhaps unfairly) ignoring the role of social and economic structures in perpetuating class divisions; for painting an unrealistically monolithic picture of culture in poor communities; and for "blaming the victim," that is, laying the blame for poverty at the feet of the poor themselves. However, W. J. Wilson's work helped revive cultural approaches to understanding poverty and poverty transfer, albeit in a much more nuanced form, by incorporating them into the structural explanations mentioned above (Wilson, 1987; Wilson 2010; Small, Harding, and Lamont 2010; Corcoran 1995). This approach posits that once poor, jobless, segregated neighborhoods (in other words, ghettos) are created by discriminatory housing policies, they tend to reinforce values, attitudes, beliefs, and behaviors that are inimical to successful "escape" from poverty.

Scholars such as Thomas Sowell (1975) and Lawrence Mead (1992) have pointed to the historical experiences of blacks as a subordinate caste in America that have left this group with a culture that makes them "uniquely prone to the attitudes contrary to work, and thus vulnerable to poverty and dependency" (Mead 1992, 148). Of importance, rather than being intrinsic to poor communities, these cultural characteristics are seen as adaptations to discriminatory structural forces. They may even promote survival within a poor community, but may simply not transfer well to the expectations of the mainstream economy. For instance, Anderson's (1999) ethnographic study paints a picture of young urban male culture in which a violent "code of the street" has evolved as a response to sustained joblessness and material deprivation. Anderson theorizes that young men in these very poor communities must engage in violence, or at least portray themselves as being willing to resort to violence, as a way to earn respect from their peers, which then helps them avoid future victimization. This "cool pose" attitude helps protect these young men in their daily lives, but it is not valued at all in a customer-service oriented modern economy. If poor people do indeed learn behaviors, values, attitudes, and beliefs from the people and the conditions in their neighborhoods, then helping them move to a community with cultural norms that are more accepted by the mainstream economy might improve their life outcomes.

Human capital approaches to poverty transfer are also closely tied to the question of neighborhood effects. If labor market success is driven by a person's stock of valuable skills, then it makes sense to look to schools as a potential player in why poverty is transferred across generations. Neighborhood of residence is important because it determines where a child will attend school and who his peers will be within that school. If students live in a neighborhood with a higher property tax base, their schools are more likely to receive higher per pupil expenditures. If a student lives in a neighborhood with high-achieving peers, that student is more likely to do well in school (Coleman et al. 1966; Case and Katz 1991). Regardless of which of these two theories of school failure one endorses, they both imply that a child's *neighborhood of residence* should have important implications for that child's development of marketable skills, which correlates with his or her future success in the labor market. Thus neighborhood of residence may perpetuate intergenerational poverty transfer through the mediating effect of neighborhood-based public school districts.

Social capital theory posits that a person's social networks provide a range of direct and indirect supports that can enhance labor market outcomes. Granovetter (1973) analyzes the importance of "weak ties" that link individuals to a wider network of information and resources than is defined by that person's network of family members, relatives, and close friends. Neighborhoods of concentrated poverty are seen as lacking bridging social capital, which can increase an individual's access to resources that would allow him or her to "get ahead" economically. Moving people out of concentrated poverty into better neighborhoods might help poor people forge ties with people of higher social economic status, and these connections might help them find jobs.

Regardless of whether the main mechanisms of poverty transfer lie in structural constraints, cultural adaptations, educational disparities, or social capital gaps, if neighborhood effects are important in any of the hypothesized mechanisms of poverty transfer, it would follow that deconcentration policies are potential weapons against poverty. Moreover, if poverty deconcentration policies *fail* to have an impact on life outcomes, we would have evidence weighing *against* all of these theoretical models of poverty transfer. For instance, moving to a better neighborhood might improve people's outcomes for a variety of reasons. It might increase their physical proximity to available jobs. It might improve their social networks with higher-income people, which in turn might help them find a job. It might increase a child's exposure to positive peer influences and role models, promoting higher aspirations, better social skills, and more aversion to deviant behavior. And it might improve a child's outcomes by allowing him or her to attend a higher-quality school with a higher-performing peer group. But if moving to a less poor neighborhood does not do anything at all (or if it makes things worse), one would have evidence that these theories of poverty transfer are deficient in some way.

A meta-analysis of the effects of poverty deconcentration policies will help shed light on whether these hypothesized neighborhood mechanisms are actually behind poverty transfer, or if poverty transfer is purely the result of growing up in a poor family.

In addition to being relevant for a variety of theoretical questions, the impact of housing mobility policies on life outcomes is also important for policy practitioners. Enthusiasm in the United States for confronting the issue of poverty and for combating it through public policy has waxed and waned over time, but it has been fairly low in the United States since at least the Reagan era. Partially, this has been fueled by large-scale belief that many of our past policies at best have failed and at worst have seriously exacerbated the problem (Murray 1984). This perception is one of several reasons that housing policy in the United States has focused overwhelmingly on home ownership in suburbs at the expense of ensuring affordable rental housing and promoting mixed-income, mixed-race neighborhoods within urban areas (Dreier, Mollenkopf, and Swanstrom 2004; Katz and Turner 2008). Meanwhile, rents have been rising faster than wages or inflation, particularly for those at the bottom of the income distribution (de Souza Briggs, Popkin, and Goering 2010; Katz and Turner 2008). An increasing share of renters are "precariously housed," spending more than 30 percent of their monthly incomes on rent, thus exceeding HUD's standard for housing security (Katz and Turner 2008). In addition to simply increasing a family's vulnerability to economic shocks, the combination of rising rents and flat incomes means that higher-income urban neighborhoods are out of reach for many low-income families. A positive finding from this meta-analysis might indicate that further investment in poverty deconcentration policies may be warranted.

Impacts of Poverty Deconcentration Policies on Individual Economic and Behavioral Life Outcomes

Research Questions

The key research question motivating this meta-analysis is whether housing programs designed to deconcentrate poverty actually improve participants' life outcomes, particularly economic achievement and avoidance of criminal, delinquent, and risky behaviors. It is important to note that this is a meta-analysis of *policy interventions*. While the neighborhood effects literature is important for understanding the theoretical foundation and the motivation behind these programs and for their hypothesized results, this chapter should not be construed as a meta-analysis of neighborhood effects. A null finding here may indicate flaws in the underlying neighborhood effects theories, but it may just as well indicate a failure of the policies to effectively alter participants' exposure to the relevant neighborhood characteristics. If the policies in question fail to induce enough of a "dosage," then one would not expect them to alter life outcomes. Thus the reader is cautioned to interpret this chapter as a meta-analysis of *program effects*, not a meta-analysis of neighborhood effects. This distinction also means that this meta-analysis will *not* include studies that measure the impact of *neighborhood characteristics* on life outcomes, but rather will assess the impact of *program participation* on life outcomes.

The conclusions from the studies of Gautreaux, MTO, and HOPE VI offer inconsistent and sometimes outright contradictory findings on the likely impact of poverty deconcentration on economic self-sufficiency and on the incidence of problematic behaviors, particularly regarding the interaction of these programs with gender. These are the questions that we will investigate in this meta-analysis. These are not the only important outcome measures that one might choose to study. For example, many of the studies of poverty deconcentration policies have found significant positive impacts on mental health indicators. Nevertheless, we are choosing to focus on economic outcomes (employment, income, welfare receipt) and problematic behavioral outcomes (crime and delinquency) because much of the motivation for housing dispersal projects was based initially on these goals. In MTO, for example, it was only after the studies began that scholars discovered the importance of mental and physical health outcomes (de Souza Briggs, Popkin, and Goering 2010). While technically it is possible to combine all of these outcomes in one meta-analysis, and while such a project would have no intrinsic threats to internal validity, it may increase the difficulty of interpreting the results and may leave some who are already skeptical of meta-analytical methods even more leery of our conclusions. Therefore we will conduct two different meta-analyses on these two "families" of outcome measures.

One important family of studies that we do *not* examine in this meta-analysis are those that assess the impact of housing choice vouchers on life outcomes *compared to individuals receiving no housing assistance*. While it is true that giving housing vouchers to previously unassisted households might allow them to relocate to lower-poverty neighborhoods, we would argue that this is a fundamentally different policy intervention than deconcentrating households that are starting out as public housing residents. The initial degree of poverty concentration is likely to be much higher for public housing residents than for unassisted households, and the impact of the subsidy on work incentives is going to be completely different depending on whether the recipient is starting out as a public housing resident or as someone receiving no housing subsidies. Consequently, this meta-analysis only examines studies that offer a comparison group consisting of public housing residents (either the treatment group at a previous time point, or a cross-sectional study comparing voucher receivers or mixed-income residents to public housing residents).

Literature Review

The existing research on mixed-income housing policies offers conflicting stories about the effectiveness of these programs in improving individuals' life outcomes. Studies of the Gautreaux program, which provided Section 8 vouchers to African American families who were eligible for public housing in Chicago and required them to move to a low-poverty and racially integrated neighborhood, have revealed significant improvement in employment rates, academic attainment, and crime rates for families that used the program to move to suburbs rather than to neighborhoods in cities (Popkin, Rosenbaum, and Meaden 1993; Rubinowitz and Rosenbaum 2000). Keels found that young boys who moved to suburbs seemed to reduce problem behaviors, while girls actually fared worse (Keels 2008). There were several weaknesses about the Gautreaux studies. The studies only followed families who actually moved, which turned out to be only about 20 percent of the sample. More important, families were not assigned randomly into different kinds of neighborhoods. Rather, the process involved a combination of self-selection and screening procedures, both of which create an endogeneity threat. Although the studies controlled for a number of important baseline characteristics, it was still possible that outcomes were driven by unobserved differences between suburban and urban movers, not by neighborhood type.

The Moving to Opportunity experiment (begun in 1994) used randomization to reduce the threat of endogeneity. Moving to Opportunity was much like the Gautreaux program, in that it granted Section 8 housing vouchers to public housing residents and conducted follow-up studies to measure the program's impact on a variety of life outcomes. The five-city experiment had two treatment groups; one experimental group, which was provided housing counseling and was required to move to a low-poverty neighborhood for at least one year, and one Section 8 group, which was offered vouchers according to the regular rules and services of the Section 8 program at that time, with no geographical restriction and no special assistance. In addition, many of the analyses employ both intent-to-treat (ITT) and treatment-on-the-treated (TT) measures of program impact. ITT compare the full sample of the experimental group to the full sample of the control group, including measures of the treatment group who never actually used their offered voucher. TT measures attempt to compare only those in the experimental group who actually used the treatment to the control group. In 2011, the third and final wave of post-randomization follow-up studies was released (Sanbonmatsu et al. 2011). The findings from the three waves of MTO follow-up are not entirely consistent across time, site, or measurement type (ITT or TT). In general, using the full sample across all five sites, the MTO experiment has found no evidence of significant improvements for either treatment group on measures of economic well-being, which is a stark contrast to the findings from the Gautreaux program (Goering and Feins 2003; Orr et al. 2003; de Souza Briggs, Popkin, and Goering 2010).

MTO's evidence on problem behaviors among youth is mixed. The early MTO evaluations from Boston showed improvement on a behavioral problem index for boys only (Goering, Feins, and Richardson 2003;

Katz, Kling, and Liebman 2001). Early findings from Baltimore showed reductions in violent crime rates for male youth, but increases in property crime (Goering, Feins, and Richardson 2003; Ludwig, Duncan, and Hirschfield 2001). Early findings from New York showed behavioral improvements for boys, but no impacts for girls (Leventhal and Brooks-Gunn 2003). In general, these early findings seemed to show that housing mobility could improve youth behavioral outcomes for boys and would be harmless at worst for girls. However, for the interim evaluations, MTO data show that young men in the treatment group showed statistically significant *increases* in problem behavior, while young women showed statistically significant *reductions* in problem behavior (Kling, Ludwig, and Katz 2005; Kling, Liebman, and Katz 2007; de Souza Briggs, Popkin, and Goering 2010). This finding is a direct contrast to Keel's finding from the Gautreaux data that young female suburban movers fared worse than young male suburban movers. Another study of the entire MTO sample showed that when adults and youth are pooled together, there are no statistically significant impacts on individual crime rates, positive or negative (Harcourt and Ludwig 2006). Clearly, MTO shows discrepancies in behavioral outcomes depending on site, time of measurement, and subgroup (age and gender). Finally, the latest released MTO final impacts evaluation (Sanbonmatsu et al. 2011) shows virtually no impact on behaviors for either gender group.

Studies of the HOPE VI program thus far have reached conclusions that are similar to MTO. Briefly, HOPE VI funds the rehabilitation or demolition and reconstruction of highly distressed public housing projects, with the goal of creating mixed-income developments. By design, not all of the original tenants would be able to relocate into the new mixed-income developments, and those tenants were either allowed to transfer to another public housing site or were given a Section 8 voucher. The HOPE VI panel study has shown improvements on subjective sense of safety, but little improvement on individual economic outcomes (Popkin, Levy, and Buron 2009). Those who moved into other public housing units showed virtually no improvement, but those who moved via a Section 8 voucher did. To date, not enough of the mixed-income developments have come online to have studied their impact. Youth from families that used the voucher also displayed significant improvements in their level of problem behaviors compared to those who relocated to public housing (Gallagher and Bajaj 2007). However, youth, particularly girls, who either used their vouchers to move to new public housing projects or remained in their current unit awaiting reassignment, showed significant increases in problem behavior.

Research Frame

We hypothesize that people who are subjected to policy interventions designed to decrease the level of neighborhood poverty concentration that they face will find it easier to find jobs; earn higher wages; become independent of the welfare system; and reduce their involvement in risky, criminal, and delinquent behaviors.

The important moderating variables for this analysis have to do with characteristics of the target population, the characteristics of the treatment itself (that is, the rules of the specific programs in question), and finally characteristics of the study design. There is considerable evidence that outcomes of housing mobility projects differ for males and for females, particularly for the young (de Souza Briggs, Popkin, and Goering 2010). Thus gender is an important moderating variable that may systematically have an impact on effect size. This is a critical issue, because much of the social dysfunction in urban communities is highly "gendered." Gang activity is more relevant to males (Anderson 1999; de Souza Briggs, Popkin, and Goering 2010), while young women bear the brunt of out-of-wedlock child rearing (Wilson 1987; Elwood and Jencks 2004). It is unlikely that this would be particularly relevant to policy, since programs will be limited by law in how much they are able to consider gender in designing policy.

Age is an important factor here as well. Not all outcomes are relevant for each age group. Deviant behavior is much more applicable to adolescents, while employment status and receipt of welfare is more relevant to heads of households and other adults. This is crucial in any discussion of intergenerational poverty transfer.

Another important set of moderating variables will be variation in the type of program used. Section 8, Hope VI, Gautreaux, and Moving to Opportunity have significant programmatic differences. In terms of putting constraints on where recipients are allowed to move, Section 8 is much less restrictive than Gautreaux or MTO, and MTO is less restrictive than Gautreaux. Hope VI is a completely different form of program altogether. Nevertheless, they all promote mixed-income neighborhoods and thus belong in the meta-analysis.

Time is also an important variable in that many of the hypothesized effects of poverty deconcentration are likely to be lagged or to fade over time. The effects of moving to a wealthier neighborhood, for instance, are not likely to be instantaneous (Clampet-Lundquist and Massey 2008). Moreover, in many of the programs, families who initially moved do not "stay put." They are free to move back into poorer neighborhoods, and in fact, research shows that they frequently do. In addition, if there is a benefit of living in a wealthier neighborhood, it may fade over time as families become farther and farther removed from the treatment. For all of these reasons, a moderating variable measuring the length of time since treatment is appropriate.

Finally, the method that studies use to control self-selection is enormously important. Trying to parse out the independent effect of neighborhood on a person's life outcomes is a classic problem of endogeneity. It is possible that people self-select into neighborhoods on the basis of underlying factors (for example, motivation) that also influence life outcomes. The problem is similar for studying the effect of housing mobility policies; if individuals self-select into housing mobility programs, then the observed effect of changing neighborhoods is contaminated with the effect of those underlying, unobserved factors. Thus, whether or not studies control for endogeneity is also an important moderating variable.

Literature Search

We conducted a comprehensive literature search for quantitative studies evaluating the program effect of housing dispersal programs on the economic well-being and problematic behaviors of the affected tenants. Those studies included in this meta-analysis had to meet a variety of criteria. First, they had to compare the policy target population with a public housing comparison group (or with the target population at an earlier time point when residents lived in public housing). Second, they had to have been programs that took place within the United States. Third, they had to offer enough quantitative analysis for us to calculate an effect size. Finally, they had to report data in such a way that extracting the necessary effect size data was feasible. While we were open to any programs that met these criteria, every study we found fit into one of four programs: the Gautreaux program; Moving to Opportunity (which was really two programs in one); Section 8 Voucher programs with a public housing comparison group; and HOPE VI, which also featured both voucher recipient treatment groups and mixed-income residence treatment groups.

We identified six types of publications that might qualify a study to be included in this meta-analysis: peer-reviewed articles; non-peer-reviewed articles; books and book chapters; government reports; private reports issued by think tanks and NGOs; and dissertations and theses. Depending on the type of publication, we employed different search strategies, including using search engines with a set of keywords, browsing and searching the websites that are relevant to the topic, and going through the bibliographies of key publications and conducting ancestry searching, as well as contacting active researchers in the area for working papers and reports. The literature search engines employed includes academic search engines, think tanks, NGOs and private research shops, government agencies, and working paper directories. The full list can be found in table 10.1.

The authors conducted the literature search using three different combinations of the following keywords: *public housing, low-income housing, HOPE VI, Section 8, Moving to Opportunity, Gautreaux, housing mobility, housing voucher, housing dispersal, housing choice, neighborhood effects, deconcentration of poverty, integration, mixed-income, segregation.*

The literature search produced thousands of "hits." The authors imposed additional, more restrictive criteria to identify the small subset of studies that would be included in this meta-analysis. First, we looked at

TABLE 10.1. LIST OF SEARCH ENGINES, ORGANIZATIONS, AND SITES SEARCHED FOR POVERTY DECONCENTRATION PROGRAMS

Academic Search Engines	Think Tanks, NGOs, Private Research Firms	Working Papers/ Conference Proceedings	Government Agencies
Academic Search Premier (EBSCO) Business Source Premier (EBSCO)	Urban Institute Brookings	SSRN NBER	HUD State/large local
JSTOR ProQuest Dissertation Search	MDRC RAND	Econlit APPAM	Federal Reserve OMB
ISI Web of Knowledge	McArthur	ASA Annual	GAO
Google Scholar	Ford Foundation	Joint Center for Housing Studies	CBO
Eric British Library Document Supply Centre BLDSC	Rockefeller National	Furman Center Shimberg Center	CRS
WorldCat IUCAT (Indiana University's Library System)	ABT Mathmatica		

the title of each "hit" that was returned by our keyword search to decide whether the studies were "potentially relevant." We excluded those studies that have a non-U.S. focus; those that study housing policies before 1974, when the Section 8 tenant assistance program was established by law; and those that are clearly not related to housing or clearly not social science (such as newspaper articles or literature). We identified 658 potentially relevant studies and assigned each a unique study ID to be used throughout the study.

Next, potentially relevant studies were assessed for "relevance" by reading only their title and abstract. Potentially relevant studies were excluded from the relevant studies if they were not empirical quantitative studies, not original studies (such as book review), focused on aggregated-level neighborhood indicators instead of individual life outcomes, or clearly did not have a connection to policy intervention. Each potentially relevant document was coded relevant or not relevant using a coding sheet. To make sure that all members of the research team used the same criteria in identifying relevant studies, a random sample of forty-nine potentially relevant studies was coded by each member of the research team independently and two different measurements of intercoder reliability were calculated. There was 91.84 percent of agreement between the two authors, with a Cohen's kappa of 0.8005.

Then we obtained the full text of all relevant studies in order to determine their "acceptability." The criteria mentioned above for assessing potentially relevant and relevant studies still applied here in case a mistake was made in the first two steps of the coding. In addition, we looked for sufficient statistical details that enabled us to calculate effect sizes to determine whether a specific relevant study should be included in this meta-analysis. We found a total of forty-four acceptable studies during our literature search. The bibliography at the end of this chapter lists the acceptable studies that are used in our meta-regression. A second set of intercoder reliability measures was calculated on the basis of the coding of forty-three randomly selected relevant studies. The two team members agreed on 97.7 percent of the coding and had a Cohen's kappa of 0.947.

Finally, the authors coded all relevant effect sizes along with necessary statistical details and study-level characteristics. The authors assessed levels of agreement in coding effect sizes and related statistical details by computing a percentage agreement measure, as the two-by-two matrix structure used for the first two intercoder reliability assessments was not appropriate. The authors coded a total of 94 effect sizes for which we measured 20 characteristics. We had a percentage agreement of 98 percent ($n = 1,880$).

FIGURE 10.1. STUDY FLOW DIAGRAM

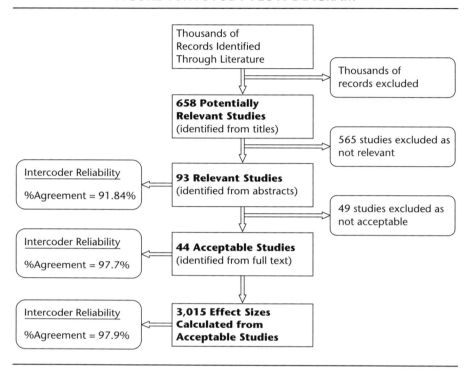

Figure 10.1 provides a study flow diagram with the number of studies identified at each step of the literature search along with the corresponding intercoder reliability measurements.

Analysis

Description of Data Set

Choice of Effect Size Type. The effect size we chose to use was Fisher's Z, a correlation, or r- based effect size that has been adjusted for small samples. All effect sizes in the studies we examined were ultimately converted to Fisher's Z. Effect sizes that were recorded as regression coefficients (least squares, probit, logit, tobit, and so on) were converted to t-scores, then into r-based effect sizes, and finally into Fisher's Z. Effect sizes that were recorded as differences of means were converted to a d-based effect size, then converted to r, and then into Fisher's Z. Finally, effect sizes that were recorded as a difference of proportions were converted to log odds ratios, then converted to d-based effect sizes, and then converted to r and Fisher's Z.

Descriptive Statistics of Effect Sizes. We identified thirty-seven studies containing a total of 1,755 effect sizes related to the effect of poverty deconcentration on individual economic well-being. Twenty-three studies with 147 effect sizes come from non–Moving to Opportunity studies. Three hundred and ninety-four of the effect sizes examined earnings in some form, 613 examined the receipt of means-tested government benefits, 714 examined employment outcomes, and 34 examined general indexes of economic well-being. The average number of effects per study was 47.4, ranging from a low of 1 to a high of 736 (standard deviation of 136.4), but with the maximum number for non-MTO studies at 26. The effect sizes themselves ranged from a low of −0.79 to a high of 1.31. The sample sizes for each effect size range from a low of 15 to a high of 17,948,607.

We identified thirteen studies containing a total of 1,260 effect sizes related to the effect of poverty deconcentration on individuals' tendency to engage in criminal, delinquent, or risky behaviors. The mean number of effect sizes per study was 96.92, with a minimum of 1 and a maximum of 692. Only two studies containing a total of 11 effect sizes were not generated by a Moving to Opportunity study. Six hundred and eighty-nine effect sizes examined general indexes of criminal or delinquent behavior; 162 examined violent crime; 159 examined property crime; and 250 examined risky behaviors. These effect sizes ranged from a low of −.14 to a high of .18. The sample sizes for these studies ranged from a low of 96 to a high of 9,133.

Meta-Analysis: Economic Outcomes

Fixed Versus Random Effects. Beginning with the analysis of economic outcomes, we will examine the impact of poverty deconcentration on overall economic well-being, combining all the economic outcome variables previously discussed. We conduct this analysis twice, once with the data from MTO and once without it, to help shed light on how MTO is dominating the findings on economic outcomes.

One of the initial tasks in analyzing data for a meta-analysis is to determine whether one should be employing a fixed effects framework or a random effects framework. A fixed effects framework assumes that the effect of the underlying treatment in question differs from study to study for reasons of sampling error only. The random effects framework assumes that there is heterogeneity in the effect size across studies, due to idiosyncrasies of program implementation, historical conditions, target populations, and other variables.

Using meta-analysis commands in Stata, it is possible to test which framework is more appropriate. The nonparametric I^2 statistic for the full set of economic outcomes suggests that 46.4 percent of the variation in our effect sizes across studies cannot be explained by sampling error alone. For our non-MTO data set, the I^2 statistic is 67.9 percent. These both suggest moderate-to-high levels of heterogeneity in effects sizes across studies. The chi-square test of the Q statistic can be rejected at an alpha $< .001$, implying that a random effects model is more appropriate than a fixed effects framework for our data analysis. This is true whether MTO studies are included or not. Thus, in both cases, we will employ a random effects framework for our analysis.

Forest Plots. We have collapsed our effect sizes to the study level to facilitate visual interpretation of the forest plots for our effect sizes. Figure 10.2 presents the effect size estimates and confidence intervals for the average study-level effect sizes for economic outcomes. The overall average effect is positive but very small, at .01. This contrasts slightly with effect-size-level forest plot analysis, which estimated the overall effect at $-.004$, but both are very near zero. One can see that the effect sizes range widely in their degree of precision, and even in their sign, but none are very large, either in the positive or negative direction. All effect sizes are less than .1 in magnitude. The same analysis conducted only for non-MTO studies (not pictured) suggests a very similar pattern, with an overall effect at .02.

The cumulative study-level meta-analysis displayed in figure 10.3 shows how the estimates of effect sizes have changed over time. This shows that earlier studies estimated larger effects for poverty deconcentration efforts, but these estimates were fairly imprecise. Over time, the estimated effect sizes have diminished while model precision has increased. This pattern is very similar whether one includes MTO studies or not.

Publication Bias. A funnel plot of effect size estimates is a useful visual diagnostic for detecting publication bias (the tendency of small studies to only be published if their results are positive). If no publication bias were present, the effect sizes should be distributed symmetrically on either side

FIGURE 10.2. STUDY-LEVEL AVERAGE EFFECT SIZES, ALL ECONOMIC OUTCOMES

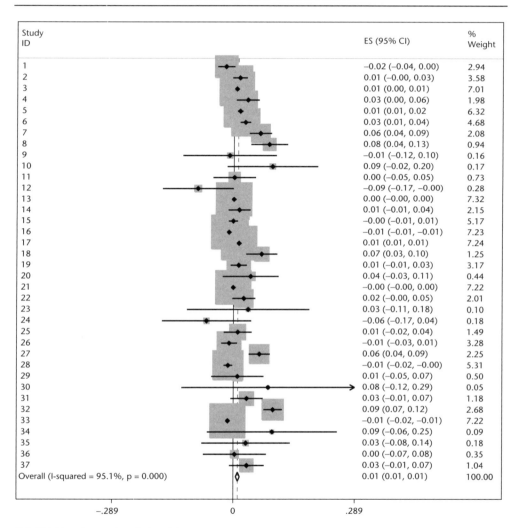

Note: Weights are from random effects analysis.

FIGURE 10.3. CUMULATIVE FOREST PLOT OF STUDY-LEVEL AVERAGE EFFECT SIZES, ALL ECONOMIC OUTCOMES

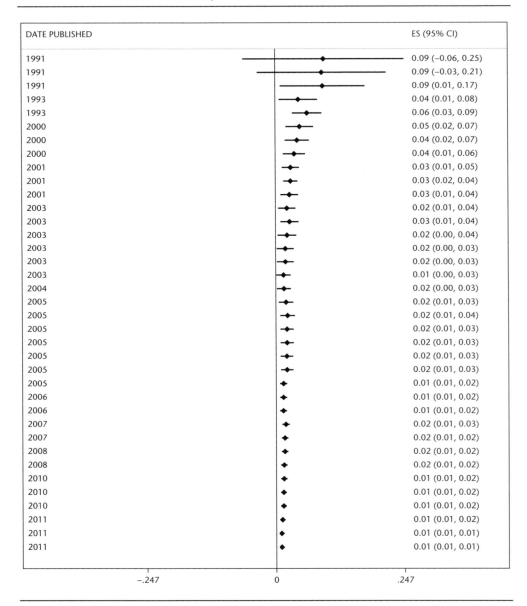

DATE PUBLISHED	ES (95% CI)
1991	0.09 (−0.06, 0.25)
1991	0.09 (−0.03, 0.21)
1991	0.09 (0.01, 0.17)
1993	0.04 (0.01, 0.08)
1993	0.06 (0.03, 0.09)
2000	0.05 (0.02, 0.07)
2000	0.04 (0.02, 0.07)
2000	0.04 (0.01, 0.06)
2001	0.03 (0.01, 0.05)
2001	0.03 (0.02, 0.04)
2001	0.03 (0.01, 0.04)
2003	0.02 (0.01, 0.04)
2003	0.03 (0.01, 0.04)
2003	0.02 (0.00, 0.04)
2003	0.02 (0.00, 0.03)
2003	0.02 (0.00, 0.03)
2003	0.01 (0.00, 0.03)
2004	0.02 (0.00, 0.03)
2005	0.02 (0.01, 0.03)
2005	0.02 (0.01, 0.04)
2005	0.02 (0.01, 0.03)
2005	0.02 (0.01, 0.03)
2005	0.02 (0.01, 0.03)
2005	0.02 (0.01, 0.03)
2005	0.01 (0.01, 0.02)
2006	0.01 (0.01, 0.02)
2006	0.01 (0.01, 0.02)
2007	0.02 (0.01, 0.03)
2007	0.02 (0.01, 0.02)
2008	0.02 (0.01, 0.02)
2008	0.02 (0.01, 0.02)
2010	0.01 (0.01, 0.02)
2010	0.01 (0.01, 0.02)
2010	0.01 (0.01, 0.02)
2011	0.01 (0.01, 0.02)
2011	0.01 (0.01, 0.01)
2011	0.01 (0.01, 0.01)

−.247   0   .247

of zero, with the estimates becoming more clustered toward the top due to the increased model precision that accompanies increased sample sizes. A meta-analysis suffering from publication bias would see a "hollow" area in the lower left portion of the funnel plot. It is not obvious from a simple visual inspection of these data whether publication bias is occurring. Figure 10.4 shows what appears to be a relatively symmetrical distribution about the mean.

The Begg test and the Eggers test are two parametric diagnostic tools for detecting publication bias. In both cases, the null hypothesis of no publication bias can be rejected at alpha <.001, suggesting that these results may be tainted by the lack of small studies publishing negative effects. Moreover, simulation results in chapter 6 of this text discusses simulation results that suggest the Egger test is a poor tool for identifying publication bias.

A better way of assessing publication bias is to include an indicator of publication source in the meta-regression. A positive coefficient indicates

FIGURE 10.4. FUNNEL PLOT OF ALL ECONOMIC OUTCOME EFFECT SIZES

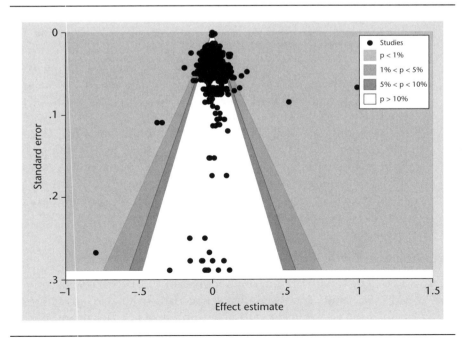

that peer-reviewed publications are more likely than non-peer-reviewed publications to find positive effects. Three of the four meta-regression models (the random effects model, the clustered random effects model, and the wild cluster bootstrap model) are designed to find identical coefficient estimates and only differ in their standard error estimates (see table 10.3 later in this chapter). The coefficient estimate from those models is 0.0157. The estimate from the generalized estimating equations model is .0071. In the most rigorous models, the GEE model and the wild cluster bootstrap model, the coefficient estimates are not statistically significant. Taken as a whole, the data indicate the possibility that there is a small degree of publication bias in the data, but not enough to present much of a danger to the validity of the conclusions. In addition, two factors about our research should attenuate this concern. First, we aggressively sought out grey literature, including working papers and dissertations, and many were included in this meta-analysis. Second, the largest studies with the most effect sizes and the smallest standard errors were actually government reports, not peer-reviewed publications, and these found very small-to-negative effect sizes, generally speaking. It is unlikely that the results are being heavily influenced by small studies with positive effects, given that most of the effect sizes come from large studies with very small or negative effects.

The funnel plot for the economic outcomes excluding MTO is perhaps a bit more revealing about the patterns of publication bias. Here (figure 10.5), there appears to be more bias, not at the extremes of the standard error range but rather in the middle. However, a Begg test for this analysis suggests that one cannot reject the null hypothesis of no publication bias at an alpha of .05. One would still reject the null hypothesis of the Eggers test, however, even at alpha <.001.

Generally speaking, the problem with publication bias is that it would bias the estimate of average effect size upward by excluding studies with large standard errors and negative or null impacts. Given the general thrust of finding very small effect sizes for these interventions, the threat of publication bias is probably not particularly serious here, but the reader should take caution nevertheless.

Data Analysis: Behavioral Outcomes

The data analysis and meta-regressions for behavioral outcomes will present results for the entire set of data instead of presenting separate results for the data set with and without MTO. Because there are so few

FIGURE 10.5. FUNNEL PLOT FOR ECONOMIC OUTCOMES EXCLUDING MTO

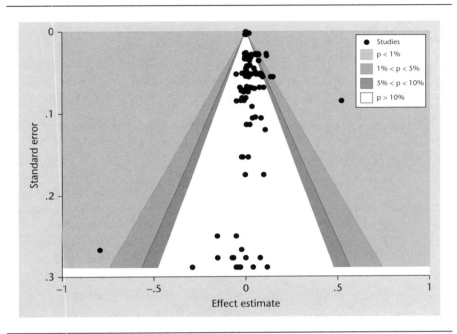

non-MTO effect sizes of behavioral outcomes in our data, it makes little sense to present a separate analysis for non-MTO studies.

Again, we must determine whether to use a fixed effects or random effects framework for our analysis. For behavioral outcomes, the I^2 statistic suggests that 28.7 percent of the variation in effect sizes across studies cannot be explained by sampling error. A hypothesis test on the parametric Q statistic is rejected at alpha $< .001$, suggesting that we should indeed be in a random effects framework.

Forest Plots. The forest plot for individual effect sizes is not particularly useful for visual interpretation given the large number of effect sizes, but the overall average effect estimated for behavioral outcomes from this method is .003. Collapsing the effect sizes to the average study level yields the forest plot shown in figure 10.6. The effects vary considerably in their standard errors, with some being quite precise and some being very imprecise. The

FIGURE 10.6. FOREST PLOT OF AVERAGE STUDY-LEVEL EFFECT SIZES FOR BEHAVIORAL OUTCOMES

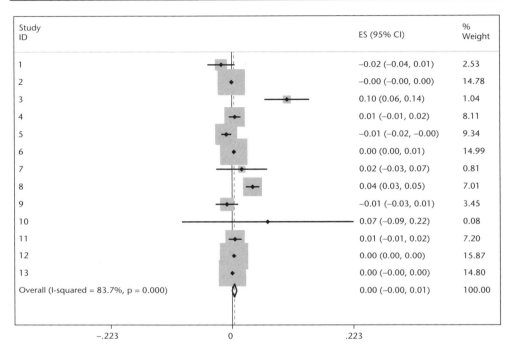

Study ID		ES (95% CI)	% Weight
1		−0.02 (−0.04, 0.01)	2.53
2		−0.00 (−0.00, 0.00)	14.78
3		0.10 (0.06, 0.14)	1.04
4		0.01 (−0.01, 0.02)	8.11
5		−0.01 (−0.02, −0.00)	9.34
6		0.00 (0.00, 0.01)	14.99
7		0.02 (−0.03, 0.07)	0.81
8		0.04 (0.03, 0.05)	7.01
9		−0.01 (−0.03, 0.01)	3.45
10		0.07 (−0.09, 0.22)	0.08
11		0.01 (−0.01, 0.02)	7.20
12		0.00 (0.00, 0.00)	15.87
13		0.00 (−0.00, 0.00)	14.80
Overall (I-squared = 83.7%, p = 0.000)		0.00 (−0.00, 0.01)	100.00

−.223   0   .223

Note: Weights are from random effects analysis.

effect sizes vary as well, with most effect sizes hovering either just above or just below zero and with a weighted average of .004. Even the largest effect sizes (which also have the largest standard errors) have fairly modest magnitudes, with the largest being only .1.

The cumulative forest plot (figure 10.7) displays the trend in average study-level effect size estimates over time. Interestingly, the earlier studies showed significant variation in effect size estimates, and these were estimated imprecisely. Over time, the estimated effect sizes appear to have gotten smaller and have been estimated more precisely.

Publication Bias. As displayed in figure 10.8, a visual inspection of the funnel plot for behavioral outcomes does not reveal any obvious publication

FIGURE 10.7. CUMULATIVE FOREST PLOT OF AVERAGE STUDY-LEVEL EFFECT SIZE, BEHAVIORAL OUTCOMES

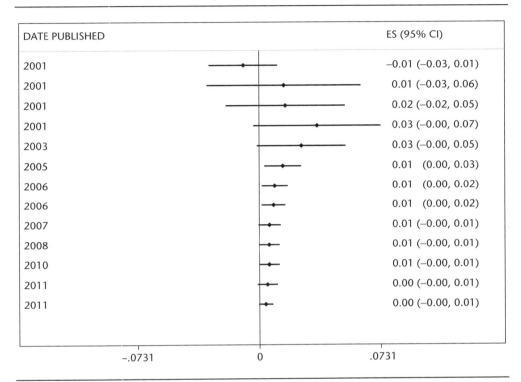

DATE PUBLISHED	ES (95% CI)
2001	−0.01 (−0.03, 0.01)
2001	0.01 (−0.03, 0.06)
2001	0.02 (−0.02, 0.05)
2001	0.03 (−0.00, 0.07)
2003	0.03 (−0.00, 0.05)
2005	0.01 (0.00, 0.03)
2006	0.01 (0.00, 0.02)
2006	0.01 (0.00, 0.02)
2007	0.01 (−0.00, 0.01)
2008	0.01 (−0.00, 0.01)
2010	0.01 (−0.00, 0.01)
2011	0.00 (−0.00, 0.01)
2011	0.00 (−0.00, 0.01)

−.0731   0   .0731

bias. The effect sizes appear to be distributed fairly symmetrically around the mean, regardless of the size of the standard error, suggesting that small studies with negative effects are just as likely to be included in our study as small studies with positive effects.

The Begg test for publication bias cannot be rejected at conventional levels of alpha ($z = .36$), suggesting that publication bias is not an issue here. However, the Eggers test can be rejected at alpha $< .05$ ($p = .02$). Again, the Eggers test has been shown in chapter 6 of this volume to be an unreliable test. Taken together, the evidence suggests that publication bias is not a large problem in this data set.[1]

FIGURE 10.8. FUNNEL PLOT OF EFFECT SIZE ESTIMATES, BEHAVIORAL OUTCOMES

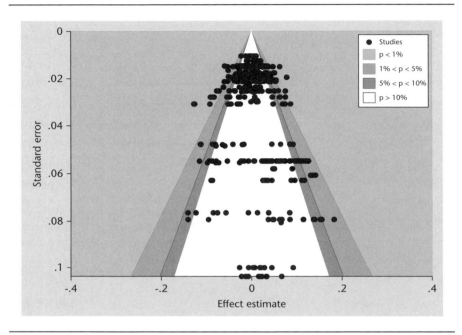

Meta-Regression Analysis

Estimation Techniques

The forest plots and funnel plots provide a convenient picture of the overall shape of distribution of effect size estimates, including estimates of overall average program effects. However, they provide little insight into how effect sizes may vary systematically due to important differences from model to model and study to study. Much as regression techniques provide insight into how outcomes vary by the values of important explanatory variables, so does meta-regression provide insight into how the effect sizes in the meta-analysis vary systematically due to differences in the important explanatory variables such as the target populations, the study design, details of program implementation, historical conditions, and even the underlying estimation technique.

We employ five different meta-regression techniques in the analyses of both behavioral and economic outcomes. First, we employ an unrestricted meta-regression that calculates an overall average effect size, similar to what we calculated in the forest plots earlier. We then calculate a weighted least squares (WLS) estimate that is designed to correct for the heteroskedasticity in our data. The variance of the effect size estimates decreases as the sample size increases, violating the assumption of homoskedasticity. We can correct for this issue by weighting each estimate by the inverse of the sample size. However, there are still problems with another one of the Gauss-Markov assumptions, namely the correlation of errors that arise from effect sizes being clustered within studies. It is likely that multiple effect sizes within a particular study will be correlated, due to similarities in data sources and estimation procedures. We adjust for this problem using WLS estimation with clustered standard errors.

A different way of dealing with the clustering of effect sizes within studies is to employ a generalized estimating equations (GEE) framework. This model adjusts parameter estimates by placing less emphasis on effect sizes from studies that generate multiple effect sizes. These GEE estimates help guard against a few studies from dominating the results of the meta-regression. The implicit assumption when using this model is that effect sizes from the same original study contain less information than if these same effect sizes came from different studies.

Finally, we employ a bootstrapping technique to correct for problems in WLS with clustered standard errors when studies must employ a small number of clusters. Cameron, Gelbach, and Miller (2008) find that standard errors are underestimated when using clustered standard errors with a small number of clusters. Our analysis of economic outcomes utilizes data from thirty-seven studies, which is fairly large. However, our analysis of behavioral outcomes employs just eleven studies. To address this problem, we use a cluster bootstrapping approach to empirically estimate a distribution of t statistics for each coefficient estimate in our model. The critical value of t for a chosen percentile of the empirical distribution of t is then compared to the original t statistic calculated for the coefficient estimate in question. If it is smaller than the original t statistic, it is possible to reject the null hypothesis.

Independent Variables

Five groups of independent variables are utilized in the meta-regression analysis to predict our dependent variables, the economic well-being, and the negative behavior effect sizes. Most variables are dichotomous in nature and are discussed in turn in the following sections.

Program Type. This set of variables represents what types of housing programs are investigated in the original studies. As discussed earlier, four major housing programs are the focus of this meta-analysis: the Gautreaux program; the Moving to Opportunity program, which includes the MTO voucher program and the MTO Section 8 program; the general Section 8 voucher program; and the HOPE VI program, which includes the HOPE VI voucher program and the HOPE VI mixed-income housing developments. To investigate the effect of these different programs, we created a dummy variable for each of these programs. For the economic well-being models, we include Gautreaux, HOPE VI Mixed Income, HOPE VI Voucher, General HOPE VI Studies, and General Section 8 Voucher on the righthand side of these models and compare those programs to the omitted MTO program (MTO voucher and MTO Section 8 combined). Since there are fewer studies that have looked at negative behaviors of the tenants, we only have observations for the Gautreaux program, the MTO program, and the HOPE VI voucher program. We omitted the MTO Section 8 program from the behavior models and compare that to studies that have looked at the Gautreaux program, the MTO voucher program, and the HOPE VI voucher program.

Outcome Type. This set of variables describes the outcome measures in the original studies to test whether the direction and magnitude of the estimated program effects are dependent on the way the outcomes are measured. Employment, earnings, welfare receipt, and some general economic well-being indices are the most common methods of measuring the economic well-being of the tenants that are affected by the housing programs. For negative behaviors, we categorize the outcomes into general crime and delinquency index; violent crimes; property crimes; and risky behaviors of youth, which includes drug use, alcohol use, smoking, and risky sexual behaviors.

Control Variables. Past studies have shown that the program effects might differ along gender lines and for different age groups. Therefore we have compared studies that looked at specific gender and age groups with those studies that looked at all gender and age groups together. It is worth noting that we followed the literature and coded children who were youths when the experiment started but turned into adults at the time of evaluations as adult.

Study Quality. We include two variables that are indicators of study quality. Invoking the program evaluation literature, we code whether the original researchers used some type of research design or econometric method to control for the endogeneity problem. We also coded a variable that indicates whether an effect size came from a study that appeared in the peer-reviewed literature. All other publication venues, including government reports, working papers, dissertations, and private foundation reports, are the reference case. Since almost all of the effect sizes that are related to negative behaviors come from the MTO studies, that is, experimental designs, we include only the study quality indicators in the economic models.

Time Since Treatment. We hypothesize that changes in economic well-being or behaviors would not follow policy changes immediately and that program impacts might fade with time. Therefore we included a "time since treatment" variable to indicate roughly how long the samples in the original studies have been exposed to the programs. It is a continuous variable that is measured in years.

Meta-Regression Results

While a number of variables across the two outcome measurements are statistically significant using at least one of our four estimation techniques, none of the variables in question in either model are statistically significant using the wild cluster bootstrap estimation technique. The wild cluster bootstrap technique is the most conservative of these estimation techniques. The reader should bear in mind that the wild cluster technique is most appropriate when the number of studies being examined is small, and given the relatively large number of studies in the economic meta-regression, the wild cluster bootstrap model may be more conservative than is necessary. However, it is more appropriate for the behavioral outcomes meta regression, given the smaller number of studies. The rest of this analysis will leave aside discussion of the wild cluster bootstrap results, but the reader should take this into consideration when examining the results from the CRVE and GEE regressions, especially for the behavioral outcomes.

These coefficients should be interpreted as the average change in the predicted Fisher's Z effect size for a one-unit change in the variable. The reader will recall that the Fisher's Z effect size is similar to the correlation coefficient (bounded between −1 and 1), so the magnitude of the coefficients should be interpreted in that context.

Results: Economic Outcomes. The results of the meta-regressions for economic outcomes are displayed in table 10.2. The first column, the unconditional meta-regression, yields an estimate of the overall impact of the treatment. For economic outcomes, the overall impact of poverty deconcentration policies on individual economic well-being appears to be negative, contrary to our research hypothesis. However, this negative impact is almost certainly too small to be of much substantive significance.

Age and Gender. Notably, neither gender nor age appears to be predictive of the effect sizes in relation to models that do not differentiate between those groups. Neither of these groupings is statistically significant in any of the models tested.

Program Type. The excluded category for our program type indicators was a dummy variable representing that the effect size was derived from a Moving to Opportunity study. While the MTO studies actually contained two treatment groups (a group that received Section 8 vouchers and another one that received vouchers but was also required to move to a non-poor neighborhood), we chose to collapse these two types of effect sizes into one category. The treatments experienced by these two groups were quite similar in design, and together they were quite different from the other program types. The magnitude and direction of the coefficients in the model here should be interpreted as the difference in average effect size moving from an MTO study to a study that examined one of the other programs.

Studies that examined the Gautreaux program found larger effect sizes than in Moving to Opportunity. This impact was fairly large compared to the other variables in the model and was highly statistically significant in the WLS, clustered WLS, and GEE models, but in absolute terms even this effect was quite small. Studies that examined Hope VI mixed-income communities also consistently found larger effect sizes that were (relatively) substantial, and this result was statistically significant across each of the three models. Studies that examined HOPE VI voucher recipients, however, found only very small positive effects, and this was not significant in the GEE model. Interestingly, studies that examined HOPE VI treatment recipients as a combined group (both mixed-income and voucher recipients combined) actually found smaller effect sizes than

TABLE 10.2. META-REGRESSION OF THE IMPACT OF POVERTY DECONCENTRATION PROGRAMS ON THE ECONOMIC WELL-BEING OF THE TENANTS

	Unconditional Meta-Regression (Model 1)	Random Effects Meta-Regression (Model 2)	Clustered Standard Errors (Model 3)	Generalized Estimating Equations (Model 4)	Wild Cluster Bootstrap (Model 5)
Constant	$-.0065^{***}$	.0024	.0024	.0063	0.0024
	(.0008)	(.0065)	(.0132)	(.015)	
Program Type (Reference: MTO programs)					
Gautreaux		$.0388^{***}$	$.0388^{***}$	$.04^{**}$	.0388
		(.0115)	(.0141)	(.0157)	
HOPE VI Mixed Income		$.0663^{***}$	$.0663^{**}$	$.048^{**}$	.0663
		(.0166)	(.0316)	(.0216)	
Hope VI Voucher		$.0050^{**}$	$.0050^{*}$	.0059	.0050
		(.0023)	(.0026)	(.0074)	
General Hope VI Studies		$-.0197^{***}$	$-.0197$	$-.0117$	$-.0197$
		(.0060)	(.0142)	(.0154)	
General Section 8 Voucher		$-.0082^{***}$	$-.0082^{***}$	$-.0075$	$-.0082$
		(.0023)	(.0028)	(.0074)	
Outcome Type (Reference: Employment)					
Earnings		$-.0001$	$-.0001$	$-.0002$	$-.0001$
		(.0007)	(.0003)	(.0003)	
Welfare Receipt		$-.0063^{***}$	$-.0063$	$-.007$	$-.0063$
		(.0017)	(.0056)	(.0045)	
Economic Well-Being Index		$.0091^{*}$	$.0091^{*}$	$.009^{*}$	.0091
		(0.0048)	(0.0042)	(.0050)	
Gender (Reference: Both Genders)					
Male		$-.0049$	$-.0049$	$-.002$	$-.0049$
		(0.0034)	(0.0024)	(.004)	
Female		-0.0037	-0.0037	$-.0006$	-0.0037
		(0.0031)	(0.0035)	(.0052)	
Age (Reference: All Ages)					
Adult		0.0018	0.0018	$-.0014$	0.0018
		(0.0029)	(0.0042)	(.0055)	
Youth		0.0030	0.0030	.0023	0.0030
		(0.0032)	(0.0057)	(.0047)	
Indicators of Quality					
Control for Endogeneity		-0.0121^{**}	-0.0121	$-.0051$	-0.0121
		(0.0054)	(0.0126)	(.0118)	
Peer Reviewed		0.0157^{***}	0.0157^{***}	.0071	0.0157
		(0.0021)	(0.0036)	(.0083)	
Adjusted R^2			0.1716		
N	1755	1755	1755	1755	1755
F		25.61	9158.12		
Wald χ^2				28938.69^{***}	

Note: *** $p < 0.01$, ** $p < 0.05$, * $p < 0.1$.

studies that examined MTO, but this result was not statistically significant once the model was adjusted for study-level clustering. Finally, effect sizes coming from studies of Section 8 voucher recipients alone (in other words, not as a part of either Hope VI or MTO) found smaller effect sizes than in MTO. This result was statistically significant in the WLS and clustered WLS models, but was not significant at all in the GEE model. In all models, the difference is substantively small.

Outcome Type. Whether a model examined economic outcomes as earnings or employment made no difference in the expected effect size in any of the models. However, compared to effect sizes for employment, effect sizes that examined welfare receipt were consistently smaller, although this result was only statistically significant in the unclustered model, and it was small. Finally, effect sizes that used a general economic index of some sort found consistently larger effect sizes, albeit only marginally so.

Indicators of Quality. Studies that controlled for endogeneity found smaller effect sizes than studies that did not. Presumably, the ability to control for self-selection processes reduced the perceived impact of the treatment. However, this result loses statistical significance in the clustered WLS and GEE models. Whether a study was found in a peer-reviewed outlet appears to predict larger effect sizes. The results differ significantly between the weighted least squares models and the GEE model. In the former, the peer-reviewed source appears to have a larger effect and is more statistically significant. In the GEE model, the magnitude falls and loses all statistical significance. In all cases, though, the magnitude is fairly small.

Behavioral Outcomes

The meta-regression results for our behavioral outcomes are displayed in table 10.3. The unconditional meta-regression estimate of the overall impact of poverty deconcentration policies on problematic behaviors appears to be positive, and this result is statistically significant, but it is also small.

Program Type. For program type in this model, we used effect sizes that examined the Section 8 treatment group within the MTO program as the reference category (as opposed to collapsing them both into one category as we did earlier). Compared to that group, the effect sizes coming from the treatment group in MTO that was required to move to low-poverty neighborhoods were systematically lower, but that difference was small,

TABLE 10.3. META-REGRESSION OF THE IMPACT OF POVERTY DECONCENTRATION PROGRAMS ON NEGATIVE BEHAVIORS

	Unconditional Meta-Regression (Model 1)	Random Effects Meta-Regression (Model 2)	Clustered Standard Errors (Model 3)	Generalized Estimating Equations (Model 4)	Wild Cluster Bootstrap (Model 5)
Constant	.0027***	.0023	.0023	.003	.0023
	(0.0007)	(0.0025)	(0.0038)	(.0036)	
Program Type (Reference MTO Section 8)					
Gautreaux		.0015	.0015	.0019	.0015
		(.0063)	(0.048)	(.0056)	
MTO		−.0045***	−.0045	−.0045	−.0045
Voucher		(.0012)	(.0038)	(.0038)	
Hope VI		.0578	.0578***	.0575***	.0578
Voucher		(.0858)	(.0035)	(.0036)	
Outcome Type (Reference: General Crime/Delinquency)					
Violent		.0062	.0062	.0061**	.0062
Crime		(.0018)	(.0038)	(.0037)	
Property		−.0135***	−.0135***	−.0135***	−.0135
Crime		(.0018)	(.0019)	(.0019)	
Risky		−.0087***	−.0087***	−.0085***	−.0087
Behaviors		(.0018)	(.0017)	(.0018)	
Time Since Treatment		−.0002	−.0002	−.0003	−.0002
		(.0002)	(.0002)	(.0003)	
Gender (Reference: Both Genders)					
Male		−.0076***	−.0076	−.0075	−.0076
		(0.0015)	(0.0054)	(.0054)	
Female		.0087***	.0087*	.0087**	.0087
		(0.0015)	(0.0045)	(.0044)	
Age (Reference: All Ages)					
Adult		0.0096***	.0096***	.0098***	−.0076
		(0.0026)	(0.0019)	(.002)	
Youth		0.0065***	0.0065***	.0065*	0.0065
		(0.0022)	(0.0018)	(.0019)	
Indicators of Quality					
Adjusted R^2			0.1677		
N	1260	1260	1260		1260
F		20.97			
Wald χ^2				2625277***	

Note: ***, $p < 0.01$, ** $p < 0.05$, * $p < 0.1$.

and it becomes statistically insignificant when the models are adjusted for clustering. However, adjusting for clustering makes the fairly large positive coefficient on the Hope VI voucher variable highly statistically significant (there were no studies in our data examining Hope VI mixed-income communities for behavioral outcomes). None of the models found a statistically significant difference between models that examined the MTO Section 8 recipients and ones that examined Gautreaux program participants.

Outcome Type. The reference category for our outcome type variable is any effect size measured as general crime or delinquency. Compared to this general index category, poverty deconcentration policies appeared to yield a greater reduction in violent crime (remember that these behaviors are reverse coded in this meta regression). However, this result becomes statistically insignificant in the clustered WLS and GEE models. However, models that use property crime as the outcome find smaller effects than the general index category. This result is substantial and holds true across all of the models except the wild cluster bootstrap model. Finally, in the WLS, weighted WLS, and GEE regression models, effect sizes calculated from models using risky behaviors as the outcome variable find smaller effects than do ones that use the reference category. This result, however, is not particularly large.

Time. The effect size does not appear to vary according to the length of time that has passed since the target population began experiencing the treatment in question. This is a somewhat surprising result, given that one would expect the impact of any treatment to decay over time.

Gender. Compared to models that do not differentiate between genders, models that examine the impact of poverty deconcentration on the negative behaviors of males tend to find smaller effect sizes, although this result is fairly small and is only statistically significant in the WLS model. Not surprisingly, the opposite is true for models that examine female target groups compared to the impact on all genders. The effect sizes for women appear to be greater, meaning that poverty deconcentration has more of a positive impact on women's behavioral outcomes. This result is statistically significant across the WLS, clustered WLS, and GEE models.

Age. Oddly, compared to models that do not differentiate between age groups, models that focus on either adult children or youth are *both* likely to find larger effect sizes. This result is small for both groups, but it is also statistically significant for both groups across the WLS, clustered WLS, and GEE models.

Estimated Average Effect Sizes for Different Variables

Table 10.4. and table 10.5 report average r-based effect sizes (Fischer's Z) from the CRVE and GEE models under different scenarios for the economic well-being models and the negative behavior models respectively. The first row of both tables reports average effect sizes under the meta-regression baseline scenarios. The second through sixth rows in table 10.4. report average effect sizes for different program types under the meta-regression baseline scenario, while the seventh, eighth, and ninth rows report average effect sizes for different outcome measures under the meta-regression baseline scenario. In defining the highest-quality original studies, we made the following changes to the baseline scenario: the use of endogeneity controls and publication in a peer-reviewed outlet. Table 10.5 is similar to table 10.4 in terms of the rows representing different programs and different outcome measures, but has an additional four rows reporting the average effect sizes under the baseline scenario for male, female, adult, and youth tenants separately.

The largest average effect size for the economic well-being models is associated with the effect of the HOPE VI mixed-income development

TABLE 10.4. RANDOM EFFECTS META-REGRESSION RESULTS USING CRVE AND GEE; DEPENDENT VARIABLE IS EFFECT SIZE OF POVERTY DECONCENTRATION PROGRAMS ON THE ECONOMIC WELL-BEING OF THE TENANTS

Scenario	CRVE Estimate	GEE Estimate
Baseline	0.0024	0.0063
Baseline Gautreaux	0.0412	0.0463
Baseline HOPE VI Mixed Income	0.0687	0.0543
Baseline HOPE VI Voucher	0.0074	0.0122
Baseline General HOPE VI Studies	−0.0173	−0.0054
Baseline Section 8 Voucher	−0.0058	−0.0012
Baseline Earnings	0.0023	0.0061
Baseline Welfare Receipt	−0.0039	−0.0007
Baseline Economic Well-Being Index	0.0115	0.0153
Highest-Quality Studies	0.006	0.0083

TABLE 10.5. RANDOM EFFECTS META-REGRESSION RESULTS USING CRVE AND GEE; DEPENDENT VARIABLE IS EFFECT SIZE OF POVERTY DECONCENTRATION PROGRAMS ON THE NEGATIVE BEHAVIORS OF THE TENANTS

Scenario	CRVE Estimate	GEE Estimate
Baseline	0.0023	0.003
Baseline Gautreaux	0.0038	0.0049
Baseline MTO Voucher	−0.0022	−0.0015
Baseline HOPE VI Voucher	0.0601	0.0605
Baseline Violent Crime	0.0085	0.0091
Baseline Property Crime	−0.0112	−0.0105
Baseline Risky Behaviors	−0.0064	−0.0055
Baseline Male	−0.0053	−0.0045
Baseline Female	0.011	0.0117
Baseline Adult	0.0119	0.0128
Baseline Youth	0.0088	0.0095

program ($Z_r = 0.0687$) from the CRVE model, while the smallest size comes from the general HOPE VI studies ($Z_r = -0.0173$). Average effect sizes are positive in seven of the ten scenarios using results from the CRVE model, and negative in three scenarios. The highest-quality studies generate an average r-based effect size that is effectively zero ($Z_r = 0.006$). The average effect sizes from the GEE model follows the patterns from the CRVE model in terms of signs, but are generally smaller in magnitude.

For the negative behavior models, the largest average effect size is associated with the HOPE VI voucher program from both the CRVE and GEE models, although we should use caution generalizing this finding because of the small number of effect sizes we have for the HOPE VI voucher program compared to other types of programs. The average effect sizes are negative for property crime and risky behaviors under the baseline scenarios, while the average effect sizes are positive for violent crime. The poverty deconcentration programs on average reduce negative behaviors for males in the baseline scenarios, while increasing negative behaviors for females, adults, and youth alike.

Conclusion

In general, we find tentative support for our hypothesis that housing mobility programs reduce negative behaviors. The magnitude of the impact is, however, rather small and statistically significant only in some models. Contrary to our research hypothesis, the overall impact of poverty deconcentration policies on individual economic well-being appears to actually be negative, although this negative impact is almost certainly too small to be of much substantive significance. Overall, the programs seem not to be very successful in achieving some of the central policy outcomes that many policy makers were hoping for: more work and earnings, greater independence from welfare, less crime and delinquency, and reductions in youth risky behaviors. Merely changing neighborhoods does not seem to produce the kind of achievement-oriented successes that the architects of these programs were aiming for. There is some evidence that HOPE VI–related programs may be more successful than MTO studies at achieving some of these goals, but given the relatively weak rigor of the HOPE VI studies included in this meta-analysis, those results should be interpreted with caution. One has to wonder why the scholarly community has not found much evidence of success in these outcomes from what appears on the surface to be a rational policy intervention theoretically. Is the underlying theory linking neighborhood to life outcomes simply wrong? Or does the failure lie in the implementation of programs? Perhaps the programs do not provide a sufficient "dosage" in terms of strength and duration of the treatment. Or maybe the current analytical methods are not equipped to capture the program effect?

Readers need to bear in mind that in this chapter we only synthesized the studies on economic well-being and crime and delinquency behaviors. We purposely left out studies that look at changes in attitudes, changes in social networks of the families in the new neighborhoods, or children's academic performance. Thus this meta-analysis is not equipped to test the human capital, social capital, or cultural theories of poverty transfer. It is also worth noting that the macro economic conditions in which different programs took place are very different. However, the macro economic conditions and housing market conditions are generally not examined in the original studies in this area, leaving the spatial-mismatch hypothesis largely untested. Future research needs to specifically test the impact of the mediating variables to be able to draw conclusions on the kinds of mechanisms that are at work.

The implicit assumption of these poverty deconcentration programs via housing assistance is that moving poor people into a new neighborhood is not a zero-sum game. The poor people who moved would benefit from the better neighborhoods, while the originally good neighborhoods these poor tenants move into do not degrade into bad neighborhoods. To achieve this, Gautreaux intentionally moved only a few public housing residents to each suburb to avoid white flight as well as not to overwhelm local infrastructure such as police force and public schools. However, other programs did not tackle this potential problem explicitly. What is the role of the characteristics of destination neighborhoods in shaping the life outcomes of the families that are affected? Did the housing mobility programs create new concentrations of poverty? More research is needed to examine the impact of these policy interventions according to the poverty rates, racial characteristics, and other features of the destination neighborhoods.

Although the programs that are examined in this chapter all aim at poverty deconcentration through new types of housing assistance, there are significant differences in program designs and program implementation. One important way in which the Gautreaux program designs differ from MTO and other programs is that the Gautreaux program was part of a legal settlement involving racial discrimination and was designed to provide those living in highly segregated neighborhoods of concentrated poverty in Chicago the opportunity to move to more racially integrated neighborhoods. In contrast, Moving to Opportunity targeted only class. It provided families with opportunities to move to more affluent neighborhoods. In fact, most MTO families moved to highly segregated, if more affluent, neighborhoods (Orr et al. 2003). It is surprising that the studies we have examined often put gender and age in their models as control variables but rarely examined the impact of race on the various outcomes of the families affected. Reanalysis of existing data and collection of new data on the racial composition of the families in these programs might shed further light on why certain programs seem to be more effective than others in promoting positive outcomes and reducing negative outcomes.

Last but not least, our meta-analysis indicates that study-level characteristics of the original research contribute to a significant portion of the variation in the estimated effect sizes. The program effects vary by program type, outcome type, age, gender, and study quality. The earlier studies tend to find larger effects, but are estimated with less precision than the later studies. Peer-reviewed journal articles are less likely to report no findings. Although the housing mobility programs are a great example of how scholarly work can have a real impact on policy, one should use caution to translate results from limited academic studies directly into designs of policy interventions.

Note

1. Due to a lack of variability in the underlying studies for behavioral outcomes, we were not able to include a peer-review variable in the meta-analysis to test for publication bias.

Studies Coded for Meta-Analysis

Aliprantis, D. *Assessing the Evidence on Neighborhood Effects from Moving to Opportunity*. Federal Reserve Bank of Cleveland Working Paper, 2011.

Anil, Bulent, David L. Sjoquist, and Sally Wallace. "The Effect of a Program-Based Housing Move on Employment: HOPE VI in Atlanta." *Southern Economic Journal* 77, no. 1 (2010): 138–160.

Boston, T. D. "The Effects of Revitalization on Public Housing Residents: A Case Study of the Atlanta Housing Authority." *Journal of the American Planning Association* 71, no. 4 (2005): 393–407.

Boston, T. D. *Environment Matters: The Effect of Mixed-Income Revitalization on the Socio-Economic Status of Public Housing Residents: A Case Study of Atlanta*. Working paper, 2005.

Brooks, Fred, Carole Zugazaga, James Wolk, and Mary Anne Adams. "Resident Perceptions of Housing, Neighborhood, and Economic Conditions After Relocation from Public Housing Undergoing HOPE VI Redevelopment." *Research on Social Work Practice* 15, no. 6 (2005): 481–490.

Carlson, D., R. Haveman, T. Kaplan, and B. Wolfe. "Long-Term Earnings and Employment Effects of Housing Voucher Receipt." *Journal of Urban Economics* (2012): 128–150.

Clampet-Lundquist, Susan E. *Hope or Harm? Deconcentration and the Welfare of Families in Public Housing*. Ph.D. dissertation, University of Pennsylvania, 2003.

Clampet-Lundquist, Susan. "Moving Over or Moving Up? Short-Term Gains and Losses for Relocated HOPE VI Families." *Cityscape: A Journal of Policy Development and Research* 7, no. 1 (2004): 57–80.

Clampet-Lundquist, Susan, Kathryn Edin, Jeffrey R. Kling, and Greg J. Duncan. "Moving Teenagers Out of High-Risk Neighborhoods: How Girls Fare Better Than Boys." *American Journal of Sociology* 116, no. 4 (2011): 1154–1189.

Clampet-Lundquist, Susan, and Douglas S. Massey. "Neighborhood Effects on Economic Self-Sufficiency: A Reconsideration of the Moving to Opportunity Experiment. *American Journal of Sociology* 114, no. 1 (2008): 107–143.

Curley, Alexandra M. *Hope and Housing: The Effects of Relocation on Movers' Economic Stability, Social Networks, and Health*. Ph.D. dissertation, Boston University, 2006.

Curley, Alexandra M. "HOPE VI: A Viable Strategy for Improving Neighborhood Conditions and Resident Self-Sufficiency? The Case of Maverick Gardens in Boston." *Housing Policy Debate* 20, no. 2 (2010): 237–294.

Gilderbloom, J. I., and Brazley, M. Newport HOPE VI Evaluation. Louisville, KY: Center for Sustainable Urban Neighborhoods, University of Louisville, 2003.

Hanratty, M., S. McLanahan, and B. Pettit. "Los Angeles Site Findings." In *Choosing a Better Life? Evaluating the Moving to Opportunity Social Experiment*, ed. J. Goering, and J. Feins. Washington, DC: Urban Institute Press, 2003: 245–274.

Katz, L., J. Kling, and J. Liebman. "Moving to Opportunity in Boston: Early Impacts of a Housing Mobility Program." *Quarterly Journal of Economics* 116, no. 2 (2001): 607–654.

Katz, L., J. Kling, and J. Liebman. "Boston Site Findings." In *Choosing a Better Life? Evaluating the Moving to Opportunity Social Experiment*, ed. J. Goering and J. Feins. Washington, DC: Urban Institute Press, 2003: 177–212.

Kaufman, Julie E. *Low-Income Black Youth in White Suburbs: Education and Employment Outcomes*. Ph.D. dissertation, Northwestern University, 1991.

Kaufman, Julie E., James E. Rosenbaum, Evanston Center for Urban Affairs, Northwestern University, and Research Policy. *The Education and Employment of Low-Income Black Youth in White Suburbs.* Working papers, 1991. EBSCOhost.

Keels, Idolly Micere. *The Effects of Neighborhoods: Residential Mobility and Long-Term Child Outcomes.* Ph.D. dissertation, Northwestern University, 2005.

Keels, Idolly Micere. "Second-Generation Effects of Chicago's Gautreaux Residential Mobility Program on Children's Participation in Crime." *Journal of Research on Adolescence* 18, no. 2 (2008): 305–352.

Kling, J. R., J. B. Liebman, and L. F. Katz. "Experimental Analysis of Neighborhood Effects." *Econometrica* 75, no. 1 (2007): 83–119.

Kling, J. R., J. Ludwig, and L. F. Katz. "Neighborhood Effects on Crime for Female and Male Youth: Evidence from a Randomized Housing Voucher Experiment." *Quarterly Journal of Economics* 120, no. 1 (2005): 87–130.

Leventhal, T. and J. Brooks-Gunn. *Moving to Opportunity: What About the Kids?* NBER working paper, 2001.

Leventhal, T. and J. Brooks-Gunn. "The Early Impacts of Moving to Opportunity on Children and Youth in New York City." In *Choosing a Better Life: Evaluating the Moving to Opportunity Social Experiment*, ed. J. Goering and J. Feins. Washington, DC: Urban Institute Press, 2003: 213–244.

Leventhal, T., R. C. Fauth, and others. "Neighborhood Poverty and Public Policy: A 5-Year Follow-Up of Children's Educational Outcomes in the New York City Moving to Opportunity Demonstration." *Developmental Psychology* 41, no. 6 (2005): 933.

Ludwig, J., G. J. Duncan, and P. Hirschfield. "Urban Poverty and Juvenile Crime: Evidence from a Randomized Housing-Mobility Experiment." *Quarterly Journal of Economics* 116, no. 2 (2001): 655–679.

Ludwig, J., H. F. Ladd, G. J. Duncan, J. Kling, and K. M. O'Regan. "Urban Poverty and Educational Outcomes" [with comments]. *Brookings-Wharton Papers on Urban Affairs* (2001): 147–201.

Ludwig, J., G. J. Duncan, and J. C. Pinkston. *Neighborhood Effects on Economic Self-Sufficiency: Evidence from a Randomized Housing-Mobility Experiment.* Unpublished paper, Georgetown University, 2000.

Ludwig, J., G. J. Duncan, and J.C. Pinkston. "Housing Mobility Programs and Economic Self-Sufficiency: Evidence from a Randomized Experiment." *Journal of Public Economics* 89, no. 1 (2005): 131–156.

Mendenhall, R., S. DeLuca, and G. Duncan. "Neighborhood Resources, Racial Segregation, and Economic Mobility: Results from the Gautreaux Program." *Social Science Research* 35, no. 4 (2006): 892–923.

Orr, Larry L., and others. *Moving to Opportunity: Interim Impacts Evaluation.* Washington, D.C.: U.S. Department of Housing and Urban Development, 2003.

Popkin, S. J. "A Glass Half Empty? New Evidence from the HOPE VI Panel Study." *Housing Policy Debate* 20, no. 1 (2010): 43–63.

Popkin, S. J., J. E. Rosenbaum, and P. M. Meaden. "Labor Market Experiences of Low-Income Black Women in Middle Class Suburbs: Evidence from a Survey of Gautreaux Program Participants." *Journal of Policy Analysis and Management* 12, no. 3 (1993): 556–573.

Rosenbaum, Emily, and Laura E. Harris. "Residential Mobility and Opportunities: Early Impacts of the Moving to Opportunity Demonstration Program in Chicago." *Housing Policy Debate* 12, no. 2 (2001): 321–346.

Rosenbaum, Emily, and Laura E. Harris. *Short-Term Impacts of Moving for Children: Evidence from the Chicago MTO Program*. Cambridge, MA: National Bureau of Economic Research, 2000.

Rosenbaum, J. E., and S. J. Popkin. 1991. "Employment and Earnings of Low-Income Blacks Who Move to Middle-Class Suburbs." *The Urban Underclass* (1991): 342–356.

Rubinowitz, Leonard S., and James E. Rosenbaum. *Crossing the Class and Color Lines: From Public Housing to White Suburbia*. Chicago: University of Chicago Press, 2002.

Rusin-White, Jennifer. "Self-Efficacy, Residential Integration and Attainment in Gautreaux Families: A Longitudinal Study." Ph.D. dissertation, Northwestern University, 1993.

Sanbonmatsu, Lisa, Jeffrey R. Kling, Greg J. Duncan, and Jeanne Brooks-Gunn. "Neighborhoods and Academic Achievement: Results from the Moving to Opportunity Experiment." *Journal of Human Resources* 41, no. 4 (2006): 649–691.

Sanbonmatsu, Lisa, and others. *Moving to Opportunity for Fair Housing Demonstration Program: Final Impacts Evaluation*. Washington, D.C.: U.S. Department of Housing and Urban Development, 2011.

Tatian, P. A., and C. Snow. "The Effects of Housing Assistance on Income, Earnings, and Employment." *Cityscape: A Journal of Policy Development and Research* 8 no. 2 (2005): 135–161.

Turney, Kristine, Susan Clampet-Lundquist, Kathryn Edin, Jeffrey R. Kling, and Greg J. Duncan. "Neighborhood Effects on Barriers to Employment: Results from a Randomized Housing Mobility Experiment in Baltimore." *Brookings-Wharton Papers on Urban Affairs* 7 (2006): 137–187.

Verma, N., and R. Hendra. *Comparing Outcomes for Los Angeles County's HUD-Assisted and Unassisted CalWORKS Leavers*. New York: Manpower Demonstration Research Corp., 2003.

Zhuang, Z. "Factors Influencing the Labor Force Participation of Low-Income Adults on Public Housing Assistance," Ph.D. dissertation, Georgia Institute of Technology, 2007.

Joe Bolinger *is a doctoral student in the joint public policy program at Indiana University-Bloomington's School of Public and Environmental Affairs and Department of Political Science.*

Lanlan Xu *is a doctoral student in public affairs at Indiana University-Bloomington's School of Public and Environmental Affairs.*

CHAPTER ELEVEN

THE RELATIONSHIP BETWEEN PUBLIC SERVICE MOTIVATION AND PERFORMANCE

David C. Warren and Li-Ting Chen

"Calls for a recommitment of Americans to values associated with government service, among them personal sacrifice and duty to the public interest, raise practical questions about the power of these values to stimulate and direct human behavior. At their core, calls for a renewal of public service motivation assume the importance of such motivations for an effective and efficient public service. Those who advocate using public service motivation as the primary steering mechanism for bureaucratic behavior perceive that it is essential for achieving high levels of performance"

(JAMES PERRY AND LOIS WISE 1990, 367).

For several decades scholars have been grappling with the idea and effects of public service motivation, from here on referred to as PSM. Broadly stated, PSM refers to a desire to serve the public interest; however, a number of different definitions have been offered throughout the years. Perry and Wise (1990) provide what is likely the most widely used definition, stating that PSM is "an individual's predisposition to respond to motives grounded primarily or uniquely in public institutions and organizations" (p. 368). Perry and Wise elaborate by defining these motives as "psychological deficiencies or needs that an individual feels some compulsion to eliminate" (p. 368). In this way, someone who joins a public organization in order to reduce social problems such as poverty or childhood obesity is exhibiting PSM. Brewer and Selden (1998), meanwhile, suggest that PSM is "the motivational force that induces individuals to perform meaningful [public, community, and social] service" (p. 417). Like other scholars, Brewer and Selden assume that PSM should be higher in governmental organizations because of the many public service opportunities that such organizations provide. A more general definition of PSM is constructed by Rainey and Steinbauer (1999), who describe PSM as a "general altruistic motivation to serve the interests of a community of people, a state, a nation, or humankind" (p. 23). Vandenabeele (2007) offers a similarly broad description, defining PSM as "the belief, values and attitudes that go beyond self-interest and organizational interest, that concern the interest of a larger political entity, and that motivate individuals to act accordingly whenever appropriate" (p. 547). While these definitions differ in their specificity, their common denominator is the concept that PSM represents an internal motivation to improve the conditions of a defined group of people, often through the vehicles of public service provision housed within public institutions and organizations. The fact that the objects of PSM, which include a desire to serve a particular organization or community, are more clearly delineated is what separates PSM from the more general concepts of altruism and prosocial behavior (Perry, Hondeghem, and Wise 2010). And although those motivated to serve the public may derive enjoyment from their activities, such pleasure is not a necessary condition, making PSM distinct from the concepts of self-interest and intrinsic motivation (Grant 2008; Perry, Hondeghem, and Wise 2010).

As definitions of PSM accumulated and evolved over the years, scholarly activity turned toward testing some of the propositions made about PSM. Of these propositions, arguably the most important is the assertion that PSM is positively related to an employee's performance and thus better performance of the public organizations in which they serve. The meta-analysis carried out in this chapter examines the growing number of empirical studies that investigate such a relationship in an effort to estimate the average effect of PSM on performance and test hypotheses about how this effect varies.

The Importance of a Possible PSM-Performance Relationship

The possibility that PSM may drive improved performance in public organizations is of much interest to practitioners and scholars for several reasons.

First, if PSM does indeed improve performance, this suggests that public managers—whether at the federal, state, or local level—may be able to use nonfinancial means to maximize performance. A greater focus on stimulating or cultivating an employee's motivation to serve the public, for instance, may pay off more than higher wages. This is especially important in public institutions, which are often more limited in utilizing extrinsic incentives such as bonuses and raises. This naturally flows toward a second reason for the question's importance: current budget deficits place added pressure on public managers' fiscal discipline. If extrinsic rewards such as higher salaries are not the only way an organization can improve performance, public organizations may realize fiscal savings and improved outcomes by focusing on nonfinancial motivators such as regular reminders of the ways in which employees' work directly or indirectly benefits targeted individuals or institutions. Third, the coming explosion of retiring baby boomers leaves governments with sizeable personnel holes to fill. Hiring the "right" replacements may involve finding talent that is both skilled *and* committed to public service. That is, hiring and promotion procedures may benefit from assessments of employees' PSM. Fourth, if performance can be increased by attracting and retaining employees with high levels of PSM, public managers may find some success in training programs or operational procedures meant to increase public-spiritedness among employees. In short, it may be possible to cultivate an ethos of PSM aimed at improving performance. Finally, the current public discourse is noticeably skeptical of the effectiveness of public institutions (Gallup 2010a; Gallup 2010b). If such attitudes depress PSM, and if PSM is related to organizational performance, the possibility of a vicious downward cycle exists.

Aside from the general, practical importance for public managers, answering questions about the effects of PSM on performance may be particularly important for certain public policies that specifically target individuals with a strong service ethic. For instance, increased understanding of PSM and its effects may have implications for public programs such as AmeriCorps that seek to connect service-minded individuals with projects intended to improve the nation's health, public safety, environment, and education systems. In turn, such programs may "serve as a catalyst for activating" PSM (Perry and Wise 1990), providing the opportunity for a virtuous upward cycle.

Theoretical Foundations of the PSM-Performance Relationship

Of all the previous work on PSM and its effects, no study more cogently develops a theoretical foundation for the PSM-performance relationship—or has had as large an impact on the ensuing empirical research—than that of Perry and Wise (1990). Perry and Wise begin by defining and discussing the three main theoretical "bases" that contribute—either individually or additively in various combinations—to PSM: rational, norm-based, and affective. The rational strand represents the attraction to public service due to an individual's desire to maximize her or his utility. Such individuals may be attracted to the prestige associated with a particular government agency or the "exciting and dramatic" process of making policy, or they may have a personal association with some policy or interest group. People who join public organizations for these reasons, therefore, may not necessarily be doing so in order to serve the public interest. Indeed, they may be attracted to public service in order to serve their own interests.

The norm-based rationale for public service engagement revolves around a normative belief that public service is an honorable endeavor. Public employees subscribing to this view may place individual accomplishments behind a sense of duty to serve the government or advance social equity goals. President John F. Kennedy's famous call to "ask what you can do for your country" as opposed to asking "what your country can do for you" is a good example of a norm-based appeal to individuals' PSM.

Finally, the affective base is described as a more emotional version of the normative base for PSM. Here, a "love of others" combines with a sense of duty toward government to form a "patriotism of benevolence" that translates into a desire to serve the public (this facet of PSM is suggested by Perry and Wise [1990] to be perhaps the least important component of a theory of PSM).

It is also important to note that the idea of PSM has its roots in—but is distinct from—intrinsic motivation. Theorists of intrinsic motivation, a natural psychological process (Deci 1975), claim that people are innately inclined to develop skills and learn; extrinsic rewards are thus not a necessary condition for motivation (Stipek 2002). In fact, DeCharms (1968), Deci (1971), and others discuss the idea that intrinsic motivation can be reduced (or "crowded out") by the introduction of extrinsic rewards. By this logic, increased external incentives such as higher salaries or better benefits packages may retard the performance of individuals if their required tasks encroach on intrinsic motivation.

Recently, Vandenabeele (2007) proposed an institutional theory of PSM to describe the origins and the consequences of PSM. This theory has its roots in self-determination theory (Deci and Ryan 2004) and assumes that institutions vary in terms of their values (interest in politics and policy making, compassion, and so on) and their responsiveness to an individual's psychological needs (for example, relatedness, competence, and autonomy). The better the institution's responsiveness, the better institutional values are internalized within the individual's public service identity. Here, identity means an internalized position within an institution. Vandenabeele further proposed two alternative hypotheses regarding the relation between public service identity and public service behavior. First, public service identity is positively related to intensive public service behavior. Second, there is an interaction effect of public service identity and institutional values on intensive public service behavior.

But how does PSM translate into improved public organizational performance? In an excellent review of the literature examining the PSM-performance relationship, Brewer (2008) suggests there is a growing consensus among scholars that there indeed exists a positive relationship between the two constructs, supported by a number of empirical studies that will be discussed later in this chapter. Before addressing empirical evidence, however, it is important to formulate a theory or theories of PSM's impact on performance. Petrovsky (2009) summarizes the relatively small amount of theoretical work on this topic, asserting that "existing theoretical arguments linking public service motivation and performance do not go too far beyond the notion that motivated employees will perform better" (p. 2). A longer version of this theoretical argument can be found from Perry and Wise (1990), who offer a series of three propositions, one of which points toward an explicit testable linkage between PSM and performance.

The first proposition asserted by Perry and Wise (1990) is that individuals with high levels of PSM are more likely to be found in public organizations. That is, people select into public service on the basis of their preferences. Indeed, the authors cite empirical research by Oldham and Hackman (1981) that supports the "attraction-selection framework." Additional context is added by Hirschman (1982), who theorizes that individuals are attracted to or repelled from public organizations (or private organizations) on the basis of factors such as extrinsic and intrinsic rewards. Indeed, Porter and Lawler's (1968) theory of motivation includes the notion that motivation is a function of both intrinsic and extrinsic reward expectations. In the case of PSM and a person's likelihood of joining (or leaving) a public organization, changes in conditions or a mismatch between expectations and experiences that change the expected intrinsic or extrinsic rewards can result in changes to an employee's desire to work for or remain in a particular organization.

A second theoretical proposition offered by Perry and Wise (1990) holds that the performance of individuals is positively correlated with PSM. A theory of a link between PSM and performance relies on several assumptions. First, employees committed to the causes of their organization are thought to be more likely to stay in their positions. Second, employees committed to their organization's goals are thought to be more likely to come up with "spontaneous, innovative behaviors on behalf of the organizations" (p. 371), giving their organizations more nimbleness in the face of change.

The third proposition provided by Perry and Wise (1990) is that organizations with a large share of employees with high PSM are less likely to depend on extrinsic rewards to incentivize performance. That is, if employees are attracted to the mission and goals of a public organization, they can be expected to perform well if the incentive structure of the organization is set up to exploit PSM. Related, performance is not expected to reach optimal levels if high-PSM individuals are incentivized with primarily extrinsic incentives (Perry and Wise 1990). This relates back to the idea of motivational crowding (DeCharms 1968, Deci 1971, and others).

These three propositions together constitute a rather elegant theoretical framework: service-minded individuals should be found disproportionately in the offices of public organizations, where they are motivated to maximize their personal performance, particularly if the organizations use complementary incentive structures. This meta-analysis focuses on the performance component of this framework, in large part due to the practical implications of the PSM-performance relationship.

Framing the Meta-Analysis of the PSM-Performance Relationship

General Research Questions

In the years since the seminal piece by Perry and Wise (1990), a number of empirical analyses have tested the proposition that PSM drives improved performance. These studies will help answer the following two general meta-analytic research questions:

1. What is the average effect of PSM on performance?
2. What variables have an impact on the effect size for the PSM-performance relationship?

A Review of the Literature

A common thread throughout most PSM-performance studies is the use of survey instruments to obtain measures of performance, almost always via self-reports of personal or organizational performance. The use of surveys and self-reported performance ratings opens the door to internal validity concerns, as survey participants may not respond honestly to questions about their own performance. However, a handful of studies have used measures of *actual* performance to examine the influence of PSM on performance. Instead of relying on self-reporting of performance, these studies capture performance using measures of actual behavior such as hours worked or the utilization of innovative management systems. An excellent example from this strand of research is found in a study of Danish physiotherapists by Andersen and Serritzlew (2009). Danish physiotherapists provide services for two types of patients: those who are disabled and "ordinary" patients. The fees paid to the physiothera-pists are the same regardless of patient type, but the disabled patients require more time per session, making ordinary patients more attractive financially. The authors use this information to hypothesize that doctors with higher PSM would devote a larger share of their time to disabled patients than would doctors with lower PSM; indeed, the analysis confirms the hypothesis. Whistle-blowing is the dependent variable in a study by Brewer and Selden (1998), which supports a relationship between PSM and whistle-blowing in the U.S. federal government. Paine (2009) surveys elected officials in Illinois local governments and used hours devoted to local government duties and hours devoted to volunteer activities as two measures of performance. Employees' innovative behavior—reported by their supervisors as opposed to being self-reported—is the performance measurement employed by Palmer (2006). And Moynihan and Pandey (2010) investigate the relationship between PSM and the actual use of performance information by local government managers.

Variation is also evident with respect to measurement of PSM (the inde-pendent variable of interest) across studies. While most use Perry's (1996) survey-based multi-item approach to measuring PSM, some studies use dif-ferent subsets of the Perry index. For instance, Park and Rainey (2008) measure PSM using survey responses to all four dimensions of Perry's scale (attraction to policy making, commitment to the public interest, compas-sion, and self-sacrifice) while Ritz (2009) measures PSM using responses to only two components of the Perry scale (attraction to policy making and commitment to the public interest).

In their review of PSM-performance studies, Perry, Hondeghem, and Wise (2010) also conclude that existing studies appear to show a significant relationship between PSM and performance. The authors provide a help-ful discussion of studies that examined the potential for mediation of the link between PSM and performance. Bright (2007), for instance, finds performance to be mediated by the degree of fit between the employee and the organization. At the same time, Leisink and Steijn (2009) find no such mediating effect of "person-organization fit." Vandenabeele (2009), however, finds both job satisfaction and organizational commitment to mediate the PSM-performance relationship. Finally, a number of other variables have been shown to correlate with PSM, including gender, education, professional identification, (DeHart-Davis, Marlowe, and Pandey 2006; Moynihan and Pandey 2007; Crewson 1997), religiosity, family socialization, and volunteering (Perry, Brudney, Coursey, and Littlepage 2008).

Of particular interest for this analysis is a recently completed research synthesis summarizing nearly twenty empirical studies on the PSM-performance relationship in the peer-reviewed literature (Petrovsky 2009). The synthesis, which employed a vote-counting approach to summarize the effect of PSM on performance, finds that PSM does indeed tend to be positively associated with higher personal and organizational performance. Another key finding is that PSM tends to correlate with attributes such as job satisfaction, organizational commitment, and organizational citizenship.

Highlighting a key area for further examination and reflecting measurement differences mentioned above, the research synthesis (Petrovsky 2009) also finds considerable design variation across studies, especially with respect to how PSM and performance are measured. On the dependent variable side, for instance, eleven studies operationalized performance using survey respondents' self-reports of their performance while three studies used self-reported observations about pay grades and job performance evaluations and four other studies used employees' self-reported perceptions of either their work unit's performance or their organization's performance. Park and Rainey (2008) measured performance a number of ways, including employees' perceptions about their work unit's (and their organization's) productivity and performance quality; Ritz (2009) measured performance by asking employees about their perceptions of their work unit's efficiency. Park and Rainey found a significant, positive relationship between their measures of PSM and performance while Ritz was less conclusive, finding a positive significant relationship in just one of two models tested. In some studies, such as Wright and Pandey (2008); Liu, Tang, and Zhu (2008); and Steijn (2008), job satisfaction is employed as a measure of performance; such studies appear to show less of a connection between PSM and performance, though one can argue that job satisfaction is a suspect proxy for performance.

Thus the existing empirical literature appears to support the idea that PSM is related to performance. However, the variation in PSM and performance measurement—along with a number of moderating and mediating variables—clouds more precise understanding of this relationship. This meta-analysis attempts to reduce some of this uncertainty through a quantitative analysis of previous empirical studies.

Refined Research Questions

Given the findings in the empirical literature discussed in the preceding section, this meta-analysis will answer the following questions:

1. Does PSM have a positive impact on performance, and if so, what is the magnitude of this effect? These two broad questions will be answered by aggregating effect sizes into a weighted average effect size using meta-analytical techniques and by an unconditional meta-regression analysis.
2. What impact do other variables have on the effect size of PSM on performance, and by how much? Here, moderating and mediating variables will be used in meta-regression analysis to test hypotheses regarding the effect of such variables on the PSM-performance relationship.
3. Is there a difference in the mean effect size between studies that measure performance using stated behavior and those that use revealed measures of actual behavior? To answer this, we will compare the weighted average effect sizes calculated for these two types of studies.

Literature Search

Conducting a rigorous meta-analysis requires an exhaustive search of both the published and unpublished literature on the question at hand. As such, our literature search included academic electronic search engines, the proceedings of any conferences that may have attracted scholars studying PSM and performance, government publication databases, think tanks and nongovernmental organizations, working paper repositories, dissertation and theses search engines, Google Scholar, and contacts with authors engaged in PSM research. Table 11.1 identifies the specific outlets used in the literature search.

When searching for literature in electronic databases, we used Boolean operators (such as AND, OR, parentheses, and quotation marks) to find

TABLE 11.1. SEARCH VENUES USED IN LITERATURE SEARCH

Academic Journal Search Engines
EBSCO Academic Search Primer
JSTOR
Web of Knowledge
Education Resources Information Center (ERIC)
British Library Document Supply Centre (BLDSC)
PsycINFO
ISI Web of Knowledge

Dissertations and Theses Search Engine
ProQuest Dissertations and Theses Database

Working Paper Search Engines
Social Science Research Network (SSRN)
EconLit

Nongovernmental Organizations and Think Tanks
National Academy of Public Administration
RAND

Conference Proceedings
American Society for Public Administration
Association for Public Policy and Management
The American Political Science Association
Midwest Political Science Association
Public Management Research Association
International Public Service Motivation Research Conference
European Group for Public Administration

Government Databases
Government Accountability Office
Office of Management and Budget
Congressional Budget Office

Other
Google Scholar
Emails to individual scholars
Ancestry search

studies that contained specific words or phrases in the title or abstract. For our research questions, we needed to identify keywords and phrases for two main constructs: PSM and performance.

Because *PSM* is a very specific term, the phrases *PSM* and *public service motivation* constituted the PSM component of our search. It is highly unlikely that any study examining PSM would fail to use the words *PSM* or *public service motivation* at least once in the title or abstract of the article.

Performance is a bit more complex because of the many types of performance that might be measured: individual performance, organizational performance, effectiveness, and so on. Fortunately, whether a study investigates individual, organizational, or some other measure of performance, the word *performance* will still appear in the article's title or abstract. In other words, simply using *performance* will capture all studies regardless of the type of performance being measured. Because effectiveness (of agencies, departments, and so on) may also be used as a measure of performance, we also include the search term *effectiveness*.

These decisions led to the following simple phrase that was employed in all searches: (*psm* OR *public service motivation*) AND (*performance* OR *effectiveness*). The AND operator was used because we are not interested in articles that study only PSM or only performance; we are interested in studies that examine the relationship between these two concepts.

In some cases, such as conference proceedings and reports from think tanks, electronic databases were not available or the use of Boolean logic was not possible. When this occurred, the following strategy was employed, using conference proceedings as an example. First, we went to the conference websites to find search engines for previous years' conferences and proceedings. If no site-specific search engine was available, we simply searched for *PSM* or *public service motivation* using the search tool in our web browser. The same strategy was used for think tanks, nongovernmental organizations, and government databases if a site-specific search engine was not available.

To minimize the risk of publication bias, we also contacted scholars engaged in PSM research by first identifying researchers from the published literature and then finding their email addresses (either from the journal articles themselves or from their institutions' websites). The authors were then contacted individually via email and asked if they had any unpublished research related to the PSM-performance relationship or if they knew of any such unpublished research.

Another important search strategy was the ancestry search, which involves combing through the bibliographies of existing studies. This ensures the capture of any important articles that search engines or other databases may have missed. Finally, Google Scholar was used as a last resort to find any pieces of published or unpublished literature not included in the more widely used search outlets.

Both authors split up search venues and employed the same search phrase and selection strategy. Studies were deemed potentially relevant if the title of the study suggested it explored any sort of relationship between PSM and performance. After potentially relevant articles were identified, the articles' titles and abstracts were read to assess relevance. Studies with abstracts describing a quantitative examination of the link between PSM and performance were coded as relevant. In situations in which we were unsure of relevance, we erred on the side of inclusion, knowing that we would be able to reject unacceptable studies in the next step of the process. All relevant articles were then read for acceptability, with particular attention paid to how the PSM and performance variables were operationalized and whether enough quantitative information was available to extract for the meta-analysis.

Here it is important to note an obstacle faced with respect to finding acceptable PSM-performance studies. While it was clear from initial searches that there were plenty of studies investigating PSM and performance, it was also evident that such studies exhibited considerable variation in terms of how performance was operationalized. Because of this, we did not have the luxury of narrowing our search strategy to only include studies that measured performance in one particular way. We also knew that some of the studies deemed acceptable might eventually be unusable in the meta-analysis if they were too dissimilar from other PSM-performance studies and did not contribute enough effect sizes to reliably measure whether such study differences were significant in affecting the PSM-performance effect size. Not knowing how many of each type of study we would find, we cast a large net. Thus, we counted as acceptable any study that contained extractable data on the quantitative relationship between PSM and any measure of performance, including stated personal performance, organizational performance, actual ("revealed") measures of performance (such as whistle-blowing), and even softer measures such as work motivation.

Intercoder Reliability Assessments

Another key aspect of performing a meta-analysis is an assessment of the degree to which authors make the same relevance, acceptability, and coding decisions. Significant disagreement on these fronts can lead to intercoder bias. Three intercoder reliability assessments were performed at various stages of the literature search. The first two assessments measured the agreement between our decisions to mark studies relevant and acceptable from a random sample of forty-eight studies while the third examined agreement with respect to the number of effect sizes coded for a random sample of ten studies and the correlation between our recorded values for eight key variables chosen for the assessment.

In the first reliability assessment, we agreed 88 percent of the time on which potentially relevant articles should be labeled relevant, leading to a Cohen's kappa of 0.74. These values—considered acceptable—were only slightly improved upon in the second reliability assessment, where we agreed on the acceptability of 89 percent of the studies with a Cohen's kappa of 0.77. The results are shown in figure 11.1.

Our third reliability assessment requires some discussion. This assessment first required us to compare the number of effect sizes and compare the values we recorded for eight variables (including sample size, coefficient

FIGURE 11.1. STUDY FLOW DIAGRAM

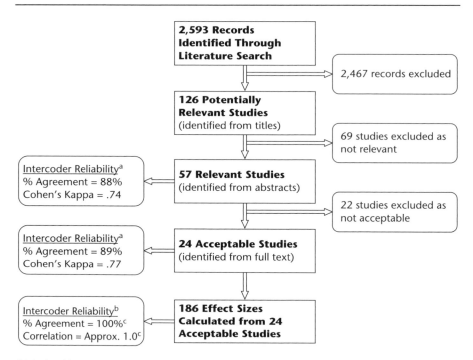

[a]Calculated from a random sample of forty-eight studies.

[b]Calculated from a random sample of ten studies. Percentage agreement is agreement on the number of effect sizes from each study. Correlation is the average correlation between the authors' recorded values for the eight variables used in the intercoder reliability assessment.

[c]It must be noted that the very high percentage agreement and correlations are likely due to discussions after a preliminary intercoder reliability assessment highlighted key areas of disagreement between the two authors.

estimate, and so on) from the same set of ten studies. While making a preliminary comparison, we found high agreement on the number of effect sizes for each study but significant differences in the values coded for the eight variables. Instead of proceeding, we stopped to discuss why we were obtaining different values and highlighted several key issues to keep in mind while coding (for instance, coding the exact sample size, being very careful to correctly enter values into our coding spreadsheet, and so on). After these discussions, coding resumed and we recorded nearly identical information from the ten studies. While this is reassuring, we decided to take advantage of the fact that we had a relatively small number of studies and effect sizes to code for this meta-analysis and made a point to spot-check each other's coding decisions. Virtually all corrections made from these later checks were related to typographical errors made on the initial coding. Given the reasonable intercoder reliability assessments for relevance and acceptability and our protocol for checking each other's coding decisions, we feel comfortable that any intercoder bias threat is small.

Data Analysis

This section presents three products of the meta-analysis. First is a discussion of the effect sizes calculated and used in the meta-analysis, along with a description of these effect sizes. Next, forest plots will illustrate the distribution of effect sizes and the average effect size of the PSM-performance relationship. Finally, we present the results of publication bias tests.

Effect Sizes

This PSM-performance study employed Fisher's Z, an r-based effect size commonly used in meta-analysis. To do this, we first extracted applicable data from acceptable studies, including data on sample size, degrees of freedom, estimated coefficients, p-values, and so on. These data allowed us to calculate a p-value for the associated test statistics. Often these test statistics were t-scores, but sometimes these were chi-squares, Z-scores, or correlation coefficients. All non t-test statistics were converted to t-scores using the p-values and degrees of freedom so that our entire data set consisted of t-scores. These t-scores were then transformed into an r-based effect size allowing for the comparison among different studies and effects. This r-based effect was then transformed into Fisher's Z in order to correct for small sample biases. For more on different types of effect sizes, see chapter 3.

The literature search and acceptability analysis returned 186 effect sizes from twenty-four studies. However, many of these effect sizes turned out to be unusable for the meta-analysis. The primary reason is that many studies used very different measures of performance that would have resulted in apples-to-oranges comparisons among effect sizes. And almost always, these different measures were specific to individual studies. For instance, Andersen and Serritzlew (2009) used the share of hours spent administering services to disabled patients as a measure of performance, providing 18 effect sizes in one study while Leisink and Steijn (2009) employed self-reported work effort as their performance measure, contributing 2 effect sizes from their analysis. Other measures of performance used by authors included job motivation, job involvement, hours worked on the job, hours of volunteer service performed, organizational commitment, and others. Furthermore, 16 effect sizes were found in four studies that used some measure of organizational performance as the dependent variable (Kim 2005, Petrovsky and Ritz 2011, Ritz 2009, Brewer and Selden 2000). Effect sizes from all of these studies were still coded because, going into this meta-analysis, we had no reason to expect a particular measure of performance to be more widely utilized in the literature; thus we cast a large net to ensure we would have enough effect sizes originating from studies that employed common measures of performance.

After filtering out effect sizes that came from studies using significantly different measures of performance, we were left with 86 effect sizes from eleven studies. All of these studies used either employees' self-reported performance levels or employees' self-reported external evaluations of their performance (for example, the results of their annual performance appraisal). The mean number of effect sizes per study was 7.8; the median was 2. Three studies provided only one effect size each (Brewer and Selden 1998, Bright 2007, Naff and Crum 1999) while one study provided 30 effect sizes (Vandenabeele 2009).

The mean sample size associated with these 86 effect sizes was 5,301, with a minimum of 179 and a maximum of 27,320. The median sample size was 3,506, and only 4 effect sizes were associated with sample sizes less than 1,000. Twenty-four (or about 28 percent) of the 86 effect sizes were negative. The unweighted average effect size was 0.028, with a standard deviation of 0.057, a minimum value of -0.074, and a maximum value of 0.186. This suggests a substantively small effect of PSM on performance, which will be confirmed by the analysis that follows.

As stated earlier, we could not use a sizeable number of effect sizes in the meta-regression analysis because of the diversity of ways in which performance was measured in the literature and the small number of effect sizes that are derived from each of these studies. However, one group of effect sizes is of particular interest for this meta-analysis and is composed of studies that share a common thread—they all employ *actual* measures of performance (or what we will call "revealed" measures of performance) rather than relying on self-reports of performance levels. These five studies (Andersen and Serritzlew 2009, Brewer and Selden 1998, Paine 2009, Palmer 2006, Moynihan and Pandey 2010), mentioned earlier, contain 31 effect sizes with a mean Fisher's Z of 0.068 and a standard deviation of

0.048. The minimum and maximum Fisher's Z values are just under zero and 0.194, respectively. While we cannot include these studies in the meta-regression, we can calculate a weighted average effect size and compare it to the weighted average effect size of the other studies. This analysis will be performed further on.

Descriptive Analysis

Test for Random Effects. Before any hypothesis tests or meta-regressions are run, we must first determine whether to operate in a fixed effects or random effects framework. If we use fixed effects, we would essentially be assuming that there is just one true effect size, with variation occurring only from sampling error. Such an assumption might be valid in meta-analyses of randomized control trials of the effects of some medicine on a partic-ular disease, as most characteristics of such experiments can be largely controlled. Unlike fixed effects, the use of random effects assumes a dis-tribution of effect sizes across studies, with each study producing a unique effect size. Thus, variation in effect sizes is produced by variation across studies as well as sampling error. Because of the variation in characteristics across studies used in this meta-analysis, the random effects framework is almost certainly preferred, though a test can be conducted to determine if this is indeed the case.

Using a meta-analysis package developed for Stata, we calculated the I^2 statistic for our distribution of effect sizes, which represents the amount of variation in our effect sizes that cannot be explained by sampling error. In other words, I^2 tells us the percentage of variation attributable to differences in study characteristics. In our case, I^2 was found to be 0.893, meaning that 89.3 percent of the variation in effect sizes cannot be explained by sampling error alone. A chi-squared test on the Q statistic—which is directly related to I^2—confirms that this variation is significantly different from zero. Thus we can conclude we should indeed be working in a random effects framework. All analysis that follows employs the assumption of random effects.

Forest Plot. The Stata meta-analysis package allows for the creation of forest plots that illustrate the variation in effect sizes, the variation in weights across effect sizes, confidence intervals around each effect size, and an average weighted effect size, symbolized by the diamond at the bottom of the plot. Examining the forest plot in figure 11.2 is revealing. First, a large number of effect sizes have confidence intervals that include

FIGURE 11.2. FOREST PLOT OF EIGHTY-SIX EFFECT SIZES FROM ELEVEN STUDIES

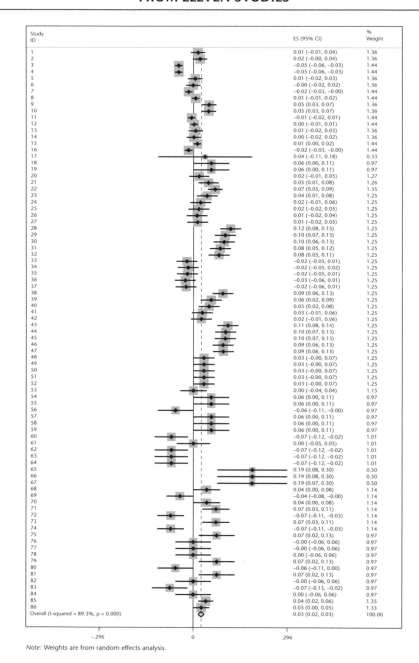

Note: Weights are from random effects analysis.

zero, suggesting many of the effects identified in the literature are not statistically different from zero. A number of effect sizes are significantly different from zero and are negative, indicative of a negative relationship between PSM and performance. However, it is also clear that many effect sizes are statistically significant and positive, suggesting a positive relationship between PSM and performance. The weighted average effect size of 0.03 is positive and statistically different from zero; however such a low Fisher's Z suggests that the effect of PSM on performance is substantively quite small.

Hypothesis Test for a Weighted Average Effect of Zero. The actual weighted mean effect size from our 86 observations is 0.025, with a 95 percent confidence interval ranging from 0.016 to 0.035. The Z-score associated with the weighted mean effect size is 5.17, meaning we can reject the null hypothesis that this effect size is zero with a high level of confidence (the p-value is less than 0.001). While we conclude the mean effect size is positive, it is important to reiterate that a Fisher's Z of 0.025 is quite small, suggesting a trivial effect size.

Forest Plot and Weighted Average Effect Size for Revealed Performance Studies. To examine whether the effect sizes produced by studies using revealed measures of performance differ from studies that use self-reported measures of performance, we produced a forest plot of the 31 effect sizes from the five studies utilizing some form of revealed performance measurement. Evident in figure 11.3 is the fact that the majority of effect sizes are positive. Furthermore, the weighted average effect size is 0.088, with 95 percent of the distribution between a Fisher's Z of 0.070 and 0.106. Thus, we conclude that the weighted average effect size for studies using revealed performance measures seems to be larger than for studies using self-reports. A caveat here: the weighted average effect size reported assumes a random effects framework; however, we are unable to reject the null hypothesis of a fixed-effects framework. While we keep our assumption of random effects for comparison purposes, the weighted average effect size assuming fixed effects for studies using revealed performance measures is 0.092, with a 95 percent confidence interval ranging from 0.075 to 0.108.

The remainder of the analysis will focus on the 86 effect sizes from the eleven studies using self-reported measures of performance.

Tests for Publication Bias. A complete meta-analysis must examine the potential for publication bias. Doing so helps us understand whether

FIGURE 11.3. FOREST PLOT OF THIRTY-ONE EFFECT SIZES FROM FIVE REVEALED PERFORMANCE STUDIES

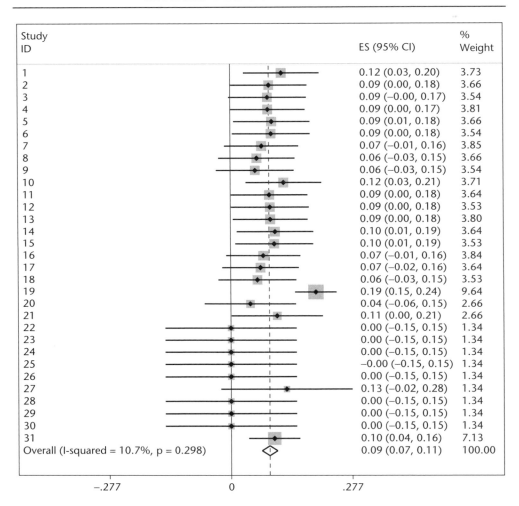

Study ID	ES (95% CI)	% Weight
1	0.12 (0.03, 0.20)	3.73
2	0.09 (0.00, 0.18)	3.66
3	0.09 (−0.00, 0.17)	3.54
4	0.09 (0.00, 0.17)	3.81
5	0.09 (0.01, 0.18)	3.66
6	0.09 (0.00, 0.18)	3.54
7	0.07 (−0.01, 0.16)	3.85
8	0.06 (−0.03, 0.15)	3.66
9	0.06 (−0.03, 0.15)	3.54
10	0.12 (0.03, 0.21)	3.71
11	0.09 (0.00, 0.18)	3.64
12	0.09 (0.00, 0.18)	3.53
13	0.09 (0.00, 0.18)	3.80
14	0.10 (0.01, 0.19)	3.64
15	0.10 (0.01, 0.19)	3.53
16	0.07 (−0.01, 0.16)	3.84
17	0.07 (−0.02, 0.16)	3.64
18	0.06 (−0.03, 0.15)	3.53
19	0.19 (0.15, 0.24)	9.64
20	0.04 (−0.06, 0.15)	2.66
21	0.11 (0.00, 0.21)	2.66
22	0.00 (−0.15, 0.15)	1.34
23	0.00 (−0.15, 0.15)	1.34
24	0.00 (−0.15, 0.15)	1.34
25	−0.00 (−0.15, 0.15)	1.34
26	0.00 (−0.15, 0.15)	1.34
27	0.13 (−0.02, 0.28)	1.34
28	0.00 (−0.15, 0.15)	1.34
29	0.00 (−0.15, 0.15)	1.34
30	0.00 (−0.15, 0.15)	1.34
31	0.10 (0.04, 0.16)	7.13
Overall (I-squared = 10.7%, p = 0.298)	0.09 (0.07, 0.11)	100.00

−.277   0   .277

Note: Weights are from random effects analysis.

studies might be absent from our sample, due primarily to two systematic phenomena: rejection by editors of journal articles that produce results running counter to those expected by the field or the decision by authors to not submit articles for publication if their results conflict with expectations (sometimes called the "file drawer problem"). One way to reduce the chance of publication bias is to include dissertations, unpublished manuscripts, and other grey literature in the literature search, as we did with this meta-analysis.

Testing for publication bias essentially involves examining the distribution of effect sizes around the mean. If no bias exists, we would expect to find an equal distribution around the mean, with the distribution tightening as the sample size increases. In fact, this is more or less the behavior we see in this meta-analysis, illustrated by the cone funnel graph in figure 11.4. It is important to note that almost all effect sizes in our sample came from studies that used surveys with more than a thousand responses, so the standard error associated with most effect sizes is small (hence the clumping of effect sizes toward the top of the cone in figure 11.4). There does appear to be a rather even distribution of effect sizes around the mean, with the exception likely the result of a large number of positive effect sizes coming from the Vandenabeele (2009) study.

Two other tests are available for detecting publication bias: the Begg and Egger tests. The former examines the correlation of the effect sizes and their standard errors with a significant finding indicating asymmetry (publication bias). Performing the Begg test with our data produces a Z-score of 1.20, which is associated with a p-value of 0.23, allowing us to accept the null hypothesis of symmetry and conclude there is no publication bias. This conclusion cannot be made using the Egger test, however, which incorporates more information about the effect size and standard errors. Using this test, we are able to reject the null hypothesis of no small-study effect, as the p-value is less than 0.001.

It should be noted, though, that chapter 6 of this text discusses simulation results that suggest the Egger test is a poor tool for identifying publication bias. Instead, publication bias is better examined by testing the peer-review parameter estimate in the meta-regression analysis. As will be discussed later in this chapter, this estimate is statistically significant with a positive sign, suggesting that peer-reviewed studies tend to report a larger effect of PSM on performance than do non-peer-reviewed studies. This does not necessarily mean the difference is due to publication bias. Indeed, the difference in the PSM-performance relationship between published and unpublished studies may be due to peer-reviewed studies being systematically better than non-peer-reviewed studies.

FIGURE 11.4. CONTOUR FUNNEL PLOT FOR EXAMINING POTENTIAL PUBLICATION BIAS

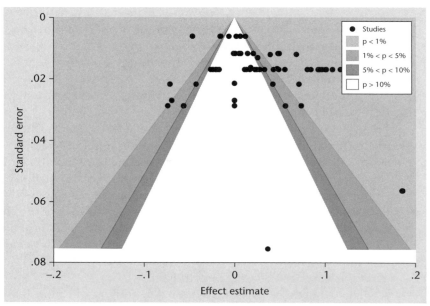

Meta-Regression Analysis

We now present results of our meta-regression analysis. Here, the effect sizes discussed previously become the dependent variable in regressions, with independent variables representing characteristics that differ from study to study. The aim of this analysis—as is the aim of any meta-regression analysis—is to test hypotheses pertaining to how the effect size varies depending on different study characteristics, leading to a better understanding of the body of literature.

Estimation Techniques

Four techniques are used in the meta-regression analysis: weighted least squares (WLS), WLS with clustered standard errors (also referred to as the standard clustered robust variance estimator, or CRVE), WLS with clustered standard errors using the wild cluster bootstrap (WCB) technique, and generalized estimating equations (GEE). Together, the use of these techniques allows us to address two violations of ordinary least squares (OLS) assumptions that result in incorrect standard errors: heteroskedasticity and non-independence of observations.

OLS estimates are heteroskedastic because we know that as sample size increases, the variance of the effect size decreases (because of reduced sampling error). But because we know the nature of the heteroskedasticity, we can generate a weighted matrix to calculate consistent and efficient estimates. Hence the use of WLS.

Observations are non-independent because most studies in our analysis include multiple effect sizes. While this characteristic leaves estimates unbiased, it results in incorrect standard errors because of the within-study correlation among effect sizes. Thus, we employ WLS with clustered standard errors, when standard errors are clustered by study.

But WLS with clustered standard errors bring with them additional problems, particularly when using a small number of clusters. Cameron, Gelbach, and Miller (2008) find that standard errors are underestimated when using clustered standard errors with a small number of clusters. For this meta-regression analysis, which utilizes just eleven clusters, this means we may be incorrectly rejecting null hypotheses. To address this problem, we use a cluster bootstrapping approach to empirically estimate a distribution of t statistics for each coefficient estimate in our model. The critical value of t for a chosen percentile of the empirical distribution of t is then compared to the original t statistic calculated for the coefficient estimate in question. If it is smaller than the original t statistic, it is possible to reject the null hypothesis of insignificance.

The use of generalized estimating equations (GEE) with an identity link function, exchangeable error correlation matrix, and a robust parameter covariance matrix is also employed in this analysis to address the non-independence problem. Unlike the clustered standard errors approach, coefficient estimates in GEE do not weight effect sizes equally, leading to different parameter estimates. This is especially important because just 30 effect sizes came from a single study while a number of studies contributed single effect sizes. For more on both WCB and GEE, see chapter 5 of this text.

Ultimately, the four techniques produce the four model estimates provided later in the chapter (in addition to the unconditional model). It is instructive to note that the coefficient estimates are the same for all but the GEE models. For WLS, CRVE, and CRVE with WCB, controlling for heteroskedasticity and non-independence of observations has an impact on efficiency of estimates but not on consistency. Coefficient estimates differ slightly in the GEE, however, due to independent observations being weighted more than correlated observations in the estimation of the parameters.

Meta-Regression Variables

Six independent variables are used in the meta-regression analysis to predict our dependent variable, the PSM-performance effect size. All variables are dichotomous in nature and are discussed in turn as follows.

PSM Index. This variable represents how the PSM treatment variable was operationalized by authors in the studies. As discussed earlier, some studies tested the relationship between an index of the four components of PSM and performance while others examined the relationship between individual PSM components and performance (and some studies produced both types of models). To investigate the effect of these different approaches, we created a dummy variable (PSM) coded zero if the treatment variable represented a single component of PSM (for example, attraction to policy making or self-sacrifice) and 1 if the treatment variable represented an index of at least three of the four components of PSM. There is no a priori reason to expect the use of index to produce higher or lower estimates of the effect of PSM on performance, but it is reasonable to expect that the use of an index versus individual components of PSM leads to significantly different estimates of the PSM-performance effect. Thus, our research hypothesis is simply that the coefficient estimate on PSM will be statistically significantly different from zero.

Common Controls. Effect sizes that were produced from models that employed the three most commonly used control variables—educational attainment, gender, and age—were coded with a value of 1. These variables have been shown to be correlated with PSM, meaning models that exclude such variables will likely produce positively biased estimates of the effect of PSM on performance. Because of this, our research hypothesis states that studies using common controls will produce smaller estimates of the effect of PSM on performance. In statistical terms, we expect the common controls coefficient estimate to be significantly different from zero with a negative sign.

Organizational Commitment. The PSM literature contains a number of studies that investigate the impact PSM has on organizational commitment or the mediating role organizational commitment might have between PSM and performance. As such, we code this variable 1 if the effect size came from an estimate that included organizational commitment in the model. We hypothesize here that studies including a measure of organizational commitment in their models produce PSM-performance effect estimates that are lower than those that do not employ such measures (thus a negative sign is expected on the organizational commitment coefficient estimate).

Job Satisfaction. Because job satisfaction is shown to correlate with PSM, we include a variable coded 1 if the effect size comes from a study that includes job satisfaction as a variable on the righthand side. As with the organizational commitment variable, we hypothesize that studies that include this variable will produce smaller PSM-performance effect sizes; thus we expect the sign on job satisfaction to be negative.

U.S. Sample. The PSM literature has expanded over time to include studies outside of the United States. In fact, the majority of our effect sizes are from non-U.S. studies. Again, we have no a priori reason to expect a particular sign, so our research hypothesis will simply state that the studies of the PSM-performance relationship in the United States will produce different effect size estimates from those performed on non-U.S. samples.

Peer Reviewed. This variable was coded 1 if the effect size came from a study that appeared in the peer-reviewed literature and represents a measure of study quality. It is assumed that peer-reviewed articles are of higher quality than other articles, leading to the research hypothesis that estimated PSM-performance effects will be different between the two types of studies.

It is important to note here that we initially wanted to include several other variables in the meta-regression analysis on the basis of the existing PSM-performance literature. One—whether the individual responding to the PSM-performance survey had a supervisory role—is an important control variable due to its nature as an antecedent of PSM. Another—person-organization fit—is shown by Bright (2007) to mediate the relationship between PSM and performance. Unfortunately, very few studies included these variables in their analyses, leaving us no choice but to exclude such variables from our analysis.

TABLE 11.2. SUMMARY OF META-REGRESSION RESULTS

Independent Variables	Uncondi- tional Meta- Regression (Model 1)	WLS Random Effects Meta- Regression (Model 2)	WLS with Clustered Standard Errors Meta- Regression (Model 3)	WLS with Clustered Standard Errors Using Wild Cluster Boot- strapping (Model 4)	Generalized Estimates of Equations (GEE) Meta- Regression (Model 5)
PSM Index		0.040***	0.040***	0.040	0.040***
		(0.014)	(0.012)		(0.013)
Common Controls		−0.047***	−0.047***	−0.047	−0.047***
		(0.023)	(0.012)		(0.012)
Organizational Commitment		−0.009	−0.009	−0.009	−0.008
		(0.019)	(0.008)		(0.09)
Job Satisfaction		0.001	0.001	0.001	0.000
		(0.020)	(0.009)		(0.010)
U.S. Sample		−0.021	−0.021**	−0.021	−0.020***
		(0.022)	(0.009)		(0.008)
Peer Reviewed		0.056***	0.056***	0.056	0.053***
		(0.015)	(0.009)		(0.007)
Constant	0.025***	−0.004	−0.004	−0.004	−0.003
	(0.006)	(0.010)	(0.007)		(0.006)
Adjusted R^2	n.a.	0.267	0.279	n.a.	n.a.
N	86	86	86	86	86
F	n.a.	5.09	41.34	n.a.	n.a.
τ^2	0.00211	0.001556			
I^2 Residual	0.893	0.837			

Notes: Standard errors are reported in parentheses.

*$p = <0.10$, **$p = <0.05$, ***$p = <0.01$.

Results

As discussed earlier, this analysis utilized four estimation techniques, thus producing a set of four model estimates plus an estimation of the unconditional model, all of which are displayed in table 11.2. While some variables listed earlier were found to be significant with the WLS and WLS with clustered standard errors approaches, that significance evaporated after we employed the WCB approach (which, again, was used because of the small number of studies in our sample). This does not necessarily invalidate the results of the clustered standard errors approach, but does warrant some caution when interpreting the estimates. Moreover,

GEE model estimates produced results nearly identical to the WLS with clustered standard errors approach.

The first model estimated is the unconditional meta-regression, in which the effect size is simply regressed on the constant (model 1). Here we see confirmation of our finding from earlier in the chapter regarding the mean weighted effect size of 0.025. The constant term is significant beyond the 0.01 level, allowing us to again confirm the first hypothesis that as an individual's PSM increases, his or her performance tends to increase. However, as mentioned previously, this mean effect of 0.025 is quite small, suggesting that the substantive importance of PSM with respect to its impact on performance is small.

Of course, the unconditional model tells us only the mean effect. The conditional model allows us to test additional hypotheses. In model 2, we see that PSM index, common controls, and peer reviewed are all significant at the 0.05 level. As predicted, the sign on the common controls variable is negative, meaning models that include age, gender, and educational attainment produce effect sizes lower than those that do not. At −0.047—almost twice the magnitude of the mean effect but in the opposite direction—the magnitude of this estimate is striking. It suggests that using important control variables may wipe out the positive effect of PSM on performance.

Two other research hypotheses are confirmed by model 2. First, the use of a PSM index as opposed to individual PSM components has an impact on the effect size. In this case, use of a three- or four-component index—with all other variables equal to zero—raises the effect size by 0.040, an amount 1.6 times the size of the naïve mean effect. Second, peer-reviewed studies produce larger effects of PSM on performance. Here, the magnitude is more than twice as big as the mean effect size. In other words, the estimated magnitude of the PSM-performance relationship is higher when a PSM index is used (as opposed to individual components of PSM) or when the study is peer reviewed.

In model 3, results are largely unchanged save for the U.S. sample variable. The U.S. sample variable is significant with a negative sign, confirming the research hypothesis of there being a significant effect and suggesting that studies of the PSM-performance relationship using U.S. samples will produce effect sizes lower than those produced from non-U.S. samples. In all models, job satisfaction and organizational commitment are statistically insignificant, resulting in the rejection of our research hypotheses. The use of these variables as controls in PSM-performance studies appears to have no impact on the effect size.

The significance of the PSM index, common controls, peer reviewed, and U.S. sample variables mentioned above should be looked on with some suspicion because of the nature of WLS with clustered standard errors. Remember that such an estimation technique underestimates the standard error of estimates when the number of clusters is small, leading to a higher likelihood of incorrectly rejecting true null hypotheses. In our case, the results of the WCB approach (model 4) reinforce this concern. For every variable estimated, the critical value of t at the 95th percentile of the empirical distribution of t is larger than the original t statistic calculated for each variable, sometimes many times larger. This suggests we may not be able to confidently reject the null hypothesis of insignificance for any of the variables in our model.

However, the GEE meta-regression estimates presented in model 5 are virtually identical to the estimates produced using WLS with clustered standard errors. This is important given that GEE theoretically do a better job of controlling for correlation among effect sizes than WLS with clustered standard errors.

These results allow for the calculation of an average effect size for the best-conducted PSM-performance studies. Here we define "best-conducted" as those that use common controls, use a PSM index (as opposed to individual components), and are peer reviewed. Using results from the WLS with clustered standard errors estimate, the average effect size for the best-conducted studies is equal to 0.045. The standard error associated with this average effect size is calculated to be 0.019, resulting in a 95 percent confidence interval between 0.026 and 0.064. In other words, there is a statistically significant positive effect of PSM on performance among the best-conducted studies of this relationship.

Conclusion

Examining over two decades of scholarly research exploring PSM and its impact on performance, this meta-analysis set out to estimate the mean effect of such a relationship. The search that provided the data inputs for the meta-analysis revealed two key facts about the PSM-performance literature. First, around two dozen studies explicitly examine the PSM-performance relationship. Second, considerable variation exists in how performance is measured across these studies. The latter point forced us to make some tough decisions about which studies to include in the meta-analysis, as the inclusion of studies that used wildly different performance constructs would have clouded understanding of the link between PSM and performance.[1]

Ultimately, eleven studies containing 86 effect sizes were used for the primary meta-analysis of the effect of PSM on self-reported performance levels. An additional five studies containing 31 effect sizes were utilized in a secondary meta-analysis on the link between PSM and revealed measures of actual performance. We find that there is indeed a statistically significant, positive relationship between PSM and performance. That is, individuals who have higher levels of PSM tend to exhibit higher levels of performance. This is true for studies that use self-reported performance measures as well as for studies that use revealed measures such as whistle-blowing or hours worked. Interestingly, the weighted mean effect size estimated between PSM and revealed performance measures is significantly larger than that calculated for studies using self-reported performance measures. However, the Fisher's Z of 0.088 for the revealed performance studies and 0.025 for the literature using self-reported performance measures suggested that while the PSM-performance relationship is statistically significant, PSM has a substantively small impact on performance.

This study also used meta-regression analysis on the 86 effect sizes from literature using self-reported performance measures to examine how the PSM-performance relationship is moderated by a number of study-level variables, such as whether a study employs common control variables or is part of the peer-reviewed literature (as opposed to a working paper or some other non-peer-reviewed publication). Three different meta-regression techniques were used: WLS, WLS with clustered standard errors, and WLS with clustered standard errors using the wild cluster bootstrap. Of the six moderating variables included in the models, four were found to be statistically significant using WLS with clustered standard errors: PSM index, common controls, U.S. sample, and peer reviewed. But when the wild cluster bootstrap approach was used, no variables were found to be statistically significant at the 95 percent confidence level.

Significance of Findings

Although the finding of a small, positive relationship between PSM and performance in this meta-analysis is significant, the most important takeaways have to do with how differences in study-level characteristics have an impact on the size of the PSM-performance effect.

First, the use of a three- or four-component index rather than individual components (such as attraction to policy making) to measure PSM is associated with a larger effect of PSM on self-reported performance. Therefore, if PSM is more accurately measured using an index akin to Perry's (1996), studies that measure PSM using only one component of PSM are likely underestimating the impact of PSM on performance.

Second, the use of the common demographic controls of gender, age, and educational attainment tends to reduce the estimated PSM-performance effect size. Thus, studies that fail to use these common controls may be overestimating the PSM-performance relationship.

Third, the negative sign on the U.S. sample variable suggests that PSM-performance analyses performed on U.S. samples will likely result in lower PSM-performance effect sizes. This suggests that PSM may actually be a more important driver of performance *outside* of the United States. Indeed, the magnitude of the negative coefficient estimate—0.021—is almost the same as the unconditional weighted mean effect size of 0.025, implying that the effect of PSM on performance is virtually zero for U.S. employees when all other moderating variables are zero.

Fourth, studies from the peer-reviewed literature tend to produce larger estimates of the PSM-performance relationship. Although there was little indication of publication bias from the tests discussed earlier in this chapter, this finding suggests one is more likely to observe lower PSM-performance effect sizes in the grey literature.

It is also important to ponder the significance of the mean effect sizes calculated in this meta-analysis. While the weighted mean effect sizes calculated for studies using self-reported performance measures and for studies using revealed measures of performance were statistically significant and positive, the magnitudes of these effects were quite small (with Fisher's Zs of 0.025 and 0.088, respectively). Thus, individuals with higher levels of PSM do perform better, but this effect is small enough to suggest that other variables may have a more substantial impact on performance. Increased monetary incentives (salary, benefits, bonuses, and so on), for instance, may generate larger increases in performance. Of course, the use of increased monetary incentives likely entails greater costs than the additional search costs of finding employees with higher levels of PSM. If the costs of screening prospective employees for PSM is de minimis, doing so would be wise despite the substantively small effect PSM has on performance.

In terms of Perry and Wise's (1990) three propositions for the linkages between PSM and performance, findings from this meta-analysis support the second proposition: the performance of individuals is positively correlated with their level of PSM. This meta-analysis also confirms the conclusion of the Petrovsky (2009) research synthesis, in which a positive association between PSM and individual performance was found using a vote-counting method.

Areas for Future Research

The results of this study suggest a number of issues to address in future PSM-performance research. Meta-regression estimates point out the need for researchers to use common control variables such as gender, age, and educational attainment in their models, as the exclusion of such variables can overestimate the effect of PSM on performance. In addition, if PSM is indeed best captured as a composite index of attraction to policy making, commitment to the public interest, compassion, and self-sacrifice, then scholars should employ such indices in their studies rather than measuring PSM with individual components. Not doing so—according to the results of the meta-regression analysis—underestimates the impact of PSM on performance.

One intriguing question emerging from the meta-regression analysis pertains to the reduced impact of PSM on the performance of U.S. employees. This chapter makes no attempt to uncover the cause of this finding, but PSM scholars would do well to further explore how PSM and its impacts differ across countries.

The difference in weighted mean effect size between studies using self-reported performance and those using revealed performance measures suggests a very real need to more accurately measure performance. This is particularly true given that the weighted mean effect size calculated for the latter group of studies was over three times the size of the former group of studies. By using better measures of performance, scholars should arrive at improved estimates of the PSM-performance relationship. As more studies employ revealed measures of performance, future meta-analyses may be able to test how the PSM-performance effect size varies depending on different types of revealed performance measures.

Finally, more research needs to examine the effect of PSM on organizational performance. The literature search conducted for this meta-analysis turned up only 16 effect sizes from four studies that used some measure of organizational performance as the dependent variable. While it is logical to assume that the presence of higher-performing individuals in an organization correlates with higher organizational performance, more empirical work is needed to confirm this assumption.

Limitations

Several limitations of this meta-analysis must be discussed. First, only 86 effect sizes could be utilized in the meta-regression analysis. While 86 observations are certainly enough to allow for testing the significance of the handful of variables used in the meta-regression models, the relatively small number of degrees of freedom makes testing a larger number of variables impossible. Moreover, the small number of studies that used revealed measures of performance (and the fact that each study used a different, unique measure of performance) made it impossible to investigate how the use of various measures of performance affected the PSM-performance relationship in a meta-regression framework.

Second, the fact that studies used in the meta-regression analysis employed self-reported measures of performance means that effect sizes from those studies may be subject to bias. In the case of the effect of PSM on performance, it could be hypothesized that the use of self-reported performance measures may result in underestimates of such an effect due to "cheap talk." That is, individuals may all report relatively high levels of performance because there is no disincentive to lie. Thus, the average individual with low PSM may self-report a performance level that is not much lower than the average individual with high PSM. Podsakoff, MacKenzie, Lee, and Podsakoff (2003) provide an excellent discussion of self-report bias in their review of common method biases.

Finally, the meta-regression estimation results from use of the wild cluster bootstrap casts some doubt on the findings generated using GEE and WLS with clustered standard errors. As discussed earlier, WLS with clustered standard errors tend to underestimate standard errors with small cluster sizes, making the incorrect rejection of null hypotheses more likely. Using the WCB, all variables were found to be statistically insignificant, indicating that the results documented in this chapter should be read with some caution.

Note

1. This would not have been a major problem if these different performance measurements appeared in several studies, as moderating variables could have been used in the meta-regression analysis to observe how different measures affected the PSM-performance relationship. Unfortunately, these measurements were often unique to individual studies.

Studies Coded for Meta-Analyses

Studies Using Self-Reported Performance Measures

Alonso, Pablo, and Gregory B. Lewis. "Public Service Motivation and Job Performance: Evidence from the Federal Sector." *American Review of Public Administration* 31, no. 4 (2001): 363–380.

Brewer, Gene A., and Sally C. Selden "Whistle Blowers in the Federal Civil Service: New Evidence of the Public Service Ethic." *Journal of Public Administration Research and Theory* 8, no. 3 (1998): 413–439.

Bright, Leonard. "Does Person-Organization Fit Mediate the Relationship Between Public Service Motivation and the Job Performance of Public Employees?" *Review of Public Personnel Administration* 27, no. 4 (2007): 361–379.

Camilleri, Emanuel. *Organizational Commitment, Motivation and Performance in the Public Sector. The Case of Malta.* Dissertations ProQuest, Theses, The Maastricht School of Management, University of Tilburg, 2004.

Camilleri, Emanuel. *The Relationships Between Personal Attributes, Organization Politics, Public Service Motivation and Public Employee Performance.* Conference presentation paper, International Public Service Motivation Research Conference, Indiana University Bloomington, June 7–10, 2009.

Camilleri, Emanuel, and Beatrice V. D. Heijden. "Organizational Commitment, Public Service Motivation, and Performance Within the Public Sector." *Public Performance & Management Review* 31, no. 2 (2007): 241–274.

Leisink, Peter, and Bram Steijn. "Public Service Motivation and Job Performance of Public Sector Employees in the Netherlands." *International Review of Administrative Sciences* 75, no. 1 (2009): 35–52.

Li, Xiaohua. "An Empirical Study on Public Service Motivation and the Performance of Government Employees in China." *Canadian Social Science* 4, no. 2 (2008): 18–28.

Naff, Katherine C., and John Crum. "Working for America: Does Public Service Motivation Make a Difference?" *Review of Public Personnel Administration* 19, no. 3 (1999): 5–16.

Park, Sung M., and Hal G. Rainey. "Leadership and Public Service Motivation in U.S. Federal Agencies." *International Public Management Journal* 11, no. 1 (2008): 109–142.

Vandenabeele, Wouter. "The Mediating Effect of Job Satisfaction and Organizational Commitment on Self-Reported Performance: More Robust Evidence of the PSM-Performance Relationship." *International Review of Administrative Sciences* 75, no. 1 (2009): 53–78.

Studies Using Revealed Performance Measures

Andersen, Lotte B., and S. Serritzlew. *Does Public Service Motivation Affect the Behavior of Professionals?* Conference presentation paper, International Public Service Motivation Research Conference, Indiana University Bloomington, June 7–10, 2009.

Brewer, Gene A., and Sally Selden. "Whistle Blowers in the Federal Civil Service: New Evidence of the Public Service Ethic." *Journal of Public Administration Research and Theory* 8, no. 3 (1998): 413–439.

Paine, Jeffrey R. *Relating Public Service Motivation to Behavioral Outcomes Among Local Elected Administrators*. Conference presentation paper, International Public Service Motivation Research Conference, Indiana University Bloomington, June 7–10, 2009.

Palmer, Jacquelyn W. *Innovative Behavior of Frontline Employees in the Public Sector*. Dissertations ProQuest, Theses, The Department of Management of the College of Business, University of Cincinnati, 2005.

Moynihan, Donald P., and Sanjay Pandey. "The Big Question for Performance Management: Why Do Managers Use Performance Information?" *Journal of Public Administration Research and Theory* 20 (2010): 849–866.

David C. Warren *is a doctoral student in public affairs at Indiana University's School of Public and Environmental Affairs.*

Li-Ting Chen *is a doctoral candidate in educational psychology and inquiry methodology at Indiana University's School of Education.*

CONCLUSION

Meta-Analysis and the Future of Research in Public Management and Policy

Mary R. Anderson and Evan J. Ringquist

"(Meta-analysis) is going to revolutionize how the sciences . . . handle data. And it is going to be the way many arguments will end"

(THOMAS CHALMERS, QUOTED IN MANN 1990, 480).

Early in the process of writing this book we identified three objectives we aimed to meet. First, we wanted to write a book that would serve as an introduction for researchers seeking to employ meta-analysis in their work. While there are several textbooks that can provide a similar introduction, the focus of this book has been squarely on the techniques as they apply to the social sciences in general, and to public management and policy more specifically. We hope that what we have provided here will be accessible to researchers striving to manage problems and build usable knowledge. The book is written with this audience in mind. Second, we aimed to integrate the techniques of meta-analysis with recent advances in econometrics, making meta-analysis more useful for the types of analyses that are likely to be conducted by public management and policy researchers. For the more technically inclined, we provided an assessment of the most common approaches used to conduct meta-analyses and develop a set of advanced techniques customized for public management and policy. Related to this, we wanted to illustrate these techniques in a familiar statistical computing environment—Stata—so that scholars might be more willing to experiment with these techniques. Third, we wanted to offer substantive examples of meta-analyses that are derived from the public management and policy field. Toward this end, we illustrated the techniques of meta-analysis described in earlier chapters by applying them to the questions of educational vouchers, performance measurement, public housing, and public service motivation.

Now that you have made it to the conclusion, we can reveal a fourth aim in writing this book: to change perceptibly the trajectory of research in public management and policy. We hope to prod movement in two directions. First, we hope to facilitate greater concern with producing *cumulative knowledge* in public management and policy, which is one precondition for making scientific progress in these fields. Of course, Aaron Wildavsky, Deborah Stone, Frank Fischer, Norma Riccuci, and a dozen other brilliant scholars properly warn us that policy analysis and public management are not "sciences" in the same way as, say, chemistry is a science. However, the value of improved scientific understanding of human and organizational behavior that lies at the heart of public management and policy is undeniable. In our view, shortcomings in public management and policy research are just as often attributable to too little concern with scientific progress as they are to too much. Second, we hope to foster continued interest in *useable knowledge*; helping practitioners and public decision makers identify meaningful signals in the noise of sometimes contradictory original research, and helping them understand the sources of systematic differences in conclusions from this research (that is, the noise).

The four original meta-analyses in chapters 8 through 11 provide examples of how researchers in public management and policy might use the techniques of meta-analysis to produce cumulative and useable knowledge. To be sure, these are only a sampling of the types of questions that can employ the techniques of meta-analysis. There are any number of important questions that could be tackled using theses techniques. For example, when we discussed this topic with several leading public management and policy scholars, they offered the following questions as ripe for examination using the technique of meta-analysis:

· Does the "publicness" of organizations affect organizational outcomes?
· Is managerial quality related to organizational performance?
· What effects does democratic oversight have on organizational performance?
· What effects have large-scale organizational reforms had on the performance of public bureaucracies?
· Does "pay-for-performance" improve organizational performance?

- Does the use of information and analysis improve organizational outcomes?
- Does the use of information and analysis affect organizational procedures?
- Why do governments contract for services? (Some competing explanations are managerial capacity, fiscal stress, and strength of public sector unions.)
- What are the effects of leadership strategies on organizational performance?
- What are the effects of "representative bureaucracy" on organizational performance?
- What are the effects of contract design on policy performance?
- What are the effects of contract design on organizational oversight and influence?
- What are the effects of early childhood education interventions on student educational performance?
- What are the effects of early childhood education interventions on student life outcomes?
- What are the effects of workforce intervention and job training programs on job attainment, retention, and progression? (Especially important is the relative effectiveness of job training versus public employment programs.)
- What are the effects of charter schools on educational performance?
- What are the effects of using health care performance indicators on organizational procedures?
- What are the effects of using health care performance indicators on health care outcomes?
- What have been the effects of civil service reforms on organizational procedures and performance?

As we hope we have illustrated throughout this text, the approach to meta-analysis developed here is not and should not be limited to public management and policy. Social scientists from fields across the spectrum will find these techniques useful for answering questions in which the evidence to date is scattered or inconclusive. For example, when asked, scholars in the fields of political science, sociology, and economics suggested these questions as ripe for meta-analytic synthesis:

- What are the effects of negative campaigns on voter turnout?
- Which personality traits are correlated with ideology?
- What is the impact of Federal Reserve policies on inflation?

- What are the effects of fiscal stimulus on economic production and growth?
- What is the relationship between economic liberalization and economic growth?
- What effect do changes in tax rates have on the elasticity of taxable income?
- What effect do changes in tax rates have on federal revenue?
- What is the relationship between public opinion and the policy actions taken by governments?
- What are the effects of voter eligibility laws on voter turnout?
- What factors contribute to the growth and success of social movements?
- What is the relationship between immigration and neighborhood social capital and cohesion?
- What are the effects of education policies on fertility rates?
- What effects does family structure have on delinquency rates?

Why Meta-Analysis?

Meta-analysis is a systematic, quantitative, replicable process of synthesizing numerous and sometimes conflicting results from a body of original studies.

- Using meta-analysis, researchers can (1) calculate an average effect size that summarizes the weight of the evidence present in the original research on a particular question and (2) account for why empirical results vary across original studies.
- Individual studies when viewed collectively can help scholars identify shortcomings in the coverage, design, or execution of original studies and help establish the extent to which these limitations occur in which contexts.
- Meta-analysis can help scholars ascertain more precise measures for key variables of interest in their research.
- Understanding and determining best practices is critical in building successful programs. Meta-analysis permits researchers to synthesize disparate findings and generate conclusions about which practices result in more or less successful outcomes.
- Finally, as scholars of public management and policy, we strive to constantly move the discipline forward (as do virtually all fields of science) by posing new theories and building on existing ones. Indeed,

the scientific method hinges on hypothesis testing and theory building. Meta-analysis is well suited to test hypotheses from these theories. When original studies are viewed collectively and in a systemic fashion, scholars can see a broader picture and begin to construct a roadmap for future research.

Meta-analysis does not produce new knowledge in the same way as original research. However, meta-analysis can produce *greater certainty* and a *better understanding* of the knowledge that we do possess. Moreover, by fulfilling this potential, meta-analysis can also produce *more useable* knowledge. Given the current state of research and publication in public management and policy, we cannot help but think that making sense of the knowledge that we have generated is at least as important as generating more new knowledge. The more knowledge we create, the greater the need to understand *collectively* what that knowledge means in terms of the big picture.

While meta-analysis is relatively rare in the social sciences, the techniques are ubiquitous in the therapeutic sciences of medicine and psychology. In many respects the fields of public management and policy have more in common with the therapeutic sciences than with the physical sciences such as physics and biology. As with the therapeutic specialist, a central task of the management and policy researcher is identifying problems and diagnosing the source of these problems in causally noisy environments. Like the therapeutic specialist, management and policy scholars are faced with choosing from among a long list of possible treatments, and these treatments are often differentially effective depending on the context of the problem. As with the therapeutic specialist, the best-designed management or policy intervention may be ineffective if not properly administered to the problem. Medical doctors call this noncompliance with treatment. Management and policy scholars know it as implementation. Finally, when weighing their options, management and policy scholars, consultants, and practitioners consider the option of doing nothing, or preserving the status quo, recognizing that, for example, the costs of remedying a particular market failure may be greater than the resulting benefits. This might be considered the management and policy equivalent of the Hippocratic Oath—first do no harm. If the success of meta-analysis in psychology and medicine derives at least in part from the ability of the techniques to deliver accurate, actionable knowledge in this environment, it is likely that many of these same benefits might accrue to public management and policy scholars who use these techniques.

Despite its significant advantages, critics have raised doubts about the value of meta-analysis from the beginning. Indeed, we find that each time meta-analysis makes an entrance into a discipline, critics raise many of the same concerns. Many of these criticisms are valid and warrant consideration, but many are not. Many of these criticisms—for example, the "apples and oranges" critique, the "garbage in, garbage out" critique, and the selectivity bias critique—can be addressed effectively through careful attention to question definition and research design. Other critiques—such as the non-comparability of regression parameter estimates and the non-independence of multiple effect sizes from original studies—can be addressed effectively through careful attention to meta-regression model design and estimation. Ultimately, we conclude that most of the criticisms can be dealt with in a logical and systematic fashion, and that the advantages of meta-analysis far outweigh the concerns.

Why Meta-Analysis Now?

We believe that the time is now right for meta-analysis to play a larger and more meaningful role in research in public management and policy. This belief flows from the following observations.

- *Maturation of the Statistics of Meta-Analysis.* The statistics of meta-analysis, particularly the techniques of meta-regression, have improved rapidly in just the past decade. The statistical advances, coupled with advances in traditional econometrics, mean that the techniques of meta-analysis are far more useful to social scientists now than they were only ten years ago.
- *Institutionalization of Meta-Analysis.* Figures I.1 and I.2 in the introduction illustrate the rapid growth in the use of meta-analysis in the scholarly literature. In addition, large professional associations are now actively promoting the increased quality of meta-analyses and the greater use of meta-analysis to inform decision making. Management and policy scholars should participate in the institutionalization of these techniques.
- *Higher-Quality Original Studies.* The quality of quantitative research in public management, public policy, and the social sciences more broadly has improved markedly in the past generation. The quality of the data is better. The quality of the models is better. The research designs are better, extending to the large increase in field and laboratory experiments. Higher-quality original studies provide better data for meta-analyses.

- *The Increased Emphasis on Cumulative Scholarly Knowledge.* As discussed in the introduction, leading scholars in public management and policy have made high-profile pleas for a greater emphasis on building cumulative knowledge in these fields. Meta-analysis provides a suite of techniques specifically designed for answering these pleas.
- *The Increased Emphasis on Evidence-Based Management and Policy.* Few scholars would disagree with the assertion that there is a greater emphasis on evidence-based management and policy than at any time in memory. From GPRA to PART to the new evidentiary requirements for research by the U.S. Department of Education to the Coalition for Evidence-Based Policy, decision makers inside of government and important stakeholders outside of government are demanding that public decision making be evidence-driven. Meta-analysis can provide accurate, generalizable, and policy-relevant information to aid in this goal.
- *Requests from Practitioners.* In the introduction we offered three recent examples of high-level federal officials imploring public management and policy scholars to help them make better decisions by telling them just what the results of our research mean for practice. Our sense is that this is the tip of the proverbial iceberg. Management and policy scholars generate large amounts of policy-relevant information, but in a form that is difficult for practitioners to understand or absorb. Meta-analysis can synthesize this information and package it in a manner more useful for policy makers.

Meta-Analysis for Public Management and Policy: An Adaptation

The accumulation of knowledge in the therapeutic sciences has, in large part, developed as a result of conducting analyses that synthesize the results from original studies. We have argued that meta-analysis can provide a similar benefit for public management and policy; however, there are adaptations that need to be considered and implemented for its use in these fields. The context and techniques of meta-analysis are meaningfully different for public management and policy than they are for medicine, and therefore we have adapted the techniques to deal with these differences. Here we want to briefly remind the reader that it is critical to make these necessary changes when conducting a meta-analysis in public management and policy. There are three considerations for adaptation: (1) differences in original studies, (2) differences in effect sizes, and (3) differences in the goals of the meta-analysis.

Original studies in management and policy are different than original studies in the fields in which meta-analysis is more common.

- Study designs differ. Unlike our counterparts in the physical and therapeutic sciences, for the most part we do not conduct our studies as laboratory experiments or field trials. As social scientists, we have less control over our subjects. Most commonly, we conduct studies that are quasi-experimental and more often are observational, lacking any real controls whatsoever over the subjects.
- Measurement differs. Validated and common measurement scales are not the norm in public management and policy studies as they are in psychology, for example. Therefore, combining effect sizes across multiple indicators can be tricky, and researchers should be prepared to account for these differences when calculating average effect sizes.
- Estimation routines differ. Social scientists generally estimate quantities of interest from some version of the general linear model that includes multiple covariates—or even multiple endogenous variables. Some might say that social scientists compensate for weaker research designs by using more complicated statistical routines. Different statistical techniques often estimate different quantities of interest (for example, intent to treat compared to treatment on the treated, or estimates derived from panel data compared to cross-sectional data). Meta-analysts must consider carefully the complexity of these models when coding moderator variables, so that the resulting meta-regressions can control for differences in average effect sizes that are a function of estimation choices.

Effect sizes from original studies in public management and policy also differ from effect sizes in other fields. These differences arise in three areas: the type of effect size, heterogeneity in effect sizes, and the number of effect sizes. Social scientists will almost always calculate r-based effect sizes from original studies, while meta-analysts in other fields generally work with odds-based or d-based effect sizes. The use of multivariate models means that these r-based effect sizes will be far more heterogeneous than those confronted by meta-analysts in other fields. Finally, unlike meta-analysts in other fields, researchers in public management, policy, and the social sciences will almost always code multiple effect sizes from single original studies. Using these effect sizes violates the assumption of independent observations that underlies virtually all of inferential statistics. Thankfully, each of these issues can be dealt with properly provided that researchers employ the statistical and modeling tools described in this book.

Finally, when adapting meta-analysis to public management and policy there are differences in the goals of the meta-analysis. Traditionally, meta-analysis has been used to calculate an average effect size as an estimate of a common population effect size, and to describe the distribution of effect sizes across studies. For public management and policy, however, the primary goal of meta-analysis should be to account for variation in effect sizes (that is, to determine the source of that variation). Of particular interest is variation in effect sizes stemming from what Rubin (1992) calls "scientifically interesting" factors; for example, the extent to which program effects and other correlations of interest vary across groups, organizations, and contexts. Therefore, paying close attention to original study characteristics, applying proper statistical tools, and determining the goal of the meta-analysis at the outset should allow researchers to advance the accumulation of knowledge in the field of public management and policy.

Our discussion of adapting meta-analysis for public management and policy would be incomplete without offering two warnings to scholars in these fields who are considering conducting a meta-analysis. First, *meta-analyses in public management and policy should never rely solely upon peer-reviewed or "published" research*. A greater proportion of research in public management and policy appears in the grey literature than in virtually any other fields. Meta-analyses that ignore this literature will provide an incomplete picture of our knowledge regarding a particular research question. In addition, the very real risk of publication selection bias means that meta-analyses relying only on published research may not only be incomplete, but biased as well. Given the poor quality of our tests for publication bias and the even poorer quality of ex-post remedies for publication bias, researchers should make every effort to include grey literature in their meta-analyses. Second, *high-quality meta-analyses are difficult and time consuming*. Conducting a meta-analysis is nothing like conducting a traditional literature review. Our rule of thumb is that it will take approximately three times as long as originally estimated to complete the project. In addition to being time consuming, conducting a meta-analysis is intellectually taxing, as you have to carefully pour over the minute details of original studies so that you might obtain the proper data for calculating effect sizes and coding moderating variables. The benefits from this investment are substantial, however. The scholarly and practical value of high-quality meta-analyses have been discussed elsewhere and will not be repeated here. Instead, we will emphasize our firm belief that *conducting a meta-analysis meaningfully improves the quality of your original research*. Carefully and critically reviewing the research of others alerts you to important questions that remain unanswered and sensitizes you to the types of mistakes made by other researchers that you will want to avoid in your own work.

We will end this section by noting that meta-analysis may be particularly useful for one group of readers: Ph.D. students preparing to write their dissertations. Virtually all dissertations in public management, public policy, and the social sciences contain the obligatory "literature review" chapter. Students often view these chapters as drudgery, and editors view them as the first thing to be chopped when preparing the dissertation for publication. Our advice to these students is to replace the standard literature review chapter with a meta-analysis of previous research on your question (or closely related questions). The resulting literature review will be more systematic and more comprehensive, and therefore will better inform the original research that follows in subsequent chapters. In the interests of full disclosure, we should also point out that conducting a meta-analysis might also delay completion of the dissertation. But a meta-analysis is more useful than a traditional literature review—both for the student and for the discipline—and it is eminently more publishable.

A World of Possibilities: The Future of Meta-Analysis in Public Management and Policy

What does the future hold for research in public management and policy? How will policy makers, managers, and scholars evaluating the effectiveness of public policy programs determine to what extent the policy prescription is meeting its intended objective? We can only speculate on the former question, as no one has a crystal ball that will allow the future to be told (though we will make an attempt shortly). However, as to the latter question, we believe meta-analysis holds a great deal of promise to refocus research in the field of public management and policy. As we have discussed previously, there are almost limitless possibilities for research using meta-analysis. Original research has produced a wealth of studies examining educational policies, health policies, and organizational reforms and practices. And yet questions remain unanswered, evidence can be inconsistent, and findings are often contradictory. Meta-analysis provides a set of techniques to bring some semblance of order to this chaos. It provides a means for policy makers, managers, and scholars to evaluate programs and policies in a systematic fashion.

So what might the future hold for public management and policy research? In light of the evidence we have presented and the review we have conducted we will offer some speculation. Simply stated, we can envision a world of possibilities. Meta-analysis provides an important addition to the social scientist's statistical tool box. In conducting research, we have all encountered studies that provide contradictory or inconsistent results about the effect of an independent variable on a dependent variable. Often, we seek to replicate and modify these studies to determine whether our results are similar to those of study A or study B, thus adding to the knowledge pool but not necessarily to the *accumulation of aggregate knowledge*. Until now, we have lacked the statistical tools and familiar statistical software setting (such as Stata) that would allow researchers in the field of public management and policy to conduct a systematic, quantitative, and replicable synthesis of these conflicting studies. We have aimed to alleviate that disadvantaged position for public policy scholars (as compared to our counterparts in medicine and psychology). The adaptations of meta-analysis presented here ought to allow researchers in public management and policy (and social sciences more broadly) to contribute to the accumulation of knowledge. As scholars, we no longer are bound to simply report that our research is consistent with the findings of study A but not study B. Rather, we can determine the extent to which the effect of a particular independent variable on a dependent variable exists and the magnitude of that effect by pooling all of the studies that examine this relationship using meta-analysis. We can also examine the role of mediator variables in contributing to these effects. In other words, we can *aggregate knowledge*.

We hope the examples of the substantive questions we explored in this book—the impact of educational vouchers on student academic achievement (chapter 8), the effects of performance management systems on the performance of public organizations (chapter 9), the effects from the poverty deconcentration efforts on the life outcomes of recipients of federal housing assistance (chapter 10), and the relationship between public service motivation and the performance of government agencies (chapter 11)—will encourage readers to approach other research questions using this technique. Public management and policy is packed full of interesting questions that remain unresolved or unanswered. Governments at all levels (federal, state, and local) are constantly passing new policies, adopting practices, and enacting programs that warrant closer examination. Meta-analysis provides the best technique, we believe, for synthesizing evaluations of these programs and practices. As we made clear earlier, the technique is not only useful to public management and policy but also to the social sciences more generally. Moreover, we can envision studies that examine programs and practices in an international and comparative context as well. For example, one might be interested in examining the role of per-pupil expenditures or teacher pay and student outcomes across several countries. Meta-analysis suits this purpose.

There is a world of possibilities for the use of meta-analysis. Scholars, researchers, and practitioners are bound only by their imaginations. Research in public management and policy is certain to move forward. If we want it to advance in a more systematic and scientific manner, then the more frequent use of meta-analysis will surely advance that goal. Conducting meta-analyses will clearly demonstrate the accumulation of knowledge and prepare a roadmap for future research. As Morton Hunt eloquently puts it, "all serious and gifted scientists, I think, are adventurers—intellectual explorers making their way into terra incognita . . ." (1997, 166–167). As we conclude this book, it is our hope that readers will feel confident in their ability to apply the techniques we have demonstrated and conduct meta-analyses of their own; to be intellectual adventurers and explorers in their own right.

APPENDIX A

CODING SHEETS

A1: School Vouchers

ID # _____
Coder # _____

Section I: Data for Relevant Studies

1. Bibliographic Information
    a. Author 1
    b. Author 2
    c. Author 3
    d. Year

2. Search Protocol That Found Study

    (1) __ IUCAT (Book)   (2) __ WorldCat (Book)
    (3) __ JSTOR   (4) __ Academic Search Premier
    (5) __ Google Scholar   (6) __ NBER
    (7) __ SSRN   (8) __ ERIC
    (9) __ ProQuest dissertations   (10) __ EconLit
    (11) __ Sociological abstracts   (12) __ Social Science abstracts
    (13) __ Web of Knowledge   (14) __ Proceedings First
    (15) __ Ancestry search _____
    (16) __ Conference program _____
    (17) __ Government website _____
    (18) __ Think tank or NGO _____
    (19) __ Personal communication _____
    (20) __ Other _____

3. Study Relevance
    a. Is study relevant?
        (1) __ Yes   (0) __ No

    b. If no, why not relevant?
        (1) __ Non-analytic   (2) __ Non-quantitative
        (3) __ Non-U.S.   (4) __ Dependent variable
        (5) __ Choice type   (6) __ Other

Section II: Study Characteristics

(Complete this section only for "relevant" studies)

Bibliographic Reference: _____

1. Source
   (1) __ Peer-reviewed article   (2) __ Non-peer-reviewed article
   (3) __ Book or book chapter   (4) __ Working paper
   (5) __ Government document.   (6) __ Private report
   (7) __ Dissertation   (8) __ Conference paper
   (9) __ Other unpublished source

2. Is this study acceptable?
   (1) __ Yes   (0) __ No

3. If no, why unacceptable?
   (1) __ Non-analytic   (2) __ Non-quantitative
   (3) __ Outcome measure   (4) __ Treatment type
   (5) __ No original analysis   (6) __ Duplicate study
   (7) __ Insufficient reporting
   (9) __ Other

ID # _____   **Coder** # _____
Effect# _____   **Page** # _____

Section III: Effects Measures

(Complete this section only for "acceptable" studies)

Treatment and Outcome Identifiers

1. Outcome Measure
   (1) __ Standard test, math   (2) __ Standard test, reading
   (3) __ Standard test, verbal   (4) __ Standard test, overall
   (5) __ Other achievement _____

2. Domain of Effect
   (1) __ Overall   (2) __ Males
   (3) __ Females   (4) __ Blacks
   (5) __ Whites   (6) __ Latinos
   (7) __ Other

3. Length of Treatment _____

4. Beginning Date of Study (year) _____

Research Design Characteristics

5. Pre-Test Control Included
   (1) __ Yes   (0) __ No

6. Endogeneity of Treatment Controlled For
   (0) __ No
   (1) __ Yes, fixed effects
   (2) __ Yes, matching
   (3) __ Yes, differencing
   (4) __ Yes, instrumental variables
   (5) __ Yes, regression discontinuity
   (6) __ Yes, random assignment
   (7) __ Yes, other _____

7. Method of Assignment to Control Groups
   (1) __ Simple random assignment
   (2) __ Random assignment after matching
   (3) __ Nonrandom, post-hoc matching
   (4) __ Nonrandom, self selection
   (5) __ Nonrandom, other
   (6) __ Multiple methods
   (9) __ Cannot tell

8. Research Design
    (1) __ Experimental
    (2) __ Regression discontinuity
    (3) __ Onegroup other quasi-experimental post-only
    (4) __ Onegroup other quasi-experimental pre-post
    (5) __ Twogroup other quasi-experimental post-only
    (6) __ Twogroup other quasi-experimental pre-post
    (7) __ Multigroup other quasi-experimental post-only
    (9) __ Multigroup other quasi-experimental pre-post
    (10) __ Other

9. Data Structure
    (1) __ Cross-sectional   (3) __ Pooled cross-sections
    (2) __ Time series   (4) __ True panel

Moderating and Mediating Variables

10. Location of the Program
    (1) __ Milwaukee, Wisconsin
    (2) __ New York
    (3) __ Dayton, Ohio
    (4) __ Florida (Opportunity Scholarship)
    (5) __ Florida other
    (6) __ Charlotte, North Carolina
    (7) __ Washington, D.C.
    (8) __ Maine and Vermont
    (9) __ Cleveland, Ohio
    (10) __ Other

11. Treatment Type
    (1) __ Secular school only
    (2) __ Secular and religious school

12. Funding
    (1) __ Public
    (2) __ Private
    (3) __ Mixed

13. Type of voucher
    (1) __ Means-tested
    (2) __ Failing schools or students
    (3) __ Special needs
    (4) __ Town tuitioning

14. Eligible students
    (1)__Elementary school
    (2) __ Middle school
    (3) __ High school
    (4) __ Elementary and middle
    (5) __ Middle and high
    (6)__Overall

15. Treatment Interaction
    (1) __ Yes   (0) __ No

16. Treatment Interaction Favors
    (1) __ Treatment   (0) __ Control

Data for Effect Sizes

17. Statistical technique
    (1) __ Difference of means   (2) __ Difference of proportions
    (3) __ Regression   (4) __ ANOVA
    (5) __ Probit   (6) __ Logit
    (7) __ Correlation   (8) __ Chi-squared
    (9) __ Multi-equation models (e.g., path analysis, SEM)
    (10) __ Mixed models (e.g., HLM)
    (11) __ Other _____

18. Raw Effect Favors
    (1) __ Treatment   (0) __ Control

19. Total Sample Size _____

20. Number of Independent Variables _____

21. Test Degrees of Freedom _____

22. Coefficient _____

23. Coefficient Standard Error _____

24. Type of Significance Test
    (1) __ Chi-squared   (2) __ F-value
    (3) __ T-score   (4) __ Z-score
    (5) __ Cannot tell   (6) __ Other _____

25. Test Statistic _____

26. P-Value _____

27. One- or Two-Tailed Test _____

28. Treatment Group Sample Size _____

29. Control Group Sample Size _____

30. Treatment Group Mean _____

31. Control Group Mean _____

32. Mean Difference _____

33. Treatment Group Standard Deviation _____

34. Control Group Standard Deviation _____

35. Pooled Standard Deviation _____

36. Effect Size _____

37. Effect Size Standard Error _____

38. Effect Size Type
    (1) __ Glass's *d*   (2) __ Hedges's *g*
    (3) __ *r*   (4) __ Fisher's *Z*
    (5) __ Log odds   (6) __ Risk ratio
    (7) __ Other _____

39. Effect Size Confidence Interval Upper Bound _____

40. Effect Size Confidence Interval Lower Bound _____

41. Effect Size Confidence Interval Level (e.g., .90) _____

Comments:

A2: Performance Management

ID # _____
Coder # _____

Section I: Data for Relevant Studies

1. Bibliographic Information
    a. Author 1
    b. Author 2
    c. Author 3
    d. Year

2. Search Protocol That Found Study

    (1) __ IUCAT (Book)   (2) __ WorldCat (Book)
    (3) __ JSTOR   (4) __ Academic Search Premier
    (5) __ Google Scholar   (6) __ NBER
    (7) __ SSRN   (8) __ ERIC
    (9) __ ProQuest dissertations   (10) __ EconLit
    (11) __ Sociological abstracts (12) __ Social science abstracts
    (13) __ PsychInfo   (14) __ Proceedings First
    (15) __ Ancestry search _____
    (16) __ Conference program _____
    (17) __ Government website _____
    (18) __ Think tank or NGO _____
    (19) __ Personal communication _____
    (20) __ Other _____
    (21) __ Business Search Premier _____

3. Study Relevance
    a. Is study relevant?
        (1) __ Yes   (0) __ No

    b. If no, why not relevant?
        (1) __ Non-analytic   (2) __ Non-quantitative
        (3) __ Outcome measure   (4) __ Treatment type
        (5) __ No original analysis (6) __ Other

ID # _____
Coder # _____

Section II: Study Characteristics

(Complete this section only for "relevant" studies)

Bibliographic Reference (APSA Style): _____

1. Source
   (1) ___ Peer-reviewed article
   (2) ___ Non-peer-reviewed article
   (3) ___ Book or book chapter
   (4) ___ Working paper
   (5) ___ Government document
   (6) ___ Private report
   (7) ___ Dissertation
   (8) ___ Conference paper
   (9) ___ Other unpublished source

2. Is this study acceptable?
   (1) ___ Yes
   (0) ___ No

3. If no, why unacceptable?
   (1) ___ Non-analytic
   (2) ___ Non-quantitative
   (3) ___ Outcome measure
   (4) ___ Treatment type
   (5) ___ No original analysis
   (6) ___ Duplicate study
   (7) ___ Insufficient reporting
   (8) ___ Non-client survey
   (9) ___ Other

4. Discipline of Publication Outlet
   (1) ___ Public administration
   (2) ___ Public policy
   (3) ___ Political science
   (4) ___ Economics
   (5) ___ Sociology
   (6) ___ Geography
   (7) ___ Education
   (8) ___ Psychology
   (9) ___ Business
   (10) ___ Natural science
   (11) ___ Interdisciplinary
   (12) ___ Government
   (13) ___ Other or Can't tell
   (14) ___ Medical or public health
   (15) ___ Criminal justice

ID # _____   **Coder** # _____
Effect# _____   **Page** # _____

Section III: Effects Measures

(Complete this section only for "acceptable" studies.)

Treatment and Outcome Identifiers

1. Type of Outcome Measure [1]
    (1) __ Single output measure
    (2) __ Multiple output measure (includes factor or component analysis)
    (3) __ Single outcome measure
    (4) __ Multiple outcome measure (includes factor or component)
    (5) __ Mixed output and outcome measures
    (6) __ Efficiency (output or outcome over cost)
    (9) __ Other performance measure _____

2. Characteristic of Outcome Measure (CHAR)
    (1) __ Dollars
    (2) __ Client or customer survey response
    (3) __ Test score
    (4) __ Administrative record (e.g., hours worked, number of clients served)
    (5) __ GIS/ IT-generated report (e.g., crimes in geographic area)
    (6) __ Third party report or evaluation (e.g., PART score)
    (7) __ Health outcomes
    (8) __ Multifactor outcome (e.g., dollars and survey response)
    (9) __ Other _____

3. Original Author's Assessment of Outcome Measure's Validity
    (1) __ Valid   (2) __ Not valid
    (9) __ Unknown

4. If Not Valid, Why Not?
    (1) __ Principal-agent theory or gaming
    (2) __ Low-correlation with desired outcome
    (3) __ Poor record-keeping or measurement error
    (4) __ Represents only one (or some) of conflicting organizational goals
    (9) __ Other: _____

---

[1] An output measure is something an organization does. Examples would be staff hours, patients seen, welfare checks processed, pounds of food delivered, and so on. An outcome variable is a harder to measure (typically) but more closely aligned with organizational goals. Examples would be percentage of population not obese, percentage of children below the poverty line receiving assistance, number of individuals food secure, and so on. These measures tend to contain elements of error outside of the organization's control.

5. Domain of Effect
   (1) __ Federal or national   (2) __ State or province
   (3) __ County   (4) __ Municipality
   (9) __ Other

6. Domain of Effect (2)
   (1) __ United States   (2) __ Non-U.S. OECD nation
   (3) __ Non-U.S., Non-OECD   (4) __ Multinational
   (9) __ Other _____

7. Performance Management System (Treatment) by Name (PMNAME)
   (1) __ Management-by-objectives
   (2) __ Total Quality Management (TQM)
   (3) __ Government Performance and Results Act (GPRA)
   (4) __ Performance Assessment Rating Tool (PART)
   (5) __ Performance Budgeting
   (6) __ Performance Contracting
   (7) __ Compstat
   (8) __ JTPA
   (9) __ Pressure Ulcer Expert Panel
   (10) __ Healthcare Effectiveness Data and Information Set (HEDIS)
   (11) __ Hospital Quality Incentive Demonstration (HQID)
   (12) __ Veteran's Health Administration reforms (VA)
   (13) __ Nursing Home Setting Targets—Achieving Results (STAR)
   (14) __ Child Support Performance and Incentive Act of 1998 (CSPIA)
   (15) __ No Child Left Behind (NCLB) or NCLB-like School Accountability
   (16) __ JobCorps
   (99) __ Other _____

8. Length of Treatment (in years) _____

9. Aggregation of Performance Measurement (AGGREG)
   (1) __ Individual
   (2) __ Teams or small groups
   (3) __ Program
   (4) __ Agency (comprising many programs, e.g., HHS, DOT)

Research Design Characteristics

10. Pre-Test Control Included
    (1) __ Yes   (0) __ No

11. Endogeneity of Treatment Controlled For
     (0) __ No
     (1) __ Yes, fixed effects
     (2) __ Yes, matching
     (3) __ Yes, differencing
     (4) __ Yes, instrumental variables
     (5) __ Yes, regression discontinuity
     (6) __ Yes, random assignment
     (9) __ Yes, other _____

12. Method of Assignment to Control Groups
     (1) __ Simple random assignment
     (2) __ Random assignment after matching
     (3) __ Nonrandom, post-hoc matching
     (4) __ Nonrandom, self selection
     (5) __ Nonrandom, other
     (6) __ Multiple methods
     (9) __ Cannot tell

13. Research Design
     (1) __ Experimental
     (2) __ Onegroup quasi-experimental post-only
     (3) __ Onegroup quasi-experimental pre-post
     (4) __ Twogroup quasi-experimental post-only
     (5) __ Twogroup quasi-experimental pre-post
     (6) __ Multigroup quasi-experimental post-only
     (7) __ Multigroup quasi-experimental pre-post
     (9) __ Other

14. Data Structure
     (1) __ Cross-sectional   (3) __ Pooled cross-sections
     (2) __ Time series   (4) __ True panel

Moderating and Mediating Variables

Characteristics of Performance Management Systems

15. Type of Agency (James Q. Wilson's Typology) (JQW)
     (1) __ Production (both outputs and outcomes observable)
     (2) __ Procedural (outputs not outcomes)
     (3) __ Craft (outcomes not outputs)
     (4) __ Coping (neither)
     (9) __ Unknown

16. Type of Agency (OMB's PART Guidance) (OMB)
    (1) __ Direct programs
    (2) __ Competitive grant programs
    (3) __ Block or formula grant programs
    (4) __ Regulatory programs or agencies
    (5) __ Capital assets and service acquisition programs
    (6) __ Credit or credit-enhancement programs
    (7) __ Research and development programs
    (9) __ Unknown or other

17. Broad Issue Area (ISSUE)
    (1) __ Education   (2) __ Job training
    (3) __ Crime and policing (4) __ Poverty and housing
    (5) __ Finance and budgeting (6) __ Public health
    (7) __ Child support   (9) __ Other _____

18. Organizational Structure (ORG)
    (1) __ Horizontal (many offices, small or no central office)
    (2) __ Vertical
    (3) __ Network (Central office with satellite offices—common in contracting)
    (9) __ Unable to determine

19. Source of Performance Management Adoption (ADOPT)
    (1) __ Legislative mandate (2) __ Executive mandate
    (3) __ Top-level management (4) __ Middle-level management
    (5) __ Researcher   (9) __ Other _____

20. Evidence for Support from Upper or Middle Management (MGMT)
    (0) __ No   (1) __ Yes   (2) __ Variable

21. Evidence for Support from Line Staff (LINE)
    (0) __ No   (1) __ Yes   (2) __ Variable

22. Evidence for Support from External Clientele Groups (CLIENT)
    (0) __ No   (1) __ Yes   (2) __ Variable

23. Evidence for Support from External Political Actors (POLS)
    (0) __ No   (1) __ Yes   (2) __ Variable

24. Evidence of Performance Linked to Financial Resources or Organizational Inputs (e.g., performance budgeting) (INPUTS)
    (1) __ Linked   (2) __ Not linked
    (9) __ Unknown or no information

25. Evidence of Performance Info Linked to Organizational Autonomy (e.g., hiring and firing, budget transfer powers) (AUTONOMY)
    (1) __ Linked   (2) __ Not linked
    (9) __ Unknown or no information

26. Evidence of use of benchmarking
    (1) __ Yes, to previous performance (2) __ Yes, within agency
    (3) __ Yes, to other organizations   (4) __ Yes, multiple
    (5) __ No   (9) __ Unknown or no information

Data for Effect Sizes

27. Statistical technique
    (1) __ Difference of means   (2) __ Difference of proportions
    (3) __ Regression   (4) __ ANOVA
    (5) __ Probit   (6) __ Logit
    (7) __ Correlation   (8) __ Chi-squared
    (9) __ Multi-equation models (SEM, SUR)
    (10) __ HLM and mixed models
    (11) __ Other _____

28. Raw Effect Favors
    (1) __ Treatment   (0) __ Control

29. Total Sample Size _____

30. Number of Independent Variables _____

31. Test Degrees of Freedom _____

32. Coefficient _____

33. Coefficient Standard Deviation _____

34. Type of Significance Test
    (1) __ Chi-squared   (2) __ F-value
    (3) __ T-score   (4) __ Z-score
    (5) __ Cannot tell   (9) __ Other _____

35. Test Statistic _____

36. P-Value _____

37. One- or Two-Tailed Test _____

38. Treatment Group Sample Size _____

39. Control Group Sample Size _____

40. Treatment Group Mean _____

41. Control Group Mean _____

42. Mean difference _____

43. Treatment Group Standard Deviation _____

44. Control Group Standard Deviation _____

45. Pooled Standard Deviation _____

46. Effect Size _____

47. Effect Size Type _____

48. Effect Size Standard Error _____

49. Effect Size C.I. _____

50. Effect Size C.I. Alpha _____

51. Interaction Effect Favors
    (1) __ Treatment   (−1) __ Control

Comments:

A3: Public Housing

ID # _____

Coder # _____

Section I: Data for Relevant Studies

1. Bibliographic Information
   a. Author 1
   b. Author 2
   c. Author 3
   d. Year

2. Search Protocol That Found Study
   - (1) ___ IUCAT (Book)
   - (2) ___ WorldCat (Book)
   - (3) ___ JSTOR
   - (4) ___ Academic Search Premier
   - (5) ___ Google Scholar
   - (6) ___ NBER
   - (7) ___ SSRN
   - (8) ___ ERIC
   - (9) ___ ProQuest dissertations
   - (10) ___ EconLit
   - (11) ___ Sociological abstracts
   - (12) ___ Social science abstracts
   - (13) ___ PsychInfo
   - (14) ___ Proceedings First
   - (15) ___ Ancestry search
   - (16) ___ Conference program _____
   - (17) ___ Government website _____
   - (18) ___ Think tank or NGO _____
   - (19) ___ Personal communication _____
   - (20) ___ Other _____

3. Study Relevance
   a. Is study relevant?
      - (1) ___ Yes
      - (0) ___ No

   b. If no, why not relevant?
      - (1) ___ Non-analytic
      - (2) ___ Non-quantitative
      - (3) ___ Outcome measure
      - (4) ___ Treatment type
      - (5) ___ No original analysis
      - (6) ___ Other

ID # _____
Coder # _____

Section II: Study Characteristics

(Complete this section only for "relevant" studies)

Bibliographic Reference (APSA Style): _____

1. Source
    (1) __ Peer-reviewed article   (2) __ Non-peer-reviewed article
    (3) __ Book or book chapter   (4) __ Working paper
    (5) __ Government document   (6) __ Private report
    (7) __ Dissertation   (8) __ Conference paper
    (9) __ Other unpublished source

2. Is this study acceptable?
    (1) __ Yes   (0) __ No

3. If no, why unacceptable?
    (1) __ Non-analytic   (2) __ Non-quantitative
    (3) __ Outcome measure   (4) __ Treatment type
    (5) __ No original analysis   (6) __ Duplicate study
    (7) __ Insufficient reporting   (8) __ Non-client survey
    (9) __ Other

4. Discipline of Publication Outlet
    (1) __ Public administration   (2) __ Public policy
    (3) __ Political science   (4) __ Economics
    (5) __ Sociology   (6) __ Geography
    (7) __ Education   (8) __ Psychology
    (9) __ Business   (10) __ Natural science
    (11) __ Interdisciplinary   (12) __ Other or can't tell

ID # ____   **Coder** # ____
Effect # ____   **Page** # ____

Section III: Effects Measures

(Complete this section only for "acceptable" studies)

Treatment and Outcome Identifiers

1. Outcome Measure
   (1) __ Income   (2) __ Welfare receipt
   (3) __ Employment   (4) __ Economic well-being (aggregated)
   (5) __ Crime or delinquency
        (general index, arrests,
        expelled from school)
   (6) __ Violent crime   (7) __ Property crime
   (8) __Risky behaviors (drug,
        alcohol, cigarettes, sexual
        behaviors, and so on)
   (9) __ Other _____

2. Domain of Effect
   (1) __ Overall   (2) __ Males
   (3) __ Females   (4) __ Blacks
   (5) __ Whites   (6) __ Latinos
   (7) __ Adults   (8) __ Youth
   (9) __ Other

3. Programs
   (1) __ Gautreaux   (2) __ MTO voucher
   (3) __ MTO Section 8   (4) __ Mixed-income development
   (5) __ Section 8 voucher   (6) __ Hope VI voucher
   (7) __ Other or multiple

4. Study sites
   (1) __ Atlanta   (2) __ Baltimore
   (3) __ Boston   (4) __ Chicago
   (5) __ Los Angeles   (6) __ Philadelphia
   (7) __ Multicity or national   (8) __ Other
   (9) __ New York City

5. Length of Time Since Policy Intervention Began Until This Study _____

Research Design Characteristics

6. Pre-Test Control Included
   (1) __ Yes   (0) __ No

7. Endogeneity of Treatment Controlled For
   (0) __ No
   (1) __ Yes, fixed effects
   (2) __ Yes, matching
   (3) __ Yes, differencing
   (4) __ Yes, instrumental variables
   (5) __ Yes, regression discontinuity
   (6) __ Yes, random assignment
   (7) __ Yes, other _____

8. Method of Assignment to Control Groups
   (1) __ Simple random assignment
   (2) __ Random assignment after matching
   (3) __ Nonrandom, post-hoc matching
   (4) __ Nonrandom, self selection
   (5) __ Nonrandom, other
   (6) __ Multiple methods
   (9) __ Cannot tell

9. Research Design
   (1) __ Experimental
   (2) __ Onegroup quasi-experimental post-only
   (3) __ Onegroup quasi-experimental pre-post
   (4) __ Twogroup quasi-experimental post-only
   (5) __ Twogroup quasi-experimental pre-post
   (6) __ Multigroup quasi-experimental post-only
   (7) __ Multigroup quasi-experimental pre-post
   (9) __ Other _____

10. Data Structure
    (1) __ Cross-sectional   (3) __ Pooled cross-sections
    (2) __ Time series   (4) __ True panel

11. Intention to Treat (1)   Treatment of the Treated (0)

Moderating and Mediating Variables

12. Did the Treatment Improve Proximity to Jobs?
    (1) __ Yes   (0) __ No

13. Did the Treatment Increase the Density of Social Network?
    (1) __ Yes   (0) __ No

14. Did the Treatment Improve Aggregate Measures of Destination Neighborhoods?

    A. Unemployment rate?   (1) __ Yes   (0) __ No
    B. Crime rate?   (1) __ Yes   (0) __ No
    C. School quality?   (1) __ Yes   (0) __ No
    D. Median Household Income?   (1) __ Yes   (0) __ No

Data for Effect Sizes

15. Statistical Technique
    (1) __ Difference of means   (2) __ Difference of prop.
    (3) __ Regression   (4) __ ANOVA
    (5) __ Probit   (6) __ Logit
    (7) __ Correlation   (8) __ Chi-squared
    (9) __ Other _____

16. Raw Effect Favors
    (1) __ Treatment   (0) __ Control

17. Type of Effect
    (1) __ Intention to Treat
    (2) __ Treatment of the Treated

18. Treatment Group Sample Size _____

19. Control Group Sample Size _____

20. Total Sample Size _____

21. Treatment Group Mean _____

22. Control Group Mean _____

23. Mean Difference _____

24. Treatment Group Standard Deviation _____

25. Control Group Standard Deviation _____

26. Pooled Standard Deviation _____

27. Coefficient _____

28. Coefficient Standard Deviation _____

29. Type of Significance Test
    (1) __ Chi-squared   (2) __ F-value
    (3) __ T-score   (4) __ Z-score
    (5) __ Cannot tell   (6) __ Other _____

30. Est Statistic _____

31. P-Value _____

32. One- or Two-Tailed Test _____

33. Test Degree of Freedom _____

34. Number of Independent Variables _____

35. Effect Size _____

36. Effect Size Standard Error _____

37. Effect Size Type
    (1) __ Glass's *d*   (2) __ Hedges's *g*
    (3) __ *r*   (4) __ Fisher's *Z*
    (5) __ Log odds   (6) __ Risk ratio
    (7) __ Other _____

38. Effect Size Confidence Interval Upper Bound _____

39. Effect Size Confidence Interval Lower Bound _____

40. Effect Size Confidence Interval Level (e.g., .90) _____

Comments:

A4: Public Service Motivation

ID # _____
Coder # _____

Section I: Data for Relevant Studies

1. Bibliographic Information
   a. Author 1
   b. Author 2
   c. Author 3
   d. Year

2. Search Protocol That Found Study
   - (1) __ IUCAT (Book)
   - (2) __ WorldCat (Book)
   - (3) __ JSTOR
   - (4) __ Academic Search Premier
   - (5) __ Google Scholar
   - (6) __ NBER
   - (7) __ SSRN
   - (8) __ ERIC
   - (9) __ ProQuest dissertations
   - (10) __ EconLit
   - (11) __ Sociological abstracts
   - (12) __ Social science abstracts
   - (13) __ PsychInfo
   - (14) __ Proceedings First
   - (15) __ Ancestry search _____
   - (16) __ Conference program _____
   - (17) __ Government website _____
   - (18) __ Think tank or NGO _____
   - (19) __ Personal communication _____
   - (20) __ Other _____

3. Study Relevance
   a. Is study relevant?
      - (1) __ Yes
      - (0) __ No

   b. If no, why not relevant?
      - (1) __ Non-analytic
      - (2) __ Non-quantitative
      - (3) __ Outcome Measure
      - (4) __ Treatment Type
      - (5) __ No Original Analysis
      - (6) __ Other

Section II: Study Characteristics

(Complete this section only for "relevant" studies)

Bibliographic Reference (APSA Style): _____

1. Source
   - (1) __ Peer-reviewed article
   - (2) __ Non-peer-reviewed article
   - (3) __ Book or book chapter
   - (4) __ Working paper
   - (5) __ Government document
   - (6) __ Private report
   - (7) __ Dissertation
   - (8) __ Conference paper
   - (9) __ Other unpublished source

2. Is this study acceptable?
   - (1) __ Yes
   - (0) __ No

3. If no, why unacceptable?
   - (1) __ Non-analytic
   - (2) __ Non-quantitative
   - (3) __ Outcome measure
   - (4) __ Treatment type
   - (5) __ No original analysis
   - (6) __ Duplicate study
   - (7) __ Insufficient reporting
   - (9) __ Other

4. Discipline of Publication Outlet
   - (1) __ Public administration
   - (2) __ Public policy
   - (3) __ Political science
   - (4) __ Economics
   - (5) __ Sociology
   - (6) __ Geography
   - (7) __ Education
   - (8) __ Psychology
   - (9) __ Business
   - (10) __ Natural science
   - (11) __ Interdisciplinary
   - (12) __ Other or can't tell

Section III: Effects Measures

(Complete this section only for "acceptable" studies)

Treatment and Outcome Identifiers

1. Outcome Measure
    (1) __ Self-reported performance
    (2) __ Self-reported external evaluations of their performance (pay grade)
    (3) __ Self-reported external evaluations of their performance (performance evaluations or appraisals)
    (4) __ Self-reported perception of work unit (e.g., department) performance
    (5) __ Self-reported perception of organizational performance (procedural efficiency)
    (6) __ Self-reported perception of organization performance (performance improvement over time)
    (7) __ Share of services provided to disabled patients
    (8) __ Self-reported work effort
    (9) __ Whistle-blowing
    (10) __ Other outcome _____

2. Domain of Effect
    (1) __ Overall (U.S.)   (2) __ U.S. federal organizations
    (3) __ U.S. or state organizations   (4) __ U.S. local (city or county) organizations
    (5) __ Overall (non-U.S.)   (6) __ Non-U.S. federal organizations
    (7) __ Non-U.S. state organizations   (8) __ Non-U.S. local organizations
    (9) __ U.S. NGO   (10) __ Non-U.S. NGO
    (11) __ Other

3. Treatment Type
    (1) __ Attraction to policy making
    (2) __ Commitment to the public interest or civic duty
    (3) __ Compassion
    (4) __ Self-sacrifice
    (5) __ Index of 1, 2, 3, and 4 above
    (6) __ Index of 1, 2, and 3 above
    (7) __ Index of 2, 3, and 4 above
    (8) __ Other _____

4. Length of Treatment _____

Research Design Characteristics

5. Pre-Test Control Included
   (1) __ Yes   (0) __ No

6. Endogeneity of Treatment Controlled For
   (0) __ No
   (1) __ Yes, fixed effects
   (2) __ Yes, matching
   (3) __ Yes, differencing
   (4) __ Yes, instrumental variables
   (5) __ Yes, regression discontinuity
   (6) __ Yes, random assignment
   (7) __ Yes, other _____

7. Method of Assignment to Control Groups
   (1) __ Simple random assignment
   (2) __ Random assignment after matching
   (3) __ Nonrandom, post-hoc matching
   (4) __ Nonrandom, self selection
   (5) __ Nonrandom, other
   (6) __ Multiple methods
   (9) __ Cannot tell

8. Research Design
   (1) __ Experimental
   (2) __ Onegroup quasi-experimental post-only
   (3) __ Onegroup quasi-experimental pre-post
   (4) __ Twogroup quasi-experimental post-only
   (5) __ Twogroup quasi-experimental pre-post
   (6) __ Multigroup quasi-experimental post-only
   (7) __ Multigroup quasi-experimental pre-post
   (9) __ Other _____

9. Data Structure
   (1) __ Cross-sectional   (3) __ Pooled cross-sections
   (2) __ Time series   (4) __ True panel

Moderating and Mediating Variables

Does the survey include the following?
10. Variable About the Level of Congruence Between Employees' and Organization's Goals or Values (person-environment fit or PSM-fit) (FIT)?
    (1) __ Yes   (0) __ No

11. Survey Asks About Employee's Perception of the Style of Leadership in Their Organization (LEADERSHIP)?
    (1) __ Yes   (0) __ No

12. Employees' Level of Job Satisfaction (JOBSATIS)?
    (1) __ Yes   (0) __ No

13. Employees' Level of Pay Satisfaction (PAYSATIS)?
    (1) __ Yes   (0) __ No

14. Level of Commitment to the Organization (COMMIT)?
    (1) __ Yes   (0) __ No

15. Gender of Respondent (GENDER)?
    (1) __ Yes   (0) __ No

16. Age of Respondent (AGE)?
    (1) __ Yes   (0) __ No

17. Educational Attainment of Respondent (EDU)?
    (1) __ Yes   (0) __ No

18. Variable for If the Respondent Has a Supervisory Role (SUPERVISOR)?
    (1) __ Yes   (0) __ No

19. Interaction of PSM with Employee Perception of the Use of Merit-Based Appraisal
    Systems?
    (1) __ Yes   (0) __ No

20. Variable for Mean PSM for the Organization?
    (1) __ Yes   (0) __ No

21. Variable for Standard Deviation of PSM for the Organization?
    (1) __ Yes   (0) __ No

Data for Effect Sizes

22. Statistical Technique
    (1) __ Difference of means   (2) __ Difference of proportions
    (3) __ Regression   (4) __ ANOVA
    (5) __ Probit   (6) __ Logit
    (7) __ Correlation   (8) __ Chi-squared
    (9) __ Multi-equation models (e.g., path analysis, SEM)
    (10) __ Mixed models (e.g., HLM)
    (11) __ Other _____

23. Raw Effect Favors
    (1) __ Treatment   (0) __ Control

24. Total Sample Size _____

25. Number of Independent Variables _____

26. Test Degrees of Freedom _____

27. Coefficient _____

28. Coefficient Standard Error _____

29. Type of Significance Test
    (1) __ Chi-squared   (2) __ F-value
    (3) __ T-score   (4) __ Z-score
    (5) __ Cannot tell   (6) __ Other _____

30. Test Statistic _____

31. P-Value _____

32. One- or Two-Tailed Test _____

33. Treatment Group Sample Size _____

34. Control Group Sample Size _____

35. Treatment Group Mean _____

36. Control Group Mean _____

37. Mean Difference _____

38. Treatment Group Standard Deviation _____

39. Control Group Standard Deviation _____

40. Pooled Standard Deviation _____

41. Effect Size _____

42. Effect Size Standard Error _____

43. Effect Size Type
    (1) __ Glass's d (2) __ Hedges's g
    (3) __ r (4) __ Fisher's Z
    (5) __ Log odds   (6) __ Risk ratio
    (7) __ Other _____

44. Effect Size Confidence Interval Upper Bound _____

45. Effect Size Confidence Interval Lower Bound _____

46. Effect Size Confidence Interval Level (e.g., .90) _____

Comments:

REFERENCES

Acemoglu, D., and J. Pischke. 2003. "Minimum Wages and On-the-Job Training." *Research in Labor Economics* 22 (1):159–202.

Alliance for School Choice. 2011. *The Facts About School Choice 2010*. http://www.alliance forschoolchoice.org/school-choice-facts (accessed November 19, 2011).

Aloe, Ariel, and Betsy Jane Becker. Forthcoming. "An Effect Size for Regression Predictors in Meta-Analysis." *Journal of Educational and Behavioral Statistics* (DOI: 10.3102/1076998610396901).

American Federation of Teachers. 2002. *Private School Vouchers: The Track Record* 2000. http://www.aft.org/research/vouchers/trackrecord.htm (accessed March 8, 2002).

Andersen, Lotte B., and S. Serritzlew. 2009. *"Does Public Service Motivation Affect the Behavior of Professionals?"* Paper presented at the International Public Service Motivation Research Conference, June 7–10, Bloomington, IN.

Anderson, E. 1999. *Code of the Street: Decency, Violence, and the Moral Life of the Inner City*. New York: WW Norton.

Anderton, Douglas, Andy Anderson, John Michael Oakes, and Michael Fraser. 1994. "Environmental Equity: The Demographics of Dumping." *Demography* 31:229–248.

Arellano, M. 1987. "Computing Robust Standard Errors for Within-Group Estimators." *Oxford Bulletin of Economics and Statistics* 49:431–434.

Ashenfelter, O., C. Harmon, and H. Oosterbeek. 1999. "A Review of Estimates of the Schooling/Earnings Relationship, with Tests for Publication Bias." *Labour Economics* 6 (3):453–470.

Associated Press. 2011. *"School Voucher Bills Flood GOP-Led Statehouses,"* August 2.

Baier, R. R., K. Butterfield, S. Gravenstein, and Y. Harris. 2008. "Aiming for Star Performance: The Relationship Between Setting Targets and Improved Nursing Home Quality of Care." *Journal of the American Medical Directors Association* 9 (8):594–598.

Bangert-Drowns, R. L. 1986. "Review of Developments in Meta-Analytic Methods." *Psychological Bulletin* 99:388–399.

Barnard, John, Constantine E. Frangakis, Jennifer L. Hill, and Donald B. Rubin. 2003. "Principal Stratification Approach to Broken Randomized Experiments." *Journal of the American Statistical Association* 98 (462):299–323.

Barnow, Burt. 1987. "The Impact of CETA Programs on Earnings: A Review of the Literature." *Journal of Human Resources* 22 (2):157–193.

Barnow, Burt S. 2000. "Exploring the Relationship Between Performance Management and Program Impact: A Case Study of the Job Training Partnership Act." *Journal of Policy Analysis and Management* 19 (1):118–141.

Bateman, Ian, and Andrew Jones. 2003. "Contrasting Conventional with Multi-Level Modeling Approaches to Meta-Analysis: Expectation Consistency in UK Woodlot Recreation Values." *Land Economics* 79 (2):235–258.

Becker, Betsy Jane. 1989. "Gender and Science Achievement: A Reanalysis of Studies from Two Meta-Analyses." *Journal of Research in Science Teaching* 26 (2):141–169.

Becker, Betsy Jane. 1992. "Using Results from Replicated Studies to Estimate Linear Models." *Journal of Educational Statistics* 17 (4):341–362.

Becker, Betsy Jane. 2005. "Failsafe N or File Drawer Number." In *Publication Bias in Meta-Analysis*, ed. H. Rothstein, A. Sutton, and M. Borenstein, 111–125. New York: John Wiley & Sons.

Becker, Betsy Jane. 2009. "Model-Based Meta-Analysis." In *The Handbook of Research Synthesis and Meta-Analysis, 2nd edition*, ed. Harris Cooper, Larry Hedges, and Jeffrey Valentine, 377–398. New York: Russell Sage Foundation.

Becker, Betsy Jane, and Meng-Jia Wu. 2007. "The Synthesis of Regression Slopes in Meta-Analysis." *Statistical Science* 22 (3):414–429.

Becker, Gary S., and Tomes, Nigel. 1986. "Human Capital and the Rise and Fall of Families." *Journal of Labor Economics* 4 (3, pt. 2):S1–S39.

Begg, Colin, and Jesse Berlin. 1988. "Publication Bias: A Problem in Interpreting Medical Data." *Journal of the Royal Statistical Society, Series A* 151 (3):419–463.

Begg, Colin, and Madhuchhanda Mazumdar. 1994. "Operating Characteristics of a Rank Correlation Test for Publication Bias." *Biometrics* 50 (4):1088–1101.

Behn, Robert D. 2003. "Why Measure Performance? Different Purposes Require Different Measures." *Public Administration Review* 63 (5):586–606.

Bel, Germa, Xavier Fageda, and Mildred Warnerd. 2010. "Is Private Production of Public Services Cheaper Than Public Production? A Meta-Regression of Solid Waste and Water Services." *Journal of Policy Analysis and Management* 29 (3):553–577.

Bell, R., and D. McCaffrey. 2002. "Bias Reduction in Standard Errors for Linear Regression with Multi-Stage Samples." *Survey Methodology* 28 (2):169–179.

Berkely, C. S., D. C. Hoaglin, F. Mosteller, and G. A. Colditz. 1995. "A Random-Effects Regression Model for Meta-Analysis." *Statistics in Medicine* 14 (4):395–411.

Berlin, Jesse A., and Graham A. Colditz. 1999. "The Role of Meta-analysis in the Regulatory Process for Foods, Drugs, and Devices." *The Journal of the American Medical Association* 281 (9):830–834.

Berman, Evan. 2002. "How Useful Is Performance Measurement." *Public Performance & Management Review* 25 (4):348–351.

Berry, William, and Stanley Feldman. 1985. *Multiple Regression in Practice*. Thousand Oaks, CA: Sage.

Bland, J. M. 1988. "Discussion of the Paper by Begg and Berlin." *Journal of the Royal Statistical Society, Series A* 151 (3):450–451.

Blau, Peter M., and Otis Dudley Duncan. 1967. *The American Occupational Structure*. New York: Wiley.

Borenstein, Michael. 2009. "Effect Sizes for Continuous Data." In *The Handbook of Research Synthesis and Meta-Analysis*, ed. Harris Cooper, Larry Hedges, and Jeffrey Valentine, 221–236. New York: Russell Sage Foundation.

Borenstein, Michael, Larry V. Hedges, Julian P. T. Higgins, and Hannah R. Rothstein. 2009. *Introduction to Meta-Analysis*. Chichester, U.K.: John Wiley & Sons.

Boudville, Neil, et al. 2006. "Meta-Analysis: Risk for Hypertension in Living Kidney Donors." *Annals of Internal Medicine* 145:185–196.

Bowman, Nicholas. 2010a. "College Diversity Experiences and Cognitive Development: A Meta-Analysis." *Review of Educational Research* 80 (1):4–33.

Bowman, Nicholas. 2010b. "Promoting Participation in a Diverse Democracy: A Meta-Analysis of College Diversity Experiences and Civic Engagement." *Review of Educational Research* 81 (1):29–68.

Boyne, George A., and Alex A. Chen. 2007. "Performance Targets and Public Service Improvement." *Journal of Public Administration Research & Theory* 17 (3): 455–477.

Bradbury, Katharine, and Katz, Jane (2009). *Trends in U.S. Family Income Mobility, 1967–2004*. Federal Reserve Bank of Boston Working Paper Series, No. 09–7.

Brewer, Gene A. 2008. "Employee and Organizational Performance." In *Motivation in Public Management: The Call of Public Service*, ed. J. L. Perry and A. Hondeghem. Oxford: Oxford University Press.

Brewer, Gene A., and Sally Coleman Selden. 1998. "Whistle Blowers in the Federal Civil Service: New Evidence of the Public Service Ethic." *Journal of Public Administration Research and Theory* 8 (3):413–440.

Brewer, Gene A., and Sally Coleman Selden. 2000. "Why Elephants Gallop: Assessing and Predicting Organizational Performance in Federal Agencies." *Journal of Public Administration Research and Theory* 10 (4):685–711.

Bright, Leonard. 2007. "Does Person-Organization Fit Mediate the Relationship Between Public Service Motivation and the Job Performance of Public Employees?" *Review of Public Personnel Administration* 27 (4):361–379.

Brooks-Gunn, J., G. J. Duncan, P. K. Klebanov, and N. Sealand. 1993. "Do Neighborhoods Influence Child and Adolescent Development?" *American Journal of Sociology*:353–395.

Bundorf, M. Kate, Kavita Choudhry, and Laurence Baker. 2008. "Health Plan Performance Measurement: Does It Affect Quality of Care for Medicare Managed Care Enrollees?" *Inquiry* 45 (2):168–183.

Burton, Paul, Lyle Gurrin, and Peter Sly. 1998. "Extending the Simple Linear Regression Model to Account for Correlated Responses: An Introduction to Generalized Estimating Equations and Multi-Level Mixed Modelling." *Statistics in Medicine* 17:1261–1291.

Callot, Laurent, and Martin Paldam. 2011. "The Problem of Natural Funnel Asymmetries: A Simulation Analysis of Meta-Analysis in Macroeconomics." *Research Synthesis Methods* 2 (2):84–102.

Cameron, A. Colin, Jonah B. Gelbach, and Douglas L. Miller. 2008. "Bootstrap-Based Improvements for Inference with Clustered Errors." *Review of Economics and Statistics* 90 (3):414–427.

Cameron, A. Colin, Jonah Gelbach, and Douglas Miller. 2011. "Robust Inference with Multiway Clustering." *Journal of Business and Economic Statistics* 29 (2):238–249.

Campanella, Andrew, Malcolmn Glenn, and Lauren Perry. 2011. "Hope for America's Children." In School Choice *Yearbook* 2010–11. Washington, DC: Alliance for School Choice.

Cappelleri, Joseph C., et al. 1996. "Large Trials vs. Meta-Analysis of Smaller Trials." *The Journal of the American Medical Association* 276 (16):1332–1338.

Card, David, and Alan B. Krueger. 1995. "Time-Series Minimum-Wage Studies: A Meta-Analysis." *The American Economic Review* 85 (2):238–243.

Case, A. C., and L. F. Katz. 1991. "The Company You Keep: The Effects of Family and Neighborhood on Disadvantaged Youths." National Bureau of Economic Research working paper.

Catalano, R. F., and J. D. Hawkins. 1996. "*The Social Development Model.*" In *In Delinquency and Crime: Current Theories*. New York: Cambridge University Press.

Cavalluzzo, Ken S., and Christopher D. Ittner. 2003. "Implementing Performance Measurement Innovations: Evidence from Government." *Accounting, Organizations and Society* 29 (3–4):243–267.

Center on Education Policy. 2011. *Keeping Informed About School Vouchers: A Review of Major Developments and Research*. Washington, DC.

Chilvers, M., and D. Weatherburn. 2001. "*Do Targeted Arrests Reduce Crime?*" *Contemporary Issues in Crime and Justice* no. 63. Government report, New South Wales, Australia.

Chilvers, M., and D. Weatherburn. 2004. "The New South Wales 'Compstat' Process: Its Impact on Crime." *The Australian & New Zealand Journal of Criminology* 37:22–48.

Chubb, John E., and Terry M. Moe. 1990. "*Politics, Markets, and America's Schools.*" Washington, DC: Brookings Institution.

Clampet-Lundquist, Susan, and Douglas S. Massey. 2008. "Neighborhood Effects on Economic Self-Sufficiency: A Reconsideration of the Moving to Opportunity Experiment." *American Journal of Sociology* 114 (1):107–143.

Cohen, Jacob. 1988. *Statistical Power Analysis for the Behavioral Sciences*. Hillsdale, NJ: Lawrence Erlbaum Associates.

Coleman, J. S., et al. 1966. "*Equality of Educational Opportunity.*" Washington: U.S. Government Printing Office.

Cook, Thomas, and Donald Campbell. 1979. *Quasi-Experimentation: Design and Analysis Issues for Field Settings*. Boston: Houghton Mifflin.

Cook, Thomas, et al. 1992. *Meta-Analysis for Explanation: A Casebook*. New York: Russell Sage Foundation.

Cooper, Harris. 1982. "Scientific Guidelines for Conducting Integrative Research Reviews." *Review of Educational Research* 52 (2):291–302.

Cooper, Harris. 2003. *Ways of Taking Stock: Replication, Scaling Up, Meta-Analysis, Professional Consensus Building*. Paper read at Workshop on Understanding and Promoting Knowledge Accumulation in Education: Tools and Strategy for Education Research, July 1.

Cooper, Harris. 2007. "*Evaluating and Interpreting Research Syntheses in Adult Learning and Literacy.*" National Center for the Study of Adult Learning and Literacy Occasional Paper. Boston, MA: NCALL.

Cooper, Harris. 2010. *Research Synthesis and Meta-Analysis: A Step-by-Step Approach*, *4th edition*. Los Angeles: Sage.

Cooper, H., and L. V. Hedges. 1994a. "Research Synthesis as a Scientific Enterprise." In *The Handbook of Research Synthesis*, ed. Harris Cooper and Larry Hedges. New York: Russell Sage Foundation.

Cooper, H., and L. V. Hedges. 1994b. "*The Handbook of Research Synthesis.*" ed. Harris Cooper and Larry Hedges: Russell Sage Foundation.

Cooper, H., L. V. Hedges, and J. Valentine, eds. 2009. *The Handbook of Research Synthesis and Meta-Analysis, 2nd edition*. New York: Russell Sage Foundation.

Copas, John. 1999. "What Works?: Selectivity Models and Meta-Analysis." *Journal of the Royal Statistical Society: Series A (Statistics in Society)* 162 (1):95–109.

Copas, John, and Claudia Lozada-Can. 2009. "The Radial Plot in Meta-Analysis: Approximations and Applications." *Journal of the Royal Statistical Society: Series C (Applied Statistics)* 58 (3):329–344.

Copas, John B., and Paul F. Malley. 2008. "A Robust P-Value for Treatment Effect in Meta-Analysis with Publication Bias." *Statistics in Medicine* 27 (21):4267–4278.

Copas, John, and Jian Qing Shi. 2000. "Meta-Analysis, Funnel Plots and Sensitivity Analysis." *Biostatistics* 1 (3):247–262.

Copas, John, and Jian Qing Shi. 2001. "A Sensitivity Analysis for Publication Bias in Systematic Reviews." *Statistical Methods in Medical Research* 10 (2):251–265.

Corcoran, M. 1995. "Rags to Rags: Poverty and Mobility in the United States." *Annual Review of Sociology*:237–267.

Cordray, David, and Paul Morphy. 2009. "Research Synthesis and Public Policy." In *The Handbook of Research Synthesis and Meta-Analysis, 2nd edition*, ed. Harris Cooper, Larry Hedges, and Jeffrey Valentine, pp. 473–497. New York: Russell Sage Foundation.

Courty, Pascal, and Gerald Marschke. 2004. "An Empirical Investigation of Gaming Responses to Explicit Performance Incentives." *Journal of Labor Economics* 22 (1):23–56.

Courty, Pascal, and Gerald Marschke. 2007. "Making Government Accountable: Lessons from a Federal Job Training Program." *Public Administration Review* 67 (5):904–916.

Courty, P., and G. Marschke. 2008. "A General Test for Distortions in Performance Measures." *The Review of Economics and Statistics* 90 (3):428–441.

Cowen, Joshua M. 2008. "School Choice as a Latent Variable: Estimating the "Complier Average Causal Effect" of Vouchers in Charlotte." *Policy Studies Journal* 36 (2):301–315.

Cragg, Michael. 1997. "Performance Incentives in the Public Sector: Evidence from the Job Training Partnership Act." *Journal of Law, Economics, & Organization* 13 (1):147–168.

Crewson, Philip E. 1997. "Public-Service Motivation: Building Empirical Evidence of Incidence and Effect." *Journal of Public Administration Research and Theory* 7 (4):499–518.

Danziger, Sheldon, and Peter Gottschalk. 1987. "Earnings Inequality, the Spatial Concentration of Poverty, and the Underclass." *The American Economic Review* 77 (2):211–215.

Darling, N., and L. Steinberg. 1997. "Community Influences on Adolescent Achievement and Deviance." In *Neighborhood Poverty: Context and Consequences for Children*, ed. J. Brooks-Gunn, G. Duncan, and J. Aber, pp. 120–131. New York: Russell Sage Foundation.

Davidson, Pamela, and Douglas Anderton. 2000. "Demographics of Dumping II: A National Environmental Equity Survey and the Distribution of Hazardous Materials Handlers." *Demography* 37 (4):461–466.

Davidson, Russell, and James MacKinnon. 1999. "The Size Distortion of Bootstrap Tests." *Econometric Theory* 15:361–376.

De Long, J. Bradford, and Kevin Lang. 1992. "Are All Economic Hypotheses False?" *Journal of Political Economy* 100 (6):1257–1272.

de Souza Briggs, X., S. J. Popkin, and J. M. Goering. 2010. *Moving to Opportunity: The Story of an American Experiment to Fight Ghetto Poverty*. Oxford: Oxford University Press.

DeCharms, Richard. 1968. *Personal Causation: The Internal Affective Determinants of Behavior*. New York: Academic Press.

Deci, Edward L. 1971. "Effects of Externally Mediated Rewards on Intrinsic Motivation." *Journal of Personality and Social Psychology* 18 (1):105–115.

Deci, Edward L. 1975. *Intrinsic Motivation*. New York: Plenum Press.

Deci, Edward L., and Richard M. Ryan. 2004. *Handbook of Self-Determination Research*. Rochester, NY: University of Rochester Press.

Dee, Thomas, and Brian Jacob. 2009. "*The Impact of No Child Left Behind on Student Achievement*." *National Bureau of Economic Research Working Paper Series* No. 15531.

Dee, Thomas, and Brian Jacob. 2011. "The Impact of No Child Left Behind on Student Achievement." *Journal of Policy Analysis and Management* 30 (3):418–446.

DeHart-Davis, Leisha, Justin Marlowe, and Sanjay K. Pandey. 2006. "Gender Dimensions of Public Service Motivation." *Public Administration Review* 66 (6):873–887.

DeLeon, Peter. 1998. "Models of Policy Discourse: Insights Versus Prediction." *Policy Studies Journal* 26 (1):147–161.

DeNavas-Walt, Carmen, Bernadette D. Proctor, and Jessica C. Smith. 2008. *Income, Poverty, and Health Insurance Coverage in the United States: 2007*, U.S. Census Bureau, Current Population Reports, P60-235. Washington, DC: U.S. Government Printing Office.

Denton, Frank T. 1985. "Data Mining as an Industry." *The Review of Economics and Statistics* 67 (1):124–127.

DerSimonian, Rebecca, and Nan Laird. 1986. "Meta-Analysis in Clinical Trials." *Controlled Clinical Trials* 7 (3):177–188.

Dickersin, Kay. 2002. "Reducing Reporting Biases." In *The James Lind Library*, ed. I. Chalmers, I. Milne, and U. Trohler (www.jameslindlibrary.org).

Dickersin, K., and I. Chalmers. 2010. *Recognizing, Investigating, and Dealing with Incomplete and Biased Reporting of Clinical Research: From Francis Bacon to the World Health Organization*. http://www.jameslindlibrary.org/essays/biased_reporting/biased_reporting.html (accessed April 19, 2012).

Dickersin, Kay, S. Chan, T. Chalmers, H. Sacks, and H. Smith. 1987. "Publication Bias in Clinical Trials." *Controlled Clinical Trials* 8:343–353.

Dickinson, Katherine, et al. 2011. *Evaluation of the Effects of JTPA Performance Standards on Clients, Services, and Costs: Final Report.* National Commission for Employment Policy Research Report No. 88–16.

Donohue, John J., and Steven D. Levitt. 2001. "The Impact of Legalized Abortion on Crime." *The Quarterly Journal of Economics* 116 (2):379–420.

Doucouliagos, C., P. Laroche, and T. D. Stanley. 2005. "Publication Bias in Union Productivity Research." *Industrial Relations* 60 (2):320–346.

Doucouliagos, Hristos, and Mehmet Ali Ulubaşoğlu. 2008. "Democracy and Economic Growth: A Meta-Analysis." *American Journal of Political Science* 52 (1):61–83.

Downey, Liam. 1998. "Environmental Injustice: Is Race or Income a Better Predictor?" *Social Science Quarterly* 79 (4):766–778.

Draper, Norman, and Harry Smith. 1981. *Applied Regression Analysis, 2nd ed.* New York: Wiley Interscience.

Dreier, Peter, John Mollenkopf, and Todd Swanstrom. 2004. *Place Matters: Metropolitics for the Twenty-First Century, 2nd ed.* Lawrence: University Press of Kansas.

Dubow, E. F., Edwards, S., and Ippolito, M. F. 1997. "Life Stressors, Neighborhood Disadvantage, and Resources: A Focus on Inner-City Children's Adjustment." *Journal of Clinical Child Psychology* 26:130–144.

DuMouchel, William, and Sharon-Lise Normand. 2000. "Computer-Modeling and Graphical Strategies for Meta-Analysis." In *Meta-Analysis in Medicine and Health Policy*, ed. Dalene Stangl and Donald Berry. New York: Marcel Dekker.

Duval, Sue, and Richard Tweedie. 2000a. "Trim and Fill: A Simple Funnel-Plot-Based Method of Testing and Adjusting for Publication Bias in Meta-Analysis." *Biometrics* 56 (2):455–463.

Duval, Sue, and Richard Tweedie. 2000b. "A Nonparametric 'Trim and Fill' Method of Accounting for Publication Bias in Meta-Analysis." *Journal of the American Statistical Association* 95 (449):89–98.

Dyson, Freeman. 1996. "The Scientist as Rebel." *American Mathematical Monthly* 130 (9):800–805.

Dyson, Freeman. 1998. "Science as a Craft Industry." *Science* 280 (5366):1014–1015.

Egger, M., P. Jüni, C. Bartlett, F. Holenstein, and J. Sterne. 2003. *"How Important Are Comprehensive Literature Searches and the Assessment of Trial Quality in Systematic Reviews? Empirical Study."* Executive Summary. *Health Technology Assessment 2003* 7 (1).

Egger, Matthias, George Davey Smith, Martin Schneider, and Christoph Minder. 1997. "Bias in Meta-Analysis Detected by a Simple, Graphical Test." *British Medical Journal* 315 (7109):629–634.

Ellis, Paul. 2010. *The Essential Guide to Effect Sizes: Statistical Power, Meta-Analysis, and the Interpretation of Research Results.* New York: Cambridge University Press.

Elmore, Richard. 1979. "Backward Mapping: Implementation Research and Policy Decisions." *Political Science Quarterly* 94 (4):601–616.

Elwood, David T., and Christopher Jencks. 2004. "The Uneven Spread of Single Parent Families: What Do We Know? Where Do We Look for Answers?" In *Social Inequality*, ed. Kathryn Neckerman. New York: Russell Sage Foundation.

Emerson, G., et al. 2010. "Testing for the Presence of Positive-Outcome Bias in Peer Review." *Archives of Internal Medicine* 170:1934–1939.

Epstein, W. 1990. "Confirmational Response Bias Among Social Work Journals." *Science, Technology, and Human Values* 15:9–37.

Eterno, John A., and Eli B. Silverman. 2010. "The NYPD's Compstat: Compare Statistics or Compose Statistics?" *International Journal of Police Science & Management* 12 (3):426–449.

Eysenck, H. J. 1978. "An Exercise in Meta-Silliness." *American Psychologist* 33 (5):517.

Farley, John, Donald Lehmann, and Alan Sawyer. 1995. "Empirical Marketing Generalization Using Meta-Analysis." *Marketing Science* 14 (3):G36–G48.

Fay, Michael, and Barry Graubard. 2001. "Small Sample Adjustments for Wald-Type Tests Using Sandwich Estimators." *Biometrics* 57 (4):1198–1206.

Fay, Michael, Barry Graubard, Laurence Freedman, and Douglas Midthune. 1998. "Conditional Logistic Regression with Sandwich Estimators: An Application to a Meta-Analysis." *Biometrics* 54 (1):195–208.

Feldman, Kenneth. 1971. "Using the Work of Others: Some Observations on Reviewing and Integrating." *Sociology of Education* 4 (1):86–102.

Field, C., and A. Welsh. 2007. "Bootstrapping Clustered Data." *Journal of the Royal Statistical Society B* 69 (3):369–390.

Fleiss, Joseph, and Jesse Berlin. 2009. "Effect Sizes for Dichotomous Data." In *The Handbook of Research Synthesis and Meta-Analysis, 2nd edition*, ed. Harris Cooper, Larry Hedges, and Jeffrey Valentine, 237–253. New York: Russell Sage Foundation.

Folz, David H. 2004. "Service Quality and Benchmarking the Performance of Municipal Services." *Public Administration Review* 64 (2):209–220.

Fraker, Thomas, Rebecca Maynard, and Lyle Nelson. 1984. *An Assessment of Alternative Comparison Group Methodologies for Evaluating Employment and Training Programs."* Princeton, NJ: Mathematica Policy Research.

Frederickson, David G., and H. George Frederickson. 2006. *Measuring the Performance of the Hollow State*. Washington, DC: Georgetown University Press.

Frederickson, H. George, and Kevin Smith. 2003. *The Public Administration Theory Primer*. Boulder, CO: Westview Press.

Friedman, Milton. 1962. *Capitalism and Freedom*. Chicago: University Of Chicago Press.

Frost, Chris, Robert Clarke, and Heather Beacon. 1999. "Use of Hierarchical Models for Meta-Analysis: Experience in the Metabiology Wand Studies of Diet and Blood Cholesterol." *Statistics in Medicine* 18:1657–1676.

Galbraith, Rex. 1988. "Graphical Display of Estimates Having Differing Standard Errors." *Technometrics* 30:271–281.

Galbraith, Rex F. 1994. "Some Applications of Radial Plots." *Journal of the American Statistical Association* 89 (428):1232–1242.

Gallagher, M., and B. Bajaj. 2007. *Moving On: Assessing the Benefits and Challenges of HOPE VI for Children. HOPE VI: Where Do We Go from Here? Brief 4*. Washington DC: The Urban Institute.

Gallup. 2010a. *Americans' Image of "Federal Government" Mostly Negative*. http://www.gallup.com/poll/143492/americans-image-federal-government-mostly-negative.aspx.

Gallup. 2010b. *Congress' Job Approval Rating Worst in Gallup History*. http://www.gallup.com/poll/145238/congress-job-approval-rating-worst-gallup-history.aspx.

Garg, Amit, et al. 2006. "Proteinuria and Reduced Kidney Function in Living Kidney Donors: A Systematic Review, Meta-Analysis, and Meta-Regression." *Kidney International* 70:1801–1810.

Garicano, Luis, and Paul Heaton. 2010. "Information Technology, Organization, and Productivity in the Public Sector: Evidence from Police Departments." *Journal of Labor Economics* 28 (1):167–201.

Gelman, Andrew. 2009. *Who Wants School Vouchers? Rich Whites and Poor Nonwhites.* www.andrewgelman.com/?s=vouchers (accessed November 21, 2011).

Gelman, Andrew, and Jennifer Hill. 2007. *Data Analysis Using Regression and Multilevel/Hierarchical Models.* New York: Cambridge University Press.

Gelman, Andrew, Matt Stevens, and Valerie Chan. 2003. "Regression Modeling and Meta-Analysis for Decision Making." *Journal of Business & Economic Statistics* 21 (2):213–225.

Ghisletta, Paolo, and Dario Spini. 2004. "An Introduction to Generalized Estimating Equations and an Application to Assess Selectivity Effects in a Longitudinal Study on Very Old Individuals." *Journal of Educational and Behavioral Statistics* 29 (4):421–437.

Gill, Jeff. 1999. "The Insignificance of Null Hypothesis Significance Testing." *Political Research Quarterly* 52 (3):647–674.

Gilmour, John B., and David E. Lewis. 2006. "Assessing Performance Budgeting at OMB: The Influence of Politics, Performance, and Program Size." *Journal of Public Administration Research and Theory* 16 (2):169–186.

Glass, Gene. 1976. "Primary, Secondary, and Meta-Analysis." *Educational Researcher* 5 (10):3–8.

Glass, Gene. 1978. "Integrating Findings: The Meta-Analysis of Research." In *Review of Research in Education, volume 5*, ed. L. S. Shulman. Itasca, IL: Peacock.

Glass, Gene, Barry McGraw, and Mary Smith. 1981. *Meta-Analysis in Social Science Research*. Beverly Hills, CA: Sage.

Glasziou, P. P., and S. L. Sanders. 2002. "Investigating Causes of Heterogeneity in Systematic Reviews." *Statistics in Medicine* 21 (11):1503–1511.

Gleser, Leon, and Ingram Olkin. 1996. "Models for Estimating the Number of Unpublished Studies." *Statistics in Medicine* 25:2493–2507.

Gleser, Leon, and Ingram Olkin. 2009. "Stochastically Dependent Effect Sizes." In *The Handbook of Research Synthesis and Meta-Analysis, 2nd edition*, ed. Harris Cooper, Larry Hedges, and Jeffrey Valentine, pp. 357–376. New York: Russell Sage Foundation.

Gmel, Gerhard, Elisabeth Gutjahr, and Jurgen Rehm. 2003. "How Stable Is the Risk Curve Between Alcohol and All-Cause Mortality and What Factors Influence the Shape? A Precision-Weighted Hierarchical Meta-Analysis." *European Journal of Epidemiology* 18 (7):631–642.

Goering, John M., and Judith D. Feins, eds. 2003. *Choosing a Better Life: Evaluating the Moving to Opportunity Social Experiment*. Washington DC: Urban Institute Press.

Goering, John M., Judith D. Feins, and Todd M. Richardson. 2003. "What Have We Learned About Housing Mobility and Poverty Deconcentration?" In *Choosing a Better Life? Evaluating the Moving to Opportunity Social Experiment*, ed. John M. Goering and Judith D. Feins. Washington, DC: The Urban Institute Press.

Goetz, E. G., and K. Chapple. 2010. "You Gotta Move: Advancing the Debate on the Record of Dispersal." *Housing Policy Debate* 20 (2):209–236.

Goldstein, Harold, Ming Yang, Ruman Omar, Rebecca Turner, and Simon Thompson. 2000. "Meta-Analysis Using Multilevel Models with an Application to the Study of Class Size Effects." *Journal of the Royal Statistical Society, Series C* 49 (3):399–412.

Gonzales, N.A., A. M. Cauce, and C. A. Mason. 1996. "Interobserver Agreement in the Assessment of Parental Behavior and Parent-Adolescent Conflict: African American Mothers, Daughters, and Independent Observers." *Child Development* 67:1483–1498.

Granovetter, Mark S. 1973. "The Strength of *Weak Ties*." *American Journal of Sociology* 78 (6):1360–1380.

Grant, Adam M. 2008. "Does Intrinsic Motivation Fuel the Prosocial Fire? Motivational Synergy in Predicting Persistence, Performance, and Productivity." *Journal of Applied Psychology* 93 (1):48–58.

Grayson, Lesley, and Alan Gomersall. 2003. *A Difficult Business: Finding the Evidence for Social Science Reviews*. ESRC Working Paper 19. London: ESRC U.K. Center for Evidence-Based Policy and Practice.

Greenberg, David, Andreas Cebulla, and Stacey Bouchet. 2005. *Report on a Meta-Analysis of Welfare-to-Work Programs*. Maryland Institute for Policy Analysis and Research, University of Maryland, Baltimore County.

Greenberg, David, Charles Michaelopoulos, and Philip Robin. 2006. "Do Experimental and Nonexperimental Evaluations Give Different Answers About the Effectiveness of Government-Funded Training Programs?" *Journal of Policy Analysis and Management* 25 (3):523–552.

Greene, Donald. 1993. *Econometric Analysis, 2nd edition*. New York: Macmillan.

Greene, Jay. 2000. "*The Effect of School Choice: An Evaluation of the Charlotte Children's Scholarship Fund Program*." New York: Manhattan Institute for Policy Research.

Greene, Jay P. 2001. "The Surprising Consensus on School Choice." *The Public Interest* 144:19–35.

Greene, Jay, Paul Peterson, and Jiangtao Du. 1999. "Effectiveness of School Choice: The Milwaukee Experiment." *Education and Urban Society* 31 (2):190–213.

Greenland, Sander, and Keither O'Rourke. 2001. "On the Bias Produced by Quality Scores in Meta-Analysis, and a Hierarchical View of Proposed Solutions." *Biostatistics* 2 (4):463–471.

Greenwald, Anthony G. 1975. "Consequences of Prejudice Against the Null Hypothesis." *Psychological Bulletin* 82 (1):1–20.

Greenwald, Rob, Larry V. Hedges, and Richard D. Laine. 1994. "When Reinventing the Wheel Is Not Necessary: A Case Study in the Use of Meta-Analysis in Education Finance." *Journal of Education Finance* 20 (1):1–20.

Greenwald, Rob, Larry V. Hedges, and Richard D. Laine. 1996a. "Interpreting Research on School Resources and Student Achievement: A Rejoinder to Hanushek." *Review of Educational Research* 66 (3):411–416.

Greenwald, Rob, Larry V. Hedges, and Richard D. Laine. 1996b. "The Effect of School Resources on Student Achievement." *Review of Educational Research* 66 (3):361–396.

Grossbart, Stephen. 2006. "What's the Return? Assessing the Effect of Pay-for-Performance: Initiatives on the Quality of Care Delivery." *Medical Care Research and Review* 63, (Supplement).

Gujarati, Damodar, and Dawn Porter. 2009. *Basic Econometrics, 5th Edition*. Boston: McGraw-Hill.

Hamilton, James. 1995. "Testing for Environmental Racism: Prejudice, Profits, Political Power?" *Journal of Policy Analysis and Management* 95:107–132.

Hanley, James, Abdissa Negassa, Michael deB. Edwardes, and Janet Forrester. 2003. "Statistical Analysis of Correlated Data Using Generalized Estimating Equations: An Orientation." *American Journal of Epidemiology* 157 (4):364–375.

Hanushek, Eric. 1989. "The Impact of Differential Expenditures on School Performance." *Educational Researcher* 18 (4):45–51.

Hanushek, Eric. 1994. "Money Might Matter Somewhere: A Response to Hedges, Laine, and Greenwald." *Educational Researcher* 23 (4):5–8.

Hanushek, Eric. 1996. "A More Complete Picture of School Resource Policies." *Review of Educational Research* 66 (3):397–409.

Hanushek, E. A., and M. E. Raymond. 2005. "Does School Accountability Lead to Improved Student Performance?" *Journal of Policy Analysis and Management* 24 (2):297–327.

Harbord, Roger M., Matthias Egger, and Jonathan A. C. Sterne. 2006. "A Modified Test for Small-Study Effects in Meta-Analyses of Controlled Trials with Binary Endpoints." *Statistics in Medicine* 25 (20):3443–3457.

Harbord, Roger, and Julian Higgins. 2008. "Meta-Regression in Stata." *The Stata Journal* 8 (4):493–519.

Harcourt, Bernard E., and Jens Ludwig. 2006. "Broken Windows: New Evidence from New York City and a Five-City Social Experiment." *University of Chicago Law Review* 73:271–320.

Hardin, James, and Joseph Hilbe. 2003. *Generalized Estimating Equations*. New York: Chapman and Hall/CRC.

Hartung, Joachim, and Guido Knapp. 2001. "On Tests of the Overall Treatment Effect in Meta-Analysis with Normally Distributed Responses." *Statistics in Medicine* 20 (12):1771–1782.

Hatry, Harry P. 2006. *Performance Measurement: Getting Results*. Washington, DC: Urban Institute Press.

Heckman, James. 1979. "Sample Selection Bias as Specification Error." *Econometrica* 47 (1):153–161.

Heckman, James J. 2000. "Causal Parameters and Policy Analysis in Economics: A Twentieth Century Retrospective." *The Quarterly Journal of Economics* 115 (1):45–97.

Heckman, James, Carolyn Heinrich, and Jeffrey Smith. 1997. "Assessing the Performance of Performance Standards in Public Bureaucracies." *The American Economic Review* 87 (2):389–395.

Heckman, James J., Carolyn Heinrich, and Jeffrey Smith. 2002. "The Performance of Performance Standards." *The Journal of Human Resources* 37 (4):778–811.

Heckman, James J., and V. Joseph Hotz. 1989. "Choosing Among Alternative Nonexperimental Methods for Estimating the Impact of Social Programs: The Case of Manpower Training." *Journal of the American Statistical Association* 84 (408):862–874.

Heckman, James J., and Jeffrey A. Smith. 1995. "Assessing the Case for Social Experiments." *The Journal of Economic Perspectives* 9 (2):85–110.

Hedges, Larry. 1981. "Distribution Theory for Glass's Estimator of Effect Size and Related Estimators." *Journal of Educational and Behavioral Statistics* 6 (2):107–128.

Hedges, Larry V. 1982. "Fitting Continuous Models to Effect Size Data." *Journal of Educational Statistics* 7 (4):245–270.

Hedges, Larry V. 1984. "Estimation of Effect Size Under Nonrandom Sampling: The Effects of Censoring Studies Yielding Statistically Insignificant Mean Differences." *Journal of Educational and Behavioral Statistics* 9 (1):61–85.

Hedges, Larry V. 1987. "How Hard Is Hard Science, How Soft Is Soft Science? The Empirical Cumulativeness of Research." *American Psychologist* 42 (5):443–455.

Hedges, Larry V. 1992. "Modeling Publication Selection Effects in Meta-Analysis." *Statistical Science* 7 (2):246–255.

Hedges, Larry V. 1994. "Statistical Considerations." In *The Handbook of Research Synthesis*, ed. Harris Cooper and Larry Hedges. New York: Russell Sage Foundation.

Hedges, Larry V. 2007. "Effect Sizes in Cluster-Randomized Designs." *Journal of Educational and Behavioral Statistics* 32 (4):341–370.

Hedges, Larry. 2009. "Statistical Considerations." In *The Handbook of Research Synthesis and Meta-Analysis, 2nd edition*, ed. Harris Cooper, Larry Hedges, and Jeffrey Valentine, pp. 37–50. New York: Russell Sage Foundation.

Hedges, Larry V., Richard D. Laine, and Rob Greenwald. 1994a. "Money Does Matter Somewhere: A Reply to Hanushek." *Educational Researcher* 23 (4):9–10.

Hedges, Larry V., Richard D. Laine, and Rob Greenwald. 1994b. "An Exchange: Part I: Does Money Matter? A Meta-Analysis of Studies of the Effects of Differential School Inputs on Student Outcomes." *Educational Researcher* 23 (3):5–14.

Hedges, Larry, and Ingram Olkin. 1985. *Statistical Methods for Meta-Analysis*. New York: Academic Press.

Hedges, Larry V., and Therese D. Pigott. 2004. "The Power of Statistical Tests for Moderators in Meta-Analysis." *Psychological Methods* 9 (4):426–445.

Hedges, Larry V., and Jack L. Vevea. 1996. "Estimating Effect Size Under Publication Bias: Small Sample Properties and Robustness of a Random Effects Selection Model." *Journal of Educational and Behavioral Statistics* 21 (2):299–332.

Hedges, Larry, and Jack Vevea. 2005. "Selection Method Approaches." In *Publication Bias in Meta-Analysis: Prevention, Assessment and Adjustments*, ed. H. Rothstein, A. Sutton, and M. Borenstein, pp. 145–174. New York: Wiley.

Heinrich, Carolyn J. 2002. "Outcomes-Based Performance Management in the Public Sector: Implications for Government Accountability and Effectiveness." *Public Administration Review* 62 (6):712–725.

Heinrich, Carolyn J., and Laurence E. Lynn. 2001. "Means and Ends: A Comparative Study of Empirical Methods for Investigating Governance and Performance." *Journal of Public Administration Research and Theory* 11 (1):109–138.

Heinrich, Carolyn J., and Gerald Marschke. 2010. "Incentives and Their Dynamics in Public Sector Performance Management Systems." *Journal of Policy Analysis and Management* 29 (1):183–208.

Higgins, Julian, and Douglas Altman. 2008. "Assessing Risk of Bias in Included Studies." In *Cochrane Handbook for Systematic Reviews of Interventions*, ed. J. Higgins and S. Green, 186–241. Chinchester, UK: John Wiley & Sons.

Higgins, Julian, and Jonathan Deeks. 2008. "Selecting Studies and Collecting Data." In *Cochrane Handbook for Systematic Reviews of Interventions*, ed. J. Higgins and S. Green, 151–185. Chinchester, UK: John Wiley & Sons.

Higgins, Julian, and Sally Green, eds. 2008. *Cochrane Handbook for Systematic Reviews of Interventions*. Chinchester, UK: John Wiley & Sons.

Higgins, Julian P. T., and Simon G. Thompson. 2004. "Controlling the Risk of Spurious Findings from Meta-Regression." *Statistics in Medicine* 23 (11):1663–1682.

Higgins, Julian P. T., Simon G. Thompson, Jonathan J. Deeks, and Douglas G. Altman. 2003. "Measuring Inconsistency in Meta-Analyses." *British Medical Journal* 327 (7414):557–560.

Hill, Kim Quale. 1997. "In Search of Policy Theory." *Policy Currents* 7 (June):1–9.

Hill, Michael, and Peter Hupe. 2009. *Implementing Public Policy, 2nd edition*. Los Angeles: Sage.

Hirsch, Arnold R. 1983. *Making the Second Ghetto: Race & Housing in Chicago 1940–1960*. Chicago: University of Chicago Press.

Hirschman, Albert. 1982. *Shifting Involvements: Private Interest and Public Action*. Princeton: Princeton University Press.

Ho, Alfred Tat-Kei. 2006. "Accounting for the Value of Performance Measurement from the Perspective of Midwestern Mayors." *Journal of Public Administration Research and Theory* 16 (2):217–237.

Holland, Paul W. 1986. "Statistics and Causal Inference." *Journal of the American Statistical Association* 81 (396):945–960.

Hopewell, Sally, Mike Clarke, and Sue Mallett. 2005. "Grey Literature and Systematic Reviews." In *Publication Bias in Meta-Analysis*, ed. H. Rothstein, A. Sutton, and M. Borenstein, 49–72. New York: John Wiley & Sons.

Horton, James. 2010. "*An Examination of the Applicability of the Citistat Performance Management System to Municipal Fire Departments*." Thesis, School of Public Affairs, Urban University of Texas at Arlington.

Houston, David, and Sybil Delevan. 1990. "Public Administration Research: An Assessment of Journal Publications." *Public Administration Review* 50 (6):674–681.

Howell, William, Paul Peterson, and Martin West. 2011. "The Public Weighs in on School Reform." *Education Next* 11 (4):11–22.

Howell, William G., Patrick J. Wolf, David E. Campbell, and Paul E. Peterson. 2002. "School Vouchers and Academic Performance: Results from Three Randomized Field Trials." *Journal of Policy Analysis and Management* 21 (2):191–217.

Hsaio, Cheng. 1986. *Analysis of Panel Data*. New York: Cambridge University Press.

Huang, Chien-Chung, and Richard L. Edwards. 2009. "The Relationship Between State Efforts and Child Support Performance." *Children and Youth Services Review* 31 (2):243–248.

Hunt, Morton. 1997. *How Science Takes Stock: The Story of Meta-Analysis*. New York: Russell Sage Foundation.

Hunter, John E., and Frank L. Schmidt. 1990. *Methods of Meta-Analysis: Correcting Error and Bias in Research Findings*. Newbury Park, CA: Sage.

Hunter, J. E., and Frank L. Schmidt. 1994. "Correcting for Sources of Artificial Variation Across Studies." In *The Handbook of Research Synthesis*, ed. Harris Cooper and Larry Hedges. New York: Russell Sage Foundation.

Hunter, John E., and Frank Schmidt. 1996. "Cumulative Research Knowledge and Social Policy Formulation: The Critical Role of Meta-Analysis." *Psychology, Public Policy, and Law* 2 (2):324–347.

Ioannidis, John P. A. 2008. "Interpretation of Tests of Heterogeneity and Bias in Meta-Analysis." *Journal of Evaluation in Clinical Practice* 14 (5):951–957.

Ioannidis, John P. A., and Thomas A. Trikalinos. 2007. "The Appropriateness of Asymmetry Tests for Publication Bias in Meta-Analyses: A Large Survey." *Canadian Medical Association Journal* 176 (8):1091–1096.

Ishak, K. Jack, Robert Platt, Lawrence Joseph, and James Hanley. 2007. "Impact of Approximating or Ignoring Within-Study Covariances in Multivariate Meta-Analyses." *Statistics in Medicine* 27:670–686.

Iyengar, Satish, and Joel B. Greenhouse. 1988. "Selection Models and the File Drawer Problem." *Statistical Science* 3 (1):109–117.

Jackson, v. *Benson*, 218 Wis. 2d 835 (1998) 578 NW 2d 602.

Jackson, Dan. 2006. "The Implications of Publication Bias for Meta-Analysis' Other Parameter." *Statistics in Medicine* 25 (17):2911–2921.

Jackson, Dan. 2007. "Assessing the Implications of Publication Bias for Two Popular Estimates of Between-Study Variance in Meta-Analysis." *Biometrics* 63 (1):187–193.

Jang, H., L. T. Hoover, and H. J. Joo. 2010. "An Evaluation of Compstat's Effect on Crime: The Fort Worth Experience." *Police Quarterly* 13 (4):387–412.

Janiszewski, Chris, Hayden Noel, and Alan Sawyer. 2003. "A Meta-Analysis of the Spacing Effect in Verbal Learning: Implications for Research on Advertising Repetition and Consumer Memory." *Journal of Consumer Research* 30 (1):138–149.

Jargowsky, P. A. 2003. *Stunning Progress, Hidden Problems: The Dramatic Decline of Concentrated Poverty in the 1990s*. Washington, DC: Brookings Institution.

Jargowsky, Paul A., and Mary Jo Bane. 1991. "Ghetto Poverty in the United States, 1970 to 1980," In *The Urban Underclass*, ed. Christopher Jencks and Paul E. Peterson, pp. 235–273. Washington, DC: The Brookings Institution.

Jarrell, Stephen B., and T. D. Stanley. 1990. "A Meta-Analysis of the Union-Nonunion Wage Gap." *Industrial and Labor Relations Review* 44 (1):54–67.

Jencks, Christopher, and Susan E. Mayer. 1990. "The Social Consequences of Growing Up in a Poor Neighborhood." In *In Inner-City Poverty in the United States*, ed. L. E. Lynn and M. G. H. McGeary. Washington, DC: National Academy Press.

Joyce, Philip G. 2011. "The Obama Administration and PBB: Building on the Legacy of Federal Performance-Informed Budgeting?" *Public Administration Review* 71 (3):356–367.

Julnes, Patria de Lancer. 2009. *Performance-Based Management Systems: Effective Implementation and Maintenance*. Boca Raton: CRC Press.

Julnes, Patria de Lancer, and Marc Holzer. 2001. "Promoting the Utilization of Performance Measures in Public Organizations: An Empirical Study of Factors Affecting Adoption and Implementation." *Public Administration Review* 61 (6):693–708.

Jüni, Peter, Anne Witschi, Ralph Bloch, and Matthias Egger. 1999. "The Hazards of Scoring the Quality of Clinical Trials for Meta-analysis." *The Journal of the American Medical Association* 282 (11):1054–1060.

Kalaian, Hripsime, and Stephen Raudenbush. 1996. "A Multivariate Mixed Linear Model for Meta-Analysis." *Psychological Methods* 1 (3):227–235.

Karoly, Lynn A., et al. 1998. *Investing in Our Children: What We Know and Don't Know About the Costs and Benefits of Early Childhood Interventions*. Santa Monica, CA: RAND Corporation. http://www.rand.org/pubs/monograph_reports/MR898.

Katz, Bruce, and Margery Austin Turner. 2008. "*Rethinking US Rental Housing Policy: A New Blueprint for Federal, State, and Local Action*." In *Revisiting Rental Housing: Policies, Programs, Priorities*, ed. Nicolas P. Retsinas and E. S. Belsky. Washington, DC: Brookings Institution.

Katz, L., J. Kling, and J. Liebman. 2001. "Moving to Opportunity in Boston: Early Impacts of a Housing Mobility Program." *Quarterly Journal of Economics* 116 (2):607–654.

Keef, Stephen P., and Leigh A. Roberts. 2004. "The Meta-Analysis of Partial Effect Sizes." *British Journal of Mathematical & Statistical Psychology* 57 (1):97–129.

Keels, Idolly Micere. 2008. "Second-Generation Effects of Chicago's Gautreaux Residential Mobility Program on Children's Participation in Crime." *Journal of Research on Adolescence (Blackwell Publishing Limited)* 18 (2):305–352.

Kelling, George L., and James Q. Wilson. 1982. "Broken Windows." *Atlantic Monthly*, 249 (3):29–38.

Kim, Johnny. 2008. "Examining the Effectiveness of Solution-Focused Brief Therapy: A Meta-Analysis." *Research in Social Work Practice* 18 (2):107–116.

Kim, Sangmook. 2005. "Individual-Level Factors and Organizational Performance in Government Organizations." *Journal of Public Administration Research and Theory* 15 (2):245–261.

King, Gary, Robert Keohane, and Sidney Verba. 1994. *Designing Social Inquiry*. Princeton, NJ: Princeton University Press.

Kisida, Brian, Laura I. Jensen, Patrick J. Wolf, and School Choice Demonstration Project University of Arkansas. 2011. *The Milwaukee Parental Choice Program: Descriptive Report on Participating Schools, 2009–2010. SCDP Milwaukee Evaluation. Report #27*. School Choice Demonstration Project.

Kling, J. R., J. B. Liebman, and L. F. Katz. 2007. "Experimental Analysis of Neighborhood Effects." *Econometrica* 75 (1):83–119.

Kling, J. R., J. Ludwig, and L. F. Katz. 2005. "Neighborhood Effects on Crime for Female and Male Youth: Evidence from a Randomized Housing Voucher Experiment." *The Quarterly Journal of Economics* 120 (1):87–130.

Knapp, Guido, and Joachim Hartung. 2003. "Improved Tests for a Random Effects Meta-Regression with a Single Covariate." *Statistics in Medicine* 22 (17):2693–2710.

Kneebone, E., A. Berube, and Brookings Institution. Metropolitan Policy Program. 2008. *Reversal of Fortune: A New Look at Concentrated Poverty in the 2000s*. Washington, DC: Brookings Institution.

Kober, Nancy. 2000. *School Vouchers: What We Know and Don't Know . . . and How We Could Learn More*. Washington, DC: Center on Education Policy. http://www.ctredpol.org/ vouchers/schoolvouchers.pdf.

Konstantopoulos, Spyros, and Larry Hedges. 2009. "Analyzing Effect Sizes: Fixed Effects Models." In *The Handbook of Research Synthesis and Meta-Analysis, 2nd edition*, ed. Harris Cooper, Larry Hedges, and Jeffrey Valentine. New York: Russell Sage Foundation.

Krueger, Alan, and Pei Zhu. 2003. "Comment: Principal Stratification Approach to Broken Randomized Experiments: A Case Study of Vouchers in New York City." *Journal of the American Statistical Association* 98 (462):314–318.

Krueger, Alan B., and Pei Zhu. 2004. "Another Look at the New York City School Voucher Experiment." *American Behavioral Scientist* 47 (5):658–698.

Kulik, J., and C. Kulick. 1989. "Meta-Analysis in Education." *International Journal of Educational Research* 13:221–240.

Kulinskaya, Elena, Stephan Morgenthaler, and Robert G. Staudte. 2008. "*Meta Analysis: A Guide to Calibrating and Combining Statistical Evidence*." In *Wiley Series in Probability and Statistics; Variation: Wiley Series in Probability and Statistics*. Hoboken, NJ: John Wiley & Sons.

Lake, Robin. 2010. "*Hopes, Fears, & Reality: A Balanced Look at American Charter Schools in 2009*." Seattle: Center on Reinventing Public Education.

LaLonde, Robert. 1986. "Evaluating the Econometric Evaluations of Training Programs with Experimental Data." *American Economic Review* 76 (4):604–620.

LaLonde, Robert, and Rebecca Maynard. 1987. "How Precise Are Evaluations of Employment and Training Programs? Evidence from a Field Experiment." *Evaluation Review* 11 (4):428–451.

Lamarche, Carlos. 2008. "Private School Vouchers and Student Achievement: A Fixed Effects Quantile Regression Evaluation." *Labour Economics* 15 (4):575–590.

Langbein, Laura Irwin, and Claire L. Felbinger. 2006. *Public Program Evaluation: A Statistical Guide*. Armonk, NY: M. E. Sharpe.

Lasswell, Harold. 1951. "The Policy Orientation." In *The Policy Sciences: Recent Developments in Scope and Method*, eds. Daniel Learner and Harold Lasswell. Stanford: Stanford University Press.

Lau, Joseph, John P. A. Ioannidis, Norma Terrin, Christopher H. Schmid, and Ingram Olkin. 2006. "Evidence-Based Medicine: The Case of the Misleading Funnel Plot." *British Medical Journal* 333 (7568):597–600.

Lau, Richard R., Lee Sigelman, Caroline Heldman, and Paul Babbitt. 1999. "The Effects of Negative Political Advertisements: A Meta-Analytic Assessment." *The American Political Science Review* 93 (4):851–875.

Leamer, Edward. 1978. *Specification Searches: Ad Hoc Inference with Nonexperimental Data*. New York: Wiley.

Lee, Youngio, and John Nelder. 2006. "Double Hierarchical Generalized Linear Models." *Journal of the Royal Statistical Society, Series C* 55 (2):139–185.

Leisink, Peter, and Bram Steijn. 2009. "Public Service Motivation and Job Performance of Public Sector Employees in the Netherlands." *International Review of Administrative Sciences* 75 (1):35–52.

LePine, Jeffrey, Amir Erez, and Diane Johnson. 2002. "The Nature and Dimensionality of Organizational Citizenship Behavior: A Critical Review and Meta-Analysis." *Journal of Applied Psychology* 87 (1):52–65.

Leventhal, Tama, and Jeanne Brooks-Gunn. 2003. "New York Site Findings: The Early Impacts of Moving to Opportunity on Children and Youth." In *Choosing a Better Life? Evaluating the Moving to Opportunity Social Experiment*, ed. John M. Goering and Judith D. Feins. Washington DC: Urban Institute Press.

Levin, H. M. 1998. "Educational Vouchers: Effectiveness, Choice, and Costs." *Journal of Policy Analysis and Management* 17 (3):373–392.

Lewis, Oscar. 1966. *La Vida: A Puerto Rican Family in the Culture of Poverty—San Juan and New York*. New York: Random House.

Li, Zhaohai, and Colin B. Begg. 1994. "Random Effects Models for Combining Results from Controlled and Uncontrolled Studies in a Meta-Analysis." *Journal of the American Statistical Association* 89 (428):1523–1527.

Liang, K., and S. Zeger. 1986. "Longitudinal Data Analysis Using Generalized Linear Models." *Biometrika* 73:13–22.

Lied, T. R., and S. Sheingold. 2001. "HEDIS Performance Trends in Medicare Managed Care." *Health Care Financing Review* 23 (1):149–160.

Light, R., and D. Pillemer. 1984. *Summing Up: The Science of Reviewing Research*. Cambridge, MA: Harvard University Press.

Lipsey, Mark. 2009. "The Primary Factors That Characterize Effective Interventions with Juvenile Offenders: A Meta-Analytic Overview." *Victims and Offenders* 4 (2):124–147.

Lipsey, Mark, and David Wilson. 1993. "The Efficacy of Psychological, Educational, and Behavioural Treatment: Confirmation from Meta-Analysis." *American Psychologist* 12:1181–1209.

Lipsey, Mark W., and David B. Wilson. 2001. "Practical Meta-Analysis." In *Applied Social Research Methods Series*. Beverley Hills, CA:Sage.

Lipsey, Mark, David Wilson, and Lynn Cothern. 2000. "*Effective Intervention for Serious Juvenile Offenders*." *Juvenile Justice Bulletin* (April):1–9.

Lissek, Shmuel, et al. 2005. "Classical Fear Conditioning in the Anxiety Disorders: A Meta-Analysis." *Behavior Research and Theory* 43:1391–1424.

Liu, Bangcheng, Ningyu Tang, and Xiaomei Zhu. 2008. "Public Service Motivation and Job Satisfaction in China: An Investigation of Generalizability and Instrumentality." *International Journal of Manpower* 29 (8):684–699.

Lubienski, Christopher, Sarah Theule Lubienski, National Assessment of Educational Progress, and National Center for the Study of Privatization in Education. 2006. *Charter, Private, Public Schools and Academic Achievement: New Evidence from NAEP Mathematics Data*. National Center for the Study of Privatization in Education, Teachers College, Columbia University. http://www.ncspe.org/publications%5Ffiles/OP111 .pdf.

Lubienski, Sarah Theule, Christopher Lubienski, and Corinna Crawford Crane. 2008. "Achievement Differences and School Type: The Role of School Climate, Teacher Certification, and Instruction." *American Journal of Education* 115 (1):97–138.

Ludwig, J., G. J. Duncan, and P. Hirschfield. 2001. "Urban Poverty and Juvenile Crime: Evidence from a Randomized Housing-Mobility Experiment." *Quarterly Journal of Economics* 116 (2):655–679.

Lynn, Laurence E., Carolyn J. Heinrich, and Carolyn J. Hill. 2001. *Improving Governance: A New Logic for Empirical Research*. Washington, DC: Georgetown University Press.

Lynn, J., et al. 2007. "Collaborative Clinical Quality Improvement for Pressure Ulcers in Nursing Homes." *Journal of the American Geriatrics Society* 55 (10):1663–1669.

Macaskill, Petra, Stephen D. Walter, and Les Irwig. 2001. "A Comparison of Methods to Detect Publication Bias in Meta-Analysis." *Statistics in Medicine* 20 (4):641–654.

Mahoney, Michael J. 1977. "Publication Prejudices: An Experimental Study of Confirmatory Bias in the Peer Review System." *Cognitive Therapy and Research* 1 (2):161–175.

Mancl, L., and R. DeRouen. 2001. "A Covariance Estimator for GEE with Improved Finite Sample Properties." *Biometrics* 57:126–134.

Mann, Charles C. 1990. "Meta-Analysis in the Breech." *Science* 249:476–80.

Mann, Charles C. 1994. "Can Meta-Analysis Make Policy?" *Science* 266 (5187):960–962.

Mann, Thomas. 2005. *The Oxford Guide to Library Research*. New York: Oxford University Press.

Marcotte, Dave E., and Sara Markowitz. 2011. "A Cure for Crime? Psycho-Pharmaceuticals and Crime Trends." *Journal of Policy Analysis and Management* 30 (1):29–56.

Massey, D. S., and N. A. Denton. 1993. *American Apartheid: Segregation and the Making of the Underclass*. Cambridge: Harvard University Press.

Mayer, Daniel P., Paul E. Peterson, David E. Myers, Christina Clark Tuttle, and William G. Howell. 2002. *School Choice in New York City After Three Years: An Evaluation of the School Choice Scholarships Program*. Mathematica Policy Research, Inc., and the Program on Education Policy and Governance, Harvard University.

Maynard-Moody, Steven, Michael Musheno, and Denis Palumbo. 1990. "Street-Wise Social Policy: Resolving the Dilemma of Street-Level Influence and Successful Implementation." *Western Political Quarterly* 43 (4):833–848.

Mazerolle, Lorraine, James McBroom, and Sacha Rombouts. 2011. "Compstat in Australia: An Analysis of the Spatial and Temporal Impact." *Journal of Criminal Justice* 39 (2):128–136.

Mazerolle, Lorraine, Sacha Rombouts, and James McBroom. 2006. *The Impact of Operational Performance Reviews on Reported Crime in Queensland*. Canberra: Australian Institute of Criminology.

Mazerolle, Lorraine, Sacha Rombouts, and James McBroom. 2007. "The Impact of Compstat on Reported Crime in Queensland." *Policing* 30 (2):237–256.

Mazmanian, Daniel, and Paul Sabatier. 1989. *Implementation and Public Policy*. Lanham, MD: University Press of America.

Mazumder, B. 2005. "Fortunate Sons: New Estimates of Intergenerational Mobility in the United States Using Social Security Earnings Data." *Review of Economics and Statistics* 87 (2):235–255.

McCloskey, Dierdre, and Stephen Ziliak. 2008. *The Cult of Statistical Significance: How the Standard Error Costs Us Jobs, Justice, and Lives*. Ann Arbor: University of Michigan Press.

McCloskey, Donald. 1985. "The Loss Function Has Been Mislaid: The Rhetoric of Significance Tests." *American Economic Review* 75 (2):201–205.

Mead, Lawrence M. 1992. *The New Politics of Poverty: The Nonworking Poor in America*. New York: Basic Books.

Meier, Kenneth, and Kevin Smith. 1995. *The Case Against School Choice: Politics, Markets, and Fools*. Armonke, NY: M. E. Sharpe.

Meier, Kenneth, Robert D. Wrinkle, and J. L. Polinard. 1999. "Representative Bureaucracy and Distributional Equity: Addressing the Hard Question." *Journal of Politics* 61 (4):1025–1039.

Metcalf, Kim, William Boone, Frances Stage, Todd Chilton, Patty Muller, and Polly Tait. 1998. "*A Comparative Evaluation of the Cleveland Scholarship and Tutoring Grant Program, Year One: 1996–97*." Bloomington: Indiana Center for Evaluation, Indiana University.

Metcalf, Kim, Patricia Muller, William Boone, Polly Tait, Frances Stage, and Nicole Stacey. 1998. "*Evaluation of the Cleveland Scholarship Program: Second-Year Report (1997–98)*." Bloomington: Indiana Center for Evaluation, Indiana University.

Metcalf, Kim K., Stephen D. West, Natalie A. Legan, Kelli M. Paul, and William J. Boone. 2003. *Evaluation of the Cleveland Scholarship and Tutoring Program. Technical Report 1998–2001*. Bloomington: Indiana Center for Evaluation, Indiana University.

Miller, W., L. A. Robinson, and R. S. Lawrence, eds. 2006. *Valuing Health for Regulatory Cost Effectiveness Analysis*. Committee to Evaluate Measures of Health Benefits for Environmental, Health, and Safety Regulation. Washington, DC: The National Academies Press.

Mohai, Paul, and Robin Saha. 2007. "Racial Inequality in the Distribution of Hazardous Waste: A National-Level Reassessment." *Social Problems* 54 (3):343–370.

Mooney, Christopher Z., and Robert Duval. 1993. *Bootstrapping: A Nonparametric Approach to Statistical Inference*. Newbury Park, CA: Sage.

Moreno, Santiago, et al. 2009. "Assessment of Regression-Based Methods to Adjust for Publication Bias Through a Comprehensive Simulation Study." *BMC Medical Research Methodology* 9 (1):2.

Morris, Carl. 1983. "Parametric Empirical Bayes Inference: Theory and Applications." *Journal of the American Statistical Association* 78 (381):47–55.

Mosher, Frederick. 1956. "Research in Public Administration: Some Notes and Suggestions." *Public Administration Review* 16 (3):169–178.

Moulton, B. R. 1990. "An Illustration of a Pitfall in Estimating the Effect on Micro Units." *Review of Economics and Statistics* 72:334–338.

Moynihan, Donald P. 2006. "What Do We Talk About When We Talk About Performance? Dialogue Theory and Performance Budgeting." *Journal of Public Administration Research and Theory* 16 (2):151–168.

Moynihan, Donald P., and Sanjay K. Pandey. 2007. "The Role of Organizations in Fostering Public Service Motivation." *Public Administration Review* 67 (1):40–53.

Moynihan, Donald P. 2008. *The Dynamics of Performance Management: Constructing Information and Reform*. Washington, DC: Georgetown University Press.

Moynihan, Donald. 2010. "*The Politics Measurement Makes: Performance Management in the Obama Era.*" *Selected Works of Donald Moynihan*, http://works.bepress.com/donald_moynihan/1/.

Moynihan, Donald P., and Sanjay K. Pandey. 2010. "The Big Question for Performance Management: Why Do Managers Use Performance Information?" *Journal of Public Administration Research and Theory* 20 (4):849–866.

Mullen, Patricia Dolan, and Gilbert Ramírez. 2006. "The Promise and Pitfalls of Systematic Reviews." *Annual Review of Public Health* 27:81–102.

Murray, C. A. 1984. *Losing Ground: American Social Policy, 1950–1980*. New York: Basic Books.

Naff, Katherine C., and John Crum. 1999. "Working for America." *Review of Public Personnel Administration* 19 (4):5–16.

National Research Council. 1992. *Combining Information: Statistical Issues and Opportunities for Research*. Washington, DC: National Academies Press.

Nelson, Daniel. 1980. *Frederick W. Taylor and the Rise of Scientific Management*. Madison: University of Wisconsin Press.

Nijkamp, Peter, and Jacques Poot. 2004. "Meta-Analysis of the Effect of Fiscal Policies on Long-Run Growth." *European Journal of Political Economy* 20 (1):91–124.

Nilsson, Robert. 2001. "Environmental Tobacco Smoke Revisited: The Reliability of the Data Used for Risk Assessment." *Risk Analysis* 21 (4):737–760.

Oakes, John Michael, Douglas Anderton, Andy Anderson. 1996. "A Longitudinal Analysis of Environmental Equity in Communities with Hazardous Waste Facilities." *Social Science Research* 25 (2):125–148.

Oldham, Greg R., and J. Richard Hackman. 1981. "Relationships Between Organizational Structure and Employee Reactions: Comparing Alternative Frameworks." *Administrative Science Quarterly* 26 (1):66–83.

Orr, Larry L., et al. 2003. *Moving to Opportunity: Interim Impacts Evaluation*. Washington, DC: U.S. Dept. of Housing and Urban Development.

Orwin, R. G. 1983. "A Fail-Safe N for Effect Size in Meta-Analysis." *Journal of Educational Statistics* 8 (1):157–159.

Orwin, R. G. 1994. "Evaluating Coding Decisions." In *The Handbook of Research Synthesis*, ed. Harris Cooper and Larry Hedges. New York: Russell Sage Foundation.

Orwin, Robert, and Jack Vevea. 2009. "Evaluating Coding Decisions." In *The Handbook of Research Synthesis and Meta-Analysis* Valentine, *2nd edition*, Harris Cooper, Larry Hedges, and Jeffrey Valentine, 177–203. New York: Russell Sage Foundation.

Osborne, David E., and Ted A. Gaebler. 1992. *Reinventing Government: How the Entrepreneurial Spirit Is Transforming the Public Sector*. Reading, MA: Addison-Wesley.

Osborne, David, and Peter Plastrik. 1997. *Banishing Bureaucracy: The Five Strategies for Reinventing Government*. Reading, MA: Addison-Wesley.

Osenberg, Craig W., Orlando Sarnelle, Scott D. Cooper, and Robert D. Holt. 1999. "Resolving Ecological Questions Through Meta-Analysis: Goals, Metrics, and Models." *Ecology* 80 (4):1105–1117.

Overman, E. Sam, and Kathy Boyd. 1994. "Best Practice Research and Postbureaucratic Reform." *Journal of Public Administration Research and Theory* 4 (1):67–84.

Paine, Jeffrey R. 2009. "Relating Public Service Motivation to Behavioral Outcomes Among Local Elected Administrators." In *International Public Service Motivation Research Conference*, Indiana University.

Palmer, Jacquelyn W. 2006. *Innovative Behavior of Frontline Employees in the Public Sector*, Ph.d. dissertation, School of Business Administration, University of Cincinnati.

Pan, Wei, and Melanie Wall. 2002. "Small-Sample Adjustments in Using the Sandwich Variance Estimator in Generalized Estimating Equations." *Statistics in Medicine* 21:1429–1441.

Park, Sung Min, and Hal G. Rainey. 2008. "Leadership and Public Service Motivation in U.S. Federal Agencies." *International Public Management Journal* 11 (1):109–142.

Parkhurst, David. 2001. "Statistical Significance Tests: Equivalence and Reverse Tests Should Reduce Misinterpretation." *BioScience* 51 (2):1051–1057.

Paul, P. A., P. E. Lipps, and L. V. Madden. 2006. "Meta-Analysis of Regression Coefficients for the Relationship Between Fusarium Head Blight and Deoxynivalenol Content of Wheat." *Phytopathology* 96 (9):951–961.

Pearson, Karl. 1900. "Mathematical Contributions to the Study of Evolution VII: On the Correlation of Characters Not Quantitatively Measurable." *Philosophical Transactions of the Royal Society of London* 195:1–47.

Pearson, Karl. 1904. "Report on Certain Enteric Fever Inoculation Statistics." *British Medical Journal* 3:1243–1246.

Pepper, J. V. 2002. "Robust Inferences from Random Clustered Samples: An Application Using Data from the Panel Study of Income Dynamics." *Economics Letters* 75:341–345.

Perry, James L. 1996. "Measuring Public Service Motivation: An Assessment of Construct Reliability and Validity." *Journal of Public Administration Research and Theory* 6 (1):5–22.

Perry, James L., Jeffrey L. Brudney, David Coursey, and Laura Littlepage. 2008. "What Drives Morally Committed Citizens? A Study of the Antecedents of Public Service Motivation." *Public Administration Review* 68 (3):445–458.

Perry, James L., Annie Hondeghem, and Lois Recascino Wise. 2010. "Revisiting the Motivational Bases of Public Service: Twenty Years of Research and an Agenda for the Future." *Public Administration Review* 70 (5):681–690.

Perry, James, and Kenneth Kraemer. 1986. "Research Methodology in the *Public Administration Review*, 1975–1984." *Public Administration Review* 46 (3):215–226.

Perry, James, and Lois R. Wise. 1990. "The Motivational Bases of Public Service." *Public Administration Review* 50 (3):367–373.

Peters, Jaime L., Alex J. Sutton, David R. Jones, Keith R. Abrams, and Lesley Rushton. 2006. "Comparison of Two Methods to Detect Publication Bias in Meta-analysis." *The Journal of the American Medical Association* 295 (6):676–680.

Peters, Jaime L., Alex J. Sutton, David R. Jones, Keith R. Abrams, and Lesley Rushton. 2007. "Performance of the Trim and Fill Method in the Presence of Publication Bias and Between-Study Heterogeneity." *Statistics in Medicine* 26 (25):4544–4562.

Peters, Jaime L., et al 2010. "Assessing Publication Bias in Meta-Analyses in the Presence of Between-Study Heterogeneity." *Journal of the Royal Statistical Society: Series A (Statistics in Society)* 173 (3):575–591.

Petersen, M. 2009. "Estimating Standard Errors in Finance Panel Data Sets: Comparing Approaches." *Review of Financial Studies* 22 (3):435–480.

Peterson, Robert A., and Steven P. Brown. 2005. "On the Use of Beta Coefficients in Meta-Analysis." *Journal of Applied Psychology* 90 (1):175–181.

Peterson, Paul, Jay Greene, and William Howell. 1998. "*New Findings from the Cleveland Scholarship Program: A Reanalysis of Data from the Indiana University School of Education Evaluation.*" Program on Education Policy and Governance, Kennedy School of Government. Boston, MA: Harvard University.

Petrovsky, Nicolai. 2009. "*Public Service Motivation Predict Higher Public Service Performance? A Research Synthesis.*" In *10th Public Management Research Association Conference*, Ohio State University.

Petrovsky, Nicolai, and Adrian Ritz. 2011. "*Do Motivated Elephants Gallop Faster? An Assessment of the Effect of Public Service Motivation on Government Performance at the Individual and Organizational Levels.*" Paper delivered at the Public Management Research Association/International Research Society of Public Management Conference, Hong Kong.

Pigott, Therese. 2009. "Handling Missing Data." In *The Handbook of Research Synthesis and Meta-Analysis, 2nd edition*, ed. Harris Cooper, Larry Hedges, and Jeffrey Valentine, pp. 399–416. New York: Russell Sage Foundation.

Platt, John. 1964. "Strong Inference." *Science* 146 (3642):347–353.

Plucker, Jonathan, Patricia Muller, John Hansen, Russ Ravert, and Matthew Makel. 2006. "*Evaluation of the Cleveland Scholarship Tutoring Program: Summary Report 1998–2004.*" Bloomington: Center for Evaluation and Education Policy, Indiana University.

Podsakoff, Philip M., Scott B. MacKenzie, Jeong-Yeon Lee, and Nathan P. Podsakoff. 2003. "Common Method Biases in Behavioral Research: A Critical Review of the Literature and Recommended Remedies." *Journal of Applied Psychology* 88 (5):879–903.

Poister, Theodore H. 2003. *Measuring Performance in Public and Nonprofit Organizations.* San Francisco: Jossey-Bass.

Popkin, S. J., D. K. Levy, and L. Buron. 2009. "Has HOPE VI Transformed Residents' Lives? New Evidence from the HOPE VI Panel Study." *Housing Studies* 24 (4):477–502.

Popkin, S. J., J. E. Rosenbaum, and P. M. Meaden. 1993. "Labor Market Experiences of Low Income Black Women in Middle Class Suburbs: Evidence from a Survey of Gautreaux Program Participants." *Journal of Policy Analysis and Management* 12 (3):556–573.

Porter, Lyman W., and Edward E. Lawler. 1968. *Managerial Attitudes and Performance.* Homewood, IL: Irwin-Dorsey.

Posner, Paul, and David M. Walker. 2004. *Performance Budgeting: Observations on the Use of OMB's Program Assessment Rating Tool for the Fiscal Year 2004 Budget: GAO-04-174.* Washington, DC: U.S. Government Accountability Office.

Primo, David, Matthew Jacobsmeier, and Jeffrey Milyo. 2007. "Estimating the Impact of State Policies and Institutions with Mixed-Level Data." *State Politics and Policy Quarterly* 7 (4):446–459.

Public Agenda. 2011. *Issue Guide: Education.* www.publicagenda.org/citizen/issueguides /education.

Radin, Beryl A. 1998. "The Government Performance and Results Act (GPRA): Hydra-Headed Monster or Flexible Management Tool?" *Public Administration Review* 58 (4):307–316.

Radin, Beryl. 2006. *Challenging the Performance Movement: Accountability, Complexity, and Democratic Values.* Washington, DC: Georgetown University Press.

Rainey, Hal G., and Paula Steinbauer. 1999. "Galloping Elephants: Developing Elements of a Theory of Effective Government Organizations." *Journal of Public Administration Research and Theory* 9 (1):1–32.

Raudenbush, S. W. 1994. "Random Effects Models." In *The Handbook of Research Synthesis*, ed. Harris Cooper and Larry Hedges. New York: Russell Sage Foundation.

Raudenbush, Stephen. 2009. "Analyzing Effect Sizes: Random Effects Models." In *The Handbook of Research Synthesis and Meta-Analysis*, ed. Harris Cooper, Larry Hedges, and Jeffrey Valentine. New York: Russell Sage Foundation.

Raudenbush, Stephen W., and Anthony S. Bryk. 1985. "Empirical Bayes Meta-Analysis." *Journal of Educational Statistics* 10 (2):75–98.

Raudenbush, Stephen, and Anthony Bryk. 1986. "A Hierarchical Model for Studying School Effects." *Sociology of Education* 59 (1):1–17.

Raudenbush, Stephen, and Anthony Bryk. 2002. *Hierarchical Linear Models: Applications and Data Analysis Methods.* Thousand Oaks, CA: Sage.

Reeves, Barnaby, Jonathan Deeks, Julian Higgins, and George Wells. 2008. "Including Non-Randomized Studies." In *Cochrane Handbook for Systematic Reviews of Interventions*, ed. J. Higgins and S. Green, 391–432. Chinchester, UK: John Wiley & Sons.

Reyes, Jessica Wolpaw. 2007. "Environmental Policy as Social Policy? The Impact of Childhood Lead Exposure on Crime." *The B.E. Journal of Economic Analysis & Policy* 7 (1):51.

Riccucci, Norma. 2010. *Public Administration: Traditions of Inquiry and Philosophies of Knowledge.* Washington, DC: Georgetown University Press.

Riley, Richard. 2009. "Multivariate Meta-Analysis: The Effect of Ignoring Within-Study Correlation." *Journal of the Royal Statistical Society A* 172 (4):789–811.

Ringquist, Evan J. 1997. "Equity and the Distribution of Environmental Risk: The Case of TRI Facilities." *Social Science Quarterly* 78:811–829.

Ringquist, Evan J. 2005. "Assessing Evidence of Environmental Inequities: A Meta-Analysis." *Journal of Policy Analysis and Management* 24 (2):223–247.

Ringquist, Evan J., Mary Anderson, and Hersung Kum. 2002. *"Assessing Evidence from School Choice: A Meta-Analysis."* Delivered at the Annual Meeting of the Midwest Political Science Association, Chicago, April 25–28.

Ritz, Adrian. 2009. "Public Service Motivation and Organizational Performance in Swiss Federal Government." *International Review of Administrative Sciences* 75 (1):53–78.

Roberts, Colin J. 2005. "Issues in Meta-Regression Analysis: An Overview." *Journal of Economic Surveys* 19 (3):295–298.

Root, Terry L., et al. 2003. "Fingerprints of Global Warming on Wild Animals and Plants." *Nature* 421 (6918):57–60.

Rose, Andrew, and T. D. Stanley. 2005. "A Meta-Analysis of the Effect of Common Currencies on International Trade." *Journal of Economic Surveys* 19 (3):347–365.

Rosenfeld, Richard, Robert Fornango, and Eric Baumer. 2005. "Did Ceasefire, Compstat, and Exile Reduce Homicide?" *Criminology & Public Policy* 4 (3):419–449.

Rosenthal, Robert. 1979. "The 'File Drawer Problem' and Tolerance for Null Results." *Psychological Bulletin* 86 (3):638–641.

Rothstein, Hannah, and Sally Hopewell. 2009. "Grey Literature." In *The Handbook of Research Synthesis and Meta-Analysis, 2nd edition*, ed. Harris Cooper, Larry Hedges, and Jeffrey Valentine, pp. 103–122. New York: Russell Sage Foundation.

Rothstein, Hannah, Herbert Turner, and Julia Lavenberg. 2004. *Information Retrieval Policy Brief*. Philadelphia: International Campbell Collaboration.

Rossi, Peter H., and Howard E. Freeman. 1993. *Evaluation: A Systematic Approach, 5th edition*. Newbury Park, CA: Sage.

Rothstein, Hannah, Alexander Sutton, and Michael Borenstein, eds. 2005. *Publication Bias in Meta-Analysis: Prevention, Assessment, Adjustments*. New York: John Wiley & Sons.

Rouse, Cecilia Elena. 1998. "Private School Vouchers and Student Achievement: An Evaluation of the Milwaukee Parental Choice Program." *The Quarterly Journal of Economics* 113 (2):553–602.

Rubin, Donald B. 1986. "Statistics and Causal Inference: Comment: Which Ifs Have Causal Answers?" *Journal of the American Statistical Association* 81 (396):961–962.

Rubin, Donald B. 1992. "Meta-Analysis: Literature Synthesis or Effect-Size Surface Estimation?" *Journal of Educational Statistics* 17 (4):363–374.

Rubin, Donald B. 2005. "Causal Inference Using Potential Outcomes: Design, Modeling, Decisions." *Journal of the American Statistical Association* 100 (469):322–331.

Rubin, Donald. 2008. "For Objective Causal Inference, Design Trumps Analysis." *The Annals of Applied Statistics* 2 (3):808–840.

Rubinowitz, Leonard S., and James E. Rosenbaum. 2000. *Crossing the Class and Color Lines: From Public Housing to White Suburbia*. Chicago: University of Chicago Press.

Rucker, Gerta. 2010. *Small-Study Effects and Heterogeneity in Meta-Analysis*. Ph.D. dissertation, Freiburg University, Germany.

Rucker, Gerta, James Carpenter, and Guido Schwarzer. 2011. "Detecting and Adjusting for Small-Study Effects in Meta-Analysis." *Biometrical Journal* 53 (2):351–368.

Rucker, Gerta, Guido Schwarzer, James Carpenter, H. Binder, and M. Schumacher. 2010. "Treatment Effect Estimates Adjusted for Small-Study Effects via a Limit Meta-Analysis." *Biostatistics* DOI: 10.1136/jme.2008.024521.

Sabatier, Paul. 1997. "The Status and Development of Policy Theory: A Reply to Hill." *Policy Currents* 7 (December):1–10.

Sabatier, Paul. 2001. "Toward Better Theories of the Policy Process." *PS: Political Science and Politics* 24 (3):147–156.

Sabatier, Paul, and Hank Jenkins-Smith. 1993. *Policy Change and Learning: An Advocacy Coalition Approach*. Boulder, CO: Westview Press.

Sampson, R. J., and Lauritsen, J. L. 1994. "Violent Victimization and Offending: Individual-, Situational-, and Community-Level Risk Factors." In *Understanding and Preventing Violence Volume 3, Social Influences*, ed. Albert J. Reiss and Jeffrey A. Roth. Washington, DC: National Academy Press.

Sanbonmatsu, L., et al. 2011. *Moving to Opportunity for Fair Housing Demonstration Program—Final Impacts Evaluation*. Washington, DC: U.S. Department of Housing & Urban Development, PD & R.

Schmidt, Frank, John Hunter, and Nambury Raju. 1988. "Validity Generalization and Situational Specificity: A Second Look at the 75% Rule and Fisher's Z Transformation." *Journal of Applied Psychology* 73 (4):665–672.

Schochet, P. Z., and J. A. Burghardt. 2008. "Do Job Corps Performance Measures Track Program Impacts?" *Journal of Policy Analysis and Management* 27 (3):556–576.

Schram, Christine M. 1996. "A Meta-Analysis of Gender Differences in Applied Statistics Achievement." *Journal of Educational and Behavioral Statistics* 21 (1):55–70.

Schram, Sanford, and Brian Caterino, eds. 2006. *Making Political Science Matter: Debating Knowledge, Research, and Method*. New York: New York University Press.

Schwarzer, Guido, Gerd Antes, and Martin Schumacher. 2002. "Inflation of Type I Error Rate in Two Statistical Tests for the Detection of Publication Bias in Meta-Analyses with Binary Outcomes." *Statistics in Medicine* 21 (17):2465–2477.

Shadish, William, Thomas Cook, and Donald Campbell. 2002. *Experimental and Quasi-Experimental Designs for Generalized Causal Inference*. New York: Houghton-Mifflin.

Shadish, W. R., and C. K. Haddock. 2009. "Combining Estimates of Effect Size." In *The Handbook of Research Synthesis and Meta-Analysis*, ed. Harris Cooper, Larry Hedges, and Jeffrey Valentine. New York: Russell Sage Foundation.

Shadish, William, Goerg Matt, Ana Navarro, and Glenn Phillips. 2000. "The Effects of Psychological Therapies Under Clinically Representative Conditions: A Meta-Analysis." *Psychological Bulletin* 126 (4):512–529.

Sharpe, Donald. 1997. "Of Apples and Oranges, File Drawers and Garbage: Why Validity Issues in Meta-Analysis Will Not Go Away." *Clinical Psychology Review* 17 (8):881–901.

Silliman, Nancy. 1997. "Hierarchical Selection Models with Applications in Meta-Analysis." *Journal of the American Statistical Association* 92 (439):926–935.

Simon, Ronald L., Christine Johnson, Jay Beaman, Rand D. Conger, and Les B. Whitbeck. 1996. "Parents and Peer Group As Mediators of the Effect of Community Structure on Adolescent Problem Behavior." *American Journal of Community Psychology* 24 (1):145–71.

Slavin, Robert. 1995. "Best Evidence Synthesis: An Intelligent Alternative to Meta-Analysis." *Journal of Clinical Epidemiology* 48 (1):9–18.

Small, Mario Luis, David J. Harding, and Michèle Lamont. 2010. "Reconsidering Culture and Poverty." *The Annals of the American Academy of Political and Social Science* 629 (1):6–27.

Smart, R. 1964. "The Importance of Negative Results in Psychological Research." *Canadian Psychologist* 5:225–232.

Smith, Dennis C. 2009. "What Can We Expect from Performance Management Activities That We Cannot Expect from Performance Measurement?" *Journal of Policy Analysis and Management* 28 (3):512–514.

Smith, Dennis C., and William J. Bratton. 2001. "Performance Management in New York City: Compstat and the Revolution in Police Management." In *Quicker Better Cheaper? Managing Performance in American Government*, ed. D. W. Forsythe. Albany, NY: Rockefeller Institute Press.

Smith, M. F. 1989. *Evaluability Assessment: A Practical Approach*. Boston: Kluwer Academic.

Smith, M. L. 1980. "Publication Bias and Meta-Analysis." *Evaluating Education* 4 (1):22–24.

Smith, M., and Gene Glass. 1977. "Meta-Analysis of Psychotherapy Outcome Studies." *American Psychologist* 32:752–760.

Smith, V. Kerry, and Ju-Chin Huang. 1995. "Can Markets Value Air Quality? A Meta-Analysis of Hedonic Property Value Models." *Journal of Political Economy* 103 (1):209–227.

Smith, V. Kerry, and Yoshiaki Kaoru. 1990. "Signals or Noise? Explaining the Variation in Recreation Benefit Estimates." *American Journal of Agricultural Economics* 72 (2):419–433.

Solon, Gary. 1999. "Intergenerational Mobility in the Labor Market." In *Handbook of Labor Economics*, Volume 3A, ed. Orley C. Ashenfelter and David Card, pp. 1761–1800. Amsterdam: North-Holland.

Sowell, Thomas. 1975. *Race and Economics*. New York: McKay.

Stanley, T. D. 1998. "New Wine in Old Bottles: A Meta-Analysis of Ricardian Equivalence." *Southern Economic Journal* 64 (3):713–727.

Stanley, T. D. 2001. "Wheat from Chaff: Meta-Analysis as Quantitative Literature Review." *The Journal of Economic Perspectives* 15 (3):131–150.

Stanley, T. D. 2005. "Beyond Publication Bias." *Journal of Economic Surveys* 19 (3):309–345.

Stanley, T. D. 2008. "Meta-Regression Methods for Detecting and Estimating Empirical Effects in the Presence of Publication Selection." *Oxford Bulletin of Economics and Statistics* 70 (1):103–127.

Stanley, T. D., and Stephen B. Jarrell. 1989. "Meta-Regression Analysis: A Quantitative Method of Literature Surveys." *Journal of Economic Surveys* 3 (2):161.

Stanley, T. D., and Stephen B. Jarrell. 1998. "Gender Wage Discrimination Bias? A Meta-Regression Analysis." *The Journal of Human Resources* 33 (4):947–973.

Stanley, T. D., Stephen B. Jarrell, and Hristos Doucouliagos. 2010. "Could It Be Better to Discard 90% of the Data? A Statistical Paradox." *The American Statistician* 64 (1):70–77.

Steenbergen, Marco, and Bradford Jones. 2002. "Modeling Multilevel Data Structures." *American Journal of Political Science* 46 (1):218–237.

Steijn, Bram. 2008. "Person-Environment Fit and Public Service Motivation." *International Public Management Journal* 11 (1):13–27.

Sterling, T. D. 1959. "Publication Decisions and Their Possible Effects on Inferences Drawn from Tests of Significance—or Vice Versa." *Journal of the American Statistical Association* 54:30–34.

Sterling, T. D., W. Rosenbaum, and J. Weinkam. 1995. "Publication Decisions Revisited: The Effect of the Outcome of Statistical Tests on the Decision to Publish and Vice Versa." *The American Statistician* 49 (1):108–112.

Sterne, Jonathan, ed. 2009. *Meta-Analysis in Stata*. College Station, TX: Stata Press.

Sterne, Jonathan, Betsey Jane Becker, and Matthias Egger. 2005. "The Funnel Plot." In *Publication Bias in Meta-Analysis*, ed. H. Rothstein, A. Sutton, and M. Borenstein, pp. 75–98. New York: John Wiley & Sons.

Sterne, Jonathan, and Matthias Egger. 2005. "Regression Methods to Detect Publication Bias and Other Biases in Meta-Analysis." In *Publication Bias in Meta-Analysis*, ed. H. Rothstein, A. Sutton, and M. Borenstein, pp. 99–110. New York: John Wiley & Sons.

Sterne, Jonathan A. C., Matthias Egger, and George Davey Smith. 2001. "Systematic Reviews In Health Care: Investigating and Dealing with Publication and Other Biases in Meta-Analysis." *British Medical Journal* 323 (7304):101–105.

Sterne, Jonathan A. C., et al. 2002. "Statistical Methods for Assessing the Influence of Study Characteristics on Treatment Effects in 'Meta-Epidemiological' Research." *Statistics in Medicine* 21 (11):1513–1524.

Sterne, Jonathan A. C., et al. 2011. "Recommendations for Examining and Interpreting Funnel Plot Asymmetry in Meta-Analyses of Randomised Controlled Trials." *British Medical Journal* 343:d4002.

Stevens, John R., and Alan M. Taylor. 2009. "Hierarchical Dependence in Meta-Analysis." *Journal of Educational and Behavioral Statistics* 34 (1):46–73.

Stipek, Deborah. 2002. *Motivation to Learn: Integrating Theory and Practice*. Boston: Allyn and Bacon.

Stock, James H., and Mark W. Watson. 2008. "Heteroskedasticity-Robust Standard Errors for Fixed Effects Panel Data Regression." *Econometrica* 76 (1):155–174.

Stock, W. A. 1994. "Systematic Coding for Research Synthesis." In *The Handbook of Research Synthesis*, ed. Harris Cooper and Larry Hedges. New York: Russell Sage Foundation.

Stretesky, Paul, and M. J. Lynch. 1999. "Environmental Justice and the Predictions of Distance to Accidental Chemical Releases in Hillsborough County, Florida." *Social Science Quarterly* 80 (4):830–846.

Supreme Court of Florida. January 5, 2006. "John Ellis 'Jeb' Bush et al. v. Ruth D. Holmes et al." No. SC04-2323.

Sutton, Alexander. 2005. "Evidence Concerning the Consequences of Publication and Related Biases." In *Publication Bias in Meta-Analysis*, ed. H. Rothstein, A. Sutton, and M. Borenstein, 175–192. New York: John Wiley & Sons.

Sutton, Alex. 2009. "Publication Bias." In *The Handbook of Research Synthesis and Meta-Analysis, 2nd edition,*. ed. Harris Cooper, Larry Hedges, and Jeffrey Valentine, 435–454. New York: Russell Sage Foundation.

Sutton, Alexander, and Therese Pigott. 2005. "Bias in Meta-Analysis Induced by Incompletely Reported Studies." In *Publication Bias in Meta-Analysis*, ed. H. Rothstein, A. Sutton, and M. Borenstein, 223–239. New York: John Wiley & Sons.

Swanborn, M., and K. de Glopper. 1999. "Incidental Word Learning While Reading: A Meta-Analysis." *Review of Educational Research* 69 (3):261–285.

Swanson, H. Lee, and Olga Jerman. 2006. "Math Disabilities: A Selective Meta-Analysis of the Literature." *Review of Educational Research* 76:249–274.

Tengs, Tammy, and Ting Lin. 2003. "A Meta-Analysis of Quality-of-Life Estimates for Stroke." *Pharmacoeconomics* 21 (3):191–204.

Terrin, Norma, Christopher H. Schmid, Joseph Lau, and Ingram Olkin. 2003. "Adjusting for Publication Bias in the Presence of Heterogeneity." *Statistics in Medicine* 22 (13):2113–2126.

Teske, Paul, and Mark Schneider. 2001. "What Research Can Tell Policymakers About School Choice." *Journal of Policy Analysis and Management* 20 (4):609–631.

Thibodeau, Nicole, John H. Evans III, Nandu J. Nagarajan, and Jeff Whittle. 2007. "Value Creation in Public Enterprises: An Empirical Analysis of Coordinated Organizational Changes in the Veterans Health Administration." *Accounting Review* 82 (2):483–520.

Thompson, Simon G., and Julian P. T. Higgins. 2002. "How Should Meta-Regression Analyses Be Undertaken and Interpreted?" *Statistics in Medicine* 21 (11):1559–1573.

Thompson, Simon G., and Stephen J. Sharp. 1999. "Explaining Heterogeneity in Meta-Analysis: A Comparison of Methods." *Statistics in Medicine* 18 (20):2693–2708.

Torgerson, Carole J. 2006. "Publication Bias: The Achilles' Heel of Systematic Reviews." *British Journal of Educational Studies* 54 (1):89–102.

Turner, Erick, Annette Matthews, Eftihia Linardatos, Robert Tell, and Robert Rosenthal. 2008. "Selective Publication of Antidepressant Trials and Its Influence on Apparent Efficacy." *The New England Journal of Medicine* 358:252–260.

U.S. Department of Housing and Urban Development. 2010. *FY 2010 Budget: Road Map for Transformation*. Washington, DC: Government Printing Office.

U.S. Government Accountability Office. 2007. *Report to Congressional Requesters: "District of Columbia Opportunity Scholarship Program."* Washington, DC: Government Printing Office.

U.S. Government Accountability Office. 2009. *Public Transportation: FTA's Triennial Review Program Has Improved, but Assessments of Grantees' Performance Could Be Enhanced*. GAO-09-603. Washington, DC: Government Printing Office.

U.S. Government Accountability Office. 2010. *Teen Driver Safety: Additional Research Could Help States Strenghen Graduated Driver Licensing Systems*. GAO-10-544. Washington, DC: Government Printing Office.

U.S. Government Accountability Office. 2012. *Designing Evaluations, 2012 Revision*. GAO-12-208G. Washington, DC: Government Printing Office.

U.S. Supreme Court. 2002. *Zelman, Superintendent of Public Instruction of Ohio, et al. v. Simmons-Harris, et al*. 536 US 639.

van Houwelingen, Hans C., Lidia R. Arends, and Theo Stijnen. 2002. "Advanced Methods in Meta-Analysis: Multivariate Approach and Meta-Regression." *Statistics in Medicine* 21 (4):589–624.

Van Slyke, David, Rosemary O'Leary, and Soonhee Kim, eds. 2010. *The Future of Public Administration Around the World: The Minnowbrook Perspective*. Washington, DC: Georgetown University Press.

Vandenabeele, Wouter. 2007. "Toward a Public Administration Theory of Public Service Motivation." *Public Management Review* 9 (4):545–556.

Vandenabeele, Wouter. 2009. "The Mediating Effect of Job Satisfaction and Organizational Commitment on Self-Reported Performance: More Robust Evidence of the PSM—Performance Relationship." *International Review of Administrative Sciences* 75 (1):11–34.

Vanhonacker, Wilfried R. 1996. "Meta-Analysis and Response Surface Extrapolation: A Least Squares Approach." *The American Statistician* 50 (4):294–299.

Vevea, Jack L., and Carol M. Woods. 2005. "Publication Bias in Research Synthesis: Sensitivity Analysis Using A Priori Weight Functions." *Psychological Methods* 10 (4):428–443.

Wachter, Kenneth W. 1988. "Disturbed by Meta-Analysis?" *Science* 241 (4872):1407–1408.

Wachter, Kenneth, and Miron Straf, eds. 1990. *The Future of Meta-Analysis*. Washington, DC: National Academies Press.

Walker, Richard M., Fariborz Damanpour, and Carlos A. Devece. 2011. "Management Innovation and Organizational Performance: The Mediating Effect of Performance Management." *Journal of Public Administration Research & Theory* 21 (2):367–386.

Wang, XiaoHu, and Evan Berman. 2001. "Hypotheses About Performance Measurement in Counties: Findings from a Survey." *Journal of Public Administration Research and Theory* 11 (3):403–428.

Weibel, Antoinette, Katja Rost, and Margit Osterloh. 2010. "Pay for Performance in the Public Sector—Benefits and (Hidden) Costs." *Journal of Public Administration Research and Theory* 20 (2):387–412.

Weimer, David, and Aidan Vining. 2009. *Policy Analysis: Concepts and Practice*. 5th ed. Englewood Cliffs, NJ: Prentice-Hall.

West, Martin R., Paul E. Peterson, and David E. Campbell. 2001. "*School Choice in Dayton, Ohio After Two Years: An Evaluation of the Parents Advancing Choice in Education Scholarship Program*." KSG Working Paper NO. RWP02-021. *SSRN eLibrary*, No. 320253.

Western, B., and B. Pettit. 2010. "Incarceration & Social Inequality." *Daedalus* 139 (3):8–19.

Western, B., and C. Wildeman. 2009. "The Black Family and Mass Incarceration." *The Annals of the American Academy of Political and Social Science* 621 (1):221–242.

White, Halbert. 1980. "A Heteroskedasticity-Consistent Covariance Matrix Estimator and a Direct Test for Heteroskedasticity." *Econometrica* 48:817–838.

Whittaker, Robert J. 2010a. "In the Dragon's Den: A Response to the Meta-Analysis Forum Contributions." *Ecology* 91 (9):2568–2571.

Whittaker, Robert J. 2010b. "Meta-Analyses and Mega-Mistakes: Calling Time on Meta-Analysis of the Species Richness-Productivity Relationship." *Ecology* 91 (9):2522–2533.

Wilborn, D., U. Grittner, T. Dassen, and J. Kottner. 2010. "The National Expert Standard Pressure Ulcer Prevention in Nursing and Pressure Ulcer Prevalence in German Health Care Facilities: A Multilevel Analysis." *Journal of Clinical Nursing* 19 (23–24):3364–3371.

Wille, Michael Patrick. 2010. *School Vouchers Source/Amount of Funds and Effects on Math/Reading Scores*. Masters thesis, Public Policy Institute, Georgetown University.

Williams, Daniel W. 2003. "Measuring Government in the Early Twentieth Century." *Public Administration Review* 63 (6):643–659.

Wilson, David. 2009. "Systematic Coding." In *The Handbook of Research Synthesis and Meta-Analysis, 2nd edition*, ed. Harris Cooper, Larry Hedges, and Jeffrey Valentine, pp. 159–176. New York: Russell Sage Foundation.

Wilson, W. J. 1987. *The Truly Disadvantaged: The Inner City, the Underclass, and Public Policy*. Chicago, London: University of Chicago Press.

Wilson, W. J. 1996. *When Work Disappears: The World of the New Urban Poor*. New York: Alfred A. Knopf.

Wilson, W. J. 2010. "Why Both Social Structure and Culture Matter in a Holistic Analysis of Inner-City Poverty." *The Annals of the American Academy of Political and Social Science* 629 (1):200–219.

Wisconsin Legislative Audit Bureau. 1995. *The Milwaukee Parental Choice Program*. Madison, WI: WI LAB.

Witte, John F. 1998. "The Milwaukee Voucher Experiment." *Educational Evaluation and Policy Analysis* 20 (4):229–251.

Witte , John F. 2000. *The Market Approach to Education: An Analysis of America's First Voucher Program*. Princeton, NJ: Princeton University Press.

Wolf, Patrick J., Paul E. Peterson, Martin R. West, M. A. Kennedy School of Government, Harvard University, and Georgetown University. 2001. *Results of a School Voucher Experiment: The Case of Washington, D.C. After Two Years*. Cambridge, MA: Kennedy School of Government.

Wooldridge, Jeffrey. 2002. *Econometric Analysis of Cross Section and Panel Data*. Cambridge, MA: MIT Press.

Wooldridge, Jeffrey. 2003. "Cluster-Sample Methods in Applied Economics." *American Economic Review* 93 (2):133–138.

Wright, Bradley E., and Sanjay K. Pandey. 2008. "Public Service Motivation and the Assumption of Person-Organization Fit." *Administration & Society* 40 (5):502–521.

Yang, Kaifeng, and Jun Yi Hsieh. 2007. "Managerial Effectiveness of Government Performance Measurement: Testing a Middle-Range Model." *Public Administration Review* 67 (5):861–879.

Zeger, Scott, and Kung-Yee Liang. 1986. "Longitudinal Data Analysis for Discrete and Continuous Outcomes." *Biometrics* 42 (1):121–130.

Zimmer, Ron, and Eric Bettinger. 2008. "Getting Beyond the Rhetoric: Surveying the Evidence on Vouchers and Tax Credits." In *Handbook in Education Finance and Policy*, ed. Helen F. Ladd and Edward B. Fiske. New York and London: Routledge.

Zorn, Christopher. 2001. "Generalized Estimating Equations for Correlated Data: A Review with Applications." *American Journal of Political Science* 45 (2):470–490.

Zorn, Christopher. 2006. "Comparing GEE and Robust Standard Errors for Conditionally Dependent Data." *Political Research Quarterly* 59 (3):329–323.

Zornitsky, Jeffrey, and Mary Rubin. 1998. *Establishing a Performance Management System for Targeted Welfare Programs*. National Commission for Employment Policy Research, 1988.

NAME INDEX

SUBJECT INDEX

Page references followed by *fig* indicate an illustrated figure; followed by *t* indicate a table.